Y0-BKH-233

Praise for Steven Honigberg's Biography!

"Leonard Rose was a cellist of enormous importance, as a soloist and chamber musician and as a deeply devoted teacher. It is not surprising that it would take another cellist to do justice to Leonard Rose's life and career—and Mr. Honigberg has done just that. This book is a wonderful combination of being informative and highly readable, and it will bring much deserved attention to one of the twentieth century's most important musical figures."

—HENRY FOGEL
President & CEO, American Symphony Orchestra League

"Mr. Honigberg's credentials as a fine musician, cellist, and writer make this an invaluable study: Leonard Rose was to all cellists who have studied with him a perfect combination of the most remarkable virtuoso and caring and profoundly knowledgeable teacher. He almost single-handedly made the American school of not only cello playing, but of string playing the foremost in the world. This biography is a work of love and care from someone who knew Mr. Rose over a period of years. Mr. Honigberg has tirelessly compiled anecdotes and facts about this notable cellist."

—LYNN HARRELL
Cello Soloist and Rose protégé

"Few cellists on the American scene made the impact of Leonard Rose. This remarkable book gives Rose his rightful due. It reminds those who knew, respected and loved the man about our loss, and it introduces a new generation to the accomplishments of this extraordinary musician. A must-read for all cellists and for all those who are interested in the history of the instrument."

—LEONARD SLATKIN
Fifth Music Director, National Symphony Orchestra

"Steven Honigberg's biography of the great cellist, Leonard Rose, treats the reader to the performance of a lifetime. His detailed account of the virtuoso's career is a ticket to watch classical music take the American stage in the twentieth century. All who love the cello, its history and great classical music, will value it."

—JOHN MONTGOMERY
Violin Maker, Dealer and Restorer

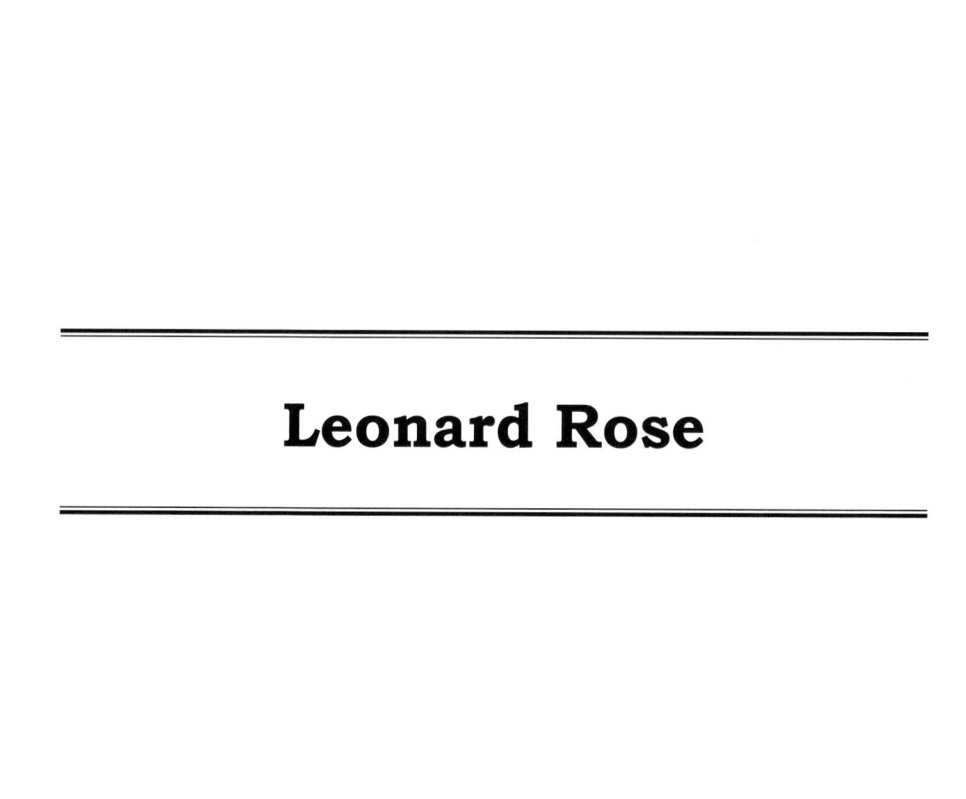

Leonard Rose

Copyright © Steven Honigberg, 2010

All rights reserved. Printed in the U.S.A.

No part of this publication may be reproduced or transmitted in any form or by any means, electronic or mechanical, including photocopy, recording or any information storage and retrieval system now known or to be invented, without permission in writing from the publisher, except by a reviewer who wishes to quote brief passages in connection with a review written for inclusion in a magazine, newspaper or broadcast.

Published in the United States by
Beckham Publications Group, Inc.
P.O. Box 4066, Silver Spring, MD 20914

ISBN: 978-0-9823876-7-2
0-9823876-7-9

Library of Congress Control Number: 2009932440

Leonard Rose
America's Golden Age and Its First Cellist

Steven Honigberg

THE **Beckham**
PUBLICATIONS GROUP, INC.
Silver Spring

ML418
.R76
5H66
2010

In Memoriam:

Channing Robbins (1922-1992)

Leonard Rose's most loyal associate and forgotten pedagogue.

The greatest teachers are the greatest artists.

Contents

Preface 1

Introduction 4

Chapter One: Peculiar American Childhood 7

Chapter Two: Felix Salmond, Leonard Rose's
                        Profound Influence 22

Chapter Three: Coming of Age in Philadelphia 37

Chapter Four: Toscanini and the NBC Symphony,
                         New York 1938 53

Chapter Five: Principal Cellist Under Artur Rodzinski 70

Chapter Six: The Cellists of Rose's New York Philharmonic 86

Chapter Seven: Joseph Schuster, Rose's Rival 95

Chapter Eight: Leonard Bernstein, an American Triumph 107

Chapter Nine: Greek Hero, Dimitri Mitropoulos 121

Chapter Ten: Titanic George Szell 132

Chapter Eleven: The Nobility of Bruno Walter 146

Chapter Twelve: Jascha Heifetz, Perfect Soloist 157

Chapter Thirteen: America's Golden Symphonic Age 166

Chapter Fourteen: Rose's Career Ignites 176

Chapter Fifteen: Rose's Discoveries 197

Chapter Sixteen: Lustrous 1662 Amati Cello..........................213

Chapter Seventeen: Visionary Ivan Galamian and
　　　　　　　　　　His Meadowmount School.......................224

Chapter Eighteen: Glenn Gould, Eccentric Genius................237

Chapter Nineteen: Istomin, Stern, Rose Assume
　　　　　　　　　　the Trio Mantle...................................251

Chapter Twenty: Darkness and Light, 1964 276

Chapter Twenty-One: Foremost Rose Disciples....................290

Chapter Twenty-Two: Rose's Chamber Music Insights...........302

Chapter Twenty-Three: Master Teacher; Juilliard Versus Curtis;
　　　　　　　　　　　　the Rise of Channing Robbins.......311

Chapter Twenty-Four: Ruminations....................................334

Chapter Twenty-Five: Death of a Legend.............................348

Book Acknowledgments 356

Appendices 360

Endnotes 457

Addendum..482

About the Author 485

Index 492

Preface

Leonard Rose's exquisite artistry as a soloist, chamber musician, and orchestral player touched the lives of thousands of musicians and music lovers—yet none so profoundly as the roughly two hundred and fifty individuals entitled to call the great cellist, "my teacher."

I am among those so privileged. In a musical household, my first encounter with Leonard Rose came by way of the family phonograph and LP collection. I repeatedly listened to recordings Rose made after leaving his position as the New York Philharmonic's principal cellist and bursting onto the solo scene. I recall peering into the jacket photo's focused, deep-set, dark eyes that looked straight at me with the gaze of a tireless performer who appeared direct, sensitive, and passionate. In adolescence, I didn't comprehend the emotions and thoughts the man's sober expression conveyed. But his playing tugged at my heart. Its soulful beauty enthralled me. The tone was large and robust; his technique was impeccable. As a young cellist, an inexplicable desire to play for and to follow this man who so naturally produced this beautiful sound consumed me.

As a mature, seasoned performer, I still wonder exactly what set and kept me on that near-obsessive path and why Rose's influence hasn't waned. My earliest experience with Rose's records charted the course of my life, but why? Was it how he sat and held the instrument? The way his left hand glided along the fingerboard? His unique bow position? A sublime vibrato that meshed with carefully planned fingerings and phrases? And why is it that subsequent generations of cellists teach and play in the manner of Leonard Rose?

His teaching career began at The Juilliard School in 1947. Four years later, Rose added six cello pupils at his alma mater, The Curtis Institute; and until 1962, he routinely commuted between New York City and Philadelphia to teach. From 1979 to 1984, I attained my childhood dream: I had the honor of studying at Juilliard in, as it turned out, Leonard Rose's final class, his final opportunity to imbue a group of young musicians with his powerful mastery of the instrument. Rose was a superb teacher—kind, patient, encouraging, and exacting. I admired him enormously.

This book examines the multifaceted American cellist and the classical music context that dominated Rose's twentieth century. Professionally, the era during which he achieved greatness and the direction he chose to pursue could not have been musically richer. While Leonard Rose is a more than worthy solo biographical subject, he felt that the story of his inordinate contact and collaboration with his era's most renowned musicians was especially valuable for posterity. So my aim in this volume was to showcase Rose among the countless musical figures he affected and those who affected him.

On a personal note, the book portrays a complex individual during a period of tremendous individualism, and explores his sympathetic nature, his unyielding devotion to the cello, and—inevitably—his failings. The man was fiercely competitive and judgmental abruptly severing ties with friends or colleagues, even family members, on occasion. Not unlike other performers of his caliber, Leonard Rose had a sizable but fragile ego that when damaged, put Rose in uncomfortable situations—including expulsion from class.

Few interpersonal experiences rival the intimacy of a master artist's lesson. Rose served as a father figure who bestowed undivided attention to those pupils who desired and warranted it. His verbal instruction may have lacked magic, but the way he played and demonstrated thrilled students. His quest for perfection hovered over every lesson. Rose instilled in us a profound respect for the compositions we studied and a rich knowledge of the heritage he passed down from previous generations. Most vital of all, he bestowed us with infinite inspiration.

In 1979, as he recovered from cancer surgery, Leonard Rose dictated his memoir from his hospital bed, intending to produce an autobiography from the material. It would not come to fruition. While he qualified as a quintessential American success story, his life was not devoid of conflict. As such, the well-mannered and dignified Leonard Rose simply could not put painful memories into words. His son, Arthur, eventually transcribed the complete memoir.* When I corresponded with Arthur and Rose's daughter Barbara in March 2004, they allowed me to read the transcript. While I wrote this book, the two cautiously granted me interviews that provided keen insights of a more personal portrait of their father. Their stories—combined with years of research, decades of students' memories, and Rose's own resonant reminiscences—bring this great American cellist to life.

After his passing in 1984, my admiration for the cellist never faded. Inspired by his eternal aura, several years ago I decided to solicit written tributes from fellow Rose students. I was curious to learn if others shared a comparable fondness for the man, and if his teaching continued to influence their lives and playing as it still affected mine. The outpouring of responses was enthusiastic and touching. Instead of satiating my curiosity; these remembrances underscored the paucity of widely available information about this extraordinary pedagogue, artist, and human being. I resolved to rectify the literary omission and historical oversight. The result—*Leonard Rose: America's Golden Age and Its First Cellist*—finally seats Leonard Rose in his proper place in the musical pantheon.

---

* Excerpted in: 1. "An aristocrat of the cello looks back at a long career" by Leonard Rose *New York Tribune August 31, 1984 section 4B*).
2. Johann Sebastian Bach, Ernest Bloch, Johannes Brahms et al. *Leonard Rose the Memorial Edition* with Leonard Rose, Irving Owen, Leon Machan, John Corigliano Sr., William Lincer, © 1997 by Pearl, B000000WS3, Compact disc.
3. Janof, Tim. 2004. Leonard rose remembered. Internet Cello Society. http://www.cello.org/ Newsletter/Articles/rose/rose.htm (accessed May 1, 2004).
4. Susan Anderson Seeking Perfection: The Life and Career of Leonard Rose (2004).

Introduction

"Pure gold." Thus *the New York Times* described the playing of Leonard Rose, the most successful American-born cellist of his generation. Rose's knowledge of the instrument was unsurpassed. Every phrase of every piece he recorded—his legacy—continues to sparkle with meaning. His Beethoven and Brahms were noble in style, favoring huge dynamic contrasts and rhythmic freedom. His Schumann and Schubert each had a semblance of epic beauty. His Bach could be transcendently romantic and powerful. His signature concerti had a consistency, accuracy, and no-nonsense approach. And, notably, he performed works by living American composers, a tendency many of his peers shunned.

In the United States in the mid twentieth century, Russian and European immigrants dominated the music profession. Rose followed an individualist's path toward stardom and shattered the stereotype that an American required training in Europe. While many stellar soloists pursued their loftiest goals at the youngest ages, which too frequently abbreviated their careers, this pragmatic American initially, upon graduation from the Curtis Institute, immersed himself in the symphonic repertoire. The result exposed Rose to a Who's Who of the century's world-class performing artists and the canon of orchestral masterpieces, providing the broadest of musical foundations on which to build his solo achievements. That decade of on-the-job education came under the batons of Arturo Toscanini, Leonard Bernstein, Pierre Monteux, Charles Münch, Fritz Reiner, Igor Stravinsky,

Artur Rodzinski, George Szell, Dimitri Mitropoulos, Bruno Walter, and others. When Rose held the principal cello position of the Cleveland Orchestra, then the New York Philharmonic, he accompanied concerti with incomparable soloists such as violinists Jascha Heifetz, Nathan Milstein and Joseph Szigeti, cellists Emanuel Feuermann and Gregor Piatigorsky and with pianists Claudo Arrau, William Kapell, Vladimir Horowitz, Artur Rubinstein, and Rudolf Serkin—all in their prime. And Rose witnessed Leonard Bernstein's famously spectacular debut on the podium from a few feet away as principal cellist of the New York Philharmonic. These experiences informed his playing as recording and concert artist, soloist and chamber musician, and renowned teacher: each aspect of his musicianship symbiotically enhanced his others.

Leonard Rose departed from the Philharmonic in the early 1950s and took the country by storm as soloist. He secured his star status with a series of dazzling, highly acclaimed cello recitals in New York's Town Hall. His individual career would place him on the most magnificent stages in the world, with ninety-eight visits to Carnegie Hall alone where he embarked on an astonishing consecutive run of fifty-five solo appearances with orchestras; and a number of these key cello concerti were recorded, all with the era's most distinguished conductors. Among these early releases are the Saint-Saëns Concerto and Ernest Bloch's "Schelomo" (with Mitropoulos), Tchaikovsky's "Rococo" Variations (with Szell), Brahms "Double" and Beethoven "Triple" concerti (with Walter).

These prodigious accomplishments and their accolades attracted the attention of a well-known contemporary, violinist Isaac Stern, who invited Rose to join him and form a trio with pianist Eugene Istomin. For three decades, the Istomin-Stern-Rose Trio established the standard by which chamber music performances are still measured. They traveled around the world on concert tours, made recordings of piano trios, and Istomin played with Rose in cello sonata performances. At their zenith, the trio garnered worldwide attention in 1970 with a series of eight concerts featuring Beethoven's complete cycle of piano trios, violin sonatas, cello sonatas, and sets of variations for cello and piano. The give-and-take of small ensemble collaborations likewise affected the cellist.

In addition to the trio, Rose worked with other extraordinary chamber musicians of the twentieth century, like Glenn Gould. The idiosyncratic Canadian pianist was one of Rose's partners at the Stratford Festival and the pair recorded a fascinating rendition of Bach's Gamba sonatas in the 1970s.

The influence of this American era's greatest musicians, Rose's prolific background as first-rank soloist and first-chair orchestra member—in concert halls and recording studios—combined to create the finest cello pedagogue in history. He was arguably the top performer, but it is as cello teacher that Leonard Rose retains name recognition. Even now, his students praise him (in print in the present volume). He was, in the eyes of his students, a perfect cellist; his music making was of unparalleled beauty. Two of his best-known pupils currently before the public, Yo-Yo Ma and Lynn Harrell, cite Rose as perpetual inspiration throughout their own phenomenal professional lives. Yet, unfairly, Rose is all but forgotten in the role of performer, while his contemporaries' fame looms large, beyond any inner circle. On his deathbed, Rose—probably resigned to the inevitable—remarked, "So what? I'm famous." These last words were neither as true as the American cellist wished nor as true as history should have it. The superb recordings barely begin to reflect Rose's rich contributions to the arts. However, that elusive fame does linger, if somewhat indirectly: hidden deep within current and future generations of cellists.

Chapter One

PECULIAR AMERICAN CHILDHOOD

Leonard Rose was someone who grew, was sustained by, developed through the entire musical experience in America— as a student, as an orchestral musician, as a solo player, as a teacher.

—Isaac Stern[1]

Leonard Rose appeared as the featured soloist with the Tucson Symphony, the oldest orchestra in the American Southwest, performing Dvořák's majestic cello concerto. Rose's very early arrival on February 15, 1955, at the auditorium exemplified the routines that he unfailingly followed throughout his career: awaking at a specific hour, practicing three hours every morning, a certain amount of rest between fixed hours, and his pre-concert 4:00 p.m. steak and potatoes. The extra time allowed him the requisite stretch, without any distractions, to get comfortable in a different venue's dressing room; smoke several cigarettes to steady himself; and warm up the muscles of his bow arm—his most critically praised skill. With a firm grip on his recently acquired 1662 Nicolò Amati instrument, he left the private room and peered at the orchestra members gathered on stage. He met a fellow cellist's eyes dead on. This older man was no anonymous colleague; he was Leonard Rose's father, Harry Rose. Less than a year before, Rose's wife Minnie, who had been his family's "Rock of Gibraltar," received a grim diagnosis of leukemia, yet his father had not found an opportunity to speak to him about the upsetting news. For that matter, Harry had seemed to lack compassion for and opportunities to talk to his son when he was growing up and learning to play the cello. In Harry's new home of Tucson, the glimpse dredged up mixed emotions and Rose's stomach tightened up in anticipation of striding to his place on the elevated wooden platform in front of the orchestra. The concerto's glorious opening statement, two-dozen notes practiced over and over for decades, ran around in his head. The 37-year-old cellist, who had boldly struck out on his own as soloist just four years earlier, loved the repertoire's most celebrated concerto and believed his performance of the emotionally charged, 45-minute work superior to any other colossus who came along. Better than Piatigorsky, Salmond, Cassadó, Silva, Miller, Schuster, Janigro, Kurtz, Garbousova, Starker, Fournier, even Casals. Its pacing was of paramount importance. The concerto required formidable strength to conquer the first movement's militaristic style and virtuoso challenges. Rose needed to reach inward for the emotional intensity to color the delicate second movement, all the while holding in reserve enough power to vigorously attack and sustain the finale. He would then bring the powerful work to a bittersweet conclusion. The longer Rose stood waiting, the colder and sweatier his hands became. He knew the origins of his lifelong stage fright. Routines helped. Routines mattered. His eyes lowered to the floor, a perfunctory inspection of his spotless black shoes. He brushed invisible lint off his tuxedo, straightened lapels and the white handkerchief that needed no straightening. For the umpteenth time, he wiped his hands on his formal black pants, perhaps leaving sweat streaks. His gaze returned to the floor while he listened: "It gives me great pleasure to introduce our soloist for this evening, America's leading cellist—Leonard Rose." Another spasm tightened the knot in his stomach further. With the applause as his cue, Rose emerged from the wings. The soloist and his Amati wading through dozens of violin players tapping their bows upon music stands in approval, while Rose wore his mask of smiling calm. Standing adjacent to the podium, the Budapest-born maestro, Frederic Balazs, shook his hand and whispered "Good luck." As the audience quieted down, Rose settled in the soloist's chair, adjusting the endpin to its proper height; he fidgeted with his jacket's tails, and then suddenly realized that his position seemed too near the edge, too near the people in the front row of the 2,600-seat University of Arizona auditorium which was filled to capacity. Rose winced. Balazs, at ease, baton in hand, was turned to his left, awaiting the traditional soloist's nod that signaled permission to set things in motion. Preparation complete, Leonard Rose made eye contact with the conductor and inadvertently glimpsed that memorable other cellist again, seated on the inside of the section's third stand. Leonard found Harry Rose's grimace all too recognizable. As his son plunged into Dvořák's vital opening statement, a familiar invincibility pushed his father—and everything else—out of his thoughts.

Leonard's Rose's parents immigrated to the United States shortly after the turn of the twentieth century. Rose's father, originally Gdal Rosovsky, was born in 1886 in Bragin, Russia, a town of about 4,000 today in the peninsula of southeastern Belarus near Mozyr, Gomel, and the Chernobyl nuclear power plant. In late-19th-century Russia, despotism reigned, spawning violence that targeted the Jewish population. Jews bore the brunt as "enemies of the Tsar" and were brutally beaten and killed. Back in 1898, Rosovsky's village population was 4,520 people, half of whom were Jews. In all probability, the Rosovskys lived in cramped quarters, as it was common for several families to live together under one roof. Equality of civic rights did not exist. Corrupt landlords, the rich nobility, the Court, and the stratum of the Tsar suppressed any dissension from the people. If means were uncovered, Jewish emigration ensued.

In 1904, Gdal Rosovsky, likely aided by American Jewish charities, journeyed to the east coast of the United States and joined other members of his family in Baltimore, Maryland, an active port of entry for Eastern European immigrants. He was 18 years of age when a customs officer interviewed him and urged that he drop the suffix "sky" to Americanize his surname. From that moment on, Gdal would be known as Harry Rose. (The name proved popular: a contemporary Baltimore city directory registered hundreds of Roses.) The young woman he would marry in 1910 crossed the Atlantic and reached Maryland two years later than he did. Leonard Rose's mother was also Russian, born in 1889. Both parents were fortunate to escape their homeland prior to the Bolsheviks's horrific attacks on religion. In October 1905 alone, they slaughtered a staggering 4,000 and wounded approximately 10,000 in 660 recorded pogroms.[2] Leonard Rose's mother or father could well have figured into the statistics.

Harry met and married Jennie Frankel while living in a vibrant Jewish neighborhood in southwest Baltimore in an area around Ramsay Street dubbed "little Jerusalem." Many labor unionists resided there who were mostly tailors like Harry, employed by the city's clothing manufacturers: Sonneborn, Schoeneman, and others. These workers, with modest incomes and struggling to eke out an existence, were intent on gaining American citizenship. Both Harry and Jennie became United States citizens a year after their respective immigrations. Long considered a Southern town, Baltimore's dominant natural feature was its harbor on the Chesapeake Bay, which enabled such manufacturers and the shipping industry to flourish. The harbor's historical significance as the site of America's violent battle with and defeat of the British in 1814, an event Francis Scott Key commemorated in poetry. Key's words would form the lyrics for the national anthem. Imbued with an appreciation for the country's liberties, Leonard's parents fit the stereotype of hardworking, patriotic, new Americans. Harry Rose, the youngest of 13 children, possessed multiple talents and excelled in a variety of careers during his lifetime. Around 1912, Harry and Jennie relocated 50 miles south to Washington, DC, where Harry continued his profession as a tailor and clothing designer for clients that included two American first ladies: the wives of presidents Calvin Coolidge and Warren G. Harding.

In the heart of the nation's capital, Harry and Jennie made their home in a rented pre-Civil War building on 5th Street, NW, a sparsely developed area dominated by an industrial bottling plant. Horse-drawn carriages, streetcars, and a 10-cent messenger service with a fleet of bicycles filled the street, going about the business of the U.S. government. Here the couple began their family: Frank Rose was born in 1912. This was an era of child laborer–peddlers, where boys on street corners and outside pool parlors hawked chewing gum and newspapers, and hustled nickel shoe shines. And Harry, product of an urban childhood, no doubt befriended some of the children on the block. With headlines blaring atrocities a few months shy of the end of World War I, Leonard Joseph Rose was born at 3:50 a.m. July 27, 1918, at George Washington Hospital near Washington circle on 23rd Street.

However, the young Leonard was not raised in Washington, DC. After Harry developed a severe case of asthma, he decided to move the family of four to Miami in 1922, hoping that Florida's climate would ease his malady.

Harry purchased a grocery store on SW 8th Street and Second Avenue. In those days, independent grocers flowed like the tide: rising up one day, falling the next. A short supply of money forced the Rose store to remain open seven days a week and Harry into sixteen-hour workdays. For approximately three years, the young family could afford no separate home, so they lived, somewhat primitively, in the back of the store in a single large room with an enclosed toilet, but no proper bathroom. Rose recalls bathing in an oversized sink basin.

Their business was rather small and managed to survive on a credit system. Even though retail chains—which would have obliterated Rose's shop—were not yet common, Harry had plenty of competition. He stocked a full line of household goods and food, including meats. When reminiscing about the store, Leonard Rose describes a huge icebox and a butcher's block with enormous knives. As a child, his impression was that his mother never set foot outside the place, forever working to fill orders and serve customers while Harry delivered purchases to customers' homes.

He showed extreme affection for his younger son during his earliest years—with particular interest after he observed the first glimmerings of the boy's musical awareness. Harry liked to recount his experiment of exposing his infant son to lullabies, then comparing the reactions. It appeared the child preferred or could discern certain selections over others. "I felt sure even then," Harry would later claim, "that someday my son would be a fine musician." Another type of music Leonard Rose heard from toddlerhood were Hebrew songs, sung by his maternal grandfather, a Hebrew scholar who was very religious. Harry, on the other hand, was not, despite the Judaism that surrounded his youth, steeped in mysticism as the Belarus rabbis were leading Kabbalists of the time. With Hebrew spoken in the home, Leonard obviously inherited his family's Jewish heritage, but similar to countless Jewish immigrants religious observance was kept to a bare minimum. Frequently, patriotism and love of country supplanted the supernatural in these new Americans. From birth until he left home at 15, Rose attended synagogue—more than likely for Yom Kippur—just a handful of times. Rose believed Harry went on the off chance "there was someone up there watching." Harry and Jennie never gave Leonard a bar mitzvah. But—perhaps motivated by guilt or in the spirit of Harry's "just in case" philosophy—he agreed with Jennie and his first wife Minnie, who insisted, to carry out the ritual with their son Arthur.

Jennie and Harry conversed in three languages: Russian, Hebrew/Yiddish, and English. Jennie, whom Rose always describes with affection, spoke English inflected with a heavy Yiddish-Polish accent. He was ashamed to admit his great embarrassment when outsiders heard her speech. On the flipside, Rose acquired a pronounced Southern drawl. Making fun of his mother's accent would come back to trouble the young Southerner when he attended school in the North. It also irked him whenever his mother exhibited signs of hysteria, sighing loudly and engaging in what he classified as typical Yiddish breast-beating. Despite these complaints, Rose loved his mother. Sharing the one-room residence attached to their workplace meant a total lack of privacy for the adults. The couple's continual quarrels left young Leonard feeling direly insecure. "What a terrible thing to do to a child!" Rose would later conclude.

Harry was talented and handsome; he belonged on stage. Back in Baltimore, before Leonard's birth, Harry was a bit-player in his spare time in productions of Maurice Schwartz's Yiddish Arts Theater.[3] Harry's voice was beautiful, and he was gifted at recitation and emoting in the dialect. His innate extroversion often thrust him into the limelight. Jennie, by contrast, was quiet, suffering, and neurotic. "Dad was a terrific ham and Mom very introverted and basically sad and self-conscious." Rose figured that he had inherited the paternal "ham" and talent, tempered with an equal dose of his mother's sensitive inner turmoil that toed the line of despair.

When Leonard reached his eighth birthday, his father arranged for him to start piano lessons with a Mrs. Felter, the woman who lived next to their store with her father, an elderly Civil War veteran. Mrs. Felter provided a special, early opportunity for the gifted boy whose family could not afford to own a piano: she permitted him to practice on hers. He was also grateful for the refuge from the close quarters of home.

The Florida Gold Coast's population soared threefold from the time the Roses arrived. Miami grew into a hotbed for speculators in the real estate market. During the summer and autumn of 1925, a frenzied real-estate craze overwhelmed the entire city. An astonishing 25,000 agents sold prospective land parcels and homes, frequently bought sight unseen. The *Miami Herald's* advertisements reflected the atmosphere: "The Wonder City," "The Fair White Goddess of Cities," "The World's Playground," "The City Invincible." The boom didn't last long. In September 1926, a devastating hurricane paralyzed the region. Amid unimaginable destruction, the storm left 400 residents dead, 6,300 injured and 50,000 homeless. By 1927, boarded-up houses lined Miami's streets and bankruptcy filings piled high. By mid-1930, when Leonard Rose was twelve, 26 Florida cities, including Miami, defaulted on the principal or interest on their bonds. Alarmingly, half the banks in business prior to 1920 failed before 1929. The Great Depression took hold and Miami, "Wonder City," was not exempt.

Still, a city took shape where a backwater had been. Miami had three organized music series in those years. One—the University of Miami Symphony, conducted by Arnold Volpe[*]— offered Rose his first experience to hear a live orchestra. "I loved those sounds." Not only did his father play in the orchestra's cello section, his older brother, Frank, was a percussionist.

When Rose was 10 and quite accomplished on piano, Harry introduced his son to the cello. It qualified as the family instrument: in addition to his father, his older first cousins, Frank Miller and Samuel Stern, were developing into fine cellists. Leonard's lessons started at the Miami Conservatory of Music

---

[*] Volpe founded this orchestra in 1926. A Lithuanian-born musician, he had been active as conductor and teacher in New York.

with Walter Grossman, who had studied with Josef Malkin in Berlin before World War I (coincidentally, Malkin would be in Rose's New York Philharmonic cello section 1944-1949). Rose wryly recounted his debut lesson with Grossman, "My first strong instinct was to finger the cello with the right hand, and hold the bow with the left. I soon got over that."

A palpable change in behavior swept over Harry when his son took so naturally to the cello. The change intensified when Leonard Rose began receiving prizes and recognition. He believed that his father "dropped me around that time."[4] Memories of this behavior haunted him throughout his professional and personal life, and affected his own parenting skills. In his introduction to the cello, it is uncertain how tough—or tender—Harry's attitude was toward his prodigious son. The older man had begun as a violinist, but because holding the instrument under his chin aggravated his asthma, he took a few lessons and reinvented himself as an admirable amateur cellist. From the lack of privacy in the family's small living space, it is easy to imagine the man commenting or correcting when the boy practiced, and to imagine the inevitable discomfort, akin to stage fright. Frank had dabbled with the cello for a few years before quitting. However, Leonard's innate talent, coupled with a purposeful drive rarely found in youth, would achieve a level that soon surpassed Frank's—and their father's. Compounding Rose's malaise with his father, he frequently felt as if an only child due to the six-year span between siblings. In that solitude, the school-age boy could lose himself in a musical world of his own creation, and that devotion facilitated his rapid progress. Whether or not triggered by his father's envy—a spectator to his son's pursuit and conquering of his own artistic aspiration—this distancing had an impact on the young musician. That Harry spent an inordinate amount of Leonard's childhood laboring at the store must have further oppressed and frustrated him. Harry's continuation of orchestra playing—he persevered into his 90s in Miami's Senior Citizens Orchestra— possibly compensated for some part of his desire. That hardly altered the reality, early on, that the more his child achieved, the less attention he paid. By adolescence, Leonard actively resented his father's seeming half-hearted encouragement. Parental inconsistency has a profound influence. The paucity of available biographical information about Harry Rose may well indicate Leonard's bitterness. The son's emotional response at the University of Arizona in 1955 definitely indicates it.

Leonard Rose, 1931
Courtesy of Arthur Rose

Rose viewed Walter Grossman as a breath of fresh air, cultivated and exciting, in spite of the fact that this German Nationalist's liberal use of "kike" upset him. Grossman offered support and plenty of attention, along with instruction. Prophetically, the cello teacher declared to Harry someday his son's name would be "up in lights." From the start, that child was determined to rise to greatness. "I had the stubborn drive to do better and better," Rose explains. "I focused on the idea. I knew what I wanted, even then."

"Walter Grossman was, at best, just a fair cellist," Rose entered in his unpublished memoir, in distant retrospect. "I remember his rather careless intonation and general insecurity on the instrument. I do have him to thank for several extremely important instrumental basic principles that are vital in my cello playing and teaching. First was the establishment of a curved thumb on the bow, for without the thumb being capable of flexing, the bow arm must be faulty. Second was a good left-hand setting on the fingerboard in the lower positions. Third were the early scales, exercises and études ..."

Miami's population had increased to around 75,000; an extremely small portion was Jewish. Rose was one of only three Jewish children in his elementary school, and anti-Semitism ran rampant in this Southern State. He recalls that his best friend's parents belonged to the Ku Klux Klan, which he deduced from observing a local KKK rally: when the Klan marched down Second Avenue camouflaged in white robes, the family's dog faithfully followed at the heels of its presumed owner.

During these grade-school years, Leonard attended the *Arbeiter Ring Schule* or the Workman's Circle School. The Workman's Circle is a Jewish cultural fraternal organization that founded, sponsored, and supported the schools centered on a curriculum of Yiddish cultural subjects. This organization, socialist in orientation, urged members to take a stand for labor rights and the environment. Rose stated, "As I remember, there were two camps within the Workman's Circle, Communists and anti-Communist Socialists. The arguments were often highly charged and there were lots of raised voices. I know we Jews didn't corner the market on heated discussions and hysteria, but we very often tried. Were we so different from the Italian immigrants? Both have strong family ties, and both groups are very emotional."

As a child, Leonard's days were crammed full. Besides school, he had classes at the Workman's Circle, practiced the piano along with cello, and dutifully completed his homework. He prided himself on his athletic prowess and running speed. The latter, he once noted, may well have resulted from evading his anti-Semitic peers.

When Leonard reached age 13, he graduated into Ada Merritt Junior High, about 25 minutes from the grocery store. That walk was often very trying for the self-conscious young boy. Not only was he regarded as the chubby Jewish kid; he was also weighted down, lugging books supplies and an unwieldy instrument. "What a target I was for the Jew-baiting bullies, and what a sensitive, frightened kid I was." At least twice, he suffered humiliation and beatings at the hands of a half dozen older teenagers. "I couldn't fight back because they were bigger. I am afraid my psyche was very damaged by those episodes. I do remember my reactions to those numerous taunts. Inevitably I said to myself, 'some day I'll show you bastards!' Nice, huh? It left its mark."

Rose's advancement on the cello was unrelenting. There seemed no doubt that he surpassed other student cellists in the junior high as well as high school divisions. Actually, Miami had a dearth of cellists, and Rose deemed the so-called "professionals" not terribly good. The junior high music teacher, Mrs. Foster, whom Rose "loved and learned a hell of a lot from" insisted he travel to Tampa to participate in the All-State Cello Competition. The contest was open to public school students below college age. With few rivals in the entire state, the 13 year old entered and won against 17- and 18-year-olds on the cusp of their graduation. Regardless of his innocent age, Rose's face and eyes projected a formality in bearing and appearance similar to the intense photos that, in adulthood, graced his record covers. And the deft position of his hands on the instrument and bow was striking for a child. Besides the accolade as "crowned champion," the competition awarded him an appearance in a recital with other winners, presented in the university auditorium. The day of the performance hardly differed from every other in Florida: the weather was extremely hot and humid. Plus, air conditioning was nonexistent. This compounded problems for string players who used all-gut strings. Modern metal strings can last for months. Within four or five days after getting a gut-A string to hold its pitch, the string already began to develop "whiskers," a sign that meant it would break shortly. Rose may have had this disconcerting thought in the back of his mind during the recital. But what he did notice was the effect of the high temperature on his own body. As his account of the special event shows, he couldn't tolerate the added warmth of formal dress. "I walked on stage in a nice suit, and after taking a bow, put down the cello and removed my coat tossing it on the piano lid. The audience got a kick out of this, and I then proceeded to play the "Allegro Appassionato" of Saint-Saëns and the "Hungarian Rhapsody" by David Popper."

...L PRODIGY ...O PLAY TUESDAY

Leonard Rose, the 13-year-old 'cellist who has won innumerable prizes for his splendid ability in playing the 'cello, will be the soloist next Tuesday evening at the concert presented under the auspices of the University of Miami Conservatory of Music. The concert, featuring the Junior Symphony Orchestra, will be held at the patio of the Miami Conservatory, 1449 N. E. Second avenue, beginning at 8 p. m. Tuesday, November 3.

Leonard is the son of Mr. and Mrs. Harry Rose and comes from a family noted for their musical accomplishments. About three years ago he became the pupil of Mr. Walter Grossman, famous virtuoso, and has exhibited such splendid musical abilities that critics are predicting an exceptional musical career for him. His playing is marked by a buoyancy and forceful enthusiasm, by a balance and flexibility of tone and smoothness which is unusual in children of his age.

Leonard Rose, 1931
Courtesy of the Curtis Institute

The eventual move from the suffocating single room to a separate, proper house proved anticlimactic; it was merely a sleeping place. With the workload at the family's grocery store unchanged, daytime hours continued in that back room where Harry managed his affairs. Leonard Rose's social life was minimal, at best. Around this time, he became aware of an acute sense of his unorthodoxness from his peers, "I had the feeling that I was a fish out of water. Somehow, I knew I had the stuff to do something none of them would ever approach. I just knew it, and felt it down to my toes." The observation that his father showed little interest in or fondness for the younger boy, once inferred as beneficial to the boy's single-minded devotion to practicing, appears to have contributed to the lifestyle of a loner. His emotions were melancholy much of the time. "I was sensitive—painfully so!"

On the other hand, Jennie and Harry developed a social life, visiting the homes of various cronies to play cards. "I guess I can't blame them after those long hot hours in the store," Rose sympathizes. He was less sympathetic, though, because he accompanied them. "I was the 'schlep along,' and my parents' friends didn't have any children. I was alone. I would watch the card games for a while, and then when I was sleepy, I'd go out and sleep in the backseat of our car. Around 11:00 p.m., my parents would drive home. I'd be awakened from sleeping in the car to go into the house and go to bed." One such night deviated from the boring routine. The vivid impression stuck with him as an adult, seeing fit to use the incident to exemplify his opinions of his mother's concern for him and his father's lack thereof. Alone in the backseat, the boy was awakened by a couple of thieves siphoning out their gasoline. Scared to death, he lay utterly motionless for fear of being discovered. Jennie, much later, berated herself for irresponsibly leaving her son unattended. Rose maintained no comparable concern came from Harry, who would have relished his role of life of the party inside the friends' home rather than worry about him outside.

Not all students who excel in music as he did simultaneously earn highest honors in academic subjects. Nevertheless, in 1933, Leonard Rose graduated from junior high as class valedictorian. The ceremony required him to deliver a speech, on stage, before faculty, families, and—conspicuously—the peers who had either tormented or shunned him. "I was absolutely petrified," Rose exclaims. "I remember going to the principal and telling him how frightened I was. That was the beginning of something that plagued me most of my adult life—nerves."

The ceremony may have marked his first conscious manifestation of "nerves," but Harry probably deserves responsibility for instilling the affliction. Rose recounted his father's harsh admonishment before the speech: "If you don't talk, people won't find out how stupid you are." Rose never forgot those words, to which years later, he caustically appended, "Today, I find it very easy to speak in front of an audience, but my father's not around to plague me anymore, but he sure as Hell was then!" The pain Harry inflicted—evident in this vicious recollection and echoed in the vindictive triumph two decades later in Tucson—may well have pushed Leonard Rose to greatness. To be sure, Harry's was not benevolent parental encouragement. Yet in reverse, he unintentionally may have spurred his son's atypical drive.

For the time, Leonard continued to surprise his cello teacher. Grossman conducted the Conservatory of Miami's Little Symphony, with which his gifted pupil performed as soloist at the White Temple Methodist Church. The building, on NE Second Avenue and erected in 1913, held the era's most notable local music series. Rose heard a number of famous musicians at the venue—including the Austrian-born violinist Fritz Kreisler. As a mature artist, the cellist would return for a pair of recitals at White Temple before the building burned to the ground in 1970. In the early 1930s, Miami was barren of young musical talent; but Rose remained undeterred. With Grossman as coach, Rose's first encounter with chamber music was a trio with violinist Lewis Eley and pianist Mildred Greenberg—whom the cellist had a crush on. The three rehearsed at the Conservatory and performed in and around Miami, an experience Rose appreciated. At 14, the young artist was presented in a series of solo recitals throughout the state of Florida, for which he proudly accepted his first concert fee of $5[*]—substantial during the depths of the Great Depression.

---

[*] At the Civic Theater in Miami sponsored by the Mana-Zucca Music Club, the 13-year-old cellist performed a solo by Georg Goltermann and David Popper's "Hungarian Rhapsody" in the afternoon on January 19, 1932.

Chapter Two

FELIX SALMOND, LEONARD ROSE'S PROFOUND INFLUENCE

Music is, for those of us who love it passionately and are caught forever in its spell, the most magical, treasurable, moving, and exciting experience life has to offer ... how fortunate we are whose lives are dedicated to music; indeed we are the richest people on earth.

—Felix Salmond

Just as Leonard Rose would come to dominate cello teaching in America during the 1950s, '60s, and '70s, Felix Salmond was the country's foremost cello force during the preceding three decades. In the life of Leonard Rose, few musicians had as dominant an influence over him as his teacher, Felix Salmond. There can be no doubt that he passed time-honored musical traditions directly to his star pupil. The older cellist played with, among others, Ignacy Paderewski, Josef Hofmann, Ossip Gabrilowitsch, Josef Lhévinne, Arthur Rubinstein, Jascha Heifetz, Joseph Szigeti, Bronislaw Huberman, Georges Enesco, with the Curtis String Quartet (along with Carl Flesch and Emanuel Zetlin, violinists and Louis Bailly, viola) and the New York Piano Trio (violinist Daniel Karpilowsky and pianist Carl Friedberg*). Both men carved out

---

* Friedberg (1872-1955) once studied with Clara Schumann and was a friend to Johannes Brahms. At one time, Rose performed the Brahms sonatas with Friedberg, then 80 years old. Friedberg told Rose how he played them for the

impressive solo careers and taught hundreds of aspiring cellists who placed their teacher upon pedestals.

The way in which Salmond taught, however, unsettled the young Rose.

Felix Salmond was already an established concert cellist when he settled in the United States at age 34. He presented the world premiere of Edward Elgar's Cello Concerto in 1919 with the composer conducting the London Symphony Orchestra. Born November 19, 1888, in London into a family of musicians, he began cello studies at the age of 12 with William Edward Whitehouse (1859-1935), a pupil of the renowned Italian cellist Alfredo Piatti. Whitehouse was professor at Cambridge University and the Royal College of Music.

Unhappy in England, possibly due to the disintegration of his first marriage or to the lack of performance opportunities, Salmond immigrated to the U.S. in 1922 where his American debut recital at Aeolian Hall in New York City made an immediate impact.[5]

Felix Salmond, Circa 1920
Courtesy of the Curtis Institute

---

composer who told the pianist that he felt his music was too often played with vulgar force, instead of subtle depth of tone.

A New York teaching appointment soon followed at the Mannes School of Music. With the inception of the Juilliard Graduate School in 1924, he was named head of the cello department and professor of chamber music, posts he held until his death in 1952. Salmond would eventually split his time between New York and Philadelphia, where he taught at the Curtis Institute until 1942. Rose would follow in his footsteps, likewise dividing pedagogical work between the same cities.

Salmond's background as a seasoned performer proved invaluable. A hot-blooded personality and extroverted cellist, Salmond taught his young cellists to put every ounce of emotion into their playing. From his memoir, Rose indicated, "he had a magnificent sound on the instrument. I think a lot of my sense of sound came from that period." Alla Goldberg conveys insights into what Rose may have learned from Salmond: "He was the most wonderful chamber music teacher who ever lived. He knew each piece that he taught by heart and could tell you every marking for each instrument. ... He must have had a photographic memory. I remember him putting his hand over my hand on the bow and pressing to give me the feeling of how to engage the string. ... He loved music and he very much wanted to instill this love in his students. Anything that I studied with him became indelible ..."[6]

Felix Salmond and Leonard Rose, Circa 1936

Rose's generation benefitted from Salmond's commitment to teaching and—according to Bernard Greenhouse[*], who attended the Juilliard Graduate School from 1933-1939—subsequent generations continue to feel his effect: "Felix Salmond was a man consummately dedicated to his art and to his students. Many of the happiest moments of my youth were the days when my lessons pleased him. He was not easy with his students, demanding of them the highest standards, as he did for himself. When I reflect now on those formative years—I realize that his artistic integrity has remained with me. ... If Felix Salmond were alive today, he would hear an amazing achievement ... in the younger generation of cellists fortunate enough to have had contact with a great master through his students."

Salmond's exterior, however, was tough and demanding, which never did appeal to Rose. His uncompromising approach to the instrument was not how he motivated Rose. Yet, if one is to believe Rose's close friend and colleague Nathan Stutch,[**] the young Rose was certainly awed in the Brit's presence: "He was a giant. So many of us revered him," Stutch recollected. "When he said this is the way it has to be done, it was at once written in stone. ... Something in his manner of teaching that was so right—as if there was no other way to do it. But he could be brutal. I would sometimes see students crying. His concepts were lofty ... I don't know that there were too many who came out of their lessons enthralled or exhilarated because his methods were *so* terribly tough."[7]

Salmond's accomplishments are dazzling. He was the cello soloist in the Los Angeles premiere of Dvořák's Cello Concerto on November 6, 1925, with the Los Angeles Philharmonic and Walter Henry Rothwell conducting. He was a champion of Ernest Bloch's "Schelomo," revitalizing the 1916 work in 1927. Salmond also presented the world premiere of Frank Bridge's Cello Sonata (written between 1913 and 1917) at London's Wigmore Hall. During the summer of 1935, Samuel Barber heard him practicing

---

[*] Bernard Greenhouse was a founding member of the 1955 Beaux Arts Trio in which he played for 32 years.
[**] Nathan Stutch's long membership in the New York Philharmonic (1946-1989) included 24 seasons as standmate with principal cellist Lorne Munroe.

his newly composed cello sonata. "It sounds like a different work," Barber wrote in a letter to his friend, Jeanne Behrend. "I had forgotten I wanted it to sound that way—dramatic. And he plays with fire."[8]

In January of 1939, 52-year-old Salmond introduced Georges Enesco's "Symphonie Concertante,"[9] for cello and orchestra with the composer as guest conductor and the New York Philharmonic Symphony in Carnegie Hall. Six years later, Salmond performed the complete Beethoven Cello Sonatas at Juilliard with pianist Leonid Hambro,[10] who became Rose's pianist in his own New York debut recital. According to Hambro:

> We rehearsed every morning and afternoon for 22 days. Salmond was maybe the most nervous performer I have ever played with. He was petrified. Even though he had powerful ideas, it manifested itself sometimes on an uneven bow or shift. He loved the way I played and he would tell me how he wanted it to go. If I played a crescendo that Beethoven did not indicate, he would yell, 'Boy, what are you doing? Where is it written a crescendo?' All along, though, he might say, 'Let's hold this note a little longer,' or 'We must delay the entrance to that.' Illusion was an enormous part of the way he and I presented these five Beethoven Sonatas.[11]

In his formative stages, the young cellist dared not question any of Salmond's musical tastes without risking stern reprimand. Salmond's style of teaching, Rose believed late in his own life, portrayed him in an insecure light. He argued that because Salmond was six feet two inches tall and he was a mere five feet eight, he could not possibly replicate his teacher's technical command. Salmond's arms were much longer than Rose's and his hands much bigger, although Rose was certain his own hands had greater flexibility. And Rose thought his fingers were better balanced. Rose revealed a peculiarity that facilitated his technical dexterity: "[because] I have a tremendous lack of webbing in my hand, I am capable of doing many extensions—stretching on the instrument—so that I can cover a vast area quite quickly."

Echoing Nathan Stutch and others, Salmond did not, in Rose's opinion, inspire curiosity or teach how to investigate possibilities other than those he dictated. No others existed. "If we took the slightest different fingering or bowing, his ego was immediately shattered," Rose wrote. One of the few pupils who stood up to him was Eleanor Aller (1917-1995), whose playing Rose undoubtedly heard in the Warner Brothers 1946 film *Deception*.[*] She exclaimed:

> I, of course, like every student went to the library and copied in Salmond's fingerings and bowings. I once had five days to prepare a concerto. I tried and tried his markings and there was absolutely no way that I could do the fingerings because I couldn't make these enormous reaches. I started to play. I don't think I got through half a page when he stopped me and said, 'Did you go to the library?' I said that I did. He said, 'Dear, you are not doing them.' I said, 'Mr. Salmond, you have an enormous hand and you can reach many things.' I held up my hand and said, 'I have a little hand. I can't do your fingerings and really, if I make it come out sounding good, what difference does it make?'[12]

When Aller's famed Hollywood String Quartet, some years later, was preparing to record the two-cello quintet of Schubert, four of the five musicians had coincidentally studied the work with Salmond. About rehearsals, Aller remarked, "On our first read-through, the feeling in the group was that one could not deviate, one inch, from what he had taught us. What we recorded is exactly the way he taught it to us. Even a glissando, about which he once said, 'You must do it, because musically it is so right,' we just did it automatically because Salmond's influence was so formidable." According to Aller, the eminent teacher was a bit inelegant with the instrument precisely because of his physical

---

[*] The popular film's plot involves the love life of solo cellist Karel Novak (played by Paul Henreid) who marries Christine Radcliffe (Bette Davis)—to the angst of composer Alexander Hollenius (Erich Wolfgang Korngold). The premiere performance of Wolfgang Korngold's Cello Concerto is featured. The superb cello playing heard throughout the film is that of Aller.

size: "There was nothing graceful about him at the cello. But that sound, once you got it in your ear, you could never get it out." She explained how students could never get away with anything at lessons. He once declared, "Eleanor, dear, if you came here to study with me, it's because you don't know how to play the cello. If you knew how, you wouldn't be here."[13]

From the moment Salmond's contemporary, the Polish-born Viennese Emanuel Feuermann, was hired as instructor of cello at Curtis in 1941, tensions flared. Salmond was miffed that the institution had not consulted him about hiring another cello teacher. A short time later, Feuermann was appointed to head the chamber music program as well.[14] With Feuermann's sudden death in 1942 in tandem with an immediate replacement—

Felix Salmond, Circa 1935
Courtesy of Wendy Salmond Oler

the renowned Gregor Piatigorsky, whom Salmond disliked vociferously—he abruptly departed after 17 years of teaching at Curtis. His daughter Wendy Salmond Oler remembers, "Daddy was a little erratic and resigned in a huff. He got his feelings hurt pretty easily. It was a mistake."[15] To be sure, there were other external pressures. Enrollment had dropped, in part because of the war, from 167 in 1941-1942 to 100 in the following school year. The pedagogue was asked to take a cut in hours and salary in light of "present conditions." Some faculty members were let go. The entire orchestra department was eliminated and with it, all wind, brass, and percussion instructors. Salmond went from six to three students. Piatigorsky, who taught at Curtis from 1942 to 1951 (whose position Rose would replace in 1951), began in 1942 with six students. Although Salmond initially accepted his pay reduction, he took as an insult that he was not offered the chamber music teaching post after the resignation of the Curtis Quartet.

As his daughter and students attest, Salmond was chronically an unhappy man. Wendy believes he was too much a perfectionist and required unreasonable attention from Helen (Salmond's second wife), who took care of all domestic matters. Others see the roots of his discontent in a terrible insecurity with himself and his profession where true satisfaction is practically impossible to attain. Salmond also enjoyed an extravagant lifestyle, which made him always desperate for money to make that lifestyle succeed. Wendy remains bewildered: "He was never satisfied with his own playing. He always thought he should play better than he was playing. The rest of the world in New York felt like he was doing a good job. So, why was he so difficult on himself?"

Wendy remembers her father's impression of the young student, her father's "favorite pupil," she asserts. "Daddy had very high ideals for Leonard. He was a very strict musician, but he was also a big dreamer. I also think that Leonard had enormous respect for my father. He thought that there was nobody on earth who was quite as good a cellist. ... I can still hear ... when he had Leonard in the living room giving him a lesson. He would have been a little bit strict. He regarded Leonard almost like a child." She describes her incomprehension at her father's infantilizing, why this "sort of the 'God' of cellists," would treat a pupil like a child. "But I do know that he felt that there was nobody on earth who played the cello like Leonard. My father felt that Leonard was the shining light for the next generation."[16]

"Rose put Salmond on such a pedestal that he never learned anything beyond him," his critical contemporary and lifelong competitor, Bernard Greenhouse, one of the last surviving links with Salmond, Feuermann, Alexanian, and Casals, believes. "Every piece that Rose played, I could give you the exact editing which he did which was Salmond's. He never went beyond it. He never had the desire to create his own way of playing. He was a perfect example of Felix Salmond's teaching." Greenhouse, who is not mentioned in Rose's sprawling memoir, began his career with aspirations of becoming a soloist. Despite superlative reviews from the *New York Times* as recitalist—"Gifted performing artist" (debut-1946); "He has a warm, smooth tone, a fine style, technique admirably developed, taste and high intelligence" (1947); "It was resourceful in its technical facility and searching in its musicianship" (1948); "... cellist of quiet and impressive sincerity. ... He is one of the most rewarding young cellists around" (1950); "His technique is uncommonly substantial, his tone always warm, full, alive" (1951)—he was unable to attract the upper echelon management necessary to initiate such a career.

When a solo career did not materialize, Greenhouse—miffed that Rose had attained what he desired—settled alongside Rose as teacher at Juilliard from 1951 to 1962. There is no question that Leonard Rose, performing his own New York recitals during the period, noticed him. Somehow, the two managed to remain gracious. Lunching one afternoon, Greenhouse strongly urged Rose to go play for Casals, which he believed —"Nobody could ever match his level of artistry"—an invaluable experience. The Beaux Arts Trio legend relates decades later, "I had a great amount of respect for Leonard Rose, and he deserves a great deal of recognition for who he was. No other American cellist came close to his success. Yet, he didn't feel that he needed any further work toward his playing. He was perfectly happy. He expressed that to me. He felt that his associations were the best and that he felt he didn't need to go beyond that." Greenhouse continues, "I don't want to take away the good from Salmond that he did for me. He was a man who had a wonderful musical approach to the repertoire. I do want to convey that at the time of my development, he was just the beginning."[17]

Rose states in his memoir that although he believed Salmond was a very good cellist, he did not rank him among the truly great cellists due to a rather limited technical control of the instrument. Yet, Salmond's occasional remarks such as, "move the bow faster" or "float the bow" were invaluable aids in fostering the young Rose's appetite for his lifelong work with sound production.

When Felix Salmond died, he left no estate except for two cellos: A Gofriller and one other, leaving his wife in a difficult financial situation for the rest of her life. Helen worked as an assistant to the treasurer of Lenox Hill Hospital until she retired. She met and married Felix Salmond when first appointed to the faculty of the Mannes School of Music in the 1920s, and died in 1985.

There is no denying Salmond's love affair with the cello. The Curtis Institute began a newsletter in 1929 called "Overtones" that was issued on an irregular basis until April 1940. Many members of the Curtis faculty would be major contributors. During its first year of existence, Salmond was the featured writer. The following excerpts appeared in the "Overtones" newsletter in November 1929:

> That the greatest composers recognized the violoncello's tone color ... in the works of Beethoven and Brahms. The five sonatas of the former master and the two sonatas and magnificent cello part in the "Double" Concerto of Brahms are striking examples of this aspect of the characteristic qualities of the instrument. Indeed, it is not too much to say that these works contain everything of which the violoncello is capable musically and technically.

Salmond's turned toward Strauss's *Don Quixote* and Bloch's "Schelomo" as his favorite works—which, in turn, became Rose's signature pieces:

> Strauss never reached greater heights of profound inspiration than in the final variation of the Don

Quixote, which is an intensely moving solo for the cello, depicting the death of the Knight. ... If Ernest Bloch had composed nothing but his "Schelomo," he would take his place among the great masters of music. It is a work of passionate sincerity, grandeur, power, and sublime beauty... All its resources for tone color in song and for dramatic expression have been seized upon by the composer with amazing skill, and despite the overwhelming power of the tuttis, there is no feeling of weakness when the solo instrument is heard. In "Schelomo," the violoncello is, in truth, the king of instruments!

Although Salmond's reputation as a soloist did not reach the heights that Leonard Rose would achieve, it is unquestionable that his teaching methods produced a number of first-rate cellists. Can there be any doubt that Salmond transferred his passion to Rose, his favorite pupil? Salmond's written words gives us this rare glimpse on what Rose may well have heard during his grueling lessons.

There were other gripes Rose needed to get off his chest. Unlike the experience of most every student at any level of musicianship, Salmond never wanted to hear Rose, or for that matter any of his students, play scales and études. From the start, Rose took note. What also angered him was his teacher's occasional but extreme condescending behavior. In the midst of Salmond's talented class—a total of six or seven—a younger student, Richard Kapuchinsky, was assigned to learn by observing Rose practice. The influence was such when Kapuchinsky started lessons with Salmond, the Brit exclaimed, "Oh, I've got another Rose!" The mood didn't last long: after acing the first two movements of the Boccherini Concerto for Salmond, the third (on which he had not yet worked with Rose) went poorly. In complete frustration, Salmond cried, "Well, boy, that's impossible. You could do that better." He glanced at Ralph Berkowitz—the faculty pianist accompanying his classes who would become Gregor Piatigorsky's regular pianist in 1940 for 30 years—and complained, "I don't understand, Ralph. He played so marvelously and now he is shoveling coal." Salmond's tantrum escalated: "Get a nurse. Get a pram. Have her give you a bottle, boy! Perhaps she could teach you the third movement of the Boccherini Concerto—I can't!" He then threw his costly Cleopatra cigar out the window. Kapuchinsky had incited fury without knowing what he did wrong.

From afar, the episode traumatized his star pupil. Unknown to the flamboyant teacher, the obstinate behavior subconsciously helped form Rose as a teacher. Upon hearing the ruckus, some graduate students, who had been waiting outside the studio for the next class, intervened. They informed the teacher that his victim was poverty-stricken, living on $3 a week eating dinners cooked on a hot plate. Kapuchinsky continues: "Salmond came out of the room and stood above me like the Empire State Building, while I'm crying, putting my cello in its case. He put his arm around my shoulder and said, 'What's the matter, boy, financial troubles?' Though Rose is not over enthusiastic about Salmond's cello playing, his admiration for the man is undeniable. Kapuchinsky was the recipient of Salmond's softer, more compassionate side: "On Monday," the cellist related, "I was called into the principal's office where they gave me lunch free everyday with the faculty and the poor students upstairs. They also offered me $21 (equivalent to nearly $320 in 2008) a week assistance."[18]

For his first lesson, Rose brought in Beethoven's Sonata No. 2. He had never played the work before and only a few bars into the opening, Salmond lifted his tall body out of his comfortable chair, approached the student, grabbed him by the arm and started shaking him, shouting in a tenor-pitched foreign accent, "You silly little boy. What do you know about playing Beethoven?" Lesson over, outside the studio door, Rose burst into tears. The experience had such a profound effect Rose vowed then and there he would never disparage a student in this manner, and he never did.

Salmond also tended to belittle famous leading contemporaries before his cello class. For example, Salmond didn't care for the playing of Gregor Piatigorsky. As a result, students, including Rose, were adversely influenced by the teacher's strong opinions. "He'd tell me that he was not a very good musician, and as a stupid boy, I'd repeat the same thing. [Piatigorsky made his American debut in 1929 with the New York Philharmonic performing

Dvořák's Concerto with Willem Mengelberg conducting. From 1930 through the spring 1940, he made 102 appearances with American orchestras.[19] It was absolutely ridiculous because Piatigorsky was a wonderful artist, as I found out later on in life."

Soon after graduation from Curtis—out from under Salmond's opinionated thumb—Rose discovered that Piatigorsky was a first-rate player; but in his memoir, he expressed a feeling that his performance relied too much on instinct and not enough on practice. Rose reflects that he, too, played from instinct, "but I think I was more careful musically." Salmond's behavior made Rose wonder about authority and the relationship between instructor and student. "Why do teachers feel that they have to be sadistic to teach? It is wrong."

Four years before Salmond died, after Rose had joined the faculty at the Juilliard School of Music alongside his teacher, the British cellist addressed the student class. The timelessness of his words is relevant to Rose's teaching philosophy. Considering Rose heard this speech, it is yet another indication how Salmond's infectious love for music was funneled to Leonard Rose. The address, delivered over ten years after Rose's final lesson with Salmond, does not diminish the everlasting effect his teacher's powerful words left upon Rose. To readers of this book, it becomes murky, as Rose aged, whether he absorbed every last point made in the following excerpted transcript:

ADDRESS TO THE STUDENTS OF THE
JUILLIARD SCHOOL OF MUSIC AT CONVOCATION
Felix Salmond
September 17, 1948

I am now beginning my 25th year at the Juilliard School. This is a long time, but it does not seem so, since I never tire of music, which has what I like to call the feeling of inevitability. It has given me deep happiness to have come in contact with, and tried to help, many highly talented young people to develop into fine professional musicians, and especially to have brought to their knowledge many of the masterpieces of chamber music.

How fortunate we are whose lives are dedicated to music; indeed, we are the richest people on earth. Let us consider for a moment the many dozens of masterworks, which we may hear during the music season in New York. I am almost 60 years old, but even today I cannot hear these great works without a feeling of awe and reverence for the supermen who created such *Beauty*.

Learn to know something of all branches of music. Go hear great singers and great players of other instruments besides your own. I am often astonished and saddened by the ignorance a young pianist, violinist, or cellist shows of any music but his own... Nevertheless, the young pianist should make it a duty to know at least some of the superb chamber music in which the piano is included. The association with good string players will be of inestimable value in helping to develop beautiful piano tone; it will also be invaluable in developing a keen rhythmic sense, than which there is nothing more important in music-making.

It has often struck me how rarely students understand that music is not constantly espressivo! There are long stretches in all big masterworks where no "expression" is called for. But all music, fast or slow, is—with the exception of free recitative—unceasingly rhythmic. Rhythm is the very foundation of a musical structure.

If you are a string player, strive constantly for two things which, when acquired, denote the highest technical perfection: beautiful tone and beautiful intonation. All too often, alas, in listening to string playing, one hears neither! Our two hands, whether used on the keyboard or on bow and fingerboard, should be the means of bringing to the listener the message of the composer and only that.

You cannot possess a piece of music until it possesses you. By this I mean that you should learn to study away from the instrument. Sing mentally and actually the piece you are learning and let it haunt you every hour of the day until you have mastered it. You will then be able to project its message with real conviction.

Don't be apathetic about anything except mediocrity, which should not interest you. Enthusiasm is the salt of life and of art; use it liberally. Try to make all you do in your daily life interesting and exciting, so that your enthusiasm for all activities is constant.

This attitude must inevitably help you to grow as a human being and as an artist.

Never forget that music is a full time job—the study of it should occupy most of your waking hours.

Now, children, in closing I wish you all happy, fruitful, and exciting years in this great school. Make the most of every hour of study; work always with burning and unflagging enthusiasm and courage. Aim for the highest standards only. Learn to be self-critical, humble, modest, happy over talent in your friends and colleagues, and unenvious of their success. And above all, be utterly uncompromising in all matters of artistic integrity. This may get you into trouble occasionally, but your soul will be your own.

I know you will find in the sublime art of music inspiration and exaltation in times of happiness; solace and hope in times of sadness or sorrow. May each and all of you be magnetized by its inexhaustible beauties, by its unique power to move and uplift, from now until life's end.

Good luck to you all!

Felix Salmond, Circa 1945
Courtesy of Wendy Salmond Oler

Chapter Three

COMING OF AGE IN PHILADELPHIA

It is my aim that earnest students shall acquire a thorough musical education, not learning only to sing or play, but also the history of music, the laws of its making, languages, ear-training, and music appreciation. They shall learn to think and to express their thoughts against a background of quiet culture, with the stimulus of personal contact with artist teachers who represent the highest and finest in their art. The aim is for quality of the work rather than quick, showy results.

—Mary Louise Curtis Bok[*]

For the talented boy from Miami, the Curtis Institute of Music in Philadelphia sounded like an ideal and logical next step. However, Leonard Rose failed at his initial attempt to enter the tuition-free school and into the cello class of Felix Salmond. As Rose exclaimed, "I was bitterly disappointed that I had not been accepted the first time I tried out." Rose could not conceal the frustration in not achieving admission into the conservatory of music. Naturally and somewhat naively he viewed himself as the "big fish" in the small pond that was Southern Florida. The audition brought home the reality that other cellists existed, at his age, who played better than he did.

On the drive up to Philadelphia in September of 1933, the farther north Rose and his father traveled, the more the 15-year-old became increasingly "frightened—until I actually became

---
[*] As stated in the 1924 to 1934 Curtis catalogues.

sick to my stomach." The first place the two stopped to sleep was some sort of rooming house where his cot was covered with horrible bedbugs. Continuing the next day, Rose's father's relentless exhortations "I hope you make it," did not boost the confidence of the inhibited youngster. "God knows he'd [Rose's father] done enough harm to me psychologically," Rose stated decades later. That it was rather painful to recall is obvious in the lifelong "nerves" he battled.

Although Salmond did not accept Rose into his own class, he recommended that the teenager remain in Philadelphia to work with Frank Miller, Rose's gifted cousin, who graduated from Curtis and was sitting last chair of the Philadelphia Orchestra earning $90 (equivalent to nearly $1,500 in 2008) a week for a 30-week season—a tremendous amount of money for a musician in those years. In the ensuing six to eight months, Rose not only studied the cello with Miller, he moved into his house. The residency posed a bureaucratic snag regarding Rose's education: Because Rose lived apart from his legal guardians, the school district of Philadelphia could not admit him. As a result, Rose never completed more than an eighth-grade education.

As young men, the camaraderie between Rose and Miller was tremendous. As their stock rose individually, as cellists, their rivalry became genuine.

Frank Miller (1912-1986) also came from a branch of the family that was poor. His father, a tailor just as Harry Rose, came to the United States from Russia at about 19 years of age. Upon his arrival, immigration officers shortened his name from Milofsky to Miller.[20] Frank was born in Baltimore, Maryland, and by age nine he was given a scholarship to attend that city's Peabody Conservatory of Music. In 1927, he auditioned for Felix Salmond and was accepted into Curtis. At conductor Leopold Stokowski's invitation, Miller joined the Philadelphia Orchestra in 1930 at the age of 18.

Miller was kind to his teenaged cousin, often engaging in athletic activities in the sand lots together then treating him to dinners. "We would often play baseball with the local kids," Rose recalled. "Frank was a terrific athlete, he was a marvelous hitter—I wasn't bad either; I was smaller, but we would have in-field practice and do all sorts of things like that." Miller also arranged for Rose to attend the Philadelphia Orchestra in concert, excursions Rose treasured. Miller's tutelage extended to three-cushion billiards and even how to eat spaghetti with a fork and spoon. They had a great time together and understandably, Rose revered Miller as a "kind of god" in the 1930s. The freedom Rose experienced away from a stifling childhood to a great extent enhanced in close friendship with Miller.

To Rose, Frank Miller the cellist was equally illuminating. Rose overheard Frank practice every day and soon began lessons with him: "In those years, Frank had tremendous command of the instrument and sounded like a house afire," Rose relates. "He immediately set off helping me with my bow arm. I used to play with a rather high setting of the hand on the bow and immediately he lowered my wrist, which, of course, was absolutely right." Daily, Rose was exposed to the intensely ambitious Miller who relentlessly practiced in addition to rehearsals with the Philadelphia Orchestra. "I am somewhat sorry that I did not stay with Frank Miller longer," Rose confesses in his memoir, "because he really gave me a first-class beginning of a technique on the instrument." Cellist Avron Coleman,[21] who studied with Miller in the 1940s, uncovers Miller's methods:

> One lesson with Frank was an all-day affair. I paid Frank $25 for what amounted to a lesson from 2:00 to 5:00 in the afternoon. We would start with a half hour of arpeggios and scales. He had one fingering for all major and minor arpeggios, which worked for them all. He loved practicing scales with odd groups of notes bowing triplets or five notes to a bow. As a result you would be changing your bow or position after an odd group. He also loved the Popper* études. He knew all 40 of them from memory, I kid you not. You could name one of them and Frank could play it in a concert performance from beginning to end from memory. He must have ferociously studied those études at one time in his life.

---

* David Popper (1843-1913) was a celebrated Czech cellist and composer for the cello. His 40 études are virtuoso exercises designed to improve every technical angle imaginable.

He knew that if all the Popper études could be played, that it could cover any problem in both hands. We ended each session with repertoire. Even if a student was not ready for it, he wanted this exposure to the demands of the repertoire.

The major focus of Rose's work with Miller was Haydn's D Major Concerto. Through Miller, Rose learned numerous ways in which to navigate the difficult technical demands of the work. In addition, Miller infused his cousin with Haydn's required charismatic style. The following May (1934), his second examination bowled over the delighted Salmond who immediately accepted him—and with the full scholarship to the Curtis Institute starting the following fall. Rose's secret desire then was to play in the Philadelphia Orchestra on the last stand—with his cousin.

Quickly the school took notice of the youngster. At the age of 16, Rose was appointed the Curtis Orchestra's principal cellist. Fritz Reiner, the conductor at Curtis from 1931 to 1941, was Rose's prototype for four years. Due to the school's schedule of three concerts per academic year, in the course of Rose's studies, he performed in a mere 12 orchestral concerts—a number Rose felt was "utterly ridiculous" and woefully inadequate experience for what lay in store for him upon graduation. He was also shocked as Reiner often used rough, unthinkable language with his adolescent peers. Once, enraged, he threw pennies toward the double-bass section calling out, "You're just furniture movers. Here!" Another time a cellist accidentally plucked a pizzicato note too hard causing the string to slap against the fingerboard. Rose recalls Reiner's cutting tone, "What do you think you're doing, playing a percussion instrument?" The Curtis Orchestra had no choice but to tolerate the Hungarian-born Reiner's caustic remarks, because these students had the immeasurable privilege to play under America's top contemporary conductors. Of course, the maestro offered plenty in the way of education, as well. Miller's feelings for Reiner differed considerably from his cousin's. Toward the end of his life, Miller recalled:

"I had played under Fritz Reiner since I was a young boy. When I was at the Curtis Institute, Reiner used to come and conduct the student orchestra. ... He used to sit down and play bits of every symphony, every solo work, and every opera on the piano. He had almost the greatest knowledge of music I have ever encountered. His tempos were always so good."

To which Rose adds:

"Of course, Reiner did teach us something absolutely essential, something of inestimable value throughout our careers. He was mean, nasty, sadistic, and sarcastic, and left us well prepared to face conductors of a similar disposition. I guess, in a way, it was a kind of preparation for my later years when I witnessed some absolutely abominable behavior from Toscanini."

In Rose's student days at Curtis, the school maintained a summer colony in Rockport, Maine, where Mary Bok (the founder of Curtis) provided many of her faculty a lovely place to live on the bay. One of the residences, the Stone House, was where Felix Salmond, his wife, and two children spent their vacations. Per Curtis policy, teachers were allowed to invite their particularly gifted students, and in the summer of 1934, Salmond took Rose. He stayed in a small room, adjoining the garage, detached from the main building. His room contained a small desk, a chair, and a bed. There was no bathroom. In this setting, he had an opportunity to become acquainted with the personal side of the teacher. The summer marked the first time Rose had seen the game of golf, and Salmond was a golfer. He would ask Rose and one of Rose's colleagues, Samuel Mayes,[*] to walk along the golf course with him while he played. This was Rose's introduction to the sport, which he would eventually play quite well. Stone House also had a ping-pong table in Salmond's bedroom. Using the Chinese penholder grip on the paddle, Rose became an excellent, agile player who could easily beat Mayes and Salmond. Rose recounts:

> In those summer months, we would come back to the Stone House around 8:00 o'clock in the evening and if their garage door was open and the car was not there,

---

[*] At 12 years of age, Mayes (1917-1990) began his studies with Felix Salmond. In 1938, he was appointed principal cellist of the Philadelphia Orchestra, under Stokowski. After 10 years, he became the principal cellist of the Boston Symphony. Mayes performed the American premiere of Dmitri Kabalevsky's "Cello Concerto" (1949), with the composer conducting.

we had Salmond's permission to use the ping-pong table. We would go to the bedroom, put the light on, and play. One night turned out to be quite embarrassing. Sammy and I had returned from the local little town of Rockport to the Stone House, with the house dark, the garage door open, and no car in the garage. That was our signal, so we went into the house and Sammy paraded into the bedroom, switched on the light, and there were the Salmonds in bed together! Well, you can bet Sammy switched off that light awfully quickly. The next day, we went to Salmond, and he knew exactly what had happened. He was very, very kind about it—I must say he had a wonderful streak to him. We apologized.

Leonard Rose in Rockport, Maine, 1934
Courtesy of Arthur Rose

That summer, as Rose did for most of his life, he got up early in the morning to practice. "I was an early riser and always a compulsive worker," Rose emphatically stated numerous times in his unpublished memoir. It was not uncommon for him to have practiced as much as four hours by noon. Rose continues: "I was the original worrier. Those old words of my father, when he drove me to Curtis always came back to haunt me: 'I hope you make it. I hope you make it!' Somehow his words always rang around in my brain."

Back in Philadelphia, on the $2 a week his parents could afford, Rose proceeded with his studies. One day after practicing at a friend's house just across from Rittenhouse Square, Rose locked himself out. The house was empty and he suddenly had no way to retrieve his instrument. He recently received a call from another friend informing him that Stokowski wanted to hear some Curtis instrumentalists. Was Rose available? Frantic, Rose climbed up the fire escape of the steep apartment building and jimmied open the window with a coat hanger so he could show up promptly at the conductor's little house, located coincidentally just behind Curtis. The colors—purples, greens, blues, and yellows—of the Stokowski house decor overwhelmed the cellist—as did the imposing maestro, 6 feet 2 inches tall with a mane of white hair, when he entered the room. "Good afternoon. What would you like to play for me, young man?" Rose began to play and Stokowski responded, "Bravo, it sounds beautiful, very good. I'd like you to read something for me." The slow movement of Beethoven's Symphony No. 5 was placed before the cellist. He sight-read it without much trouble. Then Stokowski put a movement of a Mozart symphony on the music stand. Rose had never seen that particular score before and had a little difficulty with it. "Leonard," the conductor said, "I've got to go downstairs for a few minutes. Why don't you look at it? I'll be up in a couple of minutes." Then Stokowski disappeared. *Where on earth did he go?* Rose thought. He placed a fingering or two in the passage in question then felt confident. Stokowski returned and the cellist proceeded to play it well. Stokowski said, "Very good. How would you like to come to the Philadelphia Orchestra?" This was Rose's second year at Curtis. Rose remembered responding, "Mr. Stokowski, I am flattered and honored and I love the Philadelphia Orchestra. I suppose I really should talk to my teacher and to Mrs. Bok." Rose floated out of Stokowski's colorful den imagining that at 17 he would realize his dream of becoming a member of the famous orchestra.

Mary Bok and Felix Salmond, however, dissuaded the young, no doubt deflated, cellist, emphasizing the importance of his education. Perhaps they also had some stern words with

Stokowski, who had conducted the student orchestra prior to Reiner. These guardians may have requested that he keep his seductive invitations away from their young talent. Around this time, Rose was smitten by the glamour of Sunday afternoon radio broadcasts that featured Arturo Toscanini and the New York Philharmonic.* There was something about those broadcasts that thrilled Rose. Rose dreamed bigger now: of becoming principal cellist of the New York Philharmonic.

During Rose's second year at Curtis, he met his future wife, Minnie Knopow, a talented and vivacious violist from Milwaukee. The youngest of four siblings, Minnie came from a Russian-Jewish musical family, and as a child, she learned to play several instruments. "There wasn't an instrument my mother couldn't pick up and play ... from the violin to the zither," Rose's daughter, Barbara, asserts. She was enrolled at Curtis to study the viola with Louis Bailly. One day Rose walked to the soda fountain where Minnie held a part-time job. They rapidly fell for each other and within a week of their meeting, Rose invited her to play string quartets with him. Barbara recounts, "My mother had poise, beauty, and a kindness which everyone recognized. ... She was generous with her time and worked for causes that she felt were worth her while ..." Later in life, Minnie became involved in music education in the Long Island school systems and her charitable work extended to unfortunate students in need of money. She was a member of the advisory board of the Great Neck Adult Education Program and a board member of the Great Neck Symphony. She also headed fund drives for the New York Philharmonic.

At Curtis, Bok told Minnie that Rose was going to be famous someday and that it was her duty to "make him practice." Minnie was not allowed to see him until he practiced for hours each day. Their love affair endured through their conservatory years and

---

* The first network broadcast of a symphony orchestra occurred in 1926, the first sponsored one came in 1929. Between 1920 and 1929 the number of families with radio receivers grew from 60,000 to 10,250,000 (Andrea Olmstead: Juilliard A History. University of Illinois Press, 1999. p100). Beginning in 1930, the Philharmonic's Sunday-afternoon concerts, conducted by Toscanini, were carried by the Columbia Broadcasting System and heard throughout the U.S. to an estimated nine million by 1934.

they married December 1, 1938. Sixteen years later, with Rose making his living as a soloist and with children aged 10 and 13, Minnie was diagnosed with chronic lymphocytic leukemia, a condition that jolted the family. During the ensuing decade in which the disease darted in and out of remission, Rose often returned home from tours distraught at seeing her weakened physical state. He despairingly blamed himself for the misery he felt he caused. In 1964, the Roses' life dramatically changed with her death on June 6. The closeness between the two is debatable. According to Rose's children, she was the glue that held the family together. Her death left Leonard without a coach, an organizer, and a secretary. "When my mother died," Barbara maintains, "my father's life died with her. ... She was his strength."[22]

Leonard and Minnie, 1939
Courtesy of Arthur Rose

Rose's son, Arthur, contends that his father could not have performed at an exceptional level of artistry without his mother's complete involvement in his musical maturity. Yet, some distinctly remember how badly Rose treated Minnie, dressing her down in front of others. "I had the feeling that Rose just didn't have much respect for her at all," was a sentiment floated before me. "Minnie was a homespun mom type and played a very subservient role in his life. And he could be downright mean to her. ..." Rose's mention of his first wife in his memoir is harsh: "I'd love to be able to fill the pages with an epic romance here, but I'm afraid that I was just a dumb, frightened jerk who couldn't wait to jump into something he had no business jumping into. I was simply too damn young. I'd had no experience with girls; I was shy and introverted as well. If I had my way, I'd pass a law prohibiting males from marrying before the age of 25!" In fervent disagreement, the children recall their father performing for their mother before critical concerts who would in turn proffer critical assessments. In fact, Rose "could not go onstage, couldn't play" if Minnie wasn't in his line of sight from the soloist position onstage.[23] Arthur's declaration of his father's massive reliance upon Minnie's musical judgments and criticisms throughout is intriguing yet wholly unsubstantiated in Rose's memoir.

Also during his second year at Curtis, in addition to gaining his first experience teaching as Salmond's assistant, Mary Bok gave Rose an extra $70 a month (equivalent to nearly $1,100 in 2008) on top of his full scholarship. The generous gesture made life quite comfortable for the teenager. Artur Rodzinski, then music director of the Cleveland Orchestra who taught operatic and orchestral conducting at Curtis from 1927 to 1929, was well aware of the school's reputation for producing outstanding performers. During the academic year, Rose tagged along with a group of classmates who were traveling to New York City to the Essex House to play for the conductor. In essence, it was an audition for his orchestra in Cleveland. "What do you have for me, Leonard?" Rose played a couple of pages of the Haydn D Major Concerto. "Very good. You play beautifully. Do you by any chance know the solo in the Brahms B-Flat Piano Concerto?" "Excuse me?" Rose asked. The cellist was too embarrassed to tell him that he hadn't the faintest idea Brahms composed a B-flat Piano Concerto! Instead, the cellist offered the opening cadenza from the Brahms "Double" Concerto. "Fine, play that." Rose loved that piece and was learning it for the first time back at school. He executed the passagework confidently and accurately. "Thank you very much. You are certainly gifted."

A short time later, the manager of the Cleveland Orchestra telephoned Rose to ask whether he would like come to the Cleveland Orchestra as assistant principal cellist for what appeared to be an attractive salary then, too. Once again Salmond demanded he hold off, reiterating that he should remain patient and concentrate on the cello class repertoire.

Rose also asserts, although without verification, that during this same period, he was similarly offered the principal cello position of the Chicago Symphony Orchestra. According to Rose: "Although I did not get an official, firm offer from the Chicago Orchestra, it was through [Efrem] Zimbalist,* and I could have had the job—there was no question of it."

Despite the lure of these exciting symphonic positions, Rose remained the dutiful Curtis student, playing on an inexpensive $400 German instrument that his father purchased years earlier. Salmond, however, knew that to succeed professionally, Rose needed a better instrument; so he had a talk with Mary Bok. The wealthy heiress agreed to buy an instrument for Rose on terms that amounted to a permanent loan, no interest and repayable at any time. "I want to illustrate again and again how very kind and caring Mrs. Bok was," Rose recalls. In 1936, Rose bought his first fine cello made by David Tecchler from William Moennig & Son for $5,000 (equivalent to nearly $77,600 in 2008). Soon after, Felix Salmond heard him in concert in Philadelphia and wrote on October 22:

> My Dear Leonard,
> Your playing yesterday gave me more than pleasure— far more. It had all the qualities I admire most in music-making: beautiful tone, perfect intonation and rhythm and above all, a subtle phrasing and feeling for style that are the hallmarks of a first-rate talent. I am more

---

* Efrem Zimbalist (1889-1985), director at Curtis from 1941 to 1968 who would eventually hire and fire Rose from the Curtis faculty was considered one of Leopold Auer's most famous violin students. Zimbalist's second marriage in 1943 was to Mary Louise Curtis Bok.

than ever convinced that you are destined to become a great player and, much more, a great artist. Be grateful every day of your life for your beautiful gift, treasure it, and work unceasingly to bring it as near perfection as humanly possible. Above all, dear Leonard, remain truly modest and humble toward your art and its great Masters and you will never stand still. Self-criticism means a constant striving for the unattainable and the more you will learn—the more you will want to know of the miracle of great music. With every sincere wish for your future, I am always, yours most sincerely,
Felix Salmond
P.S. Your cello is superb.

During 1937, his third year at Curtis, Rose began to explore the chamber music literature with—among others—violinist Oscar Shumsky, who would remain a lifelong colleague and friend. Shumsky recalled that it didn't take very long before Rose's presence was felt in the school's closely knit family of students. "Rumor had it that the new kid in the block was a terrific cellist ..." Rose reciprocates the compliment as mutual admiration abounded. In 1982, Rose stated, "To this day, I don't think I have ever heard a greater violin talent." Twice a week on average, the young virtuosos would meet with a violist and another violinist to read string quartets. Shumsky was living at the time with his parents, also Russian-Jewish immigrants, in Philadelphia. The musicians usually assembled between 4:00 and 5:00 in the late afternoon to sight read for a couple of hours. After dinner, they would start fresh and sometimes not stop until 3:00 or 4:00 in the morning. In the 1930s, Frank Miller brought Rose to Shumsky's home for what was Rose's first exposure to Schubert's two-cello quintet. In a truthful sense, Shumsky became Rose's chamber music mentor. Rose described him as having "one of those marvelous minds and he had that quality even then. He knew all of these pieces and had studied the scores and led [the quartet] in such a masterly fashion."

Shumsky's bow arm, Rose believed, was one of the finest he had ever seen. As such, he seemingly helped inspire the cellist's long fascination with bow technique and sound. One illustrative concept was how Shumsky* demonstrated basic principles of changing directions with the bow and stressed to Rose that the bow did not actually go straight across the strings, rather, it glides in figure 8s: the square aspect of the bow was something that mentally shouldn't exist. Another instance, he emphasized the sensation of "pulling the bow," a phrase heard time and again by generations of Rose students. And long hours they discussed the art of vibrato. These two men became musical soulmates. Upon Rose's death, Shumsky wrote, "Let it be remembered that he loved his instrument and served its music with honor."[24]

On the evening of November 17, 1936, Leonard Rose had his first thrill of stepping onto the stage to solo with an orchestra in York, Pennsylvania. Rose performed Haydn's D Major Concerto and collected $200 for the engagement. One month later came the most important concert of his young life with Fritz Reiner and the Curtis Orchestra: the Brahms "Double" Concerto with violinist Eudice Shapiro (1914-2007).

As the only female student of Efrem Zimbalist, the gifted violinist's collaboration with Rose would not last beyond a few intensive years at school where their piano trio often traveled to Baltimore to perform in private homes. Shapiro remembered Rose as "a very quiet boy. But I knew that he was going to be a foremost cellist. He had to, with that kind of sound."[25] In Shapiro's final year at Curtis, after exhaustive coaching lessons with Felix Salmond, the two artists performed the Brahms "Double" Concerto at the Pennsylvania Museum of Art with the Curtis Orchestra. The concert was broadcast on the CBS Radio Network December 20, 1936. Although of antiquated sound quality, Rose relished owning a copy of this recording, a treasure he listened to from time to time throughout his life.

In Rose's early Curtis days, recording devices were made in the 78-rpm format that could only run a few minutes per side. Columbia Records, Victor Talking Machine Company, and the Brunswick-Balke Collender Company were industry leaders. A

---

* Shumsky (1917-2000) was on the faculty of the Juilliard School from 1953-1978 and taught at Curtis from 1961-1965. Shumsky and Rose's final performance together was in Toronto in 1983 where they performed Kodály's Duo for violin and cello and then joined the Orford String Quartet in a performance of Brahms' String Sextet in B-Flat.

Presto Recorder, introduced to the United States in the fall of 1934, and its "Presto Disc" was quickly becoming the industry standard, however short-lived. Curtis used this new technology to record the 1936 Brahms concert. That year, Presto equipment was being installed in radio stations nationwide. With the aural document, Rose proudly comments that it served as proof that at age 18, "I played the instrument extremely well ... it is a very difficult concerto and this was not only an acceptable performance, but in many ways a remarkable performance, especially considering our youth." Arthur Statter, a trumpeter in the orchestra, recalled, "As soon as I heard him play, I said that this guy must be the greatest cellist alive. I am talking about the very first notes I heard him play. He had what we call a rubato. Nobody could master the rubato the way Leonard Rose did."[26] Unmistakably, Rose's playing held this powerful effect on colleagues and listeners from the inception of his career.

In his fourth and final year at Curtis, Rose met Samuel Chotzinoff, who was hired to teach a class in music journalism at the school. Unknown to Rose, David Sarnoff—president of the Radio Corporation of America (RCA), which owned the subsidiary Red and Blue networks of the National Broadcasting Company (NBC)—had embarked on an ambitious project of organizing a world-class symphony orchestra expressly for Arturo Toscanini, and specifically to exploit radio's ability to attract an audience of millions. Toscanini's tenure with the New York Philharmonic which had ended—marking a key transition in his career and transforming the maestro's reputation as primarily an opera conductor to one almost exclusively devoted to symphonic repertoire—was about to be resuscitated.[27]

Chotzinoff, born in Vitebsk, Russia, in 1889 (died 1964), began his life in the musical world as piano accompanist to Efrem Zimbalist in 1912 and continued in that role on tour with Alma Gluck (1915) and with Jascha Heifetz (1918), with whom he recorded several works in the early 1920s. From 1925 to 1931, Chotzinoff was a music critic of the *New York World* subsequently writing reviews for the *New York Post*. Mary Bok summoned Rose and asked him if he would like to play for Chotzinoff's class. Afterward, she told the cellist, the class would make various observations and criticisms that the Russian musician would monitor. Rose, not initially thrilled with the criticism part of it, agreed. At the appointed hour, Rose entered, sat down, and played unaccompanied Bach and Robert Schumann's Cello Concerto. "Thank you very much," Chotzinoff said. "My class will be over at four o'clock. Could you possibly come back to see me at that time?" When he returned, he asked what Rose planned after graduation. The young cellist responded with uncertainty but that he had to get a job somewhere: "Don't forget," Rose points out from his memoir, "in those years, we didn't have all those competitions that exist today [1982]; but word had gotten around that I was that rare bird—a real hot shot young cellist. There weren't so many of those then; there were damned few. Today, there are many, many more, but this goes back to 1938, and there were very few really talented young cellists." Chotzinoff stunned Rose, "How would you like to play with Toscanini next year? I think I can arrange that." Artur Rodzinski, who Toscanini hired to form, train, and co-conduct the newly formed NBC Symphony, was auditioning 60 to 70 applicants a day in New York. Before he was through, he would hear an astounding 400 to 500 musicians for 100 orchestral positions.[28] Rose, though, already auditioned for Rodzinski at the Essex House two years earlier, when he made a formidable impression. So formidable, in fact, that Rodzinski offered him the assistant principal position in Cleveland. He was an obvious choice. Chotzinoff would have no trouble convincing Rodzinski about Rose who had no idea that his juggernaut rise to fame had just begun.

"Oh my heavens, yes, I would love to do that!" Rose managed to say.

The next call Rose took was from Toscanini's personnel manager, H. Leopold Spitalny[29] who informed him, "Look, kid, you will have to come to New York and join the union." Rose took the advice and even prior to graduation, moved to Manhattan with Minnie. Yet in New York, where Leonard and Minnie lived in a friend's apartment, Rose grew uneasy about Spitalny's plan to become an immediate union member before the strictly enforced six-month probation union status. Rose noted in his memoir that his anxiety reached a point of severe emotional distress. He had no option but to follow his instincts that Spitalny, a powerful figure, would take care of matters. Although still subsisting on the $2 a week his mother sent him, there was little to do that summer but go out with Minnie and pitch horseshoes. "That didn't cost anything because we used to go out to the park ... and I became pretty good at it. I practiced."

Chapter Four

TOSCANINI AND THE NBC SYMPHONY, NEW YORK 1938

Playing with Toscanini was a musical rebirth. The clarity, intensity, and honesty of his musical vision—his own torment—was like a cleansing baptismal pool. Caught up in his force, your own indifference was washed away. There was a purpose and self-fulfillment in your work. It was not a job, it was a calling.[30]

—Samuel Antek, violinist, NBC Symphony

Arturo Toscanini was born on March 25, 1867, in Parma, Italy. Neither his ancestors nor his parents were musical, yet because his community was filled with notoriously exuberant opera fans, the young boy was deeply affected. In 1878, he was accepted as a scholarship student to the Parma Conservatory—the year in which Brahms's First Symphony premiered, the year of the first Bayreuth festival, and six years before Stravinsky's birth. Beginning in Toscanini's second year at the Conservatory, the cello was his principal instrument, which he studied with Leandro Carini.

Toscanini's studies on the cello developed well. He not only taught himself some important cello melodies in orchestral scores, he studied many other key works at the piano. Between 1881 and 1885, he played in the theater's famous string section at the Teatro Reggio in Turin, which Verdi called the finest in Italy. In the spring of 1884, the then-17-year-old Toscanini, appeared as cellist, conductor, and composer on a program that Conservatory students presented at the school. He played the introduction and polonaise for cello by E. Dunkler then conducted the orchestra in his own andante and scherzo. No fewer than 10 newspapers reviewed the performance and praised him, especially as cellist.

Almost 20 years before Toscanini's death, a *Fortune* magazine poll survey revealed that one-quarter of the United States population knew his name and that he was an orchestral conductor. His appearances on the cover of *Life* magazine (1938 and 1943) and *Time* magazine (1948) spoke to his unprecedented popularity. Therefore, it comes as no surprise that Toscanini was indisputably the world's most famous musician at the time Leonard Rose played in the NBC Symphony. Toscanini, a conductor of uncompromising ideals and convictions, incited commotion everywhere he went. More than 30 books have been published about the man since the first in 1929, which marked the mere beginning of a seemingly endless public infatuation with the Italian maestro.

Rose was the twelfth of twelve cellists in the NBC Symphony, turning pages on the last stand of the section during the orchestra's 1938-1939 season. In the splendor of Art Deco that flaunted Deer Island granite, Indiana limestone, and a striking new feature for the time—an escalator—the 70-story RCA building was the largest private building project undertaken in the era. It was also the centerpiece of 21 buildings that made up the Rockefeller Center between Fifth and Sixth Avenues in midtown Manhattan. Rose's subway ride from his apartment at 1921 E. 97th Street led him to a dramatic sunken public roller skating rink overlooked by Paul Manship's giant gilded bronze sculpture Prometheus that rested above a pool of water. This spanking new facility was completed November 1939 and housed the largest radio studio in the world known as 8H because the entrance to the studio was on the eighth floor. The space was large enough to accommodate a 130-piece orchestra and seat 1,250. Although Toscanini's favorite autumn colors adorned the studio, the towering drapes that covered the walls, the cigar box–recording booth behind the stage, and the generally drab materials that went into the construction of the studio contributed to what has been described as the room's "dry" and "antiseptic" acoustic.

Toscanini historians, however, point out that he preferred these conditions because all the notes, no matter how fast, could be heard cleanly and clearly.

Rose's stand partner, a Russian Jew by the name of Gdal Saleski,* was chosen one season earlier, making him a charter member of the orchestra. The two of them hit it off immediately, especially after Saleski learned that Rose could understand some Yiddish. Saleski affectionately called Rose "Ketzeleh," which means kitten. The name was appropriate; after all, Rose was only 20 years old and had no professional orchestra experience. Rose soon found out that his formal training at Curtis had not provided the best possible preparation for his prestigious seat. Rose states, "Curtis seemed to believe that nearly all its carefully selected students would become solo virtuosi, the successors to Casals, Heifetz, and Rubinstein. This approach, with its emphasis on solo literature, is not only simplistic, it can be quite damaging. In any school of music at any time, only a very few students will be destined for any sort of a solo career at all ..."

In its second season, the NBC Symphony grew from 92 to 94 musicians. Twenty-one of its members formerly held first-desk positions in other prominent orchestras.[31] The talent assembled was possible in part due to the extraordinary salaries offered to certain players (concertmaster Mischa Mischakoff reportedly received $450 a week in 1937—equivalent to nearly $6,700 in 2008). It was also an attractive job—and in Manhattan no less, where a musician could earn money in other city venues.

At 69, Toscanini did not initially want to return to America after his triumphant tenure as director of the New York Philharmonic—his farewell concert at Carnegie Hall April 29, 1936 having sold out in a matter of hours.[32] After leading the Metropolitan Opera (1908-1915) and the New York Philharmonic (1929-1936), which earned him the critical acclaim of "prophet," "priest," and "vehicle of revelation" from *New York Herald Tribune* critic Lawrence Gilman, among others, Toscanini felt mentally and physically worn out.[33] RCA's David Sarnoff, who presided over the 142 broadcasting stations that furnished access to

---

* Gdal Saleski (1888-1967), who had been a member of the New York Symphony, wrote *Famous Musicians of Jewish Origin*, published in 1927.

virtually all of the 88 percent of American homes with radios, had different plans. Luring Toscanini back to New York by presenting the opportunity to lead a custom-made, world-class, symphony orchestra specifically for broadcasting to potentially 25 million homes was too compelling for Toscanini to turn down. In Milan, Sarnoff's right-hand man, Samuel Chotzinoff, made Toscanini the offer he couldn't refuse. After having agreed in principle on the concept, Toscanini stated that he would return on the condition that the ensemble equal or surpass the standard set by the orchestras in New York, Boston, and Philadelphia. Chotzinoff, with assistance from the Cleveland Orchestra's music director, Artur Rodzinski, had 10 months to assemble an orchestra before the Maestro's first broadcast on Christmas night 1937.[34]

Leonard Rose had been chosen to join this elite group of men and at his tender age, was curious about the evolution of the cello. He stumbled upon and purchased one of the first books on the subject, a volume by Polish writer Wilhelm Wasielewski, originally published in German in 1888 and translated into English in 1894. Rose appreciated Wasielewski's discussion not only of the history of the cello, but his description of the various national schools where it was played and their notable cellists: the Italians, the French, and the Germans. In the section on Italian cellists, Rose learned that Toscanini, the Parma Conservatory pupil, had been hailed a child prodigy. Excited by his new knowledge, he approached the conductor during an intermission. "Maestro," Rose began timidly, "I found something most interesting about your cello playing in a book." In his heavily accented English, Toscanini replied, "Yes, what did you find? No, no! Don't tell me. You must show me. I must see it for myself!" Rose brought him the book and watched as the old man's face instantly lit up with surprise and delight.

Toscanini's fame and respect from musicians had a lot to do with an almost zealous approach to commitment in every piece of music; precision and passion dominated his every concert. In recordings made late in his life, he hardly strayed from the composer's markings. Some listeners have complained that Toscanini was an interpreter with the dedication of a fundamentalist. If the composer neglected to write in an *accelerando* or a *ritardando,* Toscanini would rarely consider the possible nuance. Yet, once after hearing a musician object to switching a *forte* passage to *piano* the conductor requested, Toscanini's shout could be heard throughout the bare acoustic of Studio 8H, "What? *Forte? Forte?* ... What means *forte?* ... Is a thousand *fortes*—all kinds of *fortes*. Sometimes a *forte* is a pia-a-a-no, *piano* is *forte*."[35] One outspoken Toscanini critic, Eduard Steuermann, described the Italian's performance ideal as "the barbarism of perfection." He continues:

> To be sure, passages are not inflated or climaxes overstressed for the sake of fascination. There is iron discipline. ... The new fetish is the flawlessly functioning, metallically brilliant apparatus as such, in which all the cogwheels mesh so perfectly that not the slightest hole remains open for the meaning of the whole. Perfect, immaculate performance in the latest style presents [the work] as already complete from the very first note. The performance sounds like its own phonograph recording ... The protective fixation of the work leads to its destruction, for its unity is realized in precisely that spontaneity which is sacrificed to the fixation.

Members of the Frankfurt School, who represent a time of the leftist Institute for Social Research (Sozialforschung), observed that Toscanini routinely compromised counterpoint and inner voices: "the Maestro ... replaces the Fuhrer-personality and religion, and also expresses the victory of technique and administration over the music; with him, people feel musically well-tended, safe and sheltered."[36] Toscanini arrived on the scene during a period when German conductors—such as Hans von Bülow, Richard Strauss, Gustav Mahler, Arthur Nikisch, and Wilhelm Furtwängler—routinely took extreme liberties. In many ways, Toscanini swung the pendulum in the opposite direction. Many of his protégés, then attached to symphony orchestras of their own—Guido Cantelli, Erich Leinsdorf, Artur Rodzinski, William Steinberg, Alfred Wallenstein, and Milton Katims—conducted in the same manner.[37] Fritz Reiner and George Szell, simultaneously forging fine careers, also agreed in principle with Toscanini. Szell openly spoke of the man's legacy: "Whatever you may think about his interpretation of a specific work, that he changed the whole concept of conducting and that he rectified many, many arbitrary procedures of a generation of conductors before him is now already authentic history." And he inspired other conductors whose authority infused Leonard Rose: Charles Münch of the Boston Symphony (1949-1962), who ranked Toscanini "of all the great ... the greatest." To Pierre Monteux of the Boston Symphony (1919-1924) and San Francisco Symphony (1936-52), he was "the greatest of all." Eugene Ormandy, of the Minneapolis Symphony (1931-36) and Philadelphia Orchestra (1938-1980), called him "the greatest conductor of all times," and his "one and only musical influence."[38] From a historical perspective, Toscanini served a vital role in correcting mannerisms of dubious taste, which the inured public accepted but Toscanini detested.

On the podium, he was earnest; and when problems arose, he threw temper tantrums: loud, legendary rages. "It was among the most horrifying sounds I have ever heard," a member of his NBC Symphony recalled. "It seemed to come from his entrails. He would almost double up, his mouth opened wide, his face red, as if on the verge of an apoplectic fit. Then a raucous blast of unbelievable volume would blare forth." Unknown to Toscanini, the Victor recording engineers kept an open microphone on some of his rehearsals, and later produced acetate discs of the more interesting tantrums for posterity. Violinist Joseph Gingold, who would become one of Rose's dearest friends, described one such occurrence during a 1938 rehearsal of Tchaikovsky's "Pathétique" Symphony: "He came to the rehearsal with the preconceived idea that the orchestra was set in its way of playing the symphony, and he was right. We came to ... the D-Major melody (in the first movement), which traditionally we had all played with a *ritardando* on the first three notes. He stopped: "Signori, perche? Why? Is written so, eh? Ancora." We started again; and again we made the *ritardando:* it was so ingrained in us we couldn't help it. And he threw a fit, shouting so loud that we all looked up in astonishment, "Se, tradizione! The first asino—the first jackass— did it that way and everyone follow him." Then he gestured toward the score: "This is my tradizione! So play like this."[39]

Leonard Rose soon experienced Toscanini's irrational podium behavior. Early in the cellist's tenure, the NBC Symphony began rehearsing a piece by Giacomo Meyerbeer that required the Metropolitan Opera Chorus' participation. Only Toscanini seemed to know the obscure work. Unhappy with what he heard, he would stop every few minutes, leap down and snake his way through the orchestra to chew out the singers, in Italian. Rose's familiarity with the language was limited, but the fear Toscanini elicited by his use of foul words was palpable. The inexperienced, somewhat naïve, 20-year-old cellist was as surprised as the rest of the personnel when Toscanini sped from his position at the front of the stage to the back, coming perilously close to smashing someone's instrument—like Eddie Bachman, the principal second violinist's Stradivarius. Rose couldn't suppress some mild amusement at the perplexing scene. The pattern continued with Toscanini growing angrier and angrier. Suddenly, the conductor snapped his ivory baton in half and tossed the score high into the air with pages fluttering in all directions. Regardless of his 70 years, Toscanini jumped to the floor of the auditorium and began to pace in front of the ensemble like a caged lion—except, according to Rose, "for the orchestra members, Toscanini wasn't caged!" Rose felt confused, despite his respect for and awe of Toscanini. In this initiation, he watched the world's preeminent conductor dart back and forth; the musicians sat idle and bewildered. Throughout the tirade, Rose persistently noticed how impressive a figure Toscanini cut with the black alpaca jacket with a high clerical collar and striped formal trousers he routinely wore to rehearsals; his striking facial features, distinguished white hair, piercing eyes; and, of course, those abominable curses. At this point, Saleski leaned over toward Rose and whispered, "Ketzeleh, mestahme hat er zich nicht gut oisekaht beint in der frie," which translates, "Kitten, perhaps he didn't take a good shit this morning!" Rose howled in laughter. He could hardly control himself. Moments later, the rehearsal was abruptly called off as Toscanini could be seen smashing chairs on his way out of the auditorium. Toscanini was simply too angry to function. The performance of Meyerbeer's *Dinorah* Overture with the Metropolitan Opera Chorus was presented as scheduled November 12, 1938.

Despite the notorious tantrums, Toscanini and his commitment to music inspired admiration. His performances of the classical and romantic repertoire were unmatched in intensity and urgency. Furthermore, he held fellow conductors, critics, musicians, and audiences spellbound by his charisma. Much of what Rose heard stimulated and motivated the ensemble, for example, when Toscanini directed: "I don't want to hear the notes any more. There must be no more notes. Only spirit here! ... Abandon yourselves to your hearts; it's not enough to interpret the signs you have on the paper in front of your eyes. Look, I'm shuddering here. You must shudder, too. ... What you're expressing is serenity, contentedness, but it's not joy yet [Beethoven's Ninth Symphony]. You have to look for it in yourselves, not in the music ..."[40] The man also possessed outstanding communication skills. If his words failed to achieve a desired result, he would pantomime, sing—in a rough falsetto at times—or try something else. If that failed, he would lay down the baton and point to his head, his staring eyes would scan his alert musicians and he would shout "T'ink!"

Often categorized as a contemporary of Stokowski (born in 1882), Klemperer (1885), and Furtwängler (1886), Toscanini fit more closely into the generation of Nikisch (1855) and Mahler (1860).[41] The earliest part of Toscanini's career coincided with Wagner—viewed as a radical modernist—Brahms, Tchaikovsky, and Verdi still composing. Also, when Toscanini gained international renown, Debussy, Puccini, Ravel, Strauss and Igor Stravinsky still created notable pieces. Around the turn of the twentieth century, he and Mahler set out to drastically transform performance practices in their respective opera houses. Mahler became artistic director of the Vienna Opera in 1897 at age 37; in 1898, Toscanini became the principal conductor of La Scala in Milan at age 31. Ultimately, Mahler gave up his position to compose. Toscanini, however, continued to impose landmark operational changes with an iron will. In 1908, these two men would meet up at New York's Metropolitan Opera: rival conductors under the same roof.*

---

* Just prior to Mahler's acceptance of three months' work at the Metropolitan in 1907 for a staggering $15,000 (equivalent to $355,000 in 2008), his eldest

About a month following Emanuel Feuermann's performance of *Don Quixote* with the NBC Symphony, in which Rose did not play (but certainly heard) due to union restrictions, a splendid opportunity landed in his lap. Television remained some years off, but a special radio feature enabled news broadcasts via short-wave radio. The signal, however, frequently lacked strength. At 9:00 Sunday morning, Rose got a call from Spitalny. "Kid," he started, "there is a radio broadcast scheduled for 5:00 this afternoon. We've had advance warning that the weather conditions are not good, and it is possible the broadcast will not come through. Here is what I want you to do. Take some music and go over to Wild's to rehearse.* I want you to be prepared to play at five. There's a good chance you'll be heard coast to coast for 20 minutes."

The majority of his sheet music remained stored in Philadelphia, so Rose frantically telephoned Felix Salmond, explaining the situation. "Mr. Salmond, can I come over and borrow some music?" His teacher responded generously, "You can come over and have anything you like." Rose was confident of his readiness, since he always practiced and maintained a number of short pieces to perform on command. After a rehearsal, Wild and Rose headed to studio 8H. The transmission from Europe predictably failed, so the pair performed several virtuoso works on air to an audience of millions on NBC national radio. At Monday afternoon's orchestra rehearsal, a surprised Rose found that many colleagues had tuned it, and was heartily congratulated.**

Toscanini took notice. In fact, information reached Rose later that Toscanini listened to and admired his solo broadcast—which contributed to another of Toscanini's infamous eruptions, this time

---

daughter, Maria Anna, died at age five. Days later, Mahler was diagnosed with a diseased heart and forbidden exercise. In February 1908, a cable from Milan announced that Toscanini had been engaged to conduct at the Metropolitan. The two conductors were to be joint musical directors.
* Earl Wild (1915-2010) staff pianist at NBC in 1937 is considered the last of the great romantic pianists/composers. Wild performed at Carnegie Hall in November 30, 2005, three days after his 90th birthday. He taught at Juilliard, along with Rose, from 1979 to 1987.
** This broadcast led to the formation of the Mischakoff String Quartet: concertmaster Mischa Mischakoff and Jacques Larner, violins; Emanuel Vardi, viola; and Leonard Rose, cello.

directly affecting the budding cellist. An upcoming appearance in Newark, New Jersey, with Toscanini precipitated an unusual Sunday morning rehearsal. Oswaldo Mazzucchi, principal, and his assistant Jascha Schwarzmann comprised the first desk of cellos. In his memoir, Rose inferred that Toscanini had taken irrational dislikes to Mazzucchi—although Rose believed him a "fine cellist who produced and had excellent musical taste"—and of Schwarzmann for a "rather nonchalant and unconcerned look about him," and that he rarely "looked alert while playing, even though, of course, he certainly was."

During preparations for the Newark concert, Rose noticed that Mazzucchi and Schwarzmann both were tired and seemed half-asleep when Toscanini, in Italian, fiercely lashed out at Schwarzmann. Rose didn't understand the words, but the blatantly insulting demeanor was obvious. The conductor lastly bellowed, "You," a solitary finger pointed at Schwarzmann, "go back there." The same finger did not retract but beckoned to Rose as he concluded, "You, come here." On the backside of this conniption, Toscanini ordered Rose forward to the first stand. In an instant, Rose became the assistant principal cellist of the NBC Symphony at 20 years of age. That Rose needed to face Schwarzmann for the rest of the season tempered any joy. Rose triumphed in this strike of good fortune, but in the reality laid a brutal and heartless maneuver hastened by Rose's outstanding radio broadcast.

Within weeks from his new seat, Rose participated in a recording session of Beethoven's Fifth Symphony.[42] He had not been with the orchestra when it played the work earlier in the season, and immediately felt betrayed by his Curtis training. Why hadn't the conservatory programmed such a well-known and regularly performed masterpiece during his four years? Now, he sat struggling directly beneath Toscanini's blazing eyes! The experience left the young cellist simultaneously exasperated and helpless in a recording he would never forget—for the wrong reasons.

If Toscanini ever lost his temper with Rose, he does not mention any nastiness coming his way in his memoir, even though the conductor's disposition grew fouler with each passing day. One day, under Rose's nose, he snarled at Mazzucchi, which a colleague translated: "You call yourself a first cellist? I wouldn't let you be a first cellist in a whorehouse!" In retrospect, Rose angrily exclaimed, "Really, no human being, let alone a professional musician, should be subjected to such abuse." Another memory Rose relates involved a passage Toscanini conducted in Haydn's "Posthorn" Symphony, which has a difficult cello solo in thumb position. It opens on the A above middle C and ascends to a high D; the cellist must use his thumb to stand a decent chance of hitting the higher positioned notes in tune. Mazzucchi had prepared his solo and played it quite well, when Toscanini halted him with the curt directive, *"Senza pollice"*—without thumb. The Italian cellist tried his best to play without his thumb, but simply could not and Toscanini, as a cellist, must have known better. Rose believed it, with whatever motive, an act of blatant sadism.

Deep down, Leonard Rose cared for neither Toscanini's Brahms nor his Beethoven, and recognized flaws in his French interpretations. While he infused these works with rhythmic vitality, Rose believed the man drove them too hard, too deliberately. Rose's own style on the cello conveyed a sense of liberty. Contrary to Toscanini, Rose believed that, inevitably, music requires interpretative contributions. He actually preferred the renditions of Bruno Walter, a frequent guest conductor with whom he would better acquaint himself later as principal cellist of the New York Philharmonic. He appreciated Walter's rhythmic nuances and defined these subtleties, a quality of a profound artist. Decades later, Rose portrayed this first professional position as that of "a scared to death young man—talented, yes, but scared! I somehow managed to stay out of his doghouse—no mean feat!"

Though Rose's succeeding job was principal chair of the Cleveland Orchestra, he rejoined the NBC Symphony in the summer of 1940 for a "goodwill" tour of South America (fiftieth anniversary of the founding of the Pan-American Union); Toscanini's first visit to the region in years. One cellist in the NBC Symphony, a German refugee, posed a problem for the organization. Management worried that the British might remove him from the ship when docked in Barbados and detain the man. An option was to hire a replacement, so NBC invited Rose; the young cellist and his wife gladly accepted. The tour brought him the pleasure of working for extra pay and again for the most extraordinary conductor of the era. Plus, with Minnie present, the couple could treat the two weeks it took the luxury ship, *Brazil*, to voyage from the U.S. to Rio de Janeiro (12-day sail) as a vacation. Indeed, a 35-millimeter movie-camera Rose purchased for the trip, feature the couple reveling in glee. One doubt lingered: How would Rose relate with Frank Miller on the trip, his beloved cousin who became the NBC principal cellist the year Rose decided to leave NBC for the Cleveland Orchestra? The saga between the cousins begins with posturing for this solo cello chair of the NBC Symphony.

In 1933, his final season in the Philadelphia Orchestra's cello section, Miller learned of the vacant principal post in Minneapolis, where Eugene Ormandy conducted. Miller auditioned privately for Ormandy, who swiftly appointed him principal of the orchestra. Four years later, Miller learned that Toscanini's NBC Symphony lacked a principal cellist. After an hour-and-a-half ordeal with the maestro where Miller anticipated "Toscanini was going to make me play every note of music that I knew," he landed the plum position.

In December 1938, Artur Rodzinski guest conducted the NBC orchestra four consecutive weeks. At intermission of the first rehearsal, Rose was compelled to inquire whether Rodzinski remembered him from two years before when he played for him at the Essex House. "Leonard Rose! Of course I remember you, and with great pleasure," patting the cellist's shoulder. With this genuine recognition, Rose exited the conductor's dressing room glowing. What Rose didn't know was that the conductor told his wife Halina, the very day he heard Rose for the first time, "I found a genius, Halusia, a real cellist."[43]

Shortly into the new year, following Rodzinski's NBC Symphony stint, Rose received a call from Boris Goldovsky, the conductor's personal assistant. The message relayed important news. Victor de Gomez,[*] the orchestra's principal cellist, resigned

---

[*] Oscar Eiler was the original principal cellist of the Cleveland Orchestra. Leopold Stokowski would agree to release Victor de Gomez from his Philadelphia contract; he would replace Eiler in June of 1919. Gomez earned $5,120 (equivalent to nearly $63,700 in 2008) for a 30-week season in the 1924-1925

due to health concerns. The maestro wanted Rose to be his replacement. This job offer arrived without warning and without a need for a second audition.

Rose was thrilled, but had the presence of mind to ask for a few days to think about it. The next day, as Rose arrived at Studio 8H, a union official greeted him at the elevators. "Spitalny wants you. Go in to see him." In his office, the personnel manager immediately blurted his point. He knew all about the previous evening's call from Cleveland. Rose's jaw dropped as he fumbled for words to ask who betrayed his privacy. "Carl Vosburgh, the manager of the Cleveland, called John Royal to find out if you were under contract. Look, I don't want you to take that job," and the man proceeded to explain Miller's appointment as the new principal. "You'll sit beside him, make $8,000 a year as his assistant, and you'll play all year long." In those days, $8,000 was a lavish sum. Rose reveals his enthusiasm and a bit of uncharacteristic optimism: "Frank Miller, the cousin who I idolized and from whom I had learned so much, was coming from Minneapolis to New York. I was going to sit with him. Just think of it, my dear cousin, my hero. I didn't want to go to Cleveland. I wanted to sit with Frank. I called Boris and explained the situation." Upon acknowledging Rose's rejection, Boris responded, "Well, we will all be very sorry, but I certainly understand."

Several days after Rose expressed his final decision, Spitalny met Rose as he entered rehearsal and insisted that he confer with him immediately. Behind the closed door, Spitalny cautioned his held news: The orchestra needed to move Rose back to second stand next season. For the second time in a week, Rose sat stunned. "Do you know what you're saying? I just turned down the solo chair at Cleveland, based on your word." Spitalny replied, "Yeah, sorry about that, but Toscanini wants Gusikoff as the assistant first cellist."

A number of explanations are possible. An obvious theory lay in the existence of professional angst. Miller may have tuned into Rose's 1938 broadcast and resented his younger relative's nationwide exposure. It is also conceivable that it was Toscanini

---

season, while the concertmaster earned $2,900; the minimum pay was $1,080 (equivalent to $13,400 in 2008).

who demanded Rose be moved back. The legendary conductor, with more than 50 years leading orchestras, insisting that Rose, a cellist with eight months of experience be removed from the first stand. It seems feasible. Rose does not acknowledge the possibility but concocted a most disturbing theory. He blamed Miller, not Toscanini, for the denial of a first stand position in that third NBC Symphony season. Crushed, Rose soon fled NBC and its maestro for his first principal job in the Cleveland Orchestra. As Rose saw it, "Obviously what had happened, and I'm sorry to have to say this, was that my cousin did not want me to sit with him. ... I have a very strong suspicion that that is what happened." The aftermath of this event resulted in decades without contact between the cellists.

Tension, no doubt, permeated the South American tour of 1940. Although Rose chose to omit from his unpublished memoir mention of their interaction, he describes Toscanini again, this time reverentially. "He was not a very tall man, rather short in fact, but very handsome and very imposing. When he walked around on board, he actually had pajamas on! I also discovered that he loved the ladies." On the ship, Toscanini chatted with his musicians, played shuffleboard contests, and lounged with them at the swimming pool. Except during the hours between four and nine each morning when in his suite, he made himself available to all.[44]

Shortly after the ship left New York, Toscanini spotted Rose. Then it dawned on him that he hadn't seen him the entire season. "What happened? Why?" he demanded. "Maestro," Rose explained, "they wanted to move me back to second stand." "Who wanted to move you?" Toscanini grumbled. Rose related the story. Toscanini showed surprise and denied that he had wanted Rose on the second stand. "I never made such a phrase," he stated emphatically. "I always wanted you there." Rose believed him. That assertion of loyalty meant a lot to Rose. It was also further proof, in the younger cousin's mind, that Miller had everything to do with his demotion.

On another occasion, Rose and Minnie observed the old man peering out over the railing. Rose reverently recalled, "He was well attired and looking absolutely lovely. I went up to him and said, 'Maestro, could I take a picture of you with my wife?' and he replied, 'Why, of course, of course!'"

An enormous crowd greeted the orchestra on its arrival in Rio de Janeiro. These were Toscanini's first appearances in Brazil since his debut season 54 years earlier. The orchestra proceeded to Sao Paulo for a single performance, then seven in Buenos Aires, where Toscanini last conducted in 1912. The tour consisted of 15 concerts in 27 days with plenty of leisure time on the open seas. Rose noted his love for the Teatro Colón (Columbus Theater) in Buenos Aires. The magnificent structure seats about 3,500 and boasts faultless acoustics. Considering how little scientists knew about acoustics when the theater was constructed in 1908, the result seems miraculous. Rose always took pleasure performing there, just as he would later as soloist with orchestra and with his piano trio. His most vivid recollection was of the orchestra's final concert in Buenos Aires. That event, like all of the performances, sold out and the Argentineans, characteristically demonstrative, simply would not stop cheering. After many minutes of ovation, audience members took up a chant, "Tos-ca-ni-ni! Tos-ca-ni-ni!" It marked one of the most thrilling receptions Rose ever witnessed; and it even frightened him somewhat because he could feel the walls trembling!*

On the flip side, another impression of Argentina haunted Rose. Led by Roberto Ortiz, the nation's military government purchased equipment including uniforms and helmets from Germany. Rose was most distressed at the sight of streets lined with soldiers in German uniforms: "There was that God-damned German helmet! We all talked about it and it was very upsetting for many of the boys in the orchestra—not just me."

Although Toscanini conducted, for no fee on occasion, one alleged legacy places the blame of his well-documented income on the contemporary disproportion between conductor and orchestra member salaries. Conspicuous was his Philharmonic salary of $110,000 in 1931 (equivalent to 1.55 million in 2008) to conduct 60 concerts in 15 weeks, with all taxes paid plus

---

* Chotzinoff told the New York *Herald Tribune* that the audience "threatened to tear down the house unless Maestro came out again" (Horowitz: Toscanini, p. 168).

steamship passage to and from New York. Then, during the Great Depression, the average musician in the orchestra earned $3,000 for a 30-week season. As for soloists of Toscanini's day, in his only appearance with the NBC Symphony, Emanuel Feuermann earned $350 in 1938 (equivalent to $5,350 in 2008) for his broadcast performance of Strauss's *Don Quixote*. Today, Yo-Yo Ma, one of the industry's biggest draws, reliably earns from $65,000 to $70,000 per night.[45]

In 1937, with a formidable litany of achievements behind him, Arturo Toscanini embarked on an unlikely seventeen-season journey with the newly invented custom-tailored NBC Symphony. Then it ended dramatically when the 86-year-old maestro's health failed. Frank Miller's veritably recounted:

> I will never forget Toscanini's final concert. It was an all-Wagner program that Toscanini really didn't want to conduct. But Sarnoff and the others persuaded him to finish out his series. We were doing a commercial series with Mobil Oil I think it was [it was Socony Vacuum Oil]. So he said all right, he would do the last concert and that's all. You know, the point is his memory had been slipping. He never conducted from music. So, during the number [the Venusberg Music from Tannhäuser], he stopped conducting and his hands fell down to his side [his left hand covered his eyes]. At that moment, in the back, two stands of violins were to play alone and it would have been total disaster, so I turned around and conducted them for several bars, you know, to keep it going because I was afraid they wouldn't play if left alone. So I watched Toscanini as I was conducting them and finally, little by little, his hands came up and he started conducting again. In the meantime, in the control room, they took us off the air [dead silence for 14 seconds] and put on [Toscanini's version] Brahms First Symphony in order to cover this period... Then they went back to us. When we finished that number, Toscanini wanted to walk off that stage. In fact, he started stamping off that stage. But as he passed me, I whispered, "Maestro, the 'Meistersinger' Overture, 'Meistersinger.'" He turned

around, went back, and conducted the "Meistersinger." But several bars from the end, he threw down the baton and walked off the stage while we were still playing the last chords. It was terrible.[46]

Chapter Five

PRINCIPAL CELLIST UNDER ARTUR RODZINSKI

Severance Hall is the most beautiful hall in the world. The acoustics are perfect. One could not wish for anything better; and the orchestra—magnificent, unusually responsive.
    —Artur Rodzinski, to the Cleveland Press, December 1932[47]

Leonard Rose, 1940
Courtesy of the Cleveland Orchestra

Demotion to second stand in Toscanini's increasingly famous orchestra put Leonard Rose into a dreadful state of mind, not unlike the one he experienced at his failure in his initial attempt to join Felix Salmond's elite cello class at the Curtis Institute. His moodiness, however, rapidly swerved in the opposite direction when he heard from Salmond, who had spoken to Mary Bok. Rodzinski initially contacted her to see whether she might persuade Rose to reconsider the Cleveland offer. At first, Rose's state of mind led him to utter little beyond, "Good God." The next moment, he telephoned the Cleveland Orchestra's management to accept. Within days, Rose signed a contract to become the principal cellist of the Cleveland Orchestra.

Two attempts to establish a symphony orchestra in this Rust Belt city on Lake Erie failed before a municipal orchestra tuned up in 1913. With a spiteful founding conductor, personnel problems and inevitable funding shortages, the preliminary stages began badly. The newly named conductor, Christiaan Timmner—a former concertmaster of Amsterdam's prestigious Concertgebouw Orchestra—immediately fired half his musicians because "They practice with a long stogie ... in their mouths. They cross their legs. They slouch down in their seats and rest their elbows on the arms of the chairs. They yawn audibly and without attempting to conceal their mouths with their hands. They ignore [my] appeals for them to come to rehearsal and became peeved when correcting their technique."[48] Their apathy seemed to reflect the city's perennial inferiority complex, and this third ensemble folded in 1915.

In December 1918, the Cleveland Orchestra inadequately debuted with only 54 players in its current incarnation, with just one oboist and bassoonist. A horrific strain of swine flu that in ten months killed 550,000 Americans (by October New York was recording more than 800 deaths a day; in Philadelphia 11,000 died in a month; 30 million lives were lost to the epidemic worldwide[49]) forced the closure of Cleveland area schools and colleges delayed the premiere performances. Ticket prices ranged from a mere 25 cents to $1. As with previous experiments to inaugurate symphonic music in Cleveland, the organization lacked money. During the 1920-1921 season, the combined weekly salaries of 81 musicians, which totaled approximately $48,000 (adjusted in today's dollars), pale in comparison to today's 100-musician average of about $329,000 per week.[50] New York, Boston, Philadelphia, and Chicago paid higher salaries and offered longer contracts than the single-year agreements in Cleveland. Furthermore, many of the orchestra members hired from New York didn't bother uprooting their families for a six-month season's employment. On top of that, their contracts in 1920 prohibited players from taking outside musical jobs (besides teaching) because management perceived other work as threatening to the orchestra's discipline and survival. These deficiencies led to musicians preferring to look elsewhere for employment.

In its 16th season as a bona fide orchestra, the orchestra's board hired Artur Rodzinski to fill the role of musical director. Fresh from a heralded four-year directorship with the Los Angeles Philharmonic, he brought irrepressible charm to the Midwest winning over members of the orchestra and board, audience, and press. He assumed the position confidently, declaring that international acclaim to the organization was forthcoming. That his intentions ultimately failed does not diminish his brilliant historical contributions to the Cleveland Orchestra's history.

Born in Split, Dalmatia (situated in modern Croatia) New Year's Day 1892 to Polish parents, Rodzinski studied law in Vienna before serving in the Austro-Hungarian army during World War I. Upon his return to Vienna, he immersed himself in music while earning income as a meat market inspector. After he studied piano for several years with Viennese professor George von Lalewicz, the teacher unexpectedly informed his father that Artur had no future in music. Undeterred, a job as chorus and opera conductor in the provincial Polish city of Lvov enticed the youngster. This led to his appointment to orchestra and opera posts in Warsaw. Rodzinski's unusual talent emerged without formal training although he emulated Stokowski, who was half-Polish; from his hairstyle—without part and straight back from the brow—to his podium stance.

In 1924, already with 12 years of performances at the helm of the Philadelphia Orchestra, Stokowski heard him conduct a concert in Warsaw which initiated a friendship. Two years later,

Stokowski invited the younger man to work as his assistant with his orchestra in Philadelphia. During this four-year apprenticeship, one of Rodzinski's duties was to lead the orchestra in private readings through contemporary scores while his mentor sat alone in the hall with jittery fingers pushing lighting buttons he was required to follow. On stage, the assistant conductor had to keep one eye on the score and one eye on a red light to stop, green to go, yellow for faster, and blue for slower. Rodzinski's responsibilities in Philadelphia also included conducting the Grand Opera Company to critical acclaim and both the student operatic and orchestral ensembles at Curtis Institute, some of whom were hired later by Rodzinski. He was grateful for this role, which allowed him time away from under Stokowski's thumb.

Leonard Rose's tenure in Cleveland started uncomfortably when he learned that Rodzinski had first given serious consideration for the principal position to Paul Tortelier.[51] The distinguished Frenchman, who would become one of Europe's leading solo cellists, began his career on the second stand of the Boston Symphony before leaving for Europe in 1940. Rose's relative dearth of experience justified Rodzinski's misgivings, if he had any. Although confident of his abilities, Rose recognized that he would be playing much of the repertoire for the first time, on top of the pressures that accompany the position. In his memoir, Rose duly credits the assistant cellist since 1926, Charlie McBride (16 years Rose's senior), for helping smooth this difficult period of adjustment. "What a worrywart," McBride recalled. "What a tremendous talent, but he was tense all the time. On the road, he couldn't sleep so I gave him Amatol every night before he'd leave for the sleepers."[52] Time and again, McBride's warnings aided his younger colleague: "Lennie, look at this place," or "Lennie, be careful here; watch the conductor there; do this; do that ..." Rose was grateful.

Musicians appreciated Rodzinski's artistic flair, yet recoiled at times by the conductor's peculiar behavior. Even as a youth, this conductor suffered from a nervous disposition, triggering a compulsion to carry around an assortment of medicines. In his 20s, the conductor once said to his wife, Halina: "Some people say I am crazy—well, difficult to live with. I am not healthy. I have constant stomach trouble, headaches, bad eyes—I'm almost blind in one eye..."[53] His health continued to deteriorate under the stress of conflicts with board members and directors—his concerns verged on paranoia.

Legend has it the man conducted all concerts with a loaded gun in his right rear pocket. Rose believed it because he had heard that Rodzinski would have "blown his brains out" if his conducting debut had not succeeded. But the concert went splendidly, so from then on, this most superstitious man, for good luck, allegedly carried the pistol to the stage every night.[*] In Halina Rodzinski's 1976 autobiography, she describes a concert routine endured for years: "Before ever setting foot on stage for a performance, Artur went through an entire course of rituals. ... He would first pat his trousers to be sure he had changed the pistol with his pants. ... He would kiss his father's photo and give me a kiss, which I returned with one on the forehead and a blessing. ... George Higgins, Severance Hall's stage manager, would lead Artur to the stage, then give his left arm a wrenching pinch which, like an injection of adrenalin, sharpened Rodzinski's senses, but it kept his arm mottled with bruises all season long. [Then came] ... the adjustment of a ring he wore, not his wedding band, but a Chinese curio with a frog ... the creature had to face him in a certain way when he raised his hand or otherwise its mysterious powers would be inoperative."

As Rose recalled, conductors are characters, and "Rodzinski was yet another character on the podium. He was a very impatient, intimidating figure with the baton in his hand. He frequently became irritated with, for example, string passages in one or another difficult work. ... He would first demand to hear the first violins alone. When they displeased him, he would call for the same passage, but more slowly. When that still fell short of standards, he would begin to call for 'last four stands alone.' Then, 'outside players alone,' then 'inside players alone,'

---

[*] Late in life Rodzinski told the tale to his son that he once met a woman married to a firefighter. When the conductor fell passionately in love with her, he decided to kill his rival, so he purchased a gun and tucked it in his right back pocket. Just as he planned to carry out the deed, the Lvov Opera's conductor fell ill, and he was summoned at the last minute as substitute in Verdi's *Ernani*. Only after the triumphant performance did he realize that the gun was still in his pocket.

punctuating all of the directives with 'terrible, terrible!' At length, he would advise: 'Gentlemen, if it is not better tomorrow, we shall play solos!' In a way, one must give him credit. What usually happened was that everyone took the music home and practiced ferociously—and, of course, sounded much better the next day."

Technically, Rose regarded Rodzinski at the highest level. One of the great things about him, Rose recalled, was that he was arguably the most economic rehearser of all the big conductors. Musicians appreciated that he did not waste time with a great deal of esoteric talk. Rose also claimed that he knew exactly how to get the orchestra to play with expressive clarity in every genre, supporting the well-known New York music critic Olin Downes (1886-1955) when he wrote in the *Times* after a Cleveland Orchestra 1941 Carnegie Hall performance: "He [Rodzinski] does what he pleases with an orchestra, and he has the instinct and temperament of a born leader."[54]

Yet, on occasion, he could become extremely anxious about certain pieces, bogging down rehearsals with long-winded explanations and tyrannical behavior. During a 1943 tour of New York, Massachusetts, New Jersey, and Connecticut, Rodzinski worked himself into a state of near hysterics; the rehearsals were shrill, edgy, and over-long. The orchestra's second tour date took place in Northampton, Massachusetts, at Smith College—an elite women's school. An unusual feature to the John M. Green Hall, built in 1910, was a balcony extending clear over the stage from the back of the house. On this night, the balcony was filled with women. Frenzied, he walked on stage. As was his custom, with eyes closed, he began conducting. About a minute and a half into the work—still conducting with his eyes closed—he turned the page, sensed something was wrong, and opened his eyes to discover a nude photograph of a luscious French woman between the pages. "One of my orchestral colleagues ... carefully inserted it inside the conductor's score," Rose mused, admitting he never learned the identity of the person responsible for the practical joke. "Bear in mind, there were people sitting almost on top of us in the boxes around the stage. ... A few people must have seen the photograph, because one could sense some snickering in the hall. The conductor, however, had no idea what was happening. He then looked down. ... A situation right out of the Marx Brothers film! 'Who did it?' Rodzinski repeatedly asked in a stage whisper loud enough for some audience members in the hall to hear. 'I'll kill him!' He hastily closed the score without dropping a beat and began to laugh. ...it broke [all] the tension."

About four weeks into Rose's first season, the orchestra presented a special concert featuring the legendary violinist Fritz Kreisler who made his Cleveland recital debut in 1889 at age 14. Fifty years later, the 64-year-old remained in command of his sparkling technique and honeyed tone. For his November 1939 "First All-Star Popular Concert" Cleveland appearance, he scheduled two concertos: the singular Brahms and the Paganini D Major in his own arrangement. The latter included an interruption by an eight-bar cello solo. As had always been Rose's pattern, he arrived early for the rehearsal. On this particular occasion, his extra effort provided a few moments to study the solo he had never seen. With Kreisler on stage, the rehearsal proceeded from the first movement, then the second. Finally, they reached the cello solo in the third.[55] As Rose ended, the mesmeric artist stopped the orchestra and called out to Rose, "Bravo! Beautiful!" and walked over to shake Rose's hand. "Needless to say, I was teary-eyed, moved by such public appreciation on the part of the great Fritz Kreisler," Rose affectionately evokes decades later. "Kreisler Thrills 8,679 at Concert," the *Plain Dealer's* headline shouted.

> ... largest and most enthusiastic audiences on record. ... No finer violin playing has been heard here in a long while. ... Few violinists other than Kreisler himself could have translated this material in a way to make it an open book before so vast a throng. ... The utter simplicity, the moving sincerity, the basic human feeling made articulate by the relaxed bow of this distinguished white-haired gentleman with a kindly face ... simple dignity which is so strong a characteristic of the interpreter.

At the concert that evening, Kreisler effusively and publicly congratulated Rose again. The cellist never forgot his boyhood idol's warmth and generosity. Elmore Bacon's comment in the Cleveland News etched itself into the cellist's memory: "Leonard

Rose played an accompaniment so beautifully as to receive Kreisler's congratulations at the close." Best of all, Rose seemed at last to win the full confidence of Rodzinski.

Rose loved Kreisler's bow arm and as a youngster tried to replicate the master's unique sound: "Many of his [physical] movements were characteristically Viennese; the pull on the bow, the way he played short notes. One has but to listen to a recording he made with Rachmaninoff to appreciate his sound."* Like many, Rose believed that the legend performed long past his prime. But the violinist protested, "Why not?" he once declared. "When I could play, no one would come hear me. Now that I can't play, they can't keep them away!" Kreisler didn't necessarily lose his technique at the end, but Rose believed that he unquestionably lost some hearing. "It's sad to hear people on stage when their best days are behind them. The general problem is that the motor apparatus simply doesn't function as well. With string players, the trills, vibrato, and finer movements of the bow begin to fail. If hearing is impaired, intonation suffers as well." Rose voiced hope that this would not happen to him. He thought he had one thing going that would prove invaluable. "I continue to practice regularly. I shall last longer than certain of my contemporaries who have apparently abandoned the habit."

Life was treating Rose well. His Cleveland colleagues liked him and he liked them. The press was generous as well. Thanks to Elmer Wiener, who acted as his publicist, Rose's picture was plastered in the Cleveland papers, whether he was swinging a golf club or playing his cello. They also portrayed him as one of Rodzinski's favorites. He eventually felt that the conductor regarded him almost like a son. Rose wrote: "He was terribly insecure, but when he finally liked someone as he liked me, he really became a kind of father to me. I think Rodzinski loved me and I must say I had a tremendous affection for him." With characteristic earnest intent, Rose states, "He knew I was loyal." The Cleveland Orchestra performed 123 concerts in Rose's

---

* In particular Rose mentions Kreisler's rendition of Grieg's Violin Sonata, Op. 45 recorded with Rachmaninoff in Berlin September 1928. The CD also features arrangements of Kreisler's "Liebesfreud" and "Liebesleid" spectacularly played by Rachmaninoff.

initial season that featured some of the era's greatest soloists: Arthur Rubinstein in Beethoven's Fourth Piano Concerto; Sergei Rachmaninoff in his own First Piano Concerto ("sureness of touch, perfect timing of effects and smoothness of line," the Cleveland *Plain Dealer* reported); Oscar Levant in Gershwin's Piano Concerto in F; Josef Hofmann in Schumann's Piano Concerto; and Jascha Heifetz in the world premiere of William Walton's Violin Concerto. One eye-catching soloist, 16 years Rose's senior, was Emanuel Feuermann. He arrived for Cleveland performances of Dvořák's Cello Concerto after a 15,000-mile journey, 17-day concert tour of South America. Captivated by his brilliance, Herbert Elwell of the *Plain Dealer* wrote that the cellist was "amazing as ever," basking in his "honeyed tone expressive enough to melt a heart of stone." There are precious few references in Rose's memoir to the celebrated cellist, but one can only imagine the intensely private cellist's awe or disgust hurled in the direction of the European's effortless technique; "for there is apparently no major difficulty he cannot face with nonchalance" the reviewer continued. "Most miraculous of all is the living personality which seems to speak from the instrument. In his hands, it has all the suppleness of a violin plus a color range stepped up 50 percent. And combined with the intimacy of this almost human voice is vigor and authority that makes solid drama instead of mere fireworks out of every bravura passage."[56]

Disturbing news stunned Rose at the end of his first season. Traveling on tour by train, he settled in for a game of penny-ante poker when Paul Gershman, the assistant concertmaster, leaned over and whispered, "I think Frank Miller has formally applied for your job!" The news floored Rose and an immediate depression set in. Gershman sensed what was happening and quickly consulted a colleague. About five minutes later, Rodzinski sauntered down the aisle. Stopping at Rose, he placed a hand on the cellist's shoulder, bent forward and quietly invited the cellist to see him in his compartment. Behind closed doors, Rose's boss reached into his pocket handing him the ill-timed letter just months before the two cousins would meet again on Toscanini's 1940 South American tour with the NBC Symphony. Addressed to Maestro Rodzinski, Miller punctuated his unhappiness in the NBC Symphony, clearly stating his interest in coming to

Cleveland as principal. "It seemed that he was quite unhappy having Gusikoff sitting with him," Rose stated in his unpublished memoir. "Evidently, Gusikoff was always trying to sabotage or otherwise unnerve him." In the moment of despair, gently setting the letter aside, the compassionate conductor put his arm around Rose's shoulders telling him, "Leonard, I wouldn't change you for 10 Frank Millers!"*

When the orchestra reached New York, Rose telephoned Miller and told him that he had been shown the letter. "Oh, Len," he said, "I wrote that same letter to four or five other orchestras." Rose snapped, "Did those four or five orchestras have your first cousin as solo cellist? God damn it, you shouldn't have written to Cleveland."

An upshot to the incident involving Miller's letter was Rodzinski's demonstrative reaction. It helped Rose feel more assured in his relations with the famed conductor. During his second season with the orchestra, Rose made his solo debut with the Lalo Concerto, a work infrequently heard today but popular repertoire at that time. He also performed the Brahms "Double" Concerto on four occasions with Cleveland's concertmaster, Joseph Fuchs (concertmaster from 1926). Nervousness—which always plagued Rose and would continue throughout his lifetime—bordered on hysteria in the months preceding his solo concerto debut. "In those years, I was particularly uptight before performances, and that's putting it really mildly. To be candid and totally honest, I would lose anywhere from 10 to 15 pounds before what I built up in my mind to be one of the most important appearances in the world." And indeed, performing his debut with the Cleveland Orchestra was the most important appearance he could possibly have. "Most of the horrendous sensations I used to feel occurred three to four months before I had to play. I began to worry. ... [Remember] I was one of the most neurotic, frightened kids imaginable ..." Rose was still a kid. He was in his third year of professional life, his second season in Ohio, and was only 22. Just before the end of the 1941 season, he became a proud father for the first time: Born to Leonard and Minnie on May 21, a dark-haired, striking baby girl, named Barbara Jean Rose.

---

* Until Toscanini's final hour, Miller remained with the NBC Symphony.

In Cleveland, the youngster continued his brush up close with greatness, accompanying Jascha Heifetz in Beethoven's Violin Concerto and a spectacular first New York hearing of William Walton's Violin Concerto in Carnegie Hall with Heifetz,[57] Joseph Szigeti performing Brahms Violin Concerto, Béla Bartók performing his own Second Piano Concerto, Joseph Fuchs performing Tchaikovsky's Violin Concerto, Eugene List performing Rachmaninoff's Concerto No. 2, and Gregor Piatigorsky performing Saint-Saëns Cello Concerto.

Jascha Heifetz   Leonard Rose
Walton Concerto Premiere 12-7-1939 with the Cleveland Orchestra
Photo by Martin Harris, PM Staff

Unknown to many of his musicians, Rodzinski had grown restless in Cleveland. Battling with the board over money matters—which he took personally—and its refusal to enlarge the roster to equal the numbers achieved in other top orchestras, increased his desire to leave. The Maestro sought richness and warmth in sound from his strings and their refusal to satisfy this need generated irrational claims of conspiracy. As early as 1938, New York Philharmonic board members approached him about replacing John Barbirolli, who was struggling in the shadow of his predecessor, Arturo Toscanini. During his Cleveland years,

Rodzinski regularly guest conducted the Philharmonic; in the 1941-1942 season, he spent a four-week period in New York when one of the concerts fell on Sunday, December 7, 1941. The Carnegie Hall listeners along with a nationwide radio broadcast audience heard Shostakovich's First Symphony (1925) and, with Arthur Rubinstein as soloist, Brahms Second Piano Concerto. A staff member handed the conductor an announcement to read at the end of the program; however, he was too upset to do so. As soon as the report of the devastating enemy attack was relayed, Rodzinski and the orchestra struck up "The Star-Spangled Banner"—for a second time that afternoon.

Rose was the featured soloist in Robert Schumann's Cello Concerto and in Strauss *Don Quixote* during his third season, 1941-1942, in Cleveland. One of his colleagues that year, cellist Seymour Barab, professed his awe of Leonard Rose: "I certainly admired his playing." When asked if Rose was a difficult boss, he replied, "Boss? You could try to emulate him, and you did all you could to make your section sound unified, but I never thought of him as a boss. Rodzinski was the boss."[58]

Rose's third season spotlighted Fuchs in the Brahms Violin Concerto, Rubinstein in Chopin's Piano Concerto No. 1, Nathan Milstein in Mendelssohn's Violin Concerto, Zino Francescatti in Paganini's Violin Concerto No.1, and Sergei Rachmaninoff in his own Piano Concerto No. 2—all legendary musical personalities of the twentieth century.

Admittedly, Rose was entranced with the Russian school of pianism: Josef Lhévinne, Josef Hofmann, and—above all— the playing of Sergei Rachmaninoff.* "What a player," Rose remembered. "I loved his music and I loved his playing! I remember his having rediscovered the Beethoven First Piano Concerto. In the last movement, the glee with which he played those passages, it was something to see and something to hear. It was

---

* Similarly, Rose admits an aversion to the German school: "I don't like to hear the hammers and fingernails go down, and I dislike the excessively percussive approach to piano playing."

unbelievable." In those days, the great Beethoven "expert" was Artur Schnabel.* Both Rachmaninoff and Schnabel were inspired and motivated artists; but as pianists, they were considered quite different. Before the slow movement of the concerto, Rodzinski turned to Rachmaninoff and asked him what tempo he would like. Rose recalled Rachmaninoff saying, "'I am not Beethoven expert. I just play ze right tempo!' We all laughed at the obvious shot to Herr Schnabel."

During this season, the conductor invited Rachmaninoff to host a series of concerts as conductor in his own "Isle of the Dead," and then as soloist in his own Second Piano Concerto. The program concluded with one of his latest works, the "Symphonic Dances" (1940), which was so new, it was still in manuscript. "Rodzinski began to rehearse the "Symphonic Dances" early, some two weeks before the scheduled concert," Rose dictated. "To his total frustration, he simply could not get the orchestra to play the final movement at a fast enough speed. He was very impatient, slapping his thigh, and screaming out, 'No, no, no, no!' He would yell at the orchestra, 'Look, I know this man's music. He will come here and complain that it's too slow.'" As rehearsals progressed, Rodzinski grew increasingly impatient and unpleasant. The orchestra slaved over the composition and managed, with great difficulty, to approach the conductor's desired tempo. The opening night concert was on a Thursday evening; and on Thursday morning, while Rodzinski drilled his players one last time, the stage door opened and in walked the gigantic six foot six composer in his overcoat, crew-cut black hair with eyes like black coals. His gloves were still on his enormous hands, which could cover a thirteenth on a keyboard, and crossed awkwardly across his chest. He walked up to the podium and sadly said, with his inimitable accent, 'Mr. Rodzinski, dot ees much too fahst.' The orchestra disintegrated with laughter. After a few vodkas, the pianist-composer was known to regale guests with stories of his youth in Russia—of the Russian golden musical

---

* To many, one Beethoven pianist towered above all others. Schnabel's (1882-1951) numerous recordings included all 32 sonatas of Beethoven—the first to accomplish this feat. The legendary Schnabel taught countless pupils who carry on his traditions. (Harold C. Schonberg: The Great Pianists from Mozart to the Present. New York: Simon and Schuster, 1963, p. 401.)

age of Rimsky-Korsakov, of Tchaikovsky, of Anton Rubinstein,* each of whom he had known intimately. He was fourteen when Borodin died and eight when Mussorgsky passed. Not long after the Cleveland appearances in 1943, Rachmaninoff himself died several days before his 70th birthday.

Tossy Spivakovsky replaced Joseph Fuchs as concertmaster in Rose's fourth season in Cleveland. The memories of Spivakovsky's interpretation of Bartók's First Violin Concerto and of the sick composer never left the cellist: "Bartók himself was present. ... I can still see the elderly, emaciated gentleman coming out to take his bow." Bartók came to America's shores in 1940 ill with leukemia, destitute, and with knowledge that Hitler was on the verge of annexing his homeland.** During his final season, Rose performed with Rodzinski, the Dvořák Cello Concerto. The season showcased several notable guest artists: cellist Raya Garbousova; violinists Carroll Glenn and Joseph Szigeti; and pianists Claudio Arrau and Arthur Rubinstein, who performed Rachmaninoff's Second Piano Concerto in tribute to his recent death.

Rose spent four "excellent" seasons in Cleveland where, as leader, he learned how to cope with orchestral life.[59] He found his colleagues congenial and socialized extensively with them. Rose summarized his interactions with his fellow musicians: "The Cleveland seemed in many ways more like a family than a professional organization, and the atmosphere was far friendlier than that in the New York orchestras where one sensed more friction between the players."

Towards the end of the 1942-1943 season, Rodzinski let it be known that he and Cleveland were incompatible and that he would relocate to accept a contract with the New York Philharmonic, succeeding John Barbirolli. As soon as he obtained the post, he

---

* In 1872-1873 Anton Rubinstein played a 215-concert American tour for which he was paid lavishly. He appeared frequently as well with violinist Henryk Wieniawski. He created a sensation by playing without the score, novel at the time.

** Béla Bartók first appeared before an American audience in 1928 playing his Opus 1 "Rhapsody" with the New York Philharmonic. A few years after his death at 64, crowds were turned away, in the midst of a blizzard, from New York's Town Hall where a sold-out concert featured his six string quartets performed by the Juilliard String Quartet.

set about trying to entice some of his Cleveland favorites to join him in Manhattan. William Lincer, principal violist, and Rose were two musicians he had to have. Rose wrote: "For Bill, the situation was quite clear. He was offered the principal violist's chair, and he accepted. For me, the situation was somewhat more complicated. I wasn't making much money in Cleveland in those years. ... I remember exactly how much I was making: $5,000 a year (1942 equivalent to nearly $66,000 in 2008) for 28 weeks. The year after my daughter was born, I was broke!" Even though the Philharmonic had only a 28-week season, Rose was promised more money. There was, however, a snag. New York's principal cellist, Joseph Schuster, decided to remain with the Philharmonic one more season before departing. Rose was not keen on being demoted to assistant principal, but Rodzinski found a way to sweeten the deal. Assuring him that Schuster had already submitted his resignation, effective the end of the following season, he promised Rose not only the solo cellist's chair beginning in the 1944-1945 season, but also a New York debut with the Philharmonic on a pair of subscription concerts during 1943-44. "It was an offer I couldn't refuse!"

In 1943, critic Arthur Loesser evaluated the departing Maestro's Cleveland tenure:

> Dr. Rodzinski's sojourn here was not a perpetual idyll of unclouded geniality. During the 10 years, reports of numerous frictions of a personal and professional nature occurred between him and his associates. There were dismissals, resignations, recriminations, unfulfilled promises, frustrations, and lacerated feelings. But none of these incidents could ever seriously impugn the general acceptance of his quality as a great musician and great conductor. The sincere and unprompted applause of the orchestra after the last two concerts is evidence of it. He is, indeed, one of a tiny handful of masters at the pinnacle of his profession.

When it was learned that Rose was departing, the Cleveland community felt his loss. In an undated Cleveland newspaper, an article of praise appeared titled "Best Wishes, Cellist Rose."[60]

Cleveland loses one of its most talented musical artists with the departure of Leonard Rose who for the last four years has been cellist of the Cleveland Orchestra. Rose is only 24, but despite his youth, is already recognized as one of the world's leading cellists. His engagement as soloist and member of the first cello desk of the New York Philharmonic is a great and highly deserved tribute to his musicianship.

Members of the Cleveland Orchestra cello section during Leonard Rose's years as principal 1939-1943:
Seymour Barab (1941-1942)
Nathan Chaikan (1940-1941)
Harry Fuchs (1937-1943)
Raymond Gerkowski (1926-1940)
Nathan Gershman (1941-1948)
Isadore Gordon (1934-1944)
Frank Grant (1925-1942)
David Greenbaum (1941-1944)
Alford Hampel (1927-1940)
Harry Hensel (1924-1940)
Charles McBride (1926-1944)
Robert Ripley (1942-1943)
Channing Robbins (1940-1941)
Anthony Sophos (1942-1944)
Nathan Stutch (1940-1942)
Robert Swenson (1931-1946)

Chapter Six

THE CELLISTS OF ROSE'S NEW YORK PHILHARMONIC

I don't want to put halos around my head, but I love music so much and music means so much to me that, even when I played on the last stand, I played my guts out; and I think that's the only way to be honest in this profession.
—Leonard Rose

The success of an orchestral section begins with its principal. The leader ought to have several important attributes in addition to possessing superlative performing abilities. One is to have infallible rhythmic instincts. Another is a willingness to accept bowing suggestions initiated by the concertmaster, the player traditionally anointed as second in command. A section leader must also be prepared to accept suggested interpretive moods and colorations from the conductor. Lastly, a section leader should communicate easily with fellow colleagues. With these attributes, optimism will abound, and the morale of the orchestra will be boosted.

With noted experience as the leader while at Curtis, on first stand under Toscanini and solo cellist in Cleveland, Leonard Rose contained these traits in spades by the time he arrived in New York. There, he worked productively with long time concertmaster John Corigliano and the many brilliant and egocentric guest conductors who appeared before him. But it was the delivery of his solo passagework during intricate orchestral scores that had his fellow colleagues abuzz. If a concertgoer carefully observed Leonard Rose as an important symphonic cello solo drew near, the viewer could see Rose getting ready to rid any uneasiness by rubbing his right hand repeatedly on his right thigh to remove any excess moisture. Closer to the solo entrance, he would lift his bow above his cello strings several inches into the air two or three times in a feathery fashion painting the air as if with silent brush-strokes. Left hand securely in place on the note, his bow would land on the precise string at the exact fraction of a second. Whether nerves or adrenaline, this was how Rose greeted the solos that came his way. The music sounded soulful and magically spun as a listener can attest in the Cleveland Orchestra's seventy-fifth anniversary CD featuring Rose, as principal cellist, performing the delicate solos in Rimsky-Korsakov's "Scheherazade" and in Shostakovich's Symphony No. 1. The distinctive quality that emanated from within was deeply felt. With seven members of his New York Philharmonic cello section and celebrated soprano Bidú Sayão, Leonard Rose's name first appeared on a 1945 recording of Heitor Villa-Lobos's "Bachiana Brasileira" No. 5 (composed in 1938) with the composer conducting. The 78 proved to be the single-disc sensation of Columbia Records for two years. It led to his signing a long-term contract with the record company in 1949. Grammy Awards didn't exist yet, but this recording's classic status was retroactively confirmed in 1984, the year of Rose's death, when it was voted into the Grammy Hall of Fame.[*]

By all accounts, Leonard Rose concentrated on his own playing as principal cellist. That was where his interest lay. He seldom felt any need to berate any members of his section or, for that matter, demonstrate authority over them, as some section leaders did. Because he was their best cellist, Rose's section liked and respected him. The Philharmonic group was known for their polished sound and solid intonation, and for its diversity. Russian, Hungarian, Turkish, and American cellists played alongside Rose, many born in the nineteenth century. For the 1939-1940 season, the Symphony League published a book, *The*

---

[*] Rose received $50 ($600 in 2008) at the time of the recording with no future royalties.

Philharmonic-Symphony Orchestra of New York, of biographical sketches of the entire orchestra by William G. King, music editor of the *New York Sun*. E. Bernard Lintott created the following drawings of Rose's colleagues.[61]

Abrascha Bass *(1928-1952)*

Abrascha Bass was Victor Herbert's[62] "favorite" cellist. Mr. Bass himself modestly admitted that "he liked me very much," and that one of his proudest memories is of the time he played the Herbert Cello Concerto under the composer's direction. Herbert sent for him and later told him he performed the work exactly as he had always wanted to hear it. Mr. Bass was solo cellist with the Herbert Orchestra for a number of years. Bass, born in Kiev, Russia, April 18, 1892, began to study music at the age of nine. At 11, he won a scholarship to the Imperial Conservatory of St. Petersburg. He came to the United States in 1905, and joined the New York Symphony in 1921. Mr. Bass retained his position when that orchestra merged with the Philharmonic in 1928.

Mario Caiati *(1928-1958)*

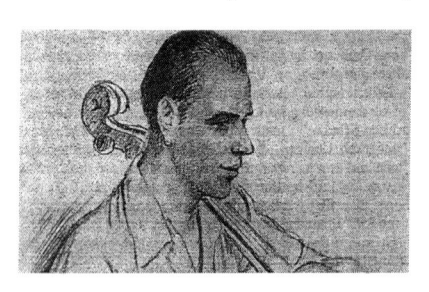

Mario Caiati was a nephew of Gaetano Merola, General Director of the San Francisco Opera Company, and of Professor Caiati of the Royal Conservatory of San Pietro a Maiella of Naples. He was born in Naples on Christmas Day, 1902. At the age of 10, he began the study of the violin and later was admitted to the Conservatory where he graduated in 1922. Before coming to the United States in 1923, he was a member of the orchestra of the San Carol

Opera of Naples. He played with the Kansas City Little Symphony before joining the New York Philharmonic Orchestra in 1928.

Naoum J. Dinger *(1925-1964)*

Noam Dinger came to the United States in 1921 to join the Cleveland Orchestra, with which he frequently did solo work during the next four years. He was engaged by the New York Symphony in 1925, and he remained with that orchestra when it merged with the Philharmonic. He was born in Smyrna, Turkey, August 5, 1898, but his parents moved to Odessa, Russia, when he was only a few weeks old. It was in that city that he obtained most of his musical training, beginning with the piano at five, and the cello when he was nine. At the Odessa Conservatory, he was a pupil of Naoum Brunberg and Enrico Brambilia. With Leonard Rose, Dinger and Carl Stern performed David Popper's Requiem for three cellos and orchestra February 13, 1945, under the direction of Artur Rodzinski.

William L. Feder *(1928-1949)*

William L. Feder's entire career was centered in New York. He was born there on January 27, 1886, and entered the National Conservatory of Music at the age of 12 to study advanced cello under Leo Schulz and to play in the students' orchestra. In 1889, he made his debut as a soloist in old Chickering Hall. He was a member of the National Symphony when it merged with the New York Philharmonic in 1921. Before that, he played with Pinto's New York Boys' Symphony, with Victor Herbert's Orchestra, and the

Russian Symphony. His strong, kindly face bears witness to his character, which caused his colleagues to have confidence and trust in him. He served as Chairman of the Orchestra Committee for ten years and was a Trustee of the Orchestra's Benefit Fund.

Alberico Guidi *(1928-1949)*

The Guidi are a Venetian family, but Alberico was born October 3, 1893, at Catania, Sicily, where his father was teaching painting and drawing. He studied the cello with Achille Rossi of Venice, the Hungarian virtuoso Dezso Kordy, and finally with William E. Whitehouse (Felix Salmond's teacher) in London. He made his concert debut at Queen's Hall in that city when he was 18. He and his brother and sister formed the Trio Guidi, which made frequent appearances in England and France. He also was a member of the Musica String Quartet and, for several years, of the Queen's Hall Symphony in London. He joined the New York Symphony as solo cellist in 1924 under Willem Mengelberg and held that position until the merger with the Philharmonic in 1928.

Martin Ormandy *(1929-1966)*

Martin Ormandy graduated from the Royal Academy of Budapest, where Zoltan Kodály, Leo Weiner, and Eugen Kerpely were among his teachers. Later he was a pupil of Diran Alexanian in Paris, and Leo Schulz and Alfred Wallenstein in New York. When he came to the United States in 1922, he joined the Capitol Theatre Orchestra, whose conductor was his brother,

Eugene Ormandy (conductor of the Philadelphia Orchestra 1936-1980). He remained with that organization until 1929 when he was engaged by the Philharmonic-Symphony.

Rudolph Sims *(1939-1966)*

The Philharmonic-Symphony Orchestra engaged Rudolph Sims only a few days before rehearsals began for the opening of the 1939-1940 season. He was born in New York City, September 19, 1892. His father, a former viola player in the Moscow Opera Orchestra, taught music in New York until his retirement. Rudolph, a pupil of Leo Schultz, gave a number of recitals in old Aeolian Hall as a child prodigy; appeared as solo cellist under conductors David Mannes and Nicolai Sokoloff; and played for the Monte Carlo Ballet during its first New York season. He spent three years in Paris at the Conservatoire de Paris as a private pupil of Paul Bazelaire. He collected early phonograph records as a hobby; and performed on a Paolo Antonio Testore cello, dated 1745. Rose became quite friendly with Sims, who was 26 years his senior and played behind him on the second stand.

Richard E. Stehl *(1928-1946)*

Two generations of Stehls were born in New York, studied music there, and practiced their art in that city. Richard Stehl began to study the cello at the age of seven, and numbered among his teachers Max Droge, Armand Ladoux, and Leo Schulz. He made a few recordings for the Columbia Phonograph Company between 1910 and 1919, both as soloist and as a member of various ensembles and orchestras. He was engaged by the New York Symphony in 1917; but shortly thereafter, went to war where he served as acting bandmaster of the 350th Regiment Band overseas. When he returned to the United States in 1919, he joined the New York Philharmonic Orchestra.

Milton Forstat (1938-1958)

Milton Forstat was born in Cleveland, September 24, 1910. He decided on a career as a professional musician when he was 12, and began to prepare for it at the Bronx House Music School, where he studied the cello under Willem Durieux and at the same time took full courses in harmony and counterpoint. In 1931, he won a fellowship in cello at the Juilliard Graduate School where his teacher was Felix Salmond. From 1928 to 1931, he played with the National Orchestral Association. Prior to his engagement by the Philharmonic-Symphony in 1938, he served as a member of the orchestras conducted each season by Mr. Stoessel at the Chautauqua and Worcester Festivals and at the concerts of the New York Oratorio Society.

The following men also played in Rose's cello section.

Nathan Stutch (1946-1990)

Nathan Stutch was co-principal cellist of the Philharmonic at the time of his retirement in 1990. He joined that orchestra in 1946, having previously played for two seasons with the Cleveland Orchestra. He studied at the Curtis Institute with Felix Salmond and Emanuel Feuermann. He was on the faculty of Manhattan School of Music from 1984-2003. "Leonard Rose changed my life," Stutch said. "He was the first person I met at Curtis. During my four years at Curtis, I spent a long time getting to know him.

There was an instant bond that was formed that lasted all of our lives. There were many sides to this man; he was a giving person and was always helpful—always. When I got out of the service and came to New York, there was a six-month period before I could get a union card. So I wasn't making any money at all. He frequently, maybe twice a week, took me to dinner and he would always pay for the meal. We used to go to his favorite restaurant on 98th and Broadway called *The Old Salt*. He loved fish. That was his favorite food. It was just the two of us. Rose used to tell me, 'You and I have something very special.' Often, we talked about music and the conceptions of the different composers. We talked about how to interpret these works."[63]

Carl Stern (1944-1964) Assistant solo cellist.

Mr. Stern remained for seven years with the NBC Symphony and then in 1944 joined the New York Philharmonic-Symphony as assistant solo cellist to Leonard Rose. The Lewisohn Stadium Symphony appointed him solo cellist the same year and he appeared as soloist with both organizations. The youngest member of a large family of New Jersey artists, Stern was born in Paterson. Entirely educated in America, he studied cello with Willem Willeke at the Institute of Musical Art. To support his belief in modern music, he formed the "String Quartet for Contemporary Music." Among first American performances given by Mr. Stern include the Shostakovich Sonata with Aaron Copland at the piano for the League of Composers. He recorded for Spa Records and played on a 1699 Guarnerius cello with a François Tourte bow [The Frenchman Tourte, 1747-1835, was considered the single most important figure in bringing the bow into its modern form.] With Leonard Rose and Naoum Dinger, Stern performed David Popper's Requiem for three cellos and orchestra February 13, 1945, under the direction of Artur Rodzinski.

George Feher (1948-1974)

George Feher, a native of Hungary, moved to the United States in 1920. After winning several scholarships, he studied with Lieff Rosanoff at the Mannes School of Music. In 1937, he was engaged by the National Symphony in Washington, DC, which he left at the outset of World War II to enlist in the Navy. From 1945 until joining the New York Philharmonic, he played with the Pittsburgh Symphony under Fritz Reiner, and with the ABC and CBS Symphony Orchestras. He taught the cello at his alma mater, the Mannes College of Music, beginning in 1945.

Josef Malkin (1944-1949)

Russian-born Josef Malkin (1879-1969) made his American debut in 1909. He later played as principal with the Boston and Chicago Symphonies, eventually forming a trio with his brothers. In 1933, the family founded the Malkin Conservatory, which Josef directed for 10 years—after which he joined the New York Philharmonic, retiring in 1949. In Europe, his credits include principal cellist with the Berlin Philharmonic [while in Berlin, Malkin worked with Walter Grossman, Rose's first cello teacher].

Anthony Sophos (1949-1957)

Anthony Sophos was born in Peabody, Massachusetts, in February 1923. He was raised in Cleveland and at 19 was appointed to the faculty of Baldwin-Wallace College in Berea, Ohio. He played in the Cleveland Orchestra under Artur Rodzinski from 1942 to 1944. He then came to New York to study with Felix Salmond at the Juilliard School. In the 1947-1948 season, Sophos was a member of Toscanini's NBC Symphony. He joined the New York Philharmonic under Dimitri Mitropoulos and Leonard Bernstein from 1947 to 1957. He was also a member of the New York Philharmonic Cello Quartet with Laszlo Varga, Nathan Stutch and Martin Ormandy, which recorded for Decca Records. Sophos left the Philharmonic in 1957 to join the CBS Symphony Orchestra.*

---

* No information was found for Heinrich Joachim (1948-1958; first teacher to Lynn Harrell) and Ralph Oxman (1943-1944) – cellists who also played in Leonard Rose's cello section.

Chapter Seven

JOSEPH SCHUSTER, ROSE'S RIVAL

Walter is trying to slow you down and you're going ahead like a racehorse. Then he called me a name and I said, don't call me that, Joe, because I'll smack you across the face. I don't take that from anybody! ... I can play that solo, too.

—Leonard Rose

Joseph Schuster

    Leonard Rose was friendly with and respected by the majority of his colleagues. However, one man in particular—the New York Philharmonic's principal cellist, Joseph Schuster, learned that a rival who crossed paths with Rose—did not experience Rose at his kindest. Fueled by youthful audacity and a compelling sense of competition—some believe it did damage to his career—Rose clashed with him during Schuster's final season with the New York Philharmonic.

Appointed by Toscanini's successor, John Barbirolli hired Schuster to head the Philharmonic-Symphony Orchestra's cello section in 1936. The orchestra's new solo cellist had been born in Constantinople in 1903 to Russian-Jewish parents, who took him to Russia when he was three. The celebrated Russian composer Alexander Glazunov (1865-1936) heard the 10-year-old Schuster while living in Sebastopol and arranged for him to receive a scholarship to the St. Petersburg Conservatory. There he studied with Josef Press, who later bequeathed his library of cello music to Felix Salmond, who in turn gave the cherished collection to Leonard Rose.*

Schuster's studies, interrupted by the Bolshevik revolution, resumed in Berlin under the eminent German cellist Hugo Becker[64] (Schuster also studied at the Leipzig Conservatory with Julius Klengel, known as the "Paganini of the cello"[65]) at the Hochschule. One of Becker's finest pupils, Schuster appeared for a while as a solo recitalist before conductor Wilhelm Furtwängler invited him to succeed Gregor Piatigorsky as solo cellist of the Berlin Philharmonic. Unquestionably, Schuster matured under the direction of Furtwängler, who Piatigorsky remembered as "perhaps the most significant [influence] in my musical life; the scope of his artistry was immense."[66] The Berlin Philharmonic was considered one of the world's premiere orchestras, and Schuster held the principal post for five years before heading to America to lead the cello section of the New York Philharmonic.[67]

The most notable musician working in Nazi Germany (prior to Herbert von Karajan) was the conductor Wilhelm Furtwängler (1867-1957). Representing the core of Romanticism, a throwback to the previous century, Furtwängler's presence—along with a unique conducting style of unorthodox body gesticulations—mesmerized performers and concertgoers alike. His musicians loved him; his interpretations were distinctive and inspiring.

---

* Subsequently, Rose edited this music—placing his interpretations in the form of fingerings and bowings into the cello part—afterward published by International Music Company under Rose's name and securing his editorial legacy for future generations.

New York Times critic Harold Schonberg (1915-2003) described Furtwängler as a conductor "who seemed often to be under hypnosis, conscious of neither the audience nor the orchestra, wrapped in sound and his inner vision. He gave the impression of operating under forces that moved him, marionette-like; and through him was distilled organized tone bent to an emotional end."[68] Although Furtwängler's interpretations represented the reverse of Toscanini's driven performances, the Italian Maestro acknowledged Furtwängler's talents and spoke of his innate skill on the podium. However, much like Bruno Walter along with German and Austrian artists before World War II, Furtwängler feigned any interest in politics, which led to his ill-fated decision to remain in Nazi Germany. Countless musicians fled, yet the conductor made music under the gaze of Adolf Hitler and his henchmen. Conducting in concert halls and opera houses adorned with the ubiquitous swastika banners, and for Hitler himself (he reportedly shook the Führer's hand after a performance of Beethoven's Ninth Symphony), roused controversy that haunted him for the rest of his life, both personally and professionally. His actions were neither forgotten nor forgiven after the end of the war.

Despite the Reich's official takeover of the Berlin Philharmonic on October 26, 1933, Furtwängler stayed, continuing a planned season that featured a number of Jewish guest artists (including Artur Schnabel and Bronislaw Huberman). When these artists staged a protest, refusing to set foot on German soil, his season crumpled under additional pressure from the Reich. It was Furtwängler's insistence on retaining his concertmaster Szymon Goldberg and principal cellist Joseph Schuster, both Jews in the most prominent positions next to him, even scheduling them as soloists that further rankled the Nazis. At the time, the conductor wrote an open letter of protest to Josef Goebbels, the propaganda minister, which the *Vossiche Zeitung* published, and which stated his belief that music and musicians needed to serve the purpose of uniting rather than dividing people. Furtwängler carefully wrote: "It must, therefore, be said plainly that men like Bruno Walter, Klemperer, and Reinhardt [the famous theater director] must be enabled to have their say in Germany in the future. ... Let our fight be concentrated against the reckless, disintegrating, and shallow spirit, but not against the true artist who in his own way, however his art may be appraised, is always creative and thus constructive."[69]

With the establishment of *Reichsmusikhammer* (National Chamber of Music) toward the end of 1933, Goebbels controlled every Jewish musician's plight. His appointment of Richard Strauss as president and Furtwängler as vice president, and their willing acceptance to this day remains contentious. Eight months later, both Goldberg and Schuster were forced to leave the orchestra.[70] It was Furtwängler's advocacy of the music of Paul Hindemith* that ultimately proved his downfall. This time, Furtwängler's open letter, published in the popular daily paper *Die Deutsche Allgemeine Zeitung*,** postulated Hindemith's music as "profound" and deigned him a man of "moral commitment." This fiery rhetoric continued by citing Hindemith as a composer "who has pure Germanic blood in his veins" and is "an out-and-out German type—German in his direct and honest craftsmanship and his open, rugged nature."[71] Soon thereafter, the powerful Nazi machine portrayed Furtwängler as a villain and ultimately squeezed and brought him down. He was forced to resign from all his posts, except for a token role in the *Staatsrat*, a state-run organization. The controversy surrounding one of the twentieth century's finest conductors still swirls. Was he pro-Nazi temporarily, then later actively anti-Nazi? Friedland Wagner, the granddaughter of composer Richard Wagner, wrote in 1944: "… inside Germany he [Furtwängler] is branded and despised as an anti-Nazi, while beyond Germany's borders he is being condemned as a Nazi." Did he dedicate himself to saving

---

* Hindemith's crime—aside from having a half-Jewish wife and a full-Jewish brother-in-law—was that his music was considered atonal, too avant-garde for the Reich. After the Hindemith debacle, Furtwängler dedicated himself to saving Jewish lives, writing letters on behalf of Jewish musicians seeking employment elsewhere. The deposed conductor helped a reported 109 individuals. This enraged Heinrich Himmler, head of the SS, who pleaded with Hitler for permission to send the conductor to a concentration camp, which never occurred.

** At that time, the *Deutche Allgemeine Zeitung* was a liberal Berlin paper with Right tendencies. Its courageous attitude was parlayed by printing anti-Nazi sentiments from famous people, including from Bruno Walter, until the editor-in-chief, Dr. Fritz Klein, disappeared, never heard from again.

Jewish lives after his defense of Hindemith? Perhaps, but there is no question that he chose to continue to make music under Nazi rule. After Furtwängler fled to Switzerland in early 1945, he was persona non grata in the United States and only found sparse work in Europe. In a few years, his failing health would derail any hope of a comeback. During a 1953 concert in Vienna, he collapsed on the podium. He would remain in Switzerland until his death in 1954.

The deal that Rose struck with Rodzinski had the cellist returning to New York, not as principal, but as assistant for a single season, with the principal position promised the following season. Schuster had problems with these terms, which gave Rose a week of solo concerts that should have been his. And Rose envied Schuster because he was departing the orchestra for a solo career, Rose's ultimate goal. What were Rose's thoughts as he adjusted his chair next to Schuster's, concert after concert, during that 1942-1943 season? Every time Schuster pulled his bow across his cello strings during precious orchestral solos, Rose was a foot and half away—passing judgment on him. Although Rose did admit that Schuster was a fine cellist, he absolutely believed he did not match his own caliber. Rose played differently from Schuster, who was accurate but his sound lacked the volume, depth, and beauty of Rose's. Furthermore, Rose must have been jealous that Schuster had already attained a level of prominence in the field that Rose still sought. But there may have been unspoken benefits to sitting alongside the man. Rose, at 24 years of age, may have recognized something in Schuster that captured his fascination and caused him to dig a little deeper in his own personal practice sessions. Rose recalls these days as trying for him and his young family.

Schuster was one of the handful of renowned cellists of his era. He was the notable solo cellist in Strauss's *Don Quixote* in Leonard Bernstein's sensational 1943 concert debut (Bernstein would later invite him to solo with his New York City Symphony). Numerous *New York Times'* reviews of Schuster's performing abilities from 1936 to 1950[72] reveal a great deal of respect for the cellist's solid musicianship and excellent intonation, but seem to dwell on the compactness of his tone and an inability to cut through the dense sounds of an orchestra, despite his exemplary

Guarneri cello purchased from Emanuel Feuermann in 1931.[73] On the other hand, a critic noted in 1936, "The new first cellist of the orchestra gave a good account of himself. His tone is much richer and has considerable more sensibility in it than that of his predecessor [Alfred Wallenstein, Toscanini's choice]."[74] In 1939, the newspaper described Schuster's tone as "broad and full, if not exceptionally brilliant."[75] In contrast, Rose's debut New York recital at Town Hall in 1945 was phrased in an entirely different manner by the *Times*: "...proved himself a master of the instrument and an intelligent musician ... possessor of a remarkable technique; draws from the cello a fine, round tone, and has interpretative gifts which more experienced artists might well envy."[76] In November of 1947, Rose's second Town Hall recital garnered yet higher praise: "Playing that remained on the highest plane of excellence throughout a noble and exacting program. ... His performances, whether considered from the technical, tonal, or interpretive angle, were of a distinguished order not easily surpassed, being equally remarkable for their communicativeness and musicianship."[77]

Schuster was a fixture on the New York scene well before Rose's arrival. He appeared annually in Town Hall recitals, performed with other famous artists, and wrote a tribute in memory of his friend Emanuel Feuermann in the *New York Times*, May 31, 1942. In Leipzig, the 15-year-old Schuster met Feuermann when he and his violinist brother, Sigmund, soloed in the Brahms "Double" Concerto with the Gewandhaus Orchestra led by Arthur Nikisch. Feuermann, who was slightly older than Schuster, possessed an impressively finished technique at a very early age that astounded Schuster. In the summer of 1926, Schuster spent a six-week vacation with Feuermann in Baden bei Wien, Austria, and swore that the young man never touched his cello once, because he didn't bother to bring it on the trip. Suddenly, on two days' notice, Feuermann substituted for an indisposed cellist in a performance of the Dvořák Cello Concerto. Schuster attended the concert along with some friends and recounted, "I can well remember that performance which he gave that day ... it was almost unbelievable for its perfection and beauty." Schuster's tribute concluded with the forecast that Feuermann's premature death marked a terrible loss to all cellists of his day and "especially to those of the coming generation."

Perhaps Schuster's most insightful appraisal in New York, published in the *Times* on January 10, 1945, came after his Philharmonic departure in another recital at Town Hall. The critic conveyed, "Schuster's performances are graced with a firm, rich tone, unusually secure intonation, and an orderly, precise technique. If he rarely achieves great poetic feeling in his readings, neither does he fail to give an accurate, tasteful account of the music at hand." Leonard Rose certainly read his rival's review.

Schuster toured America and abroad for many years. He continually transcribed for the cello works written for other instruments, for use at his own recitals. Cellists still present some of these transcriptions in concert. In addition to several concerto recordings, he participated on a 1961 recording of Fauré's Piano Trio, Op. 120, with violinist Feri Roth and pianist André Previn.[78]

Rose was hardly happy as Schuster's assistant. During the Brahms B-flat Piano Concerto, amidst the second movement's cello solos—which Rose himself previously performed in Cleveland[*]—Rose recounts what happened sitting second to Schuster. "The beautiful top line ... is one of the glorious moments in all of music. The second cello has a descending scale-line pattern; and when Bruno Walter began to conduct, I tried to follow Joe but it was very difficult. Joe was very nervous, and I felt that he was trying to push the tempo and Walter was trying to hold it back and I was caught in the middle. Somehow we managed to get through that performance, and Joe turned on me and snarled, 'Why didn't you follow me?' I replied, 'Look, Joe, I was caught in between. Walter is trying to slow you down and you're going ahead like a race horse.' Then he called me a name and I said, 'Don't call me that, Joe, because I'll smack you across the face. I don't take that from anybody! ... I can play that solo, too.' So, it wasn't the happiest of times."

Conflict persisted between the two men throughout that season. Rose remembers another incident that he, peculiarly, considered a stroke of luck: "Rodzinski scheduled on one program the Miaskovsky String Symphonietta and the Shostakovich First Symphony [February 1944 also included Tchaikovsky Symphony No. 6 "Pathétique"]. The Miaskovsky had very difficult long cello solos including cadenzas, and—of course—there are some very difficult bits and very exposed solos in the Shostakovich First. While the Miaskovsky was certainly an offbeat piece, no one knew that I had played it with Fritz Reiner [Rose belittled his alma mater for not having played Beethoven's Fifth but made no mention of gratitude for having experienced the Miaskovsky] at Curtis while I was first cellist there. I not only knew those solos, but I practiced the hell out of them just in case I would have to play them. I also had played the Shostakovich. ... I was ready."

Rose continues: "Schuster came to all four rehearsals. I arrived early for that first performance on Thursday night. As mentioned before, I have always been an early bird—I like to be well warmed up and I like to practice before I walk out on stage, even when playing in the orchestra. On this particular Thursday

---

[*] Rose's rendition from an August 25, 1951 performance with pianist Dame Myra Hess, Bruno Walter conductor can be heard at the Philharmonic Archives. Rose's interpretation is breathtakingly beautiful.

evening, I was met at the stage door by Maurice von Prague, the personnel manager, who said to me, 'Lennie, I've got some news for you. You have to play the solos tonight. Schuster cut his hand.'" The report jolted the cellist. "I didn't have time to get nervous, which was a very good thing. I got hold of the music backstage and I looked at a few places to make sure of them. Well, to make a long story short, I played all three performances, Thursday night, Friday afternoon, and the Sunday afternoon broadcast over the Columbia Radio network. There were said to be 13 million people listening. I played marvelously. The New York press picked it up and said, 'We are looking forward to this young man becoming first cellist.'"

Rose somewhat self-centeredly felt victorious, albeit at the expense of his colleague: "It was a huge triumph for me and the boys in the orchestra were absolutely so happy for me, they were practically carrying me on their shoulders. I remember I had a call from Eugene Ormandy in Philadelphia who heard the broadcast, got excited, and had to call me. It was all very thrilling for me. Schuster came back the next week. I guess you could say his tail was very much between his legs. He was sheepish as hell and, I think, the poor man couldn't wait to get the season over with." It eventually ended and Rose assumed the role of principal cellist of the orchestra the following year.

There is no mention of Schuster past this incident in Rose's memoir, yet Schuster appeared as soloist with the Philharmonic just weeks after his *Don Quixote* performance with Bernstein. On December 25 and 26, 1943, he performed Schubert's "Arpeggione" Sonata arranged for cello and orchestra by his contemporary, celebrated Spanish cellist Gaspar Cassadó[*] in Carnegie Hall, under the direction of the American conductor and pioneer Howard Barlow (1892-1972). During Schubert's Centenary Celebration in 1928, Cassadó premiered his own newly arranged version of the work in Vienna with the Berlin Philharmonic conducted by Furtwängler. The year also marked Cassadó's first United States appearance when he attended the premiere (Willem Mengelberg leading the Philharmonic) of a work he composed for orchestra,

---

[*] Cassadó was renowned, born in Barcelona, Spain (1897-1966), the apparent heir to fellow Catalonian Pablo Casals.

"Rapsodia Catalana," a piece based on songs and dances from his homeland. Eight years later, Cassadó was presented his New York debut with the Philharmonic performing Haydn's Concerto in D Major with John Barbirolli.

Although there is no mention of Cassadó by Rose, it seems certain he was aware of the cellist's reputation when he arrived in New York to perform in 1949. The man—who was in his fifties and had 30 years of concertizing behind him—was known throughout Europe as an outstanding composer for the instrument as well (he composed close to 70 transcriptions for cello and piano, one of which Rose regularly performed). What should have been a landmark musical event though became a nightmare. On March 6, during Rose's seventh season with the Philharmonic, the *New York Times* printed a letter concocted by Diran Alexanian titled "Protest by Casals." Its offensive tone instantaneously damaged Cassadó's career. The personal note, penned by Casals, is surprisingly venomous: "During the war, Cassadó made himself a brilliant career in Germany, Italy, and Franco Spain," Casals wrote. "Without scruple, he presents himself in America and is *received*. This is deplorable. The presumption of Cassadó knows no limit. When knowing that I am undergoing exile for having played the opposite card, he uses my name to cover himself. A revolting cynicism! I hope at least that the musicians of America will know how to act in this case. ... It is not a question of hatred, but one of dignity and justice."[79] Obviously, the older man's resentment (Casals was 72) had been building toward his compatriot while in exile. That he vented in America's most important newspaper was unfortunate. The ensuing public outcry devastated any chance his once treasured pupil, friend, and colleague had in continuing a burgeoning career in America. Cassadó, who hailed Casals as his "spiritual father," tried in vain to defend himself, publishing his own letter calling out Alexanian's devious scheme as "monstrous for a colleague. ... The inquisitorial tone of both letters accusing me of crimes I did not commit gave me much distress," Cassadó retorted. "During the Spanish civil war, I did not take sides. ... I am sure that if Mr. Casals realized the machinations involved, his nobility would have prevented his having a part in it."[80] In defense of his friend, American-born conductor and violinist Yehudi Menuhin (1916-1999)—one of the twentieth century's finest musicians—lashes Casals and his staunch supporters in his autobiography, writing of unnamed followers who helped him establish music festivals in Prades after the war: "... making wonderful music with Casals but also using his prestige for their own purposes, including punishment campaigns against suspect musicians. ... They demanded heroism of such as Cassadó; they were not heroes themselves, but protected from the dilemmas he had faced, buttered their prosperous bread and called for vengeance on the erring"[81] With the force of negative press from the universally beloved Casals, Cassadó's boycott—bolstered by threats of physical violence—prevented him from performing in New York which led to his demeaning deportation from Ellis Island. As competitive as Rose was and as an avid reader of newspaper reporting, he and the musical establishment surely were aghast.

The somewhat clumsy and disjointed arrangement of "Arpeggione" was recorded in 1956 by Cassadó with the Bamberg Symphony under the direction of Jonel Perlea. The austere and noble approach of the cellist, who may have been a bit past his prime, is a testament to his legacy.

As for Diran Alexanian (1881-1954)—the influential disciple of Casals born in Constantinople who played chamber music with Brahms and violinist Joseph Joachim—he is credited with having a profound influence on numerous elite cellists: Maurice Eisenberg, Pierre Fournier, Raya Garbousova, Antonio Janigro, George Neikrug, Gregor Piatigorsky, George Ricci, David Soyer, Paul Tortelier, Mischa Schneider, and his violinist brother Alexander. Rumor has it that even Feuermann rarely played in New York without first seeing Alexanian. Bernard Greenhouse, who had a significant association with Alexanian during World War II, found him "extremely analytical but also innately musical."[82] Rose's dislike for the man, possibly swayed by his gall of orchestrating public humiliation against Cassadó, is searing:

> I have the most difficulty ... from strict disciples of Alexanian. Alexanian did so much great harm to so many students. His concept of the bow was of rigidity, and his students tended to make a sound resembling coarse grain sandpaper. The instruction for the left

hand was equally crippling. Alexanian students tended to great tightness and general constipation musically. A pity!

Defending Alexanian, Greenhouse thought him a "first-class teacher" and believed that Casals never would have placed him at the École Normale de Musique in Paris (1921-1937) as his assistant to fill in for him when away on tours if he didn't think very highly of him. "I can tell you that he was a magnificent musician. That's where Rose makes his mistake. While there was the possibility of him disturbing his students about the mechanics of playing the cello he never disturbed them about music. His concept of music was analytic; but at the same time, if you were willing to put his musical interest beyond the instrument, then you came out of it a much more secure musician with a different concept of how to develop your own creativity in music-making."[83] Raya Garbousova (1909-1997), acquainted with many famous musicians of her day, knew musicians "in desperation when he died. His knowledge was tremendous."[84]

After his departure from the Philharmonic, Schuster was invited back as guest soloist February 24 and 25, 1945, to perform Robert Schumann's Concerto under Rodzinski. It was a work he recorded (along with Bruch's "Kol Nidrei" and Johann Christian Bach's Concerto in C minor) in the 1950s with the Los Angeles Orchestra Society. The finest Hollywood players comprised this orchestra, later known as the Columbia Symphony Orchestra (1947-1965), under Franz Waxman, a German refugee who was better known as a supreme Hollywood film composer who wrote over 150 scores and captured two Academy Awards. Rodzinski's solo invitation to Schuster could not possibly have sat well with Rose, his newly anchored first cellist.

Reflecting on Joseph Schuster's lack of a stellar career, Rose succinctly and perhaps unjustly states in his memoir: "Unfortunately for Joe, while he played well, he didn't play that well." Schuster died in 1969.

Chapter Eight

LEONARD BERNSTEIN, AN AMERICAN TRIUMPH

> *We have both grown older, You and I*
> *And I am not sad, and You must not be sad.*
> *Unfurrow your brow; look tenderly again*
> *At me, at us, at all these children*
> *Of God here in this sacred house.*
> *And we shall look tenderly back to You.*
> *O my Father: Lord of Light:*
> *Beloved Majesty: my Image, my Self!*
> *We are one, after all, You and I;*
> *Together we suffer, together we exist.*
> *And forever will recreate each other.*
> *Recreate, recreate each other!*
> *Suffer, and recreate each other!*
>
> —Leonard Bernstein
> (closing prayer of his *Kaddish* Symphony)

Within weeks of Rose's initiation with the New York Philharmonic, lightning struck in the name of Leonard Bernstein. Rose, seated as principal cellist during Bernstein's historic birth, played a part in Bernstein's debut. Oddly, although the men would ultimately perform and record together, Rose would leave no personal reminiscences of Bernstein in his memoir. This author believes, lurking beneath the surface, an undocumented chasm pervaded their personal and possibly their musical relationship.

**William Polisi John Corigliano Imre Pogany
Leonard Bernstein Leonard Rose
November 14, 1943, Leonard Bernstein's Debut**
Courtesy of the New York Times

Leonard Rose and Artur Rodzinski[*85] were mutually living their dreams: on top of the symphonic world with the oldest functioning symphony orchestra in America (precisely at that time, Rodzinski, in collaboration with 80-year-old composer Richard Strauss, created his popular "Der Rosenkavalier Suite" derived from his 1910 opera). Rose's tenure would continue until 1951, when he would leave the Philharmonic with honor and accolades en route to stardom as cello soloist. However, Rodzinski's tenure in New York began and ended in scandal. On January 13, 1948, five years to the day after he started, he resigned after losing control of artistic rights, repertoire choices, and guest conductors, which he alleged were dictated by the man who many deemed the most powerful and corrupt man in America's music business— Arthur

---

* In March 1928, Rodzinski first conducted the New York Philharmonic. From his next appearance in November 1934, Rodzinski became a fixture in the New York scene; guest conducting the Philharmonic and the NBC Symphony.

Judson—Rose's future manager. By 1930, the cunning Judson created Columbia Concerts Corporation, which controlled many of the era's leading artists and orchestras; he also figured prominently in the creation of Columbia Broadcasting System, which sated the American public's airwaves with classical music. Ultimately, a public battle between the two men would spell the conductor's doom.

The gravest mistake Rodzinski made before he took the podium in New York was to fire 14 members of the orchestra. The saga unfolds: While Fritz Reiner conducted, Rodzinski obsessed from Carnegie Hall's third tier and listed those musicians who "sawed, blew, or banged listlessly, sat slouched, without any sign of tension or involvement."[86] The list included his one-time friend, concertmaster Mishel Piastro,* who Toscanini hired in 1931. Six other first-desk players inexplicably received notification of their dismissals as well. The gloomy proceedings were leaked to the *New York Times,* which shook the organization. Jimmy Petrillo, head of the American Federation of Musicians, responded by counseling the entire orchestra not to sign contracts for the coming season. A stinging letter from the union was forthcoming, accusing Rodzinski of "defamation of character and jeopardizing the livelihood of brother musicians." Even from Cleveland came a message of commiseration—which included the signature of Leonard Rose. Furthermore, the crisis prompted first lady Eleanor Roosevelt to write to the conductor pleading that he reinstate the discharged men. The situation nearly veered out of control—delaying or even canceling the imminent season; eventually, just five men were rehired.

Rodzinski's next order of business was to select an assistant conductor to fill a position that had been vacant for a decade. He wanted an American. More importantly, he sought someone he could mentor who would assume the duties he once carried out for Stokowski. Just as Toscanini made his dramatic debut in June 1886 when the originally scheduled conductor was

---

* Shortly before his death in 1970, Piastro insisted he still didn't know why he was fired. His replacement, John Corigliano—Rose's concertmaster and recording partner, and father of composer John (Paul) Corigliano—was Piastro's stand partner since 1935.

suddenly nowhere to be found, Rodzinski's own successful New York debut occurred when he took over from an ailing Stokowski. That concert led directly to his first post in 1929 as music director of the Los Angeles Philharmonic.

To initiate his search for an assistant, Rodzinski contacted the finest music schools in the country. After no special candidate surfaced, he accepted Serge Koussevitzky's invitation to Tanglewood, the Berkshire Music Center in western Massachusetts founded by the Russian-born Jewish conductor in 1940, to meet a particular student Koussevitzky raved about. Of the five students accepted into the program, a brilliant one he felt confident was destined for a career was Leonard Bernstein. Upon meeting Bernstein, and with Rodzinski's curiosity piqued, the conductor invited the youngster to come visit him at a 232-acre property Rodzinski recently purchased outside Stockbridge.* At the farm, the two men got a chance to tend to the animals, dine, and talk. According to Halina Rodzinski, "In the evenings after dinner, Artur and Lenny would talk for hours, with Artur prodding information from Lenny about his background, his family, his education. Artur was duly impressed and wanted to unburden his future young apprentice from having to make a living copying manuscripts [Bernstein did all kinds of odd musical jobs for $25 a week for the Harms publishing company—a company that had given George Gershwin and Jerome Kern their first start and which would eventually publish Bernstein's first works]." According to Bernstein biographer Humphrey Burton, Rodzinski eventually told the youth, "I have gone through all the conductors I know of in my mind and I finally asked God whom I should take and God said, 'Take Bernstein.'" Rodzinski engaged Bernstein on his 25th birthday.

Toward the end of the sixth week of the New York Philharmonic's 102nd season, guest conductor Bruno Walter fell so ill with the flu he could not rouse himself from bed. A live CBS broadcast from Carnegie Hall with Walter and the Philharmonic was slated for the following afternoon. Rodzinski

---

* The *White Goat Farm,* had horses, chickens, ducks, and cows. Rodzinski, a health nut and hypochondriac, produced some 20 quarts of goat's milk a day—for himself and to sell.

received an emergency call in the morning, but resisted the temptation to make the four-hour automobile trip from his farm. "Call Bernstein," the conductor responded. "That's why we hired him. This is his chance, and I won't rob him of it. You've got to let him conduct." The music programmed for November 14, 1943, consisted of Robert Schumann's "Manfred Overture," Miklos Rozsa's Theme, Variations and Finale, and Strauss's epic tone poem *Don Quixote*, featuring principal cellist, Joseph Schuster, with Rose acting as principal cellist the entire program (Wagner's Prelude to *Die Meistersinger* was also performed but not aired).

Bernstein never conducted any of the pieces in rehearsal, let alone in concert. What ensued is legendary, one of the most remarkable events in musical history. Orchestra players remember seeing Bernstein's eyes closed and his body naturally swaying to the music. According to Philharmonic violinist Jacques Margolis, Bernstein was instructed to follow the orchestra, which had already performed the program twice under Walter's direction. Yet the *Wunderkind* managed to coax the orchestra to play differently. As Margolis recalls, "You just couldn't believe a young man could create that kind of music. Here were players in their fifties and sixties [Rose was 25] with long experience. And here this little snot-nose comes in and creates a more exciting performance [than Walter]. The orchestra stood up and cheered. We were open-mouthed. That man was the most extraordinary musician I have ever met in my life." The fateful event catapulted Bernstein onto the global musical scene. In the midst of World War II, the next morning's *New York Times* placed the story of his conquest on the front page in the same size print as "JAPANESE PLANE TRANSPORT SUNK." Another headline read: "YOUNG AIDE LEADS PHILHARMONIC, STEPS IN WHEN BRUNO WALTER IS ILL."[87]

The critic wrote:

> There are many variations of one of the six best stories in the world: the young corporal takes over the platoon when all the officers are down; the captain, with the dead admiral at his side, signals the fleet to go ahead; the young actress, fresh from Corinth or Ashtabula, steps into the star's role; the junior clerk, alone in the

office, makes the instantaneous decision that saves the firm from ruin. The adventure of Leonard Bernstein, 25-year-old assistant conductor of the Philharmonic, who blithely mounted the podium at Carnegie Sunday afternoon when conductor Bruno Walter became ill, belongs in the list. ... Mr. Bernstein had to have something approaching genius to make full use of his opportunity.

Within three days of his debut at Carnegie Hall, eight crews of photographers took approximately 110 pictures of Bernstein, and he had been interviewed by reporters from *Life, Time, Newsweek, Pic, Look, Vogue, PM, Pix, Harper's Bazaar,* the *Times,* the *Herald Tribune,* the *Jewish Forward,* the *Jewish Day,* the *News,* the *Post* and the *New Yorker*.[88] Bernstein's debut triggered invitations from all over the country to conduct, and an instant invitation to guest conduct the Philharmonic in a two-week spot in the company of Bruno Walter, Wilhelm Steinberg, and Artur Rodzinski—unheard of for a young American at that time. His arrival in the musical spotlight—a focus that became more brilliant as he matured—would mark the catalyst that changed how American audiences viewed and valued classical music. After years of artistic struggle marked by self-loathing and dissuasion from his parents, Bernstein emerged an American hero. Three months after his debut, he resigned his assistantship to the flabbergasted Polish conductor.

Although Bernstein studied conducting at the Curtis Institute with the staid Fritz Reiner, his dominant influences were Dimitri Mitropoulos, whom he met in 1937 and whom he would emulate on the podium; and Serge Koussevitzky who became his father figure. His habit, which he carried through to the final performance of his life—wearing Mitropoulos's crucifix of black ebony (given to Bernstein in the 60s) and ritually kissing a pair of cufflinks Koussevitzky gifted him each time he stepped from the wing onto stage—testified to his love for and loyalty to these mentors. The singular George Gershwin, a self-made millionaire and one of America's most naturally gifted composers, also deeply influenced Bernstein. Although he never met the man whose jazzy compositions were setting a new trend in concert halls, Gershwin's celebrity as a pianist and songwriter enamored him. A recent discovery in the Library of Congress's Bernstein Collection reveals that in response to Gershwin's early death, the 17-year-old musician, who was then working as a counselor at a summer camp in the Berkshires, immediately set to work arranging Gershwin's "Rhapsody in Blue" scoring it for accordion, ukulele, voice, among other available instruments.[89] Indeed, Bernstein's lifelong fascination with this work is clear-cut from his first period of creativity. Another notable supporter was Aaron Copland, the so-called dean of American composers and 18 years Bernstein's senior. Copland guided Bernstein's multiple talents at times when Bernstein needed direction. Bernstein's affection for Copland and his music throughout his life are well documented.

After the debut, pictures of Bernstein graced the covers of countless magazines, which printed his outspoken views. His weekly mail exceeded 500 letters, as invitations for engagements poured in. The once penniless copyist, pianist, and composer's annual income quickly rose from an estimated $100,000 to $500,000 (equivalent to nearly $6 million in 2008). His talent and box office appealed to the gamut led by jazz great Tommy Dorsey, who asked him to compose original pieces and make arrangements for his band. His handsome, debonair look attracted the attention of Paramount Pictures in Hollywood, which approached Bernstein for a series of screen tests. "He was frighteningly gifted," Helen Coates remarked, who from 1932 taught and tutored the adolescent Bernstein at the piano. "He could read, sing, and memorize anything. He used to come to me right from school. Since I never knew when he'd go home, I never scheduled anyone after him. He'd bring me his report cards, poems, questions on world topics. ... He talked about everything." From 1944 until his death, Bernstein employed her as his personal secretary. In addition to handling his mail, Coates answered the telephone, budgeted his time, arranged his appointments, kept his scrapbooks, and protected him from well-meaning intruders. "I couldn't believe that all this was happening to me," Bernstein reportedly told friends.

Rose openly expressed his disappointment, in his unpublished memoir, at not being the solo cellist in *Don Quixote* at Bernstein's debut (possibly due to the conductor's effusive hugs and kisses thrown Schuster's way, photographs of which incidentally, did not make the papers). Two months after this momentous occasion though, Leonard Rose began carving out his own piece of musical history when he debuted as soloist with the New York Philharmonic in Lalo's Cello Concerto. "I heard that debut concert with the Philharmonic," cellist Avron Coleman recalled. "We had never heard a sound like that. There was Feuermann and Piatigorsky, but there was something unique about that tone quality. The musicality and the continuity of the bow arm were fantastic. It was so pleasurable. You couldn't say that you didn't derive great emotional pleasure from listening to him. That playing was something new. He was extremely romantic." The *New York Times* noted his exceptional abilities, "Mr. Rose has a lovely tone, which was of particular use here. He has a perfection of phrasing that also was of much service …, was given with a delicacy of tone, technique, and feeling that is rare. The last movement, like the whole work, was played with reserve and taste."

Bernstein's intelligence was both unreserved and penetrating; success came easy and effortlessly to him. His love of languages became a lifelong passion that made it possible for him to conduct erudite interviews in other tongues. In some way needing constant adulation, he engaged people in and out of the music field. He loved to read and write poetry as well. His political concerns were liberal, sometimes dubiously so. When Bernstein's Chilean wife, Felicia Montealegre, came up with the idea to host a fundraising event for the militant Black Panther movement, Bernstein found trouble. He was mistaken at seeing no harm in the cause. The demigod was immediately hassled by the press prompting irate patrons to boo as he made his way toward the podium. For his part, Bernstein never let on that it was his wife's idea and vociferously denied supporting the Black Panthers. Bernstein would later accuse the FBI of carrying on a calculated campaign of harassment against him and his wife following the meeting.[90]

Bernstein was always vitally engaged in the world he belonged to. There could be no better proof than when he conducted Beethoven's Ninth Symphony to mark the reunification of Germany and the dismantling of the Berlin Wall on Christmas Day 1989, leading orchestras, choruses, and soloists from Berlin,

Dresden, New York, London, Paris, and Leningrad. Until just a few months before his death in October 1990, he remained highly social (his love for late night parties legendary) and visible, guest conducting *his* favorite orchestras.

Arguably, Bernstein may be the most important American musical figure of the twentieth century because of the way he changed the musical landscape through his celebrity and many creative bursts, among them the formation of the New York City Symphony; his staunch advocacy of American composers, which included his eclectic genres of music for the serious and popular stages (soon after the success of *On the Town,* interviewers began to call him a "genius" and a "swoon boy." Hundreds of teenagers flocked around the stage door waiting for him to appear.[91]); graceful discourses about the art of music; 600 recordings; and his groundbreaking televised *Young People's Concerts* that brought him world-wide fame. Bernstein, the creator and educator, lived long enough to see the series, which aired for over a decade on television encompassing 53 concerts from 1958-1973, produced on videotape, dubbed into a dozen languages, and syndicated to 40 countries. The inexhaustible American conductor Leonard Slatkin,[92] the National Symphony Orchestra's fifth music director (1996-2008), met Bernstein only once, three years before his death. He categorically states: "Bernstein was the 'Casals of the conducting world. There is Bernstein—and there is everybody else. We wouldn't be where we are if it wasn't for the path that he blazed. He was the first American to establish American conductors as being viable on the international scene. He brought a level of passion and commitment to music that people didn't associate with Americans at the time." When Slatkin met Bernstein (August 8, 1987), the younger man was conducting the composer's "Facsimile," a work written for film director and choreographer Jerome Robbins (1918-1998), which probes for meaning in Bernstein's complex spiritual world following World War II. With Bernstein seated in the audience at Tanglewood with the Boston Symphony, Slatkin recalls his anxiety-ridden performance. Upon meeting backstage, Bernstein gently and indelibly said, "Well, it wasn't what I intended when I wrote it. I didn't care for it, but I understand how you came to your conclusions."[93] Slatkin firmly believes Bernstein understood that for his music to survive, his scores needed to undergo alterations that Bernstein, as conductor, had done with other composers. Slatkin's affinity for the music of Bernstein is undeniable as his recording and repeated programming of Bernstein's "Jeremiah" symphony (1942) attests: "Any composer who expresses at such an early age in such an early work an individual voice is going to be heard. As time passes, 'Jeremiah' [awarded the New York Music Critics Award for 1944] will be played quite a bit more often. It is a work of such individuality that I think it will eventually find a permanent spot in the repertoire."[94]

Of course a talent of this magnitude, this tornado of a personality, left many organizations and human beings humbled in its destructive wake. Because Bernstein's ambition contained no boundaries, his insatiable appetite for success increased. Author Karen Horney points out that it all snowballed and morphed into "a demoniacal obsession, almost like a monster swallowing up the individual who has created it."[95] As if possessed by a devastating force, Bernstein's life was marked by excesses and, at times, by abuse—of drugs, alcohol, cigarettes, friends, and lovers. This also spilled over into performance. On occasion, his self-indulgent tempos rankled his soloists in concerti performances, orchestral colleagues, and—most often—Harold Schonberg, his severest critic at the *New York Times*. One episode involved Glenn Gould and the Brahms D Minor Piano Concerto in April 1962, when Bernstein earnestly announced to the audience that there had been a difference of opinion over tempos but that the show would go on. Apparently Gould's deliberateness did not please Bernstein, although upon review, Gould's tempos were not so slow as to warrant this disclaimer. Gould fumed at the accusation and in the final performance, surprised every musician on stage by opening the final movement twice as fast.[96] Another episode involved the admired pianist Murray Perahia (b. 1947). During a set of concerts and subsequent recording of the Schumann Concerto in the 1970s, the panic-stricken Perahia was nearly brought to tears by Bernstein's failure to direct the orchestra with the pianist's desired faster tempos. After pleading with executives, Perahia succeeded in halting the recording's release, which cost the company $50,000 dollars (Equivalent to nearly $200,000 in 2008).[97]

Bernstein's penchant for getting his way, at the expense of his health, often affected concerts as well, where he was spotted gulping scotch and smoking between bows. Jerry Hadley, the major American operatic tenor who died at age 55 of a self-inflicted gunshot wound in July 2007, described the aging Maestro: "Many times I saw him before a concert looking like the wreck of the Hesperus, with a cigarette in one hand and a drink in the other. Yet as soon as he reached the stage, 35 years would melt away and he would become this ageless sylph who loved music; his whole body would pulsate. He was the most utterly human, most exasperating, petulant, the most maddening person to be around, and the most stimulating and fulfilling musician I have ever encountered."[98] People who knew Bernstein wince when recalling his childlike demands, crude commentary, and need for constant glorification. According to longtime friend and eminent American composer David Diamond (1915-2005), "He treated many people badly at the end. In the last 10 years, his behavior could be shameful—to everyone for whom he should have shown the greatest respect. You see, the man had lost all judgment. Lenny was completely without shame. He was demoralized, de-everything. His self-destructive personality had taken over and it was obvious in everyone's eyes and it was painful for all of us, terribly painful. Everything was done to excess, there was self-indulgence in every possible way."[99] Could this have been the result of a lifestyle of overwhelming fame, satiated with money, sycophants and an ever-present "empire" of young men for whom he was guru?

Mstislav Rostropovich (1927-2007), a beloved colleague who was on par with Bernstein's genius, eloquently states what the majority echoes: "He had such a great combination of intelligence and *spontaneous* temperament, spontaneous interpretation. His understanding was so deep, he felt so deeply inside music. I think he appealed more to the public in his art than any other musician of his time."[100] As for the darker side, perhaps Bernstein's behavior can be compared to the everlasting spirit of Beethoven, whose forceful character and grand fame fueled impudence and abuse toward his fellow man. Who knows what Beethoven, who died at 56, might have evolved into had he lived to Bernstein's age of 72.

Leonard Bernstein   Leonard Rose   1960

Born 30 days and 450 miles apart, both to poor Russian-Jewish immigrants, Leonard Bernstein and Leonard Rose would have significant contact from Bernstein's debut until 1960—a banner year for Bernstein: named "Musician of the Year" and awarded honorary degrees from Northwestern, Hebrew Union College, Brandeis, Temple, and Dartmouth. 1960 also brought him an Emmy for "Bernstein and the New York Philharmonic" and the Page One Award of New York's Newspaper Guild. The year before, his book, *The Joy of Music*, derived from his "Omnibus" programs, became an instant bestseller, subsequently published in five languages, and showered with awards. He penned the book during a year in which he took the Philharmonic on a 10-week tour that included two weeks in Moscow (one of the orchestra's most highly publicized performances took place at Moscow's Grand Hall of the Tchaikovsky Conservatory of Music when Bernstein conducted Shostakovich's Fifth Symphony, getting the reticent composer afterward onto the stage for prolonged adulation.) plus appearances in Milan, Athens, Berlin, Brussels, Helsinki, Paris, and elsewhere: an astonishing 50 concerts in 70 days.

In October 1960, after a summer Philharmonic tour of the continental United States, Hawaii, Canada, and Berlin, Bernstein opened the Philharmonic season with the first of a concert series dedicated to "Robert Schumann and the Romantic movement." Late in the month, the 42-year-olds were engaged to perform then record Robert Schumann's Cello Concerto with the Philharmonic. Their interpretation, a half-century later, remains colorful, deeply felt—masterfully unfolding in a natural manner. Rose's cello playing is striking, especially in the virtuosic cadenza he executes before the coda (Purists, take note that Rose executed two minor cuts and does add a cadenza before the coda in the finale). Bernstein's love for the work is unquestionable, for it was his most frequently conducted and recorded work with cello: with Maurice Gendron[101] (1959), Leonard Rose (1960 and recorded), Jacqueline du Pré (1967 and issued later as a "live" recording), Mstislav Rostropovich[102] (1975 and recorded), and with Mischa Maisky (1985 and recorded).

Rose, Bernstein, and the Philharmonic would collaborate on two other occasions: Samuel Barber's Cello Concerto in January 1959 and 11 months later, Rose and Isaac Stern presented four performances of Brahms's "Double" Concerto. As Rose remembers, the first three performances went well; but the fourth, broadcast live from Carnegie Hall before millions of listeners, had a predicament.

> The orchestra played its four bars of introduction and then I played this extensive long cello cadenza. It went fine and then there is another four-bar interlude in the orchestra followed by a similar violin cadenza. At the end of this cadenza, the cello joins the violin, and together we finish with scale passages and six big chords directly to the largest tutti of the work. On this occasion, on the chord before the last one, my A string snapped. This is on the air with the New York Philharmonic! I immediately looked over to Laszlo Varga, who had been my successor at the Philharmonic, and I see he has his cheap English cello—it wasn't terribly good and very small. I knew I couldn't play on it because my Amati was much larger and I got frantic—what was I going to do? Here we were on the air and the orchestra is playing this long tutti lasting at least a minute and 10 or 20

seconds long. I had a flash of an idea and leaned over to Lotsie and said—everybody is watching me of course: Leonard Bernstein, the whole audience, they all knew what had happened—'Lotsie, give me your A string, *Quick*!' So, I got the A string from Lotsie and put it into the tail piece of the instrument, but these steel A strings that we all use now tend to curl where they go around the peg. All of this while the orchestra is playing. At first I could not insert the end of the A string into the hole of the peg so I could tune it up. I realized we were getting closer and closer to the next entrance where I had to play—a huge entrance. Finally, with God's help, I got the end of the string into the hole of the peg and got it tuned up one bar before I was to come in. I made the entrance and those listening on the air noticed nothing. The audience in the hall saw a real live drama. It was very tense for everybody. When I finally started to play, everybody let out a sigh of relief, but particularly me. If I had been Heifetz—he used to break strings left and right—it would have made the AP."

With so many productive years left to both men, why Bernstein and Rose discontinued collaborating after 1960 is unclear. Did they experience interpretive differences during that Schumann recording session? Did their two enormous egos clash? Certainly the music of Gustav Mahler, which became Bernstein's obsession (at times, Bernstein liked to tell people he was Mahler reincarnated) beginning in 1960, the centennial of Mahler's birth, may have been part of the reason. Perhaps Rose became weary of the amount of press Bernstein generated wherever he went; a Bernstein sighting always seemed to be an event of importance. Sadly, we will never know. Rose left no personal recollections of the conductor in his memoir. Yet, Leonard Rose carries the distinction as the only full-fledged soloist to have played numerous times in an orchestra under the direction of the budding Bernstein.

Chapter Nine

GREEK HERO, DIMITRI MITROPOULOS

> *Maestro, are you a religious man?*
> *Yes, I am.*
> *Do you go to church?*
> *No, I don't go to church. People who go to church are selfish.*
> *What do you mean?*
> *Mitropoulos's hand touched his crucifix, "People who go to church go to pray for themselves. I stay home and pray for everybody."*
> —Leonard Rose

Powerful words from Dimitri Mitropoulos, whose fame was worldwide, and who figured prominently on Leonard Rose's press materials: "I consider Leonard Rose the superlative cellist of today. He is the finest I have ever worked with, possessing all the qualities that make a great artist."

Rose recorded Ernest Bloch's Hebraic Rhapsody, "Schelomo," twice during his career; the first time in 1951 with the Philharmonic-Symphony Orchestra of New York conducted by Mitropoulos, the second in 1961 with the Philadelphia Orchestra conducted by Eugene Ormandy. Cellists influenced by his 1951 version regard the collaboration as the work's quintessential recorded interpretation. Rose, 32 years old when the extraordinary session occurred, describes its details: "Because of the expense, the pressures of recording in America were colossal in those days. We had played performances already so that the orchestra was well rehearsed. They allowed me a total of one hour and 20 minutes to make that recording—that's it. What we did quite literally was to play straight through." The *New York Times* foreshadowed the immense impact the recording would have when reviewing Rose's performance of the piece the same week it was taped: "Mr. Rose limned the musical outlines sympathetically, whether lyricism, intensity, or passionate outcry was called for. He projected his instrument's capacity for changing tone-color ranging from moody darkness ..."

His later "Schelomo" interpretation from 1961, which varies in subtle ways—I believe—presents a more mature artist, a deeper tone, and superior pacing. This lush stereo recording also captures the glorious sounds of Ormandy's Philadelphia Orchestra to go along with Rose's extraordinary Amati cello. In 1951, Rose was playing a Gofriller cello.

Mitropoulos, born in Greece in 1896, made his name as a composer and pianist well before he conducted. Yet on the podium, he achieved his fame. An impressive-looking man, with chiseled Mediterranean features and in exceptional physical shape, his conducting actions were demonstrative. Mitropoulos's identifiable style showed off his athletic grace leading more with his body than with his hands. As Rose remembers, "Mitropoulos had an individual kind of technique." Sometimes at a short breath or break in the flow of the music, he startled his musicians with a leap up off the podium, momentarily airborne. His habit of crouching near to the ground to get his orchestra to play softly was as unusual as it was unique.

His players appreciated—and even loved—his gentle manners. In an age when ego-driven directors ranted, raged, and were generally insulting, Mitropoulos was atypical. The downside, however, induced disrespect and a malaise that left Rose seething. "Because he was very nice, they [the orchestra] tended to crucify him, they didn't play very well for him, and were incompetent at rehearsals. He was too nice to them." Rose laments, "That orchestra had to be bullied. They had to feel fear." Unfortunately, the New York Philharmonic in that incarnation deserved its reputation for lacking discipline. Infighting, even backstage fistfights, was not uncommon.

World War II caused factions to form in the orchestra. "The New York Philharmonic, especially in the years when we were at war and right afterwards," Rose dictates in his memoir, "was an orchestra full of cliques. There was a German-Nazi clique, there were some Germans who were anti-Nazis, there was a large Italian-Fascist clique—all Mussolini lovers—there were some wonderful Italian boys, like Bill Polisi, Imre Pogany, and others I can think of who were anti-Fascist—great guys! There was a small White Russian clique in the orchestra—a very small Communist group; and then there were the rest of us; a lot of Jewish boys. We played our best for those conductors who were very tough like Rodzinski, Szell, and Toscanini."

Mitropoulos grew up in a small Greek village where his ancestry was particularly devout: his grandfather had been a priest and two of his uncles were monks. As a result, the young artist was equally drawn to religion and music. With the principles of St. Francis of Assisi steering his life, rumor had it that he considered joining an order of monks, and later the priesthood, in the Greek Orthodox Church.[103] On and off the podium, his beliefs translated into tenderness and actions of zealous generosity. His outright refusal to dismiss any musicians, regardless of their skill level, ultimately subjected him to criticism. Unlike the conductor stereotype, Mitropoulos did not feel superior to the members of his orchestra. He once stated, "All of us are no less equal in the service to music than we are in the face of God and our fellow man."[104] Leonard Rose fondly recalled "a very kind man, a very good human being who was also very generous with money. He would think nothing of writing out checks for liberal causes."* A letter to Katy Katsoyanis, a woman with whom he corresponded in autobiographical detail for 35 years, documents his largesse as it extended to colleagues, "... We have days of desperation, even considering abandoning the orchestra [Minnesota]; and then at the last minute, as by a miracle, the funds are found. The generous Dimitri has come in, not only never during the nine years asking for an augmentation of salary, but offering to

---

* In one notorious example, Mitropoulos urged orchestra members to support Henry Wallace's (33rd Vice President of the United States 1941-1945) third-party presidential candidacy in 1948—much to the chagrin of the Philharmonic board.

take a reduction, besides secretly paying the men the difference between their salary and what they asked for ..."[105]

Musically, Mitropoulos's vision was penetrating, faithful to the score, injecting an unusual personal style. His recordings reveal brilliance and exuberance. The conductor's strengths were the big Romantics: Tchaikovsky, Rachmaninoff, Berlioz, Brahms, and Strauss. Yet, he loved a broad repertoire: Mozart, Beethoven, Mendelssohn, Prokofiev, Shostakovich, Krenek, Schoenberg, Berg, Webern, and an array of French composers. During the 1949-1950 season, Mitropoulos courageously programmed "Chamber Symphony," Op. 21 (1928) by Anton Webern, a 12-tone composer and Schoenberg devotee. Webern's atonal works seemed shocking to conservative audiences, and controversy emerged within the orchestra. Incapable of fighting, Mitropoulos silently stood onstage after one of his players, disgusted by the composition, tossed his part at the conductor's feet before dashing off the stage. He never again programmed Webern in New York.

New York Philharmonic Leonard Rose (looking up)
Dimitri Mitropoulos 1940s

Mitropoulos debuted in America with the Boston Symphony Orchestra in 1936.[106] The response from critics warranted a return visit to the States the following season for engagements in Boston and Minneapolis. In 1938, Mitropoulos was named music director of the Minneapolis Symphony, succeeding Eugene Ormandy. He produced the first recordings of his career (on Columbia Masterworks) during his 10 seasons with that orchestra, and extensive tours elevated the orchestra's standing on par with the country's best. Mitropoulos' nature enabled him to become a popular figure in Minneapolis. He took an avid interest in educating local high school and college orchestras; this mentoring was celebrated in some city neighborhoods. Katsoyanis received encouraging words from him in December 1938: "Here is why America is better. There is everywhere an encouraging breath—for work, for morality."[107]

All was not well, however, with Mitropoulos. His darker side encompassed confusion, self-doubt, extreme loneliness, and depression. In a series of correspondence from Minneapolis two years later, he reveals: "[writing about another conductor] … He has the most important technical resources for being a conductor, which—unfortunately, in spite of all my efforts—I will never acquire. That's why I never believed that I could have any claim to being one of the really great artists. What makes me appear to approach them is the intensity of my expression, my logical rhythmic construction, and the convincing forcefulness I have sometimes. …" In June of 1940, a demoralized conductor wrote, "I am alone, completely alone, practically locked up in my room reading books and scores. If I manage to survive this time, then I'll never be in danger again of needing the company of any human being."

Although Mitropoulos's artistic life would continue to flourish, angst about his sexual preference—a religious taboo—and a strong sense of mortality plagued him. Toward the end of his life he wrote: "… but what else do we do in life but draw constantly on our courage and then arrive exhausted at the grave that waits for us … in order to run around chasing trifles like fame, which is nothing but the cowardly snob appeal of a puerile human ambition. … Alas, don't you think that all our life is like a funny, childish illusion?"[108]

From his first appearance in New York with the Philharmonic-Society in the 1940-1941 season,* his career with the orchestra gained momentum. In the 1947-1948 season, the management of the Philharmonic hired him to conduct 15 dates, which increased to 32 dates in the 1948-1949 season. The following year, Leopold Stokowski and Dimitri Mitropoulos (conducting 44 concerts) became co-directors. In Rose's final full season, Mitropoulos was named the sole director and conducted half of the season—an astonishing 59 concerts. By comparison, music directors today conduct as few as 25 and at most 45 concerts a season.

Leonard Rose's introduction to the Greek conductor came in 1938, when the cellist was a member of the NBC Symphony Orchestra.[109] Six seasons passed before Rose saw the man again. Rose's appearance as soloist in Robert Schumann's Concerto with Mitropoulos and the Philharmonic on November 4 and 5, 1948, incited *Times* critic Olin Downes to rave: "... Leonard Rose, the accomplished first cellist of the orchestra, played one of the dullest of celli concerti [Schumann] so beautifully that he held up the show. ... Mr. Rose played with such skill, with so much capacity to make indifferent music significant, and such taste, that the audience rightly called him back ..." Rose vividly tells of the experience: "There was a very amusing incident that happened during one of the rehearsals for that performance. Mitropoulos never had a score in front of him; he had a miraculous memory. He stopped for some musical reason in the last movement, and with a typical gesture, started tapping his forehead. He did this when he was trying to visualize where he wanted to start. He not only knew the music, but had memorized all the [identification] letters and all the numbers and knew exactly where they were. For instance, he would say, 'Gentlemen, let's start 22 bars before letter P.' I didn't have any music there either and I didn't know where 22 bars before letter P was, so I looked up at him and asked, 'Maestro, where the hell is 22 bars before letter P?' He said, 'Oh, my dear, it's where you have the diminished seventh passage coming down.' Of course, I knew immediately where it was, but the fact is he knew where it was and he knew where

---

* December 19, 1940: Beethoven Leonore Overture No. 2; Beethoven Symphony No. 4; Strauss Symphonia domestica.

22 bars before letter P was. I memorized the music but not the letters. That memory was particularly striking in 12-tone serial music."

"To Leonard Rose
The excellent young man, artist, musician and cellist. For remembrance of our collaboration, very appreciated. Dimitri Mitropoulos 1944"
Courtesy of Arthur Rose

In 1950, Rose had an opportunity to uncover the system behind Mitropoulos's prodigious memory. In April of that year, Rose decided to perform a new work, Alan Shulman's Cello Concerto. Rose recalls:

> I felt that it was time in my career to get a little adventuresome. I asked Mitropoulos whether he would consider letting me play a first performance with him. He exclaimed, "Oh, I love first performances!" Before the performances, I went up to Mitropoulos's apartment on 57th Street. My pianist went with me and I played through the piece. ... When my pianist left, Mitropoulos said to me, "Stay and have some tea with me." In his apartment, I had noticed little slips of paper in a neat little pile, and it looked like "A to B—32," "B to C—28." I asked, "Maestro, what are these little slips of paper?" He said, "That's one of the ways I remember the score. I learn the piece and I memorize the number of bars in between letters. Then I can pinpoint any place I want and know what to tell the orchestra." He was astounding! He really knew! There was only one time when I saw Mitropoulos forget and it was in a very complicated 12-tone work—Arnold Schoenberg's "Variations" [Rose's final Philharmonic season]—and he couldn't remember how one variation started. Every artist has a fear of forgetting, and so the man became human for a moment. At his invitation, I stayed for tea. During the visit he asked me, "Are you playing a recital this year?" I said, "Maestro, no, it costs too much money, and I don't feel I really need to now." He replied, "Look, I'd like to pay for the recital. This is not an empty offer, I'd really like to." At the time, a recital would have cost around $2,000 (equivalent to nearly $20,000 in 2008), and if you sold some tickets, you'd be lucky to get $500 back, so it would cost something like $1,500-$1,700. He was that kind of a person, he meant it, and it was very touching.

One year after Rose's departure from the Philharmonic, the conductor (at the age of 56) had a serious heart attack. His recovery was slow and it is likely that he never again regained his full strength. His declining health may have also ignited an effort to replace him. Another trigger for change, that caused Mitroupoulos' firing, was instigated when an April 1956 *New York Times* article concocted by Howard Taubman dissected the orchestra's shortcomings. His condemnation of Mitropoulos left him shattered. Titled "The Philharmonic—What's Wrong with it and Why," Taubman wrote: "During the 1955-1956 season, the New York Philharmonic-Symphony rarely sounded like an orchestra of the first order ... [it] seems to this observer another step in a process of deterioration. ... Such a situation must not be allowed to occur." The full-page spread contained an idiosyncratic seven-point critical essay, followed by Taubman's "constructive" directives. The assault began: "On a sheer technical level, its standards have fallen. ... The orchestra does not play with precision. Attacks and releases, which are hallmarks of a smartly trained ensemble of the first rank, are often careless. The texture of chords is frequently raveled; with upper, lower, and middle voices in inept balance. ... The orchestral tone has a tendency to coarseness. ... Demoralization is setting in. The players admit as much."

Six seasons removed from his position as leader of the cello section, the Philharmonic's 1957-1958 season jointly starred Dimitri Mitropoulos and Leonard Bernstein as co-principal conductors of the orchestra. That year, Bernstein experienced extraordinary success on Broadway with his *West Side Story*, of which the cast recording sold over a million copies. Catapulted like no other conductor before him, Bernstein was named the sole music director the following season, prompting him to prop up one of his idols: "Mr. Mitropoulos is a great genius and I hope I'll be worthy to follow him." Mitropoulos believed Bernstein's appointment indicated that America had grown up and he harbored no malice toward his younger, less experienced colleague, who had become the first American-born and trained musician to achieve such acclaim.

With Leonard Bernstein Musical Director in the 1958-1959 season, Mitropoulos continued to guest conduct the orchestra despite a second heart attack January 1959. Two months after the incident, Mitropoulos knew something was terribly wrong.

He wrote, "Since I am out, I have had not one day when I was feeling well—moments of short breath, very uncomfortable, then moments of anxiety and depression. I tried to study but my brain does not work—not only my muscles, but even my brain was affected by this treatment they gave me in order to calm me down while I was in the hospital [for four weeks]."[110]

On November 2, 1960, while rehearsing at the La Scala Orchestra in Milan, Italy, during the stately opening movement of Mahler's Third Symphony, Mitropoulos died with baton in hand, as he had foreshadowed in some of his final letters. He fell face forward into his musicians; the exact moment in the piece when he died is known because the second bassoonist drew a cross in his score at the 86th bar, noting: "*In questa misura è morto il Maestro Mitropoulos*" (In this measure died Maestro Mitropoulos). In his memory, Bernstein performed a movement from Mahler's "Resurrection" symphony that week at the four Philharmonic concerts.

Around the world, especially in Greece, Mitropoulos was viewed as a champion of the arts. Upon the return of his ashes to Ellinikon Airport, an honor guard of airmen assembled on either side of the plane's door while the band played a funeral tune written for airmen who fell in battle. From a military car, his remains were transported to the ancient theater of Herodes Atticus. On the stage, his coffin was dramatically draped with Greek colors and set between two torches. The first wreath was the king's. The vice-premier then laid a wreath and delivered a brief speech. The stage was completely covered with laurel. In the end, the State Orchestra, without a conductor, played the funeral march from Beethoven's "Eroica" symphony. Dimitri Mitropoulos had become a Greek hero.

Could there be any doubt that Rose learned a great deal in his 1951 "Schelomo" collaboration from Mitropoulos? It is unquestionable that Leonard Rose benefited from Mitropoulos's generosity of spirit and musical intellect. The conductor's abilities to communicate the essence of every piece he conducted, which was done with utter devotion, rubbed off on the impressionable young cellist. Mitropoulos's recordings remain imbued with freshness, his innate sense of drama unmistakably clear. In the era the two men shared, they collaborated on six occasions, all with the New York Philharmonic: Brahms "Double" Concerto with violinist John Corigliano (1944); Schumann Concerto (1948-1949); Shulman Concerto (1949-1950); Saint-Saëns Concerto (1950-1951); Bloch "Schelomo" (1951); and Saint-Saëns Concerto (1951) Edinburgh Festival, Scotland.

Chapter Ten

TITANIC GEORGE SZELL

We musicians are very fortunate; for we make our living doing the thing we like best to do. We should not approach it as a job, but as the thing we want most to do for our own pleasure.[111]

—George Szell

Another unique celebrity figured prominently in the life of Leonard Rose; conductor George Szell, who led the Cleveland Orchestra from 1946 to 1970 as music director. When Rose eventually concluded the orchestral segment of his career in 1951, Szell publicly declared his desire to be the first to engage him as a concerto soloist; and he did. The cellist's memories of this meticulous master, however, were mixed. Although he believed the leader possessed some remarkable qualities, his scheming tendencies and excessive need to control unsettled Rose. As he exclaims in his memoir, "I found out that one of the great difficulties with him ... was that he always had to have the feeling that he was in the driver's seat all the time no matter what. He wanted to conduct everybody. If anything, he over conducted. He used to cross every 't' three times and dot every 'i' at least three or four times ..."

George Szell built the Cleveland Orchestra from a respectable second tier ensemble into one of America's "big five" orchestras. Reviews of local concerts, from New York and from arduous worldwide tours* gushed of the orchestra's level of distinction. However, Rose objected to the notion that Szell received so much credit for this considerable achievement. He felt that Artur Rodzinski, the conductor who provided his start, raised the Cleveland Orchestra to notoriety. In his mind, what Szell achieved was the orchestra's reconstitution after Erich Leinsdorf's ineffective three seasons, between his tenure and Rodzinski's. During that unfortunate period, the orchestra lost many of Rodzinski's finest musicians to military service. Regardless of positive or negative opinion, within five years Szell implemented 84 personnel changes and molded the orchestra to reflect his personality—which focused on precision and perfection.

At 49 years of age, Szell's career was established before he ever set foot in Severance Hall as Cleveland's fourth music director. Hailed as a *wunderkind* and "the new Mozart," the young musician possessed astonishing aptitude at the piano. Around 12 years of age though, he was drawn to waving a baton. He was born June 1897 in Budapest, Hungary, but the family moved to Vienna early in his childhood. Like many Jews of his day, the family quickly converted to Catholicism to avoid Austria's unspoken anti-Semitic discrimination (Szell's parents would later perish in a Nazi concentration camp). Hungarian conductor Artur Nikisch—praised by Hans von Bülow, Anton Rubinstein, Joseph Joachim, Johannes Brahms, and Franz Liszt—made a huge imprint upon the impressionable artist. Also during his youth in Vienna, he heard and admired performances under the leadership of Gustav Mahler and his own contemporary Bruno Walter. Equally, his meeting and subsequent friendship with Germany's preeminent composer Richard Strauss altered the course of his life. Strauss helped him obtain a job in Otto Klemperer's orchestra that enabled him to appear as guest conductor. As a result, in 1929, Szell was promoted to general musical director of the German Opera and conductor of the Philharmonic in Prague. A year later, a concert by Toscanini and the New York Philharmonic similarly affected his evolution as conductor. The Hungarian enumerated

---

* Most notably a 44-day European tour in 1957—33 works by 20 composers in 22 cities—most orchestra members lived aboard the train in which they traveled; and in 1965, six weeks in Russia—a 10-city, 44-concert tour.

the maestro's accomplishments to a journalist at the *New York Times:* "The clarity of texture; the precision of ensemble; the rightness of balances; the virtuosity of every section, every solo-player of the orchestra—then at its peak—in the service of an interpretive concept of evident, self-effacing integrity, enforced with irresistible willpower and unflagging ardor, set new, undreamed-of standards literally overnight."[112]

To pay homage to his early, ardent supporter, Szell later championed and recorded a number of the composer's works with the Cleveland Orchestra: *Don Juan*—March 1957; *Don Quixote* with Pierre Fournier, cello and Abraham Skernick, viola—October 1960; *Sinfonia domestica*—January 1964; *Till Eulenspiegels lustige Streiche*—December 1954; *Tod und Verklärung*—March 1957; the Concerto No. 1 for Horn with Myron Bloom—October 1961.

Because of a dearth of trained American conductors, notable Europeans were in demand in the United States around World War II. Szell initially arrived in the States at the behest of the St. Louis Symphony in 1930 to guest conduct and potentially take over that orchestra. He failed to land that job, but found work guest conducting, including with the Los Angeles Philharmonic at the Hollywood Bowl in the summers of 1939 and 1940, and Toscanini's NBC Symphony in 1941.[113]

With the outbreak of World War II, Szell and his wife moved to New York City where he took a back seat in a crowded field that included Toscanini, Rodzinski, Walter, Mitropoulos, and the emerging Leonard Bernstein. Succeeding in establishing a reputation as an "exacting conductor" in New York, he was placed in charge of Germanic repertoire at the Metropolitan Opera from 1942 to 1946. This occurred at precisely the time when the Cleveland Orchestra was considering him for their directorship. Possibly in emulation of Rodzinski, who axed 14 members of the New York Philharmonic (or perhaps a statement about the musical talent available during the war), Szell swiftly fired 25 members of the Metropolitan Opera Orchestra, an action that sent a powerful message and created long-lasting resentment among some of the musicians.

Like a strikingly beautiful butterfly, George Szell had the press under his spell. Barry Farrell for *Time* magazine described

Szell's conducting style: "Szell is formal and correct—his beat firm, his style understated. His baton moves stolidly, but his left hand—often called the most graceful in music—is a sculptor's hand, shaping and molding each sound, grasping the fortissimos, summoning the dominant voices and, for excited counter-rhythms and violent colors, fluttering like a bird caught in a storm."[114]

After an impressive debut with the Cleveland Orchestra in November of 1944,* Szell became its top candidate. In January 1946, Szell—now an autocrat in high gear—negotiated his own terms regarding personnel, programming, schedules, tours, recordings, broadcasts, soloists, guest conductors, and leaves of absence—all conditions he demanded be met before he would consider taking the position. His annual salary of $40,000 (equivalent to nearly $440,000 in 2008) dwarfed the $18,000 his predecessor Leinsdorf earned (Rodzinski, however, was paid $60,000 for his 1946 season in New York). The instrumentalists' minimum weekly salary concurrently was a paltry $85 a week for 30 weeks (equivalent to nearly $940 in 2008)—in a large amount of the cases, not an adequate amount to support a family. When Szell was appointed Cleveland's new musical director on January 25, 1946, he fearlessly told the press: "A new leaf will be turned over with a bang! People talk about the New York, the Boston, and the Philadelphia. Now they will talk about the New York, the Boston, the Philadelphia, and the Cleveland."[115]

Immediately, Szell coolly replaced 20 players. Musicians quickly found out that "Mr. Szell" (to everyone but his closest friends) was an intimidator who could crush a professional musician with a few choice words. His relentless perfectionism, which tolerated no errors, often left his musicians under extreme pressure to play flawlessly in spite of misgivings that the man lacked poetic charm and grand inspiration. Disturbingly, off the podium, he did little to inspire confidence among the members of his orchestra he spent many hours with, fueling his reputation as a supreme artist, but a cold and unforgiving human being.

Rose quickly formed an opinion, "He did the classics really very beautifully; although for my taste, I wish he had concerned

---

* Beethoven Symphony No. 6, Strauss *Till Eulenspiegel*, and Smetana's String Quartet No. 1 in E Minor "From My Life" (Szell's arrangement).

himself a little bit more with wonderful sound. But ... [he] was a conductor who got the sound he wanted, which was rather on the dry side—a little bit *Germanic* for my taste." Rose adds, "It's too bad he didn't have a bit of Stokowski in him." Rose recalls the first time Szell entered stage left at Carnegie Hall to take his place on the podium in front of the orchestra. Some players didn't take notice and continued their warming up and conversation. "Silence!" Szell yelled nearly shaking Carnegie's famous gold and white walls. Silence followed. "Then the boys began to play," Rose continued, "because they knew that this guy wouldn't stand for any nonsense. ... If they thought they could get away with something with Szell, well they had another thing coming." Shortly before Rose performed the Dvořák Concerto in January 1945,[116] with Rodzinski and the Philharmonic, Szell was slated as a guest conductor: "I was backstage practicing the concerto in the room right across the way from him. All of a sudden, Popeye—that's what we called Szell with his thick glasses ["Dr. Cyclops" according to author Donald Rosenberg], affectionately and sometimes not so affectionately—stuck his head in the room and said, 'When are you doing that?' I said, 'I'm playing it here in two weeks.' He said, 'Come with me.' So I followed him with my cello into the conductor's room, whereupon he sits down at the piano—no music—and plays part of the introduction just before my first entrance. ... We played through the entire piece!" After completing the 45-minute concerto, Szell turned to Rose and said, "'Bravo—you are a marvelous player.' That was some introduction.... After the performance, he wrote me a note in which he said, 'Dear Leonard—your performance gave me very great pleasure. I don't think anyone can play that piece any better than you, including the gentleman in the south of France." Szell was referring to Casals, with whom he recorded this same concerto in April 1937 with the Czech Philharmonic.*

Rose considered the conductor a master musician, as evidenced by another time he played with Szell as pianist. He recounts that experience in the home of Rosalie Leventritt: "He and I played two sonatas together—Brahms F Major and Beethoven D

---

* Szell also recorded the Dvořák Concerto in 1962 with cellist Pierre Fournier and the Berlin Philharmonic.

Major. He was a remarkable pianist with a marvelous facility. As a matter of fact, his whole concept of music was the same, whether he conducted or whether he played the piano—that is, with all the advantages of a wonderful technician." Rose reiterated, "I preferred a warmer sound, both from the orchestra and from the piano."

In December 1944, during a Cleveland Orchestra performance of Strauss' *Till Eulenspiegel* an inexplicable mistake occurred within Rose's cello section. "I hadn't the faintest idea what made things go haywire. After the concert, I approached him in his dressing room. ... 'What in the hell happened in the *Till?*' He sat down and began to play the complicated score on the piano in an unbelievably brilliant manner. I couldn't believe my eyes. He calmly explained what had gone wrong, and when he noticed the expression of surprise on my face he said, 'I was a *wunderkind* on the piano, you know, and used to play this on recital programs.'"

One of his first plans, in Cleveland, was to select a leader of the orchestra—a concertmaster. Szell had already rid himself of the previous one, Joseph Knitzer (1913-1967; 1934 winner of the Naumburg Award), and of a second, the newly hired Samuel Thaviu* (many believed unfairly) after only one year. In what seemed a coup d'état, he hired Joseph Gingold away from the same position with the Detroit Symphony. When Gingold initially balked, Szell bullied he had 20 minutes to contemplate the offer. Accused of pirating from the Detroit orchestra, Szell indignantly stated that he asserted his right and did not care what people wrote or said about him.[117]

Joseph Gingold, born in 1909 in Brest Litovsk, Russia, moved to the United States in 1920. After his New York debut recital, at 17 years of age, he went to Brussels to study with legendary violinist Eugene Ysaÿe. Back in Manhattan, he played in pit orchestras for Broadway shows, where he received his first paychecks. The violinist thereafter successfully auditioned, becoming a charter

---

* Longtime concertmaster for the Pittsburgh Symphony Orchestra under Fritz Reiner, Thaviu (1910-2000) also played for the Chicago Symphony Orchestra before becoming a faculty member of the Northwestern University School of Music. According to Thaviu's widow, Szell lacked the "guts" to inform Thaviu he replaced him nor did he tell him why.

member of the NBC Symphony under Toscanini. Two years later, he left NBC to accept the position of concertmaster in Detroit. Many in the Cleveland Orchestra considered the Russian a heroic figure. His personality was suited to deflect the conductor's wrath at critical moments, colleagues liked him, and he played the violin with warmth and elegance. Szell's apparent trust in his concertmaster was schizophrenic; he abused or unjustly scapegoated him for ruining a performance from time to time by deviating from the expected. Rose, who met Gingold in the NBC Symphony, maintained a lifelong friendship with his colleague, from that overlapping season with Toscanini (Gingold remembers the intense cellist standing alone during breaks[118]), to playing chamber music—in addition to the Brahms "Double" Concerto—together at a summer festival run by composer Roy Harris in the late forties. The two remained close teaching alongside each other at Ivan Galamian's Meadowmount School of Music in the fifties and sixties. They also shared a deep-rooted, passionate tie to the Cleveland Orchestra. Rose recalls: "Joe loved music, he loved his job, and he was a great concertmaster; but Joe told me how Szell would be looking at other players in the orchestra and would suddenly call out—'Joe, that is sharp!'—which would instantly embarrass the hell out of Joe. I think Szell had a rather large sadistic streak in him ..."

In April 1959, Rose and Szell rehearsed the Dvořák Cello Concerto with the orchestra, when Szell made a remark to Joe on some minor point. "You son of a BITCH!" Rose hissed. While the musicians tacitly gave their former principal cellist the largest ovation imaginable, Rose stormed off the stage. Szell announced an impromptu intermission and raced after him. Backstage, the two made peace and the rehearsal resumed. Rose's allegiance to certain lifelong friends, like Gingold, was passionate and unwavering. By acting out, he took an enormous risk on his friend's behalf that may have caused Szell to engage French cellist Pierre Fournier for future public concerts and studio recordings.

A bundle of dichotomies, this superb musician and insensitive man relished the rehearsal process, "Rehearsals should not be a grind. They should be enjoyable periods when we play for the sole reason that we like to play."[119] Szell, the idealist, did not constantly follow his own advice.

Rose continues his assessment of the conductor in his unpublished memoir: "Certainly it was a pity that he wasn't capable of more warmth and consideration. ... He was a great scholar, but I don't think that he was particularly a great performer." Rose believed that he gave some of his best performances during dress rehearsals. Gingold, who endured under Szell from 1947 to 1960, dutifully vowed to prepare every note of his orchestral parts as if he were standing before an orchestra and audience playing as a soloist. Ultimately, he believed the conductor did not respect his integrity as a team player. Gingold described his freedom to a colleague, once his tenure with Szell had concluded: "For the first time in 14 years, I sleep well every night." But even after the violinist's departure, Szell's sadism did not abate. In 1960, the conductor presumptuously wrote to him: "Now that you are no longer with me, do you find your playing slipping?"[120] Nevertheless, Gingold enjoyed his freedom and life in academia, where he shone in his post at Indiana University's School of Music in Bloomington until his death. There, he molded numerous young violinists into fine musicians.

On a recommendation in 1962, Rose's talented teenaged pupil Lynn Harrell went to audition for Szell, though no openings existed in Cleveland. Harrell's rendering of the Dvořák concerto's first movement and Beethoven's A Major sonata impressed the conductor sufficiently to place him in the Cleveland cello section instantly after Michael Grebanier left (he assumed the principal chair of the Pittsburgh Symphony). Initially, Harrell found playing with a 100 other musicians daunting: "Only a year after coming to Cleveland [1964], expecting to sit back and enjoy things, I had the worst time of my career. My friends and colleagues, some of who were still in music school, thought I had it made with a regular salary and only myself to take care of. I had concerts all over the world with one of the greatest orchestras. ... Who could have guessed the desolation and emptiness I felt? I played on the third stand, never heard and never noticed. I felt invisible, and this existence began to feel like a boring, terrible, slow death. How was I to endure 40 years of this?"[121]

Harrell confessed that his lack of education in symphonic literature and scarcity of experience playing with and listening to colleagues plagued him, so "I just stared at the page and played along with everyone else. One day, Szell became frustrated beyond belief at my donkey-like sleepwalking and told me to stay during the intermission of a rehearsal. He grabbed my right arm and started to play as he thought I should play. Although the sound was terrible, the passion was there. He barked at me; 'You don't contribute. You don't do anything. You're not prepared. You just float along down the stream. You never know how the music goes.'" The powerful conductor had pried open Harrell's eyes. He would gradually realize the greatness in music and respect the creative forces behind each piece. He learned to immerse himself into the psyche and personality of each composer. Two years later, Szell appointed him the orchestra's youngest principal cellist in their history. "George Szell," Harrell wrote in 1994, "taught me humility. Through these experiences he brought me joy." Although the notorious nastiness brought Harrell to tears on several occasions, Szell had an incalculable impact upon the cellist's music-making. When presented with his first concerto opportunity with the orchestra (Schumann in Cleveland and at Carnegie Hall, January 1970), Szell devoted 30 hours at the piano with Harrell. Harrell started on the Dvořák Concerto with Szell when the conductor died.*[122]

No one denies the Cleveland Orchestra's ascension to America's "big five" American orchestras under Szell's leadership—but at what price? He may have been right when he stated in the 1960s "We start rehearsing where the vast majority of orchestras finish performing."[123] At the same time, his musicians comparatively were vastly underpaid, felt taken advantage of and were sick and tired of the tyrant's acerbic tongue and unrelenting manner. Conversely, the conductor increasingly resented his musicians,

---

* In Szell's memory, Harrell said," I didn't realize at the time that he was so right, but I've come to realize it more and more: rhythm, rhythm, rhythm; and this doesn't just mean playing like a metronome. It means a characteristic feeling of motion should be understood and portrayed clearly, whether it's absolutely steady, slightly accelerating, getting slightly more intense and fast, or diminishing and calming down" (Lynn Harrell, personal interview with Janof, www.cello.org 06-17-1996).

who pushed for more rights—higher salaries, the advent of a pension, sick leave with pay, more weeks of employment, overtime pay, and improved touring accommodations, abolishing Szell's right to arbitrarily fire a musician, etc.—thus going beyond what he believed was reasonable and just. In protest, he threatened to resign. His musicians became further mistrustful because of the manner in which he treated some of his soloists.

For example, Szell refused to work a second time with the phenom Canadian pianist Glenn Gould, after the pianist's awkward tempos and eccentric seating requirement—Gould kept the orchestra and Szell waiting while stagehands sawed off portions of the legs of a "normal" piano bench in order to get it down to the size he wanted. Szell stormed off the stage in 1961 when violinist Henryk Szeryng[124] refused to conform to the conductor's tempos. Szell got into screaming matches on stage with Russian violinist Nathan Milstein, frightening some members of the orchestra. Szell rudely walked out on the second week of guest-conducting the San Francisco Symphony, embarrassing that organization. The Metropolitan Opera would no longer have him back after he walked out on them too. Another astonishing story involves Szell with pianist, composer, and conductor André Previn, who was scheduled to record Strauss's "Burleske" with the Cleveland Orchestra. Upon meeting in the conductor's hotel suite, Szell asked Previn why he wanted to record the piece and was then pleased to hear Previn's persuasive answer. With no piano in the room, Szell only needed to "hear" Previn play it pounding it out on a tabletop. The surprised Previn had no choice and was soon stopped by Szell, "No, no, no. It needs to be faster." According to Previn, in a 1981 biography, "At that point, I felt incredibly stupid. I said, "Well, maestro, the reason it sounds so slow is that I'm simply not used to this table. My dining room table at home has much better action. Szell looked at me coldly and said, 'I don't consider that funny, young man. You may go.' I laughed about the incident all the way home; but the next morning, Szell called Columbia and said he would not be making any records with Mr. Previn because I was not a serious-enough musician. The whole 'Burleske' project just went down the drain."

George Szell did not walk out on Leonard Rose when he was scheduled for three performances of Strauss's *Don Quixote* with the New York Philharmonic in November 1945. However, with what occurred during their first rehearsal, it is a small miracle that he did not. Szell had begun his Cleveland tenure and when he arrived in New York late on a Saturday night, Rose got a call. The conductor wanted him to come early the next morning to have a private rehearsal.

> We gathered, tuned up, and I began to play; and the first crack out of the bat—my first entrance—he stopped me and said, 'Could it be shorter?' Good God! I hadn't even played one complete phrase. Well, that immediately was an attack upon me. ... I didn't know this bird; I didn't know what happened in that man. I was young and while I was playing, he stopped me so often I was getting more and more discouraged; and I must say I probably was not playing nearly as well. ... We came to the D-minor soliloquy ... the first major lengthy statement that the cello has to make.* I had definite ideas about how this should be played, and suddenly this guy comes along and says, 'Don't slide here, don't slide there, can this not be shorter?' This sort of thing—all personal things; I was 27 years old. Szell was 48 and a well-recognized master but a pain in the ass. There is a lovely little Jewish word, *nudnik*, meaning 'pest,' and the guys in the orchestra used to call Szell *phudnik*: a nudnik with a Ph.D. He so unnerved me. ... I couldn't take it anymore. I absolutely felt I was going to burst. I finally lifted the cello and slammed it down on to the couch and said, 'Goddamn it, I can't play this performance with you. You're going to have to get yourself somebody else.' He quickly got up from the piano as though I had set off a Roman candle under his ass and said, 'Why, is my performance so different than you've ever played before?'

---

* In the tone poem's story, here Sancho falls asleep. The tenor tuba then the contra-bassoon plays long glissandos to depict Sancho snoring. Then this wonderful D-minor soliloquy—which is the Don—signified by the solo cello, begins to talk and fantasize about his life. Here Strauss writes in German: *Frei declamirend, sentimental im Vortrag* (free presentation, sentimental in execution).

I said, 'Don't hand me that crap... What do you want me to do all of a sudden, with the first rehearsal tomorrow and we're four days away from our first performance. Do you want me to change everything? Realistically, I can't do it ....' I was a nervous wreck throughout the entire set of performances [the live broadcast from November 4, 1945, is featured on *Leonard Rose: The Memorial Edition CD*].[125]

In contrast, Rose's experience with conductor Bruno Walter in the identical piece of music was utterly different. Rose found Walter a compassionate man who commanded respect through an ability to lovingly coax the best from his instrumentalists. Walter loved everything Rose did with the piece. About three years after Rose played *Don Quixote* with Walter (February 19 and 20, 1948), along came Szell who programmed the work with Rose December 7, 8, and 10, 1950. Once again, Rose received a curt call from Szell, insisting on a piano rehearsal the following morning. Rose confides in his memoir:

I was a lot more secure at that point. ... And I was very much onto him and his psychological tricks with people. ... We gathered for the rehearsal, and Szell sits down at the piano and I knew what to expect. No matter what I did with that first entrance of mine, he was going to make some sort of comment. And, sure enough, because I remembered completely what he had said five years before at the rehearsal, first crack out of the barrel, he said, 'Could it be a little shorter?' I said, 'Oh yes, of course it can be shorter, but you know Bruno Walter asked me particularly to play it a little bit longer.' He said, 'Oh, really? Try it a little longer.' And then, of course, I knew I had him, because he had tremendous respect for Walter. So I played it a little longer, and he said, 'You know, that sounds very well.' I played it for everything it was worth. Every time he asked me for something that I didn't particularly like, I would say, 'Well you know, Walter requested...' This wasn't particularly true, but it worked like a charm, and I was pretty much able to do what I felt should be done in that particular place. I must say that I enjoyed that set of performances much more than the first ones.

About one year later, the New York Philharmonic presented their annual concert to benefit the orchestra's pension fund. The next day, Szell, with Rose and the Philharmonic, made a recording of Tchaikovsky's "Variations on a Rococo Theme." Except for the opening theme, which is played extremely slowly, the collaboration sparkles. The three outstanding soloists who donated their services that evening were cellist Rose, violinist Nathan Milstein (performing Lalo's *Symphonie Espagnol*), and pianist Dame Myra Hess (performing Beethoven's Concerto No. 4). This flurry of activity with the cellist at its center prompted the influential conductor to write:

"I consider Leonard Rose one of the outstanding cellists of our time."

These were meaningful words for Rose; the public held George Szell in highest regard, unaware of his bipolar behavior with musicians.

Szell continues to be regarded as the force behind the rise of the Cleveland Orchestra. During his tenure, a sweeping overhaul of the business organization enhanced far more than the orchestra's musical status alone. Szell oversaw the advent of full-year employment for his musicians, including a summer season named the Blossom Festival, a comparable rise in pay and implementation of a pension fund, vast renovations to Severance Hall, and the resumption of radio broadcasts and prestigious recording contracts. His substantial legacy of recorded works shows his penchant for taut rhythm and obsession with clarity of balance and texture. He viewed his ideal orchestra as one large chamber group in which the prominent voices must be heard—at all costs. He successfully taught his musicians to listen carefully to one another and prided himself on the result. On the anniversary year of his 50th season as conductor during the 1963-1964 season, Szell tried to define the qualities a conductor needed to have: "He should be equipped with the gift of leadership and should be a pedagogue, a diplomat, a poet, and a lion-tamer all rolled into one. First and foremost, he should have the magnetism which compels others to do his exact bidding whether they like it or not, but preferably he should be able to make them like it."[126] Szell's first sign of health trouble occurred in 1965, after surgery to remove a benign obstruction in his urinary tract, musicians noticed the onset of hearing loss. Bone cancer and complications due to a heart attack took his life July 30, 1970. Leonard Bernstein, who named Szell senior guest conductor and musical advisor of the New York Philharmonic during the 1969-1970 season, was crestfallen. He hoped that Szell would one day take over the Philharmonic from him.

Leonard Rose and George Szell Concerto Collaborations 1945-1966:

Beethoven: "Triple" Concerto and Brahms's: "Double" Concerto, with Isaac Stern, violin; and Eugene Istomin, piano April 14, 15, and 16, 1966; William Schuman *A Song of Orpheus*, January 9 and 11, 1964, recorded January 11, at Severance Hall; Dvořák: Concerto in B minor, April 16 and 18, 1959; Saint-Saëns: Concerto No. 1 and Tchaikovsky: "Variations on a Rococo Theme," (Cleveland Orchestra) February 28, 1956; Brahms: "Double" Concerto, (Chicago Symphony Orchestra - Ravinia Festival) with Erica Morini, violin July 5, 1952; Tchaikovsky: "Variations on a Rococo Theme," (New York Philharmonic) January 7, 1952, recorded January 8 (Columbia 30th Street Studio, New York); Dvořák: Concerto in B minor, (Cleveland Orchestra) November 22 and 24, 1951; Strauss *Don Quixote*, December 7, 8, and 10, 1950; Strauss: *Don Quixote*, Op. 35 (New York Philharmonic) November 1, 2, and 4, 1945.

Chapter Eleven

THE NOBILITY OF BRUNO WALTER

Bruno Walter left something with me, for which I shall be and will be eternally grateful.
—Leonard Rose

Above all other conductors for whom he played, Leonard Rose most admired the musicianship of Bruno Walter. In March 1944, the New York Philharmonic celebrated Walter's fiftieth anniversary as a conductor with a performance of Beethoven's Symphony No. 9. After the concert, he received what the *New York Times* described as "one of the greatest ovations in the memory of old patrons of Carnegie Hall." The thunderous ovation overwhelmed the 68-year-old Walter, whose life would span another 18 years. It also made an enduring impression on his 25-year-old cellist on the first stand. "It was moving to see how much music meant to him. I can think of at least three occasions when I saw him shed tears...."[127]

The son of Joseph and Johanna, Bruno Schlesinger (later changed to Walter) was born in Berlin in September of 1876, into a modest middle-class Jewish family. Even though Catholicism dominated, Jews lived their lives as they wished. Since 1867, their rights residing in the Austrian-Hungarian empire were protected under emperor Franz Josef who guaranteed "freedom of religion and conscience," a clause written into the empire's constitution. Walter's tranquil upbringing included typical Jewish observances in addition to ritual recitation of morning and evening Hebrew prayers. Although no documents survive, it is probable Walter was bar mitzvah'ed. Something, not clearly documented in his autobiography, caused Walter to grow totally disillusioned with Judaism. In his late teens and into his twenties, Walter's self-worth plummeted; caused in part by spiritual issues. Since assimilation was an accepted and shared ideal of the day, Walter converted to a Christian denomination, though scholars are uncertain as to which one. Unlike Gustav Mahler, Arnold Schoenberg and Leonard Bernstein, who openly struggled with Jewish identity throughout their lives, the young man turned his soul over fully—with ardent devotion—to Christianity. Long after his conversion from Judaism, the Nazi regime forcefully persecuted him for his Jewish birth. A spiritual being who believed that his long life in music was a "moral force" connected to the cosmos, earth and goodness of mankind, the conductor's journey eventually led to a dedication to Rudolf Steiner's (1861-1925) anthroposophy—a philosophy developed at the end of the 19th century based on European idealism of Aristotle, Plato, and Aquinas.

During his 1938 American visit, the 20-year-old Rose first performed with Walter in his season as assistant principal cellist with the NBC Symphony. As Rose recalled, "Walter performed a Mozart concerto conducting from the keyboard [K. 466]. He was still in his prime as a pianist and it was marvelous."[128] The NBC Symphony invited Walter to guest-conduct five concerts that season. Writing in the *Times*, Olin Downes reported that Walter's debut amounted to one of its most "distinctive" concerts, and that the music "flashed and soared, without suspicion of the weight or cumbrousness of the mortal coil."

Bruno Walter began appearing as a regular New York Philharmonic guest conductor during its 100th-anniversary season in 1941-1942. Although speculation subsists that Walter initially rejected the appointment Artur Rodzinski accepted in 1943—because Walter considered himself too old—he came on board in 1947, at the start of Rose's sixth season, as the Philharmonic's musical advisor. As he remarked at the time, "I accept the position because I feel I have a moral obligation to put my services at the disposal of the [Philharmonic-Symphony] Society."[129] Although the majority of the concerts during his two seasons as musical advisor went to Leopold Stokowski, Charles

Münch, and Dimitri Mitropoulos, Walter remained an iconic personality and was regarded as one of the world's musical Goliaths.

Born six weeks before the premiere of Brahms First Symphony, Walter was exposed to extraordinary musical experiences from an early age. As a 12 year old, he was inspired to become a pianist after he heard a staggering recital by Josef Hofmann, the man who decades later directed the Curtis Institute when Rose attended. His ambition altered upon his initial encounter with the music of Richard Wagner. "I was no longer in this world," Walter wrote. "After the performance [*Tristan und Isolde*], I roamed the streets aimlessly enchanted by what I heard. When I got home, I didn't say anything and begged not to be questioned. My ecstasy kept singing within me through half the night; and when I awoke on the following morning, I knew that my life had changed."[130] He also noted a performance of Richard Strauss's *Tod und Verklärung*, conducted by the composer that was equally transcendent.

Primarily, Walter's meeting and subsequent association with the composer and better-known conductor Gustav Mahler ultimately guided his career. When Walter attained work at the Hamburg Stadttheater, he came into direct contact with Mahler. Immediately, Walter was alarmed by his imperiousness on the podium: "Never had I dreamed that a brief, cogent word, a single compelling gesture, backed by absolute clarity of mind and intention, could fill other people with anxious terror and compel them to blind obedience."[131] Critic Ferdinand Pfohl was not as charitable: "Mahler was a tyrant with the orchestra; he sat at his podium looking dark and threatening."[132] After a brief interview in which Mahler asked Walter about his familiarity with opera repertoire and his ability to sight-read, Walter became the composer's rehearsal pianist; then a coach/conductor for his singers; and, finally, conducted segments of operas Mahler wished to hear from the auditorium. Most importantly, the composer sensed that one day Walter, 16 years his junior, would come to champion his music: which is exactly what happened. Three and a half years before Mahler's death, in a letter dated December 1907, he wrote to his colleague: "Neither of us need waste words on what we mean to each other. I know of no one who understands me as well as I feel you do, and I believe that for my part, I have entered deep into the mind of your soul."[133]

However, the apprenticeship began uneasily. Walter was conflicted over the manner in which Mahler handled his musicians. The younger, gentler man did not possess a domineering bone in his body and through the course of a decade or so discovered his ultimate strength: communicating with musicians on a more personal level would suit his personality best. This humane approach to music and a deep educational instinct proved to be one of his greatest and lasting qualities as a conductor, and the one that Leonard Rose most admired. "I had such a profound respect for Bruno Walter and his art," the cellist reminisced. "First of all, he was so very kind. He dealt with the orchestra with a great deal of love—quite refreshing after Toscanini! It was fascinating to see this wonderful, marvelous, human being—this great artist—study and restudy a score that he had performed hundreds of times and find something new in it. It wasn't always the same. It was always wonderful and relaxed. He took time to express himself."

Walter, indeed, liked to take "time," when he felt it necessary, in his interpretations; for he was strongly influenced in his early years by Hans von Bülow, Walter's boyhood idol, and the most famous conductor of German orchestral music of that era. Von Bülow was notorious for taking extreme liberties with tempo in concert. As Rose dictated, "Walter understood one of the basic truths about music: that the surest way to destroy a passionate sentiment in the score is to rush the tempo. Walter was not afraid to take time, and that was one of the things that made his performances unique." Leonard Rose witnessed how that approach angered Toscanini. In 1938, with the NBC Symphony, Rose observed Walter rehearsing the Brahms First Symphony and "Toscanini came into the hall and took a seat upstairs. Walter, on the podium, never realized Toscanini was anywhere in the building, much less listening attentively. At the end of the third movement, Walter made a charming *calando* (decreasing speed and tone). In a rage of fury and indignation, Toscanini bolted out of his chair and stormed from the studio. I felt very badly for Walter. I did not admire *that* in Toscanini. I felt frankly that Toscanini was a spoiled brat at times. Yeah, you can be great and all that, but do you have to be mean as hell? Walter surely did not deserve such an outburst."

The most frequent grievances against Walter as a conductor were that he could be too sentimental and that his beat was unclear. The legendary Hungarian conductor Sir Georg Solti refutes this notion writing in his autobiography, *Memoirs*: "Walter had a strange, not very clear beat, but he was proof that the beat is not an essential part of a conductor." Isaac Stern believed that Walter "was just as much an autocrat in his gentle way as Toscanini was in an explosive way." Perhaps an article written by Mary Komorn-Rebhan (in Walter's chorus) entitled *Was wir von Bruno Walter lernten* (What We Learned from Bruno Walter), written in Vienna in 1913, sheds light upon the man and his conducting style: "Something compelling emanates from him that raises each member above his abilities; he takes fear away from every individual and gives him courage and self-confidence, suggesting to him, as it were, that he can perfectly well do everything required of him."[134]

In 1907, not long after the completion of his Eighth Symphony, Mahler was diagnosed with a congenital heart condition that took the life of his mother 18 years before. Accepting an offer to conduct the Metropolitan Opera in New York City, Mahler decided to work far less for more money, and devote more time to composition. With his vast experience with opera productions, his mark upon the Metropolitan was instantaneous. By 1909, Mahler was appointed director of the New York Philharmonic. His numerous accomplishments included bringing the organization up to present-day standards—most importantly a larger season of 46 concerts compared to the previous 18. He also arranged for the first tour outside the city with a full complement of 92 players. Tragically, in the spring of 1911, Mahler became desperately ill and died in Vienna at the age of 51. (Currently in the U.S., about 1 million adults live with congenital heart defects).[135]

Walter's European career flourished after Mahler's death, leading to his first U.S. tour in 1923 that included conducting orchestras in New York, Detroit, Boston, and Minneapolis. About that time, he accepted the chief conductor position of the German repertoire of the Covent Garden Opera in London, and divided his time as music director of the State Opera of

Charlottenburg in Berlin. In 1929, Walter succeeded Wilhelm Furtwängler as director of one of the oldest and most celebrated of Germany's concert institutions in Leipzig, Germany—the Leipzig Gewandhaus Orchestra. Walter was 53 years old at the time and indicated in his autobiography that if the rise of Nazism had not displaced him, he would have been content to stay there the rest of his life.

At his final concert in Leipzig, Walter was engulfed by swastika flags; raised at the pier, from the town hall in Cuxhaven, displayed at every inn and restaurant. The Leipzig Nazis made it known that Walter's days as a conductor in their town were ending. On the morning of the concert, the Nazi police forbade both the dress rehearsal and the concert, consequently crushing Walter's association with the institution. A short time later in Berlin, an infamous concert barred Walter from conducting just hours before the downbeat that shockingly took place under the baton of Richard Strauss. The incident sullied Strauss's renowned reputation in an increasingly volatile music world. Despite furious telegrams sent to Hitler deploring the way Walter was being treated—signed by among others Toscanini, Reiner, and Koussevitzky—Walter fled Germany that very day for Vienna where he believed he would be safe to continue his work. Disruptive and destructive incidents forced the Walters's hand again in Austria; and in 1939, the couple fled to Paris and then permanently to the U.S., leaving everything behind.

Strauss's miscalculation in taking over for the ousted Walter turned into a major Nazi victory. He then obligingly became head of the State Music Bureau at age 69 in November of 1933—the Reich Kulturkammer—licensing authority for performers in the arts, which barred Jewish artists. Years later, Walter, who claimed he held no lifelong grudges, wrote: "I dislike Strauss as a person, and I abhor everything for which he has stood in recent years; but Strauss is a genius and some of his works are masterpieces. I cannot in all honesty boycott masterpieces...."[136] Walter steadfastly pontificated that true geniuses should be remembered for their works of art, rather than their shortcomings as human beings. When Walter escaped Austria, all his correspondences with Strauss were left behind. They were later found and are presently preserved at the New York Public Library.*

Walter's admiration for the composer, as well as conducting his works, remained unaffected in the long run by the incident. In February 1948, Walter programmed his tone poem, *Don Quixote*, with the Philharmonic and Leonard Rose as solo cellist. "Oh, what a wonderful time I had with him!" Rose fondly recalled. "Whatever I did, he loved. Bruno Walter was so human—when I would play a phrase, he would turn to me and say, 'Ach, beautiful, beautiful!' There was one suggestion he made to me that I think is still very effective. The last episode in that work is the death of the Don and contains some of the most gorgeous writing one can imagine. In this final scene, you hear the motif on the main theme where the Don expires from a D up on the C string to a low D marked with a glissando—a broken glissando. Piatigorsky told me that he played the piece something like 17 times with Strauss himself conducting and had been told, by Strauss, that he wanted a broken glissando coming down—a kind of chromatic glissando. So I did that at the rehearsal for Bruno Walter, and he said, 'My dear, this is where the Don dies, and I would do it just like an expiration—just like ah-ah-ah-ah.' ... I must tell you something else that he said to me after one of these performances. We were talking about the marvelous music and he looked at me and said, 'My dear, you are the Don. I've never heard the *Don Quixote* played the way you play it.' He had such a wonderful approach to this piece and I regret that I never had the opportunity to record it with him."

However, Leonard Rose did record as soloist with Bruno Walter and the New York Philharmonic—after the revered Maestro conducted other cello luminaries such as Emanuel Feuermann and Pablo Casals, played recitals with famed violinists Jacques Thibaud and Arnold Rosé, and on the piano accompanied the greatest singers of his day, including the Norwegian soprano Kirsten Flagstad and German sopranos Elisabeth Schwarzkopf

---

* Among the complex of buildings that New York's Lincoln Center comprises, the New York Public Library for Performing Arts contains the intimate Bruno Walter Auditorium, and the library itself holds the The Bruno Walter Papers, including some 7000 letters to and from Richard Strauss.

and Lotte Lehmann. Walter also conducted the world premiere performances of Prokofiev's First Violin Concerto, Prokofiev's Third and Fifth Piano Concertos with the composer at the keyboard and Rachmaninoff's *Rhapsody on a Theme of Paganini* with the composer as soloist.

On March 21, 1949, Rose recorded Beethoven's "Triple" Concerto with violinist John Corigliano Sr. and pianist Walter Hendl. The 31-year-old cellist had never played the work before and benefited a great deal from the conductor's guidance. "When I recorded the "Triple" Concerto, there was no tape," Rose commented. "We recorded the work directly on acetates, which meant that we had to play as nearly perfectly as we could for four minutes and 20 seconds for each side—these were the old 78s. I was in terrific form there at the recording session and it was maddening to get through all these difficult places only to have—I'm sorry to say—the pianist screw up some passage at the end and having to do the whole thing over again. I think recording like this had certain advantages, because you couldn't monkey around. ... I must add that Walter showed a profound understanding of that fiendish cello part." In a 1995 interview, the pianist Hendl recalled his own eager anticipation when the conductor announced the project: "I had never made a record. So when he announced plans to record the "Triple," I was all

Leonard Rose   Isaac Stern   Bruno Walter 1954

for it, and Lennie Rose, the cellist, was worried about it ... and Corigliano, the concertmaster, didn't care; he was the eternal pro. So we had quite a struggle with that. ... Walter was extremely pleased."[137] Five years later, Rose recorded for the second and final time with Walter. His recording of the Brahms "Double" Concerto with violinist Isaac Stern and the Philharmonic would receive the coveted 1957 *Prix du Disque* in Paris as the most outstanding symphonic recording of the year.

John Corigliano Leonard Rose Bruno Walter William Lincer 1947
Courtesy of the New York Philharmonic

As predicted, Walter did become Mahler's most persuasive advocate. Mahler himself intimately introduced his creations to the young Walter. Seated at the piano, the composer played his First Symphony and also his Second Symphony for him as he was putting the finishing touches to the score. Walter heard Mahler conduct the Third Symphony during the summer of 1896 and the first performance of the Fourth. In their 17-year friendship, Walter described Mahler as at the "very peak of his exalted being" during the creation of his Eighth and Ninth symphonies—the Ninth Bruno Walter premiered in June 1912 with the Vienna Philharmonic Orchestra. Less than a month after Mahler's death on November 20, 1911, Walter also presented the world premiere of the venerable *Das Lied von der Erde* of which the conductor wrote: "I was profoundly moved by that unique, passionate, bitter, resigned, and blessing sound of farewell and departure, that last confession of one upon whom rested the finger of death."[138]

Leonard Rose's role in the unveiling of Gustav Mahler's music in America under Walter's hand as principal cellist of the New York Philharmonic is significant: 1944—Symphony No. 4—recorded in 1945. Afterwards, Walter wrote to Mahler's widow Alma: "... I have been trying for years and years to record his symphonies, so that there is a point of reference for the next generation of young conductors." 1945—Symphony No. 9; 1947—Symphony No. 5: Rose was part of an historic recording of Mahler's Symphony No. 5 with Walter conducting the Philharmonic in Carnegie Hall February 10, 1947. Critic Doug Rea finds Walter's account "full of color, a feeling akin to nature, with a tight, dynamic sound that is a thrill to listen to." 1948—*Das Lied von der Erde*; 1948—Symphony No. 2; 1950—Symphony No. 1 (Rose first played this under Walter with the NBC Symphony in 1939). Despite Walter's tireless efforts, the cellist recalls that Mahler's works were not popular with orchestra players, audiences, and critics at this time. "Mahler is not a profound musician," wrote critic Olin Downes in 1932 after Walter performed Mahler's Symphony No. 5 with the New York Philharmonic. "Everything is a pose or a big noise."[139] In spite of these negative assessments, Walter—along with Dimitri Mitropoulos, Willem Mengelberg, and Otto Klemperer—programmed quite a lot of Mahler well before Leonard Bernstein conclusively brought international popularity to the composer.

Walter was both a teacher and mentor to Leonard Rose. An example of his tutelage occurred with Rose's colleague, Leonard Bernstein. Even though Walter was running a high fever, wrapped in blankets and bed-ridden, he roused himself in time to consult with Bernstein the day of the dynamic young conductor's debut. His gesture—out-of-the-box generosity—indelibly impressed Bernstein as well as Rose. "He was so kind, so gentle, and so authoritative at the same time," recounted Bernstein. Is it not conceivable that Bernstein might not have fared as effectively in his debut without the one-hour session he spent with Walter? When Rose wanted some musical advice or opinion, he often sought Walter. Rose remembered one particular situation: "I wondered why, for example, in the middle period of Beethoven—in particular the Opus 69 Sonata—after the trills (of which there are a number in the piece), sometimes Beethoven wrote grace notes (after the trills) and other times did not. I asked two gentlemen the same question—one was Walter and the other Casals. Both great artists gave me the identical answer: In the middle-period, Beethoven, he wanted all the trills to have grace notes and the reason why he only wrote certain ones in the score was that the grace notes written always had an accidental—a sharp or a flat—and he simply assumed that the performer would add the grace notes when they weren't notated. Walter always added grace notes after trills in the middle period Beethoven symphonies."

In 1957, Walter suffered a heart attack which resulted in a sharp cut back of public appearances. When Walter retreated to Los Angeles, a Los Angeles–based Columbia Symphony Orchestra (organized chiefly for Walter) captured, on record, his autumnal interpretations of the classics. Walter gave his final public performance in December 1960, and made his final recordings three months later. Walter died in Beverly Hills, California, on February 17, 1962, at which time Leonard Bernstein—undoubtedly speaking for Leonard Rose and countless others—eulogized Walter as "one of the saints of music ...."[140]

Chapter Twelve

JASCHA HEIFETZ, PERFECT SOLOIST

"*One of the most astonishing things was that no matter how fast he played, it never sounded speedy. He could go like the wind, but every note was under control.... It was clear beyond discussion that no other violinist had quite this mastery, this control, this constant flow of polished fire. He was one of the four or five giants in the history of performance on the violin.*" [141]

—Isaac Stern

For 50 years, Jascha Heifetz was the standard by which all other violinists were measured. Two months after his astounding Carnegie Hall debut in 1917, in which critic Sigmund Spaeth from the *Evening Mail* declared, "He is a perfect violinist," his version of Bazzini's *Ronde des lutins* [Dance of the Goblins] became a sensation.[142] "Perfect," for better and for worse, would serve like a mantra throughout his life.

"Jascha was the king," Rose adamantly noted. "As a pure fiddler, none was greater. His instrumental equipment was fantastic. The left hand was sheer lightning in its pyrotechnical accuracy. The sound was electrifying and searing. In his great days, his sound was completely unique and thrilling. He was probably the most imitated of all instrumentalists. No one else was like Heifetz. He stood alone."

During Rose's tenure as principal in Cleveland and in New York, he became well acquainted with Heifetz' playing. From close range, just a few feet away, he observed "the king" in his prime, with the orchestras accompanying such notable violin concerti as the Beethoven (1940 and 1945), Gruenberg (1947), Korngold (1950), Sibelius (1951), and Walton (1939 and 1951). Heifetz' near-universal influence extended to Leonard Rose who hung a cherished, 1940 autographed picture of the violinist on his studio wall in his Forest Hills home, along with photographs of Toscanini and publicity snapshots of his own hands.

Heifetz occupied Rose's thoughts, as evidenced by frequent comments in his memoir. The quantity of his spoken remarks about his string-player colleague show a special interest in the man and his music-making. "With his left-hand virtuosity and vibrato," Rose continued, "there was nothing like Jascha before and since. I am reminded of that old baseball phrase, 'Slide Kelly, SLIDE!' Heifetz's glissandos were there in all their glory—I loved them even though I think he used them without too much thought or taste. The right arm worked for him because he was the one and only Jascha. The bow grip—the so-called Auer schooling—was possible only for Heifetz because of his colossal talent. Only with the talent of Heifetz could one use such poor bow school."

Leopold Auer, a Jewish immigrant from Hungary and one-time Imperial Concertmaster of the St. Petersburg Symphony Orchestra, became Russia's foremost violin teacher.[143] Heifetz would study with him for about six years in a class of 25 to 30 pupils. Contrary to Rose's analysis, about Auer's weakness as a teacher, Heifetz pointedly credited his youthful period with the teacher when he learned the "art of bowing."* Under Auer's supervision, he developed his incomparable tone.

At seven, the boy made his public debut in Kovno, 62 miles west of Vilnius, Lithuania, then a part of Czarist Russia. Two years later, Auer accepted Heifetz into his class, enabling his parents and two younger sisters to move to St. Petersburg, Russia, under the set of guidelines *svoboda*, or "free artist." Without this status, any Jew caught without these necessary documents after

---

* "I do not believe," Rose noted in his unpublished memoir, "that Leopold Auer was in Ivan Galamian's class as a teacher. I say that because I know some of the basics that Auer taught and they were, in my opinion, not correct. For example, the very holding of the bow as taught by Auer was completely out of balance."

an imposed six o'clock curfew was subject to immediate arrest by the czar's police.

In the early 1900s, a small number of Jewish music students from the Pale[*][144] made their way northeast to St. Petersburg, to one of the world's finest music schools: the St. Petersburg Conservatory. Their families hoped that the children, most of whom were prodigies, would save them from poverty and the bleak conditions of the ghetto. In 1903, when Heifetz was three, his father gave him a quarter-size violin. Ruven Heifetz, Jascha's father, who played the violin in and around the Lithuanian capital, methodically taught the boy a firm way in which to master scales and arpeggios. By the end of the boy's first year of training, he precociously played in the violin's highest positions. As an older man, Heifetz unhappily lamented a childhood lost to his father's Draconian measures, none of which was disclosed. He quietly cursed his parents who often expressed that his violin playing never quite met their expectations. In contrast, to support the family, his parents exploited the boy, his education sacrificed and abandoned. A man who lived in Vilnius when Heifetz did described the boy "striding through town in a long, flowing cape, his violin in one hand and his father's hand in the other. Street urchins stood aside, pointing at him, their mouths agape."[145] As a boy, Heifetz was a freak of nature, an epithet that would follow him throughout his career.

In 1911, the Auer pupil made his official concert debut, followed by a spectacular success in Berlin at the Academy of Music in 1912. Later that year, the renowned conductor Artur Nikisch invited the 12-year-old to play Tchaikovsky's Violin Concerto, a work dedicated to Auer, with the Berlin Philharmonic. Soon Heifetz was touring to cities across Russia, generating legitimate excitement. Rave reviews poured forth from peers and press alike. Gregor Piatigorsky witnessed that period: "I eagerly awaited the recital of Heifetz. I had never heard him; but

---

* Catherine the Great created the "Pale" in 1791 to appease Russians who wanted to rid the empire of Jews (as they wouldn't convert to the Orthodox Church). Jews were allowed to live in the Pale of Settlement, the border region of Imperial Russia. It encompassed 25 provinces—much of present-day Latvia, Lithuania, Belarus, Poland, Ukraine, and parts of western Russia. Key imperial cities of Moscow and St. Petersburg were off-limits to Jews.

although only two years his junior, since my early childhood, the name Heifetz in Russia was legend. What supreme mastery over his instrument! It seemed that forces other than human had placed him there. He stood as if cut in marble; but I had to stop watching his perfect coordination and listen with my eyes closed to the unearthly beautiful sound of his violin.'"*146

Heifetz' supreme abilities on the violin baffled and stunned his critics. His speed, sound, and precise intonation were unrivaled. He had perfectly proportioned hands, a superb musical memory, and an unflappable temperament. Rose was awed by the man's elegance from the moment he walked onto the stage, *always* programmed as the final number, as stipulated in his contracts, with his 1742 Joseph Guarneri—the instrument used in 1845 to premiere Mendelssohn's Violin Concerto. Without cheer, Heifetz would acknowledge the conductor with a tiny nod of his head, then begin, hardly moving his torso. "When I was 10," Leonard Slatkin recounted, "I went to a recording session of Heifetz when my father was the concertmaster of the orchestra and my mother first cellist. Heifetz actually drew a line, a physical line on the floor; and for the four hours of the session, he never moved off that line. He just stood there. It was unbelievable."[147] With his violin perched high on his left shoulder, at close range, Rose studied Heifetz' rapid vibrato and eye-opening interpretations. A music critic in 1946 described the violinist as "a modern miracle."[148] His reserved Lithuanian persona, coupled with his Olympian technique, set him apart from the violinists of his era. In an attempt to understand Heifetz' mystique, the 1978 Nobel Laureate in Literature, Isaac Bashevis Singer explained, "In Vilnius," he wrote, "there was a style in the houses and a style in the people. Even the waiters read books."[149] During Heifetz' childhood, Vilnius was considered the "New Jerusalem"; the city teemed with Jewish scholars, sages, and holy men. Tragically, more than 90 percent of its Jewish population was massacred in World War II, the highest loss of any European-Jewish

---

* The cellist collaborated with Heifetz for 35 years. They recorded over 30 works, concertized, and made motion pictures together. Piatigorsky cofounded the Heifetz-Piatigorsky concerts.

community in the Holocaust. The overwhelming statistic—a fate Heifetz escaped—must have perpetually haunted him.

Leonard Rose repeatedly observed the violinist's ferocious intensity and his sustained high level of perfection, yet he also gazed on in incredulity as the violinist displayed no emotion whatsoever on his face. Indeed, Heifetz was drilled by his father from infancy to wear no reaction in his face, only in his music. Heifetz would be criticized for this and he suffered as a result. The increasingly bitter violinist never understood and never liked what some people called him—"highbrow, snooty, cold"[150]—labels that clung like leeches.

One year after his explosive American debut at Carnegie Hall, a review by W.J. Henderson in the *New York Sun* devastated him. Henderson wrote that the youngster's playing lacked depth and tended toward superficial brilliance. The article opined that the violinist did not immerse enough of himself in his music. Upon reading those words, the pampered boy, who still lived with his parents and knew nothing about how to cope with life's negative reactions, considered suicide.[151] Around that time, Heifetz discovered a poem entitled "If" by Rudyard Kipling (written in 1896), which thereafter remained with him at all times in some pant pocket for moral support. The poet's reference to *Triumph* and *Disaster* would invariably follow Heifetz' every success or failure and prompted the increasing cynical musician to quip, "Treat those two imposters just the same."[152]

Leonard Rose also knew Heifetz from the recordings he owned and loved. Unbelievably, their initial in-person contact came in the chamber music of Franz Schubert. Soon after Rose's appointment to the NBC Symphony, he was invited to attend a surprise 39th birthday party in Heifetz' honor at the home of the violinist's brother-in-law, Samuel Chotzinoff. Rose described the guests: "[The] personnel for Schubert's two-cello quintet was Jascha Heifetz, first violin; Efram Zimbalist, second violin; William Primrose, viola; me—age 20 and scared to death—first cello; and Marie Rosanoff, second cello. Fortunately, I knew the piece. It was very interesting—fabulous!"

As clearly as Rose perceived Heifetz' gifts, he also identified the man's tormented soul. For all his musical genius, Rose thought he "was nevertheless a very disturbed and, I am afraid, terribly lonely man." Auer's strongly worded statement from his 1921 autobiography entitled, *As I Teach It* supports Rose's premonitions. Auer states: "The majority of those who wish to become musicians, in spite of the fact that they may possess unusual gifts, have no idea of the difficulties they will have to surmount, the moral tortures they will be called upon to endure, the disillusions they will experience...." According to Rose: "In New York, Heifetz gave a marvelous performance of the Beethoven Concerto[*] on Thursday, and an even greater one on Friday afternoon. The third engagement, Sunday, was live on national radio broadcast and I noticed a slip in the cadenza. While the performance was good, it was certainly undistinguished for him. Because I had known Heifetz for some years, I made it a point to be one of the first to speak with him backstage. While he was putting his violin away, I told him how it was always a great thrill for the orchestra when he appeared as soloist, and how much I had enjoyed the recently concluded performance. I must confess that I was not altogether sincere in that last assertion. I wanted to see how the great man would respond. To my complete surprise, I noticed that there were tears in his eyes. He said, 'I'm glad you liked it. I hated it. Those damn microphones scare me to death!' It proved he could actually be human—at times."

Proving that he was human after all, at a relatively young age (after the 1955-1956 season), the violinist decided he had had enough and sharply curtailed his concert activity. When questioned, Heifetz simply replied, "I have done it before. I have no need."[153] After his second divorce in 1963, Heifetz retreated in solitude to his Beverly Hills mansion and his beloved Malibu Pacific home where he relished the serenity of the ocean and engaged the sea, staring endlessly into its waves for hours at a time. He began teaching classes of exceptionally talented violinists in Los Angeles at the University of Southern California that continued for a decade (1962-1972); some of the classes were filmed and aired on educational television. Sadly, his imperious manner ultimately deemed his teaching a failure. Domineering and condescending tendencies were often too much for most students to tolerate. Inevitably kept at arm's length from the strict

---

[*] January 1945 with the Philharmonic under Rodzinski.

master, some students might be dismissed for trivial reasons beyond logic from the inflexible man. Isaac Stern noted his odd tendency to "ask violin students, who gathered the courage to play for him, to do scales in odd keys—not only C Major, D Major, or A Major, but also F–sharp minor or E–flat Major. He wanted to test whether they had learned the proper, basic skills..."[154] Heifetz' pedagogical style had its origins in how his father first taught him. As mentioned, his education was aborted at an early age; one certain mode he was comfortable with was stringent dogma with scales—imitating his father. Indeed, Heifetz expected every student to know all scales in thirds, sixths, tenths, and in fingered and parallel octaves, as well as with *legato* and *staccato* bowing at his command. Yet, like Heifetz' teacher, he rarely accepted prodigies himself, as he blamed his lost youth—in part—for his torment. Paradoxically, he was unable to give up this daily diet of scales, which sustained him well after his farewell performance.

Heifetz took the stage for the final time in 1972, a recorded concert in Los Angeles for the benefit of a scholarship fund at USC. Sensing that he was losing the ability to enjoy the music and rise to the standard of perfection he had once set, Heifetz stored his concert clothing to its resting place. When Heifetz reached 73, he suffered a subcutaneous hemorrhage in his right shoulder that never completely healed from the ensuing surgery. In 1981, he refused worldwide invitations to celebrate his 80th birthday, in what—he discerned—would have been an uncomfortable public display.

According to confidant Ayke Agus, Heifetz became "insecure, often abrasive, and sometimes inconsiderate" into his old age. That his parents placed him on a pedestal that in the end damaged him, coupled with a half century of fame that he ultimately perceived as destructive, Heifetz voluntarily grew more and more isolated. Contact by phone was practically impossible. In his home, guests dared not mention politics, religion, or even music lest they be admonished with curt and disparaging words. He let it be known that in his presence, he dictated the topic of conversation. Yet, there were those, including Ms. Agus, who were hypnotically drawn toward the old man's allure, no matter how belligerent.

Aware and protective of his fame, he rejected honorary degrees from universities. He also experienced agonizing episodes of depression, which caused him further difficulty in relationships. "Chauvinistic," "irrational," and "tyrannical" is how Agus describes her idol in his final years spent in seclusion in Beverly Hills yet, during their daily music-making, the iconic violinist could break down and cry in the beauty of the moment.

After a series of falls and eventual brain surgery, Jascha Heifetz died in Los Angeles at the age of 86 in December 1987. The world, alive with instrumental virtuosos who heard Heifetz in his glory years, lost its greatest violinist. During an era when he was classical music's most imitated performer, did Heifetz' influence rub off on the playing of Leonard Rose? During the cellist's life when he was somewhat malleable, yes, Heifetz mattered. I believe Rose absorbed more than a fleeting glimpse of Heifetz' artistic brilliance during the time he shared the stage with the violinist in concert. Indeed, similar to that of Fritz Kreisler, Nathan Milstein, and Oscar Shumsky whose violin playing Rose revered, Heifetz loomed large. Arguably Rose's stylish, polished slides were influenced by the Lithuanian violinist. "No one else was like Heifetz," Leonard Rose dictated. "He stood alone." Rose's three-word summation is a worthy epitaph.

A decade after his death, Heifetz' complete commercial recordings were released on 65 compact discs. The advances in recording technology enabled listeners to compare Heifetz's multiple recordings, of the violin repertoire's masterpieces (Similarly, Leonard Rose recorded quite a few works multiple times): Beethoven Concerto (1940 and 1955); Brahms Concerto (1939 and 1955); Brahms "Double" Concerto recorded (with Feuermann in 1939 and Gregor Piatigorsky in 1960); Bruch Concerto (1951 and 1962); Bruch "Scottish Fantasy" (1947 and 1961); Glazounov Concerto (1934 and 1963); Mendelssohn Concerto (1949 and 1959); Mozart Concerto No. 4 (1947 and 1962); Mozart Concerto No. 5 (1934, 1951, and 1963); Prokofiev Concerto No. 2 (1937 and 1959); Saint-Saëns "Introduction and Rondo Capriccioso" (1935 and 1951); Sibelius Concerto (1935 and 1959); Tchaikovsky Concerto (1937, 1950, and 1957); Vieuxtemps Concerto No. 5 (1947 and 1961); Walton Concerto (1941 and 1950) and Wieniawski Concerto No. 2 (1935 and 1954).

Musically, Heifetz was thrilling to listen to, "because he was such a unique marvel," Rose mused in his unpublished memoir. "But I don't think he thought of very much but himself. Heifetz came first. Certainly, he didn't think too much about the composer whom he happened to be playing at the moment. The particular style of Beethoven, Brahms, or Mozart—they didn't matter very much—only Heifetz mattered. Yet, with his talent—how much did it matter? ... to reiterate, I think he was also one of the most tortured human beings I ever knew."

Chapter Thirteen

America's Golden Symphonic Age

The era I grew up in was the golden age of great conductors. Music directors directed music. Conductors were their own men. They were personalities as strong in their areas as the Paderewskis, and Rubinsteins, and the Horwitzes, and the Heifetzes. It was a spectacular period to which Leonard Rose made a very fine contribution and fitted in with that level of music-making, which was so much higher than it is today.

—Lorin Maazel[*][155]

Leonard Rose played for 13 seasons in three orchestras: a year in the NBC Symphony, four years as first cellist of the Cleveland Orchestra, and for eight years in the same position in the New York Philharmonic. While Rose was the Philharmonic's principal cellist, he and his family lived on Austin Street in Forest Hills, Queens (population around 35,000 in the mid-1940s), where Rose's sister-in-law and her children occupied the ground floor of the building, and Rose, his wife, son, and daughter shared a small fourth-floor apartment. To meet the demands of challenging orchestral music and maintain his high personal standards as a soloist, Rose felt he needed to practice whenever the opportunity presented itself. Unfortunately, his fellow tenants were unhappy with the frequent sounds from his

---

[*] Two days shy of his 13th birthday, Maazel made his Cleveland Orchestra conducting debut at a pension fund concert in Public Music Hall. Rose witnessed it as he was in his final months as the orchestra's first cellist.

cello—although he could not take the blame for the Long Island Rail Road, which regularly rumbled by just 30 yards away from the building, continuously rattling the windows. Upstairs from the Roses, the Dolangers had no sympathy for the cellist. As his son, Arthur, recalls, "When my dad practiced, they would bang on the floor trying to shut him up. Mr. Mallen [the building's landlord] would come knocking on the door with complaints from the Dolangers and from others that Dad was disturbing the neighbors. These were the conditions he was subjected to."[156] In his memoir, Rose discusses his struggles first to make a living, and later, a career. "We lived in Forest Hills from 1943 to 1949, our entire family in two rooms. I absolutely had to practice every day. Even if we had two three-hour rehearsals in one day, I still felt obliged to squeeze in a couple more when I got home." (Rose walked 3.5 blocks from the 8th Avenue Independent line to his apartment house. To Carnegie Hall, he exited at 53rd and 7th Avenue where he "would have to walk up" dozens of steps with his cello.)

For years Rose remained friends with Arthur Statter, a schoolmate of his at Curtis. Statter knew the family well and was aware of their cramped quarters since the cellist joined the Philharmonic. The trumpet player wanted to help. At Roy Harris's chamber music festival in the summer of 1949, he suggested that if he ever needed money for the down payment on a house, he would lend him $2,000 (equivalent to $18,000 in 2008). Toward year's end, Statter's telephone rang.

"Hello," Rose's words were characteristically direct. "I need your help."

"Where are you?" Statter asked.

"Back in New York. I found a house [Tudor-style in an upper-middle class primarily Jewish suburban neighborhood]. I'm calling from a real estate office in Great Neck, Long Island, and I need $2,000 for the closing."

The man raced to the bank for a cashier's check that enabled Leonard Rose to become a homeowner for the first time. In Statter's memory, "It took years before he eventually gave me back the money, but he did. So what was on his mind when I said goodbye to him for the final time in the hospital 35 years later? He remembered that I was the great benefactor who came up with $2,000. He was eternally grateful."[157]

Immediately following their move to Great Neck, Arthur Rose (who attended kindergarten) wanted to play the cello. "What kid doesn't want to follow in the path of their father?" he suggests decades later. "Gloria Strasner came to our house to give me a lesson. She showed me, this is how you hold the cello, this is how you hold the bow. My father was watching us from the side of the room. When I tried playing a note and couldn't, my father stormed in and put an abrupt end to the session: 'That's it. No more. That's the end of the lesson.' He grabbed the cello and the bow. There was no more cello. I remember it like it was yesterday." At that tender age, it was a terrible blow to the boy who wished to emulate his father.

The Rose Family: Great Neck, Long Island, Circa 1954
Courtesy of Arthur Rose

Recalling his painful childhood—and his troubled role as father to two estranged children—Rose pontificated in a 1972 interview, "Parents who pressure their children do more harm than good." Rose continued with the *Hartford Courant*, "The harm is often psychological and can't be undone. The pushing leads to a sense of failure that lasts a lifetime. ... There are enough conflicts between son-father, mother-daughter in the normal scheme without adding the complex relationship of teacher-pupil in music."[158]

The family's financial struggles hardly abated. Leonard Rose earned $175 per week during the Philharmonic's 1944-1945 season (equivalent to nearly $2,100 in 2008) with an additional $200 to solo with the orchestra that year. Bruno Zirato, the orchestra's associate manager, arranged for Rose a $25-per-week step-up raise each succeeding year. The New York Philharmonic may have qualified as America's leading orchestra, yet in no year did it employ Rose longer than 28 weeks (these were consecutive weeks with no vacation periods).

Rose was working in a period when despotic conductors ruled with iron fists and could fire a musician on the spot for falling short of expectations. In the ensuing years, stricter union regulations, courtesy of the AFM (American Federation of Musicians), nullified this policy. Nonetheless, it is no wonder people who perform in orchestras, show significant conflicts regarding their chosen profession. Enduring orders from occasional, sullen conductors and from various surly management personnel on what to play, how to play, when to play, where to play, how to conform—in addition to being judged by fellow colleagues—is not akin to a blissful existence. In a survey of professional orchestra musicians and professionals in other fields in the United States, Great Britain and Germany, the musicians scored the highest in the possession of personal, self-directed, internal motivation. However, for general job satisfaction, they rated seven out of thirteen, below federal prison guards and above industrial production teams. More distressing was the response to whether or not their jobs encouraged personal growth and development; orchestra members ranked ninth. The study's bleak conclusion draws attention to an inevitable lack of control, and potential lack of self-esteem musician's face in their work environment.[159]

Still, decades after his orchestral career concluded Rose seemed indebted for the opportunity to work with his era's greatest conductors. Rose describes how "the years I spent in the Philharmonic, exposed to such people as Toscanini, Walter, Szell, Mitropoulos, and Stokowski helped me in my art. They helped show me different approaches to the great composers. I think this was so important." His maestros came from divergent backgrounds which imbued Rose's orchestral experience with individuality and flare. Leonard Slatkin reiterates, "Each of these conductors was absolutely committed, sincere, and believed in their approach to the score. In the 1940s and 1950s, parts of the repertoire were not yet settled. That's why these conductors could afford to have a greater diversity of interpretation."[160]

After 13 seasons, Rose naturally formed strong opinions about how orchestras operated, his colleagues, and the conductors for whom he played. "I've noticed," Rose reminisced, "that a high percentage of the comical events in my career date from my years in orchestra. I suppose it takes a certain amount of bitterness to create humor, and orchestras have more than enough of that...."

The symphony has undergone radical changes since Rose's day in the limelight. For one, the emergence of 52-week employment, insurance benefits, the advent of pensions and paid vacation time has ensured the ultimate in stability for the contemporary crop of talented musicians. For another, the upheaval in medicine, life expectancy, and lifestyles has caused a retirement revolution throughout the professional world. Rose and his cohorts renewed year-to-year contracts. Tenure currently requires two seasons or less and can amount to a lifetime appointment. Mandatory retirement age for an orchestral performer in Rose's era was 60, then later at 65; there is no ceiling today, which has a downside. What if a once marvelous player's skills show signs of decline at a relatively young age? The music director, under ever increasing scrutiny today, still holds the singular responsibility to make these difficult decisions, risking alienation.

In 1982, Rose was 64 years old and contemplating retirement from the concert stage. Rose worried about his own decline. "I do not want to play when I can't. That really is on my mind. There's no danger of it now, because I still work. I am a willing worker, and I believe in practicing. I am not happy if I don't do my three hours of work in the morning. That has to be done, and then I can go on and do other things. When I am on tour, I practice. When I come home, I practice. I practice every morning and then I run like hell to the Juilliard to teach. That's the way I spend my life. In between, I manage to see my wife." Xenia, Rose's second wife, was an exceedingly tolerant woman.

As long as Rose practiced, retirement remained, out of the question. Of his youthful orchestral routine, he recalls, "In my years with the Philharmonic, and to this day, I work as much as I can before solo appearances. Then, I practiced so much that I could have been awakened at 4:00 o'clock in the morning, in the middle of wintertime, put out in the middle of ice and snow and I could sit down and play the pieces perfectly. That's how prepared I was—if anything, over prepared." Rose supposed he was that way, startlingly, because "I was frightened of making an ass out of myself, frightened of failure."

Before Rose's terminal illness, he steadily worked as soloist and chamber musician. Yet, his repetitions sound like a man obsessive over his longevity: "I am still a concertizing cellist and, of course, I am going to play as long as I can. As long as I continue to play well, I will go on. I know it cannot be forever, but a great player at advanced ages can do well. It is more common with the piano." Rose cited contemporaries Arthur Rubinstein (1887-1982) and Vladimir Horowitz (1904-1989) as examples. "The same is not true on a stringed instrument. One must feel well. On the piano—well, they don't make their own intonation. They can hit wrong notes, clinkers, as indeed we can too; but intonation is not a critical factor. Also, not such a critical factor on the piano is sound or tone. I am not by any means saying that the piano is easy. However, I think from those two viewpoints, intonation and sound on the stringed instrument is far more difficult. It is proof that even Casals in old age did not play the way Casals played as a young man."

Rose was, as expected, impressed when he heard 81-year-old Casals play Bach for the first time. "The moment, however, he started playing anything more complicated, the vibrato was already slow, the intensity of the playing was not there. This cannot be helped. This is natural. So I am going to continue to play as long as I can and still play well. If I feel that I am not playing as well as I should—the moment I feel this—I will retire. I don't mean the occasional less [than] good performance. Hell, that will happen to anybody! One might be a little more nervous; one might not feel very well that particular evening. That's human, but I don't want to happen to me what I saw happen to Fritz Kreisler, when he couldn't hear any more, literally playing out of tune."

Physical ailments in music know no boundaries. It affects the career paths of students and shortens the careers of professional orchestral, chamber, and solo performers. Conductors are not immune to career-ending disabilities as well. Similar to a professional athlete who doesn't quite know when to call it quits (albeit at a younger age), a musician—especially a grand elder statesman with a demanding schedule booked years in advance—can have trouble leaving the stage. Jascha Heifetz seems an exception because he withdrew 14 years before his death. Rose played with other musicians who he believed should have retired earlier. Violinist Josef Szigeti, for one, after a recording session in which Rose's Philharmonic participated. The once-proud soloist's work soured as his arthritic condition worsened. Rose likewise felt that Piatigorsky should have bowed out after the cellist's diagnosis of terminal cancer. He based this observation on a performance where Piatigorsky and Isaac Stern performed the "Double" Concerto of Brahms in Los Angeles. Perhaps he heard all about it from Stern who reported back to Rose.

What about teachers? Should instruction stop upon a teacher becoming too deaf, too old, or too ill? This author has heard about world famous teachers who have fallen asleep during lessons, no doubt deflating any aspiring youngster. Who will advise aging chamber music groups to retire after years of subpar performances—critics, sponsors, managers? Certainly there are a few chamber ensembles out there, with large reputations, who should call it quits but won't. Of course, plenty of highly respected musicians leave the concert stage gradually and gracefully. After a lifetime before the public, these questions quietly plagued Leonard Rose.

However, he did not retire. Rose maintained 60 to 70 concerts a season before forced to bring his career to a close in April of 1984 due to the sudden onset of leukemia; one casualty, one date that was never realized placed him before his beloved New York public in the spring of 1985 as soloist with the Philharmonic, after a surprising 20-year absence (Yo-Yo Ma filled in). Yet, anyone who heard the cellist play in those final years remembers, sadly, that they witnessed a mere shadow of his great self. "Occasionally scratchy and roughly articulated... and some shaky intonation..." John Henken wrote in the *Los Angeles Times* in January 1983, following Rose's Saint-Saëns Concerto performance with the Pacific Symphony. It all seemed heartbreaking. The formerly noble performer's musician trailblazing trademarks—accuracy, consistency, and sound—began to lose its sparkle.

Sickness may have played a role in Rose's deterioration as a performer. It was in 1976 when 58-year-old Rose first complained about a sporadic urgency to urinate. Two years later, he had a horrific 2.5-inch tumor removed from his right kidney. Needless to say, Rose didn't practice much during this period of medical attention. Doctors told him they caught the malignancy early enough, before it could metastasize. As a precaution, surgeons removed his prostate gland. Some people assert he was never the same after these operations. In 1982, Rose fell and fractured his arm while running on wet pavement. The fall caused a clean break of the humerus of his right arm. He notes in his memoir how the cancellation of several months of touring lost him an estimated $50,000 in income (equivalent to nearly $112,000 in 2008).

There was a single concert, however, he would absolutely not cancel. Wishing to relive his triumph in Richard Strauss's *Don Quixote* under George Szell and Bruno Walter, Rose was hired for a performance of the work in Greensboro, North Carolina. With his bow arm in a plaster cast, he temporarily extended his cello's endpin to its maximum length so that he could manage some left-hand practice. The cello, in this position, would lie over the sling. When the cast came off, Rose started a rigorous regimen of physical therapy. Even still, he had a slight tremor any time he extended his right arm or his bow arm. This persisted until a couple of weeks before the concert. Rose could not play at the bow's tip so he made frantic provisions and altered his long-established bowings. The concert took place as scheduled. A member of the orchestra's cello section then, remembers how small and frail Rose appeared when he walked out on the stage. "What a transformation when he began playing," the cellist recounts. "Physically he seemed to change into Superman! He appeared 10 times larger, very relaxed and powerful. It was in this dress rehearsal that I'll never forget."

Possibly remembering Bruno Walter's words, 'My dear, you are the Don' or recapturing his old magic from a performance with the Hartford Symphony in October 1966, eliciting this review—"... He played as if enrapt. The spell he seemed to feel was passed on to the audience in his absolutely impeccable technique, the singing of his instrument, the spaciousness of every statement, and his deep emotional investure of the music. Put them all together and the word is elegance. In the last glissando and the final perfect note, all that is believable in Don Quixote—if not Strauss—was passionately and dramatically summed up by Mr. Rose. It was magnificent upon the ear and heart."[161] Rose played as if he knew this would be his final portrayal of the chivalric model.

Today, Rose would be astonished at the evolution of orchestral life: Contract committees – Artistic Advisory, Standing Audition, Music Director Search, Pension, Chamber Music, Youth Fellowship, Local Internet, Hotlines, Grievances, Travel/Touring, and Parking committees abound. These were nonexistent in Rose's era.

Rose addressed the issue of attitude: "I very much resent," he dictated earnestly, "the very common attitude of players in an orchestra, who become blasé and frustrated. You find more frustrated people in the orchestra for a simple reason. They started a career wanting to be Heifetz, Casals, or what have you; and what did they turn out to be? Hackers in an orchestra—frustrated, bitter hackers—literally hating music!"

The mental makeup of a professional symphonic player has also drastically changed since Rose's era when musicians filled their unemployed weeks with other jobs to supplement their income. The process of becoming an orchestral player nowadays requires tireless perfection of every angle of the audition process. The fact that orchestral excerpt coaching programs are offered in many music conservatories today attests to the knowledge one must have before stepping on stage to audition. A parallel can be drawn with the modern college admissions' race, with test prep seminars unheard of a few decades ago. Current competition is fierce, occasionally pitting hundreds of players against each other for a single opening. To preclude discrimination by race, sex, or age, the audition occurs before a panel, behind a black curtain or screen.

Rose's era was quite different. By and large, principals were hired by private audition, exclusively at a conductor's invitation. As mentioned, Rose never did audition for principal cellist in Cleveland and Rodzinski brought Rose with him to New York. Section players could be hired by this method as well. Seymour Barab, who played in Rose's cello section in Cleveland's 1941-1942 season, explained: "It was not as though it was hard to get into the orchestra at that time. There were two people who auditioned for the position that I got. My previous job, the Indianapolis Symphony, where I played for two years, that too had only two applicants for the position. So people moved around from one orchestra to another. One year in Indianapolis, one year in Los Angeles, and then one year in Cleveland. In other words, if you moved at all, you tried to get to a better orchestra." Indeed, Rose's entire experience playing in orchestras was at the hands of what Lorin Maazel referred to as the "golden period" of conducting; exclusively with Bernstein, Golschmann, Mitropoulos, Monteux, Münch, Ormandy, Reiner, Rodzinski, De Sabata (Rose claims that De Sabata "... might have been one of the greatest conductors I ever played with."), Steinberg, Stokowski, Szell, Toscanini and Walter.[*]

Rose's point about his contemporary orchestras cannot be discounted. He concluded: "The general psychology of the average orchestral player is that they are not the most perceptive group, particularly in their judgment of the caliber of conductors. Most of them are half asleep anyway, not trying all that hard unless they have a real sadistic tyrant on the podium. Most players in the orchestra are ready to call a conductor great if he lets them go a half hour early from rehearsal."

---

[*] Rose also played under Igor Stravinsky, whom he recalled as "not particularly good on the podium. I might add that his opinion of his own music was not overly astute either."

Chapter Fourteen

Rose's Career Ignites

"My first engagement as a soloist, was to play with the Chicago Symphony. ... It was like going into the mouth of a lion because the critics out there were NASTY!"

—Leonard Rose

Rose, typical of every gifted instrumentalist, aspired to a career in the limelight—front and center, not lost in a sea of 100 or so collaborators. He paid his dues, in the role of principal cellist of the country's finest symphonic orchestras. Patrons, critics, conductors, and impresarios had taken note of his emergence. His dream remained unbroken: to strike out on his own.

Naturally, he worried about abandoning his exalted position in New York. A soloist's career offered no guarantee of concert dates or of sufficient income from fees to support his family.

One day, in January 1950, in the interval between the orchestra's two three-hour rehearsals, Rose went out to lunch with his friend, principal violist William Lincer.[*] Upon their return, Rose was summoned to the associate manager's office.

"Lennie, come with me," Bruno Zirato directed.

---

[*] The Brooklyn-born musician (1907-1997) was one of his generation's outstanding violists who remained as principal with the Philharmonic until 1972. His tenure at Juilliard began in 1969, his teaching studio adjacent to Rose's. Lincer was solo violist in Strauss's *Don Quixote* at Bernstein historic 1943 debut.

Rose was in awe of the tall, elegant gentleman, who spoke several languages fluently and had worked as Enrico Caruso's personal manager (generations of singers have been inspired by the legacy of the 250 recordings left by Caruso—Rose periodically referred to Caruso as his favorite singer). One of his Philharmonic duties involved keeping the musicians happy, especially when it came time to renew personnel contracts. Rose had no idea what the man wanted. Zirato tactfully slid a small newspaper clipping from his pocket and handed it to Rose. It read, "Piatigorsky Packed by Hurok." It hardly surprised Rose to learn that the Russian cellist, now living in Southern California, had been signed to a soloist's contract by Sol Hurok.

Born Solomon Izrailevich Gurkov, Hurok emigrated from Russia and eventually risked his own savings to import concert artists and ballet companies on U.S. tours that he organized, booked, and marketed. This powerful music manager would become the foremost impresario of his era—by his own estimation handling 4,000 individuals (among them Marian Anderson, Arthur Rubinstein, Isaac Stern, Emil Gilels, Vladimir Ashkenazy, Daniel Barenboim, and Mstislav Rostropovich) as well as the Bolshoi Ballet and Kirov Academy Ballet troupes.

"Lennie, I don't think you know what this means," Zirato said.

"Bruno," Rose responded. "What are you trying to do—get rid of me?"

"I urge you to go see Judson today," Zirato insisted.

The cellist certainly was aware that a solo career could not be launched, regardless of talent, without artists' management. In the better part of the 1920s and 1930s, Arthur Judson simultaneously held posts as manager of the Philadelphia Orchestra, New York Philharmonic, and for five of these years the Cincinnati Symphony. His penchant for signing soloists to contracts with his Columbia Artists Management and supplying nationwide public appearances, especially with orchestras he managed, fueled controversy that he held a near-monopoly on the industry's artists and repertoire. More importantly and somewhat obscured by his detractors, Judson was a visionary and a pioneer, skillfully guiding the birth of classical music radio broadcasts. In 1926, he established the Judson Radio Program

Corporation, which eventually led to the Columbia Broadcasting System (CBS). His keen and ruthless business sense drove him to absorb five of his primary management rivals. In 1930, he formed Columbia Concerts Corporation. Arthur Judson was the big time and Rose knew it.

Well aware that the meeting held the potential to alter the course of his life, the 32-year-old cellist felt anxious as he knocked on the manager's door at the appointed hour. "You know, Piatigorsky just left me and is going with Hurok," the imposing man bellowed as Rose stepped into the office. "Are you ready to leave the Philharmonic next season?" Rose swallowed hard. He recently purchased his Gofriller cello and owed many more payments. What unfolded before him was a dream come true. He had long hoped to become a Judson artist and, at last, the opportunity presented itself.

"I like you and I like your playing. What do you say?"

"Mr. Judson," Rose haltingly answered, "I want most of all the chance to be a soloist—but I need another year." The men agreed: his solo career would officially begin at the close of the 1950-1951 Philharmonic season. It was one of the greatest days of Rose's life. His elation was palpable to all who knew and loved him.

In his final season as principal cellist, Rose kept plenty busy in New York. He added a precious new concerto to the repertoire performing the world premiere of Alan Shulman's Cello Concerto, expressly written for him and the Philharmonic, and conducted by Mitropoulos April 13 and 14, 1950 (the CD accompanying this book contains the April 14 performance). Seven months later, Rose played the New York premiere of Alfredo Casella's Concerto for Trio and Orchestra in Town Hall with violinist Joseph Fuchs and pianist Nadia Reisenberg. The following month, Rose appeared in Strauss' *Don Quixote* for the second time with George Szell and the Philharmonic (December 7, 8, and 10). Still preceding his "official" solo career, Rose and violinist John Corigliano presented Brahms's "Double" Concerto with Bruno Walter leading the Philharmonic February 1, 2, and 4, 1951. Two months later, Rose performed Bloch's "Schelomo" April 5, 6, and 8 with Dimitri Mitropoulos. The same year, a Decca Gold Label Series LP featured Beethoven's String Serenade in D Major, Op.

8 with Rose, violinist Joseph Fuchs, and his sister, violist Lillian Fuchs.

Because the subsequent season opened with the Philharmonic's first European tour since Toscanini's prewar voyage, Rose asked to go. He longed to play in Edinburgh, Scotland, and expressed delight that the orchestra's management and Judson indulged his desire to temporarily hold onto his position. He was even more thrilled that Mitropoulos agreed to program the Saint-Saëns Cello Concerto with Rose (the two recorded the work in April 1951). BBC broadcasts carried Rose's performance to millions of radio listeners in Great Britain and Western Europe, and the *Glasgow Herald* hailed Rose's indomitable cello authority: "Mr. Rose possesses a tone of rare beauty and purity and a technique absolutely sure in agility and intonation."

Upon his return to New York, Rosalie Leventritt, the principal behind the prestigious Leventritt International Competition established in memory of her husband Edgar (died 1939), hosted a party to celebrate the impending solo career of Leonard Rose. "Dear old Rosalie Leventritt!" Rose dictated for his memoir. "She once said, 'Leonard, if there is anything you need, I want you to call me. I want you to remember that this is not an empty offer.'" The generous woman, in fact, assisted Rose in financing his New York debut recital at Town Hall in October 1945. "I always loved her," he continued. "She was an extraordinary person who loved the arts and [who] helped young artists like me."

In the fall of 1951, Judson launched Leonard Rose on a seven-week, coast-to-coast tour, booking Rose with nine symphony orchestras, including those in Chicago, Milwaukee, New York, and Cleveland and recital dates in Wichita, Kansas; San Antonio, Texas; Tulsa, Oklahoma; Utica, New York; Miami, Florida; and Springfield, Missouri. This tour followed a television appearance on the NBC-TV Recital Hall Series (a film with Leonid Hambro accompanying him in Tchaikovsky's "Variations on a Rococo Theme"); a Dallas recital with his colleague Walter Hendl; a Library of Congress recital in Washington, DC; with Frank Sheridan; and a recital at the Washington Irving High School in Manhattan.

Spectacular reviews poured in:

The most interesting discovery was that Leonard Rose ... has a big, fine tone, a polished technique, and the gift of direct communication.
—Claudia Cassidy, *Chicago Daily Tribune*, October 26, 1951

A sensitive and vigorous artist with a fluid tone, tremendous technique, and the ability to range from the brooding, Oriental imagery of Bloch's "Schelomo" to the icy precision of Haydn.
—Don Granger, *Wichita Eagle*, November 20, 1951

The Saint-Saëns revealed Rose's sheer technical mastery and at the same time, his ability to project the emotion of the music, warm and appealingly human ... in the Bloch his artistry was shown in full measure.
—Maurine Halliburton, *Tulsa World*, December 10, 1951

His tone is warm and velvety with no shocking changes of timbres for upper and lower strings.
—John Rosenfield, *Dallas Morning News*, December 16, 1951

A fine, flowing line ... Rose commands not only a superb technique, but is blessed with some of the soundest musicianship in the field.
—Paul Hume, *Washington Post*, February 16, 1952

The Chicago Symphony Orchestra, under the baton of Bohemian-born music director Rafael Kubelik (1914-1996), was Rose's first engagement as soloist. During World War II, the obstinate anti-Nazi spent months in hiding in the Czech countryside so as not to be caught by the Gestapo. After his defection to the United Kingdom, Bruno Walter helped him secure a career in America. Kubelik chose Chicago in 1950 over an offer from the BBC to succeed Sir Adrian Boult as chief conductor. However, his tenure in Chicago lasted only three seasons and ended in shambles, clouded by unremitting vicious attacks by the *Tribune's* music critic Claudia Cassidy (1899-1996). Also, the board of directors chased him away for introducing too many (70) contemporary works.

Rose performed the Beethoven "Triple" Concerto with violinist Joseph Fuchs and pianist George Schick and three nights later played Tchaikovsky's "Variations on a Rococo Theme" with the Chicago Symphony in Milwaukee. An elated conductor immediately wired Judson: "A magnificent artist. Proud to have had him open his first transcontinental tour with us." "It was a lot of work," Rose recalled of his rigorous introduction to solo touring, "but I was ready."

One month into that inaugural tour, Cleveland welcomed him back, this time in his superior role as soloist. As mentioned, Szell guided Rose to his Carnegie Hall studio in 1945. That long-ago event, when Szell accompanied him on piano in a reading of Dvořák's Concerto, was unforgettable for Rose and apparently as well for Szell. The tough conductor was impressed—enough to state publicly that he intended to hire Rose to solo as early as possible. On November 22 and 24, the two men repeated the Dvořák Concerto, this time with Szell on Cleveland's podium. Arthur Loesser at the *Cleveland Press* enthused: "A player of superlative attainments. ... a rich, smooth tone quality of ample volume, an extraordinary unstrained nimbleness of finger, and a fine lyrical style that never becomes mawkish."

Among the benefits that came with a Judson contract was the nationwide series of concerts he headed called Community Concerts. It provided his roster of artists outlets to present a broad selection of repertoire many times. These dates also reduced travel distances by filling idle stretches between major dates. Schuyler Chapin (1923-2009),[162] who then handled Jascha Heifetz's Midwestern bookings, wrote, "The concert business was changing in the fifties; the colleges were becoming important buyers of talent. Student funds often paid for these concerts, held in new theaters and multipurpose auditoriums that sprang up on campuses after the war."[163] Community Concerts provided the cellist with welcomed relief from the anxiety of performing in the major cities. Yo-Yo Ma believes that is where his mentor excelled. "Leonard Rose didn't love pressure," Ma asserts. "He played the freest when he didn't feel the pressure of judgment. He traveled and played absolutely everywhere. ... Don't just go and play in big cities—go to the people." Ma, speaking from the height of his fame, enlightens Rose's attitude toward after-concert receptions. "These receptions were as important to him if not more important than the concerts. These were his human moments; and that's why I still hear the stories about Leonard Rose's artistry. People come up to me to say they remember him and that he was so lovely. We know him from the classroom; I hear stories about him from the road. I never complain about going to a reception. ... That's because of Leonard Rose."[164]

Schubert's "Arpeggione" Sonata was repeated close to 30 times in recital, most of them at Community Concerts, before he recorded the work in 1953. "An artist always learns something on stage that he cannot learn in the studio," Rose explained, "and the works he will play best are the ones he has had more opportunities to present." Columbia's list boasted some of the most stellar names in the business including Heifetz, Rudolf Serkin, Claudia Arrau, Zino Francescatti, Lily Pons, Richard Tucker, Van Cliburn, and Leonard Rose. This newest client, Rose, faced a problem: the fees for these community concerts were painfully meager.

After one such appearance, a grateful sponsor expressed curiosity about how Rose managed to eke out a living from the $600 per concert, from which he subtracted travel expenses and his accompanist's fee. Rose reacted with shock. He informed the man that he received only $400, not $600. The next day, the sponsor phoned Judson's agency, and sure enough, Rose's rate should have been $600.

In Manhattan, a furious cellist headed to 57th Street—a block where the center of power for the classical music industry was concentrated.

"What's this all about?" Rose demanded.

Bill Judd, a senior partner, responded, "Well, Lennie, you have that differential in your contract."

"What do you mean?" Rose spoke incredulously.

Judd skimmed through the papers and exclaimed, "Oh my God. We forgot to give it to you." He immediately reworded the document that Rose had to sign. The executive elucidated on the costs to dispatch salespeople to the participating communities and organize and prepare for these concerts. To defray the expense, the agency took $200 off the top from all their artists—the so-called "differential." In Rose's case, the amount came to one-third of his fee from the local association that left $340 (equivalent to nearly $2,800 in 2008) after subtracting Judson's commissions. From that remainder, the cellist needed to pay his recital pianist, for transportation, lodging, and meals for both of them. Rose confessed, "It didn't leave me very much. They say it's a necessary thing to have—this differential. I think Community Concerts did a great deal for music in this country because it brought music to a widespread audience before the days when phonograph records were readily available." Small towns particularly benefited from these rare opportunities to enjoy classical music. Yet, the advantages these towns had, hosting leading soloists, did not necessarily enrich artists like Rose. "I think there is something indecent with having to pay $260 in commissions," Rose adds. Nevertheless, he played his heart out at every new venue, whether at a college campus, in a high-school auditorium, gymnasium, library, or community house, constantly honing his skills as soloist.

Despite the agency's complicated accounting methods, Rose estimated that he fared as well financially during that first year away from the Philharmonic as he had while under the security of the orchestra's contract. Building a solo career and earning a respectable soloist's income required long absences from home and family, occasionally for solitary months at a time. Simultaneously, his teaching expanded as his reputation attracted more students to his classes at America's two most prestigious conservatories.

In January 1952, amid Rose's initial season as a bonafide soloist, George Szell conducted a Philharmonic pension concert in Carnegie Hall with Rose performing Tchaikovsky's "Variations on a Rococo Theme." Rose awakened the next morning to revel in the *New York Times'* words: "Leonard Rose, the Philharmonic's former first cellist, led off the soloists with a sweetly sung but virile performance ...."

Two months later, the Philharmonic again featured him as soloist. On March 1, Rose presented the Saint-Saëns Concerto with Franco Autori (1903-1990): music director of the Buffalo

Philharmonic from 1936 to 1945 and associate conductor of the Philharmonic for a decade beginning in 1949. On March 27 and 28, the orchestra showcased him in the Dvořák Concerto with Mitropoulos conducting. The New York *Telegram and Sun's* Louis Biancolli reported on Rose's elevated status: "[Rose] played as he never played before—which means several strides ahead of almost any other cellist you might name."

The momentous inaugural year peaked when Rose purchased a 1662 Amati cello: a cello once played on by the influential Russian music patron Count Matvei Wielhorski (1794–1866) and by the last czar of Russia, Nicolas II (1868-1918). Rose would perform on this magnificent Cremonese instrument for the rest of his life. His first meaningful concert on the golden cello took place July 5th at the Ravinia Festival in Highland Park, Illinois, in Brahms's "Double" Concerto. George Szell conducted the Chicago Symphony with the Austrian-born violinist, Erica Morini (1904-1995). Morini's recordings of the great concertos of Mozart, Beethoven, Brahms, and Tchaikovsky remain highly prized. Harold Schonberg, then chief critic of the *New York Times,* once described her as "the greatest woman violinist who ever lived." (Rose would perform the same concerto with Morini ten years later with the Hartford [Connecticut] Symphony conducted by Austrian Fritz Mahler, whose father was a cousin of the composer Gustav Mahler) Seymour Raven of the *Chicago Tribune*, however, disliked the match: "I wish I could say the collaboration was a notable success, but I did not find it so. Miss Morini's playing was not of Mr. Rose's size, and where it offered to be, it became strident and labored ..."[165]

After his Ravinia appearance, Rose settled in at Ivan Galamian's Meadowmount School of Music in upstate New York. The scenic location became the soloist's home the following 12 summers, to teach, as well as relax and vacation with his family. Inevitably, he practiced that 1952 summer, no doubt preparing for his second year under Judson's management.

A typical Rose recital program from the period included sonatas by the Belgian composer César Franck and Norwegian Edvard Grieg—works he recorded in June of that year with pianist Leonid Hambro (1920-2006). Continuing an established tradition of his era, the cellist demonstrated a commitment to recital audiences presenting cello concertos with piano accompaniment. So it is no surprise that one of his sample programs contained the Saint-Saëns Concerto in A minor, Op. 33 and Tchaikovsky's "Variations on a Rococo Theme."*

During this period, he grew increasingly fascinated with Schubert's 1871 "Arpeggione" Sonata.

"I remember when I made the first recording of the Schubert Sonata [May 1953]," Rose dictated." Near the end of his life, he clung to memories of his spectacular recording of the very difficult work, which remained deep within: "I am very happy that my recording ... was played straight through. I made the first movement once with Leonid Hambro, listened to the playback, and decided that it sounded a little bit slow. We then played straight through, nonstop, and that is what you hear." Cellist Robert Battey, who is a music critic for the *Washington Post*, elaborated on his recording of "Arpeggione" in a survey of Rose's discography: "The golden sound, the scrupulous attack and release on each note, the inevitability of the phrasing, the purity of intonation, and the bold, virile shifts all announced to the world that a new solo artist of startling expressive powers had arrived."[166] In that same two-day period in May 1953, in New York City, he also recorded Italian sonatas by Boccherini's (in A Major) and Sammartini.

Concerto dates were the highlight of Rose's annual schedule. In March 1952, he played Bloch's "Schelomo" and the Saint-Saëns with the Cleveland Orchestra under Rudolph Ringwall; and in November, reprised "Schelomo" with the Philharmonic and Mitropoulos, a work the pair magnificently recorded 18 months earlier. "There were beauties galore in Mr. Rose's playing," Lester Trimble of the *New York Herald Tribune* wrote of the Bloch performance. "Phrases delightfully turned, passages sung surely and poetically in the upper registers; a level of technical perfection truly admirable."

---

* The program also consisted of Sammartini: Sonata in G Major; Bach-Siloti: Adagio from Organ Toccata in C Major; Haydn: Minuet; Frescobaldi-Cassadó: Toccata; Saint-Saëns: The Swan; Hillemacher: Gavotte; Ibert: The Little White Donkey; Chopin: Nocturne in C-Sharp Minor; Popper: Hungarian Rhapsody.

A Saint-Saëns Concerto engagement dispatched Rose to Louisiana in 1953. Martha Blackman, a young cellist in the New Orleans Philharmonic, felt euphoric: "I had come from a Southern city where nobody knew what a cello was. ... I took a job selling Magnavox LP record players. ... I got to sit for hours at a stretch playing all of Rose's records. ... After the concert, I felt staggeringly transported by what I had heard and seen. I wished to shake his hand and tell him that I had incredible admiration for his elegance and consummate mastery on the cello."

In 1954, arguably his greatest season as soloist, Rose performed in 28 states and Canada. He appeared with 11 different orchestras: the New York Philharmonic, Philadelphia Orchestra, orchestras in Minneapolis, Grand Rapids, Peoria, Tucson, Dallas, Amarillo, Edmonton, the Florida Symphony, and Thomas Scherman's Little Orchestra Society. Rose continued his dizzying itinerary of community concerts in such odd locales as high school auditoriums in Danbury, Connecticut; Forest Hills (Queens), New York; Millburn, New Jersey; Brattleboro, Vermont; at Carleton College in Northfield, Minnesota; Lawton Community Concert Association in Oklahoma, and Ban Johnson Field House in Marietta, Ohio.

In the course of these strings of concerts—with frequent, prolonged absences from his home and young family, and with perpetual loneliness and frustration of a musician on the road—Rose learned life-shattering news: His wife, Minnie, was diagnosed with leukemia. Her diagnosis clashed with his drive to become the greatest living cellist. The dedicated performer lacked financial security and had little choice but to continue his quest if only to provide financially for Minnie and their two children. Leonard Rose never looked back, although later wished he had halted his concerts to tend to his ailing wife. Marvelous reviews continued to pile up on Judson's desk; the critics were unanimous in their praise.

> Leonard Rose wowed a sizeable audience. ... With his deft technique and a tone wonderfully warm even for such a rich instrument, the top-rank cellist provided the Dvořák Cello Concerto with an unusual amount of flavor

and beauty, which backed up the nationwide claim that he is probably the finest cellist now going.
—John Bustin, Austin, *Texas Daily American*, January 19, 1954

Rose is quite somebody to hear. ... Nobody else plays the cello for stronger, richer tone, or fingers it more flexibly and 'personally,' or avoids better the breaks. ... Mr. Rose phrases with honest, divining musicianship ... played with eloquence and command.
—John Rosenfield, *Dallas Morning News*, February 1, 1954

The Dvořák predominated over other concertos. Before one performance of the work with the Philadelphia Orchestra in April, he traveled to Cincinnati where audiences heard the same piece in mid-February, prompting Arthur Darack of the *Cincinnati Enquirer* to write: "Rose is a cellist who has the ability to make the cello sound the way cellists claim it can but almost never does until Rose or Piatigorsky come along and substantiate these claims. ... Rose has a clean, spacious sound to his cello and a technique which produces the tone so vibrantly that I forget the scarcity of the cello concerto literature and think how terrific Leonard Rose is."

A May recital in Cleveland brought critics from the city's two dailies to their feet and led to the following reviews:

Cello art that is rare, inspiring, and thrilling from the flashing bow of Leonard Rose was a most auspicious opening for the music series. ... Rose revealed all of those musicianly qualities that have brought him right to the top of the cello field. ... Beauty of tone and ease and certainty of execution attainable only by the virtuosi marked his playing before a large audience that was really thrilled. Rose's cello sang its way, and revealed complete technical perfection and musical understanding. ... The Rose art came to life with a new meaning. Perfect collaboration with the piano and an art of interpretation that was supreme provided a masterpiece.
—Elmore Bacon, *Cleveland News*, May 8, 1954

The enchanting sweetness of Rose's liquid tone, his musicianly poise and insight, his fantastic facility, all were subjects of the greatest admiration and sources of rare musical pleasure.
—Herbert Elwell, *Cleveland Plain Dealer*, May 8, 1954

Cleveland, a metropolis close to Leonard Rose's heart, was a place the cellist performed time and again throughout his career. Lorin Maazel—who collaborated with him in *Don Quixote* (1973), Dvořák Concerto (1973-1974), Elgar Concerto (1976), Bloch's "Schelomo" (1976) and Tchaikovsky's "Variations on a Rococo Theme" (1978)—regarded Rose as without equal. "Leonard Rose had always been, to my mind, one of the three leading cellists. He had a warmth of sound and a delicacy of phrasing and passion for music, which he managed to communicate very effectively. He played from his heels up."[167]

Despite Minnie's frightful battle with leukemia, when he collaborated with Isaac Stern in Brahms's "Double" Concerto, the 36-year-old cellist reached new heights. On November 29, 1954, the two string players with Bruno Walter on the podium and the New York Philharmonic recorded the masterpiece. They would eventually receive the 1957 Prix du Disque in Paris, ensuring Rose's stature as one of the generation's most celebrated musicians.

Unknown to the public, Rose embarked on an exciting new venture, rehearsing with pianist Eugene Istomin and Stern in private, which ultimately became the classical music world's most famous trio. Rose acknowledges his friend's assistance in his unpublished memoir: "I was invited by Isaac Stern to record the Brahms "Double" Concerto with him. This was a great event in my life, and I must say I think we made a very beautiful recording. That one recording put me on the map in Europe." Rose explains the records rarity: "The Brahms "Double" Concerto normally plays something like 33 minutes. In those days, on the LP, the maximum they could get on was 31 to 31.5 minutes. Sometimes by shrinking the grooves a little closer together, they could get a little more time; but this was marginal. I recall the Columbia recording people asking Bruno Walter if he could possibly take the slow movement a little bit more moving so they could make sure of getting it all on one side; in fact, the great Bruno Walter did conduct it a bit more moving. I was surprised at this, because generally, his tempos tended to be leisurely; and certainly, in the performances of this little movement, the tempo was slower. I must say, listening to the recording today, the *andante* does sound a bit hurried to me. But Bruno Walter was marvelous with whom to make music. I was touched by the whole episode and grateful because it meant so much in my career."

Walter's belief in Rose was unequivocal. The maestro penned an illustrious letter of acclamation that Rose proudly displayed for decades. "Leonard Rose's profound musicianship, technical perfection, his emotional warmth and the rare beauty of his tone have been a source of pure joy for me in all the years of our musical association. The cause of the cello's musical literature can be in no better hands than his."

In 1955, the Istomin-Stern-Rose trio debuted at the Ravinia Festival. During the trio's two-week residency, the men performed concertos with the Chicago Symphony (Rose, the Saint-Saëns and the Brahms "Double" with Stern), and performed sonata and trio programs. Even though it was not an unqualified success, due in part to an intense heat wave that brought 100-degree temperatures and extreme humidity to the Midwest, the three maintained their single-mindedness to be successful. Rose also appeared as soloist with the St. Louis Symphony performing the Saint-Saëns concerto with French conductor and music director of that orchestra from 1931 to 1958, Vladimir Golschmann. In December, Rose would complete his 19th and 20th concerto appearances with the Cleveland Orchestra in "Schelomo" and "Variations on a Rococo Theme" with Rudolph Ringwall.

An unusual opportunity came Rose's direction in 1955, when he shared a recital stage with the Russian-born pianist Boris Goldovsky (1908-2001), chiefly known as the director of the New England Conservatory of Music opera department and the founder of the New England Opera Theater. At Sanders Theater in Cambridge, Massachusetts, the duo performed Beethoven: Variations on a Theme from Mozart's "Magic Flute"; Beethoven: Sonata Op. 69; Kodály: Sonata Op. 4; and Brahms: Sonata Op. 99.

In September 1955, Izler Solomon (1910-1987), an American conductor and champion of twentieth-century American works, conducted Rose in Bloch's "Schelomo" and Bruch's *Kol Nidre*. "Does he ever play badly?" Harold Schonberg remarked in the *Times* after hearing Rose before an audience of 4,000 at the Empire State Music Festival. "His tone was mellow and beautifully centered, without any rasping on the low strings and always straight in pitch. His phrasing, needless to say, was that of a sensitive musician who does not need to massage his cello like a baker with a roll of dough to make his point. ... It was masterly playing," Schonberg concluded.

In spite of much travel, Rose's itinerary did bring him to New York frequently, which gave him the chance to keep up rosters of students at both Juilliard and at the Curtis Institute in Philadelphia. Although Judson's community-venue obligations dwindled as Rose soared to stardom, Rose still performed in auditoriums in Akron, Ohio, Toaz Junior High School in Huntington Station, New York, and at San Mateo High School auditorium in California. These programs offered Bach: Aria in C minor; Francoeur-Trowell: Sonata in E Major; Schumann: Fantasy Pieces, Op. 73; Beethoven: Sonata in A Major; Kabalevsky: Concerto Op. 49; Bloch: Prayer; Ibert: The Little White Donkey; Saint-Saëns: The Swan; and Popper: Hungarian Rhapsody.

At Washington Irving High, a huge public school in Manhattan, he left those in attendance thunderstruck. Concerts on Rose's home turf enabled students from his Juilliard class to observe their idol in action. Daniel Morgenstern, one of his pupils at the time, described years later what he witnessed to be superhuman that night: "I had never heard the Rococo Variations before. I was literally jumping out of my skin. To this day, it is an inerasable memory. The up-bow strokes at the beginning, it was as if he made a complete circle with his arm. It was so elegant. ... He was there to demonstrate great cello playing." Rose's Curtis friend, Arthur Statter, vividly recalled the make-up of the crowd: "It was filled with musicians. At the end of the recital, everybody stood up. ... He played a half hour of encores. The last thing he played was a piece by Sarasate called "Zapateado". Everybody there felt that this was the greatest of all string players."

By 1956, Rose stood at the pinnacle of the cello world, and was renowned throughout the states. This was also the year he met the newest star on the scene, Russian émigré Mstislav

Rostropovich, who developed a deep affection for the American cellist. Rostropovich wrote of their initial meeting: "I already knew the name; therefore, this meeting was very exciting for me. Since then, we met many times in many cities throughout the world. ... At first, my daughter was his pupil. ... I was especially amazed at the depth of this musician's honesty and integrity."

Rose's association with conductor George Szell proceeded apace with a February appearance with the Cleveland Orchestra that saw a reprise of works in the cellist's repertoire. To date, he had yet to collaborate with the Boston Symphony Orchestra. That changed in March 1956, when the climax of Rose's five Dvořák Concerto performances with the Boston Symphony culminated in Carnegie Hall, where no doubt his wife and children (Barbara age 15, Arthur age 11) rejoiced with their father. On the podium was legendary Charles Münch, music director of the Boston Symphony from 1948 until 1962 and founder of the Orchestre de Paris. A few days before, Harold Rogers of the *Christian Science Monitor* wrote of Rose's auspicious debut in Boston: "We hope that his success will bring him many engagements in Boston. ... His tone is warm and strong, possessing an opulence that has nothing of sentimentality. His technique is secure, commanding accurate intonation. ... He can play with a bite in his tone, or smooth it into silken serenity ... brought Mr. Rose back to the stage four or five times."

To benefit the Hartt Scholarship Fund, he traveled to Connecticut to solo with the Hartt Symphony. The scholarship was merit and need-based, which enabled talented students to attend the Hartt School of Music. It also led to the distinctive honor of bestowing to Rose an honorary degree of Doctor of Music by the conservatory in 1965.

Not many cellists presented contemporary American compositions, yet at the start of 1956, Rose was preoccupied as he readied himself to premiere Peter Mennin's cello concerto, expressly written for him by his friend and eventual president of the Juilliard School. Reviews of the premiere performance at the Juilliard School from the *Times,* the *Herald Tribune,* and the *New Yorker* in February reflect his superlative effort. He performed the work a second time later that year with the Cincinnati Symphony Orchestra.

The night he played in New York's Town Hall, literally days following his premiere of the Mennin Concerto, drew comparable praise from John Briggs in the *Times*: "Last night, Rose's playing was a delight both to the eye and to the ear. He has such complete mastery of his instrument that he has no need of the body English resorted to be certain of his colleagues in difficult passages. There is no huffing and puffing, no swaying to and fro. Mr. Rose sits calmly and plays."

In 1957, the cellist continued his association with his era's most noteworthy artists when he performed the Brahms "Double" Concerto with the then heralded violin prodigy Yehudi Menuhin and the National Symphony, under the baton of Howard Mitchell (1910-1988), a cellist who was music director of the nation's National Symphony for 20 years, in Washington DC's cavernous Constitution Hall. Undoubtedly, Rose was still relishing his recent *Grand Prix du Disque* for the recording of the work he made with his musical soulmate, Isaac Stern. Aspiring Indianapolis cellist Lloyd Smith had the opportunity to hear Rose for the first time in a 1957 recital in his hometown. "His playing was so special to me that I found myself in tears almost immediately. What struck me so decisively was the gravity of his playing: full and sympathetic comprehension of the music, backed up by a flawless technique …."

The following year, Stern was aware that the cellist never toured Europe, except as member of a group of 100 in his Philharmonic days. The violinist intended to rectify that situation, and approached Columbia Records management with a proposition: because of their award-winning record, he wanted to perform the work with Rose in Europe. According to the cellist, "Isaac Stern singlehandedly arranged three concerts of the Brahms "Double" for me. His help in my career has been nothing short of miraculous." These events attracted the attention of John and Johanna Beek, founders of the continent's most reputable concert agencies. The couple instantly signed Rose to future overseas engagements. At home in New York, the kids leaned heavily on Minnie, who obliged with every ounce of energy she could muster; her condition somewhat stabilized in remission.

The duo's London debut engendered kudos from the press. Beneath the headline, "The Peak of Splendour," the *London Daily* summarized: "I do not remember a playing of this beautiful work so brilliant in style and temperament, so revealing of the music's splendours." Next stops on their itineraries were concert venues in Paris, Zurich, and The Hague.

No tour of Europe could have closed in a more glorious setting than what Rose experienced in Brussels. Leonard Rose's continental debut recital coincided with the *Exposition Universelle et Internationale de Bruxelles,* the first major post-war World's Fair, attracted representatives and exhibitions from 48 nations. New architecture was constructed for the event, on 500 acres of manicured gardens, landscaped with vegetation from across the globe. Belgium's extraordinary spectacle drew 51 million visitors to take in the culture and inventions of different countries, flashing their brilliant displays. In this setting, with its waterfalls and dazzling technology, stepped Leonard Rose to play his first European recital on October 1—appropriately showcased at the United States Pavilion. The cellist, along with pianist Ivor Newton, chose to perform works of French, German, Russian, and American composers: Bach: Aria in C minor; Francoeur: Sonata in E Major; Schumann: Fantasy Pieces Op. 73; Barber: Sonata; Debussy: Sonata; and Tchaikovsky "Variations on a Rococo Theme." Under the headline "We Can Only Speak of Perfection," critic Het Laatste Nieuw reported: "Leonard Rose's recital was not only equal to all the great recitals so far heard in the American theatre, it was a high point of the musical events organized here. This artist outshines all we have heard here in cello playing since 1944."[168]

In addition to this historic tour, Rose had his hands full all year preparing one of the most difficult cello concertos in the repertoire: Samuel Barber's composed in 1945. Rose would perform the piece in January 1959, the only time in his career, with the Philharmonic under the baton of Barber's friend Leonard Bernstein. Rose recalls a near-disastrous incident in front of the audience and for listeners to the radio broadcast during this performance. All was well, but not without some embarrassment to the cellist:

> I used to have a habit: ... holding the bow in my left hand and holding it there as I wait for the orchestra to play its

interlude. ... When [Bernstein] gave a sweeping upbeat to the violins, his baton caught my bow in between the stick and the hair pulling it out of my hand. ... We were on the air. ... I hadn't the faintest idea whether or not my bow was broken, but it sure sailed about ten feet into the audience. I had, like a schmuck, to get up off the chair, in front of the audience, and go and get my bow. Fortunately, the bow was all right. But if you want to know things that can tend to take a couple of years off one's life, it's times like this under very trying circumstances.

The *New York Times* lauded him in general and his execution of the concerto. Despite this, the cellist chose not to champion the work and never performed it again. According to Howard Taubman, "He always had the technical skills as well as the musicianship; and in recent seasons, he has achieved freedom as an interpreter. His playing of the Barber Concerto had the big singing tone as of old; it had, in addition, an appealing ease and flexibility. Mr. Rose's performance, which proclaimed him a cellist of the first order ...." *Herald Tribune* critic Francis D. Perkins wrote, "... quite a lot of it lies in the cello's higher regions, but Mr. Rose is not the kind of cellist whose tone is tenuous or whining in this register; here [Rose's tone] had an appealing, delicately hued timbre, while lyric warmth of the lower notes was persuasively illustrated in the poetic andante."

The solo cellist always carried a large number of concertos from the repertoire he could perform on a moment's notice. The week prior to the demanding Barber Concerto performances in Carnegie Hall, he played the Saint-Saëns Concerto and Bloch's "Schelomo" with the Kalamazoo Symphony in Michigan under the direction of Dr. Herman Felber, who was in his final year of a 25-year helm. The local paper noted: "[Rose's] submergence in the music he presents is complete. Masterful technique, profound understanding, and a musical sense of amazing proportions give breadth and depth to his interpretations."

As Rose aged, his engagements increased in intensity and his fees escalated.* A reporter inquired about how much repertoire he carried at one time. He relates:

> S. HUROK presents
> **Leonard Rose**
>
> "PURE GOLD... A MASTER CELLIST."
> —NEW YORK TIMES
>
> "THE MOST SUCCESSFUL AMERICAN-BORN CELLIST!"
> —ERICSON, N. Y. TIMES

Oddly enough, I once asked the same question of Casals, when I chatted with him in Israel in 1973 at the King David Hotel. He told me, to my utter amazement, that his repertoire consisted of one recital program and two concerti. I usually keep at least two recital programs and up to six concerti under my fingers—plus, of course, such standard warhorses as the Brahms "Double" and Strauss *Don Quixote*, just in case.

---

* He earned a respectable $7,000 (equivalent to nearly $18,300 in 2008) for a two- to three-concert week with orchestra in the 1980s (Anderson: Seeking Perfection: The Life and Career of Leonard Rose). Rose left Columbia Artists in 1969-1970 to sign with Sol Hurok. Hurok Management ultimately became ICM, who booked Rose for the remainder of his life.

Rose's dominance on the solo circuit hardly ebbed in the 1960s and 1970s. Critical reaction continued to glorify his stature: "Rose has a tone to match his technique and musicianship—the ideal cello tone, in fact. It is naturally large and never forced; it has nobility, a silkiness and as many hues as a rainbow," wrote Walter Arlen in a February 1966 *Los Angeles Times* article about a recital at UCLA's Royce Hall in a program of Martinu: Sonata No. 2, Bach: Suite No. 3, Schumann: Fantasy Pieces Op. 73, and Brahms: Sonata, Op. 99. He "put on the kind of authoritative musical show that was absolutely convincing … the outcome was perfect cooperation," Joan Reinthaler reported in the *Washington Post* about a 1972 recital with pianist David Golub at the Rockville, Maryland Jewish Community Center where they performed Beethoven: A Major Sonata, Boccherini: Sonata No. 6, Bruch: *Kol Nidrei*, Martinu: Sonata No. 2 and Tchaikovsky: "Variations on a Rococo Theme."

By age 52, with a trip to Fairbanks, Alaska, Leonard Rose boasted in his 20 years of solo work, he had performed in every one of the 50 states.[169]

Leonard Rose with the Israel Philharmonic June 1963 Performing Dvořák's Cello Concerto; Zubin Mehta conducting.

Chapter Fifteen

Rose's Discoveries

I am fundamentally a Romanticist, and cannot feign any great interest in the intriguing sounds or exciting new aural parameters that some of today's composers produce. I question whether these works will ever stand the test of time the way Beethoven or Brahms have.

—Leonard Rose[170]

In his memoir, Rose made his likes and dislikes known. It suited the romanticist to focus on the standard concerto repertoire, the bulk of which dated from the Romantic era. And with his busy schedule and uncompromising expectations, he felt he lacked the time to do justice to contemporary works. He earned the distinction of America's first cellist through the familiar music that concertgoers came to love from visiting European performers. Moreover, in the mid-century, the nation's audiences tended to share Rose's preferences. His opposite number, Mstislav Rostropovich, during this period in Soviet Russia, began presenting what would become a lifetime 150 premieres—more than any cellist in the instrument's 400-year history. Rostropovich, nine years younger than Rose, needed and relished close contact with compatriots Shostakovich, Prokofiev, Kabalevsky, Khachaturian, Miaskovsky, Boris Tchaikovsky, Tishenko, Vainberg, and others, to excel in his studies as composer and conductor in addition to his intense practice on the cello and piano. Rose's experience at Curtis had not similarly exposed him to living composers. Yet when he committed himself to learn a contemporary work, his accomplishments and the critical response were extraordinary.

The composers he regularly encountered belonged to the Juilliard faculty. Initially self-taught, Peter Mennin[171] (1923-1983) started writing for orchestra at 11 years old and completed his first symphony before the age of 19. Four years later, Mennin's Third Symphony satisfied his PhD requirement at the Eastman School of Music, where he studied with Howard Hanson (1896-1981), one of the country's notable composers, critics, and school administrators. The New York Philharmonic performed the work the following year, catapulting him to national success that led directly to the youth's appointment to the composition faculty at the Juilliard School.

Tough artistic and administrative challenges lay ahead for Mennin, who became Juilliard's president in 1962, a post he held for an unprecedented 21 years until his premature death. He oversaw the establishment of the school's home at Lincoln Center and was responsible for the creation of Juilliard's Drama Department as well as a permanent program for conductors. In his roles of working musician and academic bureaucrat, he chaired the National Music Council and served on ASCAP's board of directors. Simultaneously, the prodigious composer developed his own densely contrapuntal, modernist voice, ultimately leaving a legacy of 30 major compositions including nine symphonies and concertos for piano, flute – and cello.

Six years before his appointment to Juilliard's presidency, the school commissioned him to write a composition to celebrate its 50th anniversary. Upon receiving the commission for the 1956 Festival, he immediately decided to craft a large-scale work for Leonard Rose. Rose and the Juilliard Orchestra premiered the Concerto for Violoncello and Orchestra with Jean Morel on the podium.* The composer made ample use of the instrument's lyrical qualities and of virtuosic capabilities—both catered to Rose's strengths.

The opening *Allegro moderato* bears a resemblance to one of his symphonies, with the orchestra engaged in polyphonic content until the cello enters with a long, plaintive melody.

---

* The CD accompanying this book features this premiere.

Various combinations ensue, culminating to an extended brilliant cadenza. The second movement, *Adagio*, contains some of Mennin's most poignantly soaring and melancholy music enhanced, in performance, by Rose's gorgeous sound, in its prime. The final *Allegro* is fierce and full of technical hurdles. Rose repeatedly referred to this movement's "nasty passages," which triggered initial doubts that he could do the work justice.

"I'm frankly becoming frightened," Rose wrote to the composer in November of 1955. "The last movement is God damned hard, and I fear that with only such a short time to the performance and so little time. ... I don't know if I can give a first-class performance. For a piece of this degree of difficulty, I should have been practicing it all summer for a performance in February, and in New York too." His panic was unnecessary: the cellist fluently played every note in performance.

Even though the experience of working with a composer was a rare occurrence in Rose's life, it no doubt contributed to shaping a better-rounded musician. While on tour, Rose kept up a close correspondence with Mennin, in which the composer sent corrections—tinkering on the work in-progress—and the soloist made suggestions. In his reiteration about the concerto's challenging passages, he peculiarly inquired about any influence his colleague Luigi Silva might have had on the composer. Silva, perhaps best known for his fiendish cello études, obsessed over near-impossible feats, according to Rose; all three men rubbed shoulders at Juilliard.

Rose rarely spoke as candidly about himself as when he wrote Mennin, "I'm a slow learner" and required long periods of time over which "to digest music, especially in such large form."[172] Indeed, to "digest" music, Rose leaned heavily upon repetition in practice, committing early on to perform from memory. The composer replied immediately to a hotel address where the touring soloist was staying, and Rose took comfort in the encouraging words. In fact, Rose's dark mood and lack of confidence lifted within two weeks. Mennin provided some easier options, and welcomed input from the man for whom the concerto was designed. Apart from the difficulty, Rose gained a deeper understanding of the work itself. In between concert dates in Montana and Arizona, Rose practiced the piece, and came around to appreciating the reason for its frenetic speed, "its restlessness very much reflects the nervous, hectic times in which we live."[173]

As soon as Rose felt mastery of the "nasty passages," he grew fond of the composition. He wrote Mennin, citing specific "brilliantly and marvelously written" sections.

Rose's public premiere was first-rate; the reviews reflected the concerto's demands and his consummate effort to meet them. The next morning, *New York Times* critic Howard Taubman reported:

> ... Mr. Mennin's concerto belongs to a different order of approach. His lyricism, particularly in the slow movement, has more direct appeal. He uses the cello in this movement to advantage, for he is mindful of the fact that it is a rich, singing instrument.... Mr. Mennin seems to go out of his way to prove his modernism by requiring the cello to play high up in moments of the cadenza for no apparent musical reason. ... Leonard Rose was a brilliant performer....

Also on February 11, 1956, musicologist Paul Henry Lang wrote in the *Herald Tribune:*

> Mr. Mennin's cello concerto is the work of a young man. ... I found the work filled with pleasant youthful élan; it is always melodious, yet nowhere does the composer fall victim to the double jeopardy of expressive melody played on a high cello. ... At a few spots, impetuosity got the better of the composer and the piece became a bit "climactic," but this is a fine score. ... Mr. Rose elicits a beautiful tone from his cello and plays with an easy fluency that is a pleasure to hear.

The *New Yorker* magazine weighed in with its assessment in its February 18 issue. The publication's critic found the concerto's idiom baffling, but conceded it "at least fresh enough to keep me guessing—I could not figure out immediately what sort of formulas he was using." The "virtuoso brilliance and dramatic fervor" came from the performer Leonard Rose.

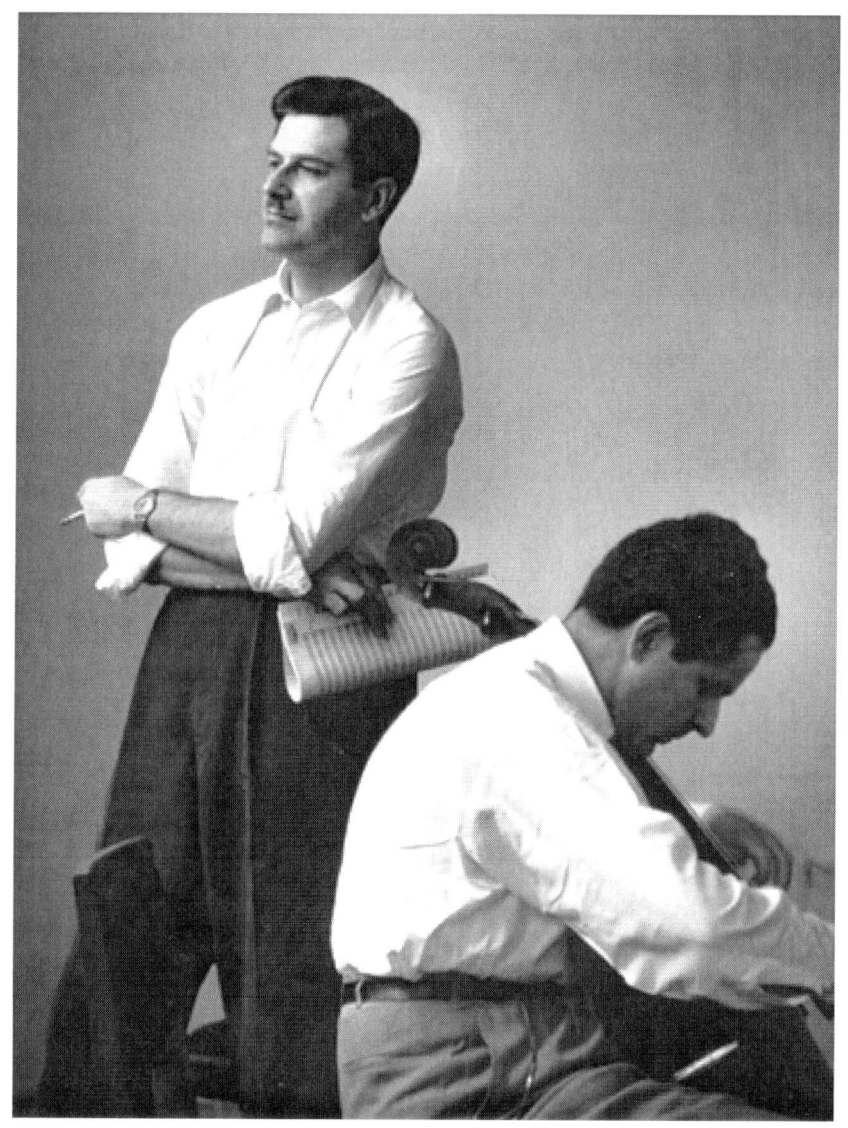

Peter Mennin   Leonard Rose 1956
Courtesy of Georganne Mennin

    The cellist performed the Mennin concerto on two other occasions that same year—November 2 and 3, 1956—with the Cincinnati Symphony Orchestra under the baton of American conductor Thor Johnson (1913-1975), music director of the orchestra from 1947 to 1958 and, along with Leonard Bernstein, among the first protégés of Koussevitzky at Tanglewood Music Center.

Rose never recorded or again performed this concerto—perhaps due to the complexity it presented to him, or to audiences. In the middle of the twentieth century, American composers were on the cusp of branching out into a multiplicity of styles. However, Peter Mennin remained rooted in a particularly knotty modernism that some concertgoers shunned. Management and performers alike shied away from programming such pieces, as a single composition could result in audience members canceling their subscriptions.

Janos Starker—the cellist against whom Rose held a perplexing personal grudge—in 1969 added Mennin to his repertoire. No doubt to Rose's vexation, his nemesis made the concerto's premiere recording with the Louisville Orchestra led by Jorge Mester. Another decade later, the rivalry ever more heated, Starker answered a query about Mennin and why he learned the challenging work. Clearly he admired and enjoyed the concerto and its idiom more than Rose initially did, yet unbeknownst to Rose, gave full credit to his predecessor for assistance in the learning process. "When [the] concerto first came to my attention, I had the advantage of listening to a first-rate performance of it by Leonard Rose."[174]

Leonard Rose appeared more than a dozen times in beloved standard repertoire as soloist with the New York Philharmonic before he chose to commission a new concerto by cellist and colleague Alan Shulman. On April 13, 1950, the New York Philharmonic with conductor Dimitri Mitropoulos and Rose premiered Shulman's Cello Concerto in Carnegie Hall.*

Shulman (1915-2002), a Baltimore native, received his early musical education at the Peabody Conservatory. Aside from his stint in the U.S. Maritime Service—from November 1942 to October 1945—he spent his life in New York City from the age of 13. In America's musical mecca, the Philharmonic-Symphony Society awarded him a fellowship in 1929; and in 1932, the

---

* The CD accompanying the present book includes the second performance from the following night.

Juilliard School of Music gave him a scholarship to study cello with Felix Salmond and composition with Bernard Wagenaar. Upon graduation in 1937, he joined the NBC Symphony under Toscanini as a charter member. Around this time, the cellist took lessons with Emanuel Feuermann and cofounded the Stuyvesant String Quartet.[175]

Leonard Rose Dimitri Mitropoulos Allan Shulman 1950
Courtesy of Jay Shulman

Shulman left a legacy of some 15 works scored for one up to eight cellos. He used the compositions for multiple cellos as teaching material in the seminars he organized for younger players. The cellist-composer began work on the concerto for his colleague in Oquossoc, Maine, in the summer of 1946, and finished it in New York City toward the end of April 1948. Wrapping up the work followed soon after the establishment of the independent state of Israel (May 14, 1948). The concerto has a Hebraic feeling, especially in its opening movement, and the composer dedicated it "to the people of Israel."

The first of the concerto's three movements opens with a cadenza and is highly emotive in character, with many distinctions of mood and intensity. The second movement, *vivace,* is designed to move, as Shulman writes, "at a terrific clip." The third movement—based, with the exception of the second theme, entirely on materials from the first movement—provides an epilogue, a summation of the work as a whole. Through its retrospective features, it "achieves peace and philosophical maturity, in contrast to the intensity of the first two movements—as if, Shulman explains, "it were my own private *Aus meinem Leben*" ("from my life," identifying the work as autobiographical).

The scoring calls for a relatively small orchestra. The composer describes the piece as "a cello concerto accompanied by the orchestra rather than a cello concerto against the orchestra." At 32 years of age, Rose performed the work with supreme artistry, as Virgil Thomson reported in the next day's *Herald Tribune*:

> ... Alan Shulman's Cello Concerto, which Mr. Rose played ever so beautifully, is a meditation about the Jewish people. Its lines are chromatic and return on themselves in the Near East style. Its harmony is lachrymose, but solid withal. Its colors are dark and a little muddy, but sometimes they glow. The cello writing is that of a professional, and the scoring is admirably calculated to throw the solo instrument into relief. This is a personal work full of feeling....

On April 14, 1950, Olin Downes of the *New York Times* concurred: "He [Rose] played superbly, with a cantilena as noble as the music permitted and with bravura, authority, and élan. The composer, later called to the stage, must surely have approved the interpretation.

In the *New York World Telegram and Sun* critic Louis Biancolli wrote:

> "... It is a beautiful piece of music, this concerto, poetically moulded, and rich in genuine feeling. Leonard Rose made each measure of the solo part say something good and true, and the orchestra rallied to its first cellist in warm and friendly style."

In 1959, Rose was among ten performers[*] chosen from 450 applicants to initiate compositional commissions from Ford Foundation grants totaling $130,000.[176] A panel of seven determined the final group and the winners themselves selected the composers. Perhaps in gratitude to the president of Juilliard, William Schuman (1910-1992) became Rose's choice. The terms of the funding dictated Rose complete seven performances with orchestra of the work—*A Song of Orpheus* composed in 1960-1961. He commercially recorded *A Song of Orpheus* with the Cleveland Orchestra conducted by George Szell on January 11, 1964, at Severance Hall.

Rose recalled in his memoir how impossible it was to get new works programmed after their premieres. "Like most contemporary works," Rose said, "it is fiendishly difficult. I actually kept the piece on my repertoire list for the next five years, but absolutely no conductor requested it. Eventually, I simply had to drop the composition."

William Schuman, born in New York City in 1910, became one of this country's most distinguished academic composers and administrators. Following study at Columbia University and with composer Roy Harris, he joined the faculty of Sarah Lawrence College in Bronxville, New York, in 1935. Ten years later, he assumed the dual responsibilities of director of publications for G. Schirmer, Inc. and president of the Juilliard School. During the 1940s, Schuman received his first of numerous honorary doctorates and the first Pulitzer Prize ever given in the field of musical composition. At Juilliard 18 years, his tenure was significant for the establishment of the Juilliard String Quartet and for the thorough overhaul of the teaching department. From 1962 to 1969, Schuman served as president of Lincoln Center for the Performing Arts, a period that saw the completion of that preeminent complex.

William Schuman was a prominent spokesman and advisor for the arts as a consultant to CBS, the Rockefeller Foundation, Broadcast Music, Inc., and the MacDowell Colony among others—

---

[*] Others notable artist/composer collaborations included Michael Rabin/Paul Creston, Leon Fleisher/Leon Kirchner, Joseph Fuchs/Walter Piston, Jacob Lateiner/Elliott Carter and Adele Addison/Lukas Foss.

while remaining active as a composer. A strict and methodical work schedule enabled him to produce an enormous amount of music for a man who wore many hats: Ten symphonies; works for piano, violin, horn, cello, and viola; five ballets and an opera; several pieces for concert band and orchestra; two dozen choral works; and numerous chamber music scores.

On September 28, 1962, the Juilliard Orchestra[*] and conductor Jean Morel presented a concert as part of the inaugural week celebrations of Philharmonic Hall at the Lincoln Center. The program included the New York premiere *A Song of Orpheus: Fantasy for Violoncello and Orchestra,* with Leonard Rose as soloist.[177] Schuman's notes elucidated:

> The song, *Orpheus with His Lute,* upon which this Fantasy is based, was composed in 1944 for a production of Shakespeare's Henry VIII. ... I was searching for an idea for the work I had agreed to compose for Leonard Rose. All the music grows out of the melodic line of the song, which is stated at the very beginning of the composition. The words of the song are written in the cello part in order to enable the soloist to perform the melody with the clarity of a singer's projection.

The composer requested that Shakespeare's text be printed in the concert program books or, if this is not possible, recited before the work is performed. Knowing the words should enhance listening pleasure. In 1989, William Schuman received this country's highest achievement award—A Kennedy Center Honor—for an extraordinary lifetime of contributions to American culture.

Twelve years after its premiere, Leonard Rose performed Samuel Barber's Cello Concerto[**] January 29, 30, and 31, 1959,

---

[*] The orchestra's roster included: violinists Donald Weilerstein, Earl Carlyss and Paul Zukofsky; cellists Stephen Kates, Robert Sylvester and André Emelianoff; bass players Gary Karr and Julius Levine; flutist Paula Robison and pianist James Levine. The work is scored for strings, woodwinds and harp.

[**] The piece received the Music Critics Circle of New York's annual award citing it as, "exceptional among orchestra compositions performed for the first time in New York City during the concert season."

with the New York Philharmonic conducted by Leonard Bernstein. The 1945 work, infrequently heard in Rose's lifetime, received its premiere in April 1946, by Raya Garbousova with the Boston Symphony Orchestra under Serge Koussevitzky. The following season, Garbousova played the concerto with the Philharmonic and Dimitri Mitropoulos. Rose, the principal cellist, soaked it up, an eyewitness to Garbousova's lucid talent and the appeal of the concerto.

On a $1,000 commission (equivalent to nearly $12,000 in 2008) from Koussevitzky, who financially promoted countless U.S. composers—as well as Garbousova's career since her American debut in 1935—Barber set out to craft this work in January 1945. Sessions with the cellist, who superbly demonstrated the instrument's range, aided his progress. A leading cellist of her day, Garbousova had an exceptional technique and played for the composer parts of cello concertos by Carl Davidov[178] (with whom she studied), and virtuoso showpieces by Duport, Popper, and Piatti. Some believe the concerto's challenging nature mirrors those encounters. Lynn Harrell, who first performed the Barber Concerto at age 60 admits, "I was afraid of it for a long time.... There are a few passages that are more difficult than in any other work for cello." Furthermore, Harrell is captivated: "Artistically, musically, *aesthetically*, it is much deeper than I thought at first. Technically, it is very daunting. Yet, it is a wonderful vehicle for the instrument and good for the orchestra. It has drama and a sense of lyricism and power that is absolutely intoxicating, and I think it should be played a lot more."[179]

Barber described his new work as "lyric and romantic with, however, some of the vivacity and rhythmic tension of 'Capricorn.'"[180] The first movement is noteworthy for its delicate interweaving of melodies between cello and orchestra and for its dazzling mid-movement cadenza. The concerto's slow movement spins a striking melody supported by muted orchestral strings. The finale, powerful and passionate, contains a haunting and dirge-like second theme that, according to a letter obtained by Barber's biographer Barbara B. Heyman, registers the composer's response to the first atomic bomb exploded over Hiroshima on August 6, 1945. It is believed that Barber, soon after the event, discarded parts of the movement, adding these sections in a minor key. The emotional content of these solemn passages gives some credibility to this assertion.[181]

Critic and composer Virgil Thomson was taken with the work:

> It is full of thought about musical expression in general and about the possibility for musical expression of the violoncello in particular. It is full of ingenious orchestral devices for accompanying the instrument without drowning it; and it is full of reasonably good tunes. ... The working up of these into a richly romantic, well-sustained structure is musical, masterful, thoughtful, and not without a certain Brahms-like grandeur.[182]

Sometime during 1947, Barber revised the concerto, altering balances he believed faulty. This revised score was published in 1950 and recorded in London the same year under the baton of the composer. Zara Nelsova (born Sarah Nelson) was the soloist on the recording with Barber; neither Garbousova[183] nor Rose—a situation that might have propelled the work and potentially altered Rose's career path—were chosen. The accompanying ensemble was the New Symphony Orchestra. During the recording, a weird incident occurred, which Barber described in a letter to his family:

> Nelsova ended with such brilliance that a cello player leapt up from the cello section onto the stage, screamed something about "giving up playing the cello after playing such as hers," took his cello and smashed it in a thousand pieces on the side of the stage, in full view of us all, bridge, fingerboard, and strings flying in all directions. There was a general howl from the orchestra, Nelsova turned pale, and then we realized that it was a joke engineered by the cello section as a compliment to the difficulty of the concerto: each man contributed a crown toward buying a two-pound cello in a pawnshop in order to smash it! Who but the English would have thought of such a prank?[184]

The concerto's reputation (along with Prokofiev's 1952 Sinfonia Concertante, which Rose never performed) continues as one of the most challenging in the cello literature. Similar to each twentieth-century work he endeavored to learn, Rose was unhappy with the amount of time needed to perfecting the cello score. He never played it again after the sensational performances with Leonard Bernstein in Carnegie Hall in early 1959.

Rose may not have contributed to the ascendancy of Barber's reputation among the finest American music for cello. However, Rose's students—Yo-Yo Ma, Ronald Leonard, Michael Grebanier, Jules Eskin, Paul Tobias, and Lynn Harrell—did so in his stead.* The breakthrough recording that launched the popularization of the work occurred in 1989 with Yo-Yo Ma as soloist with the Baltimore Symphony Orchestra, under David Zinman. In 1981, Ronald Leonard—the only other cellist besides Garbousova—performed it with the Los Angeles Philharmonic (Leonard reprised it in 1998). Jules Eskin's rendition in 1998 was the first since her premiere with the Boston Symphony; and Michael Grebanier's 1992 interpretation is the only on record with the San Francisco Symphony.

Thirty years after Rose's Barber performances, Paul Tobias resurrected the work as soloist with the New York Philharmonic. In addition, Tobias wrote passionately and persuasively, swaying cellists of his generation on the subject of the concerto's merit in publications such as *The Strad, Strings* and *Journal of the Conductor's Guild*; Tobias likewise recorded the work in 2003. Lynn Harrell's 2005 version with the National Symphony Orchestra introduced the work to Washington, DC, audiences. Through recordings and live performances—alongside sparkling performances by Lorne Munroe (1992, NY Philharmonic), Carter Brey (2005, NY Philharmonic), Steven Isserlis, Ralph Kirshbaum, Raphael Wallfisch, and other younger virtuosos—the Barber

---

* As well as the author, with Concertante di Chicago and in Idaho with the Sun Valley Symphony in 1999.

Cello Concerto has attained its deserved status as one of the great concertos in the repertoire.*

A twentieth-century composition, albeit an early conservative one, was a Rose signature piece throughout his career: Ernest Bloch's "Schelomo," Hebraic Rhapsody for Cello and Orchestra. A sensation from its inception, Bloch created the concerto-like composition just two years prior to the cellist's birth. Rose performed the work countless times and recorded it twice: as mentioned, in April 1951 at age of 32 with the Philharmonic-Symphony Orchestra of New York under Dimitri Mitropoulos, then 10 years later with the Philadelphia Orchestra with Eugene Ormandy.

Dutch-born cellist Hans Kindler (1892-1949), the founding conductor of the National Symphony Orchestra in Washington, DC, premiered "Schelomo" May 3, 1917, under the direction of the composer. Written during the Swiss-born American's self-proclaimed "Jewish Cycle" (1912-1926), the tone poem is built upon legendary King Solomon who reigned over Israel from 971 BCE to 931 BCE. According to Bloch, the cello—representing King Solomon's voice—portrays the ruler's extraordinary wisdom, wealth, and power. In the Philadelphia Orchestra's program book for Kindler's 1922 performance, the critic who wrote program notes for the New York Philharmonic Society and Philadelphia Orchestra, Lawrence Gilman, defined the effect this story had upon a listener:

> The violoncellist and the seconding orchestra are, by turns, lyricist and tragedian, poet and seer. The great king—amid his gorgeousness—reflecting in disillusionment upon his silver and his gold, the treasures of his provinces, the abundance of his gardens and his orchards, the fulfilled desires of his heart and eyes; and the Preacher, somber and mournful in his acrid wisdom, uttering bitter admonitions as he contemplates the

---

* Inexplicably, the Rose era's prolific cellists—Casals, Piatigorsky, Rostropovich, Fournier, Tortelier, Starker and Du Pré avoided the concerto. The work has never been programmed with the Cleveland Orchestra and not since Garbousova's 1949 and 1952 appearance, with the Chicago Symphony Orchestra.

vanishing mist that is all delight, the sorrowing echoes of beauty and splendor. ... in the final descent into the depths, the brooding of the violoncello filling the music with the darkness of shut doors and shadowed windows resolving dust.

Although Zara Nelsova recorded the work under Bloch's direction, many musicians and critics of the day declared that no cellist grasped, performed, and recorded "Schelomo" as compellingly as Leonard Rose.

Rose performed a few major works of his century beyond his own country. In a comfortable, conservative musical idiom, he performed Dimitri Kabalevsky's Cello Concerto No. 1, Op. 49, but somewhat radically, did so in 1955 at the height of the Cold War. The concerto, dedicated to the children of the USSR, received its U.S. premiere two years earlier by Rose's friend and colleague Samuel Mayes, with the composer conducting. In three movements, the concerto is largely a quiet work with very few moments of "loud" music. The opening theme returns toward the end of the 20-minute concerto with a dazzling display of cello virtuosity. The concerto has been praised for its "disciplined and brilliant architecture."[185]

Learning some contemporary works seemed experimental to Rose. The Kabalevsky mattered little to him. No existing documents indicate that he performed or even taught this concerto after 1955. It begs the question, why did Leonard Rose choose to perfect and to perform the Russian composition? Possibly his good friend, Samuel Mayes, convinced him of the work's merit. It is likely the cellist quickly realized the work, more nationalistic than contemporary, did not match his romantic persona.

On November 13, 1950, pianist Nadia Reisenberg, violinist Joseph Fuchs and Leonard Rose presented the New York premiere of Alfredo Casella's Concerto for Trio and Orchestra (world premiere occurred in Berlin, November 17, 1933) with the Little Orchestra Society* at Town Hall, with Thomas Scherman as conductor.

---

* The Little Orchestra Society was founded in October 1947, with the mission of presenting concerts to audiences of all ages and all economic levels. The

Alfredo Casella forged a unique path in music as a pianist, conductor, composer, director, and writer on music. Many of his articles were published in Italy, France, Russia, Germany, and America. Born in Turin, Italy, in 1883, he studied composition with Gabriel Fauré at the Conservatory in Paris.

Casella spent a good deal of time guest conducting. He appeared with orchestras in Chicago, Detroit, Cincinnati, Cleveland, and Los Angeles; his American debut in 1921 with the Philadelphia Orchestra displayed his talents as conductor, composer, and pianist. Casella conducted the Boston Pops from 1927 to 1929. The Philadelphia's Musical Fund Society acknowledged his gifts with a substantial award in 1928, and later the Coolidge Prize.[186]

In the United States in the 1920s, Casella made an unfortunate decision to return to Fascist Italy, where he remained until his death. Yet he appeared oblivious to much of what Fascism advocated. In fact, Casella married a French Jew and supported the music of Arnold Schoenberg—a Jewish modernist whose music was labeled "degenerate" by the Third Reich.

The Italian's Concerto for Trio and Orchestra falls into his neoclassicist period, likely influenced by Igor Stravinsky. Neither does Rose mention this premiere in his memoir nor does he speak of any acquaintance with Casella. The concerto and its composer seemingly exited Rose's repertoire as quickly as it entered.

---

ensemble continues to perform and abide by its philosophy under Dino Anagnost's leadership.

Chapter Sixteen

LUSTROUS 1662 AMATI CELLO

According to Messrs. William E. Hill & Sons this is one of three Nicolò Amati violoncellos which has not been reduced in size.
—*The Strad*, September 1951

    In 1952, Leonard Rose acquired a rare 1662 Nicolò Amati instrument,[187] one of just a handful of cellos known by this violinmaker. The famous luthier, Rembert Wurlitzer,[188] from whom the cellist bought it, proclaimed it one of the finest Cremonese instruments that ever passed through his hands. For the next 32 years, Leonard Rose and his Amati became synonymous with exquisite beauty, passion, and power.
    Violoncellos were created as early as the mid-1500s. These six-string, larger precursors to today's cellos possessed sizable bass timbres; some of them constructed by Andrea Amati (1525-1611, Nicolò's grandfather). As custom dictated through much of the 17th century, most of these early cellos had a small hole drilled in the center of the back near the top to insert a peg that held a cord or chain to pass around the player's shoulders, enabling the violoncellist to play while standing. In these times, a player seldom needed to ascend higher than the second or third positions on the fingerboard. So standing did not inhibit technique. The preferred bass stringed instrument, at this time, remained the six-stringed viola da gamba, which Bach notably composed for.

The Romans founded Cremona, Italy, long associated with violinmaking, in 218 B.C. Because of its proximity to the Po River, the city became an important center for trade and industry. Andrea Amati, who was the first of four generations who crafted string instruments, is considered the founder of the Cremona School[189] of which Stradivarius takes celebrity status. Certain Cremona traditions have remained, like an adherence to strict guidelines as to the size of the instrument, some unique tools have predominated, types of wood have not changed, the method of varnish application preserved, and substance of the varnish, as mysterious and secretive 350 years ago as it is today. In Amati's day, orders for many instruments besides violins and cellos abounded, which included lutes, viols, viola da gambas, violoncelli da spallas, citterns, citoles, guitars, and harps.

As throughout Europe, church records kept at that time are the basis of much of our understanding of the Amati family. Since the 1530s, the family had been connected to the Church of S. Faustino e Giovita built in 1126 and located in central Cremona on what is today the Via Guarneri del Gesu (the street named like others in town for its illustrious luthiers). Record keeping began in earnest around 1585. Through these records, researchers uncovered a timeline of baptisms, confirmations, marriages, burials, and family registries, which have led to a better understanding of the history of violinmaking.[190] In some instances, due to missing records, particular assumptions have been made.

In 1630, a devastating plague descended on all of what is now Italy, taking with it much of its population: the wealthy and poor, bishops and magistrates, and some well-known instrument artisans. Girolamo Amati (one of Andrea Amati's sons) and his wife were among the dead.* Cremona emerged a ghost town with two-thirds of its population perished, but the distinguished 34-year-old luthier Nicolò Amati survived. From 1630 until 1641, due to the impact of the epidemic and rebuilding of life in and around Cremona, records from the *Stati d'Anime* ("State of Souls") Church were lost. During these critical years, it has

---

* It is believed that Alessandro Stradivarius (father of Antonio) fled before devastation hit the town.

been deduced that contrary to common practice, the workshop of Nicolò Amati filled with apprentices who were not family members, rather trainees from outside the family who flourished under his guidance. In other words, Amati's assistants descended not from the Cremonese—with the exception of Giacomo Gennaro. Some outsiders were future masters in their own right: Andrea Guarneri, Giovanni Battista, and Francesco Ruger.[191]

By 1644, the 48-year-old Amati developed a "grand pattern"— an instrument with new measurements capable of producing a more powerful sound that contributed to the emergence of the modern violin. This discovery would aid the development of the cello, albeit more slowly, as a prodigious instrument as well. As chamber music in the Baroque period developed (chiefly in Italy and Germany), composers began writing more for the violin virtuoso. There were significant contributions from the extraordinary Italian violinist and prolific composer Arcangelo Corelli (1653-1713), considered the founder of modern violin technique, admired in his day as Paganini, Heifetz, or Perlman were in their day. Antonio Vivaldi—composer of the ubiquitous "Four Seasons" who studied violin with Corelli—Georg Friedrich Händel, and Johann Sebastian Bach all emulated Corelli in their life's work. In 1719, German composer Georg Philipp Telemann (1681-1767) enhanced the violin repertoire with a dedication of a collection of violin concertos to the *Konzermeister* and virtuoso Pisendel. During his lifetime, the famous Italian violinist, teacher and composer Giuseppe Tartini (1692-1770, whose style of bowing still serves as a model for all violinists) composed more than 130 concerti and 170 sonatas for the instrument. Yet another example was the Italian, Pietro Antonio Locatelli (1695-1764), who wrote the *Art of the Violin* in 1733 in addition to composing 12 violin concerti and 24 caprices.

Amati resided in an enormous house by 1645 with his wife, relatives and servants—10 in all. Questionable and still unsolved today places Antonio Stradivarius in the area and an apprentice to Amati. Even though they had some of the worst-kept records in Cremona, historians have deduced that Stradivarius was living in the Parish of S. Cecilia. When Antonio married Francesca, who lived four houses away from the Amatis in 1665, there is no concrete evidence that he actually became an apprentice to

Amati, which would have meant—as custom dictated—he would reside in Amati's home. Toby Faber posits an intriguing theory in his book *Stradivari's Genius*. Although Stradivarius's earliest known violin, which dates from 1666, bears the label "Antonius Stradivarius Cremonensis Alumnus Nicolaii Amati, Faciebat Anno 1666" (Made by Antonio Stradivarius of Cremona, pupil of Nicolò Amati, in 1666). Faber claims: "it would have been natural, if a little cheeky, for the young Stradivarius to paste a label in his early experiments that overplayed his link with the great Amati, and equally natural for the older Luthier to demand that he drop the reference the moment he found out about it." In support of his theory, Stradivarius's violin one year later abandons any reference on its label to Amati. Faber contends that between 1667 and 1680, Stradivarius lived in Casa Nuziale, owned by the woodcarver and inlayer Francesco Pescaroli. Could Stradivarius have originally been a woodworker and hired by Amati to decorate some of his famous violins? His expertise in this area is obvious in the ornate, black volutes, flowers, dragons, and snakes carved into the sides of some of his own instruments between 1679 and 1700.

When Leonard Rose was 17, his patron bought him a Tecchler* cello for $5,000 with the understanding that he would reimburse the Curtis Institute, at his convenience. When Rose became solo cellist with the New York Philharmonic while playing this Tecchler, it became apparent that he required a better, bigger-sounding instrument. One day an acquaintance, Gerald Warburg, the son of a prominent international banking family,[192] who took a few lessons with Emanuel Feuermann and owned both a Stradivarius cello and a Goffriller cello, invited Rose up to his studio to see his instruments. Rose recalls:

---

* Rose's Tecchler dated from 1711. Very little is known about the Roman maker, David Tecchler (1666-1748). It was formerly thought that he came from Salzburg, but new research suggests that it's more likely he originated from Augsburg, or perhaps Lechbruck, near Füssen. His original name was probably Dechler, Deschler or Teschler. The first reliable record of his life puts him in Rome in 1696, where he remained until his death. Today, his cellos in particular are highly valued.

He came to the Philharmonic and I got to know him. He said, "Bring your Tecchler over." So I went over with my cello and he brought out his Stradivarius and Goffriller.* I played on both of them. He asked, "How do you like them?" I replied, "I prefer the Goffriller." It had a wonderful dark sound, almost too dark really, but I had been playing on such a light-sounding tenorish instrument. He said, "Look, why don't you leave your Tecchler here and just play on the Goffriller?" I did just that, and when I came back to the Philharmonic, the conductors noticed a difference because it was a richer sounding instrument...

After Rose tested it for two or three months, the season ended. Rose telephoned Warburg and told him that he was in love with the Goffriller. An agitated man recounts the conclusion to his story:

I asked if I could come up to see him to talk about it. He agreed. Incidentally, that studio he had was just for him to practice, and he had a safe for his instruments. A safe for a cello has to be pretty damned big and it was. The studio was beautifully furnished with the most gorgeous antiques I had ever seen. The contrast between my dinky two-bedroom apartment in Forest Hills and the Warburg mansion farther out on the island, his summer home, was quite a shock. Since few people drove during the war years, I took the train out to see him... "Gerald, I think I would like to buy the Goffriller. What, are you asking for it?" He replied, "Well, that cello should bring me $10,000." I told him that I didn't have that kind of money. I was doing quite nicely then and thought I could sell the Tecchler cello for about $5,000, which is what I paid for it. I said to him, "Would you consider letting

---

*Matteo Goffriller (1659-1742) established the Venetian style, distinguished largely by a deep red varnish, which now characteristically shows a crackled and wrinkled finish. His son, Francesco (1692-c.1740) also produced successful instruments, one of which, built in 1733, served Pablo Casals as his concert instrument for over 50 years.

me sell the Tecchler, give you the $5,000, and then pay you $1,000 a year until I pay off the Goffriller?" And this idle millionaire looked at me, and said, "Oh, Leonard, let's have a good clean deal." Imagine—I didn't have a pot to piss in and this guy had pots of gold, and he wanted *a good clean deal*! He was a selfish, insensitive human being ... Well, I guess Gerry never did a day's work in his life, except practice the cello a little bit. The truth is he was a twentieth-rate cellist—not even tenth rate—and was really very ungifted. I finally did buy that instrument; I sold the Tecchler cello for $5,000 and I had to borrow the other $5,000 from a wealthy cousin of mine who lived in Baltimore. My agreement with him was that I would pay him $40 a week out of my New York Philharmonic salary. The Philharmonic would make out two checks each week—one to me minus withholding tax and one in his name, and I sent those checks to him in Baltimore, always with a thank-you note, all to pay for the instrument.

"I wasn't jealous of Gerald Warburg's wealth," Rose's tone softens. But comparing the mansion and its practice studio to his modest home obviously rankled. "I was playing front-line appearances all the time, feverishly trying to practice, getting annoying messages from neighbors ... Living was cramped and I was uptight all the time. I wonder which of us was happier. Who was doing more toward humanity? I daresay that, with his millions, he wasn't doing anything. At least, I was trying to do something. It was tough living in that apartment."

By the time the Italian economy nosedived in the late 18th century, causing the Cremonese violinmakers to go out of business, London-based firm W.E. Hill and Sons already established the first modern violin market specializing in sales of 18th-century instruments from Cremona. Musicians quickly found the Hills' learned eye and opinions about their fine merchandise beyond reproach. One theory the Hills perfectly understood was that even if the wood was expertly crafted and well assembled, the instrument suffered its death if poorly varnished. Today, questions about the varnish used by these masters continuously arouse speculation.

For example, what ingredients produced four generations of the Amati golden-yellow glow? Various fantasy-like theories exist: Could Amati have collected and boiled rainwater with a mix of annatto, potash, and other substances before cooking the brew over an open fire to produce this color? Perhaps he stirred the pot with a piece of maple, the instruments drying for months or even years while soaking up nutrients from the areas abundant olive and citrus trees. Why has Cremonese varnish lasted this beautifully for centuries without obvious deterioration? One theory of longevity points to the use of two separate varnishes. The first, a slow-drying oil-based varnish that penetrated the pores of the wood, giving the instruments much of their color. The overcoat, spirit-based and quicker to dry, contributed further brilliance and color but would also be subject to chipping and wear. In recent times, electron microscopes detected powder between the wood and varnish that has been identified as *Pozzolana* earth, a volcanic ash that is thought to be waterproof. The ash enabled the varnish to harden and homogenize the wood, allowing the instrument to take on polish.[193]

Varnish recipes were notoriously well guarded. David Laurie relates a story about the Parisian luthier, Jean-Baptiste Vuillaume[*] (1798-1875), who earned a fortune by producing masterful copies of Cremonese instruments, especially Stradivarius's. Setting aside Thursdays for the reception of admirers at the rue des Ternes, he sat in public view, applying his varnish to newly constructed violins and selling bottles of the same to any interested customers. Inside his mansion later in the day, a good friend of Vuillaume's, Laurie, witnessed him removing the worthless varnish before it had time to dry. Upon inquiring what he was doing, Vuillaume shot back, "Did you really think I would let my valuable secrets go so easily?"[194]

Perhaps the magic lay in the wood they discovered and carved. At the time, government authorities in Venice tightly controlled wood supplies. If a citizen was caught cutting down

---

[*] Vuillaume's violins won him a silver medal at the 1827 Paris Exhibition and gold followed in 1839 and 1844. He became a famous instrument dealer, responsible for making critical modern updates on instruments. He was equally well known for his exact copies of originals by Amati and Stradivarius. Today, only experts can distinguish Vuillaumes from Stradivarius'.

his favorite maple tree, he could be tossed in jail. Instead, authorized woodcutters felled trees in the highlands, dumping logs into the Po River, where they were carried downstream to the city's center. According to biochemist Joseph Nagyvary,[195] "The Venetian Navy got the best wood for building ships. Only after bureaucrats had taken inventory and assessed taxes could wood merchants buy their supplies—and at this point, the wood had been sitting in water for weeks or even months at a time." Electron micrographs of a handful of shavings from Cremonese instruments reveal residues of bacteria and fungi consistent with wood that sat in water. Using x-ray fluorescence spectroscopy, scientists found the wood slivers to contain unusually large amounts of minerals, including potassium, sodium, aluminum, copper, iron, and especially calcium and magnesium, consistent with Nagyvary's theory. Yet another valid theory asserts a mini Ice Age that reached its peak in Europe between 1645 and 1715 slowed the growth of trees in northern Italy, which resulted in denser wood—which proved handsome, durable, and unusually resonant.

No single instrument from the Cremonese golden age appears today as it did when first crafted. The demand for increased power and brilliance in modern performances required alterations. Bodies have been cut to smaller standards, new and stronger bass bars added, thicker sound posts attached, carbon fiber for tailpieces, their adjusters (both tailpiece and string) and endpins added. Longer and thinner strings made of steel, tungsten, and titanium rather than gut (Rose mentioned the disadvantages of gut strings he used as a student in 1931) are in vogue; and newly angled necks and updated fingerboards have been in use, developed more than 100 years ago. Even the frequency of the A string changed, increasing from about 420 vibrations per second in 1800 to 435 Hertz by the mid-nineteenth century and to as high as 460 Hertz today (an A in Amati's time, therefore, would have sounded a whole step lower today). Miraculously, not only have a portion of these instruments survived wars, pillage, forgery, worms and the test of time,* they have also withstood these

---

* These instruments, however, have not been able to overcome the mutilations performed by so-called expert luthiers. "These ruthless men just sawed off the

severe adaptations. However, with every loss, by catastrophe or encased in glass tombs in museums or whether hopelessly lost in the possession of hoarding family members determined to keep these instruments for as long as possible—robbing us all of their magnificence*—for not turning the instruments back into the pool, these rarefied objects achieve new status. It is no wonder they have been vaulted into million-dollar possessions for businessmen, collectors, and museums alike.

During Rose's European trip in September 1951 with the Philharmonic, he was introduced to Mr. Hill from W.E. Hill and Sons shop. "Oh, Mr. Rose, I know all about you and what a marvelous cellist you are," Rose recalled the luthier saying. Rose asked to see some instruments. "There is one I must show you," quipped Hill, "that would be worthy of an artist like yourself." He took Rose into his back room, dubbed "The Inner Sanctum," and brought out a Nicolò Amati (Alfred Hill owned the cello around 1900 selling it in 1905 to Mr. Kirkhope from Edinburgh). Rose gasped at its beauty. Even though it was strung with strings Rose disliked, he found himself immediately taken by its glorious appearance. "Mr. Hill," Rose asked. "It's absolutely magnificent. How much is it?" He told Rose, "For you, you can have this cello for $10,000 cash." As Rose remembers: "Well, that was like stealing an instrument; but there was one problem. I didn't have 10,000 dollars. I had been so busy paying off other cellos I didn't have 10,000 quarters saved up. I had to say a sad farewell to that cello and went off to Paris and stayed there for a few days before finally sailing home, marking the end of my first trip to Europe."

A year later, Felix Salmond died. His wish was for Rose to inherit his Gofriller cello, which Rose believed possessed a richer sound than his own Gofriller. With precisely that intention, Rose put his instrument up for sale at William Moennig & Son, and had an immediate buyer. According to Rose: "With my Goffriller sold, I began to negotiate with Mrs. Salmond over her late husband's cello. She wanted $20,000, which was way more than

---

top and another off the bottom, and the result is a thing with the inner bout of a giant and the upper and lower bout of a dwarf." Charles Reade wrote in the *Pall Mall Gazette* of 1872.

* Gregor Piatigorsky's two Stradivari cellos, 1714 "Batta" and 1725 "Baudiot", have been out of circulation for over three decades.

I dared spend. Moreover, Simone Sacconi (1895-1973, author of *The 'Secrets' of Stradivari*), instrument repairman and builder, warned me that the scroll was not a Goffriller at all, but was probably made by Carlo Tononi* (1675-1730). He gave a ceiling value of $12,000, which was already $1,000 more than I had."

What followed was a rather uncomfortable sequence of price haggling. Mrs. Salmond went down to $18,000 and despite Sacconi's discovery, Rose went as high as $16,000. But a magnificent cello came into the custody of Wurlitzer who immediately telephoned Rose: "Len, you owe it to yourself to come down to my shop and see what I have." Lo and behold, there was the identical Amati cello Rose had seen in London the year before. It was fate.

Leonard Rose at the Kennedy Center, Washington, DC, 1977
Courtesy of Raymond Scavelli

---

* The loss or destruction of scrolls during transit is not uncommon. A scroll from another maker can significantly lower an instrument's value.

"I have been asked many times," Rose quips, "how I acquired my Amati. My answer is a blunt one: I paid, and paid, and paid ..."

In 1962, in honor of the Amati cello, which turned 300 years old, the Roses hosted a sizable celebration at their home. For those who knew Leonard Rose and his playing on long-playing records, in performance and in his teaching studio, this "Rose" Amati cello will forever be linked to the great American cellist— no matter how far off into the future it survives.[*]

---

[*] The "Rose" Amati (on numerous occasions, the cellist mentions in his unpublished memoir that he hoped the instrument would acquire his name) was sold in 1985 for $375,000 (worth an estimated $1.5 million today [John Montgomery—violin maker, dealer, restorer—8-16-2007] to the prize-winning American cellist Gary Hoffman (b. 1956).

Chapter Seventeen

VISIONARY IVAN GALAMIAN AND HIS MEADOWMOUNT SCHOOL

Ivan Galamian was a virtuoso teacher whose system of teaching was both ingenious and logical. He applied that system to all of his students and it worked, no matter how much or how little talent the student had—a true sign of a great pedagogue.

—Itzhak Perlman[196*]

After joining the faculty of the Philadelphia inner city Curtis Institute in 1944, 41-year-old violinist Ivan Galamian was determined to locate a tranquil summer home—along with 50 student violinists. He found the spot in the picturesque rolling farmland that surround the Adirondack Mountains in upstate New York. There, he purchased 200 acres near Elizabethtown and dubbed this new home the Meadowmount School of Music. Under his guidance, for 37 summers the school became the most successful training ground for world-class violinists. A few of Galamian's stellar alumni include David Nadien (b. 1926), Michael Rabin (1936-1972), Arnold Steinhardt (b. 1937), Erick Friedman (1939-2004), Jaime Laredo (b. 1941), David Cerone (b. 1941), Itzhak Perlman (b. 1945), Miriam Fried (b. 1946), Pinchas

---

* After his fourth of eight summers at Meadowmount, Perlman made his Carnegie Hall debut on March 5, 1963, at age 17. Half his time at the summer camp coincided with Rose's.

Zukerman (b. 1948), Kyung-Wha Chung (b. 1948), Glenn Dicterow (b. 1948), Peter Zazofsky (b. 1954), and Joshua Bell (b. 1967).

In its first years, the program's reputation and popularity gradually grew. To enhance Meadowmount's single-focus curriculum, Galamian expanded its chamber music component and added another string instrument to the instruction offered. He brought two respected artists on board: Leonard Rose first arrived at the camp in 1952 and Joseph Gingold—whom Rose knew well—in 1955. Since 1938, when Gingold was a member of the NBC Symphony with Rose, the two established a special collaboration in chamber music concerts in the summer of 1948 at Colorado College and in 1949, at Utah State College.[197] Gingold would teach violin and chamber music at Meadowmount until Galamian's death in 1981. Those summers at Meadowmount occupied a special place in Rose's life, providing a personal respite and family time, as well as teaching—and surprisingly—learning opportunities.

Born in Tabriz, Persia, (now Iran) on January 23, 1903, Ivan Galamian moved to Russia as a young child. In Moscow, the family struggled under the Bolshevik regime. During the violinist's youth, after Lenin repositioned the government from St. Petersburg to Moscow, families like the once-affluent Galamians were stripped of every one of their belongings. Sundry records indicate that Galamian was held overnight in a jail under the oppressive Communist government for no other reason than this bourgeois status. Galamian's immersion in music, as a member of the Bolshoi Theater Orchestra, kept him focused, off the streets and alive. At 16, he graduated from the School of the Philharmonic Society in Moscow, where he was a student of Konstantin Mostras, a pupil of Leopold Auer. The family managed to emigrate to Paris in 1922 where, at age 19, Galamian privately studied with Lucien Capet[198] and made a well-received European concert debut in December 1924.[199] The young man eventually took the technique of Capet, then the authority on the art of bowing, and transformed that art into his trademark. This technique shaped not only many latter-day violinists, it influenced Leonard Rose and subsequent generations of cellists. The newly opened Conservatoire Russe de Paris, directed by Sergei Rachmaninoff, attracted a large number of exiled Russian musicians. Galamian was offered a position as

Capet's assistant then became full professor from 1925 to 1929. In his role as teacher, Galamian had his first opportunity to visit the U.S. in 1937 to shepherd one of his prized students, 15-year-old Roland Gundry, through his New York recital debut at Town Hall. The trip profoundly affected Galamian, who vowed "to become the greatest violin teacher in America." Partly influenced by his friend Gregor Piatigorsky who owned a home in upstate New York, Ivan Galamian and his wife Judith Johnson founded and modeled Meadowmount School of Music after a famous Russian school for violin students instituted by Piotr Stolyarski in Odessa in 1911.

By 1926, after a dalliance as a soloist, Galamian decided to concentrate exclusively on teaching partly due to—he confided to Rose—stage fright so severe it resulted in dreadful back pain. Asked about his teaching career, Galamian once remarked, "One must make a choice—either a solo career or a teaching career. You cannot do both equally well. One or the other will suffer ..."[200] His friend, Leonard Rose, would have categorically disagreed.

At Meadowmount, the quality of violin training and the students' technical achievements overwhelmed the cellist. Never had he seen such talented musicians learn so much repertoire so quickly and well. At once he discovered that Galamian not only expected that his most talented students learn a new concerto every few weeks, but they were also expected to play it to concert-level standards from memory. He was above all impressed with the uniformity of bowing. "The bow arms were all so beautifully crafted," Rose recalled. "It was extraordinary!"

Ivan Galamian's philosophy was a simple one, and a theory that Rose also religiously adhered to: practice, lots of it. The approach caused some violinists not so fondly, to compare their summer experiences as if interned in a "prison camp." Étude books, studies and violin concerto repertoire, all neatly stacked Galamian editions, lined the library shelves of Meadowmount's main house. Students knew to consult these books well prior to lessons—Galamian did not tolerate wasted time. While students are young and eager, he theorized, they require drills in **exercises, exercises, exercises**! Galamian heavily emphasized technical work: methodology dictated how to practice. He devoted the first hour to the basics: articulation, shifting, vibrato exercises for the left hand, and various bow strokes. The second hour was to practice difficult passages from repertoire, in addition to arpeggios, and scales. The third hour was for études or Paganini caprices; the fourth hour on the assigned concerto; and the fifth hour for practicing Bach or the student's recital repertoire.[201] Many achieved a prodigious mastery of their instrument; if lack of discipline had been a weakness, Meadowmount cured those students.

Inevitably, Galamian had his share of detractors. Critics blamed the near-monomaniacal focus that left nothing to chance. Perhaps this produced the meticulous playing (increased the likelihood of flawless playing); however, it also left nothing to choice: the discipline inhibited young individuals' experimentation and creative expression of finding their own voice. The restrictive practice routine and inherent competitiveness pushed many students to suffer from emotional strain. A few would suffer emotional breakdown. Perhaps most tragic, some students wound up having to leave their instrument of choice after developing repetitive stress injuries, sometimes called occupational overuse syndrome, a physical disability not defined until the late 1980s—although notable musicians, such as pianists Leon Fleisher and Gary Graffman, were afflicted well before then.

A 1968 *Time* article recounts a typical Meadowmount exchange, "Mr. Galamian, I'm having trouble," a student exclaims. "What shall I do?" Peering sternly into the students eyes, Galamian calmly responds, "When you have played it two thousand times, it will be much easier." The magazine continues to report how Galamian's treatise of "suffering through exercises" as a way to liberate students from the technical demands, thus enabling their growth as artists. Leonard Rose shared the thrill as he witnessed Galamian's successes, although failures occurred. The theories did not work for all his aspiring violinists.

"Leonard Rose arranged for me to get a full scholarship to go to Meadowmount," comments cellist Toby Saks.[202] "Early in my first summer, I was all alone in the main house when suddenly I heard incredible violin playing coming from downstairs. I crept down the steps and it happened to be Michael Rabin[203] playing all of the Paganini Caprices for Mr. Galamian. I couldn't believe what I was hearing. I was in awe. [On September 5, 1958, Rabin—

whose relationship with Galamian was mutual adoration—recorded Paganini's 24 Caprices.]" The summer session, which lasted eight weeks, was brutal and often effective. From 8:00 a.m. until noon students practiced in tiny rooms, easily able to eavesdrop on nearby neighbors' progress. After the lunch break, for which all participants filed into the main house to eat family style, students continued work with one or more chamber groups followed by a final compulsory individual hour of practice in the evening. One couldn't walk three feet without hearing 15 people playing up a storm on all sides practicing like crazy. It was a heady atmosphere of determined work and a considerable amount of competitiveness. It was a setting suitable to Rose's personality. As Guarneri Quartet violinist Arnold Steinhardt reveals, "Sometimes during the morning labor [individual practice], we could expect a visit from Galamian himself. He would amble down the hallways, snapping his fingers loudly, ever on the lookout for those who played badly or—God forbid—not at all.[204]

Violinist Arturo Delmoni related:

> I was 10 years-old when I first went to Meadowmount. As a prank, one day a friend of mine locked me out of my room. I didn't know what to do. I decided to go see Ms. DeLay, who was also my teacher, to tell her about it.* On my way, I saw Mrs. Galamian who was checking to see if people were practicing. ... She reported this to Mr. Galamian who punished me by sending me into the cellar of the main house to practice all day on a Sunday, which happened to be on one of those unspeakably beautiful days in the Adirondacks. ... There I was practicing in the cellar with all the spider webs, flies, and dust. All of a sudden, who would appear but Mr. Rose. He peered in and asked, "What are you doing down there?" So I told him ... He asked, "So Galamian made you do this?" He

---

* Dorothy DeLay (1917-2002) was Galamian's assistant for 22 years. A legendary teacher in her own right, among her many students were Itzhak Perlman, Cho-Liang Lin, Anne Akiko Meyers, Nadia Salerno Sonnenberg, Shlomo Mintz, Nigel Kennedy, Robert McDuffie, Sarah Chang, Mark Kaplan, Rachel Lee, Midori, Gil Shaham, and Kyoko Takezawa.

looked at me with an expression of total disbelief and tremendous empathy.[205]

Leonard Rose satisfied Galamian's desire for a chamber music program at Meadowmount when he accepted the invitation to come to his school to teach the cello and to coach chamber music ensembles. During his first year away from the Philharmonic, traveling as a soloist, he complained about feeling overextended and informed Galamian in 1952 that he had been away from home more than he intended, had two small children, and needed some time to mull it over. He then figured since solo opportunities occurred less frequently off-season, he agreed to the stipulation he have the freedom to appear in whatever concerts came his way. Rose remembered, "We soloists didn't have all that much to do in the summertime. So I went to Meadowmount and I too took with me my super talents from Curtis and Juilliard."*

At this point, Rose had little experience as a teacher and expressed some insecurity in the role. Saks recalls asking to hear Rose demonstrate: "Mostly, I wanted him to play for me. He would always say, 'Do you really want me to play that for you?' And I would always say YES. So he would play—as though he were in concert ... I always felt I had his undivided attention in these lessons. This attention from the great Leonard Rose was *so* flattering. The better I was prepared and played, the more he got involved."[206]

An extraordinary synergy existed between Rose and Galamian. Both men came from stringent Russian backgrounds and in lieu of Rose's dysfunctional relationship with his father, he likely adopted Galamian as a father figure. Galamian's age coincided with Rose's father's age more than his brother's, and their professional association altered the course of Rose's pedagogical focus. In addition, Rose always considered his friend a true gentleman "who was very kind to me, a lovely human being who was very unselfish. I heard so many stories about this man—that he was making a fortune at Meadowmount. I never believed it. I believed that this was one of the most meticulously

---

* Rose invited up-and-coming players such as Ronald Leonard, Jules Eskin, William Stokking, Michael Grebanier, later Lynn Harrell and Yo-Yo Ma.

honest people I had ever known in my life. I was on the board and I knew that the fees he charged to operate the camp were not at all exorbitant." Dorothy DeLay confirmed Galamian's altruism: "... I wanted to see what he was doing. I sat in his studio sometimes and watched the process. I once said to Mr. Galamian, 'Why do you come up here and break your back working so hard, when you can stay in New York, work half as much and make more money?' He thought for a while and said, 'Because I am proud of it [these kids].' He had never talked that way to me before, and I thought, *that's wonderful, that's really wonderful!*"[207]

One day, Rose mustered the necessary courage to ask Galamian about his methods. An invitation to his studio followed: "I went in and when he took [played] the fiddle, it became apparent that he must have been an absolutely marvelous fiddler. In fact, he could outplay most of his students—not the brilliant young talents, of course—but how he could teach them!" Rose's hour-and-a-half session with Galamian in the summer of 1952 was "one of the most enlightening times I have ever experienced in my life. To this day, I utilize 90 percent of the information that he extended to me." In subsequent summers, Rose and his family arrived at Meadowmount in advance of the camp's opening to relax and romp with his son and daughter; and as he did with Jaime Laredo and Michael Rabin in the early 1950s, he sat and observed Galamian's private lessons. The two men continuously discussed pedagogical techniques and how to convey certain crucial points across to students, especially about the bow—specifically what was right and what methods to avoid. Rose remembered one exchange: "'Tell me, Vanya, did you ever make mistakes in teaching?' He said, 'Many times—mistakes such as wrong concepts.' But not wrong for long, because this man was a brilliant teacher."

Galamian inspired confidence, employing a calm demeanor for some students, while he struck fear in others. One terrified young lad who studied intensely under Galamian's gaze, the renowned Itzhak Perlman, relates: "Sometimes, there was so much smoke in the room I couldn't see where he was. I would timidly ask, 'Mr. Galamian, are you there?'" This distinctive fear made students such as Perlman practice with even greater

Michael Rabin   Leonard Rose   1950s
Courtesy of Arthur Rose

resolve to garner Galamian's approval.* As Perlman put it, "At home the smoke from the lesson would come out of my violin as if he were still there with me in my practice. I would experience the same fright all over again."[208] Admittedly, this anxiety seemed to dwell with Perlman all of his youth. Pinchas Zukerman (Meadowmount, 1962-1966) quickly understood that the man's main objective was discipline: "He was a man of very few words, and with him it wasn't what you could do, it was what you should do. That is very important because in my case, I was coming in to show him how I could play the violin, and I learned very quickly that this was not going to fly. I once played one of the

---

* Galamian's immense prestige rested in part on the fact that seven of his students won the Leventritt Award, once the most important U.S. violin competition: Betty Jean Hagen, Sergiu Luca, David Nadien, Itzhak Perlman, Arnold Steinhardt, Kyung Wha Chung, and Pinchas Zukerman.

movements from a Vieuxtemps Concerto for three months—until I got the rotation he wanted me to have going in the bow arm."[209] Galamian's insistence that his students maintain a consistent, large, beautiful tone lay in the abilities of the student to learn to make smooth changes with the bow in proper positioning of the right hand fingers at the frog and proper rotation of the right shoulder at the tip. Zukerman takes personal offense with those who believe Galamian taught by rote. "Forty-five years later, I'm remembering his lessons ... He was really a philosopher, a man of the world ... He had figured out that teaching was cumulative. Every lesson learned was a step up for the next piece. He wanted you to know your fingerboard—where you were, what position you were playing in. No guessing—cut the fingerboard in half with scale work. He used to say to me, 'Pinky, later do what you want; but for now, you listen to me and do what I say.'" Galamian once remarked, "As a teacher, my first task is to teach the students how to practice. Once they understand this, they begin to make progress."

Diane Mather remembers listening to Rose, who was known to start practicing at Meadowmount as early as 5:00 a.m., as she approached Rose's studio. "All the girls were just so crazy about him," Mather remarks. "We all fell in love with him. He was *so* handsome." Then 40 years old and the only cello teacher at Meadowmount, all of the students benefited from Rose when he was around. Although available the entire summer in 1958 (Mather's first summer at Meadowmount), he left for four consecutive weeks in 1960 to play concerts with Glenn Gould in Canada. Nevertheless, it was at Meadowmount that Mather dedicated her full attention to becoming a cellist. She describes her mentor as:

> So inspiring, so incredible. The time that I studied most intensely and regularly with Mr. Rose was the summer of 1958 when he reworked my bow arm. I remember being told by the girls to wear a sleeveless top to the lesson so that he could see what my right arm and elbow was doing. At the end of my last lesson that summer I thanked him, and he said, 'You're welcome, sweetheart.'

His words just rang in my ear. I slowly walked back to the main house and when I lay down in the hammock, I was almost in tears. I thought, *Oh, Mr. Rose, I am going to practice and practice and become a great cellist just for you.*

As frequently occurred, Rose is credited for helping Mather secure a professional position. Mather played in the Cleveland Orchestra from 1963 to 2001.[*]

At Meadowmount, cellist Robert Newkirk[**][210] observed how constantly driven his teacher was. He explains: "Rose was very competitive even to the point that when we were playing bridge with Galamian, he really enjoyed winning. I could see it in his face. I also played golf with him in Elizabethtown. He was very nice to me, but very competitive. My impression was whatever Leonard Rose did, in his mind he had to be the best. I really believe that. That is what he impressed me with, but it wasn't in an arrogant sort of way. There was no doubt that he was a perfectionist, for whatever that meant to him."

Delmoni's impression of Rose dramatically shifted a few summers later. One afternoon, the student felt depressed and moped on the stoop of his dorm, which was adjacent to Rose's teaching studio. Unexpectedly Rose emerged from his door, approached him, and asked, "'What's the matter?' I told him my sad saga about a girl who had just broken up with me. He sat there and talked to me like a brother. 'Don't worry,' he told me, 'there are lots of fish in the ocean.' He made me feel like it was all going to be all right. I was so touched because I wasn't his student. I was a fiddle player." Upon the teacher's return from a brief errand, Delmoni heard a knock on his door. It was Rose. "Out of the blue, because he had seen me smoking, he handed me this most beautiful pipe. I was so touched. I walked around with my head ten times as big as it was for days thinking that Leonard Rose had done this for me." Throughout Rose's life,

---

[*] 1963-1967, first assistant principal; 1967-1969, assistant principal.
[**] Newkirk studied with Rose from 1956 to 1961 at Curtis and at Meadowmount.

this type of person—shy, talented, sensitive and vulnerable, no doubt, a reflection of himself —triggered this rarely revealed compassionate side.

Galamian, on the other hand, had not one drop of compassion for his students' predicament. He viewed camp relationships as an unwelcome distraction, while Rose perhaps appreciated its benefits for his cellists' "vibratos." In strict confidence, Rose—for fear of Galamian's reaction—advised one of his own students to proceed cautiously with Meadowmount romances and, if caught, not to mention his name. At the start of each summer, the school's founding director presented some firm rules to all the gathered students. In addition to the practice guidelines already mentioned, from which there could be no deviation, Galamian's uncompromising words went something like this: "Boys and girls, I vont you to understand von ting ... STAY OUT OV ZEE BOOSHES! Do you understand vot I mean? STAY OUT OV ZEE BOOSHES!" During mealtimes, he enlisted his wife, Judith, to keep a close eye on students suspected of hanky-panky. If she noticed a student missing, she would hit the dirt roads and hunt for them. Once she discovered a couple beneath the foundation of one of the cabins. The behavior meant expulsion from Meadowmount because Galamian made clear in his opening remarks he forbade even holding hands. Rose elaborated: "To me, he stated in his lovely Russian-French accent that if one of his little 14- or 15-year-old girls became pregnant, he would have to close up his school. He was terribly fearful of that; but on the other hand, with young people—they would do whatever they wanted to in the wintertime and suddenly had terrible restrictions placed on them in the summer. That was the only reservation I had and it got to the point where it was almost a sick situation. In my opinion, you can't stop kids from holding hands, for Heaven's sake!"

Rose's duties at Meadowmount also included coaching chamber music groups. Violist Ann Barak recalls what Rose said to her group after playing through a movement of Ravel's string quartet: "After some silence, he gently said, 'Well, that was pretty good. But it wasn't wonderfully well in tune and it wasn't marvelously well together. Why don't we start from the beginning and examine this?' That's how he began. He gave us a sort of left-handed compliment so as not to put and scare us off. Then he taught us how to think about making music together. He was so marvelous."[211] At other times, students remember Rose playing chamber music with them. Delmoni recalls, "The most beautiful chamber music experience I ever had in my life was when Mr. Rose played cello at Meadowmount, I played viola, Mr. Gingold second violin, and Perlman played first violin in the A minor Brahms String Quartet. It was unforgettable."[212]

1950s Chris Miller   Galamian (?) Toby Saks Judith Galamian Rose (Holding hands!) *Courtesy of Diane Mather*

Meadowmount was paradise for Rose—away from the stressful commute to and from a crowded New York City, the nerve-wracking concerts, incessant phone calls, correspondence, and management itineraries. Likewise, Meadowmount treated Rose well. The bucolic environment, where Rose strolled to work, was able to play bridge and golf with his colleagues, and spend private, quality time with his family, who always traveled with him. He appears stress-free, well rested, and smiling in photos taken during the era. For the 12 summers he taught cello and coached chamber music at Meadowmount, Rose enjoyed himself, his colleagues, perfecting repertoire, and teaching his talented kids.

Because of an ever-increasing demand, Rose's departure from the school in 1963 came as a surprise and setback that initially devastated Ivan Galamian.

The Curtis Institute, where Galamian taught, bestowed an honorary doctorate to the violinist in 1954—the first of numerous acknowledgments of his outstanding pedagogy. He was made an honorary member of the Royal Academy of Music, London (1965) and a year later, Oberlin College (Ohio) presented him with an honorary degree, as did the Cleveland Institute of Music in 1968. In 1966, he received a Master Teacher Award from the American String Teachers Association. Even though Ivan Galamian ran a tight ship at his school, most Meadowmount alumni express tremendous gratitude for the experiences. In a period when few music camps catered to serious professional-caliber youth, Ivan Galamian realized his singular vision of preparing instrumentalists to populate our concert stages and teaching studios. For those students, as well as the teachers who worked alongside him, his flame always burns brightly. Ivan Galamian died in New York City in 1981.

Galamian and Rose at Meadowmount 1953

Chapter Eighteen

GLENN GOULD, ECCENTRIC GENIUS

To me, the ideal audience-to-artist relationship is a one-to-zero relationship. I'm not at all happy with words like "public" and "artist". ... The artist should be granted anonymity. They should be permitted to operate in secret as it were unconcerned with or better still, unaware ...[213]

—Glenn Gould

Leonard Rose maintained a significant performing association with Glenn Gould that began at the Stratford Festival in Ontario, Canada, from 1959 to 1969 that extended to a unique Bach recording project released in 1974. Rose was, whether through artistry alone or some other quality, one of the few artists Gould felt comfortable working with.

Glenn Gould is chiefly known for his 75 records and groundbreaking early videos; and although inaccurate that the "concert was dead," he chose to concentrate on technology, abandoning live performances he felt were meaningless. In the 18-and-a-half years away from the stage and in the studio, results were often spectacular and sometimes disappointing. Agree or disagree, he established himself one of the great pianists of his era—certainly within his specialties. Historians concur that Gould was as unusual as he was rebellious.

If Glenn Gould was a genius, he was a troubled genius due, in part, to a disorder. His lack of social skills—a conversational style that included frequent monologues – a one-sided verbosity about topics that bored the listener and his failure to monitor whether the listener was interested or engaged in the conversation – his failure to develop peer relationships in addition to his reclusive nature – a misperception of body temperature – intense preoccupation with a narrow subject – hand movements such as flapping or twisting. These telltale signs indicated that Gould suffered from Asperger's Syndrome. Named after the Austrian pediatrician Hans Asperger (1906-1980), it has only become a standard diagnosis since 1992, well after Gould's death, when it was included in the tenth edition of the World Health Organization's diagnostic manual, *International Classification of Diseases*. Hundreds of books, articles, and Web sites now describe AS from which Gould unknowingly suffered. Anxiety from confusion and depression often accompany the disease into adulthood, which is alleviated with drug use—in some cases, with a lethal combination of liquor, Valium, and antidepressants. Not much was known at the time Rose knew Gould about disorders leading the cellist to dub Gould's eccentricities and obsessions a "crackpot genius" in his memoir.

In 1961, Gould along with Leonard Rose and violinist Oscar Shumsky were appointed co-directors of the Stratford Festival, one of the most prestigious and creatively adventurous festivals in the Canadian music scene at the time. It was a post they shared until 1964. The skepticism that met having three titan musicians share leadership, Gould believed, was unwarranted. He wrote, "Triumvirates, as most everyone was quick to point out, never work. Some hinted darkly that a season or two would find us like Caesar's heirs, locked in strife over a once benign republic. But, strange to say, we have, in these three seasons, added to an admiring musical acquaintance, a warm personal friendship."[214] It's dubious whether the "warm" friendship was reciprocated by Rose; but well after Stratford, Gould and Rose teamed up in an unlikely and remarkable recording featuring Johann Sebastian Bach's three sonatas originally composed for viola da gamba (the instrument of Bach's era) and harpsichord. Admittedly, Rose more or less followed the tempos and articulation that Gould dictated in advance through the telephone. In 1980, Laura Sewell arrived at her lesson announcing she had just purchased the recording. Rose stopped her with a look of alarm and said,

"Oh, don't listen to that recording. Glenn and I rehearsed all of it over the phone." Evidently Gould placed numerous calls to Rose exclaiming, "Listen to this passage, Leonard. What do you think of this articulation and tempo here?" Gould proceeded to play long sections while Rose hung helplessly on the other end of the line. Was Gould's interpretation totally divergent from Rose's? Is it possible that Gould knew his communication with Rose would affect the manner in which the cellist then approached, practiced, and perfected the works? Certainly, Rose didn't just go along with Gould for the ride, as he claims. According to Sewell, Rose looked slightly amused when he was telling her about it, adding with a twinkle in his eye, "Well, let's just say that we did it Glenn's way."

The recording, from a known Bach specialist and a cellist whose reputation lay in the romantic literature, has been discussed and analyzed for more than 30 years. The resulting collaboration is fascinating and their interpretations oddly compatible. It leaves any Rose devotee wishing the cellist had found time, means, and inspiration to record Bach's six suites for solo cello.

Gould had not recorded any chamber music for nearly six years before he settled in front of the microphones with Rose in December 1973 in the ballroom on the top floor of Eaton's department store in Gould's beloved city of Toronto. Because the pianist kept a nocturnal schedule, recording sessions took place from 11:00 p.m. to 5:00 a.m. and sometimes beyond. According to Gould scholar and German musicologist Michael Stegemann, "It is questionable whether this recording would have been made at all if it had not formed part of Columbia's planned recording of all Bach's keyboard works. Equally debatable is the question whether any other [celebrated] cellist would have subordinated his own interpretative ideas to Gould's to the extent that Rose was prepared to do." With the recording finished, the ecstatic pianist could not contain his enthusiasm in a letter to Rose dated September 22, 1974: "Our disc in its various manifestations—as unedited tape, edited tape, acetate and, at last, the final product—has been at the top of my personal hit parade for many months now. The whole project was a great joy and an experience which I hope we can repeat in the future."

Gould unreservedly believed that Leonard Rose was grossly under-represented as a recording artist and urged Rose to make every effort to record the entire major cello repertoire. His reference to the "future" is in response to the cellist's inquiry about Gould's availability to record Beethoven's complete works for cello and piano. Gould, however, was booked with numerous recording, film, and radio projects for years to come and saw no possibility "in the near future." Yet he made a stunning proposal to Rose that, due to failing health, he would sadly be unable to honor. Gould wrote, "I would love to do the project with you if we could do it over a period of three years, beginning during the season 1976-1977, which would mean a wrap-up date in the vicinity of 1980, and I'm not at all sure that that sort of schedule is fair to you." Unfortunately, in June of 1976, Gould was forced to reduce his recording activities to a bare minimum due to the onset of a complex psychomotoric disorder that impaired his abilities to perform in the recording studio.

Glenn Gould   Leonard Rose 1974

Glenn Gould was born September 25, 1932, in Toronto. The original family name had been Gold but his father, who was in the fur business, changed it to Gould in 1939 lest he be mistaken as Jewish during World War II. In fact, Gould's great-grandfather, born in Maine to English immigrants (Reverend Isaac Gold) became an ordained Methodist Minister. Gould was raised a Presbyterian and stopped attending church by the age of 18. His mother told the boy, who could read and memorize music before words, that he learned music while in the womb. As his first teacher, she taught her son Bach; and as a 10-year-old, he already had Book One of the Well-Tempered Clavier at hand. He used to play a game with his mother identifying piano chords from across the house. Gould would shrug when a visitor thought these skills extraordinary. He always considered his affinity for detail a normal part of his personality.

It was in a chamber music setting in 1953 that Gould made his Stratford Festival debut. The 20-year-old pianist, not yet known outside Canada, performed in three of the inaugural season's 16 concerts. An article Gould wrote in 1962 titled "Reminiscences and Prediction," recalled these first concerts as disastrous, "poorly organized, featuring a terrible piano and played for about 50 people in a flapping, noisy tent." Stratford, Ontario, a community of 29,000 located 90 miles west of Toronto, is surrounded by flat and fertile farmland. The town features a large city hall, dome-shaped towers, and gleaming limestone buildings that lie close to the tree-lined Avon River. The town, settled in the 1830s, had no cultural precedent until 1951 when a wealthy businessman formed an exploratory committee to create an annual drama festival, focusing on the plays of Shakespeare. In July 1953, the Stratford Festival was officially launched. Soon thereafter, it achieved international acclaim and has become one of Canada's most recognized cultural venues. Over half a million people visit Stratford from May to early November. In Gould's day, theatergoers plus the pianist's growing reputation resulted in standing-room audiences eager to soak in every Gouldian musical moment.

In July 1954, prior to Gould's association with Rose, the pianist performed at Stratford with violinist Alexander Schneider and cellist Zara Nelsova featuring trios of Bach, Brahms, and Beethoven. The Canadian cellist recalled: "He [Gould] was so young and eager to play. He had some strange ideas about

Beethoven, but we talked him out of most of them.... We rehearsed in the morning, and his face had a yellow complexion, a really sickly color. Obviously, he wasn't ready for the day yet, which for Glenn started in the afternoon. He told us he'd been up all night reading Tolstoy, that he had to read every classic he could get his hands on ... There were many disagreements and arguments from the beginning ... Sasha [Schneider] immediately objected when Glenn kept his piano score closed and [Gould] told Sasha he was used to playing everything from memory."[215] According to Peter Ostwald's biography, *The Ecstasy and Tragedy of Genius*, Schneider was bothered by Gould's arrogance in matters of interpretation. Asking the young pianist how many times he had performed the Beethoven trio, Gould replied that it would be his first time. Schneider shot back, "Well, I've played the trio at least 400 to 500 times." Gould stood firm, retorting, "My position has always been that quality is more important than quantity."[216] The pianist did bring the scores to the concert, but wound up sitting on them. Schneider, who recognized something in Gould that was "a little crazy, [and] had a remarkable, hypnotic effect at the piano," alerted Columbia Records to attend his New York debut the following season.

Few attended Gould's first American recital January 2, 1955, at the Phillips Gallery in Washington, DC. Yet those few, on that wet, dreary wintry day, would never forget Gould's traversal of works by Orlando Gibbons, Jan Pieterszoon Sweelinck, Beethoven (Sonata Op. 109), Berg, Webern, and Bach. The concert stirred *Washington Post's* chief music critic, Paul Hume:[217]

> January 2 is early for predictions, but it is unlikely that the year 1955 will bring us a finer piano recital than that played yesterday ... Few pianists play the instrument so beautifully, so lovingly, so musicianly in manner, and with such regard for its real nature and its enormous literature. Glenn Gould is a pianist with rare gifts for the world. It must not long delay hearing and according him, [receive] the honor and audience he deserves. We know of no pianist anything like him of any age.

Nine days later, again only the curious (about 35 people) attended Gould's New York debut in Town Hall. Yet among them was the head of the classical division at Columbia Records who immediately signed him to a recording contract. He did not disappoint, exploding onto the scene in 1955 with a rendition of Bach's *Goldberg Variations* that stunned listeners with its boldness, passion, extreme tempos, and exceptional dynamic range. In no time, the album reached the top of the classical music charts, where it has stayed, astonishingly, for over 50 years. Gould created a sensation with a style all his own: dry, taught rhythmic control, spectacular in its crispness and clarity. Over the next 25 years, Gould's obsessive focus on Bach spawned recordings of nearly all the other Bach keyboard solos including: the French Suites, the Well-Tempered Clavier, Two and Three-Part Inventions, Partitas, Preludes, and Fugues, the English Suites, Toccatas, concertos for Keyboard No. 1—5 and 7, The Art of the Fugue, Italian Concerto, Sonatas for violin (with Jaime Laredo), and the "gamba sonatas" with Leonard Rose.

According to Rose: "He had one of the most beautiful piano sounds I ever heard, to go along with a prodigious technique and phenomenal memory. Glenn was one of those lucky few who could study a piece just by looking at it; he could learn a piece lying in bed with the music in front of him, and then go to the piano and play it." In August 1960, the two men performed Beethoven's Cello Sonata in A Major, Op. 69 and with Oscar Shumsky, Beethoven's "Ghost" Trio, Op. 70, No. 1. Toronto's *Globe and Mail* reported that more than a 1,000 people seeking tickets were turned away from the sold-out concert. Unfortunately, Gould had a penchant for performing with disregard to other players. Eric McLean from the *Montreal Star* observed, "I became more and more convinced as the concert progressed that Messrs, Shumsky, and Rose were playing this music Gould's way, not because they believed in it, but simply to save the performance."[218] The concert, broadcast on the CBC Radio series *Stratford Music Festival,* was released in 1988 on Melodram, an Italian pirate CD label.

In July 1961, Gould and Rose performed Brahms Sonata in E minor and with Shumsky, Brahms Piano trio in C minor. David Gross, a pianist who played recitals with Rose in the late 1950s, and the page-turner for this concert, recalls Gould's apprehension with him sitting so nearby, claiming it was too distracting. Gross suggested that he sit in the wing of the stage, a dozen or so feet from the pianist—unseen by the public—which was not only acceptable, but "enthusiastically" received by Gould. Gross relates: "When it came time to turn the page, I would get up, walk across the stage, turn the page, and quickly walk back to my chair offstage." No signal was relayed to Gross nor did he have a score. Something was awry throughout the finale of the Brahms sonata. "When the fugue started and the cello came in," Gross recalls, "I didn't hear Rose at all. Gould kept playing and as I came over to the piano to turn the page, I glanced over ... Rose seldom sweat in concert—and he was drenched. Even in the places where it should have been *piano*, Gould was playing loud. Rose was playing for survival. When they came off the stage, the two crossed in front of me and Rose was madder than a hatter and said, 'Glenn, what the ...' Gould stopped him immediately and said, 'I know, I know. I played way too loud but you know, in the fugue, all the music is in the piano. The cello is irrelevant and there was a big wave that overcame me and I just had to go with it.'" Someone came backstage to tell Rose how much they enjoyed the concert. Rose responded, "How would you know, how could you possibly have heard me?"

John Kraglund, in Toronto's *Globe and Mail* wrote in his review titled, *Gould Overpowers His Colleagues*: "Mr. Gould's greatness as a solo performer is undisputed. I must confess I am less enthusiastic about him as an ensemble player, for he tends to dominate the performance without full consideration for the composer or the other performers." More specifically he noted, "Mr. Gould's efforts to drown out both the piano and the cello with his stamping feet," and his "tendency to force the pace." George Kidd for the *Telegram* wrote: "... The combination [of Gould, Shumsky, and Rose] was an exciting one and the audience greeted its beauty with applause that ceased only when the lights were turned on ... Mr. Gould was in his usual splendid form, complete with his glass of water, his folding chair, and a left arm that tended too often to conduct. He was also in his usual voice and clouded the last movement of the trio with noises that spoiled much of the beauty that had been heard earlier. These noises are no longer amusing. Neither are they necessary."[219]

Oscar Shumsky   Glenn Gould   Leonard Rose   1960s
Courtesy of the Stratford Festival

Rose tolerated Gould's "noises" and fondly recalled one of their collaborations:

> There are all too many people who are ready to criticize him; but at one concert (Beethoven's A Major Sonata), the television people from the CBC decided they wanted to make a production out of this performance. On the appointed day, Glenn and I arrived in Toronto. At one point in the rehearsal, which was before the cameras, the producer came out and said, "Leonard, that stand, that music stand is giving us fits. Do you, by any chance, know the piece from memory?" The taping of the performance was the next day and while I assured the producer that I did know the piece from memory, I said, "Glenn may need the music." Upon which Glenn said, "Oh, Leonard, do you want to play the piece from memory—I'll have it from memory tomorrow." And,

of course, he did! He had that kind of mind. Glenn is definitely a kind of genius and I don't toss these kinds of words around lightly (this performance can be viewed on YouTube).

Gould never married and had no family of his own. Eventually, he became a recluse—existing in a gloomy apartment, doing the bulk of his communicating by telephone. His producer, Andrew Kazdin,[220] who was unceremoniously dropped after many years of devoted work for Gould, depicts him as a "creative liar" who was destructive to all in the end. Kazdin believed that even when Gould exhibited incredible knowledge on certain subjects, his self-absorbed and often erroneous convictions on other issues were downright alarming. The writer and music critic Tim Page[*,221] visited Gould at the time, in 1982. Page etched an image of a dying man, portraying the artist as living the life of a hermit, shutting himself off in "monastic seclusion." The once handsome, charming, and naïve young man who stirred excitement and invincibility had become stern, sour, overweight, balding (the motor hand problem condition set in as well), and was living in a tiny studio with windows blackened. Technology—tapes, tape machines, video players, a television, a record player, and his infamous telephone, which Gould used by calling person-to-person, usually in the middle of the night, to the tune of four-figure phone bills—crowded the room. Gould had not visited a Toronto store or restaurant in some years. Aides did the shopping; other items were delivered. He no longer attended movies or concerts. He slept by day and worked by night. He did not live in the apartment that was his mailing address. His phone was answered by a service. Gould chose to relocate his studio to the Inn on the Park after discovering that it was the only hotel in the area that offered all-night room service.[222] The hypochondriac pianist, who never liked to be touched, carried around a briefcase full of pills, which included vast quantities of vitamins, valium, pentobarbital, librax, aldomet, clonidine, indocin, hydrochlorothiazide, septra, fiorinal,

---

[*] Page edited the *Glenn Gould Reader*, provided the text for one of several volumes devoted to Gould photographs and memorabilia, wrote liner notes for reissues of his recordings, and published other articles about Gould.

phenylbutazone, chlorothiazide, allopurinol, trifluoperazine (antipsychotic), nembutal (depresses the activity of the brain and nervous system), sedatives, and tranquilizers. Long before Page's visit to Toronto, Gould had become dependent on pills. His life was on a dangerous roller coaster of constant cycles of uppers and downers.

In 1964, after nine brilliant years on the concert stage his self-imposed retirement at age 31 made headlines (of the 250 or so concerts between his 1955 New York debut and his retirement, 90 featured Beethoven concertos[223]). No musician of his stature ever walked away from the kind of fame he attained. Gould explained how performing before the public had been the worst period of his life. "At concerts, I felt demeaned," Gould complained, "like a vaudevillian."[224] Gould tired of the routine, constant travel (he detested airplanes), subpar hotels, unacceptable beds, septic artist rooms, average pianos, post-concert receptions, and audiences he felt no connection with. Moreover, he believed that a "tremendous conservatism overtakes any artist forced to perform the same music again and again, until it becomes difficult, if not impossible, to move on."[225] In the ensuing years, he determinedly but mistakenly predicted the "public recital was a dying remnant of the Romantic age, the termination of which is long overdue." Recitals haven't died out, yet, many of his theories were prescient. Gould did not live long enough to see the advent of CD players, personal computers, downloading personal music choices, iPods, YouTube, etc. Prophetically, he theorized that:

> Technology is in the process of creating an audience which is becoming aware of a more subtle and varied range of musical impression than was its counterpart of a generation or so ago. I think—reasonable to say—that in another generation or two, the public concert as we know it today, if it exists at all, will exist as a reflection of those tastes and preferences which are being developed by the electronic culture and which will be encountered primarily in the home and in circumstances which permit the listener a rather significant degree of involvement.[226]

Gould firmly believed that at the center of the technological debate, there was a new kind of listener; a listener who is more involved in the musical experience. His obsessive albeit distorted view with technology is cutting edge: "For this listener is no longer passively analytical; he is an associate whose tastes, preferences, and inclinations even now alter peripherally the experiences to which he gives his attention, and upon whose fuller participation the future of the art of music awaits."[227]

Critics generally extolled Gould's public performances except for his extra musical idiosyncrasies—hunching, singing, grimacing, twitching, swaying, foot-stamping, arm-waving, and time-beating—that disrupted from the flow of a performance. Rose relates another odd habit in his unpublished memoir. "He insisted on having a glass of water on the piano when he was playing in case he got thirsty. The water could not be cold—it had to be lukewarm ... and at one of these concerts when we had finished a movement, he somehow managed to tip the glass of water onto the keys. I didn't know what happened, but all of a sudden, I heard my name being called in a sort of whisper. 'Leonard, do you have a handkerchief?' I always carry a handkerchief in my right pocket to wipe my brow, and I handed it to him and turned around to see—an entirely wet keyboard!" George Kidd recorded the event in *The Telegram:*

> For years, I've been waiting for Glenn Gould's inevitable glass of water to spill over the shining keyboard, and it finally happened. Now he can toss aside this personality gag, which was never very funny anyway. The accident happened in the opening sections of the [Mendelssohn] trio in D minor ... But the pianist continued with the movement ... The audience tittered and Mr. Gould smiled. Then he held up the empty glass. The mood was shattered by the clowning, but it [the mood] was picked up again as the trio started on the second movement.[228]

The weather at Stratford was unbearably hot, sometimes even intolerable. As Rose recalled, Gould was immune to the heat:

I remember when Glenn had driven in his absolutely huge Lincoln—I never saw such a car of that size. Of course, everything was power: power windows, power everything! In the middle of the summertime, Glenn always suffered from being cold. Even when it was 90-95 degrees, he would have on his galoshes, a hat, and a couple of coats. And, of course, when he'd drive us around, he would not have the air conditioning on. If we would dare sneak a window open by pressing a little button, before you knew it, there would be a "pip" and Glenn would close the window with his controls on the left-hand side. This was another one of his mannerisms.

Arriving at Gould's home with Shumsky and Rose for a rehearsal of a Brahms trio, Gross recalled: "The door was answered by his physical therapist (Gould was 19 years old) and we were kept waiting 10 minutes in sweltering heat before he made his appearance. It was close to 100 degrees out and Gould had the heat turned up full blast." The musicians somehow tolerated this behavior from Gould:

When they started to rehearse, I was sitting on a couch about 10 feet from the piano and noticed all the bass notes were wrong. ... Gould prized this ancient Chickering [piano] with some historical value, and was afraid to tune its original bass strings, which were about four tones flat, but not uniformly so. ... Of course, the string players were rather annoyed that they had to put up with the cacophony. Gould didn't seem to care one wit.[229]

Glenn Gould died, nine days after his 50th birthday (October 4, 1982), after suffering a major stroke a week earlier from which he never regained consciousness. Leonard Rose was visibly distraught, vociferously lamenting his colleague's death to students. The irony is overwhelming. According to Kazdin: "His brain—which imbued him with the rare gift of absolute pitch, which held within itself the brilliant, the unique musical interpretations that poured forth over his career; which could memorize the most complex scores of Schoenberg and Hindemith; which was probably the only single repository of all the pieces of the jigsaw puzzle into which he had fragmented his life—this brain, his greatest asset, is what killed him."[230]

In 1977, NASA sent two unmanned interplanetary spacecrafts, Voyager 1 and Voyager 2 (now billions of miles from the sun), into orbit where they are eventually destined to reach the edge of our galaxy. In the hope that some life form somewhere would intercept these crafts, a variety of human messages were placed on board that would communicate the existence of intelligence on our planet.[231] They each carried a 12-inch (30-centimeter), gold-plated copper phonograph disk containing 115 images and greetings spoken in 55 languages, selected to portray the Earth's diversity of life and culture. Included on the disk was a short prelude by Johann Sebastian Bach performed by Glenn Gould.

Leonard Rose   Oscar Shumsky   Glenn Gould
Courtesy of the Stratford Festival
(Photograph reproduced from the 1961 Stratford Festival souvenir booklet)

Chapter Nineteen

Istomin, Stern, Rose Assume the Trio Mantle

At first, we had played trios with Pablo Casals in Prades. He was the inspiration for us. We then decided to try to emulate the legendary Cortot-Thibaud-Casals trio.
—Pianist Eugene Istomin[232]

Isaac Stern   Leonard Rose   Eugene Istomin
October 31, 1970

Leonard Rose's unquenchable desire to engage the chamber music literature emerged at an early age. From his first experiences as a 14-year-old in Florida, to his formative years at the Curtis Institute working with violinist Eudice Shapiro and pianist Richard Goodman when they frequently performed in Baltimore homes, playing works learned independent of faculty and later still at Curtis with violinist Oscar Shumsky and pianist Harry Kaufmann. Throughout his life, Rose demonstrated a love for piano trio literature. His eventual collaboration with violinist Isaac Stern[233] and pianist Eugene Istomin[234] would thrust him into international stardom.

A half-century before the inception of Leonard Rose's stellar trio, its ancestor was taking shape in Europe. In 1905, the 28-year-old Catalonian cellist Pablo Casals, upon completion of his 2nd U.S. tour as soloist (president Theodore Roosevelt heard him in recital at the White House), initiated a musical collaboration with the Swiss-born pianist Alfred Cortot and the French violinist Jacques Thibaud—also in their 20s. Casals said: "Perhaps the happiest memories of my Paris days are those associated with the small informal music sessions at which my friends and I would periodically get together and play for our own pleasure. We usually gathered in the small parlor at Thibaud's house. Our group included Ysaÿe, Thibaud, Kreisler, Monteux, Cortot, Bauer, Enesco, and myself. How we all longed for that moment! Then we would play together for the sheer love of playing ..."[235] The outbreak of World War I in 1914 brought these gratifying chamber music evenings played by its era's historically significant artists to a standstill.

Cortot, Thibaud, and Casals were three well-known soloists. As a chamber music entity performing throughout the Western hemisphere before air travel was the norm, they achieved unprecedented recognition. Because of Casals' fame and longevity, his association with the next generation was unavoidable; Casals passed the torch to his trio's successors and protégés: Leonard Rose, Eugene Istomin, and Isaac Stern. Like the Istomin-Stern-Rose trio, their predecessors carefully perfected repertoire, toured, and made recordings during several decades of performance. That these early twentieth-century musicians forged a new path is unquestionable. They established the standard—brilliance in ensemble, interpretation and execution—by which audiences judged piano trio performances, and some were captured on the industry's earliest recordings.[236]

The trio's demise, however, was tragic. During World War II, Casals' discovery that Cortot was a Nazi appointee as secretary of music of the Vichy State Council—and when in office signed an order banning Jews from all orchestras in France—ended their relationship. For a while placed under house arrest and later forbidden, for a brief period, to perform in France after the war, Cortot became an outcast in his own country and died in 1962. Thibaud, who also danced to the Nazi's tune, playing in occupied and unoccupied France during the war, was killed while on tour in Japan, September 1, 1953, when his plane crashed into a mountain, leaving no survivors.* The news devastated his many colleagues and plunged the musical world into mourning.

Cellists of Rose's generation and all who followed owe an enormous debt of gratitude to Casals. The Spaniard forged a new style of play, immediately mimicked, and his innovations have influenced, literally, a century of cello playing. Specifically, he purposely omitted the audible left-hand shifts between notes and telegraphed slides that had been tradition. Finger extensions, coupled with the newfound freedom in the use of the bow arm, created the precursor to modern cello performance. Musicians regard Casals, who produced a tone as beautiful and soulful as it was considerable, as the first cellist who gripped audiences with a full-throated sound—able to soar above an orchestra. Prior to Casals, Bach's cello suites were performed in fragments or relegated to private exercise. Casals's precedent setting performances of the suites in their entirety firmly fixed the six masterpieces in the standard repertoire. In February 1940, Emanuel Feuermann wrote about Casals's (then 63 years old) contribution in an issue of *Musical America*:[237] "We cellists are especially lucky to have a figure in our time who ... has revived and revolutionized its technique and scope. Pablo Casals has created a new way to use the cello for musical expression. He was not satisfied with the standing of the instrument as he found it,

---

* Thibaud's 1720 'Baillot' Stradivarius violin was also a casualty.

so he obviously set out to make it more adequate for his ideas of interpretation. At once, the entire attitude toward the instrument changed."

A fierce opponent of the dictatorship formed in his homeland led by the nationalist general Francisco Franco in the spring of 1939, Casals went into self-imposed exile to Prades, a small, scenic town in the south of France close to the Spanish frontier. Making headlines, the icon vowed, as Franco allied himself with Nazi Germany and with Fascist Italy, that he would not play his cello anywhere in the world—and that included the U.S. which still had diplomatic relations with Franco's long ruthless regime. Leonard Rose shared a commitment to Casals's cause: with members of the NBC Symphony (concertmaster Mischa Mischakoff, violinist Jacques Larner, and violist Emanuel Vardi), Rose's quartet performed at the New School for Social Research in 1939, sponsored by the Musician's Committee to Aid Spanish Democracy.[238] Although Casals would continue to practice his cello, his self imposed retirement was for real—for the better part of a decade. Then, musicians pleaded with him to relent. At first, the somewhat reclusive 74-year-old hesitated; shortly thereafter, he found the prospect of musicians coming to him acceptable.* Prades, Casals's adopted home for 17 years, became the site of music festivals he directed. Casals devoted the 1950 inaugural festival exclusively to the music of Bach to commemorate the bicentenary of the composer's death.

It was in this town, with one large café and one church nestled among the Pyrenees ranges with an enormous, quasi-mystic, 6,800-foot Canigou Peak (a sacred mountain for Catalan people) where Isaac Stern met Pablo Casals. This meeting profoundly affected the 31-year-old star violinist who would later refer to the cellist atypically as his primary influence. In Prades, Stern ultimately developed a long-lasting musical association with pianist Eugene Istomin. As the festival matured, Casals

---

* Artists at this premiere festival included Stern, Serkin, Horszowski, Szigeti, Mannes, Conrad, Istomin, Lefebure, Haskell, and others. At each of six orchestral programs (with 38 players), Casals played one of Bach's unaccompanied cello suites. On the following chamber concerts, Casals performed, on cello, Bach's three sonatas for viola da gamba and keyboard (New York *Times* January 8, 1950).

joined Stern and later Istomin in piano trio performances. With these young artists, the older man rekindled his passion for the piano trio literature. Under the master's wing, Istomin's playing demonstrated the deep effect Casals's influence had upon him.[239] With Casals, the pianist recorded the trios of Brahms (with violinist Yehudi Menuhin), Beethoven (with violinist Alexander Schneider and Joseph Fuchs), and Schubert (with Schneider). Under his watchful eyes, the pair grew so close that, upon the old man's death, Istomin married Casals's widow, with the cellist's advance blessing.

During the Prades Festival debut in 1950, Leonard Rose was still principal cellist of the New York Philharmonic. In the period when Istomin and Stern were becoming musical soulmates, their search for a cellist led them straight to Rose, who had successfully launched his solo career in the interim. Leonard Rose became acquainted with Isaac Stern in the late 1940s when the two engaged in informal chamber music evenings. A fast friendship developed. Stern remembered their first encounter and reminisced: "There are times when you meet someone for the first time and in ten minutes, you have been friends for 20 years."[240] When the violinist invited Rose to record the Brahms "Double" Concerto with the Philharmonic and Walter in late 1954, Stern's decision to include the cellist in his trio was all but sealed. Rose, the elder statesman of the three, was well acquainted with the playing of both men, as each made multiple appearances with the Philharmonic during Rose's tenure. Already a seasoned chamber music player, Rose later went on record stating the intrinsic value he adored in chamber music: "Some of the most beautiful music written is in the chamber literature. It's a dull word, but it doesn't necessarily mean the music has to be dull. Playing chamber music gives you an inner excitement, which I think communicates itself to the audience."[241]

The history of trios scored for violin, cello, and piano dates back to the early eighteenth century. Over time, renowned musicians illuminated the genre: Carl Friedberg, Daniil Karpilowsky, and Felix Salmond; Artur Schnabel, Alfred Wittenberg, and Anton Hekking; Artur Schnabel, Bronislaw Huberman, and Emanuel Feuermann; Artur Schnabel, Carl Flesch, and Jean Gerardy (who was replaced by cellist Hugo Becker and then with cellist Gregor

Piatigorsky); Leopold Mannes, Bronislaw Gimpel, and Luigi Silva; Alfredo Casella, George Enesco, and Diran Alexanian; Emil Gilels, Leonid Kogan, and Mstislav Rostropovich; Lev Oborin, David Oistrakh, and Sviatoslav Knushevitsky (Oistrakh Trio); Menahem Pressler, Daniel Guilet (Isidore Cohen), and Bernard Greenhouse (Beaux Arts Trio); Wilhelm Kempff (Arthur Rubinstein), Henryk Szeryng, and Pierre Fournier; Leonard Pennario (Jacob Lateiner and Arthur Rubinstein), Jascha Heifetz, and Gregor Piatigorsky; Daniel Barenboim, Pinchas Zukerman, and Jacqueline Du Pré.

In the twentieth century, none was more glamorous than the Hollywood-based Heifetz-Rubinstein-Feuermann trio formed in the summer of 1941. Heifetz, long established on the American recording scene, motivated RCA/Victor's producers to work with his eminent colleagues. Though renowned in Europe, they arrived in the States more recently and had barely just dawned their own brilliant recording careers.* Their legacy included several trio recordings; in a three-day span in September 1941, they recorded Beethoven's "Archduke" trio, Schubert's B-flat trio and Brahms B Major trio. The freak accident from which Feuermann died, a routine hemorrhoidectomy that forced a second operation by an incompetent doctor in May 1942, brought the group to a heartbreaking, premature end.

Eight years would pass before Heifetz agreed to play with another cellist. This time, the ensemble—Heifetz, Rubinstein and Piatigorsky—was dubbed the "Million Dollar Trio." In 1949, in a series of sold out public performances at Ravinia Park,[242] in Highland Park, Illinois, the trio garnered headlines in national magazines and newspapers. In his unpublished memoir, Rose refers to these concerts as "an epic event without question." Instantly, the group captured the fascination of fellow musicians—surely Istomin, Stern and Rose—as well as a flock of music lovers. In another short period, six days in 1949, the trio recorded Mendelssohn's trio in D minor, the Ravel, and Tchaikovsky trios.

---

* Arthur Rubinstein shunned recordings until the electronic era's advent and its superior technology for capturing piano tone. In the late 1990s, BMG (RCA) released an Arthur Rubinstein boxed, 94-disc set, "A Life in Music."

The success of the "Million Dollar Trio" at Ravinia Park prompted its management, six years later, to repeat that format—concerto appearances with the Chicago Symphony Orchestra followed by chamber concerts—with the three young American virtuosos. The Istomin-Stern-Rose trio debuted in 1955.

The response, unfortunately, was somewhat disappointing, hindered by the sweltering heat and humidity the area experienced from July 28 to August 12, when the men performed. Their schedule of outdoor performances was grueling: July 28, Istomin performed Beethoven's Fourth Piano Concerto with the Chicago Symphony; August 2, Istomin in Chopin's Concerto No. 2; August 4, Rose in the Saint-Saëns Cello Concerto (96 degrees, but dew points in the 70s made it feel like 100 degrees). August 5, Stern performed in the Brahms Violin Concerto; August 6, Stern and Rose in the Brahms "Double" (2.03" of rain after 1.11" inches the day before). On August 9, the Istomin-Stern-Rose trio began four consecutive days of chamber music performances. August 9, the trio performed Beethoven: piano trio in B-flat; Bach: Chaconne for unaccompanied violin; Kodály: Duo for violin and cello; Mendelssohn: piano trio in D minor. August 10, the trio performed Brahms: Violin Sonata in C Major; Beethoven: Cello Sonata in A Major; Schumann: "Abegg" Variations for piano; Brahms: piano trio in B Major. August 11, they performed Beethoven: Seven Variations on a Theme from Mozart's "Magic Flute" for cello and piano; Beethoven: C minor Violin Sonata; Brahms: Cello Sonata in F Major; Brahms: piano trio in C minor. August 12, they performed Beethoven: piano trio in C minor Op. 1, No. 3; Mendelssohn: piano trio in D minor; Schubert: piano trio in B-flat.

The title of Claudia Cassidy's *Chicago Tribune* review of August 10, "Trio Battles Acoustics," said it all. The outdoor acoustics resulted in a sound that was "muffled and dispersed. Piano sounded dead, the violin diminished, the cello all but nonexistent." The critic explained the extra musical conditions better in Rose's performance: "Crickets and locusts with what must have been castanets swung into action last night, joining roaring trains, cruising planes, and Ravinia's wet blanket acoustics in frustrating any valiant hope of hearing Leonard Rose's performance of Saint-Saëns Cello Concerto." The Brahms

"Double" fared no better. Under the headline, "Stern and Rose Play Brahms in 100% Humidity," Seymour Raven wrote: "The musical story could be read in the soloists' anxious faces as they played, and in 'what can you do?' glances of figurative resignation they exchanged during bars of rest. There was just no producing a tone, by violin or cello, nor any relying on tenacity of tuning. It was just too wet in that otherwise troubled acoustical air in the Ravinia pavilion."

The less-than-spectacular reports, obviously due to the weather, did end on an important note, giving the men some optimism: "The playing took awhile getting into focus during the Beethoven. Mr. Stern's violin predominated, Mr. Istomin's piano sounded remote, and Mr. Rose's cello was rather spread out, especially in the lower tones. But in the Schubert, they got hold of the thing, as though their ears were finally bringing back what was sounding out in the pavilion. It was good to see the felicitous Schubert playing rewarded by an audience of about 3,400." Even though the weather precluded the same immediate excitement as the Heifetz-Rubinstein-Piatigorsky ensemble, the new trio—in its infancy—realized they had something special to offer the public.

As Stern recalled: "We were three men in a room, trying to work in unison, while acknowledging the primacy of a higher authority: the composer. It's putting all your skill and craft at the service of an ideal. I think it's more demanding intellectually than playing solo." Istomin also felt trio work a worthy pursuit in spite of the inauspicious debut. The pianist stated: "I come out of the trio spiritually refreshed. Then there is some subtle, intangible difference in my work. We're all too much egotists to give in much, but it happens we don't have to." And Rose puts it in plain words, "We all knew each other and took the matter quite seriously, rehearsing many long hours."

An invitation to inaugurate the Israel Music Festival in September 1961 put the Istomin-Stern-Rose trio on the map for good. This time, the trio's performances were highly anticipated and regarded. "That festival truly launched us as a group," the cellist recalled. "Media from all over the world was present. We created a sensation."

The trio played nine concerts on their 1961 trip: in Tel Aviv, Jerusalem, and the Galilee and Negev regions. The travel was strenuous and exhaustion contributed to a disaster that nearly derailed the entire tour: during one of their first concerts in Tel Aviv,[243] in the Ravel trio, Rose suddenly felt the return of an old injury. Twelve years earlier, toward the end of the Philharmonic season in April 1949, he began to feel a sharp pain in his right shoulder. Several people advised him to consult an osteopathic physician who treated conductor Fritz Reiner and other musicians with similar problems. Minutes after his arrival, the doctor proceeded to manipulate Rose's head violently. Without a single X-ray, he firmly locked Rose's shoulders between his legs, grabbed his chin with one hand then yanked and kneaded the muscles between head and shoulder. As a result of the procedure, the cellist's pain flared up so severely that he could not straighten up and spent the night slumped in a chair. By morning, he suffered excruciating spasms on the right side of his neck.

The following 10 days, Rose rested in the hospital, contemplating a daunting operation on four to five vertebrae. Dr. Irving Glick, however, recommended a less intrusive option. He urged Rose to wear a brace for two to three months until the condition healed itself. The brace the doctor prescribed was not the standard soft collar, but a cumbersome metal one. Even though it held the head absolutely steady, Rose continued to experience shooting pains down the length of his bow arm. "I wore that brace for three long, hot summer months and the pain did get better," the cellist dictated. "I had to retrain myself in playing the instrument. There is no question that it was in good part occupational because I used to be a very vigorous player. I still am a vigorous player, but I used to move my head a great deal. Every time I would attack a chord or a strong note, my head would go forward, and I weakened something back there."

Rose's daughter, Barbara, describes the family's wise planning packing that brace to Israel. Barbara assisted her father with his physical therapy in hotels: "We used to sit there with those rubber, squishy balls. He would squeeze and squeeze them so that he wouldn't lose any strength in his hand. He couldn't feel what he was doing. He would drop things and we would have to pick it up and give it to him. And yet he was so kind. He would say, 'Pussycat, please pick it up for me. I can't get it. Just put it in my hand, honey.'"[244]

Somehow, Rose, who did a brief stint in an Israeli hospital, managed to play every performance. "Under any other circumstances," Stern wrote in his autobiography, "Rose would have canceled the concerts, but he most gallantly played them all, and played gorgeously." Except for the cellist's temporary disability, it was a brilliant period for the trio.

"That was the beginning of some wonderful times," Rose's memoir acknowledges in recollecting the Istomin-Stern-Rose ensemble's heyday. "Some wonderful tours and marvelous recordings; it was great for everyone concerned. We all enjoyed each other very much. Oh, we had our differences; our rehearsals were something to behold because at times, there were some very heated discussions about what we were going to do about a certain phrase—were we going to slide here, were we going to use a certain kind of bowing there, and so forth. Inevitably, we used to laugh at each other because it finally dawned on us that what we were talking about were such minor differences—for example, of tempos or of particular feeling of a phrase. I think that one of the things that makes our trio so marvelous, is that our musical backgrounds were so similar."

Isaac Stern   Eugene Istomin   Leonard Rose 1964

Istomin summed up the trio's personal and professional relationship:

> The two string players, their sounds blended together very beautifully. They knew it and they reveled in that arrangement. I had a good ear for blending with strings. I'm a string player by nature, I think, even more than a piano player. We just liked playing together. Indeed, we were close friends. We were also three very different types. We needed to be separate. Sometimes we collided. We had our tiffs, of course as any marriage does. So because of the very closeness, there were things that were abrasive. That happens when you live together; and we lived together more than people thought. When we went onto the stage, however, we were of a union that was absolutely perfect.[245]

The trio debuted in New York performing Beethoven's "Triple" Concerto in Carnegie Hall April 23, 1962, with the Symphony of the Air under the direction of Alfred Wallenstein, the former principal cellist of the New York Philharmonic appointed by Toscanini in 1929. Louis Biancolli of the *New York World-Telegram and Sun* glowingly wrote:

"What transpired was a dream performance. One might attend concerts regularly for a lifetime and possibly twice or three times at the most come face to face with such a faultless reading ... They were made for each other."

Harold Schonberg liked what he heard as well, writing in the *Times*: "... Stern, Rose, and Istomin can play together with the best of them ... Each is a sincere musician. Each is an instrumentalist of superior capacities ... They are twentieth-century musicians, which means that they take little leeway in phrase or tempo, playing the notes without a superimposition of ego, and constantly on the watch against sentimentality. It was sharp, clear, music making they presented, mainly without going in for heroics, tender without sloppiness."

Two-and-a-half weeks later, on May 11, 1962—six months after 84-year-old Pablo Casals's historic, nationally broadcast concert at the White House in Washington, DC, (Columbia Records made and distributed a recording of it commercially)—the Istomin-Stern-Rose trio performed at the same venue for president and Mrs. John F. Kennedy, the magnetic author and French *ministre d'état* to Charles de Gaulle, André Malraux, and distinguished guests which included the reclusive Charles Lindbergh (who flew to fame across the Atlantic ocean 35 years earlier), playwrights Tennessee Williams, Arthur Miller, Thornton Wilder; authors Anne Morrow, John Hersey, Saul Bellow; choreographers George Balanchine and Agnes De Mille; conductor Leonard Bernstein; actresses Julie Harris, Susan Strasberg; painters Josef Kline and Mark Rothko; and directors Elia Kazan and Lee Strasberg. One of 166 guests seated at table No. 11, adjacent to the back of the president, Rose possibly knew of Kennedy's diplomatic failure when in the previous month he approved a misguided mission sending 1,400 anti-Castro Cuban exiles to stir up what he and military advisors thought would instigate a revolution at the Bay of Pigs. Instead of sending Castro to his doom, many of the exiles were crushed with unforeseen strength. Kennedy's leadership skills were in question while the president berated himself for heeding the advice of the military. Because of the failed mission, on May 5—less than a week before the Istomin-Stern-Rose appearance, at a meeting in the U.S. of the National Security Council—it was formally agreed, with unpopular repercussions, "U.S. policy toward Cuba should aim at the downfall of Castro."[246] This, of course, led to the showdown over Cuba with the Soviet Union in October 1962, when the world watched in horror as the two superpowers were on the brink of nuclear war.

    More than any other twentieth-century U.S. first families, the Kennedys regularly hosted America's leading artists and arts organizations in performances the press dubbed "Kennedy Command Performance" at the grand white mansion at 1600 Pennsylvania Avenue. Even though the president was somewhat of a musical Philistine, the couple's wish to encourage public acceptance of the arts was wholly laudatory. These state dinners satiated 32-year-old Jacqueline Kennedy's flair for fashion as well. On this particular evening, enchanting their guests, she wore a regal pink, floor length, strapless taffeta evening gown adorned with long vintage white opera gloves, a pink starburst hairpin, matching earrings and pink high-heeled shoes. The president, with his exceptional broad, toothy smile, sported a pink carnation pinned above his glossy black tuxedo's jacket left breast pocket. The president believed that a life dedicated to the arts was the decisive sacrifice, the "ultimate in self-discipline." He told his gathered guests, which included Istomin, Stern, and Rose (along with Rose's wife, Minnie and Stern's wife, Vera):

> We do not manage our cultural life in this country, nor does any free society, but it is an important part. It is one of the great purposes ... There are so many more people playing a musical instrument now, going to symphonies, going to the theater, to art galleries, painting, than anyone realizes; and it is our hope that Americans will begin to look about them and realize that here in these years, we are building a life which develops the maximum in each individual.[247]

The trio's program, performed after dinner, was truncated due to an especially painful episode involving Kennedy's degenerative back condition, a birth defect exacerbated on the battlefield in World War II that required spinal surgery in 1954. It never did heal properly; the president was sometimes forced to use crutches away from the public eye. "This is becoming a sort of eating place for artists," the president joked in his pre-dinner toast to his guests seated at twelve tables in the State Dining Room and to five tables in the Blue Room, decorated in a stunningly beautiful old-fashioned garden scene. The dinner served were delicacies of stuffed bar Polignac, potatoes parisienne, and pheasant aspic salad. "But they never ask us out!" Kennedy concluded to laughter.[248] At the end of the trio's traversal of Franz Schubert's romantic 45-minute trio in B-flat, the president gaffed by thanking "Isaac Stern and his two accompanists."[249] Upon the guests' departure, the president apologized to Istomin and to Rose while chatting and sharing drinks with the three men in a private setting upstairs. Rose, a great admirer of president Kennedy, recalls the occasion as one of the highlights of his life.[250] Eighteen months later, Kennedy was assassinated while riding in an automobile vulnerable to a sharpshooter in the streets of Dallas, Texas. The three artists instantly stopped all touring and in the days immediately following, convened in New York to perform the slow movement from this same Schubert trio on television in tribute. (The trio performed at the Kennedy Center in Washington, DC, honoring the memory of its namesake, in a concert Nov. 22, 1983, on the twentieth anniversary of his death.) A photo taken of Rose and president Kennedy at the White House that May 1962 evening hung for decades in Rose's three-story Tudor-style Georgian-furnished house in Hastings-on-Hudson, New York, eliciting him to comment, "I have never been happier."

President Kennedy   Istomin   Rose   1962
Courtesy of Marta Istomin

By the close of the decade, the Istomin-Stern-Rose trio became the toast of chamber music scene as well as one of the highest-paid and most critically acclaimed groups in classical music. Howard Klein wrote in the *Times* May 1964 (one month before Minnie's death), "... one of those rarest of chamber-music evenings. Technical mastery was brought to such sublime heights in service to the music that one did not hear the music so much as one heard pure spirit."[251] "Monday night's United Nations Concert in Constitution Hall was one of the most brilliant in the six-year history of these annual events ... Their generosity toward one another as they blended three powerful musical temperaments into a matchless trio ..." Paul Hume of the *Washington Post* wrote in October 1966.[252]

It's hard to imagine in the twenty-first century that popular magazines were once devoted to literary and art criticism. One defunct magazine, The *Saturday Review*, had a lifespan from 1924 to 1986. A cover photo and feature article, "Three Men on a Hobby," in October 1970 profiled each musician of the trio and their mindset in depth, as the ensemble marked its tenth consecutive season with an unprecedented series of Beethoven concerts around the world. During this Beethoven bicentenary year, the Istomin-Stern-Rose trio spent six months together, playing approximately 30 works in 50 concerts—all by Beethoven—in Israel, London, Paris, Switzerland, Buenos Aires, and at Carnegie Hall. Interviewed and clearly relishing his fame, Rose said, "I have always wanted the opportunity to participate in a cycle of this sort. It is, of course, thrilling to perform all the trios. I've always wanted to perform the five cello sonatas and the three sets of variations on one particular occasion, and now the occasion is at hand. I would say that it is the fulfillment of a lifetime ambition." Rose's ego could not be contained: "I dare say that some of our first read-through performances are a lot better than most people achieve when they finally get up to play. I think the whole history of our trio has been one where we have decided in the past 10 years to let the public in on some of the fun that we have had privately over really a 30-year period."

Beethoven's "Triple" Concerto was featured on some of these occasions in 1970 as well. Rose fondly recalls one conducted by Pablo Casals at the revered man's festival in Puerto Rico in which the performance was videotaped.[253] The aging Spaniard spent his final 16 years in Puerto Rico, his mother's birthplace. His annual festival* of concerts ran from 1957, some of which aired on San

---
* Similar to that which he founded in Prades.

Juan's educational television station. Preserved and sadly in inadequate storage, some of these performances featured the world's most prominent artists.

The early objective to record the bulk of the standard repertoire for the genre consumed the three men. From 1964 through 1970, the Istomin-Stern-Rose trio dedicated a significant part of their lives to recording the 11 Beethoven trios, the three Brahms trios, both of Mendelssohn's, and the two of Schubert's. Neither the Cortot-Thibaud-Casals nor the Heifetz-Rubinstein-Piatigorsky trios accomplished this feat. Ironically, it may have been because of the silhouette of Casals, who lived until October 1973, that they persevered to surpass his trio legacy. "Casals, by his example and his nature," Istomin stated, "reminded us of something we had forgotten, or hadn't dared contemplate: the importance in music of color and variety, of feeling, warmth, involvement—in other words, of ultimate human values and meaning."[254]

In 1970 Stern declared, "Perhaps in a way this is a tiny crusade of ours, to do the best we possibly can to present this music in the best way we possibly can, as close to the highest performance level that can be attained, so that those who come after us can keep that as a landmark and continue the belief and the faith." Twenty-three years later, well after Rose's death and two decades after the trio garnered a Grammy for their recordings of the complete piano trios of Beethoven, the violinist reminisced:

> I think what is most astonishing for me, when I listen to the old recordings, was how we listened to each other. And how, in some magical way, even the speed of our vibratos became similar. We could give and take to each other a phrase—one to the other, whoever was first, whichever way the music was written. And it would seem like the same thread ran through the material with the same needle stitching it together. That was the needle of our perception, and I think very much based on the fact there was a deep affection between us. It created not performances, but a period of life that was spent in

the service of music and is available for others to hear, study, and decide for themselves its validity.[255]

After 1970, the trio's travels trailed off with the exception of the continuation of their Beethoven commemoration throughout Asia in 1971. In some years, the trio performed just one to two weeks of concerts per season. Which begs the questions: With 14 years of productivity remaining to the ensemble, why did their recordings come to a halt after 1970? Why didn't the trio attempt to record the works of Haydn (except for the trio in E flat, Hob XV 10 recorded in 1968), Mozart (except for K. 502), Arensky, Dvořák, Rachmaninoff, Ravel, Schumann, Shostakovich or Tchaikovsky? And why, with the substantial resources these men possessed, didn't they commission new compositions for their ensemble's instrumentation? The consensus seems a lack of time: the ensemble's touring schedule simply could not accommodate the extra days and hours necessary to learn and record fresh material. Furthermore, during their arduous tour of 1970, internal unrest surfaced.

Notoriously, Eugene Istomin's ego was fragile. Istomin—who never concealed his frustration toward Rose who vociferously believed the cello would be better heard in performance if the pianist had lowered the grand piano's lid to half stick—told the writer of "Three Men on a Hobby," "I have no compunction in overwhelming, sometimes overbalancing, a partner in a given situation if I feel that a climax, a crescendo, would be aborted by my lessening drive and propulsion. At the same time, when I am musically compelled to submerge myself ... When I am required by musical necessities to come down, I will; and when I am required to go up, at whatever cost, I will. That's my idea of balance."

By 1970, 50-year-old Stern became an eloquent spokesman for all of classical music. Since he played a major role in saving Carnegie Hall from demolition, his ability to orate and persuade, and his behind-the-scenes manipulation, made his name synonymous with serious music and string playing. Wherever he went, his rhetoric was eagerly absorbed:

> **Wednesday Evening Series**
>
> **November 11**
> Trio in G major—"Kakadu" Variations, Op. 121 A
> Sonata for Piano and Violin in D major, Op. 12 No 1
> Sonata for Piano and Cello in C major, Op. 102 No 1
> Trio in D major, Op. 70 No 1 ("*Ghost*")
>
> **November 18**
> Trio in Eb major, Op. Posthumous
> Sonata for Piano and Horn in F major, Op. 17
> Sonata for Piano and Violin in A minor, Op. 23
> Variations for Piano and Cello in F major, Op. 66—"Ein Mädchen oder Weibchen" (*Zauberflöte*)
> Quintet for Piano, Oboe, Clarinet, Horn, and Bassoon in E-flat major, Op. 16
>
> **November 25**
> Sonata for Piano and Violin in A major, Op. 12 No 2
> Variations for Piano and Cello in G major—Theme from Judas Maccabaeus
> Sonata for Piano and Violin in E-flat major, Op. 12 No 3
> Trio in C minor, Op. 1 No 3
>
> **December 2**
> Variations for Piano and Cello in E-flat major—"Bei Männern, welche Liebe fühlen" (*Zauberflöte*)
> Sonata for Piano and Violin in G major, Op. 30 No 3
> Sonata for Piano and Violin in C minor, Op. 30 No 2
> Trio in B-flat major, Op. Posthumous
> Trio in E-flat major, Op. 1 No 1
>
> **Saturday Evening Series**
>
> **November 14**
> Sonata for Piano and Cello in G minor, Op. 5 No 2
> Sonata for Piano and Violin in A major, Op. 47 ("*Kreutzer*")
> Trio in B-flat major, Op. 11
>
> **November 28**
> Sonata for Piano and Violin in F major, Op. 24 ("*Spring*")
> Sonata for Piano and Cello in A major, Op. 69
> Trio in G major, Op. 1 No 2
>
> **December 5**
> Trio Variations in E-flat major, Op. 44
> Sonata for Piano and Violin in A major, Op. 30 No 1
> Sonata for Piano and Cello in F major, Op. 5 No 1
> Trio in Eb major, Op. 70 No 2
>
> **December 12**
> Sonata for Piano and Cello in D major, Op. 102 No 2
> Sonata for Piano and Violin in G major, Op. 96
> Trio in B-flat major, Op. 97 ("*Archduke*")

Istomin-Stern-Rose Carnegie Hall 1970

How else can you equate whether you've made this *piano* or this *sforzando*, or this passage didn't come out or that idea didn't get across, in relation to the deaths of thousands of people here or the destruction of a country there? You cannot compare these problems with the small limits of your own worries ... Music in essence is what happens in between the printed notes, not on the notes themselves. How, in that milli-milli-millisecond of time in going from one note to another note. ... This, then, is our search and the trust we've accepted and the basic reasoning behind all this effort.[256]

Stern, at 50, had already begun to cultivate what became known as his "Kosher Nostra"—the mentoring and thrusting of artists he deemed worthy onto the world's concert stages—a fellowship he established that his detractors claimed bordered on clannishness and outright favoritism.[257] The constant surveillance and mentoring of many young fiddlers likely took away his interest and amount of time he allotted for his trio, which affected his own preparedness that led to a gradual drop-off in performance level, unbearably painful to some post-1980; Rose openly complained about constant interruptions, telephone calls to Stern during rehearsals in addition to consternation about Stern's casual approach to some engagements.

Arturo Delmoni met up with Leonard Rose after a trio concert in San Diego in the 1970s. The scene, as he described it, "was pathetic. I was in Mr. Rose's dressing room and no one else was there with us. Yet there were hordes of people in Stern's dressing room to congratulate him in his underwear. Stern played rather poorly that day and Rose played, as always, impeccably beautifully. But Stern was the big cheese and Mr. Rose wasn't. So, he said, c'mon let's go have some dinner. He said it in kind of a sad way." On this particular occasion, very few had anything to say to Rose after the concert.

In even this finest, most successful collaboration, tensions lurked beneath the surface. In the early years, the trio suppressed them. Slowly though, compromise became impossible and differences overwhelmed the men. In his memoir, Rose surmised: "Isaac benefited from timing. He burst onto the scene when Heifetz was already in decline, when [Mischa] Elman was nearly finished, when [Joseph] Szigeti was getting old, and when [Nathan] Milstein, who still played marvelously, objected to air travel. Everyone knew that Isaac Stern was the real driving force of the trio, and enjoyed the greatest individual reputation of the group."

Rose continues the talk of his trio: "Nevertheless, the official name is the Istomin-Stern-Rose trio. Eugene insisted upon this title with his name listed first. His 'official' reasoning was that the major composers always listed their trios for pianoforte, violin, and violoncello." Rose's aggravation comes through his prose, "I am absolutely convinced that Eugene's so-called 'official' reasoning was far from the actual truth. There is no question in my mind that it was Eugene's ego that came into play, and which created unnecessary difficulties. It got to the point that at Eugene's insistence, each trio contract had to stipulate the name "Istomin-Stern-Rose" trio, in that order, and all advertisements read similarly. Isaac seemed not to care in the least; and except for my annoyance at Eugene's phony rationalization, I too couldn't have cared less. I remember remarking once to my colleague, 'Doesn't matter how it's listed, my name always comes last.'"

A discordant reality is that the pianist and cellist possessed a greater familiarity with the trio literature, and that the "real driving force of the trio," Stern needed to lean on the others before some pieces made musical sense. At times, this annoyed both Istomin and Rose. Stern admitted that his nonchalance about preparation and performance routine wore thin with his partners. Clearly, Stern had grown exasperated with Rose's concert habits when he described Rose as "a driven neurotic who couldn't get away from his nerves. He had to practice so many hours a morning—every morning. At four o'clock in the afternoon on the day of a concert, he had to have a steak and whatever came with it. No other food. Invariably, he was at the hall an hour before the concert, when he would begin with a series of little exercises to warm up."[258]

Eugene Istomin, except to those closest to him, remained private with his opinions about his esteemed colleagues. His voice did rise in indignation, however, when complaining of the trio's limited repertoire, which did not stretch, with the exception of Ravel's 1914 trio, into the twentieth century.

Rose's version of the trio's problems with instrumental balance troubles on their 1970 Beethoven tour revealed much about the men's relationship. Marta Istomin vividly remembered a dreadful piano that presented her husband a plethora of problems one particular concert in Switzerland. To be fair-minded, Stern and Rose always had the advantage of playing all the concerts on their beloved instruments whereas Istomin was forever at the mercy of strange pianos. This particular event stuck in Rose's craw:

> One of Eugene's problems was his complete conviction that a trio was really a piano concerto with violin and cello incidentally tagging along. The piano lid was always on the longest support completely open, regardless of the particular brilliance of the piano used, or the acoustics of the auditorium. Most often, our balance was okay, but at other times—particularly in the Tonhalle in Zurich—

the piano and auditorium were so brilliant, the strings were literally overwhelmed. Despite letters that Isaac received from people in the Zurich audience protesting the overwhelming piano sound, Eugene was loath to consider lowering the piano lid half stick. Eugene was always quick to quote Rudolf Serkin [his teacher at the Curtis Institute], who allegedly said he couldn't really control the piano sound unless the lid was fully open. I think that's just so much crap. Yes, the piano has more notes to play than the strings, but it is a trio with three performers, not a piano concerto with two subordinate sidekicks. After Isaac spoke to Eugene about it, Eugene very grudgingly relented and lowered the piano lid to half stick. The following concert of that particular series turned out to be terrible.

Private battles spilled over onto public stages. Rose's account continues.

In the most petulant and disagreeable manner, Eugene played the entire concert never playing more than a mezzo piano, totally underplaying and sabotaging the performance. There is no question that Eugene was under great strain during that period. After all, he played in every work. It was a hell of a lot of music, and except for causing the violin and cello to play to the greatest extent of sound—almost having to force—Eugene played masterfully. The strain Eugene was going through had its effect on the three of us.

Rose laments, "There were episodes that should not have happened."

As it turned out, an upsetting incident in 1970 made it practically impossible for Rose to continue, in good faith, with his colleagues. In retrospect, the cellist—who juggled, without the benefits from a sabbatical, a full class of students at Juilliard, concertized worldwide, and in just six years diagnosed with his first cancer—relates: "First we recorded the trios.* Then Isaac and Eugene recorded one or two violin-piano sonatas, and Eugene and I recorded the A Major and D Major cello-piano sonatas [1969]. Completely unbeknownst to me—perhaps Isaac knew—Eugene went to see the artists' and repertoire decision maker at Columbia Records** and said he wanted to record the "Emperor" Concerto. He was told that Columbia had a recent "Emperor" recording done by [Rudolf] Serkin, and a slightly older one of [Robert] Casadesus, and that Columbia didn't need another recording of that concerto." Rose was oblivious at the time and possibly never found out the truth to the simmering battle between Istomin and Columbia Records, which erupted. The resulting casualty was Istomin's broken contract with Rose. Justly or not, the pianist proceeded to stop, in its tracks, the cello and piano cycle of recordings of Beethoven. Rose related the event with understandable resentment: "Whereupon good old Eugene retorted in a huff, 'in that case, I won't record the Beethoven Sonatas with Rose.' Charming, eh? Lousy and an unforgivable thing to do to a colleague, and without even telling or asking me."

Why couldn't Rose hammer out, with Lieberson, an agreement to finish this project with some other celebrated pianist? The incident still rings with earmarks of a calamity. A cycle of Beethoven cello and piano works recorded by Leonard Rose with any pianist is a glaring omission in his discography.

Yet the show did go on. *Times* critic Harold C. Schonberg observed that the trio had not lost a step and remained in fine form in a 1974 Carnegie Hall performance: "The Istomin-Stern-Rose trio went about it with beautifully relaxed teamwork ... results were equally beautiful in Beethoven's E flat trio (Op. 70 No. 2). ... There was some overpowering impressive playing. ... It was a wonderful concert—beautiful music, beautifully played."[259] Rose seemingly came full circle; his respect for Istomin's musicianship

---
* Op. 1, No. 1 1970; Op. 1, No. 2 1969; Op. 1, No. 3 1966; Op. 11 1969; Op. 44 1970; Op. 70, No. 1 1969; Op. 70, No. 2 1970; WoO 38 1970; G. 154 1970; Op. 97 1965; Op. 121a 1968.

**Goddard Lieberson, 1911-1977: a pioneer in the recording industry, who was the president of Columbia Records from 1956 to 1971 and from 1973 to 1975.

never waned. In a letter dated August 24, 1981, Rose, in a grateful and reflective mood, sent this note to Istomin:

> My Dear Eugene,
>
> I cannot resist writing to you—Just listened to our C minor Mendelssohn [from July 1966]. The overall performance is glowing, beautiful, and spirited. It's important for me to tell you how overwhelmed I was with <u>your</u> playing. The brilliant technical mastery and sensitive musical ideas were touching.
>
> Much love, Lennie[260]

The letter piques curiosity as to why Rose expressed such vehemence in his criticism toward Istomin in his memoir. In the midst of many happy years of music making, these few incidents were the ones Rose chose to remember and wanted to make public during his lifetime.

In 1983, the relationship between the trio's string players was rocky at best. Rose continues:

> I have always loved Isaac for many reasons, but in particular, his friendship and loyalty. I still love him and always will, despite what I am to relate. About a year ago, Isaac told me he had a letter from Eugene to the effect that Eugene wanted to record the Beethoven Sonatas. Isaac Stern—being so powerful, important, and a very great artist—could have recorded the Beethoven Sonatas with Jesus Christ himself, if he were available. The same is certainly not true of me in 1983. I attempted to request that Isaac not record these sonatas with Eugene, reminding Isaac of Eugene's literally screwing me out of recording the cello sonatas in 1970. I spoke to completely deaf ears. Isaac and Eugene finished the recordings a few months ago. Oh, I blame Eugene for his total lack of collegial consideration years ago; but, Isaac, where was your loyalty when I wanted it so badly? I shall never again mention it to you, but I'm hurt!

Rarely did anyone see this side of Leonard Rose, so raw with emotion.

Nearly a decade after Rose's death, Stern grew emotional when speaking about his colleague for a videotaped oral history at the University of Maryland. With tears in his eyes, the brokenhearted Stern affectionately recalls:

> To this day, he is there because of the special quality he had as a performer—his utter devotion to the task at hand—his one mindedness at being prepared, knowledgeable, informed, and above all, respectful of music. He had a nobility of sound. He knew how to make a phrase come to life. He illuminated the idea. What I remember most about Lennie was the pleasure of rehearsals. We would sometimes have differing ideas, but they were very small nuances. Most of the time, we had a similar approach. It was always done with respect and affection between the two of us. We were very close friends. Always.[261]

Rose   Stern   1950s
Courtesy of Arthur Rose

Today, almost every major city in the country boasts at least one resident piano trio—thanks, in part, to the standards and leadership of the Istomin-Stern-Rose trio. It is not surprising that the majority of today's leading piano trios had some link with these three great artists. One example is the prolific Kalichstein-Laredo-Robinson trio, which celebrated its 30th anniversary in 2007; all three members collaborated with and had long-lasting friendships with their predecessors. "This was the greatest trio there ever was," violinist Jaime Laredo, disclosed. "I heard them in concert and owned every single one of their recordings. We wanted to emulate the Istomin-Stern-Rose trio. They were our inspiration."

What made the Istomin-Stern-Rose trio so great? Allen Hughes, writing in the *New York Times* (May 16, 1969), succeeds in explaining their extraordinary success: "They have the distinct advantage of being able to play their respective instruments better than performers who devote themselves chiefly to chamber music. Istomin, Stern, and Rose are better because they can draw upon virtuoso tonal luster that gives their group playing an almost magical sheen. Thus, even when they do exactly what habitual chamber music players do, it sounds about ten times better than usual."

In a proud moment, Isaac Stern comprehended as well the rank his trio attained in the musical pantheon: "All of us are soloists, and in solo performance have come to know, recognize, and look for that ecstasy, that moment when there is the unity between the music, the performer, and the audience. It is this power of projection *individually* that is rarely found—I think I can say in all candor—in chamber music performers."[262]

Chapter Twenty

DARKNESS AND LIGHT, 1964

I can't believe this. THIS is the greatest talent I have ever had.
     —Leonard Rose on nine-year-old Yo-Yo Ma

  In 1964, Leonard Rose's life took a dramatic turn.
  Dominating all, his wife Minnie lost her valiant 10-year battle with leukemia. A whirlwind of adjustment and transformation charged with emotion defined the final two decades of Rose's life: A new wife, a new flair, new friends, new outlook, and some musicians judged a different, deeper player. Additionally, his attitude on teaching was renewed, due to the nine year old who entered his life. Not all change was positive. His continuous struggle with depression over his wife's death and guilt from his swift remarriage led to an irreparable break with his children.
  His music making during the period, in spite of the turmoil, was at its zenith. In a September 1963 concert with the London Symphony at Royal Festival Hall, Rose performed the Brahms "Double" Concerto with Isaac Stern on the first half and Strauss's *Don Quixote* to complete the program. Rose's classifying it as "one of the highlights of my life and my career," proves the point.[263] Conductor Pierre Monteux[264]—a short, rotund, and mustached figure—renowned for having conducted the world premieres of Stravinsky's *Petrushka* (1911), *Le Sacre du Printemps* (1913), Ravel's *Daphnis et Chloe* (1911 and 1913), and Prokofiev's Third Symphony (1935), in his last year of life, at 89, told Rose in the wing of the stage, "My dear, I can't go any longer—you go out,

you go." The enthusiasm of the audience did not cease until Leonard Rose came out to take one final bow—his thirteenth in all. Donald Mitchell from the *London Telegraph* wrote, "An incomparable, spellbinding account of Strauss. ... This was undoubtedly a great performance. ... There was not a moment when any player seemed less than wholly caught up in the magic of the occasion." The *London Times* reported, "It was one those occasions, rare in our concert life, when conductor, orchestra, and soloists not only gave their best, but seemed all of one mind." Eugene Istomin was the first to greet Rose backstage: "Lennie, do you realize the reception you got tonight is reserved only for people like Rubinstein, Horowitz, or Casals!" Rose had just received news that his wife's leukemia, in remission for a decade, had returned with a vengeance. In the evening's music, the death of the Spanish Don, which Strauss portrayed so powerfully, affected Rose profoundly and he openly wept in his dressing room: "I remember the pangs so well—Isaac was with me and hugged me."

Casals   Rose   Monteux   Istomin   Stern   1963
Courtesy of Marta Istomin

Rose drove to Heathrow Airport in London to pick up his wife and daughter, whom he had just seen in Israel. He knew something was wrong as he stood waiting while a long, steady stream of passengers emerged from the plane. A moment of panic gripped him when he realized they were not on that plane. A few days later, he phoned home from Lucerne, Switzerland, and learned of Minnie's grim prognosis. He spiraled into a tailspin. His trio partners suggested gallantly playing sonata recitals in lieu of scheduled trios, offering Rose his full share of money—permitting him to fly home. Their generosity touched the cellist, but he would not accept it. He wanted to complete the tour. When he settled in at home, he saw his wife doubled over in pain, at times, in unbearable coughing fits. Side effects from radiation treatments that followed only worsened her state. The summer of 1964 was an endless and difficult one for Rose and his children: Barbara who had just turned 23 and Arthur 19.

Rose's good friends Nathan Stutch and Ann Barak visited the house daily after Minnie's death: for Leonard, for the children, and anything else that needed doing. According to Barak, as Rose drove her home shortly thereafter, he exclaimed, "Well, that's it. I will never marry again unless I find a very rich woman who can help my career. Otherwise, the love of my life is gone. That's it."

His despondency worsened as the monotonous days blurred together. On September 29, 1964, about 5:30 in the afternoon, Rose finished practicing, wrote as many letters as he possibly could, and felt restless and lonely: his daughter moved in with her boyfriend, and his son lived at college. Alone in his house, Rose started to call up friends.

One friend he hoped to see was Stutch, who took a few lessons with him at Curtis and was his colleague in the Cleveland Orchestra and New York Philharmonic. Barak reconstructed, decades later, the events of that day that changed Rose's life.

"Hello, Leonard."

"What are you guys doing tonight? I thought maybe I would take a ride into Manhattan. Maybe we can have dinner together and go to a movie or something," Rose said.

"Great! You know Nate isn't here. He is in Canada with the Philharmonic. But, c'mon over. I have two steaks in the freezer and it's no problem."

"Nate's not there? Oh, then I can't come."

"What are you talking about?"

"It wouldn't be right. I can't do that. It would be wrong."

"Well, what are you going to do then?" Barak pressed.

"I think I'll take a ride into the Village and go to the deli to pick up a corned beef sandwich and a couple of beers. I'll have that then come home, take two sleeping pills, and go to sleep."

Barak was determined to get Rose out of the house that he refers to in his memoir in a disconsolate tone as "uncomfortable; there were too many bad memories ...." Earlier in the day, she invited her close friend Xenia Petchek, one of the top researchers for the television news program, the Huntley-Brinkley Report, to come over to her place after work for dinner. From a wealthy family—her father, Walter Petchek, was a key attorney for CBS—Xenia resolved to support herself and had recently moved out of her parents' Park Avenue apartment to live by herself. She landed a job on the Huntley-Brinkley Report and worked her way up the ladder.

Xenia Petchek, born in New York City, graduated from Sarah Lawrence (BA '57) then spent a year and a half trying to become an actress before working at NBC News. In that capacity, she was on the team that edited the footage of Richard Nixon's 1962 concession speech and farewell address from his defeat in that year's California gubernatorial race. She worked three days without sleep the weekend of the JFK assassination. She would return to school after meeting Rose; and in 1974, she received a Master's degree in education from the Sarah Lawrence-NYU Project.[265] By 1979, aided by Rose's support, Petchek established a full-time private practice in psychotherapy.

With the 1964 United States presidential election looming, NBC had just acquired their first Univac computers, which filled an entire room, floor to ceiling. All personnel were required to learn how to operate the machines. On this particular Saturday, Xenia along with the rest of the staff, wrestled with the massive machinery. By mid-afternoon, she phoned Barak to tell her it was literally giving her a headache. Once she finally figured out how to feed the election data into the machine, it spat out 'Khrushchev wins primary in Arizona!' Xenia wouldn't be up for a social evening and cancelled her date. She told her friend she preferred to head home and relax, alone.

When Rose phoned Barak 20 minutes later, she started scheming. She described the interesting, beautiful Xenia and proposed she introduce him to her. Hesitant, he allowed Barak to set it up. Xenia had always wanted to meet Rose. She was a music lover who had admired the cellist from a distance. She attended his every New York concert and recognized what a handsome man and gifted artist he was. Although she couldn't arrive in time for dinner, she agreed to join Barak and Rose for dessert. Rose agreed to the plan.

The anxious Rose arrived at Barak's dressed in his finest black three-piece suit, holding a bottle of 30-year-old Scotch—presumably a hostess gift. But he headed directly to the kitchen, opened the bottle, and poured himself a large glassful. Barak watched, stunned and then confronted him. Chagrinned, Rose admitted he felt nervous. It was his first blind date since he was a teenager and he worried about how to act and what to say, especially if he liked her, or didn't.

A knock on the door signaled Petchek's arrival—perfect timing as the two were finishing their meal. From the first glimpse, Rose found her ravishing. She was 29. He was 46. As Rose remembers, "Standing before me was this absolutely adorable, beautiful, blond, young lady."

Barak introduced the two then left them alone to get acquainted in the living room. Barak knew her matchmaking effort succeeded when Petchek discreetly asked her advice about taking "Lennie" home with her to see the tree she looked at from her kitchen window. Rose mentioned to Petchek that he brought his car and offered her a lift home. She accepted. Once inside the car, he suggested they go for a drive—to her delight. "She was full of enthusiasm—that girl!" Rose recalled.

> We drove all the way out to Jones Beach [approximately 30 miles]. We got out of the car and smelled the air. Then I said, "Would you like to see my house?" She agreed, so we drove there and saw my house, after which I drove her home. She asked, "Would you like to come up for a while?"—which pleased me very much. I stayed until

4:30 in the morning. We had a wonderful time talking. I must say I was terribly attracted to her and I think she was attracted to me, too.

Barak remembered how the following day, she spent hours on the phone. He called, she called, he called, she called. ... Barak conveyed Rose's enthusiasm for Petchek. "Oh my God. I don't know what to do. She's fantastic. I never met anybody like her." He also expressed concerns about entering into a sexual relationship; the reverberation of which would damagingly affect his family on the heels of Minnie's death. Petchek was equally infatuated telling Barak, "Oh my God. He's fantastic..."

The couple quickly fell in love. But Rose's concert season had crept up suddenly and he despaired without his new companion at his side. According to Rose: "I began the season of 1964-1965 not very happily I must say, because I was still suffering a great deal of depression and guilt. During the interim period, I decided that I needed some help. Death does terrible things to a person and I'm afraid it did terrible things to me."

During this intense period of flux, the ax fell on some of his cello students. Steve Custor (a member of the Los Angeles Philharmonic), who studied with Rose from 1960 to 1964, was one of three students from his Juilliard class dropped without explanation. Custor's recollection was that it "was somewhat hard to accept at first, but I understand why he didn't want to speak to us about such a difficult situation. He was very depressed in the last lessons I had with him, looking very tired and not very involved." Yet another variation on this theme of change, he would—the same year—take on a very young new student, who would recharge him.

In January of 1965, Rose's schedule took him to Europe and suddenly he couldn't work as usual. The continued suffering affected his playing. Characteristic of major depression, at one point he literally couldn't get out of bed. He realized he needed to cancel the whole European tour. One canceled concert was a performance of the Dvořák Concerto in February 1965 with the London Symphony at Festival Hall, Sir Adrian Boult conducting. On short notice, the 20-year-old Jacqueline Du Pré filled in.

"I came back home and I wanted to marry Xenia and that's precisely what I did," Rose declared. "I also started seeing my therapist with a good deal of regularity, and lots of things came to the surface. ... One of the reasons why I was feeling such guilt was that I had the idea that I had literally killed my first wife. This plagued me so terribly that I couldn't function."

"When they got married," Barak recalled, "the people of Great Neck were horrified. 'Leonard Rose was a pariah.' 'Oh, how could he get married only a few months after Minnie died and her body isn't even cold yet!'" Barak scolded Rose, "Oh, for God's sake. Do you give a rat's ass what they think?"[266]

His answer turned out to be a double-edged sword. In the process of marrying Xenia Petchek, Rose alienated his children, other relatives, and close friends. Whether guilt played a role in alienating these vital people, whether he no longer enjoyed his old social circle, or whether the resumption of his career consumed him are among many unanswerable questions. Did the depression impel him to propose so quickly or did he view a secure relationship as its cure? He was happily in love and consequences be damned.

As if on permanent honeymoon, all Petchek really wanted was to travel the world as wife of the famous Leonard Rose. But at the age of 31, she began to crave a life of her own. A "happily ever after" romance was not to be. Not until 1990, did Xenia reveal their troubled marriage in her book, *A Return to thy Loving Self*, in which she identified herself as a "pathological mourner."[267] The book not only chronicled her severe feelings of pain and isolation after her famous husband's death, it also shed light on their own troubled marriage. Petchek, who remarried after Rose and died from liver cancer in 2001 at the same age as Rose, opens her book with an astonishing proclamation: "There was never a question on the part of either of us that, given the opportunity to marry each other again, we would not have done so."[268]

However, she did transform his life; and it was not only her immeasurable admiration for his music making that Rose cherished. What she brought into the marriage meshed with his immediate needs for self-worth and fulfillment. Her personality somewhat colder and more domineering than Minnie's contributed to Rose's alienation of his own children, but she actively broadened his horizons and improved his lot. She encouraged her new husband to see a psychiatrist who helped free the cellist from extreme anxieties and self-doubts. For a man obsessed with maintaining a standard of perfectionism and nearly debilitated by chronic depression, which may have been aided by dependence upon nicotine, psychotherapy proved beneficial. Petchek also introduced Rose to the joy of collecting eighteenth-century English furniture. It became a passion: He devoured books on the subject and frequented antique sales and auction houses. In addition, Petchek taught him Scrabble, which they frequently enjoyed together after dinner. In the old days, if Rose had any strength left in his body, he would have practiced before bedtime.

Amidst the sadness of Minnie's deteriorating condition in 1964, Isaac Stern—whose opinions Rose held in high esteem—brought a nine-year-old Chinese boy to Rose. A professor at the École Française Bilingual School while the family lived in Paris, Yo-Yo Ma's father became a teacher to the Stern children. At a very young age, Ma and his sister played for the violinist. In the fall of 1964, at Stern's New York apartment during a break, Rose recounts,

> Isaac said to me, "Someone is coming to play for you after the rehearsal. Yeah?" I said, "Who?" We finished the rehearsal, I looked around, and there's this little half-pint oriental boy, with his little cello tucked under his arm with his father beside him. I said to him, "Well, come over here. Unpack your cello and play for me." So he unpacked his little cello—and it was very small because he was very small. We found a low hassock for him. He sat down on this little hassock and played some of the Goltermann[269] Fourth Concerto, a student concerto really, and a movement or two of a Bach Suite—everything from memory, everything correct, really quite well in tune although the sound was very small. Eugene [Istomin] said to me afterwards, "Lennie, how can you tell if he's gifted?" I said, "You wait!" I knew the boy had something.

One could successfully argue that Yo-Yo Ma's rise to stardom was inevitable, no matter with whom he studied; but under Leonard Rose's scrutiny, he may have risen more quickly. Terribly inhibited, in part due to a rigidly structured upbringing, Ma later recounted:

> I was a pipsqueak of a kid and overwhelmingly shy. I was afraid to speak to Mr. Rose above a whisper. I'd try to hide behind the cello. He was always calm, soothing, and gentle. He tried to get me to overcome my timidity by constantly urging me to sing out on the instrument. There was this kind of sympathy from my teacher to me. It was like he was saying to me, "I too was shy. I went through the same thing."[270]

Yo-Yo Ma's father, born in Shanghai, dedicated much of his life to music; he learned the violin and, eventually, Nanjing University appointed him professor. Also an educator, he taught Chinese history, mythology, and Chinese calligraphy to his son whom he required to learn two characters a day. Ma's father patiently and systematically taught his son to memorize two measures of Bach—daily. As a result, Ma could play the first three Bach suites when he was just a child. Ma's father accompanied Yo-Yo to his early lessons with Rose, taking copious notes. The boy's mother, more temperamental than his father, came from Hong Kong. His parents met and married in Paris where Yo-Yo was born in 1955.

As a teenager, Ma experienced a series of transformations: rebelling at Manhattan's Professional Children's School, defying authority at Meadowmount, and then sabotaging his education at Juilliard where he was once found face-down drunk in a practice studio.[271] In the fall of 1968, the 13 year old showed up for a lesson sporting a leather jacket and boldly enlightening Rose with his new favorite swear words.

> But Mr. Rose took it in stride and saw me through this phase. At some level, he must have been very happy to find me opening up in that way; and, for some reason, he kept his faith in me. In the early years of our lessons, he

would explain every piece in advance and demonstrate his interpretation; but as time went on, he gave me leeway to experiment myself. When I was 15, after I had given a concert in Carnegie Recital Hall, he said, "Well done. Now I'm going to give you a piece—Beethoven's C Major Sonata—to work on entirely by yourself. I'm not going to suggest bowings, fingerings, or anything. You just go ahead, learn it, and play it for me." I'll always be grateful to Mr. Rose for that.[272]

In July 1982, Rose recounts in his unpublished memoir:

This morning I was practicing and my telephone rang. It was my good friend, Raya Garbousova,[273] who is absolutely darling and was, in my opinion, one of the very great talents, and certainly, the greatest woman cellist I have ever known. She called to say that she had a very great thrill, because she had driven to Ravinia the night before to hear Yo-Yo play the Haydn D Major Concerto with the Chicago Symphony. Also, in the afternoon, Yo-Yo played the Fifth Suite of Bach. She said the playing was so absolutely first rate, so artistic, with so much personality.

Rose makes his lone reference in his memoir to the cellist whom he accompanied 41 years earlier during his initial season as principal cellist of the Cleveland Orchestra. "I said, 'Doesn't he remind you of Feuermann, that kind of talent?' She responded, 'Absolutely!' That was something. Here is Raya now 70 years old, and I will soon be 64. We're both not children, but we both have had fine careers." Rose enthuses, "And this is my boy, this is my student. He studied with me. ... He is going to set the world on fire. He deserves everything he has gotten, and I think he's got the world by the tail!"

Yo-Yo Ma undoubtedly has set the world on fire as classical music's most recognizable figure. In middle age, his technical prowess and communicative gifts are unparalleled. Much like Rose at age 50, two generations of cellists have been influenced by Ma's performances, CD recordings, demonstrative approach to the instrument, and stage mannerisms, even though Ma avoids any semblance of a teaching career. Audiences, at present, routinely set eyes on budding young virtuosos performing with heads held high, torsos leaning back, and facial expressions marking each shift in musical mood in imitation of Ma. Nevertheless, it is the cellist's signature, even if gestures have grown exaggerated in recent years, possibly due to enduring physical duress—when Ma was 25, he had an operation for scoliosis, a curvature of the spine. Today, Ma walks with a noticeable limp. Despite these body distortions that are bigger than need be, Ma's performances and recordings remain breathtakingly honest and committed.[274]

"I am convinced that Yo-Yo Ma will go down in history as one of the greatest cellists of all time," Rose dictated toward the end of his life before Ma's international stardom. "For me, he has all the talent, musicality, and technique of some of the greatest players the world has ever known." Rose gushes in his memoir: "A Yo-Yo Ma comes along so rarely. If a great teacher gets one of those in a lifetime, that's a lot."

Adhering to traditional pedagogy, Rose initially assigned Ma études. "All of those extremely difficult études of [David] Popper, many of which are just plain boring musically, and those equally boring études of [Friedrich Wilhelm Ludwig] Grützmacher[275] Opus 38, Book 2! I would give one of those a week to him and he would come back at the end of the week with the piece perfectly from memory, not one bar out of place." Ma reveals, "He spent years trying to get me to play with a bent thumb. I couldn't really do it. My hands are shaped differently. I couldn't get this beautiful sound and vibrato that he got because [holding up his hand] I have thin fingers." Ma's unique approach to the instrument took years to ripen, occurring long after his final lesson with the master. "It wasn't that I didn't try to model myself the way Rose played, I simply didn't have the tools to do it. I didn't have the physical capability." Initially, Ma played with "a lot of sausages" (unrefined swell within a lengthy bow stroke) in sound production and discloses that, "he insisted on making sure I could play a legato line" before progressing to the next assignment. Rose's enthusiasm for his protégé who was 27 years old in 1982, and who has since reshaped the cello landscape is astute:

He has such a staggering command of the instrument, which he has proven time and again. He has a repertoire list that he can play at the drop of a hat—at least 20 concerti; and what he doesn't know ... he can learn the most complicated and difficult piece in just a few days and learn it from memory. He has one of the most prodigious memories I have ever encountered in my life; on par with Rostropovich, which is colossal,* and with the memory of Glenn Gould, which is also extraordinary. ... The thing I absolutely adore about Yo-Yo is that he is one of the nicest human beings in the world. His playing reflects it!

"If I have seen farther than others, it is because I was standing on the shoulders of giants," said Ma, in reflection of his own resplendent time in the limelight—quoting Isaac Newton (1642-1727), one of the foremost scientific intellects of his time. "I'm one of the beneficiaries of the landscape that was built by Leonard Rose," Ma said earnestly. "Mr. Rose gave each of us a large piece of brick and mortar in the cultural building landscape. What are we doing with that brick? How are we building on top of his work? How do we actually add to the process as opposed to the process of the zero sum game?"
Ma continues.

There is one pie and if you have a slice of the pie, you get a slice of pie from me. If this is the background, we should actually do something to better our domain, to get our domain to have more possibilities. Rather than think of a single-pie theory, let's think about recipes. Share the recipe. "Here is a new piece—only I can play it." Baloney! The more people who play it, the better

---

* One of Rostropovich's party tricks was to reel off a numbered list of 100 objects, which other guests noted on paper. They allowed him to glance at the list for only a short time, but hours later Slava rendered guests speechless by reciting the 100 items in any order (Elizabeth Wilson: Mstislav Rostropovich, Faber and Faber Limited; 2007, p. 36).

this piece will survive. There will then be more demand for our services. Only when someone has lived through something like this can you actually begin to try to change it. How do we actually add to the process as opposed to the process of the zero sum game? I think that is our work, and that is his legacy.[276]

Ma informed this author, "He had the most beautiful form and sound I have ever heard." Knowingly, Rose smiles in his eternity.

With a formidable technique on the instrument from the start, Ma had steady lessons with Rose and Channing Robbins (Rose's colleague in the Cleveland Orchestra and associate at Juilliard for 34 years) beginning in 1964 from the age of nine to 16. At Ma's introduction, the 46-year-old master cellist's life was in a devastating state of flux. At precisely that time, the tragic return of Minnie's leukemia was shaking Rose and his children's world upside down. Minnie's subsequent death coupled with Rose's deep depression and then rapid love affair with Xenia coincided with Ma's introduction to Rose. Clearly, Rose felt proud of the child who added a positive counterweight to balance his bleakness in this year of change. The single reservation Rose harbored about the boy, in which he knew he could be of everlasting value, was the transferring of his own innate musical soul to Ma.

Despite Rose's tragic and joyous events during the tumultuous 1964-1965 season, he managed to produce some of his most notable recordings to date: **Schuman:** A Song of Orpheus, Cleveland Orchestra with George Szell (Severance Hall: January 11, 1964); **Brahms:** "Double" Concerto, Op. 102, Isaac Stern, violin, Philadelphia Orchestra with Eugene Ormandy (Town Hall, Philadelphia, April 14, 1964); **Beethoven:** "Triple" Concerto, Op. 56, Isaac Stern, violin, Eugene Istomin, piano, Philadelphia Orchestra with Eugene Ormandy (Town Hall, Philadelphia, April 16, 1964); **Schubert:** Piano Trio No. 1, Op. 99, with Isaac Stern, violin, Eugene Istomin, piano (Columbia 30th Street Studio New York City, August 15-17, 1964); **Brahms:** Piano Trio No. 2 in C Major, Op. 87, with Isaac Stern, violin, Eugene Istomin, piano (Columbia 30th Street Studio New York

City, December 28. 1964); **Dvořák:** Cello Concerto in B minor, Op. 104, Philadelphia Orchestra with Eugene Ormandy (Town Hall, Philadelphia, March 22, 1965).

Chapter Twenty-One

FOREMOST ROSE DISCIPLES

Without craftsmanship, inspiration is a mere reed shaken in the wind.

—Johannes Brahms

It was not uncommon in the early to mid-twentieth century for serious, talented young musicians to forgo the traditional schooling in favor of highly specialized private instruction. Among noted string players who followed this career path (or similar) were celebrated instrumentalists Emanuel Feuermann, Janos Starker, Paul Tortelier, Jacqueline Du Pré, Yehudi Menuhin, Isaac Stern, and Michael Rabin; Rose curtailed his own formal education after the 8th grade. Despite his limited experience in the conventional classroom, as he lay in a hospital bed five years before his death, Rose contemplated how few memorable teachers he was exposed to in his lifetime. His appreciation for rare pedagogical excellence was at the forefront of his mind. "I think one would be extremely fortunate to be able to count them on the fingers of one hand," Rose says. "That's how few good teachers that one generally has in school, in any subject." After a pause, he warmed to the idea of hailing himself a great teacher. "Now, if one gets into something as esoteric as the violin or the cello or other musical instruments, there are even fewer. A great teacher has to teach many aspects of music, not only the instrument. After all, what excuse do we have for playing an instrument? The excuse is to make beautiful music and to say something to people."

Ronald Leonard, former principal cellist of the Los Angeles Philharmonic (1975-1999; Naumburg Award winner 1955), studied at age 15 with Samuel Mayes, Rose's Curtis buddy, who at that time held the principal post with the Boston Symphony Orchestra. Because orchestral literature and responsibilities inundated Mayes, he suggested the best way for the teen to excel, to advance to the next level, was to seek out his venerated friend, Leonard Rose.

In Ronald Leonard's first year of conservatory training in 1951 at Curtis, Rose only managed to offer him four lessons. He had just begun his solo career and for that initial group of students, his schedule had little time to squeeze in the commute to and from Philadelphia. "Some things about it did not work out well because his assistant, Ehrling Bengstrom, had a completely different approach to music-making than Rose ..." Over the next few years, their relationship deepened as the elder cellist took a keen interest in that student class. Ron eagerly anticipated his lessons, however sporadic, with the famous man. "I think he loved talking to and getting to know his students. He really enjoyed this interaction." Rose's emotional involvement in the lives of early students was unique that markedly waned in his last years. In certain ways, Ron felt closer to the 33-year-old pedagogue than his own father.

When demonstrating, if Rose happened to play one note out of tune, the teacher would shift gears to practice the offending measure—cursing until he got it right. "Imagine a youngster witnessing this. Now THAT was certainly eye-opening." As for his student's intonation, Rose would quietly address him, "You know, Ronnie, dear, it is beautiful, but this note [Rose plays] is a little out of tune. Can you hear that?" His protégé would backtrack and make another attempt and Rose stopped him immediately, always with the utmost politeness, "The next note, I'm not quite sure of that one either."

His introduction to the music making of his teacher was the 1951 recording of Bloch's "Schelomo." The youth fell in love with the piece, and felt inspired to learn it that same year. In his first lesson on the challenging work, in the second bar, he mistakenly played an F-natural instead of an F-sharp. Rose looked him in the eye with a bemused expression, diffusing any tension and exclaimed, "You really aren't Jewish are you!"—Rose kidding his student about his Catholic upbringing. Ron relates, "But I think he paid me one of the highest compliments of my life after I performed "Schelomo" at Meadowmount [accompanied by two pianos] when afterward he came up to me and said, 'C'mon now, which side of the family has the Jewish blood?'"

Dispelling an impression that Rose, early in his teaching career, failed to communicate orally his method and style often enough, Ron recalls how he "verbalized his bow technique to me beautifully. The picture he drew stated clearly that as the hand goes forward the arm starts in the opposite direction, and that I needed to realize that it is the sensation of the push and a pull motion that I should concentrate on. It was simple. He told me exactly how he thought I should hold the bow, what the thumb should do, where they [the fingers] go, what the thrust was, etc." The recognized cellist confided, "I have wonderful memories of my whole experience with Leonard Rose. Maybe I was lucky that I hit him at a time when he had just started his solo career; maybe he was trying to prove to the world that he was a great teacher and not just a great cellist. He really gave it his all."*

At 10 years of age, after hearing Rose's debut recording, a 78 rpm of Heitor Villa Lobos's *Bachianas Brasileiras* No. 5 with soprano Bidú Sāyao, Michael Grebanier was drawn to the cello. The San Francisco Symphony's principal cellist in retrospect and repeating what countless cellists—possibly thousands—have said, "I had never heard cello playing like that. I was not much of a Piatigorsky fan nor was I a fan of the legendary and iconic playing Feuermann represented. Rose had that sound and style from the very beginning that grabbed me."

In 1954, Grebanier could hardly contain his exhilaration upon entering the Curtis Institute to study with Rose. Yet like Ronald Leonard before him, the teen quickly grew disillusioned and somewhat frustrated with the scarcity of lessons Rose succeeded in scheduling. Why, Grebanier pondered, did Rose have any desire to teach at Curtis, located so far away from

---

* Statements from Leonard and others in Chapter 21 all come from interviews with author from 2005-2007.

his Long Island home, on top of Juilliard responsibilities and burgeoning solo career?

The 19-year-old cellist's talent emerged in the early years with his teacher when he took first prize in the 1957 Naumburg Competition receiving an all-expense–paid debut recital at New York's Town Hall. Grebanier recalled his mentor's mood from long ago: "Even though Rose didn't think I was going to win, he nevertheless thought the contest a good experience for me to try. After having won, he was quite pleased and even got Rembert Wurlitzer to lend me a Gofriller cello. He also had me run through the recital at his home in Great Neck and at Meadowmount. In terms of repertoire, Rose wanted me to include [Tchaikovsky's] "Rococo" Variations, which I dutifully programmed."

Although Rose ultimately discouraged this ambitious pupil, and countless others from the solo route, he helped Grebanier secure excellent work: "When he spoke to me about becoming a soloist, he would say something like, 'You know, you have to be realistic.' But for orchestral positions, they routinely called him for recommendations." Toward the end of the 1957 academic year, Grebanier left Curtis to join the Pittsburgh Symphony. During his tenure there, Rose advised him to audition for George Szell whom he then worked for four seasons. Flashing his infantile side, Szell would not release Grebanier from his contract when he wanted to leave to become principal in St. Louis. Neither man deterred, Rose would—once again—telephone to advise Grebanier of the upcoming opening for principal of Pittsburgh. When only four people showed up, the organization hired Grebanier on the spot.

From his position in the Bay area, the cellist told me how Rose alone was the sole inspiration for his deep love for the cello. "I can't play like Leonard Rose because I am me; but his ghost is with me to this day. Not that I listen to his recordings much anymore, but certain things he said to me have stuck. I think he is at the top when speaking about the pantheon of cellists." According to the esteemed cellist, Rose possessed a unique sound that he was able to convey to students; a superior sound that nobody has since matched.

Lynn Harrell, one of contemporary America's most acclaimed solo cellists, and arguably the instrument's most eloquent spokesman, started lessons in Juilliard's Pre-College division from the age of nine with Phyllis Kraeuter, winner of the 1926 Naumburg Award. His father, the distinguished baritone Mack Harrell, who taught alongside Rose on Juilliard's faculty until 1956, wanted the boy to study with Rose. At their first lesson, Harrell showed up with his cello—and a baseball glove. The teacher judged him not quite mature enough and, startlingly, suggested to this musically renowned parent that the youngster perhaps concentrate more on baseball.* Instead, the singer took his son to study with Henrich Joachim, a former colleague of Rose's in the New York Philharmonic, a position Joachim retained. In 1956, suffering from lymphatic cancer, Lynn's father accepted a job at Southern Methodist University in Dallas, where his family settled. In Texas, Harrell studied with Lev Aronson (1912-1988), a Holocaust survivor, who was principal of the Dallas Symphony from 1948 to 1968. Aronson, an inspiring and clever teacher, designed methods to ignite Harrell's colossal abilities. A gift that prompted Channing Robbins to publicly state, "Once in a generation do you see talent like this."

Rose was engaged to solo with the Houston Symphony while Harrell lived in Dallas, on Belmead Street, during the period he worked with Aronson. The youth's mother, Marjorie Fulton—a violin graduate of Curtis—telephoned Rose with a request that he listen to the boy a second time. According to Rose's memoir, "Lynn then played with an extremely small sound. ... I said to him, 'You don't sound like you're 6 feet 4 inches, you sound like you're 4 feet 6 inches.'" Rose then took his cello and really socked into it. Rose shouted, "Play the damned piece—stop tickling it!" A gradual transformation started to take place. In 1960, one day before Harrell's 16th birthday, his father died from his disease

---

* Harrell was eleven. In 1938, Mack Harrell made his concert debut at New York's Town Hall. After winning the Metropolitan Opera Auditions, he debuted with the company in 1939. At the Met, he sang a wide repertory and in his thirteen seasons appeared in 156 performances, twenty-three roles, and eighteen works. Stricken with polio at the age of three, Harrell was a promising violinist when he was a high school student in Greenville, South Carolina. Harrell started studying voice in his 20s. His voice was considered one of remarkable lyrical beauty.

at age 51. Tragically, less than two years later, his mother was killed in an automobile accident, leaving Harrell orphaned.

Harrell's life was in chaos. Attending Juilliard in the 1960-1961 school year, studying with Rose and Robbins, Harrell struggled psychologically and financially, failing his classes. Rose was confused: "I didn't know what to do with him. I didn't want him to stay around New York, and he had some friends in Philadelphia." Prior to suggesting Harrell go to Curtis, he was taken in periodically by Rose and his wife Minnie, sharing a room with Rose's son.[277]

From 1961 to 1963, Harrell attended Curtis and in summers, Meadowmount, continuing his studies with Rose. At Curtis, like everyone else, he saw Rose infrequently. Harrell's voice drops to a whisper when recounting lingering dark sentiments of feeling abandoned by Rose. In the meantime, Harrell moved around to different family friends' houses with one suitcase and his cello. Eventually the youngster was taken into the home of Orlando Cole, another star pupil of the Salmond era who became Rose's assistant after Ehrling Bengstrom left. Cole provided the self-doubting youth "the security to express the passion of music." Cole knew it could be difficult to overcome the inhibition of the teen years, so he let Harrell know that it was all right to "let your hair really hang out." Cole made Harrell feel as though he was with a family that revolved around an icon of great music, both logistically and emotionally. "This experience made a deep and lifelong impression on me."

During the interim, he continued to revere Rose's cello playing. Harrell remarks on the "playing, the sound, and the vibrato. It was such a beautiful sonority. Instrumentally, he played the cello with such a wonderful sense of depth and breadth of sound quality. He could get a fat, deep, singing tone out of the cello."[278] For the young Harrell: "There hasn't ever been a cellist who played better than Leonard Rose." He exerted a powerful influence on him in these early years, but as maturation approached, he found his own voice: "There were plenty of years where all I wanted to do was play like Rose, like Casals in that passage, like Rostropovich there, Jacqueline du Pré, Starker, Fournier, Miller.[279] All of my great predecessors were inspirations for me. I absorbed that, and then I discovered that even trying to copy them—because I couldn't imagine anything better than that—it started to change. It felt more like me. It was a gradual emergence of my musical personality."[280]

Of course, Rose was displeased when others took credit for teaching Harrell: "He was really a pupil of mine, and I resent these people who lay claim to having been his teacher." He dictated: "I remember the lesson when I told Lynn what to do with the thumb when he went up in the thumb position, where to place the thumb; the importance, for example, of the octave-frame work between the thumb and the third finger. Teaching him how to check on the thumb in the upper register of the cello."

At the invitation of George Szell, Harrell joined the Cleveland Orchestra at 19, and three years later, promoted him to first chair. While in Cleveland, he met James Levine who worked as an intern with the orchestra and who later became its assistant conductor. His friendship with Levine eventually served a major role in establishing Harrell's career as a solo performer. In a *New York Times* article from January 1976, Harrell told writer Raymond Ericson that Levine "has been the biggest influence on my career. I met him first in Aspen, where my father was teaching. Jimmy was 14, precocious and already accompanying my father's voice lessons. We got together to play some chamber music. He knew so much more than I did, and he was willing to help." Harrell's career skyrocketed following a 1972 dual recital with Levine in New York. Aided by the pianist-conductor's friendship and collaboration, Harrell emerged from the ranks as a top recording artist for RCA Records. A prestigious Avery Fisher Prize ensued.*

"In the beginning, Rose insisted upon hearing a system of scales with certain rhythms and bowings," Harrell says in explaining what Rose expected from his crop of students at the

---

* Avery Fisher (1906-1994) made his fortune as a pioneer of radio-phonograph amplifiers, tuners, and speakers; and he established Philharmonic Radio in 1937. A second highly successful company sold for $31 million in 1969. As a philanthropist, Fisher was influential, sitting on the boards of the New York Philharmonic, Chamber Music Society of Lincoln Center, and Vermont's Marlboro Festival. Lincoln Center's Philharmonic Hall was rechristened Avery Fisher Hall in 1973 after he donated a staggering $10.5 million. Harrell received the award named for Fisher in 1975.

time. "He also had me play études, double stops, sixths, thirds, octaves, and many other technical things, which he was able to demonstrate beautifully. You should have heard him play Popper [étude] No. 9 or No. 13; it was staggering!" Harrell found Rose's orchestral references particularly illuminating. "He would often compare a piece to a passage in an orchestral work. For example, he would say that the sound quality of a certain passage should have the sumptuous quality of Mahler rather than the overt romanticism of Tchaikovsky." Rose's experience, of course, led him to use such analogies, as it was beneficial that a student know the orchestral repertoire when working with him. "With Leonard Rose," Harrell tersely says, not necessarily agreeing with, "there was this sense that you could conquer the world through your playing."[281]

After nine seasons with the Cleveland Orchestra, America's current dean of cellists launched a solo career that has carried him through five continents as one of the leading exponents of the instrument. If Rose and Harrell had a falling out, which some people concur due in part to Harrell's ascent to stardom, Rose came full circle when he refers to Harrell as one of the finest cellists of the world and "I am very happy to say that he was a student of mine."[282]

For his 13th birthday, the 1966 Tchaikovsky Competition's silver medalist Stephen Kates (1943-2003) received a copy of a Leonard Rose recording. An early concept of a glorious cello sound permeated the youth's ears. Upon graduation from high school, Kates entered Rose's 1961 class. "He treated me with a sense of purpose and maturity," Kates would orate at a Leonard Rose memorial concert in 1985. "The lessons were inspirational—not always easy—often tough and demanding. He was not one to compromise when he sensed that there was talent. He wanted results—if one could just dig a little deeper." Tightening vibrato was Rose's first concentrated work with Kates. "He really forced me to listen to myself in ways that I was not used to," he admitted. Rose had the greatest influence upon this protégé in the area of sound-color. "After demonstrating, giving his students a perfectly beautiful example to go home with, he would say, 'Now see if you can make it sound like that someday.' He was a man of few words, but of great action as a teacher."[283] The talented cellist, who had a modest solo career in addition to what would become a stellar 28-year teaching association with the Peabody Conservatory in Baltimore, was restless; and in 1963, after just two years, Rose expelled him from the class. According to Jeffrey Siegel,[284] who accompanied Kates, the youngster insisted on playing the Dvořák Concerto with undue rhythmic liberties, wild fluctuations of speed and dynamics counter to those marked in the score. Kates insistently and perpetually defied Rose's suggestions lesson after lesson until Rose, saturated with frustration, angrily quipped, "Perhaps you would be happier studying with someone else?" Behind closed doors that day, he asked Kates why he continued to ignore his directives:

"Because this is the way Rostropovich plays it," the student replied.

"Then, why don't you go study with Rostropovich?" Rose shot back.

"Well," Kates stammered, "it is difficult to study with him because he is touring all of the time. When you were my age, wasn't there one cellist whom you admired more than any other?"

"No," Rose said, contritely contemplating Kates's fate.

"Well, I feel sorry for you."[285] And with that comment, Kates—at the time something of a cellist's bad boy—unintentionally struck a nerve that may have epitomized the inner life of Leonard Rose. When Rose was Kates's age, he was not exposed to a large variety of musical interpretations. In fact, Rose's fear of and later his stilted professional relationship with his teacher, Salmond, may have circumscribed his musical adventurism. As a student, Rose would have unquestioningly practiced with a goal of perfect sound and flawless technique, yet he wouldn't have been drawn to or curious about different interpretations the way Kates—and most cellists of the generation—did. Although Kates may have exhibited careless etiquette in his provocative dialogue, it reveals something about Leonard Rose's emotionally rigid and precocious musical, disciplined nature that had been his motif in his teaching life to that point. The last thing Rose desired was to set free one of his most talented undergraduates. Leaving him no other option—which left the pedagogue in a state of anguish—the incident reveals Rose's tough rigidity, or possibly his acute jealousy of Rostropovich, regarding a wide variety of interpretations perhaps reflecting on his own childhood, which lacked exposure to a diverse range of cello playing.

Kates had a few lessons with Rostropovich; he also studied with Laszlo Varga, Gregor Piatigorsky (a member of the Tchaikovsky Competition jury when Kates won his medal), and Claus Adam after the triumphant return from Moscow.* It was nevertheless Rose who made the deepest impression upon Kates. "Time will ultimately judge the mark he left by the legacy of his playing and teaching for those who were thrilled by his concert appearances and those who came from all over the world to study with him." Kates concluded, "He was indeed America's great cellist. I, for one, am appreciative for the privilege of being one of the lucky ones who studied with him and had the chance to prosper from his greatness."[286]

In 1974, Owen Carman began his graduate studies at Juilliard with Leonard Rose. The Michigan State University professor emeritus and eventual director of the summer program Ivan Galamian founded, the Meadowmount School of Music, was 14 when he first heard Rose's 1965 recording of the Dvořák Concerto. "It was in its purest form there and instantly identifiable as Rose, if no one told you who was playing." At once, the man's sensitive phrasing and sincerity enraptured Carman.

After graduating from Curtis, Carman had prepared sartorially for the realization of the dream of his first lesson with Rose. "I was dressed in my finest wide-cuffed pants, blue shirt and tattersall bow tie. This had to be the greatest moment of my life. Here he and I were... he dressed impeccably with watch fob and a fancy white shirt, tie and suit cradling his marvelous Amati cello imparting pearls of wisdom to a kid from Kalamazoo!"

"You are going to learn how to sit with the instrument," Rose told a flabbergasted Carman. Epitomizing an exemplary Rose student, Carman jettisoned all he had previously been taught. As the teacher explained why he sat and oriented his body to

---

* Adam, born in Indonesia (1917-1983), moved to New York in 1929 where he later studied with Emanuel Feuermann. In 1948, he formed the New Music Quartet and then joined the Juilliard String Quartet (1955), which he left after 20 years to devote his attention to composing.

the instrument the way he did, Carman followed his advice and altered his posture and position. Rose's second topic described that he intended to teach him to expand his playing and to make the expansive results more convincing. Only then would the graduate student stand out in his approach to the standard concerto, sonata, and short-piece repertoire. "After having been given an assignment and still dazed by my first experience, I rode cloud nine all the way home," Carman recalls.

In this phase, Leonard Rose was a mature, confident performer and pedagogue—and quite wealthy, too. In fact, he told Carman that he could play chess, golf, and buy apartment buildings with cash. During the youngster's Juilliard days, he asked Rose about the truth of a rumor: After a performance, an audience member came up excitedly and exclaimed, 'Mr. Rose, that was excellent!' To which he replied, "Young lady, that wasn't excellent; but it was very, very good." Rose said that he wasn't boasting, simply telling the truth. Anticipating a compliment one day, after what he felt a fine reading of Tchaikovsky's "Rococo" Variations, Rose looked Carman over and declared, "You know, Owen, I'm a marvelous teacher." Startled and without hesitation, Carman reflexively imitated the teacher's habit of raising one eyebrow. At the time, a fellow Rose student was imitating Rose in every way: dressing in three-piece suits, gold watch, and fob, mimicking his speech down to its nuances. His popular act entertained peers, but aggravated Rose. Carman continues, "He got a little perturbed and asked me if I was mocking him. Nothing of the sort, I told him … I guess Rose thought imitation of him was laughing at him. Quite the opposite!"

In his final year with Rose, Carman entered the conservatory's competition, one he thought he would win. That he failed to make it beyond the first round crushed his spirit. "I was so upset at my next lesson, I was almost in tears. He sized up my feelings and without hesitation made me feel instantly better saying 'If you weren't so sensitive, you wouldn't be such a good musician.' With Leonard Rose saying that to me, it meant more to me than if I had won the competition."

Toward the end of the academic year, Rose summoned Carman to appear at his studio door as he was finishing the teaching day. "My blood chilled and I wondered what I had done wrong," Carman fretted. At the appointed hour, Rose told him that he received a call from Michigan State University; they wanted a recommendation for a faculty cellist. "You are from Michigan, aren't you?" Rose asked. "Go get that job." Rose mentioned no one else for the position. Carman held the title for 25 years.

Carman candidly speaks his sentiments:

> Of course, no matter what he played, very few people would mix him up with someone else. So unique was his tone, phrasing, and glissandi. His admirers were not limited to cellists, but anybody who had a true appreciation of a fine tone. I can think of only a handful who have come close to turning a simple phrase as magnificently as Rose did. There were other great artists of the past who could do this; but today, it is almost a lost art.

Chapter Twenty-Two

ROSE'S CHAMBER MUSIC INSIGHTS

To try and sound like a fine string player in phrasing, legato, and beautiful sound were musical and pianistic goals I took out of his studio and continue to strive for four decades later.
—Pianist Jeffrey Siegel

Leonard Rose recognized his thorough knowledge of symphonic and chamber music literature laid the groundwork for his solo career. This study, he believed, was essential regardless of a student's ultimate direction. Rose elucidated in his memoir:

> Consider, for example, the young, presumably budding virtuoso. He should know as much music of the great composers as possible. If he is to perform a Beethoven sonata, he is more likely to play it well if he knows that composer's trios, quartets, and symphonies. More significantly, perhaps—especially for those young players who [will] never achieve the virtuoso status—chamber music teaches people to play with and listen to each other. Invariably, those who play chamber music will do well in the orchestra. After all, what is orchestral playing but glorified and amplified chamber music!

The breadth of his chamber music experience, and variety of repertoire he was familiar with had deep roots. Following Felix Salmond's Curtis model and unlike most instrumental teachers, rarely did Rose like to teach without a pianist present. Cello sonatas—or duos for cello and piano in the classical, romantic, and contemporary repertoire—stress give and take, pacing, balance, and coordination between players. It was a life Rose was steeped in as a touring and recording artist; in addition, his fame as a member of the Istomin-Stern-Rose trio made him, in the eyes of all students, a chamber music star. In fact, with such chamber music expertise, Leonard Rose was the ideal teacher of the idiom. Perturbed when his students couldn't find a willing partner for lessons, he chided keyboardists (and their teachers) who complained about tarnishing their reputation in the hallways of the school, as "mere" accompanists. He snaps: "How shocking that is! Musicians learn from all experiences, and a lot of these pianists would do damned well to learn how to play with other people. Playing sonatas and especially playing in a class [like mine] can be of great value because I teach music, and the pianists can and do learn a hell of a lot ..." A recurring topic in his spoken memoir, Rose reminisced, "I learned from every musical experience I had when I was young playing just about everything."

Five years before the American pianist rode in a ticker-tape parade in New York City from the Battery to City Hall on Broadway in a sleek convertible, waving to throngs of well-wishers in windows of skyscrapers, Van Cliburn, winner of the 1958 Tchaikovsky Competition, played in Rose's chamber music class. The teacher wrote that the boy was pleasant and easy to work with, but noted that the gangly six foot four Texan teenager showed up ill prepared. "I was scared to death of him," Cliburn confesses more than half a century later. For a dozen or so years after his cold war triumph in Russia, he was the most celebrated classical musician in the world. Assigned to Rose for chamber music at Juilliard, he was well aware of the cellist's reputation as a soloist. The pianist came to admire him when he heard Rose perform a concerto with Cliburn's hometown Dallas Symphony. In awe of the man's presence, Cliburn said, "He was so famous and important. You know that was intimidating." Rose reacted with displeasure: "I told him that he was ignoring truly great music which he'd enjoy the rest of his life." Cliburn, barely 16 at the time, recalls his careless attitude: "You know, I had to really be on my own and make my own mistakes."

The cellist mentioned the problem to his teacher, Rosina Lhévinne, who during this time in her 70s and eventually into her 80s made a remarkable series of appearances.* She suggested that he play sonatas with the skillful pianist, this prior to her pupil's triumph at the 1954 Leventritt competition and receipt of the Frank Damrosch Prize at Juilliard for postgraduate work. For two years, Rose intermittently played with and instructed Cliburn—who would later be labeled by the formidable Russian pianist Sviatoslav Richter as a "genius"—in Beethoven's A Major sonata and the two Brahms cello sonatas. The pianist, not yet 20, would make a total transformation with these chamber masterworks in the company of the famous cellist (not yet 40) touring the world. "I was so enamored with his sound. It was so gorgeous," Van Cliburn attests. "In fact, it was distracting. ... Yet, he was so kind. He would say, 'Now you really need to work on this.' I think he tried to inspire some ego in me, which was good. He would give me confidence by praising me." Cliburn continues, "My personality at the time—if you gave me a little praise—that would inspire me. ... He had the right technique for me. Had he discouraged me, I would have been finished." Even though Van Cliburn's destined path steered him away from chamber music, he learned an appreciation for the skill under Rose's tutelage. "Still to this day, I remember the [Brahms] F Major cello sonata we played together. When they started my competition [Van Cliburn International Piano Competition, 1962] here in Fort Worth, it was I who demanded that they have chamber music in the second round. Leonard Rose would be one of those artists who stirred my great love for the literature."[287]

---

* At 81, Lhévinne (1880-1976) joined Rose for a performance of the Beethoven A Major Sonata. In his memoir, Rose recounts: "This remarkable pianist didn't really know the cello repertoire very well, but was most amenable to my suggestions and coaching. In fact, she offered me this gracious compliment: 'You're just like Felix Salmond. You know the literature so well, and can express what you feel and think.' Rosina's performance of the Beethoven was quite good, save for the passage in broken octaves."

The well-known violinist Jaime Laredo met Rose at Meadowmount at 13. "I had gone up two weeks early before the camp opened to take lessons with Galamian. The Rose family was already there having a vacation ..." The cellist who "was bigger than life and one of my heroes" electrified the young Laredo. That summer of 1954, Rose coached Laredo's ensemble on Beethoven's "Razumovsky" String Quartet Op. 59 No. 1. "It was unforgettable," Laredo reminiscences. "He used the word 'tradition'. If there was any kind of disagreement he would say, 'And what's wrong with tradition?' Salmond, Walter, Szell, and Mitropoulos—he talked a lot about his mentors in those days. It was very inspiring as a young kid to hear all of this." A wonderful thrill occurred in a subsequent summer when Rose, weary of coaching for the day, took out his recently acquired Amati from its case to join the student group in a read through of Schubert's two-cello quintet.

At Meadowmount, on the heels of his triumph at the 1959 Queen Elisabeth Competition in Belgium, the violinist spent numerous hours in the company of Leonard and Minnie. In discussions about career options, the Roses unabashedly offered advice and their assistance.

Addressed first as "Mr. Rose," Laredo and Rose later became friends informally, enjoying string quartets at Rose's Great Neck house, and some of Rose's famed celebratory New Year's Eve musical marathons. Then, the relationship shifted to a professional one for a number of concerts when Laredo, on viola, expanded the Istomin-Stern-Rose trio's repertoire to piano quartets. Concurrently, Laredo invited the cellist to perform with his own younger colleagues at Laredo's 92nd Street Y chamber music series in New York.

More via the professional than personal association, Laredo caught a glimpse of Rose's psyche. Some days, he observed the cellist as jovial and witty, other days that notorious sourness surfaced, initially startling the musician. "He was bitter in some ways," Laredo recounts. "He had an incredible career, but I think he thought it should have been bigger." Underlining the calamitous events surrounding Rostropovich's intangible influence that led to Stephen Kates's expulsion from Rose's class, Laredo adds, "When Rostropovich came to this country [Carnegie

Hall debut, 1956], Lennie was very hurt." Laredo confirmed that as Rose aged, he grew ever more critically self-conscious and faultfinding. "I don't think he needed to do all that practice, but he did." The younger man cites one incident that exemplified the perfectionist behavior. In 1977, while Laredo performed with him, Rose's finger slipped off the fingerboard at the piece's very start. "Big deal," Laredo shrugged. "Yet he couldn't stop talking about it afterwards. He apologized over and over again. It was so unnecessary. He made himself very unhappy about it."

Along years of collaboration, Laredo developed a deep love for Leonard Rose the man and his instrumental abilities. Like virtually all musicians who worked with him, Laredo praised Rose's incomparable depth and spectrum of his tone: "He had that lush, beautiful, mellow sound. ... There are so many times when I think about him as a person, as a cellist, as a musician ..."[288]

Emanuel Ax, the assisting pianist in Rose's Juilliard studio on Mondays from 1967-1971, declares, "I was a huge Rose fan. ... He would talk [to his students] a lot about how to make things emotionally right, something other teachers didn't stress. He was also incredibly courteous and pleasant to all his students and to me."[289] Witnessing the Istomin-Stern-Rose trio perform all of Beethoven's significant chamber works in their 1970 Carnegie Hall concerts was a mind-boggling and inspirational occurrence in Ax's musical development.

The pianist described Leonard Rose as "humble vis-à-vis the music; and I thought he knew his self-worth, at least in the studio. I loved the fact that he was always so immaculate, so beautifully dressed, and so elegant. He was a role model of all the great professional musicians, the great artists. He always had this kind of aura that was special—someone to look up to." Acquainting himself with Rose's complicated side, the pianist described Rose's unique—somewhat disturbing—conversational style among those closest to him. "So you would hear this wonderfully slow, measured speech, 'Manny, so nice to see you. I just spent some time with a f-----g pederast.' You know, this would be sort of a cultured speech but at the same time, he would come out with these things." After his 1974 triumph at the first Arthur Rubinstein International Piano Competition in Tel Aviv, Ax had several opportunities to work with Rose, once in the Brahms Piano Quartet in C minor. "I remember asking at some point if we could try something without slowing down in a particular place. Mr. Rose said, 'Of course we could do that, Manny, but where's the tradition? The tradition is to slow down.' There wasn't an argument, but I just remember that he put a lot of value on the idea that things that were once done by the great artists of the past should be passed down."

Jeffrey Siegel, another "house pianist" who accompanied a portion of Rose's classes in the early 1960s, recalls Rose asking to produce a less 'notey' sound. Rose could allow flexibility in students' interpretative freedom up until he deemed they got out of hand. Rhythm was crucial with Rose, particularly in a concerto, which he taught in a chamber-like approach. Siegel remarks, "He would constantly remind the student, particularly in "Schelomo," that the orchestra part was tricky and ensemble a constant problem. He pointed out places where the cellist ought to look at the conductor, playing a strong down-beat at another spot, bending a phrase for the oboe here, etc.—practical advice for a young soloist from someone who had played these works many times with many orchestras and conductors, good and bad, under many conditions." In Beethoven and Brahms sonatas, Siegel learned from Rose's requests for his student "to listen more carefully to how the pianist articulated a given phrase and to try and imitate—but more often it was his suggestion that the pianist try to imitate the legato sound of the cello." Above all, the pianist believed Rose so naturally musical that he was incapable of thinking, feeling, or playing a phrase—even one note—without beauty. "Everything he did interpretatively always sounded right—the musicality was undeniable."[290]

Pinchas Zukerman believes that the passage of time has not been kind to Rose and laments, "cellists who play today don't know the first thing about who he was." The celebrity musician respectfully maintains that the music profession did not spoil his colleague, that he never took fame for granted. "He kept his value system. He kept his belief in music playing properly and truthfully." Rose had mutual admiration for Zukerman's talent and commented in his aborted memoir: "It was only the most imaginative students of Galamian who were able to really move me. Pinchas Zukerman is a great artist—there are others who are great fiddlers—but Pinky thinks and he's artistic and he makes differences in what he does."

In the summer of 1961, when the violinist was 12, Zukerman met the cellist (43 years old) in Tel Aviv on the Istomin-Stern-Rose trio's inaugural tour of Israel. The youth headed to Meadowmount the following summer where he had further contact with the cellist. In America, the Israeli violinist lived in Eugene Istomin's spacious New York home and, as page-turner for the trio's Metropolitan Museum concerts, observed Rose's arrival—habitually an hour and a half early to practice. The routine made an impression: "He would play the difficult passages over and over again until it was absolutely perfect." In concert, the youth watched Rose do things at the tip of the bow, "that most cellists wish they could do once in their life. I asked him, 'Why do you practice so much?' And he said, 'It's the only way I know how to play properly.' And I thought, wow, that's a lesson and a half right there."

Zukerman, who performed and recorded trios in the 1960s and 1970s with star cellist Jacqueline du Pré and her husband, pianist Daniel Barenboim, raves—as seemed "de rigueur"—about Rose's sound: "The control! When he started at the frog, his bow didn't move. That sound! It was like a trumpet! How the hell did he make that sound? His bow could move so slowly. The sound was so ravishing."

In 1974, Zukerman—playing the viola along with Stern and Rose—ceaselessly rehearsed, performed, and subsequently recorded Mozart's masterful Divertimento for string trio. "That piece we worked on forever," he remarked. "Every day ..., something that Lennie, Isaac, and Eugene believed in. Those guys didn't just walk into a [recording] studio after playing a work once or twice. They lived with the music. They lived with that music for a very long time."

Zukerman maintains that his relationship with the cellist did not chill. His feelings for the icon are clear-cut and unabashed: "There is no question that Lennie Rose had an influence on the cello; but I think not only on the cello, but for the 25 years he had his solo career. I think he really had a huge influence on all string playing..."[291]

Turning his attention to his recital partnerships, Rose comments: "Every pianist with whom I've ever worked has been duly acknowledged either as 'pianist' or 'at the piano'; I have never referred to that colleague as my 'accompanist.'"* When on tour together, Rose and his pianist traveled by air both in first class or both in economy class. Never one to mince words, he added, "To me, it would be offensive to get two first-class tickets (for me and the cello) and one coach (for the pianist). I am shocked and disappointed that there are cellists who do so." Among those who benefited from his graciousness in chamber music classes at Juilliard and at Meadowmount were pianists John Browning (1933-2003), David Golub (1950-2000), and Joseph Kalichstein (b. 1946).

However comfortable Leonard Rose felt coaching chamber music ensembles in his studio, he opposed the concept of master classes as musicians of his caliber taught. As a result, he held relatively few in his career. The cellist believed the public classes of minimal value because "they frequently become a case of the master exercising his ego over the student." Moreover, the added dimension of an audience into the pedagogical process affected both. His opening remarks inevitably bemoaned the fundamental worthlessness of the master class, and his closing resembled a lengthy and fundamental sermon on the mechanics of bowing. According to cellist Scott Ballantyne, the format dictated that Rose was "expected to give each student criticism in public. He had genuine distaste for this. He suffered intense pre-performance anxiety himself and personally empathized with the students." But any witness to a Rose master class will confirm that the spectators' eyes remained fixed on the debonair and mannered professional, especially craning their necks when he demonstrated his prowess. Those pupils on display, whose dream to study with Leonard Rose depended on his every move, were scrutinized by onlookers, adding to the intensity of the class. Usually, Rose zeroed in on the young cellists' right arm technique, aware that this is how he could instantly influence their style of play. "The push and pull of the bow is important."

---

* Rose's pianists: Mitchel Andrews (1951-1959); New York debut and two recordings with Leonid Hambro; Jacob Maxim (1960-1963); Samuel Sanders (1964-1974); Gary Graffman (1971-1973); David Golub (1975-1980); Andrew Wolf (1980s) and Joseph Kalichstein (1981-1984).

His eloquence and tone of voice conveyed precisely the sound he sought. Rose coaxed, "You are saying to your cello, 'Come on baby, speak,' not 'SPEAK, damn you!'"

In 1980, Rose presented a master class at the Eastern Music Festival, where most of the cello faculty were current or former pupils of the man. As a hopeful 18-year-old student, Damian Kremer appeared front and center before him in an afternoon session: "Of course I was nervous, and I think as a result, I was squeezing with my bow hand." Rose, always polite, spoke to the aspiring cellist about balance and flexibility in the bow hand, and the importance of using a relaxed, natural arm weight when pulling the bow. Kremer admits not comprehending the absolute lesson at the time, but decades later employs these principles as the basis for his teaching. Rose wanted his protégés' sound to be robust and rich, able to soar to the seats in the farthest recesses of any concert hall. Indeed, he proved it possible to have a very large and luscious tone on the cello. As Rose grew older, he tended to reminisce more in his master classes. Harking back to his Cleveland days with Artur Rodzinski on the podium, when Sergei Rachmaninoff was the celebrity at the keyboard, Rose told his rapt listeners, "I'm a sucker for Rachmaninoff. I just love that piece!"

Even though his stories delighted the audiences, Rose was typically quiet, not one to boast and certainly never out to emphasize the students' weaknesses. Instead, he could be heard exclaiming, "The sparks have to fly. You know what I mean? The music must have electricity." Continually urging a cellist to sing out, he cries, "I know the composer wrote *piano* [soft] there, but don't do it. Your heart will tell you otherwise." As a two-hour class drew to a close at Ithaca College, Rose offered one reason why he agreed to occasional master classes, although he insisted he had no faith in the concept. "If they have any value at all, it's that they give students a chance to be nervous and to rise above it. The performers who say they aren't nervous are all liars. It's only a matter of degrees. If healthy habits are formed, your chances of giving a good performance are infinitely better."[292]

Chapter Twenty-Three

MASTER TEACHER; JUILLIARD VERSUS CURTIS; THE RISE OF CHANNING ROBBINS

By the way he lived his life, he gave us a blueprint for how to live ours. He found us, he trained us, he got us jobs, he made us what we are, and he gave us much of what we have.

—Raymond Davis, longtime principal cellist, the Seattle Symphony

The Juilliard School of Music, Leonard Rose's teaching home from 1946 until his death, was founded in 1905 by Frank Damrosch. He was a leading figure in music education for the New York City Public Schools and the son of Leopold Damrosch, founder of the New York Philharmonic. Initially the Institute of Musical Art, the school operated its first years at the Lenox House located on Fifth Avenue and 12th Street. When the mansion sold, trustees decided to build their own school; in 1910, the Institute relocated to 122nd Street and Claremont Avenue—today's Manhattan School of Music. The property faces Grant's Tomb, Riverside Park, with the picturesque Hudson River beyond it. Until the 1930s, the land to the north of the area was a wasteland scarred by railroads tracks, rotting timbres, mounds of untreated garbage, and tarpaper squatter settlements.[293] Augustus Juilliard, who made his fortune selling plug hats and frock coats of the finest broadcloth (made with plied warp and filling yarns), and provided the material needed for sails used on clipper ships, was a devoted arts patron. With his death (1836-1919), he bequeathed an enormous sum to the creation of the world-renowned conservatory that would bear his name. The city's musical landscape would metamorphose, attracting some of the most highly regarded teachers and performers in the world.

Juilliard's gift, between $12.5 and $13.5 million (in excess of $160 million in 2008)—the largest donation to date for the development of classical music in America—funded the Juilliard Graduate School, which opened in Midtown Manhattan in 1924. The Institute of Musical Art and Graduate School would merge, but not before additions were made to the original 1910 building on Claremont Avenue. Architects Shreve, Lamb, and Harmon, the firm simultaneously constructing New York's enormous Empire State Building, designed the new building. Furthermore, a substantial $350,000 donation (approximately 4.5 million in 2008) by John D. Rockefeller* beautified the grounds with walkways, shrubbery, and foliage. The Olmstead brothers, responsible for landscaping all of Central Park and many of the nation's finest urban parks, supervised two additional acres of adjacent land. The school's new limestone façade style was freely adapted from the neoclassical Adams architecture of 18th-century Bath, England. The interior was furnished in a French Renaissance manner; the chamber music auditorium: a distinguished space that seated 400. Juilliard's teaching studios were large and state-of-the-art, each adorned with a brass doorplate engraved with the name of the faculty member and years of teaching service. The public entered a foyer of rose-tan and white marble with gray, black, and dark red patches. The lobby led directly into a 1,000-seat auditorium, in which there were two spectacular stairway banisters of striped South American snake wood. An unusual feature—especially for a school venue—was the maroon and gold pressroom off the foyer. Two brand-new Remington typewriters sat on a table, from where critics could report on concerts and special events. In this stunning setting, the president of the Juilliard School, William Schuman, invited Leonard Rose to join its faculty in the summer of 1946.

---

* John D. Rockefeller (1839-1937) was America's richest man at the turn of the 20th century.

When Rose began at Juilliard, he was still committed to the New York Philharmonic, so his initial teaching schedule was light—about four hours per week. After most Friday matinee performances, the exhausted cellist would travel, by subway, uptown from Carnegie Hall to Juilliard. Rose's heavy cigarette smoking (students from the era describe a hazy blue studio by the end of their lesson) and attraction to caffeine revived him sufficiently to play up a storm for students in the ensuing hours. "In fairness," Rose states in his memoir, "I knew very little about teaching during those years. Most of what I did was on a strictly imitative basis. I played, I could demonstrate, and I had good instincts." It was his dedication to improving—recalling Galamian's pronouncement that musicians could play or teach, but not excel at both—that made Rose's evolution as an instructor dramatic. As if driven by Felix Salmond's declaration that he owed to "future generations of cellists" that he become a great teacher, Rose painstakingly educated himself. Rose discovered, "Like learning an instrument, teaching takes practice. It would be some time before I could convey to my own satisfaction technical details, good bow arm strokes, vibrato, and the like."

Rose's 1940s' students unveil his early pedagogy. "I must have spent the first six months on lessons being corrected on intonation on first finger, first position on the D string," Barbara Pepper relates. "To this day, I find myself, as teacher, harping endlessly on the same subject." Victor Sazer, a newly returned veteran from World War II, found the man to be the "most intense person I have ever known and a perfectionist, perhaps to a fault." Rather close in age, the two developed a friendship that included long talks about world affairs, politics, and life in general. "Once after a concert," Sazer remarks, "after he played a concerto with the New York Philharmonic, he asked me to stick around to join him for coffee. After he changed clothes, he said he just wanted a minute to go over one little place in the piece that he had just performed brilliantly. He went over and over the passage and then decided to try another and another. Well, a couple of hours later, we had our coffee."

Mary Mayhew requested to study with Salmond at her audition who, in turn, steered her to Rose. "He was so soft spoken," Mayhew says of Rose. "Once he couldn't get my attention while I was playing Bach's Suite No. 3." Rose stopped Mayhew and asked her not to continue; he was performing the piece a few nights later at Town Hall and it made him too nervous to hear it at that moment. The lesson ended whereupon Mayhew could hear her teacher, beyond his studio's closed door, playing through the suite.

Cuban-born Jorge Sicre began his studies in this country with Rose's older colleague, Oswaldo Mazzucchi, principal cellist of Toscanini's NBC Symphony. After Mazzucchi's death, Sicre auditioned for Rose whom he had heard and admired in concert. At Juilliard, the pair worked on Edouard Lalo's 1876 Cello Concerto. Sicre didn't care for the work and recalls letting Rose know his opinion. Sicre recalls, "He said, 'Georgie, you are going to play it cover to cover perfectly and then I will let you hate the piece. But for right now you like the piece.'"

When Rose returned from the Philharmonic's 1951 European tour to embark on his career as soloist, William Schuman informed him that he wanted to ease Rose's financial state of affairs by offering him a "guarantee" for 360 hours per year, an average of about 12 teaching hours per week. The lengthy one-to-two month solo tours that Rose took then left his students adrift. "We waited for his return," Geraldine French Jennings remembers, "for, in those days, he made up all of the lessons we had missed. This made for a concentration of lessons—and you had better have kept up your practicing while he was gone!" Few women cellists belonged to major orchestras and concertized in the 1950s—in fact, some world-class ensembles forbade women as late as the 1980s—and Rose followed suit by not encouraging them for those fields. Regardless, he strongly supported them in pursuit of teaching positions in colleges as well as playing in professional chamber groups. Another student from the period, David Everhart, recounts Rose's insistence that every assignment be memorized, including études. Once during a lesson on Gabriel Fauré's Élegie, Rose halted Everhart, grabbed his cello and played, speaking loudly over the music, "David, David—every note you play must be beautiful."

"My ultimate fantasy, which I felt was unattainable, was to have lessons with Leonard Rose," Martha Blackman recalls. A chance backstage encounter in 1953 after Rose's solo performance with the New Orleans Symphony led to Blackman discussing cello technique over dinner with her future teacher. Rose asked if she was familiar with certain exercises for finger independence. At which point he pulled out manuscript paper from his pile of music and wrote out an exercise for her. Enthralled, Blackman initiated talk of moving to New York to study with him. Rose made it clear that every new pupil needed to audition. At the residence where the Symphony housed him, Blackman showed up with her cello the following day weak-kneed. Noticing her anxiety, Rose promptly prepared a snack. The two then went into the living room where, according to Blackman, "Instead of demanding that I play, he took up his cello and calmly stated that he had not quite finished practicing his recital pieces. Would I mind if he went through them first? When he finished he handed me his instrument and asked if I would like to play on it." From there, the teacher transitioned into an elegant discourse on the use of the bow hand, going into intricate and specific detail. Blackman also listened to his philosophy about left hand use—his belief that finger articulation exercises be precise and somewhat audible when removing fingers from the string as when placing them down. Practicing scales without the bow and hearing the finger articulation on the way up and using pizzicato on the way down for the same effect was a golden nugget she pocketed.

In the same decade, Toby Saks's mother took notes in the piano part for her daughter's early lessons. Harking back to the scores, scribbled on almost every line were the words: "relax," "catch," "rhythm," "steady," "easy." In high school, Gilda Barston was invited to present a lecture about her methods of cello teaching. "In my next lesson," she explained how "Rose wrote down, step by step, on how he taught." She describes a 1950s lesson: "We started with scales in three octaves with rhythmical variations and different articulations. He didn't like to do four octaves and he didn't to like to play arpeggios. Then we moved to an étude where we worked hard on intonation. We ended the lesson with repertoire." Barston remembers his insistence on using her own imagination and working with her individual creative side—not mimicking Rose's. She did, however, voice some displeasure: "I worked on the Saint-Saëns Concerto my first summer at Meadowmount. I would play the first page and he would say, 'Now that you are warmed up, let's work on it. Let's start over.' For weeks we never would get by the first page. He had so much to say.... We never did get through the work." Leonard Rose was not known for gratuitous compliments, but tended to be positive and encouraging. "I felt that for at least 75 percent of my lessons," Saks says, "he enjoyed himself. I know that these lessons gave him pleasure.... He must have liked to hear how his students were playing at such a high level..."

Raymond Davis recalls leaving each lesson filled with discovery and hope, and with a set of new tools for the next assignment. On the flip side, Rose's notorious darker side occasionally emerged as in a 1957 story related by Daniel Morganstern, who maintains a lifelong reverence for the cellist. Leveling his gaze, Rose told the young man: "If you think you are going to be a cellist like I am, you can forget it. Because in my generation, there were some very good cellists like Frank Miller and Sammy Mayes who didn't make it. I am the only one who made it. So if that's what you want to do, forget it. You're a smart boy. Why don't you become a doctor?" Morganstern's relationship with Rose turned cantankerous when the youth left him for Luigi Silva's studio. "Rose was basically a tremendously generous person, but if he felt betrayed, that was it," Morganstern comments. He eventually realized the gravity of his mistake in alienating Rose, whom he felt had more to offer than Silva, and made courageous overtures to win him back. At 35 years of age, he returned to Rose's studio, a point at which the pedagogue uttered, "You know, people change and it's a good thing they do. I'm very grateful that you came back to me because I never could have come back to you."

"Rose tried very hard to protect his back." Einar Holm recalls. The teen cellist observed the meticulous manner with which Rose put on his suit jacket, combed his hair, and checked his gold chain that ran from his belt area into his pants' pocket before leaving his Juilliard studio for the bathroom. Holm explains: "Along the way, Rose felt that competition with other cellists and teachers in a most painful way. I recall feeling so much sorrow when Rose spoke to me about his two Juilliard colleagues: 'What I like about _____ is that he knifes me while I'm looking, while _____ knifes me in the back.'" Students added to Rose's torment when behind his back, upon his return from touring, he found some wanting to or already having changed studios.

In 1961, Juilliard offered Rose the fairly generous teaching annual salary of $5,000 (equivalent to nearly $36,000 in 2008), approximately $14 ($100) an hour.[294] Twenty-two years later, in 1983, Rose was infuriated when discovering the school would provide a meager annual pension of $2,000 (about $4,400 in 2008).

The inability to see students weekly necessitated a concentrated teaching style, and Rose compressed an enormous amount of information into each hour. Scott Ballantyne remarks, "We used to say that an hour with Rose was worth 15 with any other teacher." During solo tours, students had to rely on his various assistants who had the responsibility of sharpening skills and, in some cases, supplying the nuts and bolts of cello playing to Rose's select class. One teenage cellist who was in Rose's section during the 1940-1941 season with Cleveland Orchestra, Channing Robbins (1922-1992), would become indispensable. If the two had not struck up an immediate friendship early on (there is no mention of the teenage Robbins in Rose's memoir), Robbins's loyalty to Rose was cemented 18 years later, when Rose chose him to be his teaching associate. This occurred after Robbins studied with Felix Salmond, then in the 1950-1951 academic year with Rose. In a 1958 letter, Juilliard's Dean, Mark Schubart, confirms that Robbins was groomed that year as he sat in and took notes on many of Rose's lessons. Additional memos indicate both Robbins and Luigi Silva shared responsibilities for several of Rose's pre-college and regular division students. Not without trial and tribulation, Rose rewarded Robbins with the coveted position. Determined not to disappoint, during the decades that Robbins worked as Rose's silhouette, he calmly and consciously prepared one expectant student after another for their ever-so-brief encounters with the master. At times, his efforts were taken for granted and in some instances, disregarded by the students and by Rose. Yet Robbins never publicly considered leaving Rose's side and sought consolation only in closest confidantes.

Channing Robbins devoted his life to serving other people: his parents, brother, sisters, Felix Salmond (whose portrait graced his studio wall after Rose's death), Leonard Rose, and above all his students. Ultimately, he labored selflessly, regardless of gratitude. Robbins was secure in his comprehension of cello pedagogy and awkwardly, funneled that vast knowledge to pupils whom he liked and who, in turn, treasured him. Those who did not reciprocate fared less successfully. Desmond Hoebig, principal cellist of the Cleveland Orchestra elaborates, "We were like his kids. He put all his love and energy into us. He was always thinking about us." Out front of these successful interactions, Robbins carried himself with dignity and decency. Beyond them, his discontent with being unnoticed was conspicuous. His sister Joyce described how he "valued character, honesty and loyalty above all else. If he believed that you had these qualities, he was in your court. He would do anything to help you. But if he suspected that you were lacking these human qualities, that you wouldn't toe the line, that you were not faithful to your musical education, or that you weren't true to all the people who had given so much to help you, he became displeased and disinterested."

Robbins was born in Los Angeles, February 3, 1922, the fourth generation in a family of musicians. In his early development as a cellist, his mother practiced with him daily—she attended every lesson—and accompanied him on the piano. In the mid-1930s, the family had little money, surviving off their 10-acre walnut ranch in San Fernando Valley. In those days, their sole income depended on the harvest and market price. These were deep Depression days, and the family of six had to survive on $1 to $2 daily.

In the 1930s, Los Angeles thrived with formations of training or youth orchestras for the purpose of instructing kids in the orchestral repertoire, then promoting their careers helping them seek professional opportunities, especially in supplying music to the motion picture industry. Ilya Bronson, principal cellist of the Los Angeles Philharmonic from 1919 through 1936, appointed Robbins to the first chair of his youth orchestra. Robbins also played in Peter Meremblum's[295] Youth Symphony, which accompanied Jascha Heifetz in Mendelssohn's Violin Concerto in the 1939 film, "They Shall Have Music." In an unparalleled year that released, among others, "The Wizard of Oz" and "Gone With the Wind," the movie scored by Alfred Newman was nominated for an Academy Award. The chamber orchestra's roster of 30 players included Robbins and his two sisters who spent six weeks rehearsing for the film. As required by California state law, they received schooling three hours daily on the movie set. They ate lunches in the commissary alongside the famous stars. Joyce comments, "We tore around the Goldwyn movie lots during our rehearsal breaks watching other films being made and swooning over the actors. Somebody's mother was always getting in our way though, and sometimes it was my own." Cameraman Gregg Toland shot the historic footage of Heifetz, who at 39 was at his peak of fame. A scene in the film clearly shows Robbins' slicked-back dark hair and angular, striking features. His height emphasized that, at 17, he was among the oldest in the orchestra. At the glamorous premiere in Hollywood's famed Egyptian Theatre, the orchestra arrived in an outlandish bus, lurid with signs and banners for the little celebrities. The children's reward: a Heifetz picture—autographed!

Leonard Rose met Channing Robbins in Cleveland during a tense moment in U.S. history.[*] Japan's attack on Pearl Harbor and the subsequent entry of America into World War II was cause for many musicians to leave their orchestra jobs for military service.

The United States reinstated the draft in November 1940, as the European situation deteriorated and in anticipation of its entry into a looming 50-nation war. The "Selective Training and Service Act," passed by a single vote and signed by President Franklin Delano Roosevelt, legally enabled the government to command some 16 million males between the ages of 21 and 36 to register with their local draft boards (Leonard Rose was 22). From 1940 until 1947, more than 10 million men were inducted into America's armed forces. At a time when hundreds of thousands of men of Rose's age were conscripted into military service, a curious coincidence kept the cellist from joining their ranks.

---

[*] About a dozen members of the Cleveland Orchestra enlisted by the 1941-1942 season. Rodzinski raised eyebrows by suggesting that war could force U.S. orchestras to replace the servicemen with female musicians. Rodzinski considered the hiring of women a "rather revolutionary innovation," and believed "they would make an excellent addition to any first-class symphony orchestra."

As enormous consequences preoccupied the nation (estimated total of the dead, the wounded, and missing: a mind-numbing 55 million), two small numbers held personal significance for each young American man. First, the individual's "number," assigned to organize the summoning procedure. Then, once summoned, a one-digit number plus a letter identified a potential soldier or sailor by his competence, health, and preparedness for service. For a variety of reasons, not everyone who received a draft notice wound up performing military duty. A weeding-out process evaluated men for mental and physical requirements. The examiners stamped the classification "4-F" on the file of those deemed unworthy, which translated into a rejection. And the board eventually designated Rose 4-F—although not with a usual explanation.

During the Battle of the Bulge (December 16, 1944 – January 25, 1945), Rose's number was called. By that time, he was married, already the father of two children, and appearing in his debut season as principal cellist with the New York Philharmonic. Rose was frightened and panicked.

Within weeks, the notice mandated he attend a lineup in front of an old Manhattan theater. After listening to cursory introductory remarks about the military, Rose and the assembled group formed lines, "trying to put on the best face we could muster." He recalls that December day as "freezing," and the unrest among his fellow draftees as palpable. Not everyone longed to serve his country on the battlefield. On Rose's local draft board was former major league pitcher Lefty Gomez (1908-1989), a boyhood idol of Rose's who had won a record six World Series games without a loss in the 1930s for the New York Yankees (he retired from baseball in 1943). Rose was happy to strike up a conversation "talking about anything except trying to stay out the Army."[*]

The group took the five-cent subway ride to Grand Central Terminal, where offices were located at the Plaza: an arcade on a lower level of the immense railroad station. There, the men were ordered to strip, except for their underwear. Long lines once again formed as each man prepared for tests of hearing, vision, strength, and other physical attributes military service required.

---

[*] Thirty-six-year-old Gomez was drafted into the U.S. Military.

The prospective soldiers also provided fingerprints, blood, and urine samples, all the while aware that if they scored a sufficient number of red marks on their documents, they would be denied acceptance for military duty. Sailing through the first battery of tests with flying colors meant Rose was well on his way to becoming a recruit: he had received not one demerit.

After dressing, the next activity created lines in front of numerous desks. Procedure mandated that psychiatrists interrogate the men, although Rose expressed doubt about these doctors' credentials. When Rose's turn came, he approached the desk and the official shouted out, "I know you. You're the new first cellist of the New York Philharmonic." Stunned, Rose could barely utter a word. *Somebody up there is watching over me*, he thought. "What are you doing here?" the so-called psychiatrist inquired, picking up a red pencil. "They shouldn't draft a guy like you." Once he began the grilling, the man who Rose would never see again asked, "So do you get nervous when you have to play?" Rose answered, "Of course I do." The man scribbled something on his paper then continued, "Do you ever have dreams?" To this odd query, Rose replied, "Yes, occasionally." Again, the man put red pencil to paper.

By the time he completed the interview, red marks covered Rose's sheet. Finally, the man explained, "You know, I think a guy like you should not be drafted. You're a young artist, and you should go ahead and make your career." Rose was dumbfounded. With the formal questioning concluded, the man surprised him with one final, bizarre query, "What kind of cello do you have?" Rose had just acquired an instrument crafted by the Venetian Matteo Goffriller. To Rose's astonishment, the interrogator announced, "Oh, I have a Goffriller viola!" That day's classification of 4-F guaranteed Rose an uninterrupted path to his ultimate success. And the draft board never summoned him for a retest, as it did some potential soldiers and sailors. "I guess he marked me down as one of the worst psycho-neurotics imaginable," Rose speculated years later.

In that 1941-1942 season, Robbins' only season with the Cleveland Orchestra, he undoubtedly read the same memo Rose did from their irascible conductor, Rodzinski: "At the beginning of next season, each string musician will be asked to play a concerto or sonata before the members of his section in addition to myself. The members of each section will then, through a secret ballot, intimate his idea as to the seating of his particular section. I, of course, reserve the right to make the final decision." It was the year in which Rose, already situated as principal cellist since 1939, presented his solo debut performing the Lalo Concerto.

Did Rodzinski's memo intimidate Robbins into departing? Instead of a second season, Robbins enlisted in the U.S. Army Air Force band stationed in Santa Ana, California, for the duration of the war. This band, a loose term for a full orchestra, included such future stars as cellists Victor Gottlieb,[296] Al Lustgarten, and violinists Felix Slatkin[297] and Ruggieri Ricci.[298] The ensemble often served as the official backup to the many Hollywood entertainers who performed for the troops at the Santa Ana Air Base. Robbins' cello was heard on newsreel radio broadcasts. The orchestra's surprising caliber pushed Robbins to new heights.

At the conclusion of the war, the G.I. Bill afforded the youth the opportunity to continue his education at the Juilliard School where, in September of 1946, he became a student of Felix Salmond. He took a one-year leave of absence during the 1948-1949 school year to tend to family matters and then graduated from the Juilliard School with a Bachelor of Science degree in June of 1951.

From the outset, the Channing Robbins and Leonard Rose team was dynamic; successful cellists sprang from their studio. Students flocked to Robbins before and after lessons with Rose seeking help, encouragement, advice and—in some cases—a different point of view. Near the end of Rose's life, when his class enrolment swelled to as high as 28 for his weekly 15 hours of teaching, Robbins shouldered the huge responsibility of drilling Rose's distinct style of cello playing into these kids. It was not uncommon for a student to take three-quarters of their lessons with Robbins, which he relished. But he also had somber misgivings about his quiet role as the vital cog in Rose's pedagogy. Out of respect and esteem for the man he admired, Robbins never interfered with Rose's glory. Sean Grissom noted how he shunned attention: "He was always uncomfortable in the spotlight. I always felt Channing wanted it but didn't want it." A few students willingly accepted Robbins' generosity, but departed without acknowledging his contribution, which quietly broke his heart. As Hoebig says, "I think there were some situations, when students who had experienced success, could sense Rose conveying 'my student has done this great work.' Robbins wound up muttering, 'Well, he was my student too.' Or, actually what he might have meant was, 'you haven't been around that much and it was I who mainly worked with him.' Those things always played into Channing's emotions and moods." Apparently it happened numerous times. Yo-Yo Ma passed through the Rose/Robbins studio from 1964 to 1971. Even though Mr. Ma has, on occasion, verbally credited the latter, Robbins expressed deep indignation to his class when he was not mentioned in David Blum's all-embracing 1989 profile of Ma, *A Process Larger Than Oneself,* featured in the *New Yorker* magazine. Yet, when Ma soloed in May of 1971, in Saint-Saëns' Concerto with the Juilliard Pre-College Orchestra, the printed program's biographical notes read: "Mr. Ma entered the Juilliard Pre-College Division in 1964 and has studied jointly with Leonard Rose and Channing Robbins since that time."

Robbins decisively believed that students should list every teacher they studied with—especially when the teachers were alive; that was the time to pay tribute. Robbins increased fixation went further. He felt that, after his death, he didn't want to give those who slighted him any opportunity to justify or rectify their actions posthumously. It disturbed him to contemplate the fine cellists he helped form praising him, when they had never done so when he was alive. So he added a clause in his will, directed at Juilliard, that "no institution or any person would be allowed to pay public homage to him in a ceremony or concert of any kind." Adhering to these wishes, no concerts or scholarships were ever established in Robbins' memory assuring that he has, sadly, become a footnote to Juilliard's magnificent history.

In 1974, the prestigious team of Rose and Robbins had reason to boast. Four cellists in the Philadelphia Orchestra, five in the New York Philharmonic, six in the Cleveland Orchestra, and seven in the Boston Symphony Orchestra were their protégés. Conductor Erich Leinsdorf's notorious remark referring to the cellists in the Boston Symphony Orchestra as the "Rose Section" further fueled Rose's ego and likely deflated Robbins'. "I think the cello is enjoying somewhat of a renaissance at this time," Rose told an interviewer. He proudly added, "and I think I am responsible for this, at least on the American scene."

Indeed, Rose and Robbins lived through a prodigious improvement in skill on the instrument that was played and taught inadequately in their youth. "I think what is happening today," Rose stated in his 1982 unpublished memoir "is that the pedagogy has improved so much on the various instruments [that] more and more people are playing the violin and the cello better and better. Especially with the cello, ... I am finding more interest and bigger techniques and good sounds and all that; but..." As a listener, Rose noted a downside to this progress, a homogeneity that led him to occasional boredom. "Unfortunately, the real artists, the true artists; the real imaginative players are as few as ever. I find myself listening to top-line players today and being bored. They don't say anything. Every note is played perfectly, but they don't use any imagination in the sound; everything sounds the same, whether they are playing Bach or Mendelssohn or Brahms..."

Rose needed to air his grievances.

"We go to hear a performer play a great masterpiece because we want to see what is in his or her mind and what is in the heart. I'm sick and tired of so-called "perfect" playing.... Who needs to listen to a violinist with flawless intonation, unchanging vibrato, and unwavering temperament? I wish to hell some of them would miss a note and say something! For me, boredom in music is unforgivable. The French have a saying, 'When you are untalented, it's for a hell of a long time.' Music should be an experience of all the emotions. You should feel sadness, happiness, love, and anger; all the emotions of which humans are capable of feeling are in music. When I play a great work of Beethoven, I feel the loving Beethoven, I feel the angry Beethoven." It was this trademark intensity that Leonard Rose and Channing Robbins most hoped to imbue in their protégés.

In his sixties, on the fifth floor at the new Juilliard headquarters in the quiet studio with its red door, yellow carpet, and sweeping view of Lincoln Center, Mats Lidström recalls, "In my final lesson [1981], Mr. Rose told me that I had arrived from Sweden as a boy, and would now return as a man.... I think

Mr. Rose was a great teacher. I think Channing Robbins was equally great.... To me, their greatness is confirmed by the fact that they constantly return and appear in my own teaching." Contrasting opinions welled from a spectrum of students who made contact with Rose. In the late 1970s, David Heiss, sat back "six feet away awash in this glorious, incredible sound." Offsetting these thrilling moments was Rose's volatile ego. When an instant standing ovation greeted Rostropovich at a recital appearance in Carnegie Hall, Heiss heard about it in the following day's lesson. The shocked youngster recalled the caustic remark from the American icon that he "had *never* received a standing ovation before playing." Principal cellist of the Atlanta Symphony, Christopher Rex, who at one time dropped to his hands and knees to examine the "Rose" bow in motion, expressed dissatisfaction with some aspects of his lessons. The experience impressed him "even though I never felt that Rose was able to properly put into words what he was actually doing." Yet Rex sensed that Rose made him feel that he was worth his time. Ulrich Boecheler, a graduate exchange student from Germany who studied with André Navarra (1911-1988), found Rose too complimentary. "I felt like saying, 'well, Mr. Rose, what do you really think?' I wanted to say, 'it's OK, I want to learn. You can be harsh with me.' I wasn't sure that I was getting the full brunt of his real honest-to-goodness opinion." Yet the German departed with the impression that Rose liked *tempos* "distinctly faster than what I was used to. I felt as though I wanted to indulge a little more here and there. He preferred that I had a better vision to see the big picture." Boecheler adds, "He wanted me to use longer bows. He liked brighter colors—a bit more playing on the A String rather than the D string." Bruce Uchimura, who wore out Rose's LP records from playing them so often as a youngster, echoes Boecheler's sentiment: "Ironically, Mr. Rose was not the most inspiring teacher. He was a nice man to his students, and often too nice.... Even when he did criticize, it was passive or at times indifferent. Naturally, he possessed an ego, but for a performer as successful and respected as Leonard Rose, it baffled me that he could be so insecure about his career and his professional colleagues. I think we all benefited greatly from Channing Robbins and his guidance and teaching." Uchimura's words resound, "But most of us wanted those things from Mr. Rose."

A strange and tragic interaction between Rose and a prized pupil occurred on the eve of 1981. After what Frederick Zlotkin described as "the most fruitful teacher-student relationship I had ever experienced," his relationship with Leonard Rose ended—abruptly. For a number of years, Rose maintained a warm connection with Zlotkin, a rapport closer than most. The young man exchanged phone calls and letters, and traveled out to Rose's Westchester County home for lengthy private lessons where he had a chance to witness a more relaxed teacher. Trouble brewed in the 1970s when Zlotkin's eyes opened to differing styles of cello playing under Robbins' guidance, including those of other legendary performers such as Feuermann, Fournier, Piatigorsky, and Starker. These insights, coupled with the knowledge of every facet of Rose's musicianship, made Robbins' tutelage unique—and quite different from Rose's. Because he had a more analytical mind than Rose, he not only taught the fingering and bow markings from these other cellists, he studied them and was able to convey, at times, their advantages. Zlotkin gained access to a treasure trove of new information Robbins was pleased to impart. Concurrently, Rose had developed genuine warmth toward Zlotkin, writing in June 1978: "I think you deserve tremendous credit for your great achievements.... Your marvelous progress gives me particular pleasure and I'm delighted I had something to do with it..."

This dramatically changed when a *New York Times* reporter interviewed Zlotkin, on the eve of a significant solo recital at Manhattan's 92nd Street YMHA: "Here he [Zlotkin] worked with Bernard Greenhouse, Leonard Rose, and Channing Robbins. Mr. Zlotkin says of Mr. Robbins that the latter's technical knowledge of the cello was 'perhaps the greatest. It was like he had incorporated everything that everybody else knew. Even if he doesn't agree with something, he will teach it to you.'"[299]

In the morning hours the day the interview saw print, Rose telephoned Zlotkin and recorded the following curt message: "This is Leonard Rose. I just read the *New York Times* article about you. I think you should be disgusted with yourself. I am." In disbelief, Zlotkin called Rose and left him a pleading message indicating the reporter misquoted him. Rose replied in writing—the same day—and never spoke to Zlotkin again.

> LEONARD ROSE
> 19 OVERLOOK ROAD
> HASTINGS-ON-HUDSON, NEW YORK 10706
>
> December 28, 1980
>
> Dear Fred –
>
> Don't tell me it was a misquote! I'm shocked beyond words –
>
> Leonard Rose

Dear Fred – Don't tell me it was a misquote! I'm shocked beyond words –
Courtesy of Frederick Zlotkin

Devastated, Zlotkin penned one last letter in early January: "...If you don't know from all I have expressed to you over the years that you were the most important teacher I have ever had, then I must erase from my memory the innumerable times I recall when you expressed your deepest satisfaction about our association. This I refuse to do because those memories are too precious. I cannot undo what others have done. All I can do is express to you once more the deep and abiding affection and respect I've always had for you."

No one can adequately explain Leonard Rose's behavior. The man was complex, needy, and possessed a dark side he failed to keep fully concealed. Perhaps it related to his own artistic struggles breaking free from his one major teacher, Salmond.

Perhaps his ego could not share credit with his subordinate. Who else engendered this emotion in Rose prior to Zlotkin? During the period, Rose tried to quit smoking. Recent studies conclude that when heavy smokers try to stop, they often experience "black" moods. Heavy drinking, also associated with nicotine addiction, can also trigger depressive effects. Was this the cause of his outrage? A contrary theory suggests Rose sometimes felt obligated to teach, mechanically driven to pass on what he had and what he had learned. In this mindset, Rose lacked an educator's passion, but taught out of a megalomaniacal sense of legacy and immortality.

According to friend and one-time accompanist David Gross who knew Rose for decades, "It never made sense to me why he would extol the virtues of Matt Haimovitz, a 13-year-old cellist,[300] on his deathbed. He told me that he was absolutely the greatest talent he had ever seen—even better than Yo-Yo." This *wunderkind,* with assistance from Rose's "Kosher Nostra" clan, had the makings of a major career when it careened to a standstill after a decade. Illogically, Rose, who obsessed over the boy's future, told Gross before his final illness, "'I am afraid to teach him.' And he was very definite about it.... I just never got the sense that he really enjoyed teaching all that much." Rose once canceled an afternoon of teaching at Juilliard to play sonatas with Gross who was passing through town. The pianist remembers Rose remarking: "'I'm so glad you came. It's so much more fun than teaching.'" Rose was not a happy man, outwardly and especially inwardly. He could not sustain his self-worth without perpetual affirmation from people around him. It appears as though Rose became increasingly resentful of permitting Channing Robbins to share in their students' successes despite a claim in his memoir, "I could not have taught at the Juilliard without the help of my marvelous assistant, Channing Robbins, who studied with both Salmond and me. I can say that we've turned out a number of good cellists together." Several dozen Rose/Robbins alumni granted interviews for this present volume. However it does seem plausible, because more than two hundred former Rose students chose not to, Rose ended bonds with others in a similarly chilly manner.

The dedicatee of this book, Channing Robbins, deserves recognition as an authentic pioneer, devoting his life to teaching all facets of the cello. His job description may have been "Leonard Rose's assistant," yet his devotion to absorbing knowledge and passing it on to "their" students—whom he continued to teach after Rose and up until five days before his own death—cannot be underestimated. Although not a performer, he raised the standard of cello playing to an even higher plane and was among the finest teachers of the second half of the 20th century—arguably surpassing his master.

The Curtis Institute, as old and illustrious as the Juilliard School, was founded by Mary Louise Curtis Bok, the only heir of magazine mogul and the *Ladies' Home Journal* founder, Cyrus H.K. Curtis. Encouraged by her husband to become active in civic and cultural philanthropies in their home city of Philadelphia, she donated the impressive sum of $150,000 in the early 1920s to establish a new Settlement Music House with the goal of "Americanization among the foreign population of Philadelphia."[301]

It wasn't long before she developed a more substantial idea than the Settlement Music House to serve the needs of the city's serious music students. Two major influences in Bok's ensuing endeavor were pianist Josef Hofmann and Leopold Stokowski, conductor of the Philadelphia Orchestra since 1912. These legendary musical personalities envisioned associations with an elite school of music based on Anton Rubinstein's venerable St. Petersburg Conservatory that steered Bok and her money toward the creation of the Curtis Institute, which opened its doors October 1, 1924.

Bok intended that the school be small, but of the highest level, to represent "the cream of the cream." Whereas Juilliard welcomed a broader array of young musicians, Bok's imperative emphasized a student's talent as the sole qualification for admission. Because she lacked experience in the methods and business of founding a school of any caliber, she relied heavily on the advice of Hofmann and Stokowski. Hofmann, the director of Curtis when Leonard Rose attended, believed that Curtis students required instruction by first-class solo artists, rather than by good teachers who happened to perform competently. This idealism created a unique environment: each pupil grew in a utopian setting with the most promising, provided with every advantage of the material world. In 1927, Bok transferred to the school 80,000 shares of Curtis Publishing Company stock worth, an astonishing $12 million, which matched the unprecedented amount Augustus Juilliard left for New York's eponymous conservatory.

As director of the school in 1927, Josef Hofmann's policies tended to be groundbreaking and noble. These included lending fine instruments—rent-free—to students who needed them and free concert tickets to promote their general musical education. And as with Rose, some pupils received extra financial assistance that enabled them to continue their studies during the summer recess in Maine where their teachers were spending the summer. Hofmann liberally offered stipends to defray living expenses to his neediest students.

In the fall of 1934, immersed in a highly specialized school, Rose awaited Felix Salmond. Like Rose, much of the Curtis student body at this time were children of Jewish immigrants, many from Russia, Poland, or Hungary. What distinguished Rose from his peers were his southern roots. "When I started to study at Curtis," Rose related, "I had a very thick, pronounced Southern accent. In the years when I lived in Miami, it was a provincial area and was the South.... We were called Florida Crackers. When I started at Curtis, kids made terrible fun of me." Nevertheless, the socially awkward teen soon managed to make friends.

Already hired to teach at Juilliard by 1951, during Rose's final year with the Philharmonic, Rose received a telephone call from Efrem Zimbalist, the famous Russian violinist who by then directed the Institute. He wanted to meet Rose. Over coffee and cigarettes, in the heart of Midtown Manhattan at Pennsylvania Railroad Station, Zimbalist proposed that Rose join his elite faculty. The cellist was thrilled at the prospect of teaching at his alma mater, succeeding the eminent Gregor Piatigorsky, and could not refuse. "We quickly agreed upon a huge, fat fee of $20 an hour (nearly $170 in 2008)—but I paid my own expenses [travel between Philadelphia and New York], of course."

total imitation "although I might become more dogmatic when a student isn't really very gifted and doesn't have anything to say. They have to say something [musically], so I impose myself upon them; but otherwise I try to encourage differences, I try to encourage the student to really investigate the works of music that they're playing and to try and think for themselves."

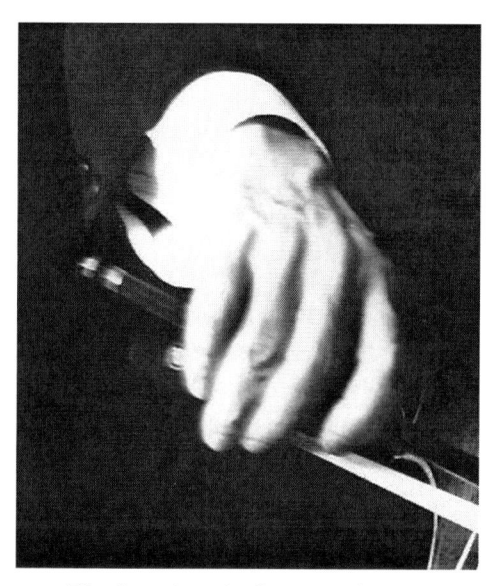

The bow hand of Leonard Rose

Leonard Rose's bow arm, considered superior to any cellist of his era, produced a golden and burnished resonance. It was precisely this quality that drew the majority who came to study with him. His unique mechanics—the natural motion of the hand, arm, and fingers coordinated in unison to make effortless circular shapes at the tip and at the frog, in effect eliminating audible bow changes—was Rose's most advanced breakthrough for the cello. Students, in awe, were known to have postured themselves on the floor in order to view the master's hand and arm from all angles—while the cellist posed, playing and verbalizing how it should be done. The longer Rose had the patience, the better a student's chances of learning the *Rose* bow arm.

Rose believed that the right hand should hang loosely on the bow, and then the fingers should fall on the bow in as natural a way as possible. He encouraged students to use the natural weight of the right arm to produce tone of larger volume and richness. The thumb should find itself between the second and third fingers—nearer to the second than the third—and should be slightly bent. Any locked joint, or specifically, any rigid position of the thumb, will create aural trouble and pain. Rose's ability and facility to keep the bow perpetually moving at the rate of his choice was remarkable: "The proper speed of the bow and change of strokes in a relaxed manner should be the aim of all young cellists," Rose declared. "The important thing is that one should aim for a slight brush stroke. I consider it of immeasurable importance to devote a great deal of time and thought to the actual planning of the bow. One hears so much forcing of tone. Instead of developing control and speed of bow stroke, too much attention is placed on the bow pressure."[305]

Furthermore, his vibrato possessed an inherently original quality. Within each phrase, his vibrato appeared to breathe with the music, never uniformly slow or fast. When Rose was at his greatest, his vibrato vividly colored the music in a dazzling array of speeds. In 1972, he described to noted author and violin teacher Samuel Applebaum (1904-1986) that his vibrato did not originate in the left fingers alone, but was realized with the lower arm, using the pad of each finger as the pivot, with the upper arm moving only passively. When vibrating, the fingers should remain close to each other, supporting each other. Importantly, the fourth finger—pinky—should not sound any different than the larger, stronger fingers. And Rose did not adhere to the school that mandated every note have vibrato.

Rose often associated the range of sonic possibilities on a stringed instrument to the barely perceptible gradations of color in a masterpiece painting. Not all reds are the same, or blues, or greens. "He [the painter] is constantly making variations of color; and for me the really artistic string players try to make differences. The sensitive musician uses sound in the most imaginative way. It is not just loud and soft, but with subtle changes of bow speed and bow pressure, and wonderful changes of vibrato from the almost unnoticeably quiet pianissimo to great intensity." The cellist felt the real artist, with intelligence and awareness, inevitably will sense the kind and type of sound, which suits the music of different composers, no matter the period. Rose believed an infinite variety of sound exists to match the differences in musical periods from Baroque through the contemporary or avant-garde.

The artist did not permit last-minute inspiration to affect performance. He believed that a musician should put as much effort as possible into the planning of a work, not only artistically, but technically too. The traditional concert, he considered, was no place to indulge improvisation. After he figured out his musical intentions, only then did he feel ready to fully express the emotional content of the work. Felix Salmond once told him that public performance was a reflection of the inner self. Rose loved the analogy. For him, part of it translated into a resolve to memorize not only concerti, but complete solo recitals as well. Rose's utterances provide insight into his preparation methods. "Conditioning oneself for public performance must take place during private practice. It is important to play before an imaginary audience. Before I play in public I very often play a program three or four times as though I were seated before an actual audience."[306] In his youth, Rose tried to envision his toughest critics sitting close and in front of him. His bow might tremble; nevertheless, he continued without pause as he attempted to conquer his fright. When Rose was "on," no other cellist could produce a nobler, more beautiful and self-assured interpretation. When he wasn't, personal troubles intruded, his execution suffered. Musicians could not perform nobly unless dignity resided in their souls, Rose believed. Conversely, Rose thought that if there were a nasty streak in one's soul that, too, would come out in performance. "Temperament," Rose pontificates, reiterating what he knew to be the inimitable ingredient in his music-making. "...What a wonderful word. To feel all those human emotions."

Most teachers refer to their influences as people who play the same instrument. Rose, however, emulated the élan of violinists Ivan Galamian, Oscar Shumsky, Fritz Kreisler, and also cellist Luigi Silva,* whom he cited as major influences in his development as a teacher. After Salmond's death in 1952, Rose attained the stature of America's leading cello instructor.

---

* Silva taught alongside Rose at Juilliard until his sudden death November 29, 1961, at the age of 58.

Due to a combination of circumstances—as a touring soloist and a teacher at the two finest conservatories in the country—his phone frequently rang with inquiries about his availability. "Strange how quickly one gains in prestige," Rose quipped. "An even greater number of talented young cellists came my way." In a teaching career that spanned 37 years, he developed a well-honed system. "I cannot conceive of not giving strict technical material to my students because I think that, basically, the teacher of a musical instrument has three main responsibilities: one, to give the student the best possible technical background; two, to give good musical guidance; and three, the most important, the teacher should teach the student how to teach themselves."

No doubt Rose absorbed a myriad of cellistic detail from his cousin, Frank Miller, and from Felix Salmond at Curtis. However, it was information obtained from his friend Ivan Galamian, whose violin students occupy many of the prestigious positions in the classical music field today that raised Leonard Rose to the uppermost tier of teaching. "The element that is the least understood and the least well taught on a stringed instrument is the right arm, the bow arm. Galamian understood it. I learned a tremendous amount from him about the bow and about the left hand. I also learned much about his organization of teaching ideas. He gave me some wonderful hints that I used all my life."

Luigi Silva, an Italian cellist fluent in French, German, and English, taught hundreds of pupils from all over the world by the time the Juilliard School hired him. In his youth, he was once advised to give up hope of becoming a cellist because his hands were too small and his constitution too frail.

Silva was not derailed. At 23, he became solo cellist at the Royal Opera in Rome. Later, he played later in the well-known *Quartetto di Roma*, then in the Mannes-Gimpel-Silva trio. Critics reviewed him as a soloist of the highest order, and applauded his fresh originality. He often performed his own transcriptions on his Pietro Guarnerius cello. Silva contributed more than 50 works to the cello repertoire, transcribing pieces from the piano, voice, violin, and orchestral literature. Hundreds of pages of notes on the art of teaching are housed at the University of North Carolina at Greensboro. "To think, to observe, to imagine, and to work hard," Silva wrote, "is the key to any success, even to cello playing."[307] Rose fondly remembered the man, "I learned a great deal from my colleague Luigi Silva. I think the best cello situation at the Juilliard was when Luigi and I taught together. His pupils were very different from mine. They could climb around the instrument with the left hand—but didn't sound very distinguished. He even said to me, 'Lennie, your students sound so much better than mine.'"

Leonard Rose derived pleasure in demonstrating for his students. Deep down, he knew that a talented student could learn more from watching him in action than from what he described verbally. "I understand the physiological problems of playing the instrument as well as anyone," Rose confidently offers. "But trying to intellectualize, that's not my cup of tea. There is a definite emotional involvement with the music; the ability to move people is not an intellectual pursuit. The basic instinct of great artists is something they feel."[308]

It saddened Rose to contemplate the general lack of expertise in cello teaching during his lifetime. The dynamic pedagogy of Soviet cellist Mstislav Rostropovich was virtually unknown in the West during the Cold War; his style emphasized spontaneity through tremendous energy and focus. Had Rose known about the Russian cellist's innovative style of teaching the instrument, he might have felt more optimistic, but Rose concluded in the late 1950s "that there are only two teachers who know how to teach the cello, [one was Margaret Rowell (1900-1995) who taught at the San Francisco Conservatory of Music, and also served on the faculties of the University of California at Berkeley, Stanford University, Mills College and San Francisco State University] and the other one is in Europe."

Rose referred to the instructive abilities of French cellist André Navarra (1911-1988). A few years prior to Rose's death, he wrote to Rowell about the joys and pitfalls of their shared career. "It is very obvious that you understand how to teach these youngsters, and avoid any tightness or tensions. The bow arms are healthy and the resultant tonal qualities lovely. It is a real joy to see, for I'm certain I don't have to tell you how many miserably taught talents I have heard in my 33 years at Juilliard, plus the 11 at Curtis. I have spent a good part of my life undoing someone else's messes." Rose emphasized that not all fine performers made fine pedagogues. "There are simply some marvelous players who should not teach. I am not an unkind person, but I think this nonsense of 'pressing the thumb into the frog [part of bow] like a thumbtack' is so destructive.

The letter to Rowell continued, "My teacher, Salmond and Casals and, perhaps, Bill Pleeth were good coaches. Inspiring musicians who really don't know a hell of a lot about teaching a good bow arm or left hand, but at least they didn't mess up a talent with very bad theories. In the final analysis, I'm afraid one must judge a good teacher by asking, 'Where are their students—whom have the teachers taught?'"

Rose often reacted defensively when the subject of his legacy cropped up. He seemed compelled to clarify his destiny: "There are people who could be somewhat envious of me and my track record, saying, 'well, yes, he's a good teacher, but he gets all the talent.' Let me tell those people something—those things work together; you judge a teacher by what he has turned out. A lot of people talk a very good line and yet they turn out very little. Well, it is true that I get a lot of very good talent; but I think, in the final analysis, the thing is to bring out the good parts of that talent and to turn out fine players. A good teacher is less likely to ruin a great talent; a poor teacher can very easily harm a great talent by imparting misinformation and stating things, which are not correct about handling and manipulating the instrument and music." Rose believed that it was extremely important for each artist to feel that his or her way is the way to play that particular work. But an artist should also be open-minded and be willing to listen to other people play differently, because "it is the differences which create greatness—that create great performances."

One question Rose doggedly asked himself toward his final years was where he saw himself in cello history. How are careers made, why do careers die? He imagined his career was built on God-given talent, dedicated practice, persistence, and good fortune. It was an enormous boon that he attained his prestige in New York, as principal of the Philharmonic whose concerts aired on national radio for millions of listeners and that he performed directly under the watchful eyes of the most important soloists, managers, and critics of his day.

Rose also voiced satisfaction that he never needed expensive publicity agents. Nor did he need to gravitate toward gimmickry, the way today's concert promoters and recording producers insist. Leonard Rose was, above all, a proud man who in no way strayed beyond his art's traditions: no crossover projects, no jazz or popular repertoire and no flashy wardrobe. In order to turn a profit in classical music, the new theory goes, an artist's appearance and extra musical attributes matter most. Shortly around the time of Rose's death, personality-driven marketing and a young performer's musician's commercial potential began to overshadow more artistic qualities. Mentors needed to guide students through a more complicated maze than Leonard Rose could have imagined.

In the unpublished memoir, Rose talks about remarkably talented young cellists, some of whom will win prizes, some of whom will get marvelous reviews, only a few of those will get much of a solo career. "... No one can really say who will or will not achieve stardom; and even after the fact, no one can definitely explain how or why. We are, of course, dealing with incomprehensible intangibles ... sometimes, one or more rave reviews help propel a performer, yet these, too, are often ignored. Indeed, one of my students had some of the most sensational critical acclaim I've ever read, and went nowhere with it." Reality suggests that some of these performers are unable to maintain the necessary levels of artistry year after year. Some become "burned out" after a few seasons; some, of their own volition, seek other professional directions. Rose implies that some musicians who win major competitions and who eventually disappear were thrust into careers for which they simply were not ready. They may have learned the required repertoire, but not had terribly much left after those few pieces were exhausted. And, of course, there is yet another possibility Rose believed with any competition; "...the winner(s) may not have truly deserved the awards."

That Leonard Rose was not the beneficiary of a major competition, he casts this singular light upon his career: "... before 1951, there were rarely more than two great cellists per decade. Casals had a very long career [until 1971 with his New York debut in 1904] Piatigorsky followed [debuted in America in 1929], then Feuermann briefly [Feuermann began annual tours of the U.S. from 1934 until his death in 1942]. I came somewhere in between them and Slava [Rostropovich debuted in New York in 1956]."

In the late 1950s, Leonard Rose was under a considerable amount of pressure in his professional and personal lives. Photographs from this period depict a man with a tense jaw, hollowing eyes, furrowed brow, rarely smiling in candid shots—a mask of determination and intensity that was donned on stage. The profession forced him to take off long stretches of time away from home. Such an absence can strain a marriage and alienate children. During the period, money was in short supply and his wife, diagnosed with leukemia, became resentful of his lengthy withdrawals from home. He didn't purposefully ignore his wife and teenage children. He was simply working too hard. It would seem fair to label the man a workaholic. As his daughter Barbara attests:

> You know, Dad was exhausted most of the time because to support all of us he had to be away on tours that lasted for months at a time. Demands were being made on him from all directions. After practicing for hours every morning, messages would pile up from all over the place. He had letters to write, phone messages to answer, students needing jobs, *and* he was expected to be a full-time husband and father. I rarely saw him just lie down on the couch and relax. In the end, he hurt himself, his family and the people who loved him the most.[309]

His son Arthur adds:

> My mother was somebody who kept a lid on my father because he was a very angry person. He was never happy doing what he did. He hated traveling. We never played music at home. He never wanted to hear music. My father considered himself to be a very shy person. Shyness goes hand in hand with insecurity. Anyone who has a giant ego has some sort of insecurity. And he had a *great* ego. He was both compulsive and obsessive

with his playing. If he screwed up on stage, it would just destroy him. It was the fear of failure that drove him.

Although Rose did not drink prior to a performance, at home and after concerts, he drank often. Occasionally, he tossed around a ball with his children; however, his physical outlets to relieve stress were limited.

Simultaneously, Leonard Rose's reputation as a performer and teacher expanded his roster of students at Juilliard and Curtis, feeding his voracious competitive drive. Maintenance of business contacts, a necessary evil, added to Rose's workload and stress. Rose, the performer, also pressured himself through his constant goal of perfectionism. The mounting stress may well have been the impetus that led the cellist to seek psychotherapy. It must have stung Rose to stand by and observe as certain concerts went to other cellists—including former students. He read magnificent reviews that were not his; he heard of recording contracts granted to his competitors. His ego was insatiable: he could never have enough concerts, never enough tours, enough recordings and, above all, enough recognition. Perhaps he was too overwhelmed by the multiple stressors to cope with what seemed a continuous onslaught of work, or perhaps competitors merely compounded the pressure he felt. There was no relief.

Of a number of cellists omitted from Rose's writings on cello history, most noteworthy is his contemporary, the Hungarian-born Janos Starker (b. 1924), whose career is considered as distinguished as Rose's.[310] Achieving worldwide recognition shortly after Rose, Starker recorded the major repertoire which included multiple sets of the Bach Suites, multiple recordings of Zoltan Kodály's Unaccompanied Sonata as well as Bartók's Viola Concerto (adapted by Tibor Serly) and a jaw-dropping 1967 album, *The Road to Cello Playing*, a solo endeavor consisting of many of the instrument's most difficult études composed by past cello virtuosos Jean-Louis Duport, Carlo Alfredo Piatti, David Popper, and transcriptions from preeminent violinist Niccolò Paganini. As his memoir demonstratively shows, not mincing words, Rose harbored contempt for his rival. "There is a cellist, whom I shall not identify by name, who has made a number of derogatory statements in public about his colleagues. Twice I read interviews in the *New York Times* in which he said that while Casals, Fournier, and Piatigorsky were good cellists, they were old-fashioned performers. He, apparently, is the only *modern* cellist."

Rose vents in his highly subjective history:

> A German newspaper had an even more outrageous quote. The gentleman was asked what he thought of Jacqueline Du Pré. 'Oh, she's a hysteric,' he announced. On another occasion, he told the world that Rostropovich plays out of tune! The only thing I can say about this *colleague* is that if his tone were as big as his mouth, he'd be outstanding. He has, alas, a very poor tone, and his remarks are both inexcusable and disgusting.

In Janos Starker's 2004 autobiography, *The World of Music, According to Starker*, he describes what may have triggered the cellist's irreversible animosity. In 1951, Starker was principal cellist of the Metropolitan Opera Orchestra. During the season, he was invited to the home of Rosalie Leventritt; the occasion marked the launch of Leonard Rose's solo career. At the celebration, Rose asked Starker whether he had any interest in the Philharmonic's position he would soon vacate. "I don't audition," Starker responded tersely, "*They* know who I am."

At Carnegie Hall later in the season, Starker strode onto the stage to audition for Rose's former job. Peering out into the audience, Starker's face registered surprise to spot Rose sitting among conductor Dimitri Mitropoulos, concertmaster John Corigliano, principal violist William Lincer, and the orchestra's manager Maurice Van Praag. For them, Starker played unaccompanied Bach and Kodály. As an audition juror, Rose then stood up and requested the extensive excerpt of solos from Brahms's Piano Concerto No. 2,* in spite of a conversation the two had at Rosalie Leventritt's party about Starker's unfamiliarity with

---

* Starker's rendition of these solos—on a recording made with the Chicago Symphony Orchestra and piano soloist Emil Gilels, under the baton of Fritz Reiner in February 1958—is superb. From 1953 to 1958, he was principal cellist of the Chicago Symphony Orchestra.

the work. Feeling this groundswell of hatred, this unattractive, cutthroat side of Rose's personality, compelled Starker to take a superior stance about a decade later, averring he was above competition. In a letter dated February 16, 1954, Starker wrote to Rose: "Through my musical life, one of my chief goals is never to consider music-making a competitive activity. If anyone reaches a high enough professional standard from there on, it should serve self-expression."

In his autobiography, Starker subtly retaliates by spreading information about Rose's unpleasant behavior and in the process, regardless of Starker's motivation, he reveals as much as any document Rose's intense insecurity regarding competitors, possibly explaining why Rose lashed out: "It struck me as somewhat unusual that a player who resigned was in charge of selecting a successor; but then I was told that he had not resigned, but taken a leave of absence. Rose was a giant of a cellist and a master teacher, but on occasion, displayed a certain insecurity. For example, he complained that Casals, then Feuermann, and then Piatigorsky played all the concerts [theoretically all concerts of past], and that there was nothing left for other cellists."[311] If one believes Starker and extrapolates, Rose implies that there was no hope, nothing left for him.

In his memoir, Rose's vitriol continues. Under the guise of musings on tone production, he dictates bitterly:

> Fascinating this business of sound. I'm amused by some players I have known who have marvelous technique and a powder-puff sound. They are very often great on recordings, because the engineers can put a microphone almost inside the instrument. In a large hall—and in one particular case, even a small hall—they sound puny and totally lacking in any communication with the audience, and completely detached from the music. As a matter of fact, for them there is no music-making without that microphone. It reminds me of the typical American-style crooner.[312] How far do you think those crooners would project without a mike? Naturally, those players who don't have any sound tend to pooh-pooh the importance of sound—one SOB in particular. What nonsense!

Yo-Yo Ma and his wife visited Rose during his final months in the hospital when Rose read a letter to Ma aloud that had just arrived from Starker. "This was such a beautiful letter," Ma says. "It was really moving. You know, life is full of miscommunications and misunderstandings, especially in a profession full of fragile egos. And here Starker wrote to him, 'My Dear Leonard – I just want you to know how much I always admired your playing, your art.... If there was ever any misunderstanding, that these were not intentional and that who knows, had we been closer, I think we could have become good friends...' Rose was visibly shaken.

Leonard Rose's children, in distant retrospect, described their father as "married to the cello," and like an overprotective spouse, emotional extremes ruled the day. It was intolerable when something came between him and his idealized view of the relationship. Jealousy of competitors, as seen through Starker's eyes, stretched into the past. Rose's behavior and thinly veiled feelings about the successes of his peers seem indicative of the manner in which he dealt with his students' successes as well. When prized pupil Lynn Harrell burst onto the scene in 1972 as a soloist, garnering glowing reviews and receiving offers of record contracts, a number of professional New York cellists had the sense Rose hovered ominously over the cellist's burgeoning workload. The fame and, more thoroughly, the comfort on stage that Rose's star students reached evinced his certain success as a teacher, an achievement he should have reveled in. He should have taken tacit credit and delight as *his* youngsters excelled. In all but a few cases, he did not. His inability to control pupils as they became more established was an incessant source of angst for the iconic cellist. Rose's multifaceted career may mirror the complex bundle of psychological inner contradictions that also defined him. On an early career path, as principal cellist in the nation's first-tier orchestras, he quantifiably was the top, unquestionably the "best" in the organization. And later, as chamber musician, the internationally acclaimed Istomin-Stern-Rose Trio placed him side-by-side with the most powerful violinist in the field, also without competition. However, his success, on the educator's path, meant sharing the limelight with his students, the union of which was anathema to him. This underlying psychology may well account for why the man, regarded as America's first great cellist, failed to attain the acclaim due him, fame that was more readily accorded to immigrants in the 20th century. "Intensity" is synonymous with Rose's career. Without it, his musical interpretations would lack the virile and elegiac beauty unique to him.

As for Starker, his autobiography mentions no ill will toward Rose. In fact, he barely mentions his late colleague at all. Although intentionally or unintentionally fueling Rose's ire, Starker admitted that he told an interviewer in the 1970s, "At this moment, there are three cellists equally active on all continents: Fournier, Rostropovich, and myself."[313] And according to Ma, Rose understood his "real sense of legacy—or the generational vision of cello playing. So he would get ticked if someone says in an interview, 'well, there are three good cellists today' and his name wasn't in there. This is where, I think, it's really the laws of unintended consequences. People say things, you are saying something, it gets printed..."[314] As if exhausted by the fight with Rose, with a tone of resignation on the subject of success, Starker waxes philosophic: "The importance of the cello remains no matter who basks in glory."

Chapter Twenty-Five

DEATH OF A LEGEND

To be an artist is like being entrusted with something precious for a brief time. It is an artist's duty to hand it on like those Greek runners who passed on the lighted torch one to another.[315]

—Jascha Heifetz

Leonard Rose knew something was terribly wrong in April 1984 when he had trouble catching his breath during the simplest tasks. His student James Lee noticed, "Toward the end of the [academic] year, you could tell that he wasn't feeling well. He would mention it too. He said he felt weak and he didn't know why... Later in the spring [he] told me, 'I don't bring my cello in anymore because I don't know what's wrong. I feel so tired all the time. I just can't carry it.' And he looked very sad saying it." The diagnosis of a terminal form of leukemia, from which his first wife died 20 years earlier, was devastating. The disease tenaciously took hold and over the next eight months, Rose's body deteriorated. His doctors expressed the prognosis in vague terms, confusing the family. Confident he would beat the cancer, Rose continued to practice his cello up until three months before his death, at which point he realized death was imminent. Rose's life would end, as Minnie's did.

It raises necessary questions: were the Roses exposed to deadly radiation during Cold War nuclear tests out West when they spent parts of two summers in Colorado and Utah in the late 1940s? Is it not conceivable that the Roses, today labeled "downwinders"—named for the winds that carried atomic debris eastward across the western plains—had vital cells damaged by these tests that are, at present, hotly debated? How many people were subjected to fallout and what happened to their health? Who became unknowing victims during the Cold War? Isn't it ironic that Leonard Rose devoted himself, performing in numerous venues, including one notable with the Cleveland Orchestra in October 1982 for the cause, "Musicians Against Nuclear Arms Benefit"? What about his health scare in his late 50s? Did he suspect something no one else knew about?

Observers commented on a decline in his spirits and in his playing. Jerome Kessler heard Rose perform two years before he died. Kessler described how Rose had just arrived from the airport and was suffering from a head cold. "He was walking down the hall looking kind of down and wishing he were either somewhere else or someone else.... I walked up to him, and said, 'Hello Mr. Rose. Do you remember me?' He said, 'Hello. Will I see you afterwards? I said, 'I hope so.' During the performance there were some technical problems not of his making. It was not an easy concert, yet the man played with passion and abandon.... It was moving and inspiring. He got some reserve somewhere and brought it all out in that concert. What a lesson!" Less than one year before Rose died, Gilda Barston heard him in the Brahms "Double" with violinist Eric Friedman and the Chicago Youth Symphony. It was clear to Barston that his skill and memory had faded.[*] "His hands froze on him during the opening. The day before that concert, we were having dinner and he had brought his cello along from the hotel.... After dinner, he actually left the restaurant without his instrument." Yet Rose continued to perform in prominent venues, struggling for sufficient volume in recital above the lush piano or in concerto with an opulent orchestral palette behind him. Equally unsettling is a live recording made of Leonard Rose's final recital from August 1983 entitled "Le dernier concert à Prades." Due to his physical and mental deterioration, the performance is substandard. Undoubtedly a bootleg—produced without the artist's permission and posthumously released—the CD shows the obvious end to a legendary career.

---

[*] Kessler and Barston, students of Rose in the late 1950s.

At the time Rose was ailing and hospitalized, his cousin Frank Miller also was in a hospital. Although Miller started the 1984-1985 season as principal cellist of the Chicago Symphony Orchestra, the prognosis of heart failure forced his immediate retirement. Frank phoned his one-time student and housemate who, gravely ill, disclosed his flagging energy, "Frank, my cello is sitting over in the corner of the room with the case open and I don't have the strength to touch it." Each man broke into tears: two cousins, who dedicated their lives to performing, were simultaneously too sick to play their beloved instruments. Miller's death on January 6, 1986, came slightly more than a year after he left the orchestral position he held for 26 years.

Rose's hospital room transformed into a virtual stage for farewells from the famous and not-so famous. During the months' long vigil, Rose had a chance to come to terms with his life, especially to reconcile with the children he fathered with Minnie.

Still Barbara (b. 1941) and Arthur (b. 1944) loved him dearly and ultimately discovered his love for them. Unfortunate circumstances, inherent to his busy career caused the estrangement. He apologized for the perceived abandonment when they needed a paternal presence.

During this end-of-life period of reflection, while Leonard Rose grew closer to his children, the distance widened between him and his second wife, Xenia Petchek. She entered his life immediately following his loss of Minnie. He had been utterly devastated, in spite of his unpublished memoir's characteristically understated, unemotional description of his first wife as a "good person who shared some very difficult years with me." His grief would compel him to move from the long-time family home in Great Neck, Long Island.

In her mother's absence, Barbara remembers that her father could not eat or sleep. "He simply broke down. His spirit was totally shattered. If it hadn't been for Xenia, I don't know where he would have been. I think she saved his life." In exchange, Rose lavished attention and affection on his new bride—his children were out of the picture. However, conflict materialized early in the marriage. Xenia reports, "I flunked my part in it. Being treated like royalty began to make me feel totally unconnected and, in time, equally isolated."[316] When she could tolerate no more, Rose salvaged the marriage with a professional suggestion. He encouraged her to pursue her former interest in becoming a psychotherapist. Without the support of "my most intimate conspirator, my caretaker and protector, my best friend and lover, all at one time," Xenia doubts she could have motivated herself through graduate school and the establishment of her fledgling career. Thereafter, their independent professional lives held together their relationship.

One day disaster struck. Leonard Rose, youthful and apparently healthy, who maintained a demanding teaching schedule, concertizing around the world, suddenly was dying—and with him, his relationship with Xenia. The pair lacked resources to cope with the dual traumas. A charitable inference could interpret Rose's behavior as a protective impulse to diminish her imminent grief. Rose was solely preoccupied with himself and his survival, pushing her away from him at the vigil's onset. All he desired was to handle his impending death with dignity and grace, without Xenia's emotional embrace. He became resentful of her youth and vigor. They argued about everything: friends, money, and Rose's children. There was no tenderness, no hugs or even touching. Life grew intolerable as the couple drifted toward separate realms.

Yet Rose sustained a temporary optimism through frequent in-person and telephone contact. "I remember talking to him in June when he was in the hospital," Gilda Barston said. "He had just gotten off the phone with Raya Garbousova and while I was talking to him, some idiot intern came in to tell him he was going to die. He was very upset, but then told me that he was going to beat this thing."

"My most poignant memory," Ron Shawger recounts of Rose's last days, was "how, even then, he was an example to emulate. I spoke with him on the phone, intending to tell him how much I cared, that I loved him.... What I figured would be a call where I would take the lead turned into something I never expected.... Rose turned the attention from my grief to him thanking me for being such a good student and for helping him out with the scheduling of his lessons. He went on at great length about the end of his life and what would happen next. He told me that although there was no hope for his health, he knew he would see me again in the next life. It was such a moving call. I mostly remember sobbing as he couldn't help but show even then what always made him a great man: his remarkable ability to put a student's interest first."

The legendary figure's mortality descended like a heavy weight upon family, friends, colleagues, and students. Because Harry Rose had thrived into his nineties, those genes—coupled with technological advances—led Rose to presume that he would live. Upon realizing he would barely attain 66 years of age, the world he inhabited grew dark and surreal. Xenia sadly recalled the dramatic contrast shown in a photograph of her husband taken just prior to his diagnosis. "The one I was looking at showed a healthy, vigorous, hearty man with thick gray hair, while the picture in my head was a pale, bald, dying man. It was impossible to believe they were the same person."

Twenty years after Rose's death, his daughter Barbara described the tough childhood of a perfectionist's child, "I was never quite good enough for anything in his eyes." Still, she justified the irregular paternal attention with a keen awareness of the breadth of Rose's responsibilities.

Despite the hectic, often solitary lifestyle his career imposed on the family, Rose provided some sweet memories for his children. The passage of time opened the floodgates. Arthur remembers playing ball, billiards, golf, and going fishing. The family of four spent summers together at Meadowmount where the son palled around with the father. He also recalls a memorable drive he and his dad took to Miami after Minnie died. Barbara tells of unforgettable chamber music evenings at their home that lasted into the wee hours of the morning, the two children hiding beneath the bed and staying up until the music ended or until they got caught. She also remembers the pleasure her father took in cooking outdoors on the grill for family and friends and the times she sat with him as he enjoyed his favorite port or sherry from big crystal decanters, which were set so neatly on the silver trays in the dining room. Her father's sweetness returns to her when she pictures him in 1960, at her bedside following the removal of her appendix. Or when she relates how particular he was about her selection of potential male suitors. "I can still see him looking so handsome in a full dress suit. I'm so proud to have been his daughter," Barbara summed up her recollections. Those good times and the belated reconciliation may have compensated for the painful years of separation from him and his love. The nadir of which was epitomized when Barbara had to purchase her own ticket at Carnegie Hall to hear her father perform.

Barbara tolerated and understood the painful estrangement from her father. "He let me back into his life in the last three months and we just covered everything." Rose received massive doses of chemotherapy as an inpatient at Manhattan's Memorial Sloan-Kettering Cancer Center where, one day, Barbara listened through the closed door to her father's final cello practice. He gathered all his strength for one more traversal through Dvořák's Cello Concerto. "I can't do this anymore," he whispered to his daughter, placing his bow upon the bed as she entered the room. "The only one I trust to take this [cello] home is you. Do you think you can handle it?" Regardless of two decades apart, Barbara assumed the role of dutiful daughter. He entrusted his instrument to her, and she arranged his transfer to a more pleasant hospice setting. For 23 years Barbara worked for the Paramedics and Emergency Personnel at the state's Department of Health and she brought him to White Plains Hospital where she was on staff. She appointed herself in charge of her father's primary care. "I think he had a lot of time to think when he was in the hospital. He told me before he died that he never allowed himself the pleasure of his childhood," Barbara says. Some missing pieces fit together for her as she solved more of the puzzle of who her father was—the man she deemed her "God" who simultaneously remained a stranger. The White Plains hospice arrangement treated him like royalty with fine meals and a room that met his every need.[*]

Barbara then handled every responsibility for her father, shuttling back and forth between his home and the hospital. "One time while I was driving him to New York City, he stopped breathing in the car. I pulled his head back and he started breathing again." The extensive training as a medical professional and opportunity to control his care may have absolved his daughter of her youthful feelings of inadequately measuring up

---

[*] The Juilliard School paid for all of Leonard Rose's exhaustive medical bills.

to his standards. The demanding perfectionist's lifelong neatness applied until the very end. "He did not want to die at home where he might leave a mess. He was unbelievably meticulous," Barbara reported. "When Dad died, his heart wouldn't give out. He was in a coma for days. He was in full command until the coma. He died in my arms.... I felt his last heartbeat in his neck ... it was 6:32 p.m. November 16, 1984."

There was no funeral service. Leonard Rose was cremated and his ashes were scattered at sea. As Felix Salmond's star student, Leonard Rose performed with other celebrated artists for his teacher's memorial concert at Juilliard May 9, 1952. In the same way, Yo-Yo Ma and Lynn Harrell, Rose's star students, along with performers Isaac Stern, Eugene Istomin, Itzhak Perlman, and Michael Tree paid tribute to Rose in a memorial concert at Juilliard, November 27, 1984, hosted by the school's president, Joseph W. Polisi.[317]

Lynn Harrell   Itzhak Perlman   Isaac Stern   Yo-Yo Ma   Michael Tree   1984
Courtesy of the Juilliard School

Before I met and played for Leonard Rose, I had built him up to iconic stature since childhood. His sound and his approach to the cello repertoire beckoned me in a magisterial way. I was swept away with his cello splendor. In his prime, Leonard Rose was the most accurate and expressive cellist alive. Living up to this larger-than-life image, after my audition at Juilliard in 1979, he wrote me a letter that has a profound effect upon me and that I refer to in times of need. His carefully chosen words ring in my head, as I am sure he intended them to:

"I expect you to become a great player. The more you learn about the cello and the miracle of great music, the more you will want to learn. We must always strive for perfection, knowing that perfection is almost impossible."

Book Acknowledgments

Writing this book has been an unparalleled experience in my life.

I wish to thank my wife of fourteen years, Jessica, and my parents, Joel and Carol Honigberg, who read, critiqued, and contributed to my work along the way.

A special thanks goes to poet and director of the International Writing Program at the University of Iowa, Christopher Merrill, who subliminally inspired me to keep going.

Archivists Richard Wandel at the New York Philharmonic, Carol Jacobs at the Cleveland Orchestra, Joanne Seitter at the Curtis Institute of Music, and Jeni Dahmus at the Juilliard School were indispensable, uncovering a treasure trove of information for me to peruse.

I would like to express my gratitude to Georganne Mennin (Peter Mennin's widow) for uncovering and then transferring her lone, pristine LP copy of her husband's cello concerto performed by Leonard Rose, tucked inside a box for 50 years, to a CD to pair with this biography.

Along the same lines, I would like to thank Jay Shulman (Alan Shulman's son) for furnishing me with a marvelous CD copy of his father's cello concerto performed by Leonard Rose for this biography as well.

And a heartfelt thanks to Charlie Pilzer, at Airshow Studios, the matchless editor who poured over these recording transfers, working hours on end to make the ambient sound first-rate.

A warm thank you to Joyce Robbins (Channing Robbins's sister), Wendy Salmond Oler (Felix Salmond's daughter), and Marta Casals Istomin for their generosity in helping me with essential information.

To the children of Leonard Rose: Arthur and Barbara. Thank you for your friendship and memories of your father. I am indebted to your good will. Thank you for your support; your love for your father has shown through despite the maze of stress that encompassed your father's life.

A word of acknowledgment to cellists Gilda Barston, Avron Coleman, Raymond Davis, Michael Grebanier, Lynn Harrell, Ronald Leonard, Yo-Yo Ma, Jorge Sicre, Nathan Stutch, and Frederick Zlotkin—who met with me face to face. I enjoyed getting to know your unique personalities if only for the briefest time.

Similarly, I would like to thank the following for consenting to take the time out of their busy schedules to meet one on one with me: Emanuel Ax, Anne Barak, Arturo Delmoni, Bernard Greenhouse, Lorin Maazel, Itzhak Perlman, Leonard Slatkin, and Pinchas Zukerman.

Thanks also to Thomas Frost, the producer of many Leonard Rose's recordings, in getting me vital information regarding the cellist's discography legacy.

Finally, without the expertise and unfailing dedication of my editor, Vanessa Weeks Page, this book may not have been done. With profound appreciation...

Also

University of Maryland: George Moquin and Bonnie Jo Dopp
The Jewish Museum: Deb Weiner
Washington, DC Research: Paul R. Lusignan, Kimberly Williams
Chicago Historical Society: Deandra Gamble
Sharon Plotkin

Cellists: Nicholas Anderson, Gerald Appleman, Scott Ballantyne, Seymour Barab, Martha Blackman, Ulrich Boeckheler, Owen Carmen, Leonard Chausow, Steve Custor, Mike D'Avanzo, David Everhart, Gregory Fiocca, Edgar Fischer, Alla Goldberg, Sean Grissom, David Heiss, Richard Hirschl, Desmond Hoebig, Einar Holm, Geraldine French Jennings, Jerome Kessler, Eric Kim, Damian Kremer, James Lee, Mats Lidström, John Martin, Diane Mather, Mary Mayhew, Daniel Morganstern, Robert Newkirk, May

Osterberg, Barbara Pepper, Dorothy Reichenberger, Christopher Rex, Toby Saks, William Salchow, Victor Sazer, Laura Sewell, Ron Shawger, Steve Sigurdson, Lori Singer, Lloyd Smith, Nina de Veritch Smith, Bruce Uchirmura, Donald White, Harry Wimmer, and Harvey Wolfe

Weather service: Stephen Kahn
Stratford Festival: Jane Edmonds and Ellen Charendoff
Glenn Gould Estate: Stephen Posen, Faye Perkins, and Brian Levine

Tuscon Symphony: Delora Pyritz
Cleveland Orchestra Archivists Amy Dankowski, Jim Menger, and Timothy Parkinson
New York Philharmonic: Barbara Hall and Bill Thomas
Chicago Symphony: Frank Villella
Boston Symphony Orchestra: Barbara Perkel, Bridget Carr
Los Angeles Philharmonic: Steve Lacoste
National Symphony archivist, Karyn Garvin and Executive Director, Rita Shapiro
San Francisco Symphony: Kathryn Cummings, Joe Evans
Eastman School of Music: David Peter Coppen
London Symphony Orchestra: Libby Rice
Pittsburgh Symphony
Carnegie Hall
St. Louis Symphony: Jeff Trammel
Juilliard: Jane Gottlieb
Curtis Institute: Sally Grant Branca

Ann Franke
Casals Festival: Anibal Ramirez
Carnegie Hall: Gino Francesconi
National Capital Cello Club Newsletter Summer 1993
Cello Society of New York

Reverend Clarke K. Oler

University of North Carolina at Greensboro: Carolyn Shankle, Sarah Dorsey

University of Hartford, Connecticut: Margaret Mair
Warren Wernick at Thomas Frost Productions

Musicians: George Adams, Van Cliburn, David Gross, Jaime Laredo, Eudice Shapiro, Jeffrey Siegel, Arthur Statter, and Michael Tree

Library of Congress
Lincoln Center Library for the Performing Arts

Luthier: John Montgomery,

Tim Janof at Cello.org Newsletter

Editors: Elizabeth Kostova, Diane Stamm, Nicole Palmer

APPENDIX A

LEONARD ROSE'S SYMPHONIC CAREER
NBC Symphony Orchestra (1938-1940)
New York Philharmonic (1943-1951)

Leonard Rose's, 1938-1939 Season:
Arturo Toscanini's sixteen weeks

October 15, 1938:   Vaughan Williams "Fantasia on a Theme by Thomas Tallis," 1910
Brahms Symphony No. 3, Op. 90
Martucci *Notturno*; *Noveletta*
Tchaikovsky Overture-Fantasy "Romeo and Juliet"

October 22, 1938   Rossini Overture *La Cenerentola*
Strauss *Don Quixote, Op.* 35 (Emanuel Feuermann, cellist)
Beethoven Symphony No. 5, Op. 67

November 5, 1938   Graener *Die Flöte von Sanssouci*, 1930
Barber "Adagio" for Strings, 1938
   First Essay, Op. 12, 1937
Debussy *Images pour Orchestre: Ibéria*, 1906
Dvořák Symphony No. 9, Op. 92, "From the New World"

November 12, 1938   Beethoven Overture *Coriolan*, Op. 62
Schubert: Symphony No. 2 in B-flat Major, D. 125
Franck *Les Eolides*
Meyerbeer Overture *Dinorah* (with the Metropolitan Opera Chorus)

November, 19, 1938	Schumann Overture "Manfred," Op. 115 Mendelssohn: Symphony No. 5, Op. 107 "Reformation" Wagner Prelude to Act III from *Die Meistersinger* Berlioz: *Roméo et Juliette, Op.* 17, Love Scene Rossini Overture "William Tell"
November 26, 1938	Smetana Overture "The Bartered Bride" Martucci Symphony No. 1 in D minor, Op. 75 Liszt *Orpheus* Ravel *Daphnis et Chloé*, Suite No. 2, 1909-1912

December 3, 1938	Beethoven Symphony No. 3, Op. 55 "Eroica"
	Wagner Forest Murmurs from *Siegfried*
	    Siegfried's Death and Funeral Music from *Götterdämmerung*
	    Overture to *Rienzi*

Leonard Rose, assistant principal;
Placed by Toscanini:

December 13, 1938	Newark, New Jersey Weber Overture *Oberon* Wagner Forest Murmurs from *Siegfried* Brahms Variations on a Theme by Haydn, Op. 56a Tchaikovsky Symphony No. 6, Op. 74 "Pathétique" Wagner Prelude to *Die Meistersinger*
December 27, 1938	Baltimore, Maryland Repeat of December 13
January 7, 1939	Mozart Symphony No. 35 in D Major, K. 385 "Haffner" Brahms-Rubbra: "Variations and Fugue" on a Theme by Handel, Op. 24 Loeffler, "Memories of My Childhood," 1925 Wagner Prelude to *Die Meistersinger*
January 10, 1939	Boston, Massachusetts Scarlatti-Tommasini "The Good Humored Ladies" Ravel *Daphnis et Chloé*, Suite No. 2, 1909-1912 Brahms: Symphony No. 3, Op. 90 Wagner Forest Murmurs from *Siegfried* Siegfried's Funeral from *Götterdämmerung*

January 14, 1939	Bazzini Overture *Saul* Shostakovich Symphony No. 1, Op. 10, 1925 Franck "Psyche Slumber," "Psyche and Eros" Strauss *Salome,* Dance of the Seven Veils
January 21, 1939	Berlioz "Harold in Italy," Op. 16 (William Primrose, viola) Catalani *La Wally*, Prelude to Act IV Ravel "Bolero," 1928
January 28, 1939	Gluck-Wagner Overture *Iphigenia in Aulis* Beethoven Symphony No. 8, Op. 93 de Falla *El Amor Brujo*, 1915 (Josephine Burzio, contralto) Rossini Overture "William Tell"

January 31, 1939	Chicago, Illinois
	Rossini Overture "The Barber of Seville"
	    Overture *La Cenerentola*
	Brahms Variations on a Theme by Haydn, Op. 56a
	Beethoven Symphony No. 3, Op. 55 "Eroica"
	Weber-Berlioz "Invitation to the Dance," Op. 65
	Wagner Prelude to *Die Meistersinger*
	    Forest Murmers from *Siegfried*

February 1, 1939	Pittsburgh, Pennsylvania Repeat of January 31
February 4, 1939	Mozart Symphony No. 38 "Prague," K. 504 Respighi "The Fountains of Rome," 1916 Weber-Berlioz "Invitation to the Dance," Op. 65 Elgar Variations on an Original Theme, Op. 36 "Enigma"
February 7, 1939	Providence, Rhode Island Repeat of the February 1

February 11, 1939	Brahms Symphony No. 4, Op. 98
	    Liebeslieder Waltzes, Op. 52 (Erich Leinsdorf and Joseph Kahn, pianists)
	    Overture "Academic Festival," Op. 80

February 18, 1939	Sibelius Symphony No. 2 in D Major, Op. 43, 1902
	    "The Swan of Tuonela," Op. 22
	    En Sag, Op. 9
	    "Finlandia," Op. 26, 1900

February 21, 1939	Newark, New Jersey Beethoven *Leonore* Overture No. 2, Op. 72a Symphony No. 7, Op. 92 Rossini "William Tell" Passo a sei, Soldier's Dance Wagner Prelude and Good Friday Spell from *Parsifal* Strauss *Till Eulenspiegel*, Op. 28

February 25, 1939	Wagner Overture "The Flying Dutchman"
	    Prelude to Act III from *Tannhäuser*
	    Overture and Bacchanale
	    Prelude and Liebestod from *Tristan und Isolde*
	Wagner-Toscanini *Götterdämmerung*
	    "Dawn and Siegfried's"
	    "Rhine Journey"
	Wagner "Ride of the Valkyries" from *Die Walküre*

March 14, 1939	Respighi "The Fountains of Rome," 1916 Wagner "Dawn and Siegfried's Rhine Journey" from *Götterdämmerung* Overture *Tannhäuser* Beethoven: Symphony No. 7, Op. 92

Guest Conductors, 1938-1939 Season:

Artur Rodzinski December 10, 1938	Glinka Overture "Ruslan and Ludmila" Tchaikovsky Symphony No. 5, Op. 64 Starokadomsky Concerto for Orchestra, Op. 14, 1937 Stravinsky "Firebird Suite," 1910
Artur Rodzinski December 17, 1938	Weber Overture "Euryanthe," Op. 81 Dvořák Symphony No. 8, Op. 88 Hindemith "Mathis der Maler," 1934 Strauss *Till Eulenspiegel*, Op. 28
Artur Rodzinski December 24, 1938	Humperdinck Prelude "Hansel and Gretel" Bach-Respighi Three Chorales Beethoven Symphony No. 1, Op. 21 Brahms-Schoenberg Piano Quartet in G Minor (arranged 1937)

Artur Rodzinski December 31, 1939	Vivaldi Concerto Grosso in G minor Scriabin Symphony No. 3, Op. 43 "Le Divin Poème," 1904 Kodály "Háry János" Suite, 1927 Strauss J. Emporer Waltz
Bruno Walter March 11, 1940	Mozart Divertimento, K. 287 Piano Concerto No. 20 in D minor, K. 466 (Bruno Walter, pianist) Symphony No. 40 in G minor K. 550
Bruno Walter March 18, 1940	Weber Overture *Oberon* Haydn Symphony No. 92 in G Major, "Oxford" Brahms Symphony No. 1, Op. 68
Bruno Walter March 25, 1940	Corelli Concerto Grosso in G minor Beethoven Symphony No. 1, Op. 21 Mason "Old English Folk Song Suite," 1933-1934 Strauss "Death and Transfiguration," Op. 24

Bruno Walter
April 1, 1940
	Berlioz Overture *Le Corsaire*, Op. 21
	  The Damnation of Faust, Op. 24: "Minuet of the Will o' the Wisps," "Dance of the Sylphs," "Rákóczy" March
	  Symphonie fantastique, Op. 14

Bruno Walter April 8, 1940	Wagner Overture *A Faust* Siegfried Idyll Mahler Symphony No. 1, "Titan"
Hans Lange April 15, 1939	Bloch Concerto Grosso for Strings and Piano Obbligato, 1925 Beethoven: Symphony No. 4, Op. 60 Delius "In a Summer Garden," 1909 Strauss *Don Juan*, Op. 20
Alberto Erede April 22, 1939	Menotti "The Old Maid and the Thief" (World Premiere)

Leonard Rose's South America tour with Toscanini and NBC Symphony 1940

June 13, 1940
Rio de Janeiro
Rossini Overture *La Cenerentola*
Beethoven Symphony No. 3, Op. 55 "Eroica"
Mignone "Congada," 1921
Smetana the Moldau
Berlioz *Roméo et Juliette,* Queen Mab Scherzo
Wagner Good Friday Spell from *Parsifal*
    Prelude to Act I *Die Meistersinger*
    Prelude to Act III *Die Meistersinger*

June 14, 1940
Rio de Janeiro
Schubert Symphony No. 9, D. 944 "The Great"
Paganini Moto perpetuo
Brahms Variations on a Theme by Haydn, Op. 56a
Ravel "La Valse," 1920
Gomes Overture *Il guarany*

June 15, 1940
Sao Paolo
Rossini Overture "The Barber of Seville"
Beethoven Symphony No. 7, Op. 92
Mignone "Congada"
Mendelssohn "A Midsummer Night's Dream," Op. 61, Scherzo
Strauss "Death and Transfiguration," Op. 24

June, 19, 1940
Buenos Aires
Mozart Overture "The Magic Flute"
Brahms Symphony No. 1, Op. 68
Franck *Les Èolids*
Respighi "The Fountains of Rome," 1916
Wagner Good Friday Spell from *Parsifal*
Prelude to *Die Meistersinger*

June 20, 1940
Buenos Aires
Rossini Overture "The Barber of Seville"
Beethoven Symphony No. 7, Op. 92
Aquirre Two Dances
Paganini *Moto perpetuo*
Brahms Variations on a Theme by Haydn, Op. 56a
Strauss *Till Eulenspiegel*, Op. 28

June 23, 1940	Buenos Aires Mozart Symphony No. 40 in G minor K. 550 Beethoven *Leonore* Overture No. 3, Op. 72b Wagner *Siegfried Idyll* Prelude and Liebestod from *Tristan und Isolde* Forest Murmurs from *Siegfried* Overture *Tannhäuser*
June 25, 1940	Buenos Aires Schubert Symphony No. 9, D. 944 "The Great" Debussy: *Images, Ibéria*, 1906 Wagner Prelude to Act I; Prelude to Act III from *Lohengrin* Strauss "Death and Transfiguration," Op. 24
June 27, 1940	Buenos Aires Weber Overture *Oberon* Brahms Symphony No. 2, Op. 73 Barber Adagio for Strings, Op. 11 Saint-Saëns *Danse macabre*, Op. 40 Tchaikovsky Overture-Fantasy "Romeo and Juliet" Ravel "La Valse," 1920
June 29, 1940	Buenos Aires Cherubini Overture *Anacréon* Beethoven Symphony No. 6, Op. 68 "Pastoral" Williams, Alberto Symphony No. 7, Op. 103 "Eterno Reposo," 1937 Smetana The Moldau Wagner Prelude and Liebestod from *Tristan und Isolde* "Ride of the Valkyries" from *Die Walküre*
July 1, 1940	Buenos Aires Rossini Overture *La Cenerentola* Beethoven Symphony No. 5, Op. 67 Mendelssohn "A Midsummer Night's Dream," Op. 61 Nocture; Scherzo Mussorgsky-Ravel Pictures at an Exhibition Wagner Prelude to *Die Meistersinger*
July 3, 1940	Montevideo Rossini Overture "The Barber of Seville" Beethoven Symphony No. 7, Op. 92 Mendelssohn "A Midsummer Night's Dream," Op. 61 Nocture; Scherzo Weber-Berlioz "Invitation to the Dance," Op. 65

Paganini *Moto perpetuo*
Smetana "The Moldau"
Debussy *La Mer*, 1905

July 4, 1940   Montevideo
Beethoven Overture *Egmont*, Op. 84
Brahms: Symphony No. 2, Op. 73
Respighi "The Fountains of Rome," 1916
Wagner Prelude and Liebestod from *Tristan und Isolde*
Prelude to *Die Meistersinger*

July 8, 1940   São Paulo
Beethoven Overture *Egmont*, Op. 84
Brahms Symphony No. 2, Op. 73
Fernandez *Reisado do pastoreio*, Batuque, 1930
Berlioz Roméo et Juliette: Queen Mab Scherzo
Rossini "William Tell," Passo a sei; Soldiers' Dance
Wagner Prelude and Leibestod from *Tristan und Isolde*
Overture *Tannhäuser*
Gomes Overture *Il guarany*

July 9, 1940   Rio de Janeiro
Beethoven Overture *Egmont*, Op. 84
Brahms Symphony No. 1, Op. 68
Fernandez *Reisado do pastoreio,* Batuque, 1930
Respighi "The Fountains of Rome," 1916
Wagner Forest Murmurs from *Siegfried*
Debussy *La Mer*, 1905

July 10, 1940   Rio de Janeiro
Cherubini Overture *Anacréon*
Beethoven Symphony No. 5, Op. 67
Mendelssohn "A Midsummer Night's Dream," Op. 61
Nocturne; Scherzo
Weber-Berlioz "Invitation to the Dance"
Wagner Prelude to *Die Meistersinger*

**Leonard Bernstein conducting the New York Philharmonic
Leonard Rose, Assistant Principal Cellist
1943-1944**

Bernstein Symphony No. 1 "Jeremiah," 1942
Brahms Variations on a Theme by Haydn, Op. 56a
Copland *El Salón México*, 1936
Delius "Paris, A Night Piece" (Nocturne), 1900

Mendelssohn Symphony No. 4, Op. 90 "Italian"
Mozart Overture to "The Marriage of Figaro" K. 492
Rózsa Theme, Variations and Finale, Op. 13, 1933✪
Schumann Overture "Manfred," Op. 115✪
Strauss *Don Quixote*, Op. 35✪ (Joseph Schuster, cellist William Lincer, violist)
Tchaikovsky Overture-Fantasy "Romeo and Juliet"
Wagner Prelude to *Die Meistersinger* ✪
✪These works comprised Bernstein's historic debut.

1944-1945

Bach, C. P. E. Concerto for Strings in D Major
Beethoven Symphony No. 2, Op. 36
Debussy Prelude *L'Après-Midi d'un Faune*
Harris Symphony No. 3, 1939
Rachmaninoff Piano Concerto No. 1 in F Sharp minor, Op. 1 (Jeanne Therrien, pianist)
Ravel "La Valse," 1920
Shostakovich Symphony No. 5, Op. 47, 1937

1945-46
NONE
1946-47
NONE
1947-48   [Bernstein was Music Director of New York's City Symphony, 1945-1948]
NONE
1948-49
NONE

1949-1950

Bartók Music for Strings, Percussion, and Celesta, 1937
Beethoven Piano Concerto No. 1, Op. 15 (Leonard Bernstein, pianist)
    Leonore Overture No. 3, Op. 72b
    Symphony No. 8, Op. 93
Bernstein Symphony No. 2, "The Age of Anxiety," 1949 (Lukas Foss, pianist)
Brahms Piano Concerto, No. 1, Op. 15 (Gary Graffman, pianist)
Copland Overture "Outdoor," 1938
Schumann Symphony No. 4, Op. 120
Shapero "Adagietto," from Symphony for Classical Orchestra, 1947
Walton Violin Concerto, 1939 (Jascha Heifetz, violinist)
Weber Overture to *Der Freischütz*

1950-1951

Copland El Salón México, 1936
Franck "Symphonic Variations" (Eugene List, pianist)
Ives Symphony No. 2, 1901
Mozart Concerto in G Major K. 453 (Leonard Bernstein, pianist)
Mozart Overture "Don Giovanni"
"Three German Dances"
Prokofiev Piano Concerto No. 3, Op. 26, 1921 (William Kapell, pianist)
Rachmaninoff Piano Concerto No. 2, Op. 18, 1901 (William Kapell, pianist)
Stravinsky Le Sacré du Printemps, 1912
Tchaikovsky Overture-Fantasy "Romeo and Juliet"

Dimitri Mitropoulos conducting the New York Philharmonic
Leonard Rose, Assistant Principal Cellist

Summer 1944

Beethoven Piano Concerto No. 3, Op. 37 (Alexander Brailowsky, pianist)
Brahms Piano Concerto No. 1, Op. 15 (Rudolf Firkusny, pianist)
"Double" Concerto, Op. 102 (John Corigliano, violinist Leonard Rose, cellist)
Symphony No. 2, Op. 73
Mendelssohn Violin Concerto in E minor, Op. 64 (Carroll Glenn, violinist)
Rachmaninoff Symphony No. 2, Op. 27, 1907
"The Isle of the Dead," Op. 29, 1909
De Lisle La Marseillaise
Schubert Symphony No. 5 in B flat Major, D.485
Schumann Symphony No. 2, Op. 61
Sibelius Violin Concerto, Op. 47, 1903 (Isaac Stern, violinist)
Symphony No. 1, Op. 39

Summer 1945

Bach Fantasy and Fugue in G Minor (Transcribed by Dimitri Mitropoulos)
Liszt Piano Concerto No. 1 (Dimitri Mitropoulos, pianist)
Milhaud Fantasie sur 'Le Boeuf Sur Le Toit', Op. 58, 1919
Rachmaninoff Piano Concerto No. 2, Op. 18, 1901 (Gyorgy Sandor, pianist)
Ravel "Valses Nobles et Sentimentales," 1912

Spring Tour 1947

Beethoven Symphony No. 2, Op. 36 (six performances)
Ibert "Escales," 1921-1922 (four performances)
Mozart Overture "Don Giovanni" (four performances)

Sibelius Symphony No. 2 in D Major, Op. 43, 1902 (four performances)
Strauss Suite from "Der Rosenkavalier," 1944 (five performances)
Tchaikovsky Symphony No. 5, Op. 64 (three performances)
Wagner Prelude to *Die Meistersinger* (two performances)
Weber Overture to *Der Freischütz* (five performances)

1947-1948

Barber Cello Concerto, Op. 22, 1945 (Raya Garbousova, cellist)
Bartók Dance Suite, 1923
Beethoven Overture *Coriolan*, Op. 62
    Symphony No. 5, Op. 67
Debussy *Images pour Orchestre*, 1906
Franck Symphonic Poem, *Le Chasseur Maudit*
Gershwin Piano Concerto in F Major, 1925 (Oscar Levant, pianist)
Gould "Minstrel Show," 1946
Handel-Casadesus Concerto for Viola and Orchestra (William Lincer, violist)
Krenek Symphony No. 4, Op. 113, 1947
Mahler Symphony No. 6, "Tragic," 1903-1904
Schumann Symphony No. 4, Op. 120
Strauss *Eine Alpensinfonie*, Op. 64, 1915
Tchaikovsky Piano Concerto No. 1, Op. 23 (Clifford Curzon, pianist)
    Violin Concerto, Op. 35 (Mischa Elman, violinist)
Verdi Overture to the Opera, *I Vespri Siciliani*
Wagner Overture to *Tannhäuser*

1948-1949

Bach-Mitropoulos Fantasia and Fugue in G minor, 1942
Bach-Respighi Prelude and Fugue in D Major
Bartók Rhapsody No. 2, 1928 (Isaac Stern, violinist)
Bloch Suite for Viola and Orchestra, 1918 (William Lincer, violist)
Borodin Symphony No. 2 in B minor
Brahms Piano Concerto No. 2, Op. 83 (Rudolf Serkin, pianist)
    Violin Concerto, Op. 77 (Joseph Szigeti, violinist)
    Symphony No. 1, Op. 68
    Symphony No. 2, Op. 73
Charpentier "Impressions d'Italie," symphonic suite for orchestra
Dvořák Two Slavonic Dances No. 1 and No. 3
Gould "Philharmonic Waltzes," 1947
    Symphony No. 3, 1946
Lalo *Symphonie Espagnole* in D minor, Op. 21 (Isaac Stern, violinist)
Mahler Symphony No. 7, 1904
Massenet Aria from Thais
Mendelssohn Violin Concerto in E minor, Op. 64 (Dorotha Powers, violinist)

         Overture "Hebrides," Op. 26
         Overture "Ruy Blas," Op. 95
         Symphony No. 3, Op. 56 "Scottish"
Mozart Overture to "The Marriage of Figaro" K. 492
Paganini Violin Concerto in D Major (Zino Francescatti, violinist)
Perpessa Prelude and Fugue for Orchestra, 1935
Poulenc *Concerto Champêtre* for Harpsichord or Piano, 1929 (Francis Poulenc, pianist)
Prokofiev Violin Concerto No. 2, Op. 63, 1935 (Zino Francescatti, violinist)
Rathaus *Vision Dramatique*, Op. 55, 1945
Satie-Debussy *Two Gymnopédies*
Schnabel Rhapsody for Orchestra, 1946
Schumann Piano Concerto in A minor, Op. 54 (Arturo Michelangeli, pianist)
         Cello Concerto in A minor, Op. 129 (Leonard Rose, cellist)
         Symphony No. 4 in D minor, Op. 120
Strauss *Also Sprach Zarathustra*, Op. 30
         Don Juan, Op. 20
Tchaikovsky Symphony No. 4, Op. 36
         Symphony No. 5, Op. 64
Verdi Overture to *Nabucodonosor*
Wagner Prelude to *Lohengrin*
         Prelude to *Parsifal*
Webern "Passacaglia," 1908

1949-1950

Bach Brandenburg Concerto No. 3 BWV 1048
     Concerto in G minor BWV 1056 (Joseph Szigeti, violinist)
Bach-Mitropoulos "Fantasia and Fugue" in G minor, 1942
Bach-Reger Aria After the Chorale-Prelude, "O Man, Bewail They Grievous Sin"
Beethoven Piano Concerto No. 4, Op. 58 (Rudolf Serkin, pianist)
         Piano Concerto No. 5, Op. 73 "Emperor" (Robert Casadesus, pianist)
         Violin Concerto, Op. 61 (Szymon Goldberg, violinist)
         Symphony No. 2, Op. 36
         Symphony No. 3, Op. 55 "Eroica"
Berg Violin Concerto, 1935 (Joseph Szigeti, violinist)
Berlioz "Minuet of the Will-o-the-Wisps," from The Damnation of Faust
    "Rákóczy" March, from The Damnation of Faust
Bliss Piano Concerto in B flat Major, 1938 (Leonard Pennario, pianist)
Brahms Symphony No. 4, Op. 98
Chabrier "Joyeuse Marche"
       "Fête Polonaise," from Le Roi Malgré Lui
Chasins Period Suite, 1949
Cherubini Overture *Anancréon*
Chopin Piano Concerto No. 1 in E Minor, Op. 11 (Leonid Hambro, pianist)

Clapp Overture to a Comedy, 1933
Conrad "The Continental," arranged for two pianos (Arthur Whittemore, Jack Lowe pianists)
Dvořák Overture "Carnival," Op. 92
Elgar Violin Concerto in B minor, Op. 61, 1910 (John Corigliano, violinist)
Falla Three Dances from "The Three-Cornered Hat," 1917
Gershwin "I Got Plenty o' Nuttin," from Porgy and Bess, 1935
Gould "Philharmonic Waltzes," 1947
Gounod "Jewel Song," from Faust
Holst "St. Paul's Suite," Op. 29 No. 2, 1912
Honegger Concertino for piano and orchestra, 1924 (Oscar Levant, pianist)
Ibert "Escales," 1921-1922
Kern "The Song is You" (Arthur Whittemore, Jack Lowe pianists)
Khachaturian Piano Concerto in D-Flat Major, 1936 (Oscar Levant, pianist)
Krenek Piano Concerto No. 3, 1946 (Dimitri Mitropoulos, pianist)
Lekeu Adagio for Strings, Op. 3
Liszt A Faust Symphony
Massenet *Pleurez, pleurez, mes yeux*, from *Le Cid*
Mendelssohn Violin Concerto in E minor, Op. 64 (Isaac Stern, violinist)
Overture "Ruy Blas," Op. 95
Mohaupt "Town Piper Music," 1946
Mozart Violin Concerto K. 216 (Joseph Szigeti, violinist) Overture to "The Abduction from the Seraglio," K. 384
Overture to "The Magic Flute" K. 620
Piket Overture "Curtain Raiser to an American Play," 1948
Poulenc Concerto "Champêtre" for Harpsichord or Piano (Leonid Hambro, pianist)
Concerto for Two Pianos in D minor, 1932 (Arthur Whittemore, Jack Lowe pianists)
Prokofiev Symphony No. 1 in D Major, Op. 25 "Classical," 1917
Purcell-Mitropoulos Prelude and Death of Dido, from "Dido and Aeneas"
Rabaud Symphonic Poem, "La Procession Nocturne"
Rachmaninoff "Symphonic Dances," Op. 45, 1940
Reger Piano Concerto in F minor, Op. 114, 1910 (Rudolf Serkin, pianist)
Rodgers "Falling in Love with Love," 1938 (Arthur Whittemore, Jack Lowe pianists)
"Lover" (Arthur Whittemore, Jack Lowe pianists)
Saint-Saëns Violin Concerto No. 3 in B minor, Op. 61 (Zino Francescatti, violinist)
Symphonic Poem, *Le Rouet d'Omphale* in A Major, Op. 31
Schoenberg "A Survivor from Warsaw," Op. 46, 1947
Schubert Symphony No. 2 in B-flat Major, D. 125
Schumann Symphony No. 1, Op. 38 "Spring"
Sessions Symphony No. 2, 1946
Shulman Cello Concerto, 1950 (Leonard Rose, cellist)
Sibelius Symphony No. 4 in A minor, Op. 63, 1911

Strauss J. "Tritsch-Tratsch" Polka
  Waltz "Emporer"
  Waltz "Voices of Spring"
Strauss R. "Elektra," Tragedy in One Act, 1909
  Symphonia Domestica, Op. 53, 1904
Tchaikovsky Serenade for Strings in C Major, Op. 48
  Symphonic Fantasy, *Francesca da Rimini*, Op. 32
Vaughan Williams Symphony No. 4, 1934
Verdi "O don fatale," from Don Carlos
Wagner *A Siegfried Idyll*
  Overture to "The Flying Dutchman"
  Introduction to Act III of *Lohengrin*
  Overture to *Tannhäuser*
  Wotan's Farewell and Magic Fire Spell, from *Die Walküre*
Weber Overture to *Der Freischütz*
Webern Symphony, Op. 21, 1928

1950-1951

Alexander "Epitaphs" for Orchestra, 1947
Babin "Capriccio," 1949
Bach Concerto for Three Piano and Strings BWV 1063 (Gaby, Jean and Robert Casadesus, pianists)
Bach-Casella "Chaconne"
Bax Overture to a "Picaresque Comedy," 1931
Beethoven Piano Concerto No. 3, Op. 37 (Sidney Foster, pianist)
  Piano Concerto No. 4, Op. 58 (Artur Rubinstein, pianist)
  Overture *Coriolan*, Op. 62
  Symphony No. 1, Op. 21
  Symphony No. 4, Op. 60
Berg "Wozzeck" Opera, Op. 7, 1922
Berlioz Excerpts from "The Damnation of Faust"
  Overture "Rob Roy"
  Overture "The Roman Carnival," Op. 9
Bizet Suite *Jeux d'Enfants*
  Symphony in C Major
Bloch "Schelomo," 1916 (Leonard Rose, cellist)
Boyce Symphony No. 1 in B-Flat Major, Op. 2
Brahms Piano Concerto No. 2, Op. 83 (Artur Rubinstein, pianist)
Bruch Violin Concerto No. 1 in G minor, Op. 26 (Yfrah Neaman, violinist)
Casadesus Concerto for Two Pianos, Op. 17, 1934 (Gaby and Robert Casadesus, pianists)
Cherubini Overture "The Water-Carrier"
Chopin Piano Concerto No. 2 in F minor, Op. 21 (Menahem Pressler, pianist)
Debussy *La Mer*, 1905

Dello Joio New York Profiles, 1951
Dvořák Violin Concerto in A minor, Op. 53 (Isaac Stern, violinist)
  Cello Concerto in B minor, Op. 104 (Edmund Kurtz, cellist)
Falla Three Dances from "The Three-Cornered Hat," 1917
Glazunov Violin Concerto in A minor, Op. 82 (Nathan Milstein, violinist)
Goldmark Overture "Sakuntala," Op. 13
Grieg Piano Concerto in A minor, Op. 16 (Richard Farrell, pianist)
Haydn Sinfonia Concertante in B Flat Major
Koutzen Morning Music, 1950 (John Wummer, flutist)
Krenek Symphonic Elegy, Op. 105, 1946 ("In Memoriam Anton Webern") for String Orchestra
Lalo Symphonie Espagnole in D minor, Op. 21 (Ossy Renardy, violinist)
Malipiero Piano Concerto No. 4, 1950 (Dimitri Mitropoulos, pianist)
Mendelssohn Piano Concerto No. 1 in G Minor, Op. 25 (Rudolf Serkin, pianist)
  Overture "Hebrides," Op. 26
  Symphony No. 3, Op. 56 "Scotch"
Milhaud Music for the Play, *Les Choéphores*, Op. 24, 1915
Mozart Adagio, K. 261; Rondo allegretto grazioso, K. 373
  Concerto for Two Pianos K. 365 (Gaby and Robert Casadesus, pianists)
  Violin Concerto No. 7 in D Major, KV 271a (Yehudi Menuhin, violinist)
  Concert-Rondo K. 382 (Rudolf Serkin, pianist)
  Overture to "The Marriage of Figaro" K. 492
  Suite from "Idomeneo," K. 366
  Symphony No. 39 in E-Flat Major, K. 543
Paganini Concerto for Violin in D Major (John Corigliano, violinist)
Perpessa "Harilaos Christus" Symphony
Prokofiev Piano Concerto No. 2, Op 16, 1913 (Jorge Bolet, pianist)
  Symphony No. 5 in B-flat Major, Op. 100, 1944
Purcell Prelude and Death of Dido
Rachmaninoff Symphony No. 2, Op. 27, 1907
Ravel *Alborado del Grazioso*, 1918
  L'Heure Espagnole Opera in One Act, 1909
  Ma Mère l'Oye, 1911
  Pavane pour une Infante Défunte
  Rhapsodie Espagnole, 1907-08
Saint-Saëns Cello Concerto in A minor, Op. 33 (Leonard Rose, cellist)
Saint-Saëns *Danse Macabre*
  Prelude to *Le Déluge*
Schoenberg "Variations" for Orchestra, Op. 31, 1926-28
Schumann Introduction and Allegro in D minor, Op. 134 (Rudolf Serkin, pianist)
  Overture, Scherzo and Finale, Op. 52
  Symphony No. 2, Op. 61
Sibelius Violin Concerto, Op. 47, 1903 (Jascha Heifetz, violinist)
Strauss "Burleske" for Piano and Orchestra, Op. 85 (Rudolf Serkin, pianist)
  Don Juan, Op. 20
  Ein Heldenleben, Op. 40

Stravinsky Ballet Music "Petrouchka," 1910-11
Swanson Short Symphony, 1950
Tchaikovsky Piano Concerto No. 1 in B-flat minor, Op. 23 (Aldo Ciccolini, pianist)
Symphony No. 6 in B Minor, Op. 74 "Pathétique"
Thomson Symphony No. 2 in C Major, 1931-1941
Vieuxtemps Violin Concerto No. 4 in D minor, Op. 31 (Yehudi Menuhin, violinist)
Weber Overture "Euryanthe," Op. 81
Overture "Ruler of the Spirits," Op. 27
Symphony No. 1 in C Major, Op. 19

1951 Edinburgh Festival

Bax Overture to a "Picaresque Comedy"
Beethoven Piano Concerto No. 4, Op. 58 (Myra Hess, pianist)
Piano Concerto No. 5, Op. 73 "Emperor" (Robert Casadesus, pianist)
Violin Concerto, Op. 61 (Zino Francescatti, violinist)
Overture *Coriolan*, Op. 62
Symphony No. 2, Op. 36
Symphony No. 4, Op. 60
Berlioz Overture "Roman Carnival," Op. 9
Three Pieces from "The Damnation of Faust"
Brahms Piano Concerto No. 1, Op. 15 (Solomon, pianist)
Cherubini Overture "The Water-Carrier"
Falla Three Dances from "The Three-Cornered Hat," 1917
Gould "Philharmonic Waltzes," 1947
Haydn Sinfonia Concertante in B Flat Major
Krenek Symphonic Elegy, Op. 105, 1946 ("In Memoriam Anton Webern")
for String Orchestra
Malipiero Piano Concerto No. 4, Op. 40, 1950 (Dimitri Mitropoulos, pianist)
Mendelssohn Symphony No. 3, Op. 56 "Scotch"
Prokofiev Symphony No. 5, Op. 100, 1944
Rachmaninoff Symphony No. 2, Op. 27, 1907
Saint-Saëns Cello Concerto in A minor, Op. 33 (Leonard Rose, cellist)
Schumann Piano Concerto in A minor, Op. 54 (Myra Hess, pianist)
Overture, Scherzo and Finale, Op. 52
Swanson Short Symphony, 1948
Vaughan Williams Symphony No. 4, 1934
Weber Overture to *Der Freischütz*
Overture "Ruler of the Spirits," Op. 27

George Szell conducting the New York Philharmonic
Leonard Rose, Principal Cellist
1944-1945

Barber Second Essay, Op. 17, 1942
Beethoven "Romance" No. 1 in G Major, Op. 40 (Joseph Szigeti, violinist)
    Symphony No. 3, Op. 55 "Eroica"
    Symphony No. 5, Op. 67
Brahms Symphony No. 4, Op. 98
Dvořák Slavonic Dances, Op. 46, No. 1 and No. 3
    Slavonic Dances, Op. 72, No. 2, No. 7
Fauré "Ballade," Op. 19 (Claudio Arrau, pianist)
Foss "Ode" for Orchestra, 1944
Haydn Symphony No. 97 in C Major, Hob. I-97
Mozart Piano Concerto K. 466 (Artur Schnabel, pianist)
    Piano Concerto K. 503 (Artur Schnabel, pianist)
Prokofiev Violin Concerto No.1 in D Major, Op. 19, 1917 (Joseph Szigeti, violinist)
Schumann Symphony No. 4, Op. 120
Smetana Symphonic Poem "Vltava" from the cycle *Ma Vlast*
Sousa March, "Stars and Stripes Forever"
Strauss "Burleske" for Piano and Orchestra in D minor (Claudio Arrau, pianist)
    Till Eulenspiegel, Op. 28
Tartini Violin Concerto (Joseph Szigeti, violinist)
Tchaikovsky Violin Concerto, Op. 35 (Erica Morini, violinist)
Wagner Prelude to *Die Meistersinger*
Weber Concertstück (Claudio Arrau, pianist)
    Overture *Oberon*

Summer 1945

Beethoven Piano Concerto No. 3, Op. 37 (Artur Schnabel, pianist)
    Overture "The Creatures of Prometheus," Op. 43
    Symphony No. 8, Op. 93
Brahms Symphony No. 2, Op. 73
Dvořák Symphony No. 9, Op. 92 "From the New World"
    Three Slavonic Dances No. 1, No. 3, No. 10
Mendelssohn Symphony No. 4, Op. 90 "Italian"
Mozart Concerto for two pianos K. 365 (Pierre Luboshutz, Genia Nemenoff pianists)
    Symphony No. 40 in G Minor K. 550
Weber Overture to *Der Freishütz*

1945-1946

Bartok Concerto for Orchestra, 1943
Beethoven Piano Concerto No. 1, Op. 15 (Claudio Arrau, pianist)
   Leonore Overture to No. 2, Op. 72
   Overture to "The Creatures of Prometheus," Op. 43
   Symphony No. 8, Op. 93
Berlioz Overture "The Roman Carnival," Op. 9
Brahms Symphony No. 3, Op. 90
Dvořák Three Slavonic Dances No. 1, No. 3, No. 10
Glazunov Violin Concerto in A Minor, Op. 82 (Michael Rosenker, violinist)
Mozart Symphony No. 41 in C Major "Jupiter" K. 551
Ravel "La Valse," *1920*
Still In Memoriam "The Colored Soldiers Who Died for Democracy" for orchestra, 1943
Strauss *Don Quixote*, Op. 35 (Leonard Rose, cellist)
Stravinsky "Firebird Suite," *1910*
Wagner *A Siegfried Idyll*
   Overture to *Tannhäuser*

1946-1947

Beethoven Piano Concerto No. 3, Op. 37 (Claudio Arrau, pianist)
   Overture *Egmont, Op.* 84
   Symphony No. 2, Op. 36
   Symphony No. 3, Op. 55 "Eroica"
Bizet Suite from *L'Arlésienne*
Dello Joio "Ricercari," 1945 (Norman Dello Joio, pianist)
Glazunov Violin Concerto in A minor, Op. 82 (David Nadien, violinist)
Liszt Piano Concerto in A Major (Claudio Arrau, pianist)
Mozart Horn Concerto No. 3 in E flat Major, K. 447 (James Chambers, hornist)
   "Funeral March," K. 477
Schubert Entr'acte and Ballet Music from "Rosamunde," D. 797
Sibelius Symphony No. 3 in C Major, Op. 52, 1907
Smetana Furiant and Polka from "The Bartered Bride"
Strauss J. Waltz, the "Beautiful Blue Danube"
Wagner Overture to *Tannhäuser*
Weber Overture to *Der Freishütz*

Spring Tour 1947

Brahms Symphony No. 2, Op. 73
Wagner Overture to *Tannhäuser*
   Prelude to Act I from *Lohengrin*
   Prelude and Love-Music from *Tristan und Isolde*

1947-1948

Beethoven Violin Concerto, Op. 61 (Erica Morini, violinist)
    Leonore Overture No. 3, Op. 72b
    Symphony No. 6, Op. 68 "Pastoral"
Brahms "Academic Festival" Overture, Op. 80
    Symphony No. 1, Op. 68
Chopin Piano Concerto No. 1 in E minor, Op. 11 (Sigi Weissenberg, pianist)
    Piano Concerto No. 2 in F minor, Op. 21 (Eugene Istomin, pianist)
Copland Symphony No. 3, 1946
Franck Symphony in D minor
Lalo *Symphonie Espagnole* in D minor, Op. 21 (Yehudi Menuhin, violinist)
Mendelssohn Violin Concerto in E minor, Op. 64 (Erica Morini, violinist)
Mozart Overture to "The Marriage of Figaro," K. 492
    Serenade in D Major K. 239
    Sinfonia Concertante K. 364 (John Corigliano, violinist William Lincer, violist)
    Symphony No. 35 in D Major, K. 385 "Haffner"
Schubert Symphony No. 8 in B minor, D. 759 "Unfinished"
Schumann Symphony No. 2, Op. 61
Strauss *Don Juan*, Op. 20
Tchaikovsky Symphony No. 6, Op. 74 "Pathétique"
Verdi *La Forza del Destino*
Weber Overture to *Der Freischütz*

1948-1949
NONE
1949-1950
NONE

1950-51

Barber First Essay, Op. 12, 1938
Beethoven Piano Concerto No. 5, Op. 73 "Emperor" (Rudolf Serkin, pianist)
    Violin Concerto, Op. 61 (Erica Morini, violinist)
    Overture to "The Creatures of Prometheus," Op. 43
    Symphony No. 2, Op. 36
Bruckner Symphony No. 8
Casella "Paganiniana," Op. 65, 1942
Chopin Piano Concerto No. 2 in F minor, Op. 21 (Guiomar Novaes, pianist)
Elgar Variations on an Original Theme, Op. 36 "Enigma"
Haydn Symphony No. 92 in G Major, "Oxford"
Martin Concerto for Seven Wind Instruments, string orchestra, percussion and timpani, 1949

Mendelssohn Piano Concerto No. 1 in G minor, Op. 25 (Rudolf Firkusny, pianist)
Overture, Scherzo, Nocturne, Wedding March from "A Midsummer Night's Dream"
Mozart Symphony No. 35 in D Major, K. 385 "Haffner"
"The Village Musicians" K. 522
Prokofiev Violin Concerto No. 2 in G minor, Op. 63, 1935 (John Corigliano, violinist)
Rossini Overture *La Scala di Seta*
Schubert Entr'acte and Ballet Music from "Rosamunde" D. 797
Sibelius Symphony No. 7 in C Major, Op. 105, 1924
Smetana From Bohemia's Fields and Groves, from the Symphonic Cycle, *Ma Vlast*
Strauss Don Quixote, Op. 35 (Leonard Rose, cellist)
Tchaikovsky Violin Concerto, Op. 35 (Erica Morini, violinist)
Symphony No. 4, Op. 36
Wagner Prelude to *Lohengrin*
Weber Overture *Oberon*

Bruno Walter conducting the New York Philharmonic
Leonard Rose, Assistant Principal Cellist
1943-1944

Bach St. Matthew Passion BWV 244
Barber Symphony in One Movement, Op. 9, 1936
Beethoven Symphony No. 5, Op. 67
Symphony No. 6, Op. 68 "Pastoral"
Symphony No. 9, Op. 125 "Choral"
Brahms Piano Concerto No. 2, Op. 83 (Rudolf Serkin, pianist)
"Tragic" Overture, Op. 81
Bruckner *Te Deum Laudamus* Mass in D minor
Haydn Symphony No. 13 in D Major, Hob I:13
Mahler Symphony No. 4 1899-1901
Mozart Symphony No. 35 in D Major, K. 385 "Haffner"
Rózsa Theme, Variations and Finale, Op. 13, 1933
Schoenberg *Verklärte Nacht* arranged for String Orchestra, 1917
Schumann Overture "Manfred," Op. 115
Symphony No. 4, Op. 120
Strauss Don Quixote, Op. 35 (Joseph Schuster, cellist William Lincer, violist)
Tchaikovsky Overture-Fantasy "Romeo and Juliet"
Wagner Prelude to *Lohengrin*
Weber Overture to *Der Freischütz*

Summer 1944

Beethoven Symphony No. 6, Op. 68 "Pastoral"
Mozart Symphony No. 39 in E-Flat Major, K. 543

Schubert Entr'acte and Ballet Music from "Rosamunde" D. 797
Strauss J. "Emperor" Waltz
　　　　Overture to "The Bat"
　　　　Overture to "The Gypsy Baron"
Wagner Prelude to Acts 1 and III from *Lohengrin*
　　　　Prelude and Love-Death from *Tristan and Isolde*

1944-1945

Bach St. Mathew Passion BWV 244
Brahms Symphony No. 1, Op. 68
Mendelssohn Violin Concerto in E minor, Op. 64 (Nathan Milstein, violinist)
Mozart Symphony No. 41 in C Major, "Jupiter" K. 551

Summer 1945

Bach Concerto for Violin with (John Corigliano, violinist)
Beethoven Piano Concerto No. 4, Op. 58 (Artur Rubinstein, pianist)
　　　　Leonore Overture No. 3, Op. 72b
　　　　Symphony No. 4, Op. 60
Berlioz Overture to "Benvenuto Cellini," Op. 23
　　　　Three excerpts from "The Damnation of Faust"
Brahms Symphony No. 1, Op. 68
　　　　Symphony No. 4, Op. 98
Gluck Orpheus (Ballet Music)
Handel "I Know That My Redeemer Liveth" from Messiah
Schubert Symphony No. 8 in B minor, D. 759 "Unfinished"
Strauss "Death and Transfiguration," Op. 24

1945-1946

Bach St. Mathew Passion BWV 244
Beethoven Piano Concerto No. 3, Op. 37 (Rudolf Firkusny, pianist)
　　　　Leonore Overture No. 2, Op. 72a
Bruckner Symphony No. 9
Corelli "Christmas Concerto"
　　　　Concerto Gross in G Minor, No. 8, Op. 6
　　　　Fatto per la Notte di Natale
Debussy Prelude *L'Après-Midi du'un Faune*
Fauré *Après un Rêve* and *Elégie* (Leonard Rose, cellist)
Haydn Minuet and Variations
Mahler Symphony No. 9, 1908-09
Mozart "Eine Kleine Nachtmusik," K. 525
　　　　Concerto for Violin and Orchestra K. 218 (Bronislaw Humberman, violinist)

Sinfonia Concertante K. 364 (John Corigliano, violinist William Lincer, violist)
Symphony No. 38 "Prague," K. 504
Symphony No. 39 in E-Flat Major, K. 543
Pfitzner Three Preludes from *Palestrina*, 1917
Schumann Symphony No. 1, Op. 38 "Spring"
Strauss *Symphonia Domestica*, Op. 53, 1904
Vaughan Williams "Fantasia on a Theme by Thomas Tallis," 1910

1946-1947

Beethoven Overture to "The Creatures of Prometheus," Op. 43
    Symphony No. 7, Op. 92
Brahms Symphony No. 4, Op. 98
    Variations on a Theme by Haydn, Op. 56a
Chopin Piano Concerto No. 1 in E minor, Op. 11 (Artur Rubinstein, pianist)
Haydn Symphony No. 92 in G Major, "Oxford"
Mahler Symphony No. 5 "The Giant," 1901-1902
Mendelssohn Violin Concerto in E minor, Op. 64 (Zino Francescatti, violinist)
Schubert Symphony No. 8 in B minor, D. 759 "Unfinished"
Strauss "Death and Transfiguration," Op. 24
Vaughan Williams Symphony No. 5, 1938-1943
Wagner Overture *Faust*
Weber Overture *Oberon*

1947-1948

Beethoven Piano Concerto No. 5, Op. 73 "Emperor" (Rudolf Serkin, pianist)
    Missa Solemnis, Op. 123
    Leonore Overture No. 3, Op. 72b
    Overture to "The Creatures of Prometheus," Op. 43
    Symphony No. 4, Op. 60
Berlioz Excerpts from "The Damnation of Faust"
Brahms Violin Concerto, Op. 77 (Ginette Neveu, violinist)
    Symphony No. 2, Op. 73
    "Tragic" Overture, Op. 81
Bruckner Symphony No. 8
Dvořák Symphony No. 4, Op. 13
    Slavonic Dances; Nos. 1, No. 2, No. 3
Haydn Symphony in C Minor
Hindemith *Symphonia Serena*, 1946
Mahler *Das Lied von der Erde,* 1908 (Kathleen Ferrier, alto Set Svanholm, tenor)
Mason Symphony No. 2 in A Major, Op. 30, 1928-29
Mendelssohn Overture "Hebrides," Op. 26
Moore Symphony No. 2 in A Major, 1945

Mozart Violin Concerto No. 5 in A Major, K. 219 (John Corigliano, violinist)
Schumann Overture "Manfred," Op. 115
Smetana "Vltava" from *Má Vlast*
Strauss *Don Quixote*, Op. 35 (Leonard Rose, cellist)
      Metamorphosen, 1945
Tchaikovsky Piano Concerto No. 1, Op. 23 (Vladimir Horowitz, pianist)
Wagner *A Siegfried Idyll*
Weber Overture "Euryanthe," Op. 81

1948-1949

Beethoven Piano Concerto No. 5, Op. 73 "Emperor" (Clifford Curzon, pianist)
           Violin Concerto, Op. 61 (Erica Morini, violinist)
           "Triple" Concerto in C Major, Op. 56 (Walter Hendl, pianist John Corigliano, violinist Leonard Rose cellist)
           Overture to "The Creatures of Prometheus," Op. 43
           Overture *Coriolan*, Op. 62
           Overture *Egmont*, Op. 84
           Leonore Overture No. 1, Op. 138
           Leonore Overture No. 2, Op. 72a
           Leonore Overture No. 3, Op. 72b
           Scena and Aria *Ah, Perfido!* Op. 65
           Symphony No. 1, Op. 21
           Symphony No. 2, Op. 36
           Symphony No. 3, Op. 55 "Eroica"
           Symphony No. 4, Op. 60
           Symphony No. 5, Op. 67
           Symphony No. 7, Op. 92
           Symphony No. 8, Op. 93
           Symphony No. 9, Op. 125 "Choral"
Brahms Symphony No. 2, Op. 73
Bruckner Symphony No. 4, "Romantic"
Dello Joio Variations, Chaconne and Finale, 1948
Haydn Symphony No. 10 in D Major (Hoboken I/10)
Mahler Symphony No. 2, "Resurrection"
Mendelssohn Overture, Scherzo, Nocturne and Wedding March from "A Midsummer Night's Dream"
Strauss "Death and Transfiguration," Op. 24
Vaughan Williams "Fantasia on a Theme by Thomas Tallis," 1910

Spring Tour 1949

Beethoven Overture *Egmont*, Op. 84
           Leonore Overture No. 3, Op. 72b
           Symphony No. 1, Op. 21

Symphony No. 3, Op. 55 "Eroica"
Symphony No. 5, Op. 67
Symphony No. 6, Op. 68 "Pastoral"
Brahms Variations on a Theme by Haydn, Op. 56a
Dvořák Symphony No. 4, Op. 13
Schubert Symphony No. 8 in B minor, D. 759 "Unfinished"
Wagner *A Siegfried Idyll*

1949-1950

Beethoven Overture *Egmont*, Op. 84
Symphony No. 3, Op. 55, "Eroica"
Bruckner Symphony No. 9
Handel Concerto Grosso, Op. 6, No. 6
Haydn Symphony No. 88 in G Major Hoboken 1/88
Mahler Symphony No. 1, "Titan"
Mendelssohn Overture to "A Midsummer Night's Dream"
Mozart Piano Concerto No. 20 in D minor, K. 466 (Rudolf Firkusny, pianist)
"Eine Kleine Nachtmusik," K. 525
Symphony No. 35 in D Major, K. 385 "Haffner"
Symphony No. 40 in G minor K. 550
Schumann Symphony No. 3, Op. 97 "Rhenish"
Weber Overture "Euryanthe," Op. 81

1950-1951

Beethoven *Leonore* Overture No. 2, Op. 72a
Scena and Aria *Ah, Perfido!*
Symphony No. 8, Op. 93
Brahms Piano Concerto No. 1, Op. 15 (Clifford Curzon, pianist)
Piano Concerto No. 2, Op. 83 (Myra Hess, pianist)
Violin Concerto, Op. 77 (Zino Francescatti, violinist)
"Double" Concerto, Op. 102 (John Corigliano, violinist and Leonard Rose, cellist)
Hungarian Dances Nos. 1, 3, 10, 17
"Academic Festival" Overture, Op. 80
"Tragic" Overture, Op. 81
Symphony No. 1, Op. 68
Symphony No. 2, Op. 73
Symphony No. 3, Op. 90
Symphony No. 4, Op. 98
Variations on a Theme by Haydn, Op. 56a

Edinburgh 1951

Beethoven Leonore Overture No. 2, Op. 72a
　　　Symphony No. 9, Op. 125 "Choral"
Brahms "Tragic" Overture, Op. 81
　　Schicksalslied, Op. 54
　　Symphony No. 2, Op. 73
　　Variations on a Theme by Haydn, Op. 56a
Bruckner Symphony No. 4, "Romantic"
Mahler Symphony No. 4 1899-1901
Mozart Symphony No. 39 in E-Flat Major, K. 543
Schubert Symphony No. 9, D. 759 "The Great"
Wagner A Siegfried Idyll
Weber Overture "Euryanthe," Op. 81

Fritz Reiner conducting the New York Philharmonic
Leonard Rose, Assistant Principal Cellist
Summer 1944

Beethoven Overture to "The Creatures of Prometheus," Op. 43
　　　Symphony No. 4, Op. 60
　　　Symphony No. 7, Op. 92
Mussorgsky Excerpts from "Boris Godounoff," orchestrated by Shostakovich (first performance)
Prokofiev "Lieutenant Kije" Suite, Op. 60, 1934
Tchaikovsky Symphony No. 5, Op. 64
Wagner Excerpts from Parsifal
　　　Excerpts from Meistersinger
　　　Overture to Rienzi
　　　Venusberg Music from Tannhäuser

Summer 1945

Beethoven Piano Concerto No. 5, Op. 73 "Emperor" (Robert Casadesus, pianist)
Mozart Overture to "The Marriage of Figaro," K. 492
Strauss Till Eulenspiegel, Op. 28
Stravinsky "Firebird Suite," 1910
Tchaikovsky Symphony No. 6, Op. 74 "Pathétique"
Wagner Overture Die Meistersinger

Vladimir Golschmann conducting the New York Philharmonic
Leonard Rose, Assistant Principal Cellist
Summer 1944

Beethoven Overture Coriolan, Op. 62
　　　Symphony No. 5, Op. 67
　　　Symphony No. 8, Op. 93

Brahms Symphony No. 1, Op. 68
Debussy *La Mer*, 1905
Glinka Overture to "Russlan and Ludmilla"
Gould Symphony No. 2 "Symphony on Marching Tunes," 1944 (first performance)
Schumann Overture "Manfred," Op. 115
        Symphony No. 4, Op. 120
Tchaikovsky Symphony No. 4, Op. 36
Wagner Overture to *Die Meistersinger*

Pierre Monteux conducting the New York Philharmonic
Leonard Rose, Principal Cellist
1944-1945

Beethoven Overture "The Creatures of Prometheus," Op. 43
        Leonore Overture No. 3, Op. 72b
        Symphony No. 1, Op. 21
Berlioz Overture to "Benvenuto Cellini," Op. 23
Brahms Piano Concerto, No. 1, Op. 15 (Leon Fleisher, pianist)
        Symphony No. 3, Op. 90
Debussy *Images pour Orchestre*, 1906
        Two Nocturnes: *Nuages*, *Fêtes*
Franck-O'Connell "Pièce Héroique"
Hindemith Symphony "Mathis der Maler," 1934
Milhaud Protée Suite Symphonique No. 2, Op. 57, 1919
Prokofiev-Byrns "Suite Diabolique"
Ravel *Rhapsodie Espagnole*, 1907-1908
Respighi Symphonic Poem, "The Pines of Rome," 1924
Sibelius Violin Concerto, Op. 47, 1903 (Michael Rosenker, violinist)
Still Symphonic Poem "Old California," 1941
Strauss *Don Juan*, Op. 20
Wagner Prelude and "Love-Death" from "Tristan and Isolde"
Weber Overture *Jubel*

Arturo Toscanini conducting the New York Philharmonic
Leonard Rose, Principal Cellist
1944-1945

Haydn Symphony No. 101 in D Major, "Clock"
Respighi Symphonic Poem, "The Pines of Rome," 1924
Sibelius "The Swan of Tuonela," Op. 22
Wagner Siegfried's Death and Funeral Music from *Götterdämmerung*
Weber Overture "Euryanthe," Op. 81

Igor Stravinsky conducting the New York Philharmonic
Leonard Rose, Principal Cellist
1944-1945

Glinka Overture to "Russlan and Ludmilla"
Stravinsky "Circus Polka," 1942
    "Four Norwegian Moods," 1942
    "Ode" in Three Parts for Orchestra, 1943
    "Scènes de Ballet," 1944
Tchaikovsky Symphony No. 2, Op. 17

1945-1946

Stravinsky Fair Scenes from "Petrouchka," 1911
    "Feu d'Artifice," *Op.* 4, 1908
    "Scènes de Ballet," 1944
    "Firebird Suite," 1910
    Symphony in Three Movements, 1942-1945

Eugene Ormandy conducting the New York Philharmonic
Leonard Rose, Principal Cellist
Summer 1945

Bach Toccata in C Major (Transcribed by Eugene Ormandy)
Beethoven Piano Concerto No. 1, Op. 15 (Rudolf Serkin, pianist)
    Symphony No. 5, Op. 67
Brahms Variations on a Theme by Haydn, Op. 56a
Glazunov Violin Concerto in A minor, Op. 82 (Erica Morini, violinist)
Handel Concerto for Orchestra in D Major (Transcribed by Eugene Ormandy)
Haydn Symphony No. 88 in G Major (Hoboken 1/88)
Moussorgsky Prelude to "Khovanshchina"
Tchaikovsky Symphony No. 4, Op. 36
Wagner Excerpts from *Die Meistersinger*
    Overture and Venusberg Scene from *Tannhäuser*
    Prelude and Love-Death from *Tristan und Isolde*

Spring Tour 1947

Beethoven *Leonore* Overture No. 3, Op. 72b
Debussy *La Mer*, 1905
Kabalevsky Overture to the Opera "Colas Breugnon," Op. 24, 1936
Shostakovich No. 6 in B minor, Op. 54, 1939
Strauss Suite from "Der Rosenkavalier," 1944
Tchaikovsky Symphony No. 5, Op. 64

Wagner "Du Bist Der Lenz" from *Die Walküre*
Elsa's Dream from *Lohengrin*
Excerpts from *Götterdämmerung*
Siegfried's Rhine Journey
Siegfried's Death and Funeral Music
Immolation and Closing Scene
Prelude to *Die Meistersinger*
Prelude and Love-Music, from *Tristan und Isolde*

**Charles Münch conducting the New York Philharmonic
Leonard Rose, Principal Cellist
1946-1947**

Beethoven Overture *Coriolan*, Op. 62
Berlioz *Symphonie fantastique*, Op. 14
Correlli "La Folia"
Debussy *Images pour Orchestre*, *Ibéria*, 1906
   La Mer, 1905
Handel-Harty Suite, "Water Music"
Honegger Symphony No. 3 for Large Orchestra, "Liturgique," 1945
Mozart Violin Concerto No. 4 in D Major, K. 218 (Joseph Szigeti, violinist)
Poulenc Concerto in G minor for Organ, String Orchestra and Kettle Drums, 1938
Roussel Suite No. 2 "Bacchus et Ariane," Op. 43, 1931
   Symphony No. 3 in G minor, Op. 42, 1929-1930
Schumann Symphony No. 4, Op. 120

1947-1948

Beethoven Piano Concerto No. 4, Op. 58 (Jacques Abram, pianist)
   Symphony No. 8, Op. 93
Berlioz Overture to "Benvenuto Cellini," Op. 23
   Symphonie fantastique, Op. 14
Brahms Violin Concerto, Op. 77 (Ginette Neveu, violinist)
   Symphony No. 4, Op. 98
Chabrier Joyeuse Marche
Dukas Scherzo from *L'Apprenti Sorcier*
Fauré Suite from *Pelléas et Mélisande*
Franck Symphony in D minor
George Introduction and Allegro
Handel Concerto Grosso in A minor, Op. 6 No. 4
Honegger *Jeanne d'Arc au Bûcher*, 1938
   Symphony No. 2, for strings & trumpet ad lib in D Major, H153, 1941
Martinu Symphony No. 3, 1944
Milhaud Symphony No. 2, Op. 247, 1944
Mozart Adagio and Fugue in C minor, K. 546
   Symphony No. 38 "Prague," K. 504

Prokofiev Piano Concerto No. 2, Op. 16 (Zadel Skolovsky, pianist), 1913
Rameau Excerpts from Suites Nos. 1 and 2 from the Opera *Dardanus*
Ravel *Daphnis et Chloé*, Suite No. 2, 1909-1912
"La Valse," *1920*
Rhapsodie Espagnole, 1908
Roussel Suite in F Major, Op. 33, 1926
Saint-Saëns Violin Concerto No. 3, Op. 61 (Michael Rosenker, violinist)
Schubert Symphony No. 5 in B flat Major, D. 485
Schumann Piano Concerto in A minor, Op. 54 (Nicole Henriot, pianist)
Tchaikovsky Variations on a Rococo Theme, Op. 33 (Leonard Rose, cellist)
Weber Overture *Oberon*

1948-1949

Bach Brandenburg Concerto No. 3 in G Major, BWV 1048
Bizet Overture "La Patrie"
Symphony in C Major
Chabrier *Bourré Fantasque*
Chausson "Poème" for Violin and Orchestra, Op. 25 (Ginette Neveu, violinist)
Fauré Suite from *Pelléas et Mélisande*
Honegger Symphony No. 4 "Deliciae Basilienses," 1946
d'Indy Symphony for Piano and Orchestra on a French Mountain Song (Robert Casadesus, pianist)
Lalo Overture *Le Roi d'Ys*
Liszt Piano Concerto No. 2 in A Major (Robert Casadesus, pianist)
Mendelssohn Symphony No. 5, Op. 107 "Reformation"
Mozart Piano Concerto in C Major, K. 467 (Robert Casadesus, pianist)
Rachmaninoff Rhapsody on a Theme of Paganini, Op. 43, 1934 (Seymour Lipkin, pianist)
Rameau Excerpts from Suites I and II from the Opera "Dardanus"
Ravel *Daphnis et Chloé*, Suite No. 1 1909-1912
Daphnis et Chloé, Suite No. 2 1909-1912
"Tzigane" (Ginette Neveu, violinist) 1924
"Valses Nobles et Sentimentales," 1912
Ropartz *La Chasse du Prince Arthur*, 1911-1912
Roussel Symphony No. 4, Op. 53, 1934
Tchaikovsky Violin Concerto, Op. 35 (Nathan Milstein, violinist)
Vivaldi Concerto Grosso in D minor, Op. 3 No. 11

Leopold Stokowski conducting the New York Philharmonic
Leonard Rose, Principal Cellist
1946-1947

Albeniz "Fête-dieu à Séville" (Transcribed by Leopold Stokowski)
Bach Brandenburg Concerto in F Major, No. 2 BWV 1047 (Transcribed by Leopold Stokowski)

Chorale-Prelude, "Christ lag in Todesbanden"
Chorale-Prelude, "Ich ruf'zu dir"
Fugue in G minor
Geistliches Lied, "Komm süsser Tod"
Geistlichs Lied, "Mein Jesu"
Passacaglia and Fugue in C minor
Preludio from the Partita in E Major for String Orchestra
Toccata and Fugue in D minor
Beethoven Symphony No. 6, Op. 68 "Pastoral"
    Symphony No. 8, Op. 93
    Symphony No. 9, Op. 125 "Choral"
Brahms "Double" Concerto, Op. 102 (first movement only: John Corigliano, violinist Leonard Rose, cellist)
    Symphony No. 1, Op. 68
    Symphony No. 3, Op. 90
Creston "Frontiers," Op. 34, 1943
Debussy Prelude *L'Après-Midi d'un Faune*
    Soirée dans Grenade, 1903
Falla *El Amor Brujo*, 1915
Glinka "Memory of a Summer Night in Madrid"
Hindemith Symphony in E Flat, No. 1, 1940
d'Indy Symphony for Orchestra and Piano on a French Mountain Song, Op. 25 (Robert Casadesus, pianist)
Kabalevsky Overture to the Opera "Colas Breugnon," Op. 24, 1936
Lalo *Symphonie Espagnole* in D minor, Op. 21 (Jacques Thibaud, violinist)
Messiaen "Hymne pour grand Orchestre," 1947
Milhaud "Saudades do Brasil," Op. 67, 1920
Moussorgsky "A Night on Bald Mountain"
    Entr'acte from the Opera "Khovanshchina"
Mozart Piano Concerto in F Major, No., 19 K. 459 (Hortense Monath, pianist)
    Overture "Don Giovanni"
Prokofiev "Scythian" Suite, Op. 20, 1914-1915
Rachmaninoff "The Isle of the Dead," Op. 29, 1909
Ravel "La Valse," 1920
Rimsky-Korsakov Overture "Russian Easter," Op. 36
Shostakovich Concerto for Piano and Orchestra, Op. 35, 1933 (Eugene List, pianist)
    Symphony No. 6, Op. 54, 1939
Sibelius "Finlandia," Op. 26, 1900
    "The Swan of Tuonela," Op. 22
Siegmeister "Harvest Evening," 1946
    "Prairie Legend," 1947
Still Festive Overture, 1946
Stravinsky "Firebird Suite," 1910

Tchaikovsky Piano Concerto No. 1, Op. 23 (Jesus Maria Sanroma, pianist)
Solitude (Symphonic Transcription)
Symphonic Fantasy, *Francesca da Rimini*, Op. 32
Symphony No. 6 in B minor, Op. 74 "Pathétique"
Wagner Finale from *Götterdämmerung*
Prelude to *Lohengrin*
Good Friday Music from *Parsifal*
Finale of Act III, *Parsifal*
Love Music from Acts II and III *Tristan und Isolde*

Spring Tour 1947

Bach Fugue in G minor
Preludio from the Partita in E Major for String Orchestra
Toccata and Fugue in D minor
Beethoven Symphony No. 7, Op. 92
Brahms Symphony No. 1, Op. 68
Creston "Frontiers," Op. 34, 1943
Debussy Prelude *L'Après-Midi d'un Faune*
Kabalevsky Overture to the Opera "Colas Breugnon," Op. 24, 1936
Novacek "Perpetual Motion"
Shostakovich No. 6 in B minor, Op. 54, 1939
Siegmeister "Prairie Legend," 1947
Stravinsky "Firebird Suite," 1910
Tchaikovsky "Solitude" (Symphonic Transcription)
Symphony No. 5, Op. 64
Wagner Finale of Act III, from *Parsifal*
Love Music from Acts II and III of *Tristan und Isolde*

1947-1948

Bach Chorale-Prelude, "Wachet auf, ruft uns die Stimme"
Prelude in E Flat minor
Sinfonia from the Church Cantata, No. 156 "Ich Steh' mit einem Fuss im Grabe"
Barber Suite from the Ballet "Medea," Op. 23, 1947
Bauer Tone Poem, Op. 19 "Sun Splendor," 1926
Beethoven *Leonore* Overture No. 3, Op. 72b
Symphony No. 7, Op. 92
Casadesus Piano Concerto, Op. 37 (Robert Casadesus, pianist), 1944
Copland "Prairie Night" and "Celebration," from the Ballet Suite "Billy the Kid," 1938
Debussy *Clair de Lune*
Nocturnes: *Nauges, Sirènes*
Dello Joio Concert Music for Orchestra, 1948

Dvorak Violin Concerto in A minor, Op. 53 (Nathan Milstein, violinist)
Symphony No. 9, Op. 92 "From the New World"
Falla *El Amor Brujo,* 1915
Fauré Ballade, for Piano and Orchestra in F Sharp Major, Op. 19 (Robert Casadesus, pianist)
Fernandez *Batuque,* Negro Dance from the Opera "Malazarte," 1939
Grieg Piano Concerto in A minor, Op. 16 (Menahem Pressler, pianist)
Griffes "The White Peacock," Op. 7 No. 1, 1919
Hindemith Concert Music for Strings and Brass, Op. 50, 1930
Khachaturian "Masquerade," 1941
Mendelssohn Symphony No. 3, Op. 56 "Scotch"
Messiaen "L'Ascension" Four Symphonic Meditations for Orchestra, 1932-1933
Moussorgsky Excerpts from "Boris Godounoff"
Mozart Piano Concerto in E Flat Major, K. 449 (Myra Hess, pianist)
Symphony No. 41 in C Major "Jupiter" K. 551
Ravel "Bolero," 1928
Daphnis et Chloe, Suite No. 2, 1909-1912
Rimsky-Korsakov Overture "Russian Easter," Op. 36
Schuman "American Festival Overture," 1939
Shostakovich Prelude in E Flat minor (Transcription Leopold Stokowski)
Sibelius Music from "Belshazzar's Feast," Op. 51, 1906
Siegmeister Symphony, 1941
Stravinsky Concerto for Strings in D Major, 1946
Thomson "The Seine at Night," 1948
Tchaikovsky Music from the Ballet "The Sleeping Beauty"
Symphonic Fantasy, *Francesca da Rimini,* Op. 32
Symphony No. 4, Op. 36
Symphony No. 5, Op. 64
Vaughan Williams "Fantasia on a Theme by Thomas Tallis," 1910
Wagner Siegfried's Rhine Journey from *Götterdämmerung*
Music from Act III *Parsifal*
Overture to *Rienzi*
Prelude and *Liebestod* from *Tristan und Isolde*
Wotan's Farewell to Brünnhilde and Magic Fire Music, from *Die Walküre*

1948-1949

Bach *Nun komm der heiden Heiland* (Transcription Leopold Stokowski)
Prelude from the Partita in E Major (Transcription Leopold Stokowski)
Baron "Ode to Democracy," 1949
Bloch "Schelomo," 1916 (Leonard Rose, cellist)
Brahms Piano Concerto, No. 1, Op. 15 (Myra Hess, pianist)
Symphony No. 3, Op. 90
Symphony No. 4, Op. 98
Cowell "American Piper," 1940s

Debussy *La Cathédrale Engloutie* (Transcription by Leopold Stokowski)
"Night in Granada" (Transcription by Leopold Stokowski)
Two Nocturnes: *Nuages, Fêtes*
Prelude *L'Après-Midi d'un Faune*
Dyson Overture to the Cantata "Canterbury Pilgrims," 1930
Gershwin Piano Concerto in F Major, 1925 (Byron Janis, pianist)
Griffes "The Pleasure-Dome of Kubla Khan," 1916
Hanson Serenade for Flute, Harp and Strings, Op. 35, 1945 (John Wummer, flutist)
Haydn Symphony No. 53 in D Major, Hob. I:53 "Imperial"
Hermann Suite from "The Devil and Daniel Webster," 1941
Hindemith "Philharmonic Concerto" (Variations for Orchestra), 1932
Khachaturian Music from the Ballet Suite "Gayaneh," 1941-1942
Symphony No. 2 "The Bell Symphony," 1944
Liszt Hungarian Rhapsody No. 2
Luening "Pilgrim's Hymn," 1940s
Maganini Suite "Three Early American Pieces," 1932
Menotti Concerto for Piano and Orchestra, 1945 (Rudolf Firkusny, pianist)
Two Interludes for the Opera "The Island God," 1942
Messiaen *L'Ascension*, four "Symphonic Meditations" for Orchestra, 1932-1933
Mozart Piano Concerto in C Major, K. 467 (Myra Hess, pianist)
Deutsche Tänze K. 605
Symphony No. 40 in G minor, K. 550
Muradeli Georgian Symphonic Dance, 1939
Panufnik "Tragic" Overture, 1945
Prokofiev Piano Concerto No. 3, Op. 26, 1921 (William Kapell, pianist)
Purcell-Wood Suite in Five Movements
Rachmaninoff Piano Concerto No. 3, Op. 30, 1909 (William Kapell, pianist)
Saint-Saëns Piano Concerto No. 2, Op. 22 (Jean Graham, pianist)
Schumann Symphony No. 2, Op. 61
Sibelius Incidental Music from Maeterlinck's Drama *Pelléas et Mélisande*
Violin Concerto, Op. 47, 1903 (John Corigliano, violinist)
Stravinsky Ballet Music "Petrouchka," 1910-11
Tchaikovsky Symphony No. 6, Op. 74 "Pathétique"
Thomson "Wheat Field at Noon," 1948
Vaughan Williams Symphony No. 6, 1946-1947
Vivaldi Concerto Grosso in D Minor, Op. 3, No. 11 (Transcription by Leopold Stokowski)
Wagner Overture to "The Flying Dutchman"
Siegfried's Rhine Journey from *Götterdämmerung*
Siegfried's Death from *Götterdämmerung*
Brunnhilde's Immolation from *Götterdämmerung*
Entrance of the Gods into Valhalla from *Das Rheingold*
Erda's Scene from *Das Rheingold*
Overture to *Rienzi*

Forest Murmurs from *Siegfried*
Siegfried's Forging Song from *Siegfried*
Prelude and Love Death from *Tristan und Isolde*
Wotan's Farewell and Magic Fire Music from *Die Walküre*

Fall Tour 1948

Bach Fugue in G minor (Transcription Leopold Stokowski)
    Toccata and Fugue in D minor (Transcription Leopold Stokowski)
Beethoven Symphony No. 7, Op. 92
Brahms Symphony No. 1, Op. 68
Copland Prairie Night and Celebration, from the Ballet Suite "Billy the Kid," 1938
Debussy *Claire de Lune* (Transcription by Leopold Stokowski)
Khachaturian "Masquerade" from the play of Lermontov, 1944
Messiaen *L'Ascension*, four "Symphonic Meditations" for Orchestra, 1932-1933
Porrini *Sinfonia per una Fiaba*, 1936
Stravinsky Ballet Music "Petrouchka," 1910-1911
Thomson "The Seine at Night," 1948
Wagner Finale of Act III from *Parsifal*
    Love Music from Acts II and III from *Tristan und Isolde*
    Prelude and Love Death from *Tristan und Isolde*
Walton Spitfire Prelude and Fugue from the Film "The First of the Few," 1942
Weinberger Polka and Fugue from the Opera "Schwanda," 1927

Spring Tour 1949

Bach Three Chorale-Preludes (Transcription Leopold Stokowski)
    Wir glauben all' an einen Gott
    Ich ruf' zu dir
    Nun komm der heiden Heiland
Brahms Symphony No. 1, Op. 68
Cowell "American Piper," 1940s
Enesco Roumanian Rhapsody No. 1 in A Major, Op. 11, 1901
Khachaturian Music from the Ballet Suite "Gayaneh," 1941-1942
Menotti Two Interludes for the Opera "The Island God," 1942
Sibelius Incidental Music from Maeterlinck's Drama *Pelléas et Mélisande*
Tchaikovsky Symphony No. 6, Op. 74 "Pathétique"
Thomson "Wheat Field at Noon," 1948
Wagner Overture to "The Flying Dutchman"
    Entrance of the Gods into Valhalla from *Das Rheingold*
    Forest Murmurs from *Siegfried*
    Wotan's Farewell and Magic Fire Music from *Die Walküre*

1949-1950

Bach-Stokowski Passacaglia and Fugue, C minor
    Es ist vollbracht, from the *Passion According to St. John*
    "Sacred Song," *Mein Jesu, was für Seelenweh*
Beethoven Piano Concerto No. 2, Op. 19 (William Kapell, pianist)
    Leonore Overture No. 3, Op. 72b
    Symphony No. 6, Op. 68 "Pastoral"
Bennett Overture to an "Imaginary Drama," 1946
Bloch Two Symphonic Interludes from "Macbeth," 1902
Borodin Polovtsian Dances, from "Prince Igor"
Brahms Violin Concerto, Op. 77 (Isaac Stern, violinist)
    Symphony No. 2, Op. 73
Britten Piano Concerto in D Major, Op. 13, 1938 (Jacques Abram, pianist)
Carpenter "Carmel Concerto," 1948
Chopin-Stokowski Mazurka in A minor, Op. 17 No. 4
Copland Children's Suite, from "The Red Pony," 1948
Diamond Overture to "The Tempest," 1946
Falla "Nights in the Gardens of Spain," 1915 (William Kapell, pianist)
Gabrieli *Canzon Quarti Toni a 15*
    In Ecclesiis Benedicite Domino, Ceremonial Music from "Symphoniae Sacrae"
Glière Symphony No. 3 in B minor, Op. 42, 1909-1911
Handel Concerto in B Flat Major, Op. 4 No. 6 for harpsichord and orchestra (Leonid Hambro, harpsichordist)
Haydn Symphony No. 88 in G Major
    Symphony No. 101 in D Major "The Clock"
Ivanov-Radkevich "Russian" Overture, 1944
Liebermann Suite on Swiss Folk Melodies, 1944
Mahler Symphony No. 8 "Symphony of a Thousand," 1906
Messiaen *Trois Petites Liturgies de la Présence Divine,* 1943
Miaskovsky "Slavic Rhapsody," Op. 71, 1946
Mozart Piano Concerto in E Flat, K. 271 (Eugene Istomin, pianist)
    "Eine Kleine Nachtmusik," K. 525
    Notturno, K. 286 for four orchestras
    Symphony No. 35 in D Major, K. 385 "Haffner"
Porrino Symphonic Poem, "Sardegna," 1932
Poulenc Concerto Champêtre for Harpsichord or Piano, 1929 (Leonid Hambro, harpsichordist)
Prokofiev Symphony No. 6, Op. 111, 1947
Revueltas Symphonic Poem "Sensemayá," 1938
Riegger Canon and Fugue in D minor, 1941
Rivier Concertino for Viola and Orchestra, 1947 (William Lincer, violist)
Ruggles "Organum," 1944-1947
Schoenberg "Song of the Wood-Dove" from *Gurrelieder,* 1911

Schubert Symphony No. 8 in B Minor, D. 759 "Unfinished"
Schumann Cello Concerto in A minor, Op. 129 (Pierre Fournier, cellist)
Strauss "Death and Transfiguration," Op. 24
Tchaikovsky Symphony No. 5, Op. 64
Thomson Suite from the Opera "The Mother of Us All," 1947
Villa-Lobos Symphonic Poem "Uirapurú," 1917
Vivaldi Concerto Grosso in G minor, Op. 3 No. 2
Wagner Prelude to *Lohengrin*
    Siegfried's Ascent of the Mountain, Awakening of Brünnhilde, and Love Scene, from Act III of *Siegfried*
    Bacchanale from *Tannhäuser*
    Opening Scene, Garden Scene and Closing Scene, from Act II of *Tristanund Isolde*
    Prelude and Liebestod, from *Tristan und Isolde*

Victor De Sabata conducting the New York Philharmonic
Leonard Rose, Principal Cellist
1949-1950

Beethoven Piano Concerto No. 4, Op. 58 (Moura Lympany, pianist)
    Symphony No. 5, Op. 67
Berlioz Overture "The Roman Carnival," Op. 9
    Symphonie fantastique, Op. 14
Brahms Violin Concerto, Op. 77 (Nathan Milstein, violinist)
Dukas Scherzo from *L'Apprenti Sorcier*
Dvorak Symphony No. 9, Op. 92 "From the New World"
Franck Symphony in D minor
Frazzi "Preludio Magico," 1937
Ghedini "Marinaresca e Baccanale," 1933
Gould Spirituals for String Choir and Orchestra, 1941
Mendelssohn Violin Concerto in E minor, Op. 64 (Miriam Solovieff, violinist)
Mozart Piano Concerto in A Major, K. 488 (Artur Rubinstein, pianist)
    Overture to "The Marriage of Figaro" K. 492
Rachmaninoff Rhapsody on a Theme of Paganini, Op. 43, 1934 (Artur Rubinstein, pianist)
Ravel "Bolero," 1928
    Daphnis et Chloé, Suite No. 2, 1909-1912
    Ma Mère l'Oye, 1911
Respighi Symphonic Poem, "The Pines of Rome," 1924
Rossini Overture to "La gazza ladra"
Sibelius Symphony No. 1 in E minor, Op. 39
Sinigaglia Overture to "Le Baruffe Chiozzotte," 1907
Wagner Siegfried's Death and Funeral Music from *Götterdämmerung*
    Siegfried's Rhine Journey from *Götterdämmerung*
    Good Friday Spell from *Parsifal*
    Ride of the Valkyries from *Die Walküre*

1950-1951

Bach-Respighi Passacaglia and Fugue in C minor
Barber Overture "School for Scandal," Op. 5, 1931
Beethoven Symphony No. 7, Op. 92
　　　　Symphony No. 8, Op. 93
Debussy *Images pour Orchestre, Ibéria*, 1906
Schumann Piano Concerto in A minor, Op. 54 (Claudia Arrau, pianist)
Wagner Brunnhilde's Immolation from *Götterdämmerung*
　　Prelude to *Die Meistersinger*
　　Good Friday Spell from *Parsifal*
　　Prelude to *Parsifal*
　　Forest Murmurs from *Siegfried*
　　A Siegfried Idyll
　　Overture to *Tannhäuser*
　　Prelude and Liebestod from *Tristan und Isolde*

Artur Rodzinski conducting the New York Philharmonic
Leonard Rose, Assistant Principal Cellist
1943-1944

Bach *Nun komm, der Heiden Heiland*
　　Meine Seele erhebt den Herren
　　Wachet auf, ruft uns die Stimme
Beethoven *Leonore* No. 3, Op. 72b
　　　　Symphony No. 1, Op. 21
　　　　Symphony No. 5, Op. 67
Berlioz *Symphonie fantastique*, Op. 14
Bloch Three Jewish Poems, 1913
Brahms Symphony No. 2, Op. 73
　　　Symphony No. 4, Op. 98
Carpenter "The Anxious Bugler," 1943
Couperin-Strauss Dance Suite
Dvořák Songs My Mother Taught Me
　　Symphony No. 9, Op. 92 "From the New World"
Elgar "Falstaff" Symphonic Study in C minor, Op. 68, 1913
Fernandez *Reisado do pastoreio*, Batuque, 1930
Franck Symphony in D minor
Gershwin "An American in Paris," 1928
Gliere Symphony in B minor, No. 3, Op. 42
Guarnieri Two Brazilian Dances
Harris "March in Time of War," 1943
Haydn Symphony No. 45 in F-sharp Minor, "Farewell"
Hindemith Symphonic Metamorphosis on Theme of C. M. von Weber, 1943

Kodály Dances from "Galanta," 1933
Lekeu "Fantaisie Contrapuntique sur un Cramignon Liégeois"
Mahler Symphony No. 2, "Resurrection"
Mendelssohn Scherzo in G Minor, from Octet for Strings, Op. 20
Miaskovsky Sinfonietta for String Orchestra in B minor, Op. 32 No. 2, 1929
Milhaud "Cortège Funèbre," Op. 202, 1939
Mozart Overture to "The Marriage of Figaro," K. 492
    Symphony No. 40 in G Minor, K. 550
Noskowski Symphonic Poem, "The Steppe," Op. 66
Rathaus Polonaise Symphonique, Op. 52, 1943
Ravel *Daphnis et Chloé,* Suite No. 2, 1909-1912
    Rapsodie Espagnole, 1907-1908
Rimski-Korsakov "Capriccio Espagnol"
Roussel Symphony No. 3 in G Minor, Op. 42, 1930
Saint-Saëns Symphony No. 3 in C minor, Op. 78
Scarlatti-Byrns Suite for Strings
Schubert Entr'acte and Ballet Music from "Rosamunde"
Schuman Overture "Billings," 1943
Schumann Symphony No. 1, Op. 38 "Spring"
Shostakovich Symphony No. 1, Op. 10, 1925
    Symphony No. 8, Op. 65, 1943
Sibelius Symphony No. 5 in E flat Major, Op. 82, 1915
Smetana Lullaby, from the Opera "The Kiss'
    Overture to "The Bartered Bride"
    String Quartet No. 1 from "Ma Vlast" (Orchestral version by George Szell)
    Symphonic Poem, "Blanik," from "Ma Vlast"
Sousa "Stars and Stripes Forever"
Still In Memoriam, "The Colored Soldiers Who Died for Democracy," 1943
Strauss J. Moto Perpetuo
    Overture to "Die Fledermaus"
    Waltz "Tales from the Vienna Woods"
Strauss R. Rondo, "Till Eulenspiegel's Merry Pranks"
    Also Sprach Zarathustra, Op. 30
Stravinsky "Firebird Suite," 1910
Suppé Overture to "The Beautiful Galathea"
Tchaikovsky Andante Cantabile from String Quartet
    Marche Slave, Op. 31
    Overture-Fantasy "Romeo and Juliet"
    Symphony No. 4, Op. 36
    Symphony No. 6, Op. 74 "Pathétique"
Wagner Excerpts from *Die Meistersinger*
Weber Overture *Oberon*

Summer 1944

Beethoven *Leonore* Overture No. 3, Op. 72b
Bland "Carry Me Back to Old Virginny"
Cohan "Over There," 1917
Franck Symphony in D minor
Gershwin "An American in Paris," 1928
Liszt Symphonic Poem "Les Préludes"
Shostakovich Symphony No. 1, Op. 10, 1925
Tchaikovsky Suite from the Ballet "The Nutcracker"
Wagner Brunnhilde's Immolation from *Götterdämmerung*

1944-1945

Bach-Respighi Passacaglia in C minor
Beethoven Overture *Coriolan*, Op. 62
   Overture *Egmont,* Op. 84
   Symphony No. 7, Op. 92
Berlioz Three Excerpts from "The Damnation of Faust"
Bizet Symphony in C Major
Bloch "Israel" Symphony, 1916
Borodin Orchestral Sketch, "On the Steppes of Central Asia"
   Symphony No. 2 in B minor
Brahms Symphony No. 1, Op. 68
   Symphony No. 2, Op. 73
   Variations on a Theme by Haydn, Op. 56-A
Bruckner Symphony No. 7
Carpenter "Sea Drift," 1933
Cherubini Overture to the Ballet-Opera "Anacreon"
Clementi-Casella Symphony No. 2
Couperin Prelude and Allegro (arranged by Darius Milhaud)
Debussy *La Mer,* 1905
Dukas Scherzo from *L'Apprenti Sorcier*
Dvořák Cello Concerto in B minor, Op. 104 (Leonard Rose, cellist)
Elgar "Pomp and Circumstance," 1901
Falla Three Dances from "The Three-Cornered Hat," 1917
Gershwin-Gould "I Got Rhythm"
Handel-Harty "Water Music Suite"
Haydn Symphony No. 93 in D Major, Hoboken I/93
Ibert "Escales," 1921-1922
Kabalevsky Overture to the Opera "Colas Breugnon," Op. 24, 1936
Lekeu "Fantaisie Contrapuntique sur un Cramignon Liégeois"
Liszt "Mephisto Waltz"
Mahler *Das Lied von der Erde,* 1908

Mendelssohn Overture "Ruy Blas," Op. 95
    Scherzo from Octet for Strings
    Symphony No. 5, Op. 107 "Reformation"
Moore "In Memoriam," 1943
Mussorgsky-Ravel "Pictures at an Exhibition"
Mozart "Eine Kleine Nachtmusik," Serenade for String Orchestra K. 525
    Symphony No. 35 in D Major, K. 385 "Haffner"
    Symphony No. 40 in G Minor, K. 550
Piston "Fugue on a Victory Tune," 1944
Popper Requiem for Three Celli and Orchestra (Leonard Rose, Carl Stern, Naoum Dinger cellists)
Rachmaninoff Symphony No. 2, Op. 27, 1907
Ravel *Daphnis et Chloé*, Suite No. 2, 1909-1912
    Introduction and Allegro, for Harp, Flute, Clarinet and Strings, 1905
Rossini Overture to *L'Italiana in Algeri*
Schoenberg "Ode to Napoleon," Op. 41-B, for Recitation, Piano and String Orchestra, 1942 (Mack Harrell, Narrator)
Schuman Symphony No. 3, 1941
Shostakovich Symphony No. 8, Op. 65, 1943
Strauss Suite from "Der Rosenkavalier," 1944
Tchaikovsky Overture 1812, Op. 49
    Overture-Fantasy "Romeo and Juliet"
    Suite, "Mozartiana, No. 4, Op. 61
    Symphony No. 5, Op. 64
    Symphony No. 6 in B minor, Op. 74 "Pathétique"
Vaughan Williams Symphony No. 5, 1938-1943
Villa-Lobos "Bachianas Brasileiras" No. 2, Toccata, 1933
    "Bachianas Brasileiras" No. 5, for Eight Cellos and Soprano, 1938
Wagner Prelude to *Die Meistersinger*
    Transformation Scene; "Good Friday Spell" from *Parsifal*
Walton "Belshazzar's Feast," 1931
Wolf-Ferrari Overture to the Opera "The Secret of Suzanne," 1909
Wooldridge "A Solemn Hymn to Victory," 1944

1945-1946

Albeniz-Arbos "Fête-Dieu à Séville," from the Suite *Ibéria*, 1906
Barrymore Symphony "Partita," 1944
Beethoven Overture *Egmont, Op.* 84
    Leonore Overture No. 3, Op. 72b
    Symphony No. 3, Op. 55 "Eroica"
    Symphony No. 5, Op. 67
    Symphony No. 7, Op. 92
    Symphony No. 9, Op. 125 "Choral"
Borodin "Polovtsian Dances," from *Prince Igor*

Brahms Symphony No. 1, Op. 68
Carpenter "The Seven Ages" Symphonic Suite, 1948
Chabrier España Rhapsody for Orchestra
Chausson Symphony in B-flat Major, Op. 20
Copland "A Lincoln Portrait," 1942 (Kenneth Spencer, Speaker)
    Suite from "Appalachian Spring," 1944
Corelli Suite for Strings (arranged by Ettore Pinelli)
Debussy La Mer, 1905
    Two Nocturnes: *Nuages*, *Fêtes*
Dohnanyi Variations on a Nursery Tune, Op. 25, 1914
Donizetti "O mio Fernando," from *La Favorita*
Enesco Roumanian Rhapsody in A Major, No. 1, Op. 11, 1901
Fauré Après un Rêve (Leonard Rose, cellist)
Fitelberg Nocturne for Large Orchestra, 1944
Franck Symphony in D minor
Gershwin "An American in Paris," 1928
    Piano Concerto in F Major, 1925 (Walter Hendl, pianist) (Oscar Levant, pianist)
    "Rhapsody in Blue," 1924 (Oscar Levant, pianist)
Gershwin-Bennett "Porgy and Bess" A Symphonic Picture, 1935
Glinka "Ruslan and Ludmila" Overture
Gould Pavane from American Symphonette No. 2, 1939
    Spirituals in five movements for String Choir and Orchestra, 1941
Gruenberg Violin Concerto, Op. 47, 1944 (Jascha Heifetz, violinist)
Haydn Concerto for Harpsichord and Orchestra in D Major, Hob. XVIII (Wanda Landowska, pianist)
Humperdinck Prelude to "Hansel and Gretel"
Ibert Festival Overture
Janáček Sinfonietta, 1926
Kabalevsky Piano Concerto No. 2 in G minor, Op. 33, 1935 (Nadia Reisenberg, pianist)
Kern Scenario for Orchestra, on Themes from "Showboat," 1945
Liadov "The Enchanted Lake," Legend for Orchestra, Op. 62, 1909
Lopatnikoff Violin Concerto, Op. 26, 1941 (Joseph Fuchs, violinist)
Mahler *Lieder eines Fahrenden Gesellen* (Marian Anderson, soprano)
    Symphony No. 1, "Titan"
Mendelssohn Violin Concerto in E minor, Op. 64 (Fritz Kreisler, violinist) (Angel Reyes, violinist) (Jascha Heifetz, violinist)
    Excerpts from the Music from "A Midsummer Night's Dream"
Mussorgsky Prelude to "Khovanshchina"
Mozart Piano Concerto in A Major, K. 488 (Artur Schnabel, pianist)
    Piano Concerto in E Flat Major, K. 482 (Wanda Landowska, pianist)
    Overture to "The Marriage of Figaro," K. 492
Piston Symphony No. 2, 1943
Popper "Vito," Op. 54, No. 5

Prokofiev Piano Concerto No. 1 in D Flat Major, Op. 10, 1912 (Hilde Somer, pianist)
Piano Concerto No. 3 in C Major, Op. 26, 1921 (Zadel Skolovsky, pianist)
Violin Concerto No. 2 in G minor, Op. 63, 1935 (Patricia Travers, violinist)
"Summer Day," (Suite for children), 1941, Op. 65 b
Symphony No. 5, Op. 100, 1944
Purcell Dido's Lament, from "Dido and Aeneas" (William Lincer, violist)
Rachmaninoff Piano Concerto No. 2, Op. 18, 1901 (Alexander Brailowsky, pianist)
Piano Concerto No. 3, Op. 30, 1909 (Marisa Regules, pianist)
Rhapsody on a Theme of Paganini, Op. 43, 1934 (William Kapell, pianist)
Ravel Piano Concerto in G Major, 1929-1931 (Walter Hendl, pianist)
Daphnis et Chloé, Suite No. 2, 1909-1912
Rogers "In Memory of Franklin Delano Roosevelt," 1945
Saint-Saëns Allegro Appassionato, Op. 43 (Leonard Rose, cellist)
Introduction and Rondo Capriccioso, Op. 28 (John Corigliano, violinist)
Schelling "A Victory Ball," Fantasy for Orchestra, 1922
Schubert Symphony No. 9, D. 944 "The Great"
Shostakovich Symphony No. 5, Op. 47, 1937
Sibelius Violin Concerto, Op. 47, 1903 (Camilla Wicks, violinist)
Symphony No. 4 in A minor, Op. 63, 1911
Sousa March, "Stars and Stripes Forever"
Spirituals "Sometimes I Feel like a Motherless Child"
"Ride On, King Jesus"
Still Poem for Orchestra, 1944
Strauss J. Waltz, "Tales from the Vienna Woods"
Strauss R. *Till Eulenspiegel*, Op. 28
Szymanowski Violin Concerto No. 1, Op. 35, 1916 (John Corigliano, violinist)
Tchaikovsky Piano Concerto No. 1, Op. 23 (Artur Rubinstein, pianist)
Violin Concerto, Op. 35 (Nathan Milstein, violinist) (Tossy Spivakovsky, violinist)
Marche Slave, Op. 31
Overture-Fantasy "Romeo and Juliet"
Polonaise from the Opera "Eugene Onegin"
Suite from the Ballet "The Nutcracker"
Symphony No. 4, Op. 36
Symphony No. 5, Op. 64
Vivaldi-Siloti Concerto Grosso in D minor, Op. 3, No. 11
Wagner Funeral Music from *Götterdämmerung*
Immolation scene from *Götterdämmerung*
Prelude to *Lohengrin*

Prelude to *Die Meistersinger*
Entrance of the Gods into Valhalla, from *Das Rheingold*
Waldweben from *Siegfried*
Act III from *Die Walküre*
Weber Overture to *Der Freischütz*
Overture *Oberon*
Wolf-Ferrari Intermezzo from the Opera "Jewels of the Madonna," 1911
Overture to the Opera "The Secret of Suzanne," 1909

1946-1947

Bach-Bloomfield Toccata and Fugue, Intermezzo in C Major
Bach-Respighi Chorale-Prelude, *Wachet auf, ruft uns die Stimme*
Barber "Capricorn Concerto," Op. 21, 1944
Beethoven Piano Concerto No. 1, Op. 15 (Maryla Jonas, pianist)
Piano Concerto No. 5, Op. 73 "Emperor" (Eugene Istomin, pianist)
Violin Concerto, Op. 61 (Mischa Elman, violinist)
Marcia alla Turca, from the Music to the Play "The Ruins of Athens," Op. 113
Symphony No. 1, Op. 21
Bizet Symphony in C Major
Brahms Violin Concerto, Op. 77 (Yehudi Menuhin, violinist)
Symphony No. 2, Op. 73
Chopin Piano Concerto No. 2 in F minor, Op. 21 (Sylvia Zaremba, pianist)
Debussy Excerpts from the Opera *Pelléas et Mélisande*, 1902
Delius Intermezzo, "The Walk to the Paradise Garden," from "A Village Romeo and Juliet," 1907
Diamond Rounds for String Orchestra, 1944
Franck Symphonic Variations (Robert Casadesus, pianist)
Handel-Harty Suite, "Water Music"
Honegger Symphony No. 3 "Liturgique," 1945-1946
Ibert "Escales," 1921-1922
Khachaturian Piano Concerto in D-Flat Major, 1936 (William Kapell, pianist)
Kodály "Háry János" Suite," 1927
Lalo Overture "Le Roi d'Ys"
Mendelssohn Overture and Scherzo from "A Midsummer Night's Dream"
Mozart Piano Concerto in B-Flat Major, K. 595 (Alec Templeton, pianist)
Piano Concerto in C Major, K. 415 (Wanda Landowska, pianist)
Symphony No. 40 in G Minor, K. 550
Prokofiev Symphony No. 5, Op. 100, 1944
Respighi Symphonic Poem, "The Pines of Rome," 1924
Rimsky-Korsakov Suite from the Opera "Tsar Saltan"
Rosenthal Orchestral Suite "Musique de Table," 1941
Rossini Overture to the Opera "Semiramide"
Saint-Saëns Cello Concerto in A minor, Op. 33 (Leonard Rose, cellist)

Schuman "Undertow" Choreographic Episodes for Orchestra, 1945
Schumann Symphony No. 2, Op. 61
Shostakovich Symphony No. 9, Op. 70, 1945
Sibelius Symphony No. 5 in E flat Major, Op. 82, 1915
Strauss Waltzes from "Der Rosenkavalier," 1944
Stravinsky Le Sacré du Printemps, 1912
Tchaikovsky Violin Concerto, Op. 35 (Joseph Fuchs, violinist)
    March Slave, Op. 31
    Overture-Fantasy "Romeo and Juliet"
    Suite from the Ballet "The Nutcracker"
    Symphony No. 5, Op. 64
Vieuxtemps Violin Concerto No. 4 in D minor, Op. 31 (Michael Rosenker, violinist)
Wagner Prelude to Act III; Dance of the Apprentices; Entrance of the Masters to *Die Meistersinger*
Weber Overture to "Euryanthe," Op. 81
Wieniawski Violin Concerto No. 2 in D minor, Op. 22 (Henryk Szeryng, violinist)
Wolf-Ferrari Overture to the Opera "The Secret of Suzanne," 1909

    Significant Repertoire: Leonard Rose's Tenure, 1943-1951

BEETHOVEN SYMPHONY NO. 1	April 13, 14, 16	Artur Rodzinski, 1944
	November 9, 10	Pierre Monteux, 1944
	October 10, 11	Artur Rodzinski, 1946
	November 17	Artur Rodzinksi, 1946
	February 24, 25, 27	Bruno Walter, 1949
	April 5	Bruno Walter, 1949
	April 29	Leopold Stokowski, 1949
	April 3	Franco Autori, 1950
	October 15	Dimitri Mitropoulos, 1950
BEETHOVEN SYMPHONY NO. 2	January 26, 27	Leonard Bernstein, 1945
	December, 19, 20, 22	George Szell, 1946
	May 3, 5, 7, 9, 11	Dimitri Mitropoulos, 1947
	March 3, 4	Bruno Walter, 1949
	January, 19, 20, 21, 22, 31	Dimitri Mitropoulos, 1950
	January 4, 5, 7	George Szell, 1951
BEETHOVEN SYMPHONY NO. 3 "EROICA"	December 14, 15	George Szell, 1944
	October 4, 5, 7	Artur Rodzinski, 1945
	December 12, 13, 14	George Szell, 1946
	February 24, 25, 27	Bruno Walter, 1949
	April 5	Bruno Walter, 1949
	October 15	Bruno Walter, 1949
	November 15	Dimitri Mitropoulos, 1949
	December 11	Dimitri Mitropoulos, 1949

BEETHOVEN SYMPHONY NO. 4	June 24 May 27 January 15, 16, 25 February 14 March 17, 18, 20 October 12, 13, 17 November 7, 12 March 10, 24	Fritz Reiner, 1944 Bruno Walter, 1945 Bruno Walter, 1948 Bruno Walter, 1948 Bruno Walter, 1949 Dimitri Mitropoulos, 1950 Dimitri Mitropoulos, 1951 Dimitri Mitropoulos, 1951
BEETHOVEN SYMPHONY NO. 5 May 28	January 3 March 11 Vladimir Golschmann, 1944 October 1 March 8, 9, 11 July 29 October 11, 12, 14 November 13, 24 December 4, 5, 6, 7, 8 April 7, 8, 10 April 28 March 18, 19	Artur Rodzinski, 1944 Artur Rodzinski, 1944 Artur Rodzinski, 1944 George Szell, 1945 Eugene Ormandy, 1945 Artur Rodzinski, 1945 Artur Rodzinski, 1945 Dimitri Mitropoulos, 1947 Bruno Walter, 1949 Leopold Stokowski, 1949 Victor De Sabata, 1950
BEETHOVEN SYMPHONY NO. 6 "PASTORAL"	November 11, 12 May 14 April 3, 4, 6 December 25, 26, 28 April 7, 8, 10 April 28 October 27, 28, 30 December 21, 22, 23, 24	Bruno Walter, 1943 Bruno Walter, 1944 Leopold Stokowski, 1947 George Szell, 1947 Bruno Walter, 1949 Leopold Stokowski, 1949 Leopold Stokowski, 1949 George Szell, 1950
BEETHOVEN SYMPHONY NO. 7	January 27, 28, 29, 30 July 16 October 5, 6, 8 November 13, 25 January 22 April 9 January 3, 4, 6 February 11, 13, 14, 16 April 14, 17, 24 March 11, 12, 14 April 6 September 22, 25, 28, 30 October 1 March 17, 18, 20	Wilhelm Steinberg, 1944 Fritz Reiner, 1944 Artur Rodzinski, 1944 Artur Rodzinski, 1944 Artur Rodzinski, 1945 Artur Rodzinski, 1945 Artur Rodzinski, 1946 Bruno Walter, 1947 Leopold Stokowski, 1947 Leopold Stokowski, 1948 Leopold Stokowski, 1948 Leopold Stokowski, 1948 Leopold Stokowski, 1948 Bruno Walter, 1949

Appendix A 405

	April 25	Leonard Bernstein, 1949
	March 15, 16	Victor De Sabata, 1951
BEETHOVEN SYMPHONY NO. 8	September 17	Vladimir Golschmann, 1944
	November 8, 9, 10, 11	George Szell, 1945
	June 17	George Szell, 1945
	January 16, 17, 18	Leopold Stokowski, 1947
	April 12	Leopold Stokowski, 1947
	January 8, 9, 11	Charles Münch, 1948
	March 10, 11, 13	Bruno Walter, 1949
	February 23, 24, 25, 26, 28	Leonard Bernstein, 1950
	February 5	Bruno Walter, 1951
	March 18	Victor De Sabata, 1951
BEETHOVEN SYMPHONY NO. 9 "Choral"	March 16, 17, 19	Bruno Walter, 1944
	April 11, 12, 14	Artur Rodzinski, 1946
	April 12	Leopold Stokowski, 1947
	April 14, 15, 17	Bruno Walter, 1949
	September 2, 4	Bruno Walter, 1951
BRAHMS SYMPHONY NO. 1	November 4, 5, 6, 7	Bruno Walter, 1943
	April 13, 14, 16	Artur Rodzinski, 1944
	September 24	Vladimir Golschmann, 1944
	January 4, 5, 6, 7	Artur Rodzinski, 1945
	March 7	Bruno Walter, 1945
	May 13	Bruno Walter, 1945
	February 14, 15, 17	Artur Rodzinski, 1946
	December 26, 27, 29	Leopold Stokowski, 1946
	April 15, 18, 19, 20, 22	Leopold Stokowski, 1947
	October 11	George Szell, 1947
	December 18, 19	George Szell, 1947
	September 20, 21, 23, 26	Leopold Stokowski, 1948
	October 2	Leopold Stokowski, 1948
	October 7, 8, 10	Dimitri Mitropoulos, 1948
	November 13	Dimitri Mitropoulos, 1948
	April 18, 19, 20, 24	Leopold Stokowski, 1949
	April 26, 30	Bruno Walter, 1949
	October 13, 14, 16	Leopold Stokowski, 1949
	January 18, 19, 20, 21	Bruno Walter, 1951
BRAHMS SYMPHONY NO. 2	October 7, 8, 10	Artur Rodzinski, 1943
	August 20	Dimitri Mitropoulos, 1944
	April 13, 15	Artur Rodzinski, 1945
	June 24	George Szell, 1945
	October 3, 4, 5, 6, 12	Artur Rodzinski, 1946

	April 29, 30 May 1, 2	George Szell, 1947
	October 9, 10, 12	Bruno Walter, 1947
	April 8, 9	Bruno Walter, 1948
	November 25, 26, 28	Dimitri Mitropoulos, 1948
	December 14	Bruno Walter, 1948
	March 5	Walter Hendl, 1949
	March 30, 31 April 2	Leopold Stokowski, 1950
	February 1, 2, 4	Bruno Walter, 1951
	August 24, 30	Bruno Walter, 1951
BRAHMS SYMPHONY NO. 3	December 23, 24, 25, 26	Howard Barlow, 1943
	November 2, 3	Pierre Monteux, 1944
	February 1, 2, 3	George Szell, 1946
	February 20, 21, 22, 23	Leopold Stokowski, 1947
	March 4	Leopold Stokowski, 1947
	March 24, 25, 26, 27	Leopold Stokowski, 1949
	January 25, 26, 27, 28	Bruno Walter, 1951
BRAHMS SYMPHONY NO. 4	February 24, 25, 26, 27	Artur Rodzinski, 1944
	April 3	Artur Rodzinski, 1944
	December 21, 22, 24	George Szell, 1944
	May 6	Bruno Walter, 1944
	March 10	Bruno Walter, 1946
	March 6, 7, 9	Bruno Walter, 1947
	April 27	Eugene Ormandy, 1947
	November 6, 7	Charles Münch, 1947
	January 13, 14, 15, 16	Leopold Stokowski, 1949
	November 15	Dimitri Mitropoulos, 1949
	December 29, 30	Dimitri Mitropoulos, 1949
	January 1, 31	Dimitri Mitropoulos, 1950
	February 4, 9, 11	Bruno Walter, 1951
BARTOK CONCERTO FOR ORCHESTRA	January 31 February 1, 3	George Szell, 1946
BERNSTEIN "JEREMIAH" SYMPHONY	March 29, 30 April 1	Leonard Bernstein, 1944
BERNSTEIN "THE AGE OF ANXIETY" SYMPHONY	February 23, 24, 26	Leonard Bernstein, 1950

BRUCKNER SYMPHONY NO. 4 "ROMANTIC"	December 9, 10 August 26	Bruno Walter, 1948 Bruno Walter, 1951
BRUCKNER SYMPHONY NO. 7	April 5, 6	Artur Rodzinski, 1945
BRUCKNER SYMPHONY NO. 8	January 22, 23 December 14, 15, 17	Bruno Walter, 1948 George Szell, 1950
BRUCKNER SYMPHONY NO. 9	March 14, 15, 17 February 2, 3	Bruno Walter, 1946 Bruno Walter, 1950
COPLAND SYMPHONY NO. 3	December 18, 19, 21	George Szell, 1947
DEBUSSY "LA MER"	November 15, 16 February 1, 2 April 27 October 13, 14 November 23, 24, 25, 26	Artur Rodzinski, 1945 Charles Münch, 1947 Eugene Ormandy, 1947 Leopold Stokowski, 1949 Dimitri Mitropoulos, 1950
DVORAK SYMPHONY NO. 9 "NEW WORLD"	January 5, 7, 8, 9 July 8 March 18, 19, 21 March 23, 24, 25, 26	Artur Rodzinski, 1944 George Szell, 1945 Leopold Stokowski, 1948 Victor De Sabata, 1950
HINDEMITH "MATHIS DER MALER"	November 9, 10	Pierre Monteux, 1944
IVES SYMPHONY NO. 2	February 22, 23, 24, 25	Leonard Bernstein, 1951
MAHLER SYMPHONY NO. 1	October 18, 19, 20, 21 March 20, 21, 22, 23 February 9, 10, 12	Artur Rodzinski, 1945 Efrem Kurtz, 1947 Bruno Walter, 1950
MAHLER SYMPHONY NO. 2	December 2, 3, 4, 5 December 2, 3, 5	Artur Rodzinski, 1943 Bruno Walter, 1948
MAHLER SYMPHONY NO. 4	February 3, 4, 5, 6 August 22	Bruno Walter, 1944 Bruno Walter, 1951
MAHLER SYMPHONY NO. 5	February 6, 7	Bruno Walter, 1947

MAHLER SYMPHONY NO. 6	December 11, 12, 13	Dimitri Mitropoulos, 1947
MAHLER SYMPHONY NO. 7	November 11, 12	Dimitri Mitropoulos, 1948
MAHLER SYMPHONY NO. 8	April 6, 7, 9	Leopold Stokowski, 1950
MAHLER SYMPHONY NO. 9	December 20, 21	Bruno Walter, 1945
MAHLER "DAS LIED VON DER ERDE"	November 16, 17, 19 January 15, 16, 18	Artur Rodzinski, 1944 Bruno Walter, 1948
PROKOFIEV SYMPHONY NO. 1	November 30	Dimitri Mitropoulos, 1949
PROKOFIEV SYMPHONY NO. 5	March 21, 22, 23, 24 April 1 October 12, 13, 15, 17	Artur Rodzinski, 1946 Walter Hendl, 1950 Dimitri Mitropoulos, 1950
RACHMANINOFF SYMPHONY NO. 2	July 30 January 11, 12 March 29, 30 April 1, 10 September 3	Dimitri Mitropoulos, 1944 Artur Rodzinski, 1945 Dimitri Mitropoulos, 1951 Dimitri Mitropoulos, 1951 Dimitri Mitropoulos, 1951
SCHÖNBERG "VERKLARTE NACHT"	February 3, 4	Bruno Walter, 1944
SHOSTAKOVICH SYMPHONY NO. 1	February 10, 11 April 23 March 27, 28, 29 December 11	Artur Rodzinski, 1944 Artur Rodzinski, 1944 Efrem Kurtz, 1947 Walter Hendl, 1948
SHOSTAKOVICH SYMPHONY NO. 5	January 27, 28 February 21, 22, 23, 24 January 17	Leonard Bernstein, 1945 Artur Rodzinski, 1946 Walter Hendl, 1948
SHOSTAKOVICH SYMPHONY NO. 8	April 2 October 12, 13, 15	Artur Rodzinski, 1944 Artur Rodzinski, 1944

STRAUSS "ALSO SPRACH ZARATHUSTRA"	February 24, 25 March 4, 26	Artur Rodzinski, 1944 Artur Rodzinski, 1944
STRAUSS "DON JUAN"	November 4, 5 March 1, 2 December 28	Pierre Monteux, 1944 Walter Hendl, 1947 George Szell, 1947
STRAUSS "DEATH AND TRANSFIGURATION," Op. 24	May 20 February 9, 11 October 20, 21, 29	Bruno Walter, 1945 Bruno Walter, 1947 Leopold Stokowski, 1949
STRAUSS "SYMPHONIA DOMESTICA"	December 13, 14, 23 April 20, 21, 22, 23	Bruno Walter, 1945 Dimitri Mitropoulos, 1950
STRAUSS "EINE ALPENSINFONIE"	November 20, 21, 23	Dimitri Mitropoulos, 1947
STRAVINSKY "FIREBIRD" SUITE	June 18 April 22 April 14, 17, 24	Fritz Reiner, 1944 Fritz Reiner, 1945 Leopold Stokowski, 1947
STRAVINSKY "LE SACRÉ DU PRINTEMPS"	November 28, 29, 30 December 1 February 15, 16, 17, 18	Artur Rodzinski, 1946 Artur Rodzinski, 1946 Leonard Bernstein, 1951
STRAVINSKY "PETROUCHKA" SUITE	February 27, 28 September 24, 27, 29 October 3 January 15, 16	Walter Hendl, 1947 Leopold Stokowski, 1948 Leopold Stokowski, 1948 Leopold Stokowski, 1949
TCHAIKOVSKY SYMPHONY NO. 2	February 1, 2, 3, 4	Igor Stravinsky, 1945
TCHAIKOVSKY SYMPHONY NO. 4	September 10 July 22 January 10, 11, 12, 13 April 1, 2, 3, 4 September 27, 29 October 3 October 9, 14, 15, 17 December 31	Vladimir Golschmann, 1944 Eugene Ormandy, 1945 Artur Rodzinski, 1946 Leopold Stokowski, 1948 Leopold Stokowski, 1948 Leopold Stokowski, 1948 Dimitri Mitropoulos, 1948 George Szell, 1950

TCHAIKOVSKY SYMPHONY NO. 5	July 2 March 1, 2, 3, 4 July 1 October 25, 26, 27, 28 November 21, 22, 24 April 16, 21, 23 April 25, 26 May 3, 5, 8 October 16, 17, 19 November 14 November 10, 11, 13	Fritz Reiner, 1944 Artur Rodzinski, 1945 Artur Rodzinski, 1945 Artur Rodzinski, 1945 Artur Rodzinski, 1946 Leopold Stokowski, 1947 Eugene Ormandy, 1947 Dimitri Mitropoulos, 1947 Leopold Stokowski, 1947 Dimitri Mitropoulos, 1948 Leopold Stokowski, 1949
TCHAIKOVSKY SYMPHONY NO. 6	February 10, 11, 13 December 7, 8 April 22 January 9, 10, 11, 12 March 4, 5, 6 February 10, 11, 13 April 21, 22, 23 November 4	Artur Rodzinski, 1944 Artur Rodzinski, 1944 Fritz Reiner, 1945 Leopold Stokowski, 1947 George Szell, 1948 Leopold Stokowski, 1949 Leopold Stokowski, 1949 Dimitri Mitropoulos, 1950

APPENDIX B

Notable Soloists during Rose's Philharmonic Tenure 1943-1951

PIANISTS:
CLAUDIO ARRAU
(1903-1991)
Nov. 8, 9, 11, 1945
Beethoven Concerto No. 1 – George Szell, conductor
Dec. 12, 13, 1946
Beethoven Concerto No. 3 – George Szell, conductor
March 8, 9, 11, 1945
Fauré Ballade, Op. 19 and *Strauss Burleske in D minor* – George Szell, conductor
Dec. 15, 1946
Liszt Concerto No. 2 – George Szell, conductor
March 15, 16, 1951
Schumann Concerto – Victor De Sabata, conductor

LEONARD BERNSTEIN
(1918-1990)
April 25, 1949; Feb. 18, 19, 1950
Beethoven Concerto No. 1 – Bernstein, conductor
Feb. 22, 23, 1951
Mozart Concerto K. 453 – Bernstein, conductor

ROBERT CASADESUS
(1899-1972)
May 28, 1944
Beethoven Concerto No. 4 – Vladimir Golschmann, conductor
Nov. 15, 16, 18, 1945
Beethoven Concerto No. 4 – Artur Rodzinski, conductor
Dec. 30, 31, 1943, Jan. 2, 1944; April 9, 1945
Beethoven Concerto No. 5 "Emperor" – Artur Rodzinski, conductor
Jan. 26, 27, 29, 1950; Aug. 29, 1951
Beethoven Concerto No. 5 "Emperor" – Dimitri Mitropoulos, conductor

April 29, 1945
Beethoven Concerto No. 5 "Emperor" – Fritz Reiner, conductor
March 11, 12, 14, 1948
Fauré Ballade, Op. 19 and *Casadesus Concerto* – Leopold Stokowski, conductor
March 13, 14, 16, 1947
Franck Symphonic Variations and *d'Indy Symphony for piano and orchestra on a French Mountain Song* – Leopold Stokowski, conductor
Dec. 16, 17, 19, 1948
Mozart Concerto K. 467, Liszt Concerto No. 2 and *d'Indy Symphony for piano and orchestra on a French Mountain Song* – Charles Münch, conductor
Oct. 26, 27, 1944
Mozart Concerto K. 491 – Artur Rodzinski, conductor
Oct. 28, 29, 1944
Saint-Saëns Concerto No. 4 – Artur Rodzinski, conductor

ANIA DORFMANN
(1899-1984)
June 25, 1944
Beethoven Concerto No. 1 – Fritz Reiner, conductor
March 29, 1947
Beethoven Concerto No. 3 – Efrem Kurtz, conductor

RUDOLF FIRKUSNY
(1912-1994)
Dec. 20, 21, 1945
Beethoven Concerto No. 3 – Bruno Walter, conductor
March 22, 23, 1945
Beethoven Concerto No. 5 "Emperor" – Artur Rodzinski, conductor
Sept. 3, 1944
Brahms Concerto No. 1 – Dimitri Mitropoulos, conductor
Oct. 28, 29, 1943
Dvořák Piano Concerto, Op. 33 – Artur Rodzinski, conductor
Jan. 14, 1951
Mendelssohn Concerto No. 1 – George Szell, conductor
Jan. 20, 21, 1949
Menotti Concerto – Leopold Stokowski, conductor
Feb. 5, 1950
Mozart Concerto K. 466 – Bruno Walter, conductor

LEON FLEISHER
(b. 1928)
Nov. 4, 5, 1944
Brahms Concerto No. 1 – Pierre Monteux, conductor

LUKAS FOSS
(1922-2009)
Feb. 23, 24, 26, 1950
Bernstein *"The Age of Anxiety" Symphony No. 2* – Leonard Bernstein, conductor

GARY GRAFFMAN
(b. 1928)
Feb. 25, 1950
Brahms Piano Concerto No. 1 – Leonard Bernstein, conductor

LEONID HAMBRO
(1920-2006)
April 22, 1950
Chopin Concerto No. 1 – Dimitri Mitropoulos, conductor
Nov. 17, 18, 1949
Poulenc "Concert Champêtre" – Leopold Stokowski, conductor

MYRA HESS
(1890-1965)
Aug. 25, 1951
Beethoven Concerto No. 4 – Dimitri Mitropoulos, conductor [1951 Edinburgh Festival]
Feb. 3, 4, 1949
Brahms Concerto No. 1 – Leopold Stokowski, conductor
Feb. 8, 9, 11, 1951
Brahms Concerto No. 2 – Bruno Walter, conductor
Feb. 6, 1949
Mozart Concerto K. 467 – Leopold Stokowski, conductor
Nov. 2, 1947
Mozart Concerto K. 499 – Leopold Stokowski, conductor
Oct. 30, 31, 1947
Schumann Concerto – Leopold Stokowski, conductor
Sept. 1, 1951
Schumann Concerto – Dimitri Mitropoulos, conductor [1951 Edinburgh Festival]

JOSEF HOFMANN
(1876-1957)
March 2, 3, 5, 1944
Rubinstein Concerto No. 3 – Artur Rodzinski, conductor

VLADIMIR HOROWITZ
(1904-1989)
Nov. 25, 26, 1943; April 23, 1944
Rachmaninoff Concerto No. 3 – Artur Rodzinski, conductor
April 8, 9, 1948

Brahms Concerto No. 2 – Bruno Walter, conductor
April 11, 1948
Tchaikovsky Concerto No. 1 – Bruno Walter, conductor

EUGENE ISTOMIN
(1925-2003)
Dec. 9, 10, 1944
Beethoven Concerto No. 4 – Artur Rodzinski, conductor
Oct., 19, 1946
Beethoven "Emperor" Concerto No. 5 – Artur Rodzinski, conductor
Nov. 21, 1943
Brahms Concerto No. 2 – Artur Rodzinski, conductor
March 6, 7, 1948
Chopin Concerto No. 2 – George Szell, conductor
Oct. 29, 1949
Mozart Concerto K. 271 – Leopold Stokowski, conductor

WILLIAM KAPELL
(1920-1953)
Nov. 10, 11, 1949
Beethoven Concerto No. 2 – Leopold Stokowski, conductor
Feb. 13, 1949
De Falla "Nights in the Gardens of Spain" – Leopold Stokowski, conductor
Nov. 21, 22, 24, 1946
Khachaturian Concerto – Artur Rodzinski, conductor
Feb. 20, 1949
Prokofiev Concerto No. 3 – Leopold Stokowski, conductor
Feb. 15, 16, 1951
Prokofiev Concerto No. 3 – Leonard Bernstein, conductor
Oct. 25, 26, 28, 1945
Rachmaninoff "Rhapsody on a Theme of Paganini" – Artur Rodzinski, conductor
March 23, 24, 1944
Rachmaninoff Concerto No. 2 – Artur Rodzinski, conductor
June 18, 1944
Rachmaninoff Concerto No. 2 – Fritz Reiner, conductor
Feb. 17, 18, 1949
Rachmaninoff Concerto No. 3 – Leopold Stokowski, conductor
Feb. 17, 18, 1951
Rachmaninoff Concerto No. 2 – Leonard Bernstein, conductor

WANDA LANDOWSKA
(1879-1959)
Dec. 1, 2, 1945
Haydn Concerto in D Major – Artur Rodzinski, conductor
Feb. 22, 23, 1945

Mozart Concerto K. 413 – Artur Rodzinski, conductor
Oct. 24, 25, 27, 1946
Mozart Concerto K. 415 – Artur Rodzinski, conductor

OSCAR LEVANT
(1906-1972)
April 18, 1946
Gershwin Concerto in F – Artur Rodzinski, conductor
Dec. 11, 12, 14, 1947
Gershwin Concerto in F – Dimitri Mitropoulos, conductor
Dec. 29, 30, 1949 – Jan 1, 1950
Honegger Concertino and *Khachaturian Concerto* – Dimitri Mitropoulos, conductor

EUGENE LIST
(1918-1985)
Feb. 24, 25, 1951
Franck Symphonic Variations – Leonard Bernstein, conductor
Jan. 9, 10, 11, 12, 1947
Shostakovich Concerto – Leopold Stokowski, conductor

NIKITA MAGALOFF
(1912-1992)
Feb. 11, 1950
Tchaikovsky Concerto No. 1 – Franco Autori, conductor

DIMITRI MITROPOULOS
(1896-1960)
Dec. 8, 9, 11, 1949
Krenek Concerto No. 3 – Mitropoulos, conductor
March 29, 30, April 1, Sept, 3, 1951
Malipiero Concerto No. 4 – Mitropoulos, conductor

LEONARD PENNARIO
(b. 1924)
Jan. 21, 1950
Bliss Concerto in B-Flat – Dimitri Mitropoulos, conductor

FRANCIS POULENC
(1899-1963)
Nov. 11, 12, 14, 1948
Poulenc "Concert Champêtre" – Dimitri Mitropoulos, conductor

MENAHEM PRESSLER
(b. 1923)
March 10, 1951

Chopin Concerto No. 2 – Dimitri Mitropoulos, conductor
March 20, 1948
Grieg Concerto in A minor – Leopold Stokowski, conductor

NADIA REISENBERG
(1904-1983)
Oct. 11, 12, 14, 1945
Kabalevsky Concerto No. 2 – Artur Rodzinski, conductor
April 13, 14, 1944
Prokofiev Concerto No. 3 – Artur Rodzinski, conductor

ARTHUR RUBINSTEIN
(1887-1982)
May 27, 1945
Beethoven Concerto No. 4 – Bruno Walter, conductor
April 22, 1951
Beethoven Concerto No. 4 – Dimitri Mitropoulos, conductor
April, 19, 20, 1951
Brahms Concerto No. 2 – Dimitri Mitropoulos, conductor
Feb. 6, 7, 9, 1947
Chopin Concerto No. 1 – Bruno Walter, conductor
Dec. 9, 10, 1943
Chopin Concerto No. 2 – Artur Rodzinski, conductor
Dec. 12, 1943
Khachaturian Concerto – Artur Rodzinski, conductor
March 23, 24, 26, 1950
Mozart Concerto K. 488 and *Rachmaninoff "Rhapsody on a Theme of Paganini"*
– Victor De Sabata, conductor
March 21, 22, 24, 1946
Tchaikovsky Concerto No. 1 – Artur Rodzinski, conductor

GYÖRGY SÁNDOR
(1912-2005)
Aug. 12, 1945
Rachmaninoff Concerto No. 2 – Dimitri Mitropoulos, conductor
Dec. 8, 1945
Rachmaninoff Concerto No. 2 – Walter Hendl, conductor

ARTUR SCHNABEL
(1882-1951)
June 17, 1945
Beethoven Concerto No. 3 – George Szell, conductor
Dec. 24, 1944
Mozart Concerto K. 466 – George Szell, conductor
March 3, 1946

Mozart Concerto K. 488 – Artur Rodzinski, conductor
Dec. 21, 22, 1944
Mozart Concerto K. 503 – George Szell, conductor
Feb. 28 March 1, 1946
Brahms Concerto No. 2 – Artur Rodzinski, conductor

RUDOLF SERKIN
(1903-1991)
June 3, 1945
Beethoven Concerto No. 1 – Eugene Ormandy, conductor
April 5, 6, 8, 1945
Beethoven Concerto No. 3 – Artur Rodzinski, conductor
Jan. 7, 8, 1949
Beethoven Concerto No. 4 – Dimitri Mitropoulos, conductor
July 16, 1944
Beethoven Concerto No. 5 "Emperor" – Fritz Reiner, conductor
Feb., 19, 20, 22, 1948
Beethoven Concerto No. 5 "Emperor" – Bruno Walter, conductor
Dec. 28, 29, 31, 1950
Beethoven Concerto No. 5 "Emperor" – George Szell, conductor
Feb. 7, 8, 10, 1946
Brahms Concerto No. 1 – Artur Rodzinski, conductor
March 8, 10, 12, 1944
Brahms Concerto No. 2 – Bruno Walter, conductor
Oct. 28, 29, 31, 1948
Brahms Concerto No. 2 – Dimitri Mitropoulos, conductor
Nov. 13, 1950
Mendelssohn Concerto No. 1, Mozart Concert-Rondo K. 382 and *Strauss Burleske*
– Dimitri Mitropoulos, conductor
Jan. 5, 6, 1949
Reger Concerto, Op. 114 – Dimitri Mitropoulos, conductor

SOLOMON
(1902-1998)
Aug. 31, 1951
Brahms Concerto No. 1 – Dimitri Mitropoulos, conductor

VIOLINISTS:
MISCHA ELMAN
(1891-1967)
Nov. 14, 15, 17, 1946
Beethoven Concerto – Artur Rodzinski, conductor
Nov. 27, 28, 1947
Tchaikovsky Concerto – Dimitri Mitropoulos, conductor

ZINO FRANCESCATTI
(1902-1991)
Aug. 27, 1951
Beethoven Concerto – Dimitri Mitropoulos, conductor
March 28, 29, 31, 1946
Brahms Concerto – Artur Rodzinski, conductor
Jan. 18, 19, 20, 21, 1951
Brahms Concerto – Bruno Walter, conductor
March 6, 7, 9, 1947
Mendelssohn Concerto – Bruno Walter, conductor
Feb. 8, 9, 11, 1945
Paganini Concerto in D Major – Artur Rodzinski, conductor
Nov. 28, 1948
Paganini Concerto in D Major – Dimitri Mitropoulos, conductor
Nov. 25, 26, 1948
Prokofiev Concerto No. 2 – Dimitri Mitropoulos, conductor
Jan., 19, 20, 22, 1949
Saint-Saëns Concerto No. 3 – Dimitri Mitropoulos, conductor
Oct. 21, 22, 24, 1943
Tchaikovsky Concerto – Artur Rodzinski, conductor

JOSEPH FUCHS
(1899-1997)
Oct. 27, 1945
Lopatnikoff Concerto – Artur Rodzinski, conductor
Dec. 7, 8, 1946
Tchaikovsky Concerto – Artur Rodzinski, conductor

SZYMON GOLDBERG
(1909-1993)
Jan. 14, 15, 1950
Beethoven Concerto – Dimitri Mitropoulos, conductor
Dec. 4, 1948
Brahms Concerto – Walter Hendl, conductor

JASCHA HEIFETZ
(1899-1987)
Jan. 11, 12, 14, 1945
Beethoven Concerto – Artur Rodzinski, conductor
April 3, 1946
Gruenberg Concerto – Artur Rodzinski, conductor
March 27, 28, 30, 1947
Korngold Concerto – Efrem Kurtz, conductor
March 8, 9, 11, 1951
Sibelius Concerto – Dimitri Mitropoulos, conductor

Feb. 16, 17, 1950
Walton Concerto – Leonard Bernstein, conductor

BRONISLAW HUBERMAN
(1882-1947)
Jan. 20, 21, 23, 1944
Brahms Concerto – Artur Rodzinski, conductor
Dec. 16, 1945
Mozart Concerto K. 218 – Bruno Walter, conductor

FRITZ KREISLER
(1875-1962)
Jan. 4, 5, 1945
Brahms Concerto – Artur Rodzinski, conductor
Jan. 10, 11, 1946
Mendelssohn Concerto – Artur Rodzinski, conductor

YEHUDI MENUHIN
(1916-1999)
Dec. 6, 7, 9, 1945
Beethoven Concerto – Artur Rodzinski, conductor
Oct. 17, 18, 20, 1946
Brahms Concerto – Artur Rodzinski, conductor
Feb. 26, 27, 29, 1948
Lalo Symphonie Espagnole – George Szell, conductor
Oct. 26, 27, 1950
Mozart Concerto No. 7 in D Major – Dimitri Mitropoulos, conductor
Oct., 19, 20, 22, 1944
Mendelssohn Concerto – Artur Rodzinski, conductor
Oct. 28, 29, 1950
Vieuxtemps Concerto No. 4 – Dimitri Mitropoulos, conductor

NATHAN MILSTEIN
(1903-1992)
June 4, 1944
Brahms Concerto – Vladimir Golschmann, conductor
March 16, 17, 19, 1950
Brahms Concerto – Victor De Sabata, conductor
Dec. 30, 31, 1944
Bruch Concerto – Artur Rodzinski, conductor
Oct. 23, 24, 26, 1947
Dvořák Concerto – Leopold Stokowski, conductor
Nov. 30, Dec 1, 3, 1950
Glazunov Concerto in A minor – Dimitri Mitropoulos, conductor
Dec. 28, 29, 1944
Goldmark Concerto in A minor – Artur Rodzinski, conductor

March 7, 1945
Mendelssohn Concerto – Bruno Walter, conductor
Feb. 17, 18, 20, 1944; Oct. 18, 19, 21, 1945
Tchaikovsky Concerto – Artur Rodzinski, conductor
Dec. 23, 24, 26, 1948
Tchaikovsky Concerto – Charles Münch, conductor

ERICA MORINI
(1904-1995)
Sept. 17, 1944
Beethoven Concerto – Vladimir Golschmann, conductor
March 10, 11, 13, 1949
Beethoven Concerto – Bruno Walter, conductor
Dec. 25, 26, 1947; Dec. 21, 22, 30, 1950
Beethoven Concerto – George Szell, conductor
Nov. 27, 28, 1943
Glazunov Concerto – Artur Rodzinski, conductor
Dec. 28, 1947
Mendelssohn Concerto – George Szell, conductor
Dec. 17, 1944
Tchaikovsky Concerto – George Szell, conductor
Dec. 24, 1950
Tchaikovsky Concerto – George Szell, conductor

GINETTE NEVEU
(1919-1949)
Nov. 13, 14, 1947
Brahms Concerto – Charles Münch, conductor
Dec. 30, 31, 1948, Jan. 2, 1949
Chausson "Poeme" and *Ravel "Tzigane"* – Charles Münch, conductor

ALBERT SPALDING
(1888-1953)
Dec. 16, 17, 1943
Beethoven Concerto – Leonard Bernstein, conductor
Dec., 19, 1943
Beethoven Concerto – Howard Barlow, conductor

TOSSY SPIVAKOVSKY
(1907-1998)
Oct. 14, 15, 17, 1943
Bartók Concerto – Artur Rodzinski, conductor

ISAAC STERN
(1920-2001)
March 1, 2, 4, 1951
Bach Concerto in A minor and *Dvořák Concerto* – Dimitri Mitropoulos, conductor
Nov. 7, 1948
Bartók Rhapsody No. 2 and *Lalo Symphonie Espagnole* – Dimitri Mitropoulos, conductor
Dec. 1, 2, 4, 1949
Brahms Concerto – Leopold Stokowski, conductor
Dec. 4, 1949
Haydn Concerto in C – Leopold Stokowski, conductor
Nov. 30, 1949
Mendelssohn Concerto – Leopold Stokowski, conductor
Nov. 6, 1948
Mozart Concerto No. 3 – Dimitri Mitropoulos, conductor
March 22, 23, 1947
Prokofiev Concerto No. 1 – Efrem Kurtz, conductor
Aug. 6, 1944
Sibelius Concerto – Dimitri Mitropoulos, conductor
Dec. 7, 8, 1944
Tchaikovsky Concerto – Artur Rodzinski, conductor
Jan., 19, 20, 1946
Wieniawski Concerto No. 2 – Howard Hanson, conductor

HENRYK SZERYNG
(1918-1988)
Oct. 26, 1946
Wieniawski Concerto No. 2 – Artur Rodzinski, conductor

JOSEPH SZIGETI
(1892-1973)
Dec. 18, 1949
Bach Concerto in G minor and *Mozart Concerto K. 216* – Dimitri Mitropoulos, conductor
March 15, 16, 18, 1945
Beethoven Romance in G Major and *Prokofiev Concerto No. 1* – George Szell, conductor
Dec. 15, 16, 1949
Berg Concerto – Dimitri Mitropoulos, conductor
Jan. 30, 31, 1947
Brahms Concerto – Charles Münch, conductor
Oct. 21, 22, 24, 1948
Brahms Concerto – Dimitri Mitropoulos, conductor
Feb. 2, 1947
Mozart Concerto No. 4 K. 218 – Charles Münch, conductor

**JACQUES THIBAUD
(1880-1953)**
Jan. 2, 3, 5, 1947
Lalo Symphonie Espagnole – Leopold Stokowski, conductor

CELLISTS:
**RAYA GARBOUSOVA
(1909-1997)**
Dec. 4, 5, 7, 1947
Barber Concerto – Dimitri Mitropoulos, conductor

**EDMUND KURTZ
(1908-2004)**
Nov. 28, 29, 1946
Milhaud Concerto No. 2 – Artur Rodzinski, conductor

CARL STERN
February 5, 1949
Brahms "Double" Concerto with violinist Michael Rosenker – Walter Hendl, conductor

**PIERRE FOURNIER
(1906-1986)**
Nov. 3, 4, 6, 1949
Schumann Concerto – Leopold Stokowski, conductor

**GREGOR PIATIGORSKY
(1903-1976)**
Nov. 26, 1944
Bloch "Schelomo" – Artur Rodzinski, conductor
Nov. 23, 24, 1944
Haydn Concerto in D – Artur Rodzinski, conductor

**JOSEPH SCHUSTER
(1903-1969)**
Feb. 24, 25, 1945
Schumann Concerto – Artur Rodzinski, conductor
Dec. 25, 26, 1943
Schubert-Cassadó Concerto – Howard Barlow, conductor
Nov. 11, 12, 1943
Strauss "Don Quixote" – Bruno Walter, conductor
Nov. 14, 1943
Strauss "Don Quixote" – Leonard Bernstein, conductor

APPENDIX C

SOLO APPEARANCES WITH MAJOR SYMPHONY ORCHESTRAS IN AMERICA

NEW YORK PHILHARMONIC

July 30, 1965 Schumann: "A Song of Orpheus"	Lukas Foss, conductor
October 21 and 23, 1960 Schumann: Concerto in A Minor [recorded October 24, 1960]	Leonard Bernstein, conductor
December 3, 4, 5, 6, 1959 Brahms: "Double" Concerto	Leonard Bernstein, conductor Isaac Stern violin
January 29, 30, 31, 1959 Barber: Concerto	Leonard Bernstein, conductor
November 28, 1954 Brahms: "Double" Concerto	Bruno Walter, conductor Isaac Stern violin
November 26 and 27, 1953 Bloch: "Schelomo" [recorded April 21, 1951]	Dimitri Mitropoulos, conductor
March 27 and 28, 1952 Dvořák: Concerto	Dimitri Mitropoulos, conductor
March 1, 1952 Saint-Saëns: Concerto	Franco Autori, conductor
January 7, 1952 Tchaikovsky: Rococo Variations	George Szell, conductor

September 3, 1951 Saint-Saëns: Concerto	Dimitri Mitropoulos, conductor
August 25, 1951 Haydn: Sinfonia Concertante Gomberg, oboe	Dimitri Mitropoulos, conductor John Corigliano, violin, Harold William Polisi, bassoon
April 16, 1951 Haydn: Sinfonia Concertante Gomberg, oboe	Dimitri Mitropoulos conductor John Corigliano, violin Harold William Polisi, bassoon
April 5, 6, 8, 1951 Bloch: "Schelomo"	Dimitri Mitropoulos, conductor
February 1, 2, 4, 1951 Brahms: "Double" Concerto	Bruno Walter, conductor John Corigliano, violin
December 7, 8, 10, 1950 Strauss: *Don Quixote*	George Szell, conductor William Lincer, viola
November 2, 3, 5, 1950 Haydn: Sinfonia Concertante Gomberg, oboe	Dimitri Mitropoulos, conductor John Corigliano, violin Harold William Polisi, bassoon
April 13 and 14, 1950 Alan Shulman: Concerto [April 14 at Princeton University]	Dimitri Mitropoulos, conductor
February 2 and 3, 1950 Handel: Concerto Grosso	Bruno Walter conductor
March 17 and 18, 1949 Beethoven: "Triple" Concerto	Bruno Walter conductor John Corigliano, violin Walter Hendl, piano
January 30, 1949 Bloch: "Schelomo"	Leopold Stokowski, conductor
November 4 and 5, 1948 Schumann: Concerto	Dimitri Mitropoulos, conductor
February, 19 and 20, 1948 Strauss: *Don Quixote*	Bruno Walter, conductor Joseph Vieland, viola

Appendix C

January 8 and 9, 1948 Tchaikovsky: Rococo Variations	Charles Münch, conductor
December 20, 1947 Saint-Saëns: Allegro Appassionato	Leon Barzin, conductor
March 10, 1947 Brahms: "Double" Concerto	Leopold Stokowski, conductor John Corigliano, violin
November 7 and 8, 1946 Saint-Saëns: Concerto	Artur Rodzinski, conductor
March 11, 1946 Fauré: Êlégie	Bruno Walter, conductor
February 11, 1946 Fauré: *Après un Rêve*	Artur Rodzinski, conductor
November 29 and 30, 1945 Bloch: "Schelomo"	Artur Rodzinski, conductor
November 1, 2, 4, 1945 Strauss: *Don Quixote*	George Szell, conductor William Lincer, viola
January 6 and 7, 1945 Dvořák: Concerto	Artur Rodzinski, conductor
January 29 and 30, 1944 Lalo: Concerto	Wilhelm Steinberg, conductor

CLEVELAND ORCHESTRA

Brahms: "Double" Concerto October 17, 1982 [Musicians Against Nuclear Arms Benefit]	Yoel Levi, conductor Shlomo Mintz, violin
August 29, 1981 Elgar: Concerto	Andrew Davis, conductor
August 4, 1979 Saint-Saëns: Concerto	José Serebrier, conductor

December 10, 1978 Tchaikovsky: Rococo Variations	Lorin Maazel, conductor
July 23, 1977 Tchaikovsky: Rococo Variations	Klaus Tennstedt, conductor
April 13, 1976 Bloch: "Schelomo" [Televised – sponsored by Standard Oil]	Lorin Maazel, conductor
April 15 and 17, 1976 Elgar: Concerto	Lorin Maazel, conductor
February 13, 1974 Dvořák: Concerto	Lorin Maazel, conductor
December 6 and 8, 1973 Dvořák: Concerto	Lorin Maazel, conductor
July 8, 1972 Saint-Saëns: Concerto	Roberto Benzi, conductor
April 11 and 12, 1970 Bloch: "Schelomo"	James Levine, conductor
July 26, 1969 Schumann: Concerto	Pierre Boulez, conductor
April 14, 15, 16, 1966 Beethoven: "Triple" Concerto Brahms: "Double" Concerto	George Szell, conductor Eugene Istomin, piano Isaac Stern, violin
January 9 and 11, 1964 Schuman: "A Song of Orpheus" [Recorded January 11, 1964 Severance Hall]	George Szell, conductor
April 16 and 18, 1959 Dvořák: Concerto	George Szell, conductor
February 28, 1956 Saint-Saëns: Concerto Tchaikovsky: Rococo Variations [Akron, Ohio]	George Szell, conductor

Appendix C

December 1 and 3, 1955 Bloch: "Schelomo" Tchaikovsky: Rococo Variations	Rudolph Ringwall, conductor
March, 19 and 21, 1953 Bloch: "Schelomo" Saint-Saëns: Concerto	Rudolph Ringwall, conductor
November 22 and 24, 1951 Dvořák: Concerto	George Szell, conductor
October 22 and 24, 1942 Dvořák: Concerto	Artur Rodzinski, conductor
March 12 and 14, 1942 Strauss: *Don Quixote*	Artur Rodzinski, conductor
January 22 and 24, 1942 Schumann: Concerto	Artur Rodzinski, conductor
April 6, 1941 Tchaikovsky: Nocturne and Suite From the Ballet *Swan Lake*	Rudolph Ringwall, conductor
March, 19, 1941 Brahms: "Double" Concerto	Artur Rodzinski, conductor Josef Fuchs, violin
March 4, 1941 Brahms: "Double" Concerto Finney Memorial Chapel, Oberlin, Ohio	Artur Rodzinski, conductor Josef Fuchs, violin
February 8, 1941 Brahms: "Double" Concerto Northampton, MA	Artur Rodzinski, conductor with Josef Fuchs, violin
January 17, 1941 Brahms: "Double" Concerto	Artur Rodzinski, conductor Josef Fuchs, violin
November 17, 1940 Lalo: Concerto	Rudolph Ringwall, conductor
October 31 and November 2, 1940 Lalo: Concerto	Artur Rodzinski, conductor

PHILADELPHIA ORCHESTRA

July 30, 1970
Beethoven: "Triple" Concerto
Brahms: "Double" Concerto

Eugene Ormandy, conductor
Eugene Istomin, piano
Isaac Stern, violin

March 21, 1967
Saint-Saëns: Concerto
Lalo: Concerto
Baltimore, Maryland

Eugene Ormandy, conductor

March 20, 1967
Saint-Saëns: Concerto
Washington, DC

Eugene Ormandy, conductor

March 17 and 18, 1967
Saint-Saëns: Concerto
Lalo: Concerto
[Both concerti in addition to Fauré's Élégie recorded March 27, 1967 at Town Hall, Philadelphia]

Eugene Ormandy, conductor

May 8, 1965
Bloch: "Schelomo"

Eugene Ormandy, conductor

April 12, 1965
Bloch: "Schelomo"

Eugene Ormandy, conductor

April 15, 1964
Beethoven: "Triple" Concerto
Brahms: "Double" Concerto
Carnegie Hall
[Beethoven recorded April 16, 1964 at Town Hall, Philadelphia]

Eugene Ormandy, conductor
Eugene Istomin, piano
Isaac Stern, violin

April 13, 1964
Beethoven: "Triple" Concerto
Brahms: "Double" Concerto
Pension Concert
[Brahms recorded April 14, 1964 at Town Hall, Philadelphia]

Eugene Ormandy, conductor
Eugene Istomin, piano
Isaac Stern, violin

November 23, 1963
Dvořák: Concerto
[Played Saturday only: performance cancelled Friday following the assassination of President Kennedy]

Eugene Ormandy, conductor

November 12, 1962
Tchaikovsky: Rococo Variations
[Recorded November 15, 1962
Town Hall, Philadelphia]

Eugene Ormandy, conductor

January 25, 1961
Bloch: "Schelomo"
Baltimore, Maryland
[Recorded January 29, 1961 with
Eugene Ormandy conducting]

William Smith, conductor

April 30, 1954
Ann Arbor, Michigan
Dvořák: Concerto

Thor Johnson, conductor

BOSTON SYMPHONY ORCHESTRA

July 25, 1965
Tanglewood
Beethoven: "Triple" Concerto

Seji Ozawa, conductor
Eugene Istomin, piano
Isaac Stern, violin

July 23, 1965
Dvořák: Concerto

Erich Leinsdorf, conductor

March 24, 1956
Carnegie Hall
Dvořák: Concerto

Charles Münch, conductor

March 23, 1956
Brooklyn, New York
Dvořák: Concerto

Charles Münch, conductor

March 22, 1956
New Brunswick, New Jersey
Dvořák: Concerto

Charles Münch, conductor

March 16 and 17, 1956
Boston, MA
Dvořák: Concerto

Charles Münch, conductor

CHICAGO SYMPHONY ORCHESTRA

December 21 and 22, 1967
Bloch: "Schelomo"

Sixten Ehrling, conductor

July 3, 1965 Ravinia Beethoven: "Triple" Concerto Brahms: "Double" Concerto	Seiji Ozawa, conductor Eugene Istomin, piano Isaac Stern, violin
July 1, 1965 Ravinia Dvořák: Concerto	Seizji Ozawa, conductor
August 6, 1955 Brahms: "Double" Concerto	Enrique Jordá, conductor Isaac Stern, violin
August 4, 1955 Ravinia Saint-Saëns: Concerto	Enrique Jordá, conductor
July 5, 1952 Brahms: "Double" Concerto	George Szell, conductor Erica Morini, violin
October 29, 1951 Milwaukee, Wisconsin Tchaikovsky: Rococo Variations	Rafael Kubelik, conductor
October 25 and 26, 1951 Beethoven: "Triple" Concerto	Rafael Kubelik, conductor Eugene Istomin, piano Isaac Stern, violin

LOS ANGELES PHILHARMONIC

July 15, 1976 Beethoven: "Triple" Concerto	Eugene Ormandy, conductor Eugene Istomin, piano Isaac Stern, violin
September 4, 1975 Brahms: ""Double" " Concerto Bloch: "Schelomo"	Judith Somogi, conductor Sidney Harth violin
July 25, 1970 Beethoven: "Triple" Concerto Brahms: "Double" Concerto	Andre Previn, conductor Eugene Istomin, piano Isaac Stern, violin
August 26, 1969 Dvořák: Concerto	Henry Lewis, conductor

Appendix C 431

August 3, 1965
Beethoven: "Triple" Concerto
Brahms: "Double" Concerto

Sixten Ehrling, conductor
Eugene Istomin, piano
Isaac Stern, violin

April 1 and 2, 1965
Schumann: Concerto

Zubin Mehta, conductor

March 2 and 3, 1961
Bloch: "Schelomo"

Arturo Basile, conductor

NATIONAL SYMPHONY ORCHESTRA

November 20, 1977
Carnegie Hall
Beethoven: "Triple" Concerto

Mstislav Rostropovich, conductor
Eugene Istomin, piano
Isaac Stern, violin

November 27, 28, 29, 1973
Constitution Hall
Tchaikovsky: Rococo Variations

Howard Mitchell, conductor

March 20, 1964
Annapolis High School, Maryland
Dvořák: Concerto

Howard Mitchell, conductor

March 17 and 18, 1964
Constitution Hall
Strauss: *Don Quixote*
Dvořák: Concerto

Howard Mitchell, conductor
Richard Parnas, viola

February, 19 and 20, 1957
Constitution Hall
Brahms: "Double" Concerto

Howard Mitchell, conductor
Yehudi Menuhin, violin

SAN FRANCISCO SYMPHONY

June 13, 1971
Stern Grove Amphitheater
Bloch: "Schelomo"

Niklaus Wyss, conductor

January 22, 23, 24, 1964
Dvořák: Concerto

Josef Krips, conductor

April 22, 23, 24, 1959
Dvořák: Concerto

Enrique Jordá, conductor

February, 19, 20, 21, 1958
Brahms: "Double" Concerto
Tchaikovsky: Rococo Variations

Enrique Jordá, conductor
Isaac Stern violin

PITTSBURGH SYMPHONY

January 6, 1980
Beethoven: "Triple" Concerto
Brahms: "Double" Concerto

William Steinberg, conductor
Eugene Istomin, piano
Isaac Stern, violin

September 7, 8, 9, 1979
Brahms: "Double" Concerto

Pinchas Zukerman, conductor
Isaac Stern, violin

January 2 and 3, 1971
Syria Mosque
Bloch: "Schelomo"

Donald Johanos, conductor

March 9 and 10, 1969
Syria Mosque
Saint-Saëns: Concerto

Walter Hendl, conductor

ST. LOUIS SYMPHONY

May, 19 and 21, 1977
Boccherini: Concerto B Flat

Jerzy Semkow, conductor

May 24 and 25, 1974
Dvořák: Concerto

Walter Susskind, conductor

June 28 and 29, 1969
Elgar: Concerto
Saint-Saëns: Concerto

Walter Susskind, conductor

June 27, 1969
Dvořák: Concerto

Walter Susskind, conductor

January 6 and 7, 1967
Bloch: "Schelomo"

Donald Johanos, conductor

October 28 and 29, 1955
Saint-Saëns: Concerto

Vladimir Golschmann, conductor

Appendix D

Summer Festivals with Roy Harris[318]
Colorado College Summer Music Festival of 1948
June 22 to August 3
Ten Concerts
Series A – 5 Concert $3.50 plus tax
Ten Concerts $6.00 plus tax

Joseph Gingold   **Roy Harris**   **Leonard Rose**
Courtesy of Harry Wimmer

July 2
Leonard Rose, Cello
Johana Harris, Piano
Beethoven – Sonata in A Major, Op. 69
Kodály – Sonata, Opus 4
Franck – Sonata

July 20
Trio Concert
Mendelssohn – Trio in D Minor, Op. 49
Ravel – Trio
Schubert – Trio in B-Flat, Op. 99
Josef Gingold, Violin, Leonard Rose, Cello, Johana Harris, Piano

July 27
Quintet Concert
Mozart – Quintet in G Minor, K. 516
Josef Gingold, Violin, Frank Costanzo, Violin, Ferenc Molnar, Viola,
Leonard Rose, Cello and Max Lanner, Piano
Brahms – Quintet in F Minor
Josef Gingold, Violin, Frank Costanzo, Violin, Ferenc Molnar, Viola,
Leonard Rose, Cello and Max Lanner, Piano
Harris – Quintet
Josef Gingold, Violin, Frank Costanzo, Violin, Ferenc Molnar, Viola,
Leonard Rose, Cello and Johana Harris, Piano

Utah State Agricultural College Summer Music Festival of 1949

July 6
Mozart – String Trio 'Divertimento,' K. 563
Josef Gingold, Violin, Milton Preves, Viola, Leonard Rose, Cello
Schubert – Piano Trio in B-Flat, Op. 99
Josef Gingold, Violin, Leonard Rose, Cello, Johana Harris, Piano
Ravel – Trio
Josef Gingold, Violin, Leonard Rose, Cello, Johana Harris, Piano

July 13
Leonard Rose, Cello
Johana Harris, Piano
Beethoven – Sonata Opus 102, No. 2
Debussy – Sonata
Franck – Sonata

July 20
Haydn – Quartet Opus 64, No. 5
Beethoven – Quartet Opus 59, No. 3
Debussy – Quartet in G Minor
Josef Gingold, Violin, James Barrett, Violin,
Milton Preves, Viola, Leonard Rose, Cello

August 2
Mozart – Piano Quartet in G Minor
Josef Gingold, Violin, Milton Preves, Viola, Leonard Rose, Cello, Johana
Harris, Piano
Schubert – Quintet in C Major, Opus 163
Josef Gingold, Violin, James Barrett, Violin
Milton Preves, Viola, Leonard Rose, Cello, Gloria Strassner, Cello
Harris – Quintet
Josef Gingold, Violin, James Barrett, Violin,
Milton Preves, Viola, Leonard Rose, Cello
Johana Harris, Piano

Appendix E

STRATFORD MUSIC FESTIVAL
ROSE PERFORMANCES

July 28 and August 1, 1959
Mozart: Violin Concerto No. 5 in A Major; Oscar Shumsky, violin; Leonard Rose, conductor
Tchaikovsky: "Variations on a Rococo Theme"; Leonard Rose, cello; Oscar Shumsky, conductor
July 29 and 31, 1959
Dvořák: Piano Quintet, Op. 81; Claudio Arrau,[319] piano; Oscar Shumsky and Hyman Goodman violins; Stephens Kondaks, viola; Leonard Rose, cello
August 1, 1959
Kodály: Duo for Violin and Cello; Oscar Shumsky, violin; Leonard Rose, cello
[In 1960 the music moved into the new, larger festival theater seating nearly 2300.]

August 7, 1960
Beethoven: Sonata in A Major, Op. 69; Leonard Rose, cello; Glenn Gould, piano
Beethoven: Piano Trio, Op. 70 No. 1; Oscar Shumsky, violin; Leonard Rose, cello; Glenn Gould, piano
July 31, 1960
Brahms: "Double" Concerto; Oscar Shumsky, violin; Leonard Rose, cello; Walter Susskind, conductor
July 24, 1960
Bach: Suite No. 3 in C Major; Leonard Rose, cello

August 13, 1961
Bach: Sonata No. 2 in D Major; Leonard Rose, cello; Glenn Gould, piano
August 6, 1961
Schumann: Concerto in A Minor; Leonard Rose, cello; Oscar Shumsky, conductor
July 16, 1961
Brahms: Sonata in E Minor; Leonard Rose, cello; Glenn Gould, piano
Brahms: Piano Trio in C Minor, Op. 101; Oscar Shumsky, violin; Leonard Rose, cello; Glenn Gould, piano

John Kraglund, writing in the *Globe and Mail* titled his review: "Gould Overpowers His Colleagues." Mr. Kraglund wrote: "Mr. Gould's greatness as a solo performer is undisputed. I must confess I am less enthusiastic about him as an ensemble player, for he tends to dominate the performance without full consideration for the composer or the other performers." Kraglund specifically notes, "Mr. Gould's efforts to drown out both the piano and the cello with his stamping feet," and his "tendency to force the pace" in the finale of the cello sonata.

George Kidd for *The Telegram* writes: "... The combination [of Gould, Shumsky, and Rose] was an exciting one and the audience greeted its beauty with applause that ceased only when the lights were turned on ... Mr. Gould was in his usual splendid form, complete with his glass of water, his folding chair, and a left arm that tended too often to conduct. He was also in his usual voice, and clouded the last movement of the trio with noise that spoiled much of the beauty that had been heard earlier. These noises are no longer amusing. Neither are they necessary."

August 12, 1962
Boccherini: Concerto in B-Flat Major; Leonard Rose, cello; Oscar Shumsky, conductor
August 5, 1962
Mendelssohn: String Octet in E-Flat, Op. 20; Oscar Shumsky, David Zafer, Lea Foli, Stuart Fastofsky, violins; Eugene Hudson and Marilyn Stroh, violas; Leonard Rose and Malcolm Tait, cellos
Mendelssohn: Piano Trio No. 1, Op 49; Oscar Shumsky, violin; Leonard Rose, cello; Glenn Gould, piano
August 4, 1962
Mozart: String Quartet in D Major, K. 593; Oscar Shumsky and Lea Foli, violins; Marilyn Stroh, viola; Leonard Rose, cello
July 29, 1962
Hindemith: Sonata, Op. 25 No. 3 for solo cello; Leonard Rose
July 22, 1962
Debussy: Sonata; Leonard Rose, cello; John Newmark, piano
Ravel: Sonata for Violin and Cello; Oscar Shumsky, violin; Leonard Rose, cello
July 14, 1962
Beethoven: String Trio in C Minor, Op. 9, No. 3; Oscar Shumsky, violin Stephen Kondaks, viola; Leonard Rose, cello
Mozart Piano Quartet in G Minor, K. 478; Lukas Foss, piano; Oscar Shumsky, violin; Stephen Kondaks, viola; Leonard Rose, cello
July 8, 1962
Bach: Trio Sonata; Glenn Gould, piano; Oscar Shumsky, violin; Leonard Rose, cello

At this concert, Gould delivered a controversial speech before the final performance of the evening (The Art of Fugue) in which he criticized the custom of automatic applause at concerts, which he considered particularly inappropriate after esoteric music like *The Art of Fugue*. Jim Curtis quoted him, on stage, referring to applause as "an easily induced mob reaction, indicating nothing but momentary hysteria." Critics were outraged. Udo Kasemets from the *Toronto Daily Star* writes: "... But that is not what Gould wants. He wants new games. And, just for kicks, why not games with audience participation? Not only did Glenn Gould make fools of the listeners, he also put his colleagues into an embarrassing light. Just prior to Glenn Gould's call to ban applause, the audience had given a standing ovation to violinist Oscar Shumsky for his excellent delivery of Bach's D-minor solo Partita. Was this, as Gould put it, 'mob hysteria'? Or an 'ugly noise?' Or a 'clever manipulation' on the performer's part to raise the 'decibel count of applause?' ... And if his purely musical contributions to concerts remain as feeble as they were yesterday, he might as well include booing in his ban of public expression."

August 2, 1964
Martinu: Sonata No. 2; Leonard Rose, cello; Rudolf Firkusny, piano
Dvořák: Piano Trio "Dumka," Op. 90; Eudice Shapiro, violin; Leonard Rose, cello; Rudolf Firkusny, piano
August 1, 1964
Beethoven: Serenade Trio in D Major, Op. 8; Eudice Shapiro, violin; Oscar Shumsky, viola;
Leonard Rose, cello
July 26, 1964
Haydn: Sinfonia Concertante in B-Flat, Op. 84; Oscar Shumsky, violin; Perry Bauman, oboe;
Sol Schoenbach, bassoon; Leonard Rose, cello
July 12, 1964
Brahms: Sonata in F Major, Op. 99; Leonard Rose, cello; Leon Fleisher, piano
Brahms: Quintet in F Minor, Op. 34; Oscar Shumsky and Mildred Goodman violins; David Mankowitz, viola; Leonard Rose, cello; Leon Fleisher, piano
July 11, 1964
Handel-Halvorsen: Passacaglia for Violin and Cello; Oscar Shumsky, violin; Leonard Rose, cello
Brahms: Sextet in B-Flat, Op. 18; Oscar Shumsky and Lea Foli, violins; David Mankowitz and Marilyn Stroh, violas; Leonard Rose and Lynn Harrell, cellos
July 5, 1964
Bach: Suite No. 2; Leonard Rose

August 1, 1965
Bloch: "Schelomo;" Leonard Rose, cello; Franz-Paul Decker, conductor

July 11, 1965
Beethoven: Cello Sonata No. 5, Op. 102, No. 2; Leonard Rose, cello; Claudio Arrau, piano
Beethoven: Piano Trio "Archduke," Op. 97; Oscar Shumsky, violin; Leonard Rose, cello; Claudio Arrau, piano

August 14, 1966
Schubert: "Arpeggione" Sonata; Leonard Rose, cello; Mario Bernardi, piano
Schubert: String Quintet in C, Op. 163; Oscar Shumsky and David Montagu, violins; Sally Trembly, viola; Leonard Rose and Ronald Laurie, cellos

July 20, 1969
Beethoven: Cello Sonata No. 5, Op. 102, No. 2; Leonard Rose, cello; Eugene Istomin, piano
Schubert: String Quintet in C, Op. 163; David Nadien and Arthur Garami, violins; David Mankovitz, viola; Leonard Rose and Malcolm Tait, cellos

July 16, 1969
Brahms: "Double" Concerto; David Nadien, violin; Leonard Rose, cello
George Schick, conductor

Appendix F

LEONARD ROSE DISCOGRAPHY

I have come to the conclusion that the best recordings are those which are made straight through without the immense editing splicing jobs, which are so commonplace these days. On those, while the technique is admittedly better, the music itself tends to lack life.
Leonard Rose

I signed with Columbia Records in, 1949, after the Villa Lobos (Bachiana Brasileira, No. 5 composed in 1938) with soprano Bidú Sāyao. It was the first time my name had been on an album, and the 78 proved to be the single disc sensation of Columbia for two years.
Leonard Rose

Johann Sebastian Bach
Sonata No. 1 in G Major BWV 1027
with Glenn Gould, Piano
Recorded May 28 and 29, 1974
Eaton's Auditorium, Toronto, Canada

"Gould's personality is the basic force behind these performances, though the fact that they are in general less wayward than usual suggests the mediating influence of Rose's less idiosyncratic musicianship ... Rose is a remarkably articulate cellist ... I was surprised to find Gould and Rose allowing themselves so much rhythmic freedom in the various andantes and adagios ... the slow sections—and particularly the D Major's Andante—are characterized by a kind of barely contained ecstasy that is quite extraordinary."
–High Fidelity/Musical America December, 1974

Johann Sebastian Bach
Sonata No. 2 in D Major BWV 1028
with Glenn Gould, Piano
Recorded December 16 –, 19, 1973
Eaton's Auditorium, Toronto, Canada

Johann Sebastian Bach
Sonata No. 3 in G Minor BWV 1029
with Glenn Gould, Piano
Recorded December 16 –, 19, 1973
Eaton's Auditorium, Toronto, Canada

Johann Sebastian Bach
Suite No. 1 in G Major, BWV 1007
Prelude – Allemande – Courante
Recorded ca. 1936 Curtis Institute
Leonard Rose *The Memorial Edition*

Johann Sebastian Bach
Suite No. 3 in C Major, BWV 1009
Prelude – Sarabande – Bourrée I – Bourrée II – Gigue
Town Hall Recital November 26, 1947
Leonard Rose *The Memorial Edition*

Ludwig van Beethoven
"Triple" Concerto in C Major, Op. 56
Walter Hendl, Piano; John Corigliano, Violin; Bruno Walter conducting the New York
Philharmonic – Recorded March 21, 1949
Columbia 30th Street Studio, New York City
[Rose 30 years old]

Ludwig van Beethoven
"Triple" Concerto in C Major, Op. 56
Eugene Istomin, Piano; Isaac Stern, Violin; Eugene Ormandy conducting the Philadelphia Orchestra – Recorded April 16, 1964
Town Hall, Philadelphia
[Rose 45 years old]

New York Times
May 15, 1970

"There is no other trio in the world that can equal the one that played at Carnegie Hall last night. Istomin, Stern, Rose are better because they can draw upon virtuoso tonal luster that gives their group playing an almost magical sheen. Thus, even when they do exactly what habitual chamber music players do, it sounds about ten times better than usual."

Ludwig van Beethoven
Piano Trio in E-Flat Major, Op. 1, No. 1
ISTOMIN-STERN-ROSE
Recorded May 13 and May 27, 1970
Columbia 30th Street Studio, New York City

Ludwig van Beethoven
Piano Trio in E-Flat G. 153 (WoO 38)
ISTOMIN-STERN-ROSE
Recorded April 2, 1970
Columbia 30th Street Studio, New York City

Ludwig van Beethoven
Piano Trio in G Major, Op. 1, No. 2
ISTOMIN-STERN-ROSE
Recorded July 11, 1969 and December 18 and, 19, 1969
Columbia 30th Street Studio, New York City

Ludwig van Beethoven
Piano Trio in G Major, Op. 12la - "Kakadu"
ISTOMIN-STERN-ROSE
Recorded June 11, 1968
Columbia 30th Street Studio, New York City

Ludwig van Beethoven
Piano Trio in C Minor, Op. 1, No. 3
ISTOMIN-STERN-ROSE
Recorded November 3, 1966
Columbia 30th Street Studio, New York City

Ludwig van Beethoven
Piano Trio in B-Flat Major, Op. 11
ISTOMIN-STERN-ROSE
Recorded July 7, 1969
Columbia 30th Street Studio, New York City

Ludwig van Beethoven
Piano Trio in B-Flat Major G. 154 (WoO 39)
ISTOMIN-STERN-ROSE
Recorded April 2, 1970
Columbia 30th Street Studio, New York City

Ludwig van Beethoven
Piano Trio in D Major, Op. 70, No. 1 "The Ghost"
ISTOMIN-STERN-ROSE
Recorded May 14, 1969
Columbia 30th Street Studio, New York City

Ludwig van Beethoven
Piano Trio in E-Flat Major, Op. 70, No. 2
ISTOMIN-STERN-ROSE
Recorded May 26 and 27, 1970
Columbia 30th Street Studio, New York City

Ludwig van Beethoven
Fourteen Variations, Op. 44
ISTOMIN-STERN-ROSE
Recorded May 7, 1970
Columbia 30th Street Studio, New York City

Ludwig van Beethoven
Piano Trio in B-Flat Major, Op. 97 "Archduke"
ISTOMIN-STERN-ROSE
Recorded October 2, 1965
Winterthur, Switzerland

Ludwig Van Beethoven
Cello Sonata No. 3, Op. 69
with Eugene Istomin - recorded, 1969 in New York City

Ludwig Van Beethoven
Cello Sonata No. 5, Op. 102, No. 2
with Eugene Istomin
Recorded, 1969 in New York City

Ernest Bloch
"Schelomo" - Hebraic Rhapsody for Cello and Orchestra
Philharmonic-Symphony Orchestra of New York conducted by Dimitri Mitropoulos
Recorded April 21, 1951
Columbia 30th Street Studio, New York City
[Rose 32 years old]

New York Times
January 31, 1949
"Mr. Rose, who is the orchestra's first cellist, limned the musical outlines sympathetically, whether lyricism, intensity or passionate outcry was called for. He projected his instrument's capacity for changing tone-color ranging from moody darkness to the nasal-sounding curlicues of the high, meditative interludes."

Ernest Bloch
"Schelomo" – Hebraic Rhapsody for Cello and Orchestra
Philadelphia Orchestra conducted by Eugene Ormandy
Recorded January 29, 1961
Town Hall, Philadelphia
[Rose 42 years old]

Ernest Bloch
Prayer (From *Jewish Life No. 1)*
with Leon Machan
Recorded December, 1941 (beginning missing)
Leonard Rose *The Memorial Edition*

Luigi Boccherini
Sonata No. 6 in A Major
with Leonid Hambro
Recorded May 12 and 13, 1953 in New York City

Johannes Brahms
Concerto in A Minor for Violin, Cello and Orchestra, Op. 102
with Isaac Stern, Violin; New York Philharmonic - Bruno Walter, Conductor
Recorded November 29, 1954
Columbia 30th Street Studio, New York City
[Rose 36 years old]

Johannes Brahms
Concerto in A Minor for Violin, Cello and Orchestra, Op. 102
with Isaac Stern, Violin; Philadelphia Orchestra – Eugene Ormandy, Conductor
Recorded April 14, 1964
at Town Hall, Philadelphia
[Rose 45 years old]

Johannes Brahms
Piano Trio No. 1 in B Major for Piano, Violin and Cello, Op. 8
Recorded September 26 and 27, 1966
Columbia 30th Street Studio, New York City

Johannes Brahms
Piano Trio No. 2 in C Major for Piano, Violin and Cello, Op. 87
Recorded December 28, 1964
Columbia 30th Street Studio, New York City

Johannes Brahms
Piano Trio No. 3 in C Minor for Piano, Violin and Cello, Op. 101
Recorded September 27 and 28, 1966
Columbia 30th Street Studio, New York City

Johannes Brahms
Cello Sonata No. 1 in E Minor, Op. 38
with Jean-Bernard Pommier
Recorded Chateau de Malesherbes, France August, 1982

Johannes Brahms
Cello Sonata No. 2 in F Major, Op. 99
with Jean-Bernard Pommier
Recorded Chateau de Malesherbes, France August, 1982

Johannes Brahms
Cello Sonata No. 2 in F Major, Op. 99
with Irving Owen
Town Hall Recital November 26, 1947
Leonard Rose *The Memorial Edition*

Frédéric Chopin
Introduction and Polonaise Brillante, Op. 3
with Samuel Sanders, piano
Recorded May 2 and 3, 1966
Columbia 30th Street Studio, New York City

Samuel Sanders was virtually unknown when Leonard Rose first heard him, but Rose was so impressed with his playing that he began performing with Sanders in 1964 in a collaboration that would last ten years. Playing with Rose set Sanders career in motion as he went on to perform with Perlman, Rostropovich, Yo-Yo Ma and others. At Juilliard, where he founded the accompanying department, Sanders was demanding, at times abrupt, and adored by his students. His scores were meticulously notated, with fingerings over every note, markings for different performers, and even markings for page-turners to know at what point to stand. Sanders always said that the musician who had taught him the most was Leonard Rose. Samuel Sanders died at age 62 in 1999.

Claude Debussy
The Little Shepherd
with Irving Owen
Town Hall Recital November 26, 1947; Leonard Rose *The Memorial Edition*

Antonin Dvořák
Concerto in B Minor for Cello and Orchestra, Op. 104
Philadelphia Orchestra conducted by Eugene Ormandy
Recorded March 22, 1965 at Town Hall, Philadelphia [Rose 46 years old]

> **Leonard Rose Impressive as 'Cello Soloist**
> **In Dvořák Concerto With the Philharmonic**
> ***New York Times***
> **January 7, 1945**
> **By Noel Straus**
>
> "...Mr. Rose played the difficult solo part with complete mastery of every measure allotted him. His tone was silken in its smoothness, and never lost its purity in rapid passage work or in the expertly encompassed flying sixth, octaves and other tricky technical hedges in the three movements. The tone, moreover, was remarkably unified in quality from the lowest to the highest of the sounds produced, a phenomenon of comparatively rare occurrence with 'cellists and not by any means entirely due to the particular instrument employed. The initial solo announcement had the forceful, impassioned and improvisational character demanded, and established the fiery, intense nature of the work admirably from the start. But when tranquility and soulfulness were asked, Mr. Rose was as successful in his treatment of sustained cantilena, which was projected with memorable lusciousness of sound, sensitively molded and most deeply expressive."

Gabriel Fauré
Élégie for Cello and Orchestra, Op. 24
Philadelphia Orchestra conducted by Eugene Ormandy
Recorded March 27, 1967
at Town Hall, Philadelphia

Gabriel Fauré
Après un Rêve
Recorded with unknown orchestra ca. 1946
Leonard Rose *The Memorial Edition*

César Franck
Sonata in A Major for Cello and Piano
with Leonid Hambro, piano
Recorded June 11, 18 and, 19, 1952
New York City

Isadore Freed
Passacaglia
with Irving Owen
Town Hall Recital November 26, 1947
Leonard Rose *The Memorial Edition*

Edvard Grieg
Sonata in A Minor, Op. 36
with Leonid Hambro, piano
Recorded June 11, 18 and, 19, 1952
New York City

Joseph Haydn
Piano Trio for Violin, Violoncello and Piano in E-Flat Major, Hob. XV:10
ISTOMIN-STERN-ROSE
Recorded August 23, 1968
Winterthur, Switzerland

Joseph Haydn
Minuet from the Sonata in C Major
Recorded with unknown orchestra ca. 1946
Leonard Rose *The Memorial Edition*

Joseph Haydn
Minuet from the Sonata in C Major
With Irving Owen
Town Hall Recital November 26, 1947
Leonard Rose *The Memorial Edition*

Édouard Lalo
Concerto in D Minor
Philadelphia Orchestra conducted by Eugene Ormandy
Recorded March 27, 1967
at Town Hall, Philadelphia
[Rose 48 years old]

"With this record, Leonard Rose gives further proof and, to these ears at least, conclusive evidence of his present status as the peerless cellist of our time."
-High Fidelity Magazine

New York Times
January 30, 1944
"Mr. Rose played the Lalo work (with conductor Wilhelm Steinberg in place of the indisposed Artur Rodzinski) with the elegance and finish it calls for. Feeling was no more conspicuous in the playing than it is in the music. The essential ideas of the work, however, largely of a Spanish delicacy and reserve, were charmingly set forth. Mr. Rose has a lovely cello tone, which was of particular use here. He has a perfection of phrasing that also was of much service ... was given with a delicacy of tone, technique and feeling that is rare. The last movement, like the whole work, was played with reserve and taste."

Wolfgang Amadeus Mozart
Divertimento in E-Flat Major for String Trio, K. 563
with Isaac Stern, violin; Pinchas Zukerman, viola
Recorded, 1974

Wolfgang Amadeus Mozart
Jean-Pierre Rampal, Flute; Isaac Stern, violin; Alexander Schneider, viola; Leonard Rose, cello: Flute Quartets: in D Major, K. 285; In A Major, K. 298; In G Major, K. 285a; In C Major, K. 285b
Recorded in New York City, 1969

Felix Mendelssohn
Piano Trio No. 1 in D Minor, Op. 49
ISTOMIN-STERN-ROSE
Recorded November 2 and 3, 1966
Columbia 30th Street Studio, New York City

Felix Mendelssohn
Piano Trio No. 2 in C Minor, Op. 66
ISTOMIN-STERN-ROSE
Recorded July, 19 and 20, 1969
Columbia 30th Street Studio, New York City

Leo Russotto
Chant Sans Paroles
Recorded with unknown orchestra August 29, 1940
Leonard Rose *The Memorial Edition*

Saint-Saëns
Concerto No. 1 in A Minor, Op. 33
Philharmonic-Symphony Orchestra of New York conducted by Dimitri Mitropoulos
Recorded April 21, 1951
Columbia 30th Street Studio, New York City
[Rose 32 years old]

Saint-Saëns
Concerto No. 1 in A Minor, Op. 33
The Philadelphia Orchestra conducted by Eugene Ormandy
Recorded March 27, 1967
at Town Hall, Philadelphia
[Rose 48 years old]

Giovanni Battista Sammartini
Sonata in G Major
with Irving Owen
Town Hall Recital November 26, 1947
Leonard Rose *The Memorial Edition*

Giovanni Battista Sammartini
Sonata in G Major
with Leonid Hambro
Recorded May 12 and 13, 1953 in New York City

Franz Schubert
Piano Trio No. 1 in B-Flat Major, Op. 99
ISTOMIN-STERN-ROSE
Recorded August 15-17, 1964
Columbia 30th Street Studio, New York City

Franz Schubert
Piano Trio No. 2 in E-Flat Major, Op. 100
ISTOMIN-STERN-ROSE
Recorded May 12 and 13, 1969
Columbia 30th Street Studio, New York City

Franz Schubert
Sonata in A Minor "Arpeggione"
with Leonid Hambro
Recorded May 12 and 13, 1955
New York City

Franz Schubert
Sonata in A Minor "Arpeggione"
with Samuel Sanders, piano
Recorded May 2 and 3, 1966
Columbia 30th Street Studio, New York City

Franz Schubert
String Quintet in C, Op. 163
with Guarneri Quartet (Arnold Steinhardt and John Dalley, violins; Michael Tree, viola; David Soyer, cello) Rose plays first cello, Soyer second:
Recorded February and May, 1975, RCA Studio A, New York City

He was absolutely ideal as a colleague. He was a gentleman through and through. He had a very wry sense of humor. Rose never pulled rank. He never reminded us whom he had played it with. One of the most touching events of my life is when I played the slow movement of the quintet at Lennie's memorial service at Juilliard.
- Michael Tree, violist[320]

New York Times
February 28, 1975
Raymond Ericson
"... [performance was] pure gold. The ensemble, on its part, made the evening special by giving what this listener considers the finest performance of Schubert's Quintet in C he has heard.... Filled it with such tension as if their very lives depended on it, while keeping a tone of spun silk. One had the sweetness as well as the drama of Schubert's swan song. The capacity audience cheered at the end of the performance, something that doesn't happen often at a chamber-music concert [in Alice Tully Hall]."

Robert Schumann
Concerto in A Minor, Op. 129
With Leonard Bernstein and the New York Philharmonic
Recorded October 24, 1960
at the Manhattan Center, New York City
[Rose 42 years old]

Robert Schumann
Fantasy Pieces for Cello and Piano, Op. 73
with Samuel Sanders, piano
Recorded May 2 and 3, 1966
Columbia 30th Street Studio, New York City

William Schuman
A Song of Orpheus
Cleveland Orchestra conducted by George Szell
Recorded January 11, 1964
at Severance Hall, Cleveland
[Rose 45 years old]

Richard Strauss
Don Quixote, Op. 35
With the New York Philharmonic conducted by George Szell. John Corigliano, violin William Lincer, viola. Recorded November 4, 1945
Leonard Rose The Memorial Edition

Piotr Tchaikovsky
"Variations on a Rococo Theme" for Cello and Orchestra, Op. 33
New York Philharmonic conducted by George Szell
Recorded January 8, 1952
Columbia 30th Street Studio, New York City
[Rose 33 years old]

Piotr Tchaikovsky
"Variations on a Rococo Theme" for Cello and Orchestra, Op. 33
Philadelphia Orchestra conducted by Eugene Ormandy
Recorded November 15, 1962
[Rose 44 years old]

Piotr Tchaikovsky
"Variations on a Rococo Theme" for Cello and Orchestra, Op. 33
with Irving Owen
Town Hall Recital November 26, 1947
Leonard Rose The Memorial Edition

Heitor Villa-Lobos
Aria from Bachiana Brasileira, No. 5
Recorded Liederkranz Hall, New York, January 26, 1945, with an ensemble of eight cellos led by Leonard Rose with soprano Bidú Sāyao, Villa Lobos conducting.

VIDEOS

1960 performance of Beethoven's, Op. 69, A Major Sonata with pianist Glenn Gould. Formerly available on Sony SHV 48412.

June 23, 1965 Canadian Broadcasting Company release of the Istomin-Stern-Rose Trio performing Beethoven's trio in C Minor, Op. 1, No. 3 and Brahms trio in C Major, Op. 87 taped before a live audience. This item is available on either VHS or DVD.

May 31, 1970 live performance of Beethoven's "Triple" Concerto with Isaac Stern, violin, Eugene Istomin, piano with the Casals Festival Orchestra conducted by Pablo Casals. The orchestra includes Alexander Schneider as concertmaster with Isidore Cohen as assistant, with Leslie Parnas principal cellist and with

Stephen Kates in the section. Available for viewing at the Casals Museum in San Juan, Puerto Rico.

Released on DVD in February 2005, Istomin-Stern-Rose, 1974 performances of Brahms's three piano trios.

April 13, 1976 televised performance of Bloch's "Schelomo" with the Cleveland Orchestra with Lorin Maazel conducting. Sponsored by Standard Oil and arranged by Unitel.

Appendix G

FELIX SALMOND AND HIS RECORDINGS

Felix Salmond, Rose's teacher, produced an enormous and beautiful tone on his cello crafted in 1700 by Matteo Goffriller of Venice. Salmond was a connoisseur of fine instruments and owned several by Italian master luthiers. The Goffriller, heard in the extant recordings, once belonged to violin phenomenon Niccolò Paganini, and was a favorite of cellist Alfredo Piatti. Sadly, Salmond's thoughtful and intriguing interpretations are preserved on but a handful of recordings—the following list of which was provided by his heirs. Bach: *Pastorale* from Organ Sonata in F Major (1948 with pianist Leonid Hambro); Bach: *Adagio* from Toccata for Organ in C Major; Bach: Prelude from Suite No. 2 (Juilliard recording); Bach: Suite No. 5 (1949 recorded at Juilliard); Beethoven: Sonata, Op. 5, No.1, Sonata, Op. 102, No. 1, Sonata in D Major, Op. 102, No. 2 (1945 with pianist Leonid Hambro at Juilliard). Beethoven: Seven Variations on 'Bei Männern, welche liebe fühlen' (1929 with pianist Simeon Rumschisky); Beethoven: excerpt Sonata, Op. 69 (with pianist Ralph Berkowitz); Bloch: "Schelomo" (1947 with Juilliard Orchestra, Edgar Schenkman conductor); Bloch: excerpts from "Schelomo" (1943 rehearsal with the Juilliard Orchestra); Brahms: Sonata in E-Minor, Op. 38; Brahms: excerpts from "Double" Concerto National Orchestra conducted by Leon Barzin (unidentified violinist, WQXR broadcast March 11, 1945); Bruch: *Kol Nidrei, Op.* 47 (recorded, 1921, Columbia 98550); Chopin: Largo from Sonata, Op. 65 (unidentified pianist, Columbia); Debussy: *Menuet* from "Petite Suite" No. 3 (1929 with pianist Simeon Rumschisky); Enesco: excerpts from *Symphonie Concertante* (1939 live broadcast with the New York Philharmonic, Georges Enesco conducting); Fauré: Berceuse (unidentified pianist, Columbia); Glazounov: *Serenade Espagnole, Op.* 20, No. 2 (recorded in, 1921-22, Columbia 98241); Goltermann: Andante (with pianist Harry Kaufman); Mendelssohn: Scherzo from piano trio in C Minor (live recording, Trio of New York); G. Pianelli: *Villanelle* arranged by Salmond (recorded, 1921-22, Columbia 98241); Pergolese: *Giorni* (with pianist Harry Kaufman); Ravel: *Pièce En Forme De Habanera*; Schubert: Piano Trio in B-Flat with violinist Jelli d'Aranyi and pianist Dame Myra Hess (1927); a brief tape of Salmond teaching a student (Harry).

Appendix H

SALMOND BESTOWS VALUABLE MUSIC LIBRARY

In 1948, after hearing Leonard Rose's Town Hall recital, Felix Salmond felt compelled to leave Rose, as a token of his esteem and affection, his entire library of musical scores. At the time, Salmond explained that his own concert career was over, that he devotes himself entirely to teaching, and that he felt his younger colleague was the "logical person" to inherit it. Some of the music once belonged to the Russian cellist, Joseph Press (1881-1924), whose friends gave it to Salmond after Press's death.

International Music Company first approached Leonard Rose in the late 1940s about publishing the entire library with updated markings—bowings and fingerings from Rose. The cellist edited the collection until 1960.

Some believe the editions are nothing more than photo-offsets of older editions on which the copyrights have expired, with a few additions and corrections. This author believes a veritable insight into Rose's style of play is in store for the curious. Rose was often asked how much money he made on these transactions. "Just about nothing," Rose said. "Editors received no royalties in the late 40s and early 50s. Mr. Haendler, owner of International, paid me a flat $25 for such concerti as the Dvořák, Lalo, Saint-Saëns, Haydn D Major (with two cadenzas, Feuermann's and mine), Schumann and Tchaikovsky "Variations on a Rococo Theme."

Why did Rose offer his services for so little? "For much the same reason that I teach," Rose countered. "That eternal quest for immortality; I want to leave something behind. I know that when I was a boy, I was always in awe of the cellists who had edited the parts that I studied—Willem Willeke for the Lalo and Dvořák, Josef Malkin for the Saint-Saëns, and others. These names meant something to me, as perhaps mine will for someone else someday..."

LEONARD ROSE, EDITOR; INTERNATIONAL MUSIC COMPANY, PUBLISHER

Bach, Johann Sebastian (1685-1750)
2171 Air from Suite No. 3 in D Major

Beethoven, Ludwig (1770-1827)
3135 Horn Sonata in F Major, Op. 17
1298 Sonata in A Major, Op. 69
1297 Sonata in G Minor, Op. 5 No. 2

Boccherini, Luigi (1743-1805)
1720 Concerto in B-Flat Major

Boellman, Leon (1862-1897)
2107 Symphonic Variations, Op. 23

Brahms, Johannes (1833-1897)
904 Sonata No. 1 in E Minor, Op. 38
621 Sonata No. 2 in F Major, Op. 99

Breval, Jean-Baptiste (1753-1823)
1883 Sonata in C Major

Bruch, Max (1838-1920)
1682 Kol Nidrei, Op. 47

Chopin, Frédéric (1810-1849)
1971 Polonaise Brillante, Op. 3

Davidoff, Carl (1838-1899)
1672 At the Fountain, Op. 20, No. 2

Debussy, Claude (1862-1918)
2422 Menuet from "Petite Suite"

Dvořák, Antonin (1841-1904)
1080 Concerto in B Minor, Op. 104
1822 Rondo, Op. 80 No. 2

Fauré, Gabriel (1845-1924)
897 Élégie, Op. 24
1779 Fileuse, Op. 80 No. 2

Franck, César
323 Sonata in A Major

Glazounov, Alexander (1865-1936)
1345 Serenade Espagnole, Op. 20, No. 2

Goltermann, Georg (1824-1898)
1438 Concerto No. 1 in A Minor
1606 Concerto No. 4 in G Major

Granados, Enrique (1867-1916)
1885 Madrigal A Minor

Grieg, Edvard (1843-1907)
591 Sonata in A Minor, Op. 36

Haydn, Joseph (1732-1809)
771 Concerto in D Major, Hob. VIIb:2

Herbert, Victor (1859-1924)
2023 Concerto No. 2 in E Major, Op. 30

Hure, Jean (1877-1930)
1723 Air in F Major

Klengel, Julius (1859-1933)
119 Concertino in C Major, Op. 7
549 Concert Piece in D Minor, Op. 10

Lalo Edouard (1823-1892)
858 Concerto in D Minor

Paganini, Niccolo (1782-1845)
491 Moto Perpetuo, Op. 11 bis

Pergolesi, Giovanni (1710-1736)
2572 Sinfonia in F Major

Popper, David (1843-1913)
1607 Gavotte No. 2, Op. 23
1759 Hungarian Rhapsody, Op. 68
1726 Papillon, Op. 3
1717 Serenade, Op. 54, No. 2
1820 Vito, Op. 54, No. 5

Rachmaninoff, Sergei (1873-1943)
1819 Dance Orientale, Op. 2, No. 2
1659 Prelude, Op. 2, No. 1
517 Sonata in G Minor, Op. 19
1646 Vocalise, Op. 34, No. 14

Rimsky-Korsakov, Nikolai (1844-1908)
1642 Flight of the Bumble Bee

Romberg, Bernhard (1767-1841)
1873 Concerto No. 2 in D Major, Op. 3
1437 Concerto No. 4 in D Minor, Op. 7
1875 Concertino in D Major, Op. 51

Saint-Saëns, Camille (1835-1921)
1648 Allegro Appassionato, Op. 43
1212 Concerto No. 1 in A Minor, Op. 33
1630 The Swan

Sammartini, Giovanni B. (c. 1698-1775)
2093 Sonata in G Major

Sarasate, Pablo de (1844-1908)
1966 Zapateado, Op. 23, No. 2

Schubert, Franz (1797-1828)
552 Sonata in A Minor, D. 821 "Arpeggione"

Schumann, Robert (1810-1856)
1242 Adagio and Allegro, Op. 70
1992 Concerto in A Minor, Op. 129

Sgambati, Giovanni (1841-1914)
1727 Serenata Napoletana, Op. 24

Shostakovich, Dimitri (1906-1975)
2087 Sonata in D Minor, Op. 40

Strauss, Richard (1864-1949)
1794 Sonata in F Major, Op. 6
1628 Don Quixote, Op. 35 (solo cello part)

Tchaikovsky, Piotr Ilich (1840-1893)
1644 Valse Sentimentale, Op. 51, No. 6
1263 "Variations on a Rococo Theme," Op. 33

Vivaldi, Antonio (1680-1743)
1853 Concerto in D Minor (Sonata #5 from Six Sonatas, F.XIV no. 5)
1374 Sonata No. 3 in A-Minor, F.XIV, no. 3
1360 Sonata No. 6 in B-Flat Major, F.XIV, No. 6
1852 Six Sonatas, F.XIV, no. 1-6

STUDIES:

Franchomme, Auguste (1808-1884)
1771 Twelve Studies, Op. 35

Klengel, Julius (1859-1903)
1597 Technical Studies, Vol. 1
2132 Technical Studies, Vol. 2

Lee, Sebastian (1805-1887)
2003 Forty Melodic Studies, Op. 31, Vol. 1
2004 Forty Melodic Studies, Op. 31, Vol. 2

Orchestral Excerpts of Symphonic Repertoire:
1321 Classical and Modern Works, Vol. 1
1322 Classical and Modern Works, Vol. 2
1323 Classical and Modern Works, Vol. 3

Endnotes

1   Isaac Stern, in discussion with George Moquin at the University of Maryland Leonard Rose Cello Competition, Feb. 27, 1993. Virtuoso violinist Isaac Stern (1920-2001) was one of the twentieth century's most celebrated and recorded musicians. He is widely recognized as an influential teacher, emissary, speaker, and humanitarian.
2   Obninskii, V. *Polgoda Russkoi Revoliutsii (Half a year of Russia revolution)*. Moscow, 1906.
3   The roots of Yiddish theater date to the origins of Judaism. The first participants were Levites, musical priests of the temple. In the early eighteenth century, groups of Purim Schmelers in the Jewish ghettos performed the story of Haman and Ester in complicated plays. In 1876, Avrom Goldfaden combined these forces. Another pioneer in Yiddish theater was Maurice Schwartz (1890-1960) who made his work more accessible, inspiring others to do the same. He eventually brought worldwide acclaim to the Yiddish theater. Schwarz felt that the aim of the writers was to evoke laughter and tears, not to make the plays so artful. When Schwartz bought the Irving Place Theater (New York, torn down 1985), he had a chance to try his ideas on the community. Among his company were some of the best actors in Yiddish Theater: Celia Adler, Anna Appel, Sonya Nadolsky, Ludwig Satz, Clara Rosenthal, Boris Rosenthal, and Max Wilner. Though at first the Yiddish art theater was very popular, interest began to slowly decline. The company disbanded in 1950; but examples of the genre are still found in U.S. cities with large Jewish immigrant populations.
4   Leonard Rose unpublished memoir.
5   Salmond's American debut recital at Aeolian Hall in New York City, March 29, 1922.
6   Alla Goldberg (born 1927) in discussion with author, May 10, 2004.
7   Nathan Stutch (born 1919), in discussion with author, New York City, March 24, 2004.
8   Heyman, Barbara B. *Samuel Barber: The Composer and his Music.* New York City: Oxford University Press, 1992, 115.

9   Georges Enesco (1881-1955) was seminal in the development of music in his own country, Romania, although much of his activity centered in Paris, where he was a violin pupil of Marsick and studied composition with Fauré and Massenet. His own students included Grumiaux, Ferras, Gitlis, and Menuhin. On January 21, 1950, during the 60th anniversary season of his violin debut, he gave a farewell concert with the Philharmonic in the multiple capacities of violinist, pianist, conductor, and composer. Enesco's *Symphonie concertante* is a noble, serious score, unique in structure and with focus on solo cello. It has two principal movements and an introductory section in which cello states the thematic material for the entire work in a long haunting refrain. The work is virtually unknown today.

10 Leonid Hambro (1920-2006), born in Chicago, was a child prodigy who made his first public appearance at age five. He later studied at Juilliard, where he held a five-year fellowship, and subsequently became a member of the faculty. In 1946, he made his Town Hall debut as a winner of the Naumburg Award. During his years as a student, he became acquainted with Felix Salmond. Through their association in the studio and later as performing partners, Hambro gained his broad knowledge of the chamber music literature. In classical circles, he was especially known as a sensitive and marvelous chamber musician, collaborating with string players such as Kreisler, Heifetz, Shumsky, Stern, Szigeti, Fournier, and Rose. In addition to his career on radio, on the concert stage and on his recordings (he made more than 100), he enjoyed a long association with Victor Borge, the comedian Danish pianist who delighted audiences for decades.

11 Leonid Hambro, BBC Centenary broadcast of Salmond's birth year, 1988. Salmond and Hambro recorded three of the sonatas: Beethoven's Sonata Op. 5, No. 1; Sonata Op. 102, No. 1; and Sonata Op. 102, No. 2. The "Long Playing Microgroove" recording states on its label: "This Recording is Not to be Sold." Proceeds from the issue aided in the establishment of a Felix Salmond Scholarship at the Juilliard School, which was awarded for the first time during the 1957-1958 academic year.

12 Eleanor Aller (Slatkin) was enrolled at the Juilliard Graduate School from October 1934-1937. In the late 1930s, she was appointed principal cellist of Warner Bros. Studio Orchestra, a position she held for 36 years. In 1972, she moved to 20th Century Fox, where she was principal until 1985. Aller is considered one of the first women musicians to succeed in the film industry. Along with her husband—violinist and conductor Felix Slatkin—she founded the Hollywood String Quartet, which made notable recordings for Capitol Records, many of which have been re-released on CD. She is the mother of cellist Frederick Zlotkin and conductor Leonard Slatkin.

13 BBC Centenary broadcast.

14	Morreau, Annette. *Emanuel Feuermann*. New Haven and London: Yale University Press, 2002, 257.
15	Wendy Salmond Oler (born 1929), in discussion with the author, June 30, 2004.
16	Ibid.
17	Bernard Greenhouse, in discussion with the author, August 25, 2008.
18	Richard Kapuscinski (1921-1991), BBC Centenary broadcast of Salmond's birth year, 1988.
19	February 10, 1940: *Musical America*—20 concerts with the Chicago Symphony, 15 with Boston, 12 with New York, 7 with Philadelphia, 6 with Los Angeles, 4 each with Cincinnati, St. Louis, and Detroit among others.
20	Frank Miller often rued his ordinary name. He preferred an Italian translation, "Francesco Milanari." That, he liked to say, sounded beautiful.
21	Avron Coleman, in discussion with the author, May 9, 2004. Avron Coleman (born 1930) performed with the Minneapolis Symphony and New York Philharmonic under Bernstein. He worked as principal cellist of the Robert Shaw Chorale Orchestra, the American Ballet Theater, and the National Ballet of Canada.
22	Barbara Rose, e-mail message to author, April 20, 2004.
23	Anderson, Susan M., "Seeking Perfection: The Life and Career of Leonard Rose," Thesis, John Hopkins University, 2004.
24	Shumsky, Oscar. "Leonard Rose," *The Strad*, July 1985, Obituary section.
25	Eudice Shapiro, in discussion with the author, October 12, 2004. Eudice Shapiro attended the Curtis Institute from 1931 to 1936; she won first prize in the prestigious American Federation of Music Club Competition in 1937. During preparation of a performance of Beethoven's "Triple" Concerto (with Frank Miller, cello, and Jeanne Behrend as pianist on April 4, 1933), the Curtis Orchestra and Reiner, the conductor reprimanded her for using spiccato, telling her the technique was unknown in Beethoven's day. He firmly believed that the music would be better served with longer détaché strokes. As a graduation present, Mary Curtis Bok paid for and presented her in recital in New York's Town Hall, in Boston, and in Chicago. While at Curtis, she also played in the Lupot String Quartet alongside Felix Slatkin, who was also in the Zimbalist class. After school, Shapiro went to Hollywood where she was concertmaster of the RKO and Paramount orchestras.
26	Arthur Statter, in discussion with the author, March 27, 2004.
27	Frank, Mortimer H. *Arturo Toscanini the NBC Years*. Portland, Oregon: Amadeus Press, 2002, 21.
28	Rosenberg, Donald. *The Cleveland Orchestra Story*. Cleveland, Ohio: Gray & Company, 2000, 188.

29 The Spitalny family of musicians hailed from Cleveland and supplied small orchestras for hotels. One son, Phil, was a clarinet player who organized an "All Girls Orchestra" that toured the U.S. Another brother (Maurice) was a gifted violinist, and an elder brother (H. Leopold) managed music for Cleveland theaters. H. Leopold eventually became music contractor for the NBC Symphony (Rosenberg, *Cleveland Orchestra*, 52).
30 Antek, Samuel. *This Was Toscanini*. New York: Vanguard Press, 1963.
31 Bettina Steinke. *The NBC Symphony Orchestra*. New York, 1938. This 120-page volume reprints charcoal portraits of each orchestra member plus Rodzinski, Monteux, and Toscanini. Biographical sketches accompany the drawings.
32 Toscanini requested that proceeds be divided among the musicians, staff, Carnegie Hall personnel, and the Musicians' Emergency Fund. The program consisted of Beethoven's Leonore Overture No. 1 and the violin concerto (with Heifetz), and four Wagner pieces. The concert was announced in the morning papers on March 16, and by 1:00 p.m., had sold out. It raised $25,000. By the time the doors opened, 5,000 people stood in line, and mayhem broke out as the crowd swept two mounted policemen back against the wall and struggled with 50 other officers.
33 In late 1931, Toscanini experienced chronic right shoulder pain. He saw doctors in Rome and Florence, had X-rays taken, and eventually went to Piazze, a village near Siena, where Dr. Rinaldi treated him. Rinaldi—confident of his cures—was a cult-like figure whose patients believed whatever he said. He seems to have been a physician and witch doctor. For Toscanini, he prescribed twenty-four daily injections of special serum. Rinaldi, as outspoken an anti-Fascist as Toscanini, was later assassinated. [Sachs, Harvey, *Toscanini*. London: Weidenfeld & Nicolson, 1978, 219.]
34 Toscanini's first appearance with the orchestra received 50,000 requests for 1,400 available seats.
35 Antek, *Toscanini*, 12.
36 Horowitz, Joseph. *Understanding Toscanini*. Berkeley and Los Angeles: University of California Press, 1987, 237.
37 Horowitz, *Toscanini*, 376.
38 All three conducted the NBC Symphony at one time or another. Münch quote from *New York Times*, January 19, 1957. Sachs, *Toscanini*, 146. Marek, George, *Toscanini*. London: Vision Press Ltd, 1976, jacket copy. Gelatt, Roland, *Music Makers Some Outstanding Musical Performers of Our Day*. Cambridge: Da Capo Press, 1979, 52. (Horowitz, *Toscanini*, 376).
39 Haggin, B. H. *The Toscanini Musicians Knew*. New York: Horizon Press, 1967, 134.
40 Haggin, *Toscanini*, 154.
41 Toscanini probably saw his first Mahler work, Symphony No. 5, in 1905. This was Toscanini's reaction upon receiving the score: "... You'll

easily be able to imagine how much joy and how much curiosity its unexpected arrival gave me. I read it immediately, or rather devoured it; but unfortunately, during this ferocious musical meal, the initial joy and curiosity gradually waned, changing in the end into a sad, very sad hilarity. No, dear Enrico, believe me: Mahler is not a genuine artist. His music has neither personality nor genius. It is a mixture of an Italianate style a la Petrella or Leoncavallo, coupled with Tchaikovsky's musical and instrumental bombast and a seeking after Straussian peculiarities without having the originality of the last two. At every step you fall, not into a commonplace, but into some triviality ..." No work of Mahler's appeared on a Toscanini program (Sachs, *Toscanini*, 88).

42 Toscanini led five recording sessions that season: February 27, March 1, 7, 29, and April 17. The orchestra recorded Mozart Symphony No. 40, Beethoven Symphony No. 5 and No. 8, Rossini's *William Tell* Overture, and Paganini's *Moto perpetuo*.

43 Rodzinski, Halina. *Our Two Lives*. New York: Charles Scribner's Sons, 1976, 160.

44 Chotzinoff, Samuel. *Toscanini: An Intimate Portrait*. New York: Alfred A. Knopf, 1956, 123.

45 Tindall, "The Plight of the White-Tie Worker."

46 Frank Miller, in discussion with Arrand Parsons, *Interlake's Profiles* series, WFMT Radio, Chicago, January 1981 (reprinted in *The Podium*, Magazine of The Fritz Reiner Society, Spring/Summer 1986, 12-13).

47 Rosenberg, Donald. *The Cleveland Orchestra Story*. Cleveland, Ohio: Gray & Company, 2000, 127.

48 Ibid, 29.

49 Ehrman, Bart D. *God's Problem*. New York: HarperCollins, 2008, 160.

50 Information furnished by finance director, Jim Menger, of the Cleveland Orchestra. The overall budget figure in 2004-2005 was $36.8 million for the 12 months that ended May 31, 2005. According to Rita Shapiro, executive director of the National Symphony Orchestra, the NSO's budget from the 2005 fiscal year totaled $27,734,939.

51 Conductor Serge Koussevitzky once asked Tortelier to play as soloist—a scandal as he was not the Boston Symphony's solo cellist. He played a work dedicated to him by Thomas de Hartmann. Eventually, Rodzinski, according to Tortelier, offered him the solo cellist position in Cleveland, but Koussevitzky voided his contract. Tortelier angrily left Boston at the end of his third season in 1940. [Paul Tortelier and Blum, David. *A Self-Portrait*. London: William Heinemann LTD, 1984, 67.]

52 Charlie McBride, in discussion with Carol Jacobs, archivist at Severance Hall, August 18, 1992. McBride (1902-1994) was a member of the cello section of the Cleveland Orchestra from 1926 to 1944.

53 Rodzinski, *Our Two Lives*, 55.

54 Olin Downes, "Rodzinski Directs Cleveland Group." *New York Times*, February 6, 1941. Program included NY premieres of Piston's "The

Incredible Flutist (Suite)," Walton's Violin Concerto with Jascha Heifetz, and Strauss's Ein Heldenleben, Op. 40.
55 November 5, 1939: The Paganini-Kreisler Concerto's arrangement was in one movement. Rose may have been referring to the rehearsal of the three-movement Brahms concerto before getting to the Paganini.
56 Herbert Elwell, "Cellist Scores In Dvořák Concerto," *Plain Dealer*, November 17, 1939.
57 Downes, "Rodzinski Directs Cleveland Group,": "...performed magnificently by him [Heifetz] ... mastery, which long phenomenal, seems to grow with the years, and by no means to be confined to exciting virtuosity. He grows as an interpreter, in the warmth of his sentiment, his scrupulousness in the treatment of detail, and indeed in every aspect of his art ..."
58 Seymour Barab (born 1921), in discussion with the author, September 2004.
59 Rose would continue an enduring relationship with the Cleveland Orchestra for the remainder of his career. Thirty-three years after he left the orchestra (1976), Rose and the orchestra under the direction of Lorin Maazel videotaped a performance of Bloch's "Schelomo," a work closely identified with the cellist, for PBS television.
60 Anderson, "Seeking Perfection," 35. Anderson found the article in Rose's files. She asks, "What are the chances that the departure of a principal player from any orchestra would generate such coverage in the local paper today?"
61 Courtesy of the New York Philharmonic Archives.
62 The celebrated Irish-born cellist, Victor Herbert (1859-1924), was conductor of the Boston Festival Orchestra in 1891, Pittsburgh Symphony Orchestra from 1894-1904, and the Victor Herbert New York Orchestra. He was soloist with the New York Philharmonic playing his own Second Cello Concerto March 10, 1894, and again on December 10, 1897. Herbert is chiefly remembered as a composer of light operas that contain wit, charm, and simple harmonies.
63 Nathan Stutch (born 1919), in discussion with the author, New York City, March 24, 2004.
64 Hugo Becker (1864-1941), a Frankfurt Conservatory professor and the Opera's solo cellist at age 20. A rigid, dogmatic teacher, Becker succeeded Hausmann (cellist of the Joachim Quartet) at the Berlin Hochschule. Grümmer, Schuster, and Piatigorsky briefly studied with him there.
65 Morreau, *Feuermann*, 13 (quote from William Pleeth [1916-1999]).
66 Piatigosrky, Gregor. *Cellist*. New York: DoubleDay & Company, Inc, 1965, 109.
67 "Schuster Will Head Philharmonic 'Cellos'" *New York Times*, February 24, 1936, Amusement Books section, 15.
68 Schonberg, Harold C. *The Great Conductors*. New York: Simon & Schuster, 1967, 270.

69	Levi, Erik. *Music in the Third Reich.* New York: St. Martin's Press, 1994, 46 [Wulf, Joseph. *Musik im Dritten Reich.* Gütersloh, 1963.]
70	Levi, *Third Reich*, 201.
71	Lipman, Samuel. "Furtwängler and the Nazis," *Commentary*, March 1993.
72	January 27, 1950, Town Hall recital; November 5, 1945, Schumann Cello Concerto with Leonard Bernstein's New York City Symphony; January 9, 1945, Town Hall recital; December 26, 1943, Schubert-Cassadó Concerto in A Major with the NY Philharmonic; November 13, 1943, *Don Quixote* with the New York Philharmonic—Bernstein's debut concert; October 25, 1943, Town Hall recital; April 11, 1943, Haydn Concerto with Bruno Walter and the NY Philharmonic; December 2, 1942, with pianist Nadia Reisenberg, presenting two concerts of the five Beethoven Cello Sonatas and three sets of Variations in Town Hall; January 10, 1942, Brahms "Double" Concerto with concertmaster Mishel Piastro with the Philharmonic; November 30, 1941, Dvořák Concerto with the Philharmonic; March 29, 1940, Town Hall recital; March 3, 1940, Boccherini Concerto in B-Flat with Barbirolli and the Philharmonic; March 17, 1939, Town Hall recital; April 3, 1937, Bloch's "Voice in the Wilderness" and Saint-Saëns Concerto with the Philharmonic; November 18, 1936, *Don Quixote* with the Philharmonic; January 19, 1936, American premiere of the Shostakovich Cello Sonata in Town Hall:
73	Morreau, *Feuermann*, 33.
74	*New York Times*, November 19, 1936. *Don Quixote* with Barbirolli and the Philharmonic in November 1936. Before Wallenstein became a respected conductor, he was a formidable cellist brought to the Philharmonic by Toscanini, having earlier served as first cellist in Chicago. According to Rose: Unfortunately, like a number of other musicians, Wallenstein felt a great loyalty toward Toscanini, but rarely gave anywhere near as much of himself to any of the other conductors. His work for [Bruno] Walter was good—but certainly subpar—and that conductor knew it. It happened that one day Wallenstein learned of his appointment as musical director of the WOR Orchestra. Preferring to conduct, he decided that resignation from the Philharmonic was in order, and went in to advise Walter of his choice. "Really? Well, well, my congratulations!' replied Walter warmly. 'Let me wish you great success—all the best of fortune. And, above all, let me wish you an Artur Wallenstein for your first cellist!"
75	R. L. "Joseph Schuster in 'Cello Recital." *New York Times*, March 17, 1939, 8.
76	"Recital Bow Made By Leonard Rose." *New York Times*, October 13, 1945, 21. Program included Schuman Cello Concerto; Beethoven A Major Sonata (with Leonid Hambro); Boccherini Adagio and Allegro (from the Sixth Sonata); Frescobaldi-Cassado *Toccata*; Bloch *Prayer*; Debussy *The Little Shepherd*; Hillemacher *Gavotte Tendre*; Fauré *Reve*; Ravel *Piece en forme de Habanera* and Cassado's *Requiebros*.

77	"Rose Stands Out In 'Cello Recital." *New York Times,* November 27, 1947, 48. Program included Sammartini Sonata in G Major; Bach Suite No. 3; Brahms F Major Sonata; Isadore Freed Passacaglia; Tchaikovsky Rococo Variations. Rose's pianist was Irving Owen.
78	"I literally met the man, rehearsed, and recorded the work. Then we left. I never played with him again. I can't tell you anything personal about him." André Previn, in discussion with the author, January 31, 2009 (Previn, born 1929).
79	"Protest by Casals," *New York Times,* March 6, 1949, to the Music Editor section.
80	"A Pair of Cellists," *New York Times,* April 10, 1949, to the Music Editor section.
81	Menuhin, Yehudi. *Unfinished Journey: Twenty Years Later.* New York: Fromm International Publishing Corporation, 1996, 242. Chaitkin, N. J. "Gaspar Cassadó: His Relationship with Pablo Casals and his Versatile Musical Life" PhD diss., University of Maryland, College Park, 2001.
82	Tim Janof, in discussion with Bernard Greenhouse, Cello.org Newsletter, 1998.
83	Bernard Greenhouse (born 1916), in discussion with the author, August 25, 2008.
84	"Great Cellists of the Past," Marshall C. St. John, 1996-1999, www.cello.org.
85	The 66-year-old Rodzinski died on November 27, 1958, three weeks before a long awaited return to the Cleveland Orchestra. Addressing the Philharmonic audience the day after Rodzinski died, Leonard Bernstein said, "I would like to pay tribute to Mr. Rodzinski because he was a great conductor." Writing in the New York *Times,* Howard Taubman stated: "If Rodzinski left turbulence in his wake, he filled his music-making with excitement. He was a passionate fighter for his convictions."
86	Rodzinski, *Our Two Lives,* 225.
87	Burton, Humphrey. *Leonard Bernstein.* New York: Doubleday, 1994, 117.
88	Secrest, Meryle. *Leonard Bernstein a Life.* New York: Vintage Books, 1994, 125.
89	Oja, Carol J., and Ryan R. Bañagale. "Bernstein the Bostonian." *Juilliard Journal* 22 (2006).
90	Secrest, *Leonard Bernstein a Life,* 323. In October of 1966, in Oakland California, Huey Newton and Bobby Seale founded the Black Panther Party for Self-Defense. The Panthers practiced militant self-defense of Minority communities against the U.S. government, and fought to establish revolutionary socialism through mass organizing and community based programs.
91	Secrest, *Leonard Bernstein,* 136.
92	Arguably America's most visible conductor, Leonard Slatkin's remarkable career has been praised internationally for his imaginative programming

Endnotes

and interpretations of a vast range of repertoire. Mr. Slatkin has made regular appearances over the last two decades with the world's major orchestras and opera companies, including the New York and Berlin Philharmonics, Chicago Symphony and Concertgebouw Orchestra of Amersterdam. Mr. Slatkin's extensive discography includes more than 100 recordings recognized with five Grammy Awards and more than 50 other Grammy nominations.

93   Leonard Slatkin, in discussion with the author, December 2005.
94   February 2005—Slatkin at the Kennedy Center in Washington, DC.
95   Secrest, *Leonard Bernstein*, 380.
96   Laszlo Varga, in discussion with Tim Janof, 2002. According to the former principal cellist, "Gould did play very deliberately, and some of us thought he did this because he couldn't play it faster. But at the last performance, he surprised us all by starting the last movement twice as fast, with a twinkle in his eye. He played it perfectly, spectacularly. For him it was just a game."
97   Burton, William W. *Conversations About Bernstein*. New York: Oxford University Press, 1995, 67.
98   Secrest, *Leonard Bernstein*, 323, 364.
99   Burton, *Conversations About Bernstein*, 28.
100 Burton, *Conversations About Bernstein*, 135.
101 Maurice Gendron (1920-1990) was born in Nice, France. After the war, he made his solo debut at Wigmore Hall in London, December 2, 1945. Benjamin Britten was his accompanist, and they performed sonatas by Fauré and Debussy. It was also in December 1945 that Gendron gave the European premiere performance of Prokofiev's First Cello Concerto, with the London Philharmonic and Walter Susskind. Gendron's New York debut was at a memorial concert for Feuermann, where he performed the Dvořák and Haydn D Major Concertos. Gendron is unique in being the only solo cellist conducted by Pablo Casals on a commercial recording. They did the Haydn D Major, and the Boccherini B Flat with the Lamoureaux Orchestra, from original scores discovered by Gendron in the Dresden State Library. Gendron became a professor at the Paris Conservatoire in 1970, and taught at other music schools around Europe. He is admired especially for his interpretations of French music.
102 According to Rostropovich: "I came there before Lenny, to warm up a little bit with my cello; and I was surprised because I saw on the conductor's podium a big mattress! So I asked: 'What is happening here—is Lenny coming here to sleep?' And the producer said: 'No, it's because he jumps. We use a mattress; otherwise, he makes a noise.'" Burton, *Conversations about Bernstein*, 134.
103 Francis of Assisi was a poor little man from the thirteenth century who astounded and inspired the Church by taking the gospel literally—not in a narrow fundamentalist sense, but by actually following all that Jesus said and did, joyfully, without limit and without self-importance.

104 Katsoyanis, Katy, and Dimitri Mitropoulos. *A Correspondence, 1930-1960.* New York: Martin Dale, 1973, 7.
105 Katsoyanis, *A Correspondence*, 52.
106 Mitropoulos made his debut with the Boston Symphony Orchestra in Providence, Rhode Island, January 21, 1936.
107 Katsoyanis, *A Correspondence*, 32.
108 Katsoyanis, *A Correspondence*, 40.
109 Mitropoulos was invited by Toscanini to conduct the NBC Symphony in its first (May 28, 1938), fifth (October 7 and October 14, 1941) and ninth (December 9, 16, 23 and 30, 1945) seasons. He was no longer invited after refusing Toscanini's 1945 invitation to conduct two concerts in Italy for the benefit and reconstruction of La Scala. Mitropoulos, who faked an illness, was uncomfortable with the event's political overtones.
110 Katsoyanis, *A Correspondence*, 160.
111 Rosenberg, Donald. *The Cleveland Orchestra Story.* Cleveland: Gray & Company Publishers, 2000, 231.
112 Rosenberg, *Cleveland Orchestra*, 240.
113 Szell conducted the NBC Symphony in its fourth season (1940-1941) January 25, March 8, March 15, and March 22 and during its fifth season January 6 and 13, 1942. After Toscanini witnessed a rehearsal of Szell's—noting the manner in which Szell went over and over passages of music—Toscanini became irate. Szell was no longer invited back by his "hero" after 1942 despite twelve more Toscanini-led NBC seasons.
114 Farrell, Barry. "The Glorious Instrument." *Time*, February 1963.
115 Rosenberg, *Cleveland Orchestra*, 229.
116 Philharmonic archival recording reveals Rodzinski and Rose surprisingly made two cuts in the concerto's on-air performance: in first movement #13 to 4 measures before #15 and in the finale #12 to 9 measures after #13 (*International Music Edition*).
117 A letter to the editor, in press stated: "Szell has shown apparent coldness, arbitrariness, and precise brutality, which are very hard to understand in a man of such intelligence. Is it true, as many charge, that these mid-European maestros can't come over here and operate with human decent contacts with the musicians they direct?" Szell had created an atmosphere in which the musicians at the orchestra were scared for their lives.
118 Joseph Gingold, in discussion with the author, Meadowmount School of Music, summer 1980.
119 Rosenberg, *Cleveland Orchestra*, 231.
120 Cellist Einar Holm, in discussion with the author by e-mail, September 25, 2005. As Holm and a cellist colleague were playing Handel's 2-cello sonata (originally for 2 violins) in the summer of 1960, for Gingold, he stopped them after the first movement. "He slowly got up, very much moving like an old man, and walked down the aisle shaking his head from side to side as he reached for something in his pocket. He was

wiping his eyes by then with his handkerchief as he reached the stage explaining, 'Children, you'll have to forgive me. The last time I heard this sonata was when I performed it with my teacher Ysaÿe.'"

121 Harrell, Lynn. "The Road That Never Ends." *Clavier* magazine. Adapted from Harrell's 1994 commencement address at the Cleveland Institute of Music.

122 Ericson, Raymond. "Cello Recitals and Lynn Harrell on the Rise Together." *New York Times*, January 23, 1976.

123 Mayer, Martin. "Szell, Still Storming After 50 Years." *New York Times*, February 2, 1964, magazine section.

124 Celebrated Polish-born Mexican violinist and pedagogue Henryk Szeryng (1918-1988) became renowned by combining a virtuoso technique with a probing musical intensity. Fluent in 7 languages, and a humanitarian, Szeryng appeared in some 300 concerts for the Allies throughout World War II. Szeryng's penetrating words are sage advice to all ambitious young musicians: If a student is really determined to pursue a career as a soloist, half of the difficulty has already been overcome. His determination will provide the self-assurance and "gutsy" approach that is necessary to survive all of the brutal competition and hurdles, and [will] help to heighten the intensity and quality of his practice. ... Remember, luck alone will not sustain a career that is not founded on exceptional achievement. In itself, winning a competition is not of paramount importance. As we have seen so often, a fourth or fifth prizewinner can eventually carve out a career equal to or even surpassing that of the first prizewinner.

125 Olin Downes wrote in the *New York Times* November 2, 1945: "The orchestra's first 'cellist, the superbly equipped Leonard Rose, and the first viola, William Lincer, proved how significant these instrumental roles can be, and should be, in the hands of distinguished artists. ... The audience was the more often impressed with Mr. Rose's richness and sonority of tone, and his fine style. In an ensemble singularly unified by Mr. Szell, these features had an unforgettable saliency..."

126 Rosenberg, *Cleveland Orchestra*, 331.

127 There was one episode Rose was not all that happy to see Walter shed tears. With the Philharmonic, Bruno Walter conducted several performances of Bach's *St. Mathew Passion* (with Mack Harrell singing the part of Jesus). Rose recalled: "The first was during the war [spring 1943] when we were receiving all those hideous reports of what Hitler was doing with his concentration camps and death camps to much of Europe, to my co-religionists. Walter was conducting one Easter and at one particular place—I think following the text of St. John in the New Testament, where it says, 'They crowned Christ with a crown of thorns'—Bruno Walter began to weep. This didn't sit very well with many of the Jewish boys in the orchestra. Everyone knows that anti-Semitic incidents around the world increase around Easter—somehow people still equate modern-day Jewry with what the Jews supposedly did to Christ. We Jews have been

blamed for everything, so why not that? However, to a lot of unhappy people in the Philharmonic—a lot of Jewish boys who knew that Bruno Walter was born Jewish, this was hypocrisy. I guess we have to forgive him for that..."

128 In 1937, Walter appeared as soloist and conductor with the Vienna Philharmonic playing this Mozart Piano Concerto in D Minor, K. 466, which can be heard on Pearl GEMM CD 9940, where the listener can get a feel for what it must have been like for Rose. Terry Teachout comments that Walter's playing "is an indispensable document of pre-modern Mozart style."

129 Shanet, Howard. *Philharmonic: A History of New York's Orchestra*. New York: Doubleday, 1975, 305.

130 Walter, Bruno. *Theme and Variations (An Autobiography by Bruno Walter)*. New York: Alfred A. Knopf, 1946, 40.

131 Ryding, Eryk, and Rebecca Pechefsky. *Bruno Walter: A World Elsewhere*. New Haven and London Yale University Press, 2001, 17.

132 Ryding and Pechefsky, *Bruno Walter*, 16.

133 Ryding and Pechefsky, *Bruno Walter*, 67.

134 Ryding and Pechefsky, *Bruno Walter*, 86-87.

135 August 2009; National Heart Lung and Blood Institute.

136 Ryding and Pechefsky, *Bruno Walter*, 313.

137 Ryding and Pechefsky, *Bruno Walter*, 326.

138 Walter, *Theme and Variations*, 187-188. Terry Teachout writes in *Bruno Walter's Way*; "To hear him conduct the hushed farewell to life at the end of *Das Lied von der Erde*, with the strings of the Vienna Philharmonic playing as softly as the lightest of spring breezes, is to be reminded of his own eloquent words: "I feel, more deeply than ever before, music as a connection to the divine."

139 Ryding and Pechefsky, *Bruno Walter*, 216.

140 The day of Walter's funeral, John Glenn made history by orbiting the earth several times in space—the first American to do so.

141 Stern, Isaac, and Chaim Potok. *My First 79 Years*. Da Capo Press, 1999, 268.

142 Sigmund Spaeth, writing in the *New York Evening Mail* October 28, 1917, reports on Heifetz' debut recital in America: "... There was never a more unassuming player who demonstrated great abilities or one more intent upon his art and as oblivious of his listeners as he stands upon the platform. ... A tone of power, smoothness, and roundness, of searching expressiveness, of subtle modulation in power and color." Among the works Mr. Heifetz debuted are: Vitali *Chaconne*, Wieniawski Concerto in D Minor, Paganini 24th Caprice, and Tartini *Variations on a Theme by Corelli*.

143 Hungarian violinist Leopold Auer (1845-1930) became one of the most famous violin teachers of his time by inaugurating a new method of violin playing and bow technique. In 1868, he became a professor at the

St. Petersburg Conservatory in Russia, holding the position until 1917. Among Auer's famous students were Mischa Elman, Jascha Heifetz, Nathan Milstein and Efrem Zimbalist. Auer wrote about his teaching methods in *Violin Playing as I Teach It* (1921) and *Violin Masterworks and Their Interpretation* (1925). He also wrote an autobiography, *My Long Life in Music* (1923).

144 Yiddish authors such as Sholom Aleichem chronicled the tribulations of Jewish life in the Pale. The immortal play and film *Fiddler on the Roof*, was based on his story *Tevye der milchiger* (Tevye the Milkman) in the fictional *shtetl* (Yiddish for "town") of Anatevka. Because of the harsh conditions of day-to-day life in the Pale, some 2 million Jews emigrated from there in the late nineteenth early twentieth century, mainly to the United States.

145 Agus, Ayke. *Heifetz As I Knew Him*. Pompton Plains, New Jersey: Amadeus Press, 2001, 86.

146 Piatigorsky, Gregor. *Cellist*. New York: Da Capo Press, 1965, 156.

147 Leonard Slatkin speaking to Kennedy Center audience, October 2006.

148 McConnaughey, Susanne. "Heifetz: Genius of the Violin." *Coronet* 20 (1946): 40.

149 Kahn, Roger. "Fiddler on the Shelf." *LIFE* magazine, October 31, 1969.

150 McConnaughey, "Heifetz," 46.

151 Agus, *Heifetz*, 149.

152 Agus, *Heifetz*, 149.

153 Kahn, "Fiddler," 61.

154 Stern, *First 79 Years*, 17.

155 Lorin Maazel, in discussion with the author, Kennedy Center, January 18, 2006. His life in music began as a violinist in the Pittsburgh Symphony, playing under some of the same conductors Rose played for. Around 1950, Maazel took over for an ailing conductor in a performance of Shostakovich's First Symphony. The dean of American conductors, Maazel was once known for his ferocious and often frigid relations with musicians and boards alike. In defense, Maazel states, "I have always given it my all. Musicians will go to hell and back if they respect a conductor—and I respect them. As a player myself, I have to." His appointments have included artistic director and chief conductor of the Deutsche Oper Berlin (1965-1971), the Cleveland Orchestra (1972-1982), the Pittsburgh Symphony (1988-1996), the Symphony Orchestra of the Bavarian Radio (1993-2002), and the New York Philharmonic (2002-2009). He was named an honorary life member of the Israel Philharmonic in 1985. He has received ten Grand Prix du Disque awards.

156 Arthur Rose, in discussion with the author, March 20, 2004.

157 Arthur Statter (1913-2004), in discussion with the author by phone, March 27, 2004.

158 "Cellist Advises Music Parents of Pushing Harm," *Hartford Courant*, April 11, 1972.

159 Yeo, Douglas. "The Modern Symphony Orchestra—Turmoil, Liberation, and Redemption." Illinois: Wheaton College, 1997.
160 Leonard Slatkin, in discussion with the author, March 2007.
161 T. H. P., "Symphony Opens Year." *Harford Courant*, October 28, 1966.
162 Schuyler Chapin (1923-2009), born in New York City, studied music with Nadia Boulanger before becoming general manager of the Metropolitan Opera, a position he held until 1976. In 1953, he joined Columbia Artists as tour manager; he also served with Columbia Records as director of artists and repertoire. He is the author of *Leonard Bernstein: Notes From a Friend* (1992) and *Musical Chairs: A Life in the Arts* (1977).
163 Chapin, Schuyler. *Musical Chairs: A Life in the Arts*. New York: G.P. Putnam's Sons, 1977, 35.
164 Yo-Yo Ma, in discussion with the author, June 28, 2008.
165 Raven, Seymour. "Ravinia Hails 3D Program of Brahms' Music." *Chicago Tribune*, July 6, 1952.
166 Anderson, "Seeking Perfection," 54.
167 Lorin Maazel, in discussion with the author, January 18, 2006:
168 Noted in Rose's biographical essay from 1968.
169 Ericson, Raymond. "Leonard Rose: Cellist With Good Life on the Side." *Battle Creek Enquirer*, June 6, 1971.
170 From Rose's incomplete memoir, 1982.
171 Mennin's works include Nine symphonies (1942-1981); *Sinfonia* for chamber orchestra (1947); *Fantasia* for strings (1948), violin concerto (1950), concertato for orchestra (*Moby Dick*) (1952), cello concerto (1956); piano concerto (1958); *Cantata de virtute*, based on *The Pied Piper of Hamelin* (1969); Symphonic Movements (1971); *Reflections of Emily*, to texts by Emily Dickinson (1979); flute concerto (1982); two string quartets (1941, 1951); and a Piano Sonata (1963).
172 November 4, 1955—letter courtesy of Georganne Mennin.
173 November 15, 1955—letter courtesy of Georganne Mennin.
174 August 22, 1980, letter to Mr. Shook from Janos Starker. Starker's recording is available on CD; first edition music, FECD-0013.
175 I had only a few lessons with Feuermann, Shulman stated in a 1985 interview. I had just bought a car—my first car—when I went up to Scarsdale in my Hudson convertible. He promptly told me to go upstairs and practice, but also said: "Give me the keys to your car." He was really a wild character. And he was gone for about half an hour. He came back and I started to play for him and he stopped me. He said, "Play like the Whitestone Bridge." I was one of these sensitive kids and when I went to Feuermann for the first time in my life, I was faced with a master class. I did not know that I was going to be playing for my peers. So after about six or eight lessons, I dropped out; and he was very angry with me. About two years later, we met at a Town Hall concert ... and we came face to face and he looked at me with a smirk and said, "Hello, composer." I think it was an affront to his ego that I left.

Endnotes 471

176 *New York Times*, March 10, 1959.
177 *A Song of Orpheus* was first performed on February 17, 1962, with Leonard Rose and the Indianapolis Symphony Orchestra, Izler Solomon conducting.
178 Born in Latvia in 1838, Carl Davidov (after which the "Davidov" Stradivarius cello from 1712 is named) was acclaimed as one of Europe's finest cellist in his early twenties. At 22, Davidov was appointed an instructor at the Leipzig Conservatory. He later taught at the newly formed St. Petersburg Conservatory while continuing to tour occasionally with the celebrated pianist Anton Rubinstein. He composed 4 cello concerti, a fantasy on Russian songs for cello and orchestra, and published a cello method book.
179 Lynn Harrell, in discussion with Leonard Slatkin and a Kennedy Center audience, February 2005.
180 Heyman, *Samuel Barber*, 252.
181 Heyman, *Barber*, 256.
182 New York *Herald Tribune*, December 2, 1947.
183 Garbousova performed the Barber Concerto with the Los Angeles Philharmonic in 1947 and Chicago Symphony Orchestra in 1949 and 1952. It is not known why Nelsova, in 1950, was chosen to record the concerto with Barber conducting. Garbousova, past her prime, did record the work in 1966.
184 December 19, 1950.
185 Analysis by Chia Han-Leon.
186 James Reel.
187 There is confusion surrounding the purchase of the instrument. The February 1955 edition of the *Arizona Star* quotes Harry Rose, Leonard Rose's father, saying that his son paid $27,000 for the instrument. Others believe Rose purchased the instrument for $18,000 but that the violin maker Erwin Hertel acted as an intermediary and gave his $1,000 commission back to Rose so that he could afford it.
188 With a rich history dating back to Europe in 1856, Rembert Wurlitzer (1904-1963) Company was a world-famous musical instrument shop that is still known for its associates around the world. Many of today's finest instruments bear Wurlitzer papers.
189 The Violin Making International School of Cremona was founded in 1938 in order to create a center of high professional qualification in the stringed instruments field.
190 The first is *Liutai Antichi e Moderni* by Giovanni de Piccolellis, first published in Florence in 1885. In 1925, the Hills made use of these records for their book, *The Violin Makers of the Guarneri Family*. The third book is Carlo Bonetti's *La Geneologia degli Amati e Il Primato della Scuola Liutistica Cremonese*, published in Cremona in 1938.
191 On the basis of research by Philip J. Kass—author of *The Stati D'Anime of S. Faustino in Cremeno: Tracing The Amati Family 1641-1686*—identifies the

following as resident apprentices in the Nicolò Amati workshop: Giacomo Gennaro (c. 1624-after 1655): (1641 to 1646 and possibly 1647); Andrea Guarneri (c.1626-1698): (1641 to 1646/47, 1650 to 1653); Francesco Mola (c. 1641-?): (1653 to 1655); Leopoldi Todesca (c. 1625-after 1665?): (1653 to 1654, 1656); Gio Batta (1653); The Malagamba brothers: (1654 to 1655, 1666); Giuseppe (c. 1634-?); Gio Batta (c.1637- ?); Giacomo (Antonio?) (c.1644-?) Bartolomeo Pasta (c. 1640-after 1685?): (1660); Giovanni Battista Rogeri; Bolognese (c. 1662-after 1705): (1661 to 1663); Giorgio Taiper (c. 1648?): (1666 to 1667); Bartolomeo Cristofori (1655?-1731): (1680) Gioseppe Segher, Padovance (c.1646-?): (1680 to 1682); Giuseppe Stucchi; Veneziano (c. 1663-?): (1681); and Giacomo Railich (c. 1650-?): (1683 to 1685).

192 Gerald Warburg's (1907-1971) father, Felix (1871-1937), commissioned Ernest Bloch's *The Sacred Service* in 1929 for $10,000 (equivalent to nearly $126,000 in 2008). The work, written from 1930–1933, was intended for a Reform synagogue in San Francisco—Temple Emanuel Congregation—whose cantor, Reuben R. Rinder, arranged for the commission. *The Sacred Service* was premiered in Turin, Italy, in January 1933. It was performed elsewhere in Italy, in London, and New York before it was presented in Temple Emanuel, in March 1938.

193 Faber, *Stradivari's Genius*, 226.

194 Laurie, David. *Reminiscences of a Fiddle Dealer*. Cape Coral, Florida: Virtuoso Publications, 1925, (Faber, *Stradivari's Genius*, 126).

195 Lemonick, Michael D. "Stradivari's Secret." *Discover*, July 1, 2000.

196 Galamian, Ivan. *Principles of Violin Playing and Teaching*, Third Edition. Ann Arbor, Michigan: Shar Products Co., 1985.

197 Rose performed with Gingold and pianist Johana Harris on July 20, 1948: Mendelssohn D Minor trio, Ravel trio, and Schubert B-flat trio; on July 27: Mozart Quintet in G Minor, Brahms Piano Quintet, and Harris Piano Quintet; Rose performed with Gingold on July 6, 1949: Mozart String *Divertimento* with Milton Preves, viola; Schubert Piano trio in B-Flat and Ravel Trio with Johana Harris, Piano; on July 20: Haydn String Quartet Op. 64, No. 5 Beethoven Quartet Op. 59, No. 3, and Debussy Quartet with James Barrett, violin, and Milton Preves, viola; and August 2: Mozart Piano Quartet in G Minor, Schubert Quintet Op. 163, and Harris Piano Quintet with James Barrett, violin, Milton Preves, viola, and Johana Harris, piano.

198 Lucien Capet's (1873-1928) influence as a teacher can still be felt through the teachings of Galamian's pupils. His *Superior Bowing Technique*, translated from French to English, is the definitive treatise on all aspects of bow technique for the violin. The Capet String Quartet (1893-1928) was arguably the most famous of its day, influencing—among others—the Budapest String Quartet. The Capet Quartet can be heard on recordings made in 1927-1928.

199 Elizabeth Green, *Miraculous Teacher: Ivan Galamian and the Meadowmount Experience*, 1993. Elizabeth A. H. Green.
200 Galamian, *Principles of Violin*, 123.
201 Barbara Lourie Sand writes about these hours of practice in her book *Teaching Genius*. Portland, Oregon: Amadeus Press, 2000. Without a doubt, DeLay (1917-2002), as Galamian's assistant for 22 years, absorbed this routine from the disciplinarian Galamian. In 1970, the two great pedagogues would split up when DeLay decided to leave Meadowmount (where she had been with Galamian since 1944) for Aspen.
202 Saks began taking lessons in 1956 with Rose when she was 14 years old: "He took me more on the basis that I played Beethoven piano sonatas for him—less on the cello playing at that time because I wasn't an advanced cellist. It was really on the basis of a recommendation from the mother of a student who was at the preparatory division. The mother lived close by in Great Neck and was very good friends with Rose and his wife Minnie. I was so touched in those days that Mr. Rose would take me home with him on the weekends so that I could be at the house and get to know his kids. It was extremely generous of him to do that."
203 The premature death of violinist Michael Rabin (1936-1972) was a shock to the world of music, as he was considered a superlative talent to emerge from Galamian's studio. In 1950, at 14, he established himself as a genuine prodigy when he recorded the Paganini caprices. His instincts to play with virtuosity, tenderness, charm, and character were all considered on par with some of the greatest violinists who lived. In his prime years, his performance consistently exuded the aura of youth.
204 Arnold Steinhardt. *Indivisible by Four*. New York: Farrar Straus Giroux, 1998, 28.
205 Arturo Delmoni, in discussion with the author, April 2004.
206 Toby Saks, in discussion with the author, March 2004.
207 Sand, *Teaching Genius*, 33.
208 Itzhak Perlman, in discussion with the author, September 20, 2005.
209 Pinchas Zukerman, in discussion with the author, October 10, 2005.
210 Robert Newkirk, in discussion with the author, March 3, 2004. Newkirk studied with Leonard Rose and Orlando Cole at the Curtis Institute and was a member of the Casals Festival Orchestra with Pablo Casals conducting. He has served on the faculties of the Meadowmount School and the Cleveland Institute of Music. He is the former principal cellist of the Kennedy Center Opera House Orchestra.
211 Ann Barak, in discussion with the author, March 7, 2004.
212 Delmoni, in discussion with the author, April 2004.
213 Girard, François and Don McKellar. *Thirty-Two Short Films About Glenn Gould*. Toronto: Coach House Press, 1995, 34 (taken from the February 1974 edition of *High Fidelity* magazine [p. 72] "Glenn Gould Interviews Glenn Gould About Glenn Gould).”
214 Gould, Glenn. "Reminiscence and Prediction." *GlennGould* 3 (1997):12.

215 Ostwald, Peter. *Glenn Gould: The Ecstasy and Tragedy of Genius.* New York: W.W. Norton & Company, 1997, 106.
216 Ostwald, *Ecstasy and Tragedy*, 107. Gould would infuriate the members of the Juilliard Quartet during their recording of the Schumann piano quartet so much that they reportedly weren't on speaking terms by the end of the session.
217 A Chicago native, Paul Hume (1915-2001) was the music editor for the *Washington Post* from 1946 to 1982. In addition to his role at the *Post*, Hume hosted a long-running classical music program on WGMS-FM radio in Washington and was guest commentator for the New York Metropolitan Opera intermission broadcasts. He was also professor of music at Georgetown University from 1950 to 1977 and adjunct professor of music at Yale University from 1975 to 1983.
218 Flowers, Brandon. "Glenn Gould at the Stratford Festival." *GlennGould* 5, (1999): 60.
219 Flowers, "Stratford Festival," 61.
220 After working extensively with Gould in New York, Kazdin was persuaded to join him in Toronto with a crew that was by far less than that of the eight member team he had in New York. Kazdin often found himself starting the machines, cueing up the playback tape, watching the score so that the crossover point in the music was not passed, executing the crossover, keeping a written log of the takes recorded, reading the score as he recorded so he could answer questions about what he had just done, and reading the meters. Kazdin felt like one of those "one-man bands." Andrew Kazdin: *Glenn Gould at Work.* New York: E. P. Dutton, 1989, 28.
221 Tim Page was the chief music critic for the *Washington Post* from 1995-2008. Once a musician in a garage rock band and later a cocktail lounge pianist, he eventually turned his attention to composing before becoming the chief classical music critic for *Newsday* and the host of a radio program on WNYC-FM in New York. He won the Pulitzer Prize for criticism in 1997 for his writings about music for the *Washington Post* and has received an honorary degree from the University of Connecticut.
222 Page, Tim. "The Last Months." *GlennGould* 7 (2001): 28.
223 Gutmann, Peter. Classical Notes—Glenn Gould, Weird and Wondrous: A guide to some of the less Conventional Volumes of Sony's *Glenn Gould Edition*. http://www.classicalnotes.net/columns/gould.html (accessed May 2006).
224 *Washington Post,* January 2, 2005.
225 Page, "The Last Months," 30.
226 Gould, Glenn. "Music at Stratford: A Personal View," *GlennGould* 3, (1964): 12.
227 Glenn Gould 1966.
228 Flowers, "Stratford Festival," 66.
229 David Gross, in discussion with the author, October 21, 2007.

Endnotes

230 Kazdin, *Glenn Gould*, 169.
231 Girard and McKellar, *Thirty Two Short Films*, 177.
232 Istomin, Eugene. in discussion with George Moquin at the University of Maryland Leonard Rose Cello Competition, July 23, 1993.
233 "One of the world's master fiddler players," proclaimed critic Virgil Thomson in January 1943 after Isaac Stern's Carnegie Hall solo recital debut. His masterful playing was brought to a nationwide audience with appearances in 1952 and 1955 on the nationally syndicated "Jack Benny Show," aired on CBS from 1950 to 1964. Stern's 1956 rendition of *Symphonie espagnol* by Édouard Lalo with the Philadelphia Orchestra conducted by Eugene Ormandy is considered among his greatest concerto recordings. Stern was known throughout the musical world as a shrewd businessman, devotee of Israel, teacher, and raconteur. As a soloist and chamber musician, he would play more than 175 performances at Carnegie Hall. His late years were marked by decline even though his musical mind remained spontaneous and intact. Listening to his early career recordings, which include all of his collaborations with Rose, is an exhilarating experience in sweetness of tone, fluidity of sound, and an astonishing musical instinct. The 2,804-seat Carnegie Hall was dedicated the "Isaac Stern Auditorium" in 1996. He died at 81 in September 2001.
234 Eugene Istomin was born in 1925 in New York City of Russian parents who were both professional singers. The gifted prodigy studied with pianists Mieczyslaw Horszowski and Rudolf Serkin at the Curtis Institute. At seventeen, he won both the prestigious Leventritt and Philadelphia Youth Orchestra awards. In 1943, Istomin made his debut with the New York Philharmonic under Artur Rodzinski, playing Brahms's Second Piano Concerto—a performance in which Rose was principal cellist. Mr. Istomin died at 77 in October 2003.
235 Kahn, Albert E. *Joys and Sorrows: Reflections by Pablo Casals*. New York: Simon & Schuster, 1970, 142.
236 In July 1926, the Cortot-Thibaud-Casals recorded Schubert's Piano trio in B flat; June 1927, Mendelssohn's Piano trio in D Minor; November 1928, Beethoven's "Archduke" trio:
237 Emanuel Feuermann, "Feuermann Inveighs Against Mechanical Methods," *Musical America* (1940): 31.
238 As reported in the *New York Times,* January 1, 1939.
239 Taper, Bernard. *Cellist in Exile*. New York: McGraw-Hill Book Company, Inc, 1962, 9.
240 Isaac Stern: University of Maryland, Testimony, February 27, 1993.
241 "The Best in Each." *Newsweek*, September 1963.
242 The Heifetz-Piatigorsky-Rubinstein Trio appeared at the Ravinia Festival for four concerts in 1949—August 9, 11, 13, and 14—performing Beethoven "Archduke," Brahms Op. 8, Mendelssohn D Minor, Ravel trio, Schubert B Flat Major, and Tchaikovsky trio. Other repertoire performed on these concerts: Bach violin Partita No. 2 BWV 1004; Bach cello Suite

No. 3 BWV 1009; Beethoven "Kreutzer" Violin Sonata; Brahms Violin Sonata No. 3; Brahms Cello Sonata No. 1; Brahms Rhapsody, B Minor, Op. 79, No. 1; Chopin Ballade No. 1 Op. 23, Franck Sonata in A Major; Glière Eight Pieces, Op. 39; Halvorsen Passacaglia; and Martinu Duo for violin and cello, 1927.

243 According to Stern, the city was Jerusalem—according to Rose, Tel Aviv.

244 Barbara Rose, in discussion with the author, February 2004.

245 Eugene Eugene in discussion with George Moquin at the University of Maryland Leonard Rose Cello Competition July 23, 1993.

246 Sierra, J. A. History of Cuba. "Timetable History of Cuba: After the Revolution." http://www.historyofcuba.com/history/time/timetbl4.htm (accessed August 2007).

247 Wooley, John T. and Gerhard Peters. *The American Presidency Project*. http://www.presidency.ucsb.edu/ (accessed September 2007).

248 Parmet, Herbert S. *JFK: The Presidency of John F. Kennedy*. New York: The Dial Press, 1983, 129.

249 Stern, *First 79 Years*, 175.

250 The Istomin-Stern-Rose Trio also performed the opening chamber music concert of the newly inaugurated John F. Kennedy Center for the Performing Arts in Washington, D.C., September 1, 1971. Their program consisted of Beethoven, Op. 70, No. 1; Brahms C minor, Op. 101; and Mendelssohn trio in D minor, Op. 49.

251 Klein, Howard. "Trio Gives Concert in Chamber Series." *New York Times*, May 4, 1964. The Istomin-Stern-Rose trio performed at Rogers Auditorium at the Metropolitan Museum of Art Schubert B-flat trio, Beethoven trio Op. 121a and Brahms trio in C minor, Op. 101.

252 Hume, Paul. "Trio's Brilliance Ensures U.N. Concert's Success." Washington *Post*, October 26, 1966. The Istomin-Stern-Rose trio performed at Constitution Hall in Washington, D.C., Brahms trio in B Major and Mendelssohn trio in D minor.

253 Housed at the Casals Museum, this black and white footage of the trio's traversal of Beethoven's "Triple" Concerto with Casals conducting is priceless in its historical perspective. It must be rescued and preserved! Rose also performed Beethoven's Sonata Op. 102, No. 2 and Beethoven's trio Op. 70, No. 2 with Stern and Istomin in June 1970. In 1975, after Casals' death, Rose performed Beethoven's trio, Op. 70, No. 2; Brahms "Double" Concerto (with Stern and Alexander Schneider conducting); Brahms Sonata No. 1; Brahms trio Op. 87; Mozart piano trio K. 502; and Schubert's trio Op. 99 with Istomin and Stern.

254 Taper, *Cellist in Exile*, 9.

255 Isaac Stern. University of Maryland, Testimony, February 27, 1993.

256 Kolodin, Irving. "Three Men on a Hobby," *Saturday Review*, October 1970.

257 Stern's "Kosher Nostra" included Pinchas Zukerman, Itzhak Perlman, Shlomo Mintz, Midori, Mischa Maisky, Murray Perahia, Yefim Bronfman,

Maxim Vengerov, Ida Haendel, Itamar Golan, Ivry Gitlis, Gil Shaham, and Daniel Barnenboim.
258 Stern, *First 79 Years*, 173.
259 Schoenberg, Harold C. "Istomin-Stern-Rose Returns." *New York Times*, December 14, 1974.
260 Courtesy of Marta Istomin.
261 Isaac Stern: University of Maryland, Testimony, February 27, 1993.
262 Kolodin, "Three Men," 49.
263 In addition to a September 26, 1963, appearance with the London Symphony at Royal Festival Hall, Rose would appear three other times: September 29, 1958; Brahms "Double" Concerto with Isaac Stern, Josef Krips conducting: October 19, 1965; Dvořák Cello Concerto, Istvan Kertesz conducting: April 11, 1972 Dvořák Cello Concerto, Andre Previn conducting.
264 Pierre Monteux (1875-1964) was the music director of the Boston Symphony from 1919 to 1924 and later the San Francisco Symphony from 1935 to 1952. From 1961 until his death, he led the London Symphony Orchestra. For many years, he also headed a summer school for conductors in Maine *L'Ecole Monteux*. In his memoir, Rose remembered back to 1944 angrily recalling the shame he felt at the abominable way Philharmonic colleagues treated Monteux during the eight concerts he conducted in November, Rose's second season with the Philharmonic.
265 Tallmer, Jerry. "At Home with Leonard & Xenia Rose," *New York Post*, April 24, 1971.
266 Story told to author, reconstructed by Ann Barak March 7, 2004. "It is the most incredible love story I have seen in my life."
267 Rose, Xenia. *Widow's Journey*. New York: Henry Hold and Company, 1990, 110.
268 Rose, *Widow's Journey*, 1.
269 German cellist Eduard Georg Goltermann (1824-1898) was a first-rate performer and composer. His eight cello concertos and many salon pieces have retained some teaching value.
270 Blum, David. "A Process Larger Than Oneself." *New Yorker*, May 1989, 50. Plus discussion with the author, June 28, 2008.
271 Blum, "Larger Than Oneself," 51.
272 Ibid.
273 Raya Garbousova (1909-1997) was born in Tbilisi, in Russian Georgia, where she enrolled in the Tbilisi Conservatory from 1914 to 1923. She later went to Leipzig to study with Julius Klengel, but after hearing her play for three hours, he would not accept her as a student because she already knew too much. Later, she studied with Hugo Becker and Casals. Casals urged her to study with Diran Alexanian, whom Bernard Greenhouse believes ruined her "natural" abilities on the cello. Ms. Garbousova's records of her personal collection are housed at Northern Illinois University Libraries Special Collections Department.

274 Author has accompanied Ma with the National Symphony Orchestra: Bloch "Schelomo" and Slatkin "Dialogue for Two Cellos and Orchestra," 2008; Shostakovich Concerto No. 1, 2006; Beethoven "Triple" Concerto with violinist Itzhak Perlman and pianist Emanuel Ax, 2005; Tchaikovsky "Variations on a Rococo Theme," 2003; Fauré Elégie, 2003; Elgar Concerto, 2002; Williams Concerto—1999; Danielpour Concerto, 1999; Tavener Concerto, 1999; Dvořák Concerto, 1996, 1999.

275 Friedrich Wilhelm Ludwig Grützmacher (1832-1903) was German cellist famous for his editions of classic works by Romberg, Beethoven, Mendelssohn, Chopin, and Schumann. His knowledge of the instrument is especially vivid in his Twenty-Four Études, op. 38, in which he displays an array of technical demands proving that he was a veritable master of his era.

276 Yo-Yo Ma, in discussion with the author, June 28, 2008.

277 Anderson, "Seeking Perfection," 46.

278 Tim Janof, in discussion with Lynn Harrell, June 17, 1996 (www.cello.org/Newsletter/Articles/harrell.html).

279 Lynn Harrell, in discussion with the author, October 19, 2006.

280 Harrell and Slatkin answer questions from Kennedy Center audience, October 19, 2006.

281 Janof, Lynn Harrell (www.cello.org/Newsletter/Articles/harrell.html).

282 Leonard Rose memoir.

283 Stephen Kates, in discussion with Tim Janof, September 1, 2002.

284 Jeffrey Siegel, e-mail message to author, November 22, 2005. American pianist Jeffrey Siegel has been soloist with the Berlin Philharmonic, the London Symphony, Philharmonic and Philharmonia, Moscow State Symphony, Bayerischer Rundfunk (Munich), the Hague Residentie Orkest, Oslo Philharmonic, Stockholm Philharmonic, Orchestra of La Scala and the NHK Symphony of Japan; in the United States, engagements include the New York Philharmonic, Chicago Symphony, Cleveland Orchestra, Boston Symphony, Philadelphia Orchestra and the Los Angeles Philharmonic.

285 In the 1970s, Kates told his student David Teie, who related it to the author in May 2004.

286 Stephen Kates, 1985 tribute to Leonard Rose, University of Maryland.

287 Van Cliburn, in discussion with the author, August 30, 2007.

288 Jaime Laredo, in discussion with the author, October 14, 2006.

289 Emanuel Ax, in discussion with the author, March 22, 2006.

290 Jeffrey Siegel, e-mail message to author, November 22, 2005.

291 Pinchas Zukerman, in discussion with the author, October 10, 2006.

292 Moss, Lee. "Cellist Critiques Pupils." *Ithaca Journal*.

293 Olmstead, Andrea. *Juilliard: A History*. Urbana and Chicago: University of Illinois Press, 1999, 40.

294 Olmstead: *Juilliard*, 164.

Endnotes 479

295 Peter Meremblum (1890-1966) founded his youth orchestra in 1936 and led it 30 years, until his passing. Meremblum came to the U.S. from Russia, with his violin, two handkerchiefs and $10 and practically no English. Just before he died, he wrote: "I never had salaries, glories, and publicity. It was for my soul; for my love and my principles..."

296 While in the Air Force Band, Robbins studied with Victor Gottlieb, once Rose's peer in Salmond's class. Gottlieb, at age 19, played in the Philadelphia Orchestra (1935) for less than a year before Salmond persuaded him to join the celebrated Coolidge String led by violinist William Kroll. Gottlieb, who married Eudice in 1938, died at age 47.

297 Felix Slatkin was active in Hollywood during the 1940s, 50s, and early 60s as an arranger, conductor, and virtuoso violinist. In the 40s, Slatkin was the concertmaster of the 20th Century Fox studio orchestra. He later conducted and recorded the Hollywood Bowl Orchestra for Liberty Records. Slatkin was Frank Sinatra's concertmaster and conductor of choice during the Capitol recordings of the 50s. Together with his wife, cellist Eleanor Aller, he founded the Hollywood String Quartet, which left several acclaimed recordings. Sinatra's 1957 ballad album, *Close to You*, with accompaniment by the Hollywood String Quartet, hit the Top Five. Slatkin died at the age 47. His sons are conductor Leonard Slatkin and cellist Frederick Zlotkin.

298 Ruggiero Ricci was born in 1920 in San Francisco. At 12 years of age, the violin prodigy toured Europe, performing with the Hallé Orchestra in England under Sir Hamilton Harty, the Cologne Orchestra in Paris under Paul Paray; the Budapest Symphony under Dohnányi; the Rome Orchestra under Molinari; and the Prague Symphony under Szell. After his service in the Army Air Force Band, he presented a New York Town Hall debut in November of 1946. Ricci is considered a supreme Paganini virtuoso.

299 Ericson, Raymond. "Santa Fe Schedule; Another Slatkin," *New York Times*, December 28, 1980. Arts & Leisure section, D17.

300 Matt Haimovitz (born 1970) is an Israeli-born cellist now based in Canada.

301 Gregor Benko and Terry McNeill: "Josef Hofmann and the 7 April 1938 Casimir Hall Recital," 1998.

302 Jules Eskin, a Naumburg award-winner, served as principal cellist of the Cleveland Orchestra before joining the Boston Symphony Orchestra (BSO) as principal in 1964. A native of Philadelphia, Mr. Eskin is a frequent soloist with the Boston Symphony and is featured on a Deutsche Grammophon recording of music by Fauré with the BSO.

303 Donald McCall was the cellist of the Lenox Quartet for 15 years and is professor of cello at the Royal Northern College of Music.

304 Dutch cellist Willem Willeke (1879-1950) had been principal cellist under Gustav Mahler at the Vienna Opera Orchestra before becoming a member of the Kneisel Quartet from 1907 to 1917. From the earliest days

of the Juilliard School's history, the Kneisel quartet was one of its main attractions and for many years, this country's leading chamber music ensembles. Willeke's successful cello students include Marie Roemaet Rosanoff, Phyllis Kraeuter (Lynn Harrell's first teacher), and Harvey Shapiro. Mr. Willeke taught at the Juilliard School until 1948.

305 Applebaum, Samuel and Sada Applebaum. *The Way They Play, Book 1*. Neptune City, New Jersey: Paganiniana Publication, 1972, 327.
306 Applebaum, *Way They Play*, 330.
307 Charming, intelligent, and generous are the words students most often use to describe Luigi Silva (1903-1961), known for his lightning fast and agile left-hand technique. Silva had been on the Juilliard faculty since 1953, the Mannes College of Music since 1949, and the Hartt College of Music of the University of Hartford since 1956 when he died in his studio on Central Park West in November of 1961. As pedagogue, Silva has edited most of the standard works of the cello literature (Piatti, Servais, Duport, Popper, etc.) plus transcriptions of such basic works as the Kreutzer études, and Paganini violin caprices.
308 Michael Fleming in discussion with Leonard Rose, *Star-Telegram*, 1981.
309 Barbara Rose, e-mail message to author, March 2004.
310 Hallmarks of performances and classes given by Janos Starker (born 1924), over the course of a long career spanning more than five decades, include peerless technical mastery, and great communicative power. In 1948, he emigrated from Budapest, Hungary, to the United States, where he subsequently held the post of principal cellist with the Dallas Symphony, the Metropolitan Opera, and then the Chicago Symphony under Fritz Reiner. Mr. Starker amassed an extensive discography of more than 165 works.
311 Starker, Janos. *The World of Music According to Starker*. Bloomington, Indiana: Indiana University Press, 2004, 118.
312 At first, "Crooning" was coined as a term of derision to describe the pallid and high-pitched sentimentality of Rudy Vallee and other early exemplars of this kind of singing. Crooners' increased popularity in the early 1930s was spurred by an unprecedented fusion of technological progress and economic collapse. In 1925, major record companies had begun to adopt the Western Electric process of making records, which brought the microphones into widespread use for the first time. No longer needing to shout into an acoustic horn, singers took advantage of the microphone's sensitivity to project an intimate style. Bamberger, Rob. "Crooners," *Washington Post*, September 2004.
313 Starker, *World of Music*, 12.
314 Yo-Yo Ma, in discussion with the author, June 28, 2008.
315 The Heifetz Collection, "A Retrospective in Six Volumes," 1917-1955.
316 Rose, *Widow's Journey*, 2.
317 For Salmond's memorial, Rose performed in Beethoven's Adagio ma non troppo from quartet , Op. 74 with Joseph Fuchs, Frank Scocozza, violins;

Lillian Fuchs, viola and the first movement and Adagio from Fauré's piano quartet in C Minor, Op. 15 along with pianist Frank Sheridan, Joseph Fuchs, and Lillian Fuchs. At Rose's memorial, Isaac Stern and Eugene Istomin performed Beethoven's Sonata for Violin and Piano in A Op. 30, No. 1 (Second movement – Adagio). Yo-Yo Ma performed Fauré's *Elegie*, Op. 24. Yo-Yo Ma and Lynn Harrell joined violinists Isaac Stern and Itzhak Perlman and Michael Tree, viola, in a performance of Schubert's Quintet in C, Op. 163, D. 956 (Second movement – Adagio).

318 Courtesy of Harry Wimmer.
319 Claudio Arrau sustained a career of 82 years; he played in public at the age of 86 and last recorded at age 87.
320 Michael Tree, telephone interview with author December 2004

Addendum

Students of Leonard Rose:

The Juilliard School Of Music 1947-1984:

Jonathan Abramowitz
Robin Abraham
Ted Ackerman
Robert Albrrecht
Herbert B. Allen
Moshe Amitay
Richard Amster
Donald Anderson
Gerald Appleman
Brace Bahng
Scott Ballantyne
Ohad Bar-David
Eric Bartlett
Gilda Barston
Batia Bergman
Toby Berlinski
Martha Blackman
Soloman Blumenkrang
Ulrich Boeckheler
Yari Bond
Katherine Brainard
Terry Braverman
John Brecher
Luba Byman
Owen Carman
Neal Cary
Francois Chanon
Li-Ke Chang
Anna Cholakian
Myung Wha Chung
Allan Cisco
Susan Cohen
Avron Coleman
Charles Curtis
Steve Custer
Raymond Davis
Marcella Decon
Thomas Demenga
Valter Despalj
Cava DeVeritch
Raphael Diaz
Michelle Djokic
Pierre Djokic
Daniel Domb
Carmen Doron
Wesley Dowdy
Barbara Draper
Lawrence Dreyfus
Mary Durell
Charles Edderg
Andre Emelianoff
Jules Eskin
David Everhart
Leonard Feldman
Gregory Fiocca
Edgar Fischer
Gary Fitzgerald
Jose Fortez
Mary Fraley
David Freed
Geraldine French
Marie Gelinas

Ruth Glasser
Wanda Glowacka
Karl-Stephen Goerner
Selma Gokcen
Mary Green
Nancy Green
Charles Griffith
Matt Haimovitz
Yehuda Hanani
Trevor Handy
Bonnie Hartman
Ellen Hassman
Elizabeth Hayden
Ulrich Heinen
David Heiss
Guillermo Helguera
Marian Heller
Richard Hirschl
Einar Holm
Desmond Hoebig
Steven Honigberg
Nella Hunkins
Ko Iwasaki
Kathe Jarke
Hans Jorgen Jensen
Daven Jenkins
Gerald Kagan
Stephen Kates
Chungsun Kim
Eric Kim
Laura Kimble
Morris Kirshbaum
Thomas Kornberg
James Kreger
Donald Larson
Warren Lash
Dorothy Lawson
Marcia Lederman
James Lee
Luis Leguia
Lawrence Lenske
Dorothy Leshin
Joel Levin
David Levine
Frank Levy
Nancy Libowitz
Mats Lidström
Enzo Liva
Roger Low
Cameron Lowe

Myron Lutzke
Charles McCracken
Laura McLellan
Maureen McSharry
Yo Yo Ma
Robert Marcus
Michael Masters
Peter Mauricci
Jonathan Miller
Frances Mitchell
Madeline Moorman
David Moore
Daniel Morganstern
Hilda Movesessian
Eugene Moye
Jacqueline Mullen
Patricia Natanek
Gerald Nelson
May Osterberg
Stephen Peirson
Joanne Perron
Fernando Penagos
Anne Pinsker
Brandoch Peters
Steven Pologe
Emilia Quinn
Kari-Lise Ravnan
Barbara Reisman
Christopher Rex
Asher Richman
Channing Robbins
Paul Ross
Olga Rostropovich
Wallace Rushkin
Milton Saier
Toby Saks
William Salchow
Susan Salh
Andrew Salvo
Sara Sant'Ambrogio
Victor Sazer
Dieuwke Schreuder
Eugene Schweitzer
Rebecca Seiver
Sara Seiver
David Sella
Laura Sewell
Geof Shank
Ronald Shawger
Richard Sher

Fred Sherry
Edwin Sholz
Mark Shuman
Jorge Sicre
Lori Singer
Wayne Smith
Nancy Steltmann
Martha Stewart
Gloria Strassner
Nancy Streetman
Robert Sylvester
Edward Szabo
Joseph Tabachnikov
Hrant Tatian
Paul Tobias

Bruce Uchimura
Christopher von Baeyer
Bruce Wang
Ellen Westerman
Grace Whang
Jeanette Whitney
Eric Wilson
Harry Wimmer
Peter Wyrick
Edith Wint
Jack Yablokoff
David Ying
Eugene Zallo
Fred Zlotkin

Students of Leonard Rose:

The Curtis Institute Of Music 1951-1962:

Fred Arico
Regula Burkhardt
David Cole
Hamisa Dor
Roger Drinkall
Jules Eskin
Anne Goodman
Michael Grebanier
Patricia Griffin
Nancy Hall
Lynn Harrell
Ellen Hassman
James Holesovsky
Edward Humeston
Margaret Jordan
Lynn Kahle

James Kennedy
Ronald Leonard
Robert Martin
Diane Mather
Donald McCall
Robert Newkirk
Dorothy Reichenberger
Peter Schenkman
Joan Shaykin
Reynold Siemens
Lloyd Smith
Noel Snyder
Frances Steiner
Yuan Tung
Marcia Whitlock

About the Author

As author and professional cellist, Steven Honigberg (b. 1962), complements his biography's subject with a musician's ear for language and the highest technical expertise. He currently plays on a 1732 Stradivarius (the "Stuart"), holds degrees from The Juilliard School, and combined with experience writing about legendary cellists, has produced a comprehensive first biography of America's "first cellist."

The cello has dominated the author's personal life since kindergarten and two of its history's most respected performers, native-born Leonard Rose and Soviet-American Mstislav Rostropovich, have entwined as recurring themes throughout his professional life.

As a protégé in Rose's final years, Honigberg retains the wealth of knowledge his subject imparted to students, as well as an abiding sympathy for the man. That intimate relationship of the past provided unparalleled access to Rose's living colleagues and classes, from his best known pupil, Yo-Yo Ma, to internationally acclaimed stars with whom the pedagogue collaborated, such as Van Cliburn, Lorin Maazel, Emanuel Ax, Pinchas Zukerman, Itzhak Perlman and more. Likewise, the biographer's exceptional music credentials served as entrée to befriend Rose's heirs.

Steven Honigberg grew up in a Chicago-area musical household where he began cello lessons at age 5 and encountered Leonard Rose via the family's LP collection.

Recordings of favorite Romantic-era literature and Rose's sonorous cello captivating the boy. He recalls a vivid childhood memory of one cover photo of his future teacher; the intense stare into the camera inexplicably attracted him, long before he could envision a move to Manhattan to learn from the intense man in the picture.

In his teens, Honigberg won a number of regional competitions that awarded him solo appearances with the Youth and Civic orchestras of Chicago; at Interlochen, he performed Bloch's *Schelomo* as concerto soloist with the World Youth Symphony. And at age 16, the Chicago Symphony's distinguished youth auditions granted him eight solo appearances with one of the nation's top-five orchestras. In the early 1980s in New York, while he completed his Masters degree at Juilliard, the author won additional awards.

One competition sponsored his formal debut at Carnegie Recital Hall. Through one at the school, he won the opportunity to perform as soloist in Strauss's *Don Quixote* with the Juilliard Orchestra.

In 1984, the author was handpicked by cellist-conductor Msistlav Rostropovich to join the National Symphony Orchestra, a position he holds to this day. Eerily similar to the Rose biography's chapter devoted to personal events of 1964, "Darkness and Light," the year 1984 marked the author's period of triumphant and tragic transitions. Within months, he graduated from college, presented his New York recital debut, appeared as soloist in Alice Tully Hall, accepted the Washington job. And – Leonard Rose died.

The entire cohort of Rose alumni concurred that his loss was immeasurable and, in retrospect, would agree his influence continued. For the author, a baton was handed off from Rose to Rostropovich, from the end of school and launch of his profession. He played in the National Symphony's cello section under Rostropovich for a decade, during which time in 1987 was the only American winner of the Scheveningen International Music Competition in Holland (1987) and cited by the influential magazine Musical America one of a select group of 1988 Young Artist(s) "to watch."

In the footsteps of his biography's subject, he constructed a career as member of symphonic and chamber ensembles, as recitalist and concerto soloist, performing in an Eastern metropolitan area during the regular season and at various U.S. summer festivals.

The affiliation with Rostropovich produced one of Honigberg's crowning literary and musical achievements, to date. In contrast to Rose's fame for perfecting the cello's standard repertoire, Slava championed contemporary works, adding some 150 new pieces from around the world to the cello canon. When Rostropovich died, Honigberg dedicated himself to a verbal and sonic memorial project, "Homage to Slava."

The author-cellist performed and recorded modern pieces for solo cello composed for Slava by such disparate creators as Penderecki, Walton, Vainberg, Ginastera, Stutschewsky, and Lutoslawski. Additionally, Honigberg recorded two cello études composed by Rostropovich. A pair of works written specifically for Steven Honigberg by American composers, David Diamond and Robert Starer, round out the memorial recording.

The author's lengthy biographical essay, "Homage to Slava," accompanied the eponymous CD, appears in print and on the web.

The author's writing career began shortly after he settled in Washington, D.C. A majority of his published work has focused on short biographies on renowned cellists. In the late 1980s and early 1990s, for a professional music trade publication, he wrote a series of columns under the heading "Remembering the Legends," – a few subjects were Leonard Rose, Pierre Fournier, and Frank Miller (who was Rose's cousin and during Rose's teenage years, a mentor). In addition, Honigberg published a feature about Gregor Piatigorsky's influence on the National Symphony's then-principal cellist, John Martin. And from an autobiographical perspective, Honigberg published "A Cellist's Life at 40," in the Potomac Review (Spring 2003).

From 1994-2002, Honigberg served as chamber music series director at the U.S. Holocaust Memorial Museum, where a primary duty required writing of some 40 overviews on the gamut of topics at the intersection of music and the Holocaust. These brief articles ran on the museum website and the author delivered them as speeches in Washington, D.C. and venues across the country.

As pedagogue, Leonard Rose believed all collaborative experiences – conductors witnessed, soloists accompanied, chamber partners, which amounted to the spectrum of the

20th-century's stars from America and abroad – each imbued him in musical knowledge or inspiration, and the sum of these experiences was what he imbued in his protégés. The author was one of the privileged handful to whom Rose passed that torch – a crucial aspect to Rose's life that requires a Rose pupil's elucidation in any life-story.

Honigberg regards himself as logical and pragmatic, nevertheless fails to adequately comprehend how Leonard Rose's LP photo lured a child who could not fathom the picture's emotional expression and, in spite of his mentor's death and time passed, how Rose's presence and active influence in his own musicianship were ongoing.

Ultimately, the mysterious feeling drove the author to seek out fellow alumni, compelled him to inquire if others shared the bizarre experience of Rose's continual effect on their artistry. In response to the curiosity, he swiftly received a hundred pages of concurring thoughts and anecdotal remembrances in praise of "America's first cellist."

The tributes to their teacher and collective disappointment that Rose deserved a full-length biography sparked Steven Honigberg to undertake the present volume. As author-cellist, he started with soliciting his own group of colleagues, recollecting a host of first-hand observations, and noting information best conveyed by a professional cellist.

The paucity of extant material about the brilliant, prolific musician was, at first, stunning. From the foundation of initial queries to his cohort, the author-cellist began several years of research and the writing of LEONARD ROSE: AMERICA'S GOLDEN AGE and ITS FIRST CELLIST.

Steven Honigberg writes in the book's Introduction, "The lives of thousands of musicians and music-lovers have been touched by Leonard Rose's exquisite artistry as a soloist, chamber musician, and orchestral member, yet none so profoundly touched as the 200-250 individuals privileged to call the great cellist, 'my teacher'."

The author lives with his wife, Jessica, and their two daughters, Lily and Clara, in Washington, D.C.

About the Bonus CD

Not in the public domain. Never released commercially.

Alan Shulman
Concerto for Violoncello and Orchestra (1948)
Leonard Rose
Dimitri Mitropoulos, conductor
New York Philharmonic-Symphony
Carnegie Hall April 14, 1950
31:26

"Dimitri Mitropoulos conducting the Philharmonic last night in Carnegie, Leonard Rose, playing the cello, and the Princeton University Chapel Choir (part of the New York premiere of Arnold Shoenberg's "A Survivor from Warsaw") gave us an evening of charm and sentiment. They gave us also, as is their custom, musical executions of the highest beauty ... Alan Shulman's Cello Concerto, <u>which Mr. Rose played ever so beautifully</u>, is also, unless I misread it, a meditation about the Jewish people. Its lines are chromatic and return on themselves in the Near East style. Its harmony is lachrymose, but solid withal. Its colors are dark and a little muddy, but sometimes they glow. The cello writing is that of a professional, and the scoring is admirably calculated to throw the solo instrument into relief. This is a personal work full of feeling..."

April 14, 1950 – New York *Herlad Tribune* – Virgil Thomson (From the World Premiere performance the evening before)

Peter Mennin
Cello Concerto (1956)
Leonard Rose
Juilliard Orchestra
Jean Morel, conductor
World Premiere February 10, 1956
26:35

"...Mr. Mennin's concerto belongs to a different order of approach. His lyricism, particularly in the slow movement, has more direct appeal... They had every reason to be grateful to the performers. Jean Morel conducted with authority and clarity ... Leonard Rose was a brilliant performer on the cello in the Mennin work."
February 11, 1956 - New York *Times* - Howard Taubman

Certification of Purchase

The bonus CD includes recordings never released commercially and not in the public domain. The CD features Leonard Rose playing the cello in an unedited live performance of Peter Mennin's 1956 Cello Concerto with Jean Morel conducting the Juilliard Orchestra and an unedited live performance of Alan Shulman's 1950 Cello Concerto with Dimitri Mitropoulos and the New York Philharmonic in Carnegie Hall.

I certify that I purchased *Leonard Rose: America's Golden Age and Its First Cellist* from_____[vendor] on_____[date] at the price of _____ and am entitled to the bonus CD.

Signature_____

Name_____

Street Address_____

City_____

State_____

Zip_____

Phone Number_____

You may send this coupon by mail or fax:

2) Mail: Beckham Publications Group
   P.O. Box 4066
   Silver Spring, MD 20914

3) Fax: 866-659-3306

INDEX

A

Adam, Claus 299
Agus, Ayke 163, 164
Alexanian, Diran 30, 90, 104, 105, 106, 256
Aller, Eleanor 27
Amati, Andrea 8, 119, 122, 184, 213-216, 219, 220, 222, 223, 299, 305
Amati, Girolamo 8, 119, 122, 184, 214-216, 219, 220, 222, 223, 299, 305, 312
Amati, Nicolò 7, 8, 119, 122, 184, 213-216, 219-223, 299, 305, 312
Anagnost, Dino 212
Andrews, Mitchel 309
Antek, Samuel 53
anti-Semitic 16, 133
Applebaum, Samuel 336
Arbeiter Ring Schule 16
Arlen, Walter 196
Aronson, Lev 294
Arrau, Claudio 5, 83, 182, 183
Asperger, Hans 238
Auer, Leopold 47, 158, 159, 162, 225
Autori, Franco 183
Awards, Grammy 87
Ax, Emanuel 306

B

Bach, Johann Sebastian 51, 106, 171, 190, 193, 196, 213, 215, 227, 237-239, 241, 242, 243, 250, 253, 254, 257, 283, 284, 314, 324, 343, 344
Bachman, Eddie 59
Bacon, Elmore 76, 187
Bailly, Louis 22, 44
Balanchine, George 262
Balazs, Frederic 8, 9
Ballantyne, Scott 309, 317
Barab, Seymour 81, 85, 175
Barak, Ann 234, 278, 279, 280, 281, 282
Barber, Samuel 25, 26, 119, 193, 194, 206-209
Barbirolli, John 80, 83, 96, 104
Barenboim, Daniel 177, 256, 308
Barlow, Howard 103
Barston, Gilda 315, 349, 351
Bartók, Béla 80, 83, 343
Bass, Abrascha 88, 206
Battey, Robert 185
Battista, Giovanni 215
Becker, Hugo 96, 255
Beek, John and Johanna 192
Beethoven, Ludwig van 4, 5, 26, 31, 33, 43, 60, 62, 63, 78, 80, 81, 82, 97, 102, 114, 117, 124, 126, 130, 135, 136, 139, 144, 145, 146, 153, 156, 158, 162, 164, 165, 178, 181, 184, 189, 190, 196, 197, 240, 241, 242, 243, 245, 247, 255- 258, 261, 265-267, 270, 272, 273, 285, 288, 302, 304, 305, 306, 307, 324
Bell, Joshua 225
Bellow, Saul 262
Bengstrom, Ehrling 291, 295
Berkowitz, Ralph 32
Bernstein, Leonard 94, 99, 103, 107, 108, 110-120, 129, 130, 134,

Index

145, 147, 155, 156, 175, 176, 193, 194, 202, 207, 209, 262
Biancolli, Louis 184, 204, 261
Blackman, Martha 186, 314, 315
Bloch, Ernest 25, 31, 32, 121, 131, 178, 180, 185, 188, 190, 210, 211, 291
Bloom, Myron 134
Blum, David 323
Boccherini, Concerto for Salmond 32, 33, 185, 196
Boecheler, Ulrich 325
Bok, Mary Louise Curtis 37, 41, 43, 44, 46, 47, 50, 71, 329, 330
Boston Symphony Orchestra 125, 191, 207, 291, 323
Boult, Sir Adrian 180, 281
Bow arm 7, 16, 39, 48, 77, 114, 173, 232, 253, 259, 313, 331, 335, 338, 340
Brahms, Johannes 3, 4, 5, 22, 31, 46, 49, 50, 53, 60, 63, 68, 76, 79, 80, 81, 101, 104, 116, 119, 124, 131, 133, 136, 138, 145, 148, 149, 154, 164, 165, 172, 178, 184, 188, 189, 192, 195, 196, 197, 208, 235, 241, 243, 244, 249, 255-258, 266, 276, 288, 290, 304, 307, 324, 344, 349,
Brambilia, Enrico 89
Brey, Carter 209
Bronson, Ilya 318
Browning, John 309
Bülow, Hans von 57, 133
Burton, Humphrey 110

C

Caiati, Mario 88
Cantelli, Guido 57
Carini, Leandro 53
Carman, Owen 299-301
Carnegie Hall 26, 55, 61, 75, 80, 81, 103, 109, 110, 112, 119, 136, 140, 146, 155, 157, 161, 167, 181, 183, 191, 194, 202, 209, 224, 261, 265, 267, 268, 272, 305, 306, 313, 325, 344, 353
Caruso, Enrico 177
Casals, Pablo 8, 30, 55, 103, 104, 105, 106, 115, 136, 152, 156, 171, 174, 195, 210, 217, 251-255, 261, 265, 266, 277, 295, 340, 341, 344, 345
Casella, Alfredo 178, 211, 212, 256
Cassadó, Gaspar 8, 103-105
Cassidy, Claudia 180, 181, 257
Catholic University 332
Cerone, David 224
Chang, Sarah 228
Chapin, Schuyler 181
Chicago Symphony Orchestra 47, 137, 145, 180, 210, 257, 344, 350
Chicago Tribune 184, 257
Chotzinoff, Samuel 50, 51, 56, 67, 161
Chung, Kyung-Wha 225, 231
Cleveland News 76, 187
Cleveland Orchestra 46, 47, 56, 63, 64, 66, 71, 72, 75, 77, 79, 80, 85, 87, 89, 92, 94, 132-135, 137, 138, 140, 141, 144, 145, 166, 185, 189, 191, 205, 210, 233, 278, 285, 288, 296, 297, 317, 318, 319, 321, 323, 349
Cleveland Plain Dealer 78, 188
Cleveland Press 70, 181
Cliburn, Van 182, 303, 304
Coates, Helen 113
Cole, Orlando 295, 332
Coleman, Avron 39, 114
Columbia Artists 177, 195
Columbia Broadcasting System (CBS) 178
Columbia Concerts Corporation 109, 178
Columbia Records 49, 87, 192, 242, 243, 262, 272
Columbia Symphony Orchestra 106, 156
Community Concerts 181, 182, 183
Coolidge, Calvin 10, 212
Copland, Aaron 93, 113
Corelli, Arcangelo 215
Corigliano, John 86, 108, 109, 131, 153, 154, 178, 344
Cortot, Alfred 252, 253

Cortot-Thibaud-Casals trio 251
Curtis, Cyrus H.K. 22, 28, 29, 31, 38, 40-44, 46-50, 55, 62, 73, 86, 92, 102, 197, 229, 233, 252, 278, 291, 292-295, 299, 302, 311, 329, 330, 331, 332, 333, 338, 329, 343
Curtis Institute of Music 37, 332
Custor, Steve 281

D

Damrosch, Frank 304, 311
Damrosch, Leopold 311
Davis, Raymond 27, 311, 316
DeLay, Dorothy 228, 230
Delmoni, Arturo 228, 233, 235, 269
Diamond, David 117
Dicterow, Glenn 225
Dinger, Naoum J. 89, 93
Dorsey, Tommy 113
Downes, Olin 75, 126, 147, 155, 204
Duport, Jean-Louis 207, 343
Durieux, Willem 92

E

École Normale de Musique 106
Eisenberg, Maurice 105
Eley, Lewis 20
Elgar, Cello Concerto 23, 188
Enesco, Georges 22, 26, 252, 256
Ericson, Raymond 296
Eskin, Jules 209, 229, 331
Essex House 46, 51, 64
Everhart, David 314

F

Faber, Toby 216, 287
Fauré, Gabriel 212, 314
Feder, William L. 89
Feher, George 93
Felber, Dr. Herman 194
Feuermann, Emanuel 28, 61, 68, 78, 92, 100, 101, 152, 203, 216, 253, 255, 256, 285, 290, 292, 299, 326, 334, 341, 345
Fisher, Avery 296
Flagstad, Kirsten 152
Fleisher, Leon 205, 227
Fortune Magazine 54

Fournier, Pierre 8, 105, 134, 136, 138, 210, 256, 295, 326, 344, 347
Francescatti, Zino 81, 182
Franck, César 184
Franco, Francisco 254
Frankel, Jennie 10
Frankfurt School 57
Fried, Miriam 224
Friedberg, Carl 22, 255
Friedman, Erick 224
Fuchs, Joseph 79, 80, 81, 83, 178, 179, 181, 205, 211, 255
Fuchs, Lillian 81, 179
Furtwängler, Wilhelm 57, 60, 96-99, 103, 151

G

Galamian, Ivan 138, 158, 184, 224-234, 236, 299, 305, 307, 313, 337, 338
Garbousova, Raya 8, 83, 105, 106, 207, 209, 210, 285, 351
Gennaro, Giacomo 215
Gershman, Paul 78
Gershwin, George 110, 112, 113
Gilels, Emil 177, 256, 344
Gilman, Lawrence 55, 210
Gingold, Joseph 58, 137, 138, 139, 225, 235
Glazunov, Alexander 96
Glenn, Carroll 83
Glick, Dr. Irving 259
Gluck, Alma 50
Goebbels, Josef 97, 98
Gofriller cello 122, 178, 221, 293
Gold, Reverend Isaac 241
Goldberg, Alla 24, 98
Goldberg, Szymon 97
Goldovsky, Boris 64, 189
Golschmann, Vladimir 175, 189
Golub, David 196, 309
Gomez, Lefty 320
Gomez, Victor de 64
Gottlieb, Victor 322
Gould, Glenn 116, 141, 232, 237, 240, 242, 245, 246, 248, 249, 250, 287
Graffman, Gary 227, 309
Great Depression 13, 21, 68

Grebanier, Michael 139, 209, 229, 292, 293, 331
Greenberg, Mildred 20
Greenhouse, Bernard 25, 30, 105, 106, 256, 326
Grieg, Edvard 77, 184
Grissom, Sean 322
Gross, David 243, 328, 344, 349
Grossman, Walter 14, 15, 20, 94
Guarneri, Andrea 100, 215
Guarneri cello 100
Guidi, Alberico 90
Gundry, Roland 226

H

Hadley, Jerry 117
Hagen, Betty Jean 231
Haimovitz, Matt 328
Hambro, Leonid 26, 179, 184, 185, 309
Händel, Georg Friedrich 215
Hanson, Howard 198
Harding, Warren G. 10
Harms publishing company 110
Harrell, Lynn 94, 139, 140, 207, 209, 229, 293, 284, 295-297, 346, 354
Harrell, Mack 294-297
Harris, Julie 262
Harris, Roy 138, 167, 205
Haydn, Cello Concerto in D 40, 46, 49, 63, 104, 180, 185, 267, 285
Heifetz, Jascha 22, 50, 55, 78, 80, 120, 157-165, 172, 181, 215, 256, 269, 318, 319, 348
Heifetz, Ruven 159
Heifetz-Rubinstein-Feuermann trio 256
Heiss, David 325
Henderson, W.J. 161
Hendl, Walter 153, 179
Henken, John 173
Herbert, Cello Concerto 88
Hersey, John 262
Hess, Dame Myra 102, 144
Heyman, Barbara B. 207
Hill & Sons, William E. 213
Hill, Alfred 221

Hindemith, Paul 98, 99, 250
Hitler, Adolf 83, 97, 98, 151
Hoebig, Desmond 318, 323
Hoffman, Gary 223
Hofmann, Josef 22, 78, 148, 329, 330
Hollywood String Quartet 27
Holm, Einar 316
Horney, Karen 116
Horowitz, Vladimir 67, 171, 277
Huberman, Bronislaw 22, 97, 255
Hughes, Allen 275
Hume, Paul 180, 242, 265
Hurok, Sol 177, 178, 195

I

intonation 15, 35, 47, 77, 87, 99, 101, 160, 171, 173, 179, 185, 191, 291, 313, 315, 324
Isserlis, Steven 209
Istomin, Eugene 145, 188, 251, 252, 254-258, 260, 261, 263, 266, 267, 270, 272, 273, 275, 277, 283, 288, 308, 354
Istomin, Marta Casals 264, 270, 277
Istomin-Stern-Rose Trio 189, 252, 257, 258, 262, 264, 265, 266, 269, 272, 275, 303, 305, 306, 308

J

Janigro, Antonio 8, 105
Jennings, Geraldine French 314
Joachim, Heinrich 94, 294
Joachim, Joseph 105, 133, 294
Johnson, Judith 226
Johnson, Thor 201
Judd, Bill 182
Judson, Arthur 108, 109, 177, 178, 179, 181-184, 186, 190
Judson Radio Program Corporation 177
Juilliard, Augustus 171, 176, 190, 198, 199, 205, 229, 311, 271, 281, 284, 288, 293, 294, 299, 300, 304, 311-314, 316, 317, 323, 330, 332, 339, 343
Juilliard Graduate School 24, 25, 92, 312

Juilliard School 34, 49, 94, 191, 198, 203, 205, 311, 312, 322, 329, 334, 338, 353, 354
Juilliard String Quartet 83, 205, 299

K

Kabalevsky, Cello Concerto 211
Kalichstein, Joseph 309
Kalichstein-Laredo-Robinson trio 275
Kaplan, Mark 228
Kapuchinsky, Richard 32, 33
Karajan, Herbert von 96
Kates, Stephen 206, 297, 298, 299, 305
Katims, Milton 57
Katsoyanis, Katy 123, 125
Kaufmann, Harry 252
Kazan, Elia 262
Kazdin, Andrew 246, 249
Kennedy, Jacqueline 262, 263
Kennedy, John F. 262
Kennedy, Nigel 228
Kennedy Center Honor 206
Kern, Jerome 110
Kessler, Jerome 349
Key, Francis Scott 10
Kidd, George 244, 248
King, William G. 88
Kipling, Rudyard 161
Kirshbaum, Ralph 209
Klein, Howard 264
Klemperer, Otto 60, 97, 133, 155
Klengel, Julius 96
Kline, Josef 262
Knitzer, Joseph 137
Knopow, Minnie 44
Kodály, Zoltan 90, 189, 257, 343, 344
Korngold, Erich Wolfgang 27, 158
Kosher Nostra 268, 328
Koussevitzky, Serge 110, 112, 151, 202, 207
Kraeuter, Phyllis 294
Kraglund, John 244
Kreisler, Fritz 20, 76, 77, 164, 172, 252, 337
Kremer, Damian 310
Kubelik, Rafael 180
Ku Klux Klan 16

L

Lalo, Cello Concerto 79, 322
Lang, Paul Henry 200
Laredo, Jaime 224, 230, 243, 275, 305, 306
Larner, Jacques 61, 254
Laurie, David 219
Lee, James 348
Lee, Rachel 228
Lehmann, Lotte 153
Leinsdorf, Erich 57, 133, 135, 323
Leukemia 7, 45, 83, 173, 186, 188, 276, 277, 288, 342, 348
Levant, Oscar 78
Leventritt, Rosalie 136, 179, 304, 344
Levine, James 206, 296
Lhévinne, Josef 22, 81
Lhévinne, Rosina 304
Lidström, Mats 324
Lieberson, Goddard 272
Life Magazine 54
Lin, Cho-Liang 228
Lincer, William 3, 84, 154, 176, 344
Lindbergh, Charles 262
List, Eugene 80
Liszt, Franz 133
Lobos, Heitor Villa 87, 292
Locatelli, Pietro Antonio 215
Loesser, Arthur 84, 181
London Daily 192
London Symphony Orchestra 23
Los Angeles Philharmonic 25, 72, 110, 134, 209, 281, 291, 318
Luca, Sergiu 231
Lustgarten, Al 322

M

Ma, Yo-Yo 68, 173, 181, 182, 209, 229, 276, 283-288, 323, 346, 347, 354
Maazel, Lorin 166, 175, 188
Mahler, Fritz 60, 61, 130, 184, 297
Mahler, Gustav 57, 60, 61, 120, 130, 133, 147, 148, 150, 154, 155, 184
Maisky, Mischa 119
Malkin, Josef 14, 94
Malraux, André 262

Manhattan School of Music 92, 311
Mannes-Gimpel-Silva Trio 338
Mannes School of Music 24, 31, 93
Margolis, Jacques 111
Mather, Diane 232, 233, 235
Maxim, Jacob 309
Mayes, Samuel 41, 211, 291
Mayhew, Mary 313, 314
Mazzucchi, Oswaldo 62, 63, 314
McBride, Charlie 73
McCall, Donald 331
McDuffie, Robert 228
McLean, Eric 243
Meadowmount School of Music 138, 184, 224, 226, 299
Mehta, Zubin 196
Mengelberg, Willem 34, 90, 103, 155
Mennin, Peter 191, 198, 199, 200, 201, 202
Menuhin, Yehudi 104, 192, 255, 290
Meremblum, Peter 318
Mester, Jorge 202
Metropolitan Opera 55, 59, 60, 134, 141, 150, 294, 344
Meyers, Anne Akiko 228
Miaskovsky String Symphonietta 102
Midori 228
Mille, Agnes De 262
Miller, Arthur 262, 295
Miller, Frank 13, 38, 39, 48, 64, 65, 68, 78, 316, 338, 350
Milstein, Nathan 5, 81, 141, 144, 164, 269
Milton, Forstat 92
Minneapolis Symphony 58, 125
Mintz, Shlomo 228
Mischakoff, Mischa 55, 61, 254
Mitchell, Donald 277
Mitchell, Howard 192
Mitropoulos, Dimitri 94, 112, 121-130, 134, 148, 155, 170, 175, 178, 179, 184, 185, 202, 203, 305, 207, 210, 344
Moennig & Son, William 47, 221
Montealegre, Felicia 114
Monteux, Pierre 58, 175, 252
Morel, Jean 198, 206
Morganstern, Daniel 316
Morini, Erica 145, 184

Morrow, Anne 262
Mostras, Konstantin 225
Mozart, Divertimento 43, 82, 124, 133, 147, 165, 184, 189, 257, 267, 308
Münch, Charles 4, 58, 147, 175, 191
Munroe, Lorne 25, 209

N

Nadien, David 224, 231
Nagyvary, Joseph 220
NASA 250
National Broadcasting Company (NBC) 50
Naumburg Award 137, 291, 294
Navarra, André 325, 339
NBC Symphony 51, 53, 54, 55, 58, 59, 61, 62, 63, 64, 66, 68, 78, 79, 93, 94, 108, 126, 134, 138, 147, 149, 155, 161, 166, 203, 225, 254, 314
Neikrug, George 105
Nelsova, Zara 208, 211, 241
Newkirk, Robert 233, 332
Newman, Alfred 318
Newton, Isaac 287
Newton, Ivor 193
New Yorker 112, 191, 200, 323
New York Herald Tribune 55, 67, 185
New York Philharmonic 14, 25, 26, 33, 44, 50, 55, 63, 80, 83, 85, 86, 87, 89, 93-96, 107, 108, 110, 114, 118, 119, 122, 124, 129, 131, 146, 92, 133, 134, 142, 144, 145, 202, 147, 150, 152, 154, 155, 166, 169, 177, 186, 188, 198, 207, 209, 210, 216, 218, 255, 261, 202, 294, 296, 311, 313, 320, 321, 323, 278
New York Piano Trio 22
New York Sun 88, 161
New York Times 30, 97, 99, 101, 104, 108, 109, 111, 114, 116, 122, 129, 134, 146, 183, 184, 194, 200, 204, 254, 275, 296, 326, 344
New York World-Telegram and Sun 261

Nikisch, Arthur 57, 60, 101

O

Oler, Wendy Salmond 28, 36
Ormandy, Eugene 58, 64, 91, 103, 121, 122, 125, 175, 210, 288, 289
Ormandy, Martin 90, 94
Ostwald, Peter 242

P

Paganini, Niccolò 215, 227, 228, 343
Page, Tim 118, 246, 247
Pepper, Barbara 313
Perahia, Murray 116
Perkins, Francis D. 194
Perlea, Jonel 105
Perlman, Itzhak 215, 224, 228, 230, 231, 235, 354
Pescaroli, Francesco 216
Petchek, Walter 279-283
Petchek, Xenia 279, 282, 350
Petrillo, Jimmy 109
Pfohl, Ferdinand 148
Philadelphia Orchestra 38, 39, 40, 41, 43, 58, 64, 72, 91, 121, 122, 177, 186, 187, 210, 212, 288, 289, 323, 329, 332
Piastro, Mishel 109
Piatigorsky, Gregor 8, 28, 29, 32, 33, 34, 80, 96, 105, 114, 152, 159, 164, 172, 177, 178, 187, 221, 226, 255, 256, 292, 299, 326, 330, 341, 344, 345
Piatti, Carlo Alfredo 23, 207, 343
Pleeth, Bill 340
Pogany, Imre 108, 123
Polisi, Joseph W. 354
Polisi, William 108
Popper, David 17, 21, 39, 40, 89, 93, 190, 207, 286, 297, 343
Prague, Maurice von 103, 133
Pré, Jacqueline du 119, 256, 281, 290, 295, 308, 344
Press, Josef 96
Previn, André 101, 141
Primrose, William 161
Prix du Disque 154, 188, 192

R

Rabin, Michael 205, 224, 227, 230, 231, 290
Rachmaninoff, Sergei 77, 78, 80, 81, 82, 83, 124, 153, 225, 267, 310
Raven, Seymour 184, 258
Ravinia 145, 184, 189, 256, 257, 258, 285
Rea, Doug 155
Reade, Charles 221
Rebhan, Mary Komorn 150
Reiner, Fritz 40, 41, 44, 49, 57, 94, 102, 109, 112, 137, 151, 175, 259, 344
Reinthaler, Joan 196
Reisenberg, Nadia 178, 211
Rex, Christopher 325
Ricci, George 105
Ricci, Ruggieri 322
Richter, Sviatoslav 304
Rimsky-Korsakov, Nikolai 83, 87
Ringwall, Rudolph 185, 189
Robbins, Channing 85, 288, 294, 311, 317, 319, 295, 318, 319, 321, 322, 323, 324, 325, 326, 328, 329
Robbins, Jerome 115
Rockefeller, John D. 312
Rodzinski, Artur 46, 51, 56, 57, 64, 70, 72, 89, 93, 94, 108, 112, 133, 147, 310, 321, 322
Rodzinski, Halina 71, 73-84, 99, 102, 106, 109, 110, 123, 134, 135, 136, 175, 321, 322,
Rogers, Harold 191
Roosevelt, Eleanor 109
Roosevelt, Franklin Delano 319
Roosevelt, Theodore 252
Rosanoff, Marie 161
Rosé, Arnold 152
Rose, Arthur 15, 42, 45, 127, 153, 168, 231, 274
Rose, Barbara 79
Rose, Frank 10
Rose, Harry 7, 9, 10, 15, 38, 352
Rosenberg, Donald 136
Rose Section 323
Rosovsky, Gdal 9

Index

Rostropovich, Mstislav 117, 177, 190, 197, 256, 287, 295, 298, 305, 325, 339, 342, 344, 347,
Roth, Feri 101
Rothko, Mark 262
Rothwell, Walter Henry 25
Rowell, Margaret 339, 340
Rubinstein, Anton 83, 133, 329
Ruger, Francesco 215

S

Sacconi, Simone 222
Saint-Saëns, Concerto Allegro Appassionato 17, 80, 131, 145, 164, 173, 179, 180, 183, 185, 186, 189, 190, 194, 257, 315, 323
Saks, Toby 227, 229, 235, 315
Saleski, Gdal 55, 59
Salmond, Felix 8, 22-34, 36-38, 40, 41, 42, 43, 46, 47, 49, 48, 61, 71, 90, 92, 94, 96, 203, 221, 222, 255, 295, 298, 302, 304, 305, 313, 317, 322, 327, 328, 330, 334, 337, 338, 340, 354
Sanders, Samuel 189, 309
Sarasate, Zapateado 190
Sarnoff, David 50, 55, 56, 68
Sayão, Bidú 87
Sazer, Victor 313
Schick, George 181
Schnabel, Artur 82, 97, 255
Schneider, Alexander 241, 242, 255
Schneider, Mischa 105
Schoenberg, Arnold 124, 128, 147, 212, 250
Schonberg, Harold 116, 184
Schubart, Mark 317
Schubert, Franz 161, 263
Schulz, Leo 89, 90, 91
Schuman, William 145, 205, 206, 288, 312, 314, 334
Schumann, Robert 51, 81, 106, 111, 119, 126
Schuster, Joseph 84, 95, 97, 106, 111
Schwarzkopf, Elisabeth 152
Schwarzmann, Jascha 62
Serkin, Rudolf 182, 271, 272
Sewell, Laura 238, 239

Shaham, Gil 228
Shapiro, Eudice 49, 252
Shawger, Ron 351
Sheridan, Frank 179
Shostakovich, Dimitri 81, 87, 93, 102, 118, 124, 197, 267
Shulman, Alan 128, 131, 178, 202, 204
Shumsky, Oscar 48, 164, 238, 243, 244, 245, 249, 250, 252, 337
Sicre, Jorge 314
Siegel, Jeffrey 298, 302, 307
Silva, Luigi 8, 199, 256, 316, 317, 337, 338, 339
Sims, Rudolph 91
Singer, Isaac Bashevis 160
Skernick, Abraham 134
Slatkin, Leonard 115, 116, 160, 170
Smith, Lloyd 192, 331
Sokoloff, Nicolai 91
Solomon, Izler 177, 189, 210
Solti, Sir Georg 150
Sonnenberg, Nadia Salerno 228
Sophos, Anthony 85, 94
Soyer, David 105
Spaeth, Sigmund 157
Spivakovsky, Tossy 83
St. Petersburg Conservatory 96, 159, 329
Starker, Janos 8, 202, 290, 295, 326, 343-347
Statter, Arthur 50, 167, 190
Stegemann, Michael 239
Stehl, Richard E. 91
Steinberg, William 57, 275
Steiner, Rudolf 147
Steinhardt, Arnold 224, 228, 231
Stern, Carl 43, 89, 93, 255, 256, 258, 260, 261, 263, 266, 267, 268, 269, 270, 274, 275, 283, 308, 354
Stern, Isaac 119, 145, 150, 153, 154, 157, 163, 172, 177, 188, 192, 251, 252, 254, 255, 260, 263, 269, 273, 275, 276, 283, 288, 290, 354
Stern Samuel 13
Steuermann, Eduard 57
Stokking, William 229

Stokowski, Leopold 38, 43, 44, 64, 72, 73, 109, 110, 126, 136, 147, 170, 175, 329
Stolyarski, Piotr 226
Stradivarius, Alessandro 59, 214, 215, 216, 217
Stradivarius, Antonio 59, 214, 215, 216, 217, 219
Strasberg, Lee 262
Strasberg, Susan 262
Strasner, Gloria 168
Stratford Festival 237, 238, 241, 245, 250
Strauss, Richard 31, 57, 60, 68, 98, 99, 111, 108, 124, 133, 137, 141, 148, 151, 152, 173, 174, 178, 195, 276, 277
Stravinsky, Igor 53, 60, 175, 212, 276
Stutch, Nathan 25, 27, 85, 92, 94, 278
Szell, George 57, 123, 132-145, 173, 178, 181, 83, 184, 191, 205, 288, 293, 296, 305
Szeryng, Henryk 256
Szigeti, Joseph 5, 22, 80, 83, 172, 269

T

Takezawa, Kyoko 228
Tartini, Giuseppe 215
Taubman, Howard 129, 194, 200
Tchaikovsky, Variations on a Rococo Theme 144, 145, 179, 181, 183, 185, 188, 189, 193, 196
Teatro Colón 67
Tecchler, David 47, 216, 217, 218
Telemann, Georg Philipp 215
Testore Cello 91
Thaviu, Samuel 137
Thibaud, Jacques 152, 252, 253
Thomson, Virgil 204, 208
Time Magazine 54, 134
Timmner, Christiaan 71
Tobias, Paul 209
Toland, Gregg 319
Tononi, Carlo 222
Tortelier, Paul 73, 105, 290

Toscanini, Arturo 44, 50, 53, 68, 80
Town Hall 41, 51, 54-68, 71, 78, 83, 86, 94, 96, 97, 100, 101, 109, 123, 133, 134, 138, 149, 150, 151, 158, 170, 174, 178, 179, 192, 203, 211, 226, 243, 261, 288, 289, 293, 294, 314
Tree, Michael 354
Trimble, Lester 185

U

Uchimura, Bruce 325, 326

V

Vardi, Emanuel 61, 254
Varga, Laszlo 94, 119, 299
Vivaldi, Antonio 215
Volpe, Arnold 13
Vosburgh, Carl 65
Vuillaume, Jean-Baptiste 219

W

Wagenaar, Bernard 203
Wagner, Friedland 98
Wagner, Richard 98, 148
Wallenstein, Alfred 57, 90, 100, 261
Wallfisch, Raphael 209
Walter, Bruno 63, 97, 98, 102, 110, 111, 112, 133, 134, 143, 146- 156, 170, 173, 174, 175, 178, 180, 188, 189, 255, 305
Warburg, Gerald 216, 217, 218
Washington Post 180, 185, 196, 242, 265
Wasielewski, Wilhelm 56
Waxman, Franz 106
Webern, Anton 124, 242
Whitehouse, William Edward 23, 90
White Plains Hospital 353
Wielhorski, Matvei 184
Wild, Earl 61
Wilder, Thornton 262
Willeke, Willem 93, 334
Williams, Tennessee 262
Wolf, Andrew 309
Wurlitzer, Rembert 213, 222, 293

Y

Ysaÿe, Eugene 137, 252

Z

Zazofsky, Peter 225
Zimbalist, Efrem 47, 49, 50, 330, 332
Zinman, David 209
Zirato, Bruno 169, 176, 177
Zlotkin, Frederick 326, 327, 328
Zukerman, Pinchas 224, 225, 231, 232, 256, 307, 308